# CHOOSING TERROR

*Choosing Terror: Virtue, Friendship and Authentic.* ... *Revolution* examines the leaders of the French Revolution—. ...re and his fellow Jacobins—and particularly the gradual process whereby many of them came to 'choose terror'. These men led the Jacobin Club between 1789 and 1794, and were attempting to establish new democratic politics in France. Exploring revolutionary politics through the eyes of these leaders, and against a political backdrop of a series of traumatic events, wars, and betrayals, Marisa Linton portrays the Jacobins as complex human beings who were influenced by emotions and personal loyalties, as well as by their revolutionary ideology.

The Jacobin leaders' entire political careers were constrained by their need to be seen by their supporters as 'men of virtue', free from corruption and ambition, and concerned only with the public good. In the early stages of the Revolution, being seen as 'men of virtue' empowered the Jacobin leaders, and aided them in their efforts to forge their political careers. However, with the onset of war, there was a growing conviction that political leaders who feigned virtue were 'the enemy within', secretly conspiring with France's external enemies. By Year Two, the year of the Terror, the Jacobin identity had become a destructive force: in order to demonstrate their own authenticity, they had to be seen to act virtuously, and be prepared, if the public good demanded it, to denounce and destroy their friends, and even to sacrifice their own lives. This desperate thinking resulted in the politicians' terror, one of the most ruthless of all forms of terror during the Revolution. *Choosing Terror* seeks neither to cast blame, nor to exonerate, but to understand the process whereby such things can happen.

**Marisa Linton** is a leading historian of the French Revolution. She is currently Reader in History at Kingston University. She has published widely on eighteenth-century France and the French Revolution. She is the author of *The Politics of Virtue in Enlightenment France* (2001) and the co-editor of *Conspiracy in the French Revolution* (2007).

'Well known to historians for her previous works, Marisa Linton offers us here a book that is sure to arouse debate. So much the better and we should thank her for it…She concludes her fine book with the call to the judgment of posterity made by those who knew they were doomed…all had made "Liberty or Death" their watchword, and kept faith with that commitment to the end'

Michel Biard, *H-France Forum* [translated from French]

'Linton has given us a potent account of how individual revolutionaries faced the Terror… Linton offers a finely texted and compelling play-by-play, as figures like Jacques-Pierre Brissot, Georges Danton, Robespierre, and Jean Tallien wrestle over each other's fates and the future of France'

Suzanne Desan, *Journal of Interdisciplinary History*

'a richly textured, well-researched, and thought-provoking account'

Jennifer Heuer, *H-France Forum*

'Marisa Linton's new book is in the best traditions of such careful, detailed, biographically-conscious evaluations'

David Andress, *Reviews in History*

'Marisa Linton's book covers five years of the revolution and integrates a great deal of recent research into an interpretation of the terror which will fascinate the general reader and encourage specialists to extend research into some of the areas she covers'

Hugh Gough, *Dublin Review of Books*

'Linton manages to provide a very convincing account of her topic of choice. One of the key strengths of the book is that Linton is never prescriptive; likewise she presents a balanced account throughout, weighing the ideological, strategic, emotional and personal inclinations of the protagonists at every turn'

Aurelien Mondon, *Modern & Contemporary France*

'In this important book, Marisa Linton shows with insight and care how [Jean-Marie] Roland's self-image as a man of virtue and honesty was shared among nearly all revolutionary politicians on the Left'

Gary Kates, *American Historical Review*

'Linton's accomplished book highlights important problems of political authority in an egalitarian age'

Sanja Perovic, *French Studies*

'One of the interesting arguments made by this book is to show precisely how the configuration of what we call the "Terror" came about as the consequence of a series of gradual and collective political choices, but equally it was a powerful political weapon which inevitably ended by burning the hands of all the protagonists who took hold of it'

Guillaume Mazeau, *H-France Forum* [translated from French]

'Linton's chronological approach allows her to offer many insights into the politicians' personal experience of the Terror'

Lynn Hunt, *French History*

'Linton's rigorously researched and documented work renders in intricate detail the personalities, motives, and interrelationships of revolutionary figures caught up in the writhing landscape of the great French political experiment… Recommended'

J.I. Donohoe, *CHOICE*

# Choosing Terror

*Virtue, Friendship, and Authenticity in the French Revolution*

MARISA LINTON

OXFORD
UNIVERSITY PRESS

# OXFORD
## UNIVERSITY PRESS

Great Clarendon Street, Oxford, OX2 6DP,
United Kingdom

Oxford University Press is a department of the University of Oxford.
It furthers the University's objective of excellence in research, scholarship,
and education by publishing worldwide. Oxford is a registered trade mark of
Oxford University Press in the UK and in certain other countries

First published 2013
First published in paperback 2015

Published in the United States of America by Oxford University Press
198 Madison Avenue, New York, NY 10016, United States of America

British Library Cataloguing in Publication Data
Data available

Library of Congress Cataloging in Publication Data
Data available

ISBN 978–0–19–957630–2 (Hbk.)
ISBN 978–0–19–873309–6 (Pbk.)

This book is dedicated to the memory of my parents,
Adele Di Lauro and David Linton.
A short time in my life, always in my heart.

'I felt before thinking; this is the common fate of humanity.'
Jean-Jacques Rousseau

# *Acknowledgements*

For nearly thirty years now, since long before I became a professional historian, I have been haunted by a question: what led a man like Robespierre (and others like him)—a man who at the start of the Revolution was a humanitarian opposed to the death penalty—to choose terror four years later? This book is my attempt to answer that question. It is far from being the definitive word on the subject. No doubt future historians will continue to pose the same question and come up with differing responses. Historians always disagree with one another—it's what we do. But two things I do know: firstly, that the answer has to be sought, not in some warp of Robespierre's personality, but in the politics of the Revolution itself; and secondly, that in addressing it there is no room for complacency. To understand the French revolutionaries is to understand ourselves better. We have cause to be grateful that we have not been confronted with the choices, in the circumstances, and with the tragic consequences, that they faced in their own lives.

I have been privileged to have had the help and support of many fine historians, whose collective knowledge of the French Revolution far outstrips my own. I would particularly like to thank John Hardman and Lynn Hunt, both of whom read sections of the manuscript and offered valuable advice. I owe an even greater debt to Peter Campbell, Annie Jourdan, Tom Kaiser, Peter McPhee, Tim Tackett, and the anonymous readers for Oxford University Press, all of whom generously gave their time and expertise to read through much—in some cases all—of the manuscript. Their advice saved me from many lapses and omissions and ensured that you, the reader, have in your hands a better book than you would otherwise have done. Any errors that remain, despite their gallant efforts, are of course my own. I am grateful to Mette Harder for sharing her as yet unpublished findings with me. Siân Reynolds and Peter McPhee both generously shared their own work with me at the prepublished stage and made me think again about two people whose experiences are central to this book, Madame Roland and Robespierre.

For a writer the most precious gift is time. I would like to thank the Arts and Humanities Research Council and Kingston University for supporting a year of research leave that helped immeasurably with the earlier stages of this project. I am particularly grateful to my colleagues in the History Research Unit at Kingston University for their unfailing support, both financial and collegial. The British Academy funded attendance at the French Historical Studies conference in Phoenix in 2010 to present my research findings.

Writing this book has given me ample evidence that the personal dimension is the most important aspect of all our lives. I give my heartfelt thanks to Peter, Elena, and Sophia for their patience in putting up with more discussions of Robespierre over breakfast than any family should have to tolerate. My daughters have had to live with a mother who, though present in body, has been all too often absent in mind, dwelling on the vicissitudes of long-dead Jacobins. That the girls have emerged relatively unscathed from the experience is due in no small measure to their resilience, their sense of humour, and their love; also their skill at deflecting the inessentials in life, and their ability to focus on the things that really matter. As they have got older I hope that the time they have spent seeing more of the world, especially with our friends in New York and Los Angeles, has compensated to some extent for their mother's weird job. As Sophia asked me yesterday, 'what is a Jacobin, anyway?' I'm so sorry, Sophia. Maybe I'll be free of them now.

# List of Contents

# Introduction
## Political Identity and the Jacobin Leaders

It was an overriding love for the *patrie* which, passing the bounds of ordinary rules about crimes and virtues, followed only its own voice, and made no distinctions between citizens, friends, philanthropists or fathers: virtue seemed to forget itself in order to surpass itself; and an action that one could not at first sight approve of, because it seemed so terrible, virtue made one admire as divine.

> Montesquieu, *Considérations sur les causes de la grandeur des Romains et de leur décadence* (1734).[1]

There is something terrible in the sacred love of the *patrie*.

> Saint-Just, speech against the Dantonists (1794).[2]

'Career of ambition, of egoism.'[3] This is how the nineteenth-century writer Charles Nodier described the qualities that motivate people to take up a career in politics. It was a realistic, if cynical, assessment: one with which we might ourselves concur. Perhaps we are all cynics about politics now. We assume our own politicians to be personally ambitious—even though they will never actually admit in public that this is why they went into politics. We expect our political leaders to hold out on us, and to not tell us the truth about themselves. We may even expect them to lie to us. We might not like it, but we tolerate it, for that is the modern world of democratic politics. But the generation before that of Nodier did not see politics in that way at all, for this was the generation that created the French Revolution, and can even be said to have invented modern politics. For the revolutionary generation politics was about something very different from ambition or egoism—it was about virtue.

We have lost sight now of what that term meant, but it was central to the way in which people understood politics in the eighteenth century. This book deals with the successive groups of political leaders who dominated the Parisian Jacobin Club between 1789 and 1794. It includes, but is not limited to, the group led by

[1] Montesquieu, *Oeuvres complètes*, Roger Caillois ed., 2 vols (Paris, Bibliothèque de la Pléiade, 1949–51), 1: 132.

[2] Saint-Just, 'Rapport sur la conjuration ourdie pour obtenir un changement de dynastie, et contre Danton...11 germinal an II' (31 March 1794), Louis-Antoine Saint-Just, *Oeuvres complètes*, ed. Michèle Duval (Paris: Éditions Ivrea, 1989), 760.

[3] Charles Nodier, *Souvenirs, épisodes et portraits pour servir à l'histoire de la Révolution et de l'Empire*, 2 vols (Brussels: Louis Hauman and Co., 1831), 1: 102.

Robespierre, Saint-Just, and others (known as the Montagnards) which dominated the revolution in its most radical phase, between June 1793 and July 1794. All of these Jacobin leaders (not the Montagnards alone) publicly identified themselves as men of virtue. This meant that they were ready to put the public good before anything else, before their own self-interest, and before personal loyalties to friends and family. It was an ideology that extended far beyond the Jacobins and even beyond the shores of France; the language of political virtue and even terror was heard in the republics of America and Western Europe in the late eighteenth century.[4] It was an ideology with which the Jacobin political leaders fully identified. Yet it was an extraordinarily difficult ideology to live up to. The attempt to do so involved the Jacobin leaders in a lived contradiction, in which the realities of their lives and the ways in which they actually practised politics could never match up to the identity they professed. The Revolution opened up the possibility of forging a career in politics. It is likely that many of the men who took up a career in revolutionary politics were motivated by ambition as well as by genuine patriotic fervour. Yet it was impossible—indeed dangerous—for them to admit this publicly. They lived with the constant risk of a perceptible gap opening up between what they said and what they did, a gap that would damage their credibility in the eyes of the public, for how could they ever prove that they were authentically virtuous, as opposed to good at faking this?

The difficulty—indeed the near impossibility—of distinguishing between a politician who was motivated by authentic virtue and one who only professed to be virtuous, was to be an integral theme in one of the most traumatic aspects of the Terror in the French Revolution. This was what I have called here the 'politicians' terror'. The politicians' terror emerged during the year that the Jacobins played a leading role in government, though the ideas that underlay it went back to a much earlier date. The politicians' terror was characterized by a series of trials of Jacobin and former Jacobin politicians. These trials were some of the most ruthless carried out during the entire Terror. In many cases conviction hinged on unreliable evidence regarding the authenticity of the accused politicians' inner motivation. The Jacobin leaders were beset on many sides by enemies, both open and covert. But in the end the most dangerous and unforgiving enemies they faced were themselves. In choosing terror, they chose a path that led to self-destruction.

This book has two aims. The first is to examine the inherent contradiction between identity and reality in Jacobin politics. The second is to uncover how this lived contradiction contributed to the self-destruction of the revolutionary leaders in the politicians' terror.

---

[4] As Hunt has observed, the 'political differences between a Jefferson or a Madison, and a Robespierre or a Saint-Just were minimal. The salient difference between them was the context in which they spoke.' See Lynn Hunt, *Politics, Culture, and Class in the French Revolution* (Berkeley: University of California Press, 1984), 43–4. There is an extensive literature on the republics of North America and Western Europe in the late eighteenth century; a recent analysis is by Annie Jourdan, *La Révolution, une exception française?* (Paris: Flammarion, 2004), Part Two. On comparative instances of the deployment of the 'discourse of terror' see Annie Jourdan, 'Les discours de la Terreur à l'époque révolutionnaire', *French Historical Studies*, 36, 1 (Winter 2013): 52–81.

## THE TERRAIN OF REVOLUTIONARY POLITICS

This book deals with the ideology of political virtue, but it does not confine itself to that ideology. Rather, it seeks to go beneath the public face of Jacobin politics to examine how that politics was constructed. My approach in this book is predicated on the belief that individual experience and agency have made a significant contribution to history, one which it is important to recover. The French Revolution had many causes, amongst which individual choices played their part. Similarly, the path to terror was not forged entirely from ideology, nor even entirely from circumstances; it was also the consequence of decisions made by certain individuals, including some of the Jacobin leaders who will feature in this book. This book does not set out to endorse the choices they made, but to understand them, and to understand the consequences of those choices. What I have tried to show here is that what makes us human, and what can make humans into monsters is not purely, or even primarily, our ideology, nor even our circumstances, but our choices.

To understand Jacobin politics, both in theory and in practice, we need to address what that politics actually entailed. As part of my approach in this book I situate the Jacobin experience within the whole terrain of politics. I argue here that Jacobin politicians operated in three dimensions, which together formed this terrain. These dimensions were closely interconnected, and can be better understood if we grasp them in relation to one another. Such an approach brings us a little closer to the ways in which Jacobin politics was actually experienced by the people involved in them.

The first dimension was that of ideology. This was the public face of Jacobinism: it was what they declared they were about. It is primarily traced through their public writings and speeches. This is what they said when, shoulders squared, dressed and coiffed as revolutionary leaders, they presented themselves at the national assemblies, and in the clubs, to make their voices heard. For the most part they believed passionately in their ideology, but they were also mindful of their audiences: these included their friends and supporters, their opponents and rivals, the unconvinced, the indifferent, the bored, and—most important of all for revolutionary politics— the spectators in the gallery. When the Jacobins' speeches, journalistic writings, pamphlets, and treatises were published, these too purveyed the public and official version of Jacobin politics, in the attempt to win over the readers.

Politics was not conducted just on the level of ideology and official discourses. It was also a practice, something that people did. The second dimension of Jacobin politics therefore was that of the practice or profession: 'doing politics'. This level was full of polemics and in-fighting, deals and tactical decisions, managing assemblies and clubs, networking and advancement. In some ways it was the inverse of the old regime, under which the way to get on was to purchase an office, be part of the patronage system, and negotiate court factions. Revolutionary politicians had to negotiate factions and corruption, while denying that such things existed under a revolution. On this level too, political participants had to be mindful of public opinion. It was vital not to outrage revolutionary public opinion, which was suspicious of anything that recalled the corruption that was endemic in the old regime.

There was also a third dimension of politics: the personal. This level was not part of the official identity of the Jacobins, but it was a potent aspect of political life nonetheless. This personal dimension was very wide. It included friendships and relationships that came in beneath the radar of the ideological dimension of revolutionary politics. This personal dimension was played out behind closed doors, in private places, houses, salons, in offices where there was no clerk to take an official record of what was said, and in personal letters. Individual circumstances, relationships with friends and family, unofficial networks, character, and choices all played a part in this dimension. Within the personal dimension we can also situate individual and collective emotions. Emotions were extremely intense in the hothouse of Jacobin politics; they had a considerable impact on individual choices, one which needs to be better understood. Positive emotions such as patriotic fervour, euphoria, friendship, and loyalty, as well as more toxic feelings such as enmity, suspicion, anxiety, stress, and fear, all contributed to the personal dimension of revolutionary politics.

These three dimensions of political life interlocked: all were part of the Jacobin leaders' political experience. This book seeks to reconstruct that experience, showing how the Jacobins shaped their identity in this multi-layered political context.

## THE INVENTION OF MODERN POLITICS

The French Revolution brought about the invention of modern politics.[5] Before the Revolution politics was the business of the king alone. The Revolution transformed that: for the first time France had politicians in a modern sense. They were answerable not to one man, but to public opinion and to the 'people'.[6] Awareness of public opinion as an audience went back to the seventeenth century. But only

---

[5] Pierre Rosenvallon, *La Démocratie inachevée. Histoire de la souveraineté du peuple en France* (Paris: Gallimard, 2003).

[6] On public opinion in the eighteenth century, see Baker, 'Public opinion as political invention', in Keith Michael Baker, *Inventing the French Revolution* (Cambridge: Cambridge University Press, 1990); Mona Ozouf, 'L'Opinion publique', in K.M. Baker (ed.), *The French Revolution and the Creation of Modern Culture*, vol. 1, *The Political Culture of the Old Regime* (Oxford: Pergamon, 1987); J.A.W. Gunn, 'Queen of the World: opinion in the public life of France from the Renaissance to the Revolution', in *Studies on Voltaire and the Eighteenth Century*, 328 (1995); Arlette Farge, *Subversive Words: Public Opinion in Eighteenth-Century France*, trans. Rosemary Morris (Oxford: Polity Press,1995). On the relationship between public opinion and the French Revolution, see Roger Chartier, *The Cultural Origins of the French Revolution*, trans. Lydia C. Cochrane (Durham, NC and London: Duke University Press, 1991), ch. 2. A good introduction to the subject is James Horn Van Melton, *The Rise of the Public in Enlightenment Europe* (Cambridge: Cambridge University Press, 2001). On how the French monarchy itself appealed to public opinion, see Thomas E. Kaiser, 'Rhetoric in the service of the King: the Abbé Dubos and the concept of public judgement', *Eighteenth-Century Studies*, 23 (1989): 182–99; and Thomas E. Kaiser, 'The Abbé de Saint-Pierre, public opinion and the reconstitution of the French monarchy', *Journal of Modern History*, 55 (1983): 618–43. For the argument that public opinion was part of the rise of the modern bourgeois public sphere, see Jürgen Habermas, *The Structural Transformation of the Public Sphere: An Inquiry into a Category of Bourgeois Society* (Cambridge: Polity Press, 1989).

with the Revolution did it come to the forefront of political life, as the sole arbiter of the correctness of the conduct of politicians and public officials. Henceforward, in order to establish their careers under the new political order, revolutionary politicians had to cultivate public opinion, play to the gallery, and establish their integrity in the eyes of the public. Their speeches, their actions, and their conduct were subjected to an unprecedented level of public scrutiny, above all by the revolutionary press. The new revolutionary journalism played a crucial role in forming public opinion. Many of the Jacobin leaders took an active role in these new media, founding their own newspapers so as to speak directly to their audiences.[7]

In common with many others of their time, the Jacobins saw politics in moral terms—as founded on virtue. They believed that the highest form of politics is based on devotion to the public good and the abnegation of self-interest. It was a concept that owed much to traditions of political thought that were derived from antiquity and reinterpreted by eighteenth-century thinkers.[8] As public servants, politicians were more subject than ordinary citizens to the rigorous demands of virtue, even extending to their private lives. In the realm of revolutionary politics, to be 'a man of virtue' required that one *be seen* to reject self-interest, venality, and personal ambition—though the reality was often rather different. The ideology of virtue was fraught with difficulties, both philosophical and practical. Firstly, many people, both at the time and subsequently, have made the philosophical observation that to act without self-interest is contrary to human nature. The Jacobins tried to argue that virtue is natural, but this argument would prove intensely problematic. Secondly, on a practical level, the ideology of virtue was conceived as a rejection of the venal practices of the old regime. In theory the Revolution had abolished the old regime, but many of the old attitudes towards venality and corruption proved impossible to erase and remained in place throughout the Revolution. The Jacobins were constantly trying to coerce the population to abandon long-standing practices—such as the offering of bribes to officials. Thus virtue proved quite as difficult to enforce on the ground as it was to formulate in theory.

The Jacobins' rhetoric of political virtue was part of a deliberate decision to reject the 'behind closed doors' way of conducting politics that they associated with the old regime. Revolutionary politics were meant to be open and transparent.[9] But when we look at how the Jacobins conducted the business of politics,

---

[7] On political journalism during the French Revolution, see Jeremy D. Popkin, *Revolutionary News: the Press in France, 1789–1799* (Durham, NC and London: Duke University Press, 1990); Jeremy D. Popkin, 'Citizenship and the press in the French Revolution', in Renée Waldinger, Philip Dawson, and Isser Woloch (eds), *The French Revolution and the Meaning of Citizenship* (Westport, CT: Greenwood Press, 1993); Hugh Gough, *The Newspaper Press in the French Revolution* (London: Routledge, 1988); William J. Murray, *The Right Wing Press in the French Revolution* (London: Royal Historical Society, 1986); Pierre Rétat (ed.), *La Révolution du journal. 1788–1794* (Paris: CNRS, 1998); Carla Hesse, *Publishing and Cultural Politics in Revolutionary Paris, 1789–1810* (Berkeley: University of California Press, 1991) and Robert Darnton and Daniel Roche (eds), *Revolution in Print: the Press in France, 1775–1800* (Berkeley: University of California Press, 1989).

[8] Marisa Linton, *The Politics of Virtue in Enlightenment France* (Houndmills: Palgrave, 2001).

[9] On the politics of transparency, see Jean Starobinski, *Jean-Jacques Rousseau: Transparency and Obstruction* (1971: this edition, Chicago: University of Chicago Press, 1988); and Hunt, *Politics, Culture, and Class in the French Revolution*.

rather than their ideology, it becomes evident that, seen in these pragmatic terms, the Jacobins still needed to operate within that more covert dimension, despite their insistence on their own transparency. We do not need to accept what the Jacobins *said* they were about as the literal truth. We need to examine the painstaking construction of political personas, and the importance of public image. This does not mean, however, that we should discount the importance of ideology: clearly it was central to what Jacobinism was about. Nor should we necessarily doubt the sincerity with which most of the Jacobins espoused their cause—though some were clearly cynical in their use of political rhetoric, and increasingly so as the political situation deteriorated. What we do need to appreciate, however, is just how complex is the relationship between ideological theory and the practice of actual politics. By being aware of the pragmatic business of politics, and the role played by individuals, we can better understand the process of creating a new political ideology, and what this entailed. The men who struck deals with each other or fell out with each other in private, were also the men who stood up in the Assembly the next day and spoke about the absolute importance of the public good in politics. To understand this process we need to go beyond how the Jacobins *spoke* publicly about revolutionary politics, and try to uncover what they actually *thought* about it. What was their motivation? What did they actually think they were trying to achieve as revolutionary politicians? Many of these inner thought processes cannot, of course, be reconstructed. In the majority of cases we have nothing beyond the public speeches to indicate what they thought on any given subject. But the business of trying to uncover their thoughts seems an invaluable one, as a way of understanding better the nature of revolutionary—and ultimately terrorist—politics. Fundamental to this problem is the inevitable gap between what they said and what they did: above all, between the absolute ideology of political virtue, of equality, and of liberty, and the contingent realities of political practice.

## WHO WERE THE JACOBINS?

The name 'Jacobins' derived from the political club of which they were members. The club was outside the formal structures of political representation, though many of the Paris club's members were also national representatives, and in the provinces many more held official posts at a local level. Strictly speaking, the term 'Jacobins' refers to men who had attended the Jacobin Club (the Société des Amis de la Constitution), either the mother club in Paris, or one of the network of provincial clubs that grew up from 1789.[10] In some ways this is quite a loose term, since many revolutionaries ceased to attend the club or to call themselves Jacobins

[10] On the provincial clubs, see Michael L. Kennedy, *The Jacobin Clubs in the French Revolution: the First Years* (Princeton, NJ: Princeton University Press, 1982); *The Jacobin Clubs in the French Revolution: the Middle Years* (Princeton, NJ: Princeton University Press, 1988); and *The Jacobin Clubs in the French Revolution, 1793 to 1795* (New York: Berghahn Books, 2000).

at certain points during the Revolution as the club itself grew more militantly radical. The focal point of Jacobinism was the Paris club.[11] Here many leaders of the
Revolution honed their skills as politicians. The Jacobins did not operate like a
modern political party. Indeed, one of the central problems is that revolutionary
leaders did not accept that parties have a valid part to play in politics. The very idea
that politicians should form a party was seen as against the public good, since party
politics were assumed to be inherently self-interested.

This book focuses on the successive groups that dominated the Paris Jacobin
Club from the time of its foundation to the fall of Robespierre. Because I take this
long perspective my remit goes beyond the group that in 1792 coalesced around
Robespierre and the Montagnards, and that is often thought of as synonymous
with 'the Jacobins' as a whole. This assumption is often made because we tend to
read the past backwards, taking our perspective from the political position at which
people ended up, their political identities fixed and frozen in death. Yet it would be
a mistake to assume that, because successive Jacobin leaders fell out with one
another and became bitter enemies, they had always held different beliefs. This
book argues something rather different—that they started out with much in
common, from shared convictions to personal friendships, but as individuals they
made different choices. One of those choices was adherence to a particular faction;
a choice which resulted in divergent paths being taken. One key thing that successive leaders of the Jacobins shared was a public commitment to the ideology of
political virtue; this remained a constant throughout the years from 1789 to 1794.
A central argument of this book is that this ideology shaped the progress of Jacobinism, and played a pivotal role in the fate both of Jacobinism itself, and of the
revolution. Other aspects of Jacobin ideology were more flexible; what came to be
known as Jacobinism emerged from a changing political terrain. Elements of it
came into being during the early years of the Revolution, in the course of infighting, splits, and secessions. Dominant ideas and groups within the club changed
during the course of revolutionary struggles. Historians have identified three phases
of Jacobinism: the first was the moderate and constitutional Jacobinism of the
period of the Constituent Assembly when the 'triumvirs' first played a leading role
in founding the club and then went on to lead it (1789–91); then there was a more
'democratic' stage during the period of the Legislative Assembly, when the Jacobins
were dominated by Brissot and his friends; finally there was the most radical phase,
when the Jacobin Club was dominated by the group of deputies that sat in the
National Convention, a group that became known as the Montagnards, and
counted Robespierre, Danton, and Marat amongst its leading figures (from late
1792 to the summer of 1794). It has been pointed out that these rigid distinctions
are too schematic. In reality membership of the club fluctuated, and throughout its
life the political views of the Jacobins were far from unanimous.[12] But we do see a

---

[11] This study is confined to the Parisian Jacobin Club, but similar issues of factionalism, fear, and
personal enmity influenced Jacobinism at a local level. See, for example, Stephen Clay, 'Vengeance,
justice and the reactions in the Revolutionary Midi', *French History*, 23, 1 (2009): 22–46.

[12] See Albert Soboul (ed.), *Dictionnaire historique de la Révolution française* (Paris: Presses Universitaires de France, 1989), article on 'Jacobins/Jacobinisme', 586.

'hardening' of the Jacobin line that coincides with the founding of the Republic and the first defeats in the war over the summer of 1792. During this time the men who led the Montagnards became the dominant figures in the Paris club, and their ideology became identified with Jacobinism—not least because the men who were open in their opposition to them either left, or were driven out of, the Paris club.

Thus the term 'Jacobin' is problematic. The identity of the successive leaders who form the focus of this book is clear enough, even though these changed amidst a series of dramatic schisms. Beyond that inner circle things get more opaque. Jacobin ideology was not monolithic, nor were all revolutionary leaders Jacobins. The Jacobins were a pressure group rather than a party of which any activist was compelled to become a member. Joining the Jacobins was a strategy, not an obligation. Forging an identity in revolutionary politics was a matter of choice and tactics, as well as ideological commitment.[13] Jacobinism was characterized by bitter struggles and disputes over ideological direction. It was shaped as much by the men who left the club, and the manner of their leaving, as by those who elected to remain and form the hard core of Jacobinism in power. Even after autumn 1792, by no means everyone who remained in the Paris club was an admirer of Robespierre's politics or his persona. Nor were all political leaders by any means habitués of the Jacobin Club. The Jacobin Club was not the sole recourse of a man who wanted to play a leading role in politics. Some drifted in and out of the Jacobin Club; some never went there. Even during the period when the Jacobins were at their most powerful, during the so-called 'Jacobin Republic' (June 1793 to July 1794), many leading revolutionaries and men in government—some of whom played a leading role in the Terror as committee members, deputies on mission— did not consider themselves to be Jacobins and did not attend the Jacobin Club. The laws that set the Terror in place were voted for by a majority of deputies in the Convention, most of whom were not Jacobins.

## THE JACOBINS AND THE TERROR

The most persistent arguments about Jacobin ideology address its relationship to the origins of the Terror. Historians in the socialist and Marxist traditions characterized the Terror as a regrettable necessity, an essential means for France to avoid military defeat at the hands of the allied invaders. The pressure of circumstances obliged the Jacobins to choose terror.[14] A very different view was taken by François Furet, who argued that the Terror was already inherent in the ideology of 1789, above all in the idea that in the name of 'liberty' and 'equality' one section

---

[13] The fascinating work of Burstin addresses some parallel themes, though his concern is with people who joined the Parisian militants by inventing themselves as '*sans-culotte*'. Burstin emphasizes the importance of what he terms '*protagonisme révolutionnaire*': Haim Burstin, *L'Invention du sans-culotte: regard sur le Paris révolutionnaire* (Paris: Odile Jacob, 2005), 114–17.

[14] This approach to Jacobinism is summarized in Marc Bouloiseau, *The Jacobin Republic, 1792–1794*, trans. Jonathan Mandelbaum (Cambridge: Cambridge University Press, 1983).

of society could exercise domination over the rest. The events of 1789 led inexorably to 1793, so that the first Revolution was simply a 'prelude to terror'. Keith Baker made a similar point when he said that the Revolution was 'opting for the Terror' in September 1789; though in his more recent work Baker has modified—or clarified—his own position, allowing space for 'revolutionary improvisation'.[15] Furet and Baker have had a considerable impact in helping to make acceptable the study of political culture and political language.[16] Of late there has been a revival of a 'force of circumstances' thesis, but this time addressed more dispassionately, and without the nationalism that characterized the attitude of historians who wrote in the shadow of France's traumatic experiences of the First and Second World Wars.[17] There is a particularly rich Anglophone tradition of historiography that has examined the provincial experience of the Terror.[18]

Amongst the most recent works on the Terror there has been a resurgence of interest in its ideological basis, exemplified in the work of Dan Edelstein, who sees the Terror as emerging from Enlightenment ideas, though the idea he singles out is not the concept of the 'general will' (to which previous historians paid much attention), but the tradition of natural law.[19] Edelstein devotes comparatively little

---

[15] Baker, *Inventing the French Revolution*. 305. For his rethinking of this question, see Keith Michael Baker, 'Enlightenment idioms, old regime discourses and Revolutionary improvisation', in Thomas E. Kaiser and Dale K. Van Kley (eds), *From Deficit to Deluge: The Origins of the French Revolution* (Stanford, CA: Stanford University Press, 2011). Norman Hampson, *Prelude to Terror: The Constituent Assembly and the Failure of Consensus, 1789–1791* (Oxford: Blackwell, 1988) sees the road to terror as a longer process but one which was essentially fixed by the end of the Constituent Assembly; Furet places the origins of the Terror earlier than either, at the start of the summer of 1789: Furet, 'Terreur', in François Furet and Mona Ozouf (eds), *Dictionnaire critique de la Révolution française* (Paris: Flammarion, 1988), 156.

[16] The works that owe a debt to Furet are too many to list here. Numerous studies of political revolutionary culture since the 1970s exist, at least in part, because of his influence in making this kind of study acceptable, even where the writers do not agree with his political conclusions. For a study that takes a particularly 'Furetist' approach to the ideology of terror, see Patrice Gueniffey, *La Politique de la Terreur: essai sur la violence révolutionnaire, 1789–1794* (Paris: Fayard, 2000); and 'La Terreur: circonstances exceptionnelles, idéologie et dynamique révolutionnaire', *Historical Reflections/Réflexions Historiques*, 29, 3 (2003): 433–50. See also Keith M. Baker (ed.), *The French Revolution and the Creation of Modern Political Culture*, vol. 4, *The Terror* (Oxford: Pergamon, 1994).

[17] The debates on the Terror are summarized in Hugh Gough, *The Terror in the French Revolution* (second edition, Houndmills: Palgrave, 2010). The vivid account by David Andress, *The Terror: Civil War in the French Revolution* (London: Little, Brown, 2005) reasserts the importance of war and counter-revolution in explaining how the Terror came about. On revolutionary violence, see Paul R. Hanson, *Contesting the French Revolution* (Oxford: Wiley-Blackwell, 2009), 159–85.

[18] Works that address terror in the provinces include Richard Cobb, *Paris and its Provinces, 1792–1802* (Oxford: Oxford University Press, 1975), and some of his collected essays in Cobb, *The French and Their Revolution* (London: John Murray, 1988); Colin Lucas, *The Structure of the Terror: the Example of Javogues and the Loire* (Oxford: Oxford University Press, 1973); William Edmonds, *Jacobinism and the Revolt of Lyon, 1789–1793* (Oxford: Clarendon Press, 1990); and D.M.G. Sutherland, *Murder in Aubagne: Lynching, Law and Justice During the French Revolution, 1789–1801* (Cambridge: Cambridge University Press, 2009). On the experience of the revolution at a local level, see Peter McPhee, *Living the French Revolution, 1789–99* (Houndmills: Palgrave, 2006).

[19] Dan Edelstein, *The Terror of Natural Right: Republicanism, the Cult of Nature, and the French Revolution* (Chicago: University of Chicago Press, 2009), 57–62. Edelstein's work can be read in conjunction with the comments by Annie Jourdan and his response to them, both at *http://www.laviedesidees.fr/Le-mystere-de-la-Terreur.html*.

attention to the impact of the war on revolutionary politics.[20] By contrast, without taking the old view that war made the use of terror morally legitimate, much recent historiography on the Terror, particularly in France, nevertheless emphasizes the need to analyse the close relationship between revolutionary politics and the war. Studies by Jean-Clément Martin, Antoine de Baecque, and Michel Biard, among others, have stressed the complex dynamics of the Terror, the ways it has been mythologized, and the diversity of regional experiences.[21] Annie Jourdan explores how far 'the discourse of terror' was a wartime rhetoric to intimidate the enemy, and contrasted with the actual business of government which was founded on a code of justice, albeit a harsh justice.[22] Guillaume Mazeau claims that 'la politique de salut public' (the politics of public safety) were intimately connected to the politics of war. He argues that the revolutionary leaders were establishing a civil republic by using terror to suppress rampant militarism and the rule of generals.[23]

All this tells us that the meaning of the Terror is still very open to changing perspectives, as each generation looks at these events through the prism of the preoccupations and concerns of its own time. For our own generation the need to understand the mentality and motivation behind terrorism has become more acute than ever. The Jacobins were the first political leaders to adopt terror as an official policy. What drove them to do so? The Terror had two aims: winning the war, and imposing conformity to revolutionary ideology. The former aim was the most important, and also by far the more successful. In part at least, terror was a way of trying to force people to do things for the new republic that they did not want to do. It was precisely because the Jacobins found they could not impose their will in any other way that they resorted to force. The Terror arose in part from a position of weakness and the lack of authority with which the Jacobins were widely regarded. This book takes the view that terror was not inevitable in 1789; nor was terror an inherent aspect of Jacobin ideology. It was contingent, and derived from circumstances, above all war, and civil war, and counter-revolution. This in itself is not an original viewpoint: other historians have reached similar conclusions. But by investigating how the business of politics worked, and the relationship between public and private political dimensions we can go further, and reconstruct the part played by individual agency and choice in the shaping of terror. In the end, each

---

[20] In his recent analysis of the Convention's decree in October 1793 'on the necessity to declare the government revolutionary until the peace', Edelstein omits any discussion of the war or its impact: Dan Edelstein, 'Do we want a Revolution without revolution? Reflections on political authority', *French Historical Studies*, 35, 2 (2012): 269–89.

[21] See in particular Jean-Clément Martin, *Violence et révolution: essais sur la naissance d'un mythe national* (Paris: Sueil, 2006); Antoine de Baecque, *Glory and Terror: Seven Deaths under the French Revolution*, trans. Charlotte Mandell (London: Routledge, 2001); also Timothy Tackett, 'La Révolution et la violence', in Jean-Clément Martin (ed.), *La Révolution à l'oeuvre: perspectives actuelles dans l'histoire de la Révolution française* (Rennes: Presses Universitaires de Rennes, 2005); and the collected essays in Michel Biard (ed.), *Les Politiques de la Terreur, 1793–1794* (Rennes: Presses Universitaires de Rennes, and the Société des études Robespierristes, 2008), especially the essay by Haim Burstin, 'Entre théorie et pratique de la Terreur: un essai de balisage'.

[22] Jourdan, 'Les discours de la Terreur'.

[23] Guillaume Mazeau, 'La "Terreur". Laboratoire de la modernité', in Jean-Luc Chappey *et al.* (eds), *Pour quoi faire la Révolution* (Marseilles: Agone, 2012), 83–114, esp. 85–9, 94–6.

revolutionary leader had to make the choice of whether to support the use of terror.

If the Terror itself provokes dissenting views, the terrorists themselves have aroused still greater contention. Using violence to assert one's will over others was hardly an unusual phenomenon, either in the late eighteenth century or since. The phrase 'reign of terror' dates back to antiquity. What made the French Revolutionaries' deployment of terror so different was that they were the first political group to enlist it as an official and legalized policy to sustain a republic, the professed ideology of which was humanitarian and liberal.[24] The terms 'terrorism' and 'terrorist' were invented shortly after the Terror, in late 1794 (ironically by men who were anxious to exculpate themselves from their own part in it), to describe this new form of politics. Many commentators have sought to understand the clash between the Jacobins' idealistic political vision and their coercive methods. As long ago as 1930 Crane Brinton explored the quasi-religious elements of Jacobinism, noting that, although Jacobins had rejected organized religion, they pursued the aim of founding a republic based on civic virtue, almost as a matter of faith.[25] It was a theme to which subsequent historians would return. One of these is Patrice Higonnet's *Goodness beyond Virtue*: rather than being a study of the Terror, or of the politics of the Jacobin leadership, this is an original attempt to rehabilitate the importance of the Jacobins' commitment to positive social values. It conducts a wide-ranging examination of Jacobinism in the multitude of clubs that sprang up throughout France, bringing to light much new material on the experience of the revolution at a local, grass-roots level.[26]

## THE POLITICIANS' TERROR

There was more than one form of terror in the French Revolution; each was directed against different groups of people. There was the violence of the crowd, which took the form of episodic—but spectacular—outbursts of popular vengeance; it occurred on the streets, where people were lynched from lampposts, or in the prisons (principally in September 1792) that crowds entered to massacre suspects after a minimal show of 'legal process'. Then there was the terror carried out under laws passed by the National Convention, directed by the revolutionary government of the Year Two. The great majority of people who were executed under this legalized, so-called 'Jacobin terror' had been engaged in open rebellion against

[24] See Arno Mayer, *The Furies: Violence and Terror in the French and Russian Revolutions* (Princeton, NJ: Princeton University Press, 2000); and the commentary by Timothy Tackett, 'Interpreting the Terror', *French Historical Studies*, 24, 4 (2001): 569–78.

[25] Crane Brinton, *The Jacobins: an Essay in the New History* (1930: this edition, New York: Russell and Russell, 1961). For a rethinking of Jacobin ideology, see Julien Boudon, *Les Jacobins: une traduction des principes de Jean-Jacques Rousseau* (Paris: Librairie Générale de Droit et de Jurisprudence, 2006), Introduction, 1–25.

[26] Patrice Higonnet, *Goodness beyond Virtue: Jacobins during the French Revolution* (Cambridge, MA: Harvard University Press, 1998); see also Jean-Pierre Gross, *Fair Shares for All: Jacobin Egalitarianism in Practice* (Cambridge: Cambridge University Press, 1997).

the Republic. Many perished under the provisions of the law of 19 March 1793, which stated that people who had engaged in armed revolt, and been captured with 'arms in their hands', should be killed within twenty-four hours. They were open enemies of the republican government. Their fate was harsh, but not out of line with the usual practice of the eighteenth century, especially in time of war.[27] Then there was terror in the Vendée: it was here, in the midst of a full-scale civil war, that the great majority of the people who died as a direct consequence of the revolution met their fate. Some perished under the law of 19 March; some were killed in the fighting; some were massacred without any form of legal process. There were atrocities and reprisals on both sides. The situation in the Vendée was grim indeed, but needs to be understood in terms of the escalating violence of the civil war, and so demands a separate treatment.[28]

In this book I do not deal directly with these forms of terror, though much of what I say here relates to wider concerns about the Terror. Rather I engage with one particular form of terror, the importance of which has been much underestimated: this was the politicians' terror. The politicians' terror was directed by Jacobin politicians against other politicians, most of whom were themselves Jacobins or former Jacobins.[29] It culminated in the extermination of a succession of factions: the Girondins, the Hébertists, the Dantonists, and the Robespierrists. Most of the people caught up in this terror, either as perpetrators or as victims (in many cases both) either were, or had previously been, members of the Parisian Jacobin Club. The numbers involved were small; but this terror was at the heart of the revolutionary project. In Paris itself, the central *locus* of the Revolution, much of the terror was directed at public officials, including the politicians. Ironically, they had more cause to fear the Terror than most of the Parisian population. It was a terror that turned inwards: its principal victims were the leaders of the Revolution themselves. Few of those victims had 'arms in their hands' when they were arrested. In many cases their 'crime' against the Revolution was much more ambiguous: it turned on their true identities. For the most part they were accused of having engaged in a secret conspiracy against the Revolution. Their identity, and the authenticity of their claims to be 'men of virtue' devoted to the public good, were subjected to intense scrutiny. Some of this terror was conducted in a cynical way—as a way of removing political enemies. But there was much more to it than that. It pointed to

---

[27] Donald Greer, *The Incidence of the Terror during the French Revolution: A Statistical Interpretation* (Cambridge, MA: Harvard University Press, 1935), 153.

[28] There are many studies of the Vendée. A good place to begin is with Martin, *Violence et Révolution*, ch. 3.

[29] Though the Jacobin leaders of the Year Two were at the apex of the 'politicians' terror', these ideas were not confined to the Jacobins, nor were they evidence of an exclusively 'Jacobin' mentality. The work of Mette Harder demonstrates that the purging of deputies continued well after the overthrow of Robespierre and adds considerably to our understanding of the scale and significance of the Convention's sacrifice of its own members. See Mette Harder, 'A "deputy's honour"—the impact of arrest and imprisonment on French Revolutionary legislators, 1789–1799', unpublished paper given at the Consortium on the Revolutionary Era conference, Baton Rouge, February 2012; and Mette Harder, 'Crisis of representation: the National Convention and the search for political legitimacy, 1792–1795' (PhD thesis, University of York, July 2010).

an inner anxiety about other people's motives; the difficulty of reading what was really in someone else's heart. It is therefore a subject that reveals a whole area of the emotional, as well as the ideological, history of the Terror.

In some ways the politicians' terror is a separate subject to that of the wider terror in the French Revolution. It was a particularly ruthless form of terror, one in which justice, legitimate defence, and hard evidence were allowed little part. It was also a horribly intimate terror. It was carried out for the most part within a relatively small group of people who knew one another well; many of them were former friends. It was in these factional trials that the Jacobin leaders played a direct role, intervening in the legal process. In taking part they were actively choosing to use terror. They were the accusers; they were witnesses to the conduct of the accused; they wrote the narrative of virtue and conspiracy. Ironically, the accused shared the same view of revolutionary politics, one based on the idea of the guilt or innocence of revolutionary leaders.

The politics of virtue and the politicians' terror affected the Terror as a whole in two significant ways. Firstly, a key instrument of terror was denunciation. It was seen as a civic duty, which could only be legitimated by the virtue of the denouncer.[30] In this respect ordinary citizens who denounced people they knew were expected to be motivated by the same devotion to the public good that was demanded of revolutionary politicians, not by personal grudges. Secondly, by being prepared to submit to the politicians' terror, by being prepared to denounce their own former friends, and ultimately by being prepared to die themselves for the cause of the revolution, the leaders of the Revolution were also legitimating their use of terror. They were ready to destroy their friends, and even sacrifice themselves for love of the *patrie*: therefore they believed they had the right to destroy other people, too.

To unravel the politicians' terror, we have to look closely at the politics and intellectual formation of the Jacobin leaders. Surprisingly—though long a classic subject with historians—the Jacobin leaders during the Terror (as opposed to the rank and file) have been somewhat neglected by historians in recent years. Many of the best biographies of individual political leaders were written many decades ago using traditional methodology.[31] There is much that remains to be explained

---

[30] See Colin Lucas, 'The theory and practice of denunciation in the French Revolution', *Journal of Modern History*, 68, 4 (1996): 768–85; and Timothy Tackett, 'Denunciatory practices in Bordeaux, 1791–92', unpublished paper, French Historical Studies Conference, Los Angeles, 2012.

[31] The most comprehensive biography of Robespierre remains J.M. Thompson, *Robespierre* (1935: republished, Oxford: Basil Blackwell, 1988). In French, see Gérard Walter, *Maximilien de Robespierre* (1961: this edition, Paris: Gallimard, 1989). To these should now be added the excellent study by Peter McPhee, *Robespierre—a Revolutionary Life* (New Haven, CT: Yale University Press, 2012). For a more hostile view, see Ruth Scurr, *Fatal Purity: Robespierre and the French Revolution* (London: Chatto and Windus, 2006). Norman Hampson, *The Life and Opinions of Maximilien Robespierre* (London: Duckworth, 1974) is a powerful, fair-minded study. For Danton, there is Norman Hampson, *Danton* (London: Duckworth, 1978). On Saint-Just, see Bernard Vinot, *Saint-Just* (Paris: Fayard, 1985); whilst in English the most recent biography is Norman Hampson, *Saint-Just* (Oxford: Blackwell, 1991); and Eugene Newton Curtis, *Saint-Just, Colleague of Robespierre* (New York: Columbia University Press, 1935) still has much of value. Many lesser known revolutionaries have fared less well of late in the biography stakes. There has been no biography of Brissot that covers his revolutionary career in depth

about the collective political strategies of the revolutionaries of 1792–4 and how they worked together. The methods used in Timothy Tackett's exemplary prosopographical study of the deputies of the Constituent Assembly have yet to be replicated for the deputies of the National Convention, though Alison Patrick's meticulous study uncovered a great deal of information on their voting habits and political alignments in debates.[32] As for the men who actually dominated government during the Jacobin Republic, there has been no attempt to improve upon the classic study from 1941 of the Committee of Public Safety by Robert Palmer, *Twelve Who Ruled*.[33] These political studies are of the greatest importance in establishing what went on in the period of the Terror; however, they focus mostly on external dimensions of politics—voting tactics, public speeches, revolutionary decrees. These are important things to know; yet there is a whole dimension of revolutionary life below this level—the personal and the emotional and informal—which needs to be grasped in order to understand how revolutionaries approached the business of politics, how they operated, and how they understood themselves and other revolutionaries. In order to write a multi-faceted history it is necessary to combine these elements, the official and the unofficial, the public and the private.

## THE POLITICAL LANGUAGE OF JACOBINISM

One very important effect of the renewed interest in ideology and politics, unleashed in part by the move away from Marxist revolutionary paradigms, has been the appearance of a considerable body of work on revolutionary language. Thanks to the work of Keith Baker and others we now have a much better idea about how revolutionary language functioned as a political discourse.[34] Specific words that

since Ellery's biography in 1915: Eloise Ellery, *Brissot de Warville: A Study in the History of the French Revolution* (1915: republished, New York: AMS Press, 1970). 1915 was also the date of the last full-length biography in English of Barnave: Eliza Dorothy Bradby, *The Life of Barnave*, 2 vols (Oxford: Clarendon Press, 1915). Other biographical works will be considered when discussing their subjects. Much information on individual deputies can be found under their respective entries in Edna Hindie Lemay (ed.), *Dictionnaire des Constituants, 1789–1791*, 2 vols (Oxford: Voltaire Foundation, 1991); Edna Hindie Lemay (ed.), *Dictionnaire des Législateurs, 1791–1792*, 2 vols (Ferney-Voltaire: Centre International d'Étude du XVIIIe Siècle, 2007); A. Kuscinski, *Dictionnaire des Conventionnels* (Yvelines: Éditions du Vexin Français, 1973); and Soboul, *Dictionnaire historique de la Révolution française*.

[32] Timothy Tackett, *Becoming a Revolutionary: the Deputies of the French National Assembly and the Emergence of a Revolutionary Culture (1789–1790)* (Princeton, NJ: Princeton University Press, 1996); and Alison Patrick, *The Men of the First French Republic* (Baltimore, MD: Johns Hopkins University Press, 1972).

[33] R.R. Palmer, *Twelve Who Ruled: the Year of the Terror in the French Revolution* (Princeton, NJ: Princeton University Press, 1941). Surprisingly, in France itself there is no sustained account of the collective history of the members of the Committee of Public Safety. There is a brief study by Jacques Castelnau, *Le Comité de Salut public, 1793–1794* (Paris: Hachette, 1941). Leigh Whaley, *Radicals, Politics and Republicanism in the French Revolution* (Stroud: Sutton Publishing, 2000) contains some invaluable work on collective biography, but ends with the overthrow of the Girondins in June 1793.

[34] Studies of revolutionary language include Keith Michael Baker, 'Political languages of the French Revolution', in Mark Goldie and Robert Wokler (eds), *The Cambridge History of Eighteenth-Century*

played an important role in revolutionary language have been investigated, including 'nation', 'citizen', '*patrie*', 'republicanism', and 'virtue'.[35] This research has transformed how we understand the nature of revolutionary politics. Above all, it has demonstrated the fundamental relationship between language and power.

My own work owes a great debt to this approach. But historians of discourse have not been without their critics. Furet and Baker in particular have been challenged for treating the political language of the revolutionaries without sufficient regard for the social and political context.[36] In this book I have investigated the relationship between revolutionary ideas and the actual practice of politics. I have tried to retain a sense of how people *chose* to use language. This involves investigating how individual Jacobins manipulated political rhetoric as part of a deliberate strategy. Revolutionary politicians did not necessarily keep to the same political language. Discourses were closely related to the changing political context—and the political context of the Revolution changed immensely over the five years from 1789 to 1794, sometimes almost from week to week. Revolutionary language was highly polemical, taking its form from specific debates and struggles that were taking place at the time. The idea of a 'discourse' suggests, perhaps misleadingly, a political theorist, developing his ideas schematically, and only in relation to the discourses of other thinkers and writers. But revolutionary language emerged from interactive situations—in the assemblies and the clubs. Emotions ran high, and political language, even in the prepared speeches, was often coloured by dramatic events, and more visceral sentiments—not least of which was the excitement of the moment, or fear of political enemies, and the reactions of spectators. Often, too,

---

*Political Thought* (Cambridge: Cambridge University Press, 2006); John Renwick (ed.), *Language and Rhetoric of the Revolution* (Edinburgh: Edinburgh University Press, 1990); Jon Cowans, *To Speak for the People: Public Opinion and the Problem of Legitimacy in the French Revolution* (London: Routledge, 2001); Lucien Jaume, *Le Discours Jacobin et la démocratie* (Paris: Fayard, 1989); and Noel Parker, *Portrayals of Revolution: Images, Debates and Patterns of Thought on the French Revolution* (Hemel Hempstead: Harvester Wheatsheaf, 1990), ch. 1, 'Political Language: Speaking for the Revolution'. Jacques Guilhaumou has made a prolific contribution to this subject, including Guilhaumou, *La Langue politique de la Révolution française: de l'événement à la raison linguistique* (Paris: Méridiens Klinckieck, 1989).

[35] On 'nation' see David A. Bell, *The Cult of the Nation in France: Inventing Nationalism, 1680–1800* (Cambridge, MA: Harvard University Press, 2001). On '*patrie*' see Peter R. Campbell, 'The politics of patriotism in France (1770–1788)', *French History* (2010), 24,4: 550–75; Peter R. Campbell, 'The language of patriotism in France, 1750–1770', *Journal of French Studies, e-France*, 1: 1 (2007) 1–43; and Edmond Dziembowski, 'Un Nouveau patriotisme français, 1750–1770, la France face à la puissance anglaise à l'époque de la guerre de Sept Ans', *Studies on Voltaire and the Eighteenth Century*, 365 (Oxford, 1998). On 'virtue' see Linton, *The Politics of Virtue in Enlightenment France*. On 'republicanism' see Raymonde Monnier, 'Républicanisme et révolution française', *French Historical Studies*, 26, 1 (2003): 87–118, and her full-length study: Raymonde Monnier, *Républicanisme, patriotisme et révolution française* (Paris: L'Harmattan, 2005). On the longevity of republicanism, and its persistence as an important idea in the period after the Terror, see Andrew Jainchill, *Reimagining Politics After the Terror: the Republican Origins of French Liberalism* (Ithaca, NY: Cornell University Press, 2008).

[36] Several historians have offered critiques of 'revisionist' historians' reification of words at the expense of social context. Amongst these, see Jay M. Smith, 'No more language games: words, beliefs, and the political culture of early modern France', *American Historical Review*, 102 (December 1997): 1413–40; and Harvey Chisick, 'Public opinion and political culture in France during the second half of the eighteenth century', *English Historical Review*, 117, issue 470 (February 2002): 48–77.

what revolutionaries said in more private situations was very different to the way they spoke in their public discourse, so that we need to compare public and private political languages and seek to reconstitute the complex and multilayered manipulation of revolutionary language. Rather than being simple 'mouthpieces of revolutionary discourse' (to use Furet's phrase), Jacobins switched between styles of rhetorical speaking, and modes of discourse, according to the context, and according to their audiences.[37] They selected their political vocabulary from a series of words and phrases that were current: they had a very wide and complex repertoire of language from which to choose. They used that language strategically and with a great deal of conscious intent, as part of the construction of a political identity.[38] This language had to be carefully negotiated: there was a gap between what the new political conventions permitted them to say, and what they actually wanted to achieve. Thus, ambition was seen as very negative in revolutionary political discourse. In order to be worthy of political office one had to appear not to want it. From the revolutionary leaders' actions and their choices we can infer that many *were* ambitious. What we never see is a revolutionary leader *admitting* to being ambitious, or motivated by the desire for his own glory. In this respect, a political career during the Revolution was very different from what it became under the rule of Napoleon, when the whole tenor of public life was much more conducive to frank avowals of personal ambition and the pursuit of glory.[39]

## BEHIND THE PUBLIC FACE

One way to uncover the more personal dimension of revolutionary leaders' lives is to pay attention to their private thoughts, mindsets, and assumptions. There are several difficulties with this, however, to do with the sources available and how we interpret them. In the period in which the revolutionaries were politically active, most of their writings were polemical, intended to convince a wider audience. For many of these men, once they devoted themselves to politics there was little time or energy to spare for any kind of personal life. To compound the problem, during the Terror it becomes exceedingly difficult to trace someone's genuine opinion as it would be incriminating and dangerous to contradict the revolutionary 'line'; most documents intended for public consumption put forward an agreed position, and used very similar language. Some revolutionary leaders later wrote their memoirs. These can be invaluable, but they were, of course, composed with hindsight. Their memoirs are self-justificatory, and not always reliable, designed to show both the integrity of their younger selves, and the perfidy of men who became their enemies.

---

[37] François Furet, *Interpreting the French Revolution*, trans. Elborg Forster (1978: this edition, Cambridge: Cambridge University Press, 1981), 60–1.

[38] On Robespierre's deployment of different rhetorical registers in the Assemblies and the Jacobin Club, see Annie Jourdan, 'Les discours de Robespierre. La parole au pouvoir', in Annie Jourdan (ed.), *Robespierre—Figure-Réputation* (Yearbook of European Studies, 9: Amsterdam, 1996).

[39] Robert Morrissey, *Napoléon et l'héritage de la gloire* (Paris: Presses Universitaires de France, 2010).

Often those same enemies did not survive long enough to write their own memoirs, so this kind of evidence can be very one-sided.

Some personal documents do remain, including letters to family or friends, private notes, and memoirs. Such documents are not transparently open: they are not an automatic window into an inner world of consciousness. All documents are written for an audience, and are fashioned with that audience in mind, whether it is for a large group of readers (as in memoirs or constituency letters); or for a single recipient (as in letters to individuals). Even private notes are still directed at an audience—the writers themselves. Such sources still represent the writers as they would wish to see themselves, and according to an image they have chosen to present. With these sources we still cannot get at the unconscious, which is why psychohistories written from such limited sources can be problematic. What we can do, however, is gain some understanding of how revolutionaries constructed their identities as political activists. By recovering how they chose to see themselves, we can unpick the assumptions behind these identities.[40] More than that, however, becomes very difficult to uncover. The question whether the inner thoughts of revolutionary leaders constitute viable territory for the historian, and if so, what kind of methods should be used, is an intensely problematic one.

## PSYCHOLOGY AND THE EMOTIONS IN REVOLUTIONARY POLITICS

Some of the greatest nineteenth-century narrative historians of the Revolution considered the private emotions of their subjects as a legitimate part of the historian's concern. Lamartine, Carlyle, and above all, Michelet recounted the history of the Revolution in a series of stories, in which the revolutionaries were depicted as rounded individuals, with private lives as well as public faces, whose lives, hearts, and minds were as relevant as their formalized ideas. Such historians depicted the personal views of the revolutionaries at the many crisis points of their lives in a poetic and dramatic form, but one which of necessity was all too often based on supposition and inference. They tended, too, to delve into the minutiae of that private dimension as a subject in itself—at the level of anecdote—with the intention of revealing the 'private lives' of 'great men' of the Revolution. In many instances they were somewhat free with the existing evidence, as it was available in documents. Such methods fell into disfavour with political historians of the twentieth century, who preferred more positivist and dispassionate approaches, which entailed confining themselves to the public lives of their subjects. For many such historians there was an insurmountable gulf between conscious thought and ideology and undercurrents of emotions, assumptions, and personal ties. To stick to only the public representations of political figures is more straightforward, and

---

[40] See the classic argument by Quentin Skinner, 'The principles and practice of Opposition: the case of Bolingbroke versus Walpole', in Neil McKendrick (ed.), *Historical Perspectives: Studies in English Thought and Society in Honour of J.H. Plumb* (London: Europa Publications, 1974).

offers fewer problems of interpretation, but the consequence is that we abandon any attempt to recover fundamental parts of their lives that had a significant impact on their political choices.

Until recently there have been very few analytical attempts to unravel the emotional aspects of revolutionary mentalities, though one notable exception is the classic work by Pierre Trahard, *La Sensibilité révolutionnaire*.[41] But of late there has been a new interest in psychological histories of the French Revolution. Indeed, the lack of such histories has become increasingly apparent. There have been relatively few attempts to deal with revolutionary psychology: this is partly because sufficient sources are lacking, particularly on the childhood and formative years of most of the figures in the Revolution, and partly because of the difficulties in formulating a method of analysing such material that is sufficiently sensitive to the historical context.[42] One notable exception to this is the work by Barry Shapiro on psychological trauma and its effects on the deputies' political decisions during the Constituent Assembly.[43] This in itself is part of the growing interest in the history of the Revolution as it involved individual experience and a changing sense of self.[44]

Other recent works have begun to open up the emotional history of the revolutionaries in different and very interesting directions.[45] One is Marie-Hélène Huet's *Mourning Glory*, an intriguing study which takes up Michelet's intellectual legacy and considers how revolutionaries articulated thoughts on death and memory.[46]

---

[41] Pierre Trahard, *La Sensibilité révolutionnaire (1789–1794)* (Paris: Boivin, 1936).

[42] The original study by Lynn Hunt, *The Family Romance of the French Revolution* (London: Routledge, 1992), examines a 'collective political unconscious'. One work to take a psychohistorical approach was Max Gallo, *Robespierre the Incorruptible: A Psycho-Biography* (New York: Herder and Herder, 1971). For a discussion of the possibilities and limits of psychohistory where Robespierre is concerned, see Peter McPhee, 'The making of Maximilien: Robespierre's childhood, 1758–69', *French History and Civilisation: Papers from the George Rudé Seminar, 2008*, 3 (2009): 26–32.

[43] Barry M. Shapiro, 'Conspiratorial thinking in the Constituent Assembly: Mirabeau and the exclusion of deputies from the ministry', in Peter R. Campbell, Thomas E. Kaiser, and Marisa Linton (eds), *Conspiracy in the French Revolution* (Manchester: Manchester University Press, 2007); together with Barry M. Shapiro, *Traumatic Politics: the Deputies and the King in the Early French Revolution* (University Park: Pennsylvania State University Press, 2009).

[44] For a wide-ranging discussion of the self and experience in French revolutionary historiography, see Lynn Hunt, 'The experience of revolution', *French Historical Studies*, 32,4 (Fall, 2009): 671–8. On changes in the idea of the self after the revolution, and the importance of imagination in this construction, see Jan Goldstein, *The Post-Revolutionary Self: Politics and Psyche in France, 1750–1850* (Cambridge, MA: Harvard University Press, 2008). On the category of experience there is Joan W. Scott, 'The evidence of experience', *Critical Inquiry*, 17 (1991): 773–97. For a contrasting view, one that emphasizes individual agency and consciousness, see Jay M. Smith, 'Between *discourse* and *experience*: agency and ideas in the French pre-Revolution', *History and Theory*, 40 (2001): 116–42.

[45] New work on emotions in the French Revolution is discussed in Sophia Rosenfeld, 'Thinking about feeling, 1789–1799', *French Historical Studies*, 32,4 (Fall, 2009): 697–706. The connections between revolutionary melodrama and sensibility in the political career of Robespierre are addressed in David Andress, 'Living the Revolutionary melodrama: Robespierre's sensibility and the construction of political commitment in the French Revolution', *Representations*, 114, 1 (Spring, 2011): 103–28.

[46] Marie-Hélène Huet, *Mourning Glory: the Will of the French Revolution* (Philadelphia: University of Pennsylvania Press, 1997).

Another thought-provoking study is William Reddy's *The Navigation of Feeling*, which depicts the Jacobins as motivated by their adoption of the eighteenth-century cult of 'sentimentalism'. Reddy argues that emotions (or rather, what he terms 'the misunderstanding of emotions') played a very specific and directional role in revolutionary politics, one that paved the way for the Terror. The Jacobin regime is shown as one in which emotions were used to control people—one must feel the right emotions, and these must be sincerely felt, or one might be subject to the guillotine—an impossible and highly tense situation. Though Reddy's emphasis on emotion is illuminating, his exclusive focus on one emotion, 'sentimentalism', which is examined without much attention to the political context, limits the applicability of his theory. Revealingly, Reddy's chapter on the Jacobin regime's repression of sentimental emotions uses evidence taken almost entirely from revolutionary leaders themselves, including Saint-Just and Madame Roland, lending support to my argument that the revolutionary leaders were themselves the group most subject to fear.[47]

There were other emotions that arguably played an even more cogent role in the Terror. Sophie Wahnich's *La Liberté ou la mort* also explores emotions and the Jacobins. In her case the emotion she focuses on is fear (*effroi*). She argues that the official state terror of the Jacobins was an attempt to control and reduce the anarchic terror waged by the *sans-culottes*, which itself was caused by the fear they felt, a fear transposed into popular violence and demands for vengeance; thus, paradoxically, the official terror decreased fear.[48] Wahnich's arguments have also produced some controversy—in this case for seeming to offer a justification of the Terror, however qualified. But without getting into the quagmire of the rights and wrongs of the Terror (and to explain is not to justify), Wahnich is surely right to stress the importance of fear as a motivating factor.[49] It is all-pervading. The documents are saturated with it. There is no understanding the contradictions, the suspicions, the betrayals that made up much of revolutionary politics without it. The war on all fronts, repeated revolts, the treachery of Dumouriez and other betrayals by military and political leaders, and the civil war in the Vendée, all provoked an atmosphere of mingled panic and fervent patriotism. Even a brief examination of the records of debates in the Convention shows that the speeches of political leaders supporting the Terror, denouncing conspiracies, and so forth, were interspersed with innumerable patriotic deputations, reports, and despatches on events at the front, in the Vendée, in Lyon, in Toulon. It was against this tense backdrop that the major political decisions of the Year Two were taken.

The fears felt by the Jacobin leaders were not just directed outwards towards foreign invaders, French *émigrés*, and avowed counter-revolutionaries. One of the themes that will be explored in this book is how by 1793 their fears also turned

---

[47] See William Reddy, *The Navigation of Feeling: A Framework for the History of the Emotions* (Cambridge: Cambridge University Press, 2001), esp. 146–7.

[48] Sophie Wahnich, *La Liberté ou la mort: essai sur la Terreur et le terrorisme* (Paris: La Fabrique Éditions, 2003), 27–37.

[49] On the role of fear in the dialectics of violence see Tackett, 'Interpreting the Terror', 574–5.

inwards, in mutual mistrust and denunciation. They feared one another—the enemy within—even more than they feared their acknowledged enemies. Some of the most dramatic and ironic moments of the Terror were the trials of revolutionary groups or factions accused of conspiracy against the very revolution that they had struggled so hard to promote.[50] As the Girondin Vergniaud had anticipated, '...the Revolution, like Saturn, would devour its own children'.[51] Often in these factional trials, accused and accusers were personally known to one another. For several years they had participated in the same cause, risked their lives on its behalf, spoken from the same platforms, and worked together as colleagues, sometimes amicably so. But by the Year Two this sense of a common purpose was fast collapsing. We gain from contemporary accounts an insight into the atmosphere amongst the Jacobins at this point. They were stressed, traumatized, exhausted from four years of revolutionary fervour, incessant work, and strain, distrustful not only of counter-revolutionaries but also of each other. Gaining power did not ease the tensions at the Jacobin Club: it meant only that some of their number were now responsible for implementing the terrorist legislation they had voted to bring about. These were men who eyed each other warily in the political forums of the Year Two, at the Convention, in the sections, at the Commune, in the Jacobin Club, and in the Committees.

Contradictions in the Jacobin notion of friendship played a critical part in the relationship between the public and private dimensions of revolutionary politics. Friendship occupied a complex position within Jacobin ideology.[52] Friendship networks, personal loyalties, and unofficial factions played a role in shaping political choices and allegiances; but the role of these friendship and personal loyalties became increasingly ambiguous. Friendship was a means of social advancement. It was a way of making connections that could give access to administrative and governmental posts. But in the revolutionary context friendships could become suspect and thus dangerous. Revolutionary politics were, therefore, dogged by problems of trust, intimacy, and confidence in others.

## AUTHENTIC IDENTITY: THE 'MAN OF VIRTUE'

At the heart of this book is the problem of authenticity. This is a step beyond saying that it is about the problem of the ideology of virtue. Almost without exception the Jacobin leaders, indeed, most of the people who were actively involved in revolutionary politics between 1789 and 1794, said that they were doing this

---

[50] On the Jacobins' fear of conspiracy see Marisa Linton, '"Do you believe that we're conspirators?" Conspiracies real and imagined in Jacobin politics, 1793–94', in Campbell, Kaiser and Linton, *Conspiracy in the French Revolution*.

[51] Pierre-Victorin Vergniaud, Speech to the Convention, 13 March 1793, *Archives Parlementaires de 1787 à 1860*, ed. M.J. Madival *et al.*, 127 vols (Paris: Librairie administrative de P. Dupont, 1862–1972), 60: 162.

[52] See Marisa Linton, 'Fatal friendships: the politics of Jacobin friendship', *French Historical Studies*, 31, 1 (2008): 51–76.

because they were 'men of virtue'. This identity and language was by no means exclusive to Robespierre. People might, however, have different reasons for saying this. They could be saying that they were motivated by virtue because it was to their advantage to do so. During the Terror they might be saying it because they were afraid. The Revolution was a process of political education, from enthusiasm to cynicism. There was a growing consciousness that, in themselves, the words of participants in revolutionary politics were relatively meaningless if not backed up by actions, and genuine emotions. This became a central anxiety for revolutionary leaders: hence the emphasis on authenticity and on demonstrating one's virtue through actions. Revolutionary leaders might seek to prove the authenticity of their identity by the way in which they lived their private and public lives; and by remaining relatively poor. Ultimately, however, the only way to prove beyond doubt the authenticity of one's identity was to be ready to die for the cause of the Revolution.

In this book I have tried to put the individual experience of revolution at the forefront. This makes for a more complex book, because the Jacobin leaders were complex human beings. They believed in virtue; they believed in patriotism; they also wanted to make a success of their careers in the new world of revolutionary politics; they were subject to personal loyalties, suspicions, enthusiasms, and dislikes. In short, they were people, as complex as all people are, as we are ourselves; pulled in different directions by myriad conflicting ideas, motives, circumstances, and intense emotions. They resist being reduced to a nice tidy theory. They are three-dimensional: viewed from varying angles, they take on very different identities. I have tried to capture something of that solidity. In asking questions about the authentic identity and motives of the Jacobin leaders one of the difficulties is that we cannot, of course, be certain whether or not we are right in our conjectures. Our subjects are dead, their thoughts gone beyond recall. All we have are the sources. Many of these sources consist of what other people—often their enemies and hostile witnesses—said about someone's motives; and what they said about themselves. This was the very problem that vexed the Jacobins themselves—the impossibility of knowing what anyone, friend or enemy, was really thinking.

We are fumbling in the dark then—but not altogether blindly. In recent years historians have begun to address these old problems in new ways, by applying different kinds of methodology that, whilst accepting the limitations of the evidence, can help us to re-evaluate the sources in terms of the ways in which people spoke, or identified themselves.[53] Thus we can look at the ways in which the Jacobins constructed their narratives of the Revolution. We can ask what stories they told, to make sense of what was happening; how people used particular narratives to forge their own identities within revolutionary politics. We can also infer some things from what the Jacobins actually did, as opposed to what they said. When we juxtapose a politician's words with their actions a very different picture may emerge

---

[53] Work on the emotions, agency, and identity cited above—see notes 42–49—has addressed this kind of area in new and interesting ways.

of what that person's goals were. With regards to the question of individual agency and how we explore it, new work on the experience of revolution can help us to understand how individuals struggled to make sense of the Revolution as a lived experience, to which they strove to give meaning. When revolutionary politics are studied at the level of individual experience it becomes apparent that people were able to negotiate and manipulate revolutionary ideology and official pronouncements in accordance with their own needs and aims.[54] When looked at on this level, the idea of the Terror as a consequence of a monolithic ideology will no longer hold water. Terror is something that individual people chose to do to one another. They might hide behind the argument that they were helpless in the face of an ideological imperative, or the weight of law. Often what decided them was something much more inchoate than an idea, or a law: often, as this book will show, they were motivated by fear, for themselves, for the Revolution. But choosing terror was still something that each individual had to do for him or herself.

The question of political identity has also been addressed by the growing number of pioneering scholars whose use of feminist and gender history methodology has helped us to reevaluate traditional political histories of the Revolution, and transformed our understanding of the relationship between male and female, public and private in revolutionary politics.[55] Their work has helped me in addressing the problem of the participation of women in Jacobin politics. One woman who played a notable role is Madame Roland.[56] Like others in her circle, she began as a stalwart Jacobin, only to see her former comrades become her bitterest enemies. The part played by Jacobin women contradicts the convention of the time that delineated women of their social background as more timid and retiring than men. Nor did they lack courage and determination. In many cases the political choices of their male relatives had a pivotal consequence on their own lives, and on those of their children. But women were also constrained by the expectations and conventions of their day. Jacobin women were obliged to negotiate their own participation in politics through these expectations. By examining their lives we can gain

---

[54] This subject is explored in various ways by the historians in David Andress (ed.), *Experiencing the French Revolution* (Oxford: Studies on Voltaire and the Eighteenth Century, 2013).

[55] Works on gender and on the role of women in the Revolution include Suzanne Desan, *The Family on Trial in Revolutionary France* (Berkeley: University of California Press, 2004); Suzanne Desan, 'The politics of intimacy: marriage and citizenship in the French Revolution', in Sarah Knott and Barbara Taylor (eds), *Women, Gender and Enlightenment* (Houndmills: Palgrave, 2005); Carla Hesse, *The Other Enlightenment: How French Women Became Modern* (Princeton, NJ: Princeton University Press, 2001); and Jennifer Heuer, *The Family and the Nation: Gender and Citizenship in Revolutionary France* (Ithaca, NY: Cornell University Press, 2005). On female *sans-culottes*, see Dominique Godineau, *Citoyennes Tricoteuses: Les femmes du peuple à Paris pendant la Révolution française* (Aix-en-Provence: Alinea, 1988); Dena Goodman (ed.), *Marie-Antoinette: Writings on the Body of a Queen* (London: Routledge, 2003); Marilyn Yalom, *Blood Sisters: the French Revolution in Women's Memory* (London: Pandora, 1995); Olwen H. Hufton, *Women and the Limits of Citizenship in the French Revolution* (Toronto: University of Toronto Press, 1992); Joan Wallach Scott, *Only Paradoxes to Offer: French Feminists and the Rights of Man* (Cambridge, MA: Harvard University Press,1996); and Sara E. Melzer and Leslie W. Rabine, *Rebel Daughters: Women and the French Revolution* (Oxford: Oxford University Press, 1992).

[56] Madame Roland and her husband are the subjects of a major new study by Siân Reynolds, *Marriage and Revolution: Monsieur and Madame Roland* (Oxford: Oxford University Press, 2012).

a very different perspective on the predominantly masculine world of politics and its human consequences.

The study of gender can also help us to address the problem of masculine political identity in revolutionary politics.[57] Here the concept of virtue played a critical part: for the most part, political virtue was closely associated with ideas about masculinity. In certain circumstances, however, feminine virtue, too, could impart to women a place within public life, albeit a limited one. The different meanings accorded to masculine and feminine virtue can tell us much about contemporary understanding of the nature of politics and of political participation.[58] One of the key images to have been explored is that of (masculine) 'heroic' revolutionary identity and the complex elements that went into its construction.[59] By drawing on these methods we can re-evaluate Jacobin ideas about what constituted proper behaviour for a political leader, and what it meant to be a 'man of virtue' in revolutionary politics.

## CHOOSING TERROR

This book engages with a fundamental problem. Why did people who had hitherto led unexceptional, 'normal' lives and shown no sign of a tendency towards violence

---

[57] On links between revolutionary imagery, gender, and concepts of the nation, see Joan B. Landes, *Visualizing the Nation: Gender, Representation, and Revolution in Eighteenth-Century France* (Ithaca, NY: Cornell University Press, 2001); and Madelyn Gutwirth, *The Twilight of the Goddesses: Women and Representation in the French Revolutionary Era* (New Brunswick, NJ: Rutgers University Press, 1992). On masculinity and *patrie*, see Joan B. Landes, 'Republican citizenship and heterosocial desire: concepts of masculinity in Revolutionary France', in Stefan Dudink, Karen Hagemann, and John Tosh (eds), *Masculinities in Politics and War: Gendering Modern History* (Manchester: Manchester University Press, 2004); and Sean M. Quinlan, 'Men without women? Ideal masculinity and male sociability in the French Revolution, 1789–99', in Christopher E. Forth and Bertrand Taithe (eds), *French Masculinities: History, Culture and Politics* (Houndmills: Palgrave, 2007) which argues that the Revolution allowed men the possibility of experimenting with new masculine identities. For a longer-term perspective see Katherine Astbury and Marie-Emmanuelle Plagnol-Diéval (eds), *Le mâle en France, 1715–1830 représentations de la masculinité* (Oxford: Peter Lang, 2004).

[58] Dorinda Outram, 'Le langage mâle de la vertu: women and the discourse of the French Revolution', in Peter Burke and Roy Porter (eds), *The Social History of Language* (Cambridge: Cambridge University Press, 1987); Carol Blum, *Rousseau and the Republic of Virtue* (Ithaca, NY: Cornell University Press, 1986), 204–15. Both Blum and Outram see revolutionary politics as being constructed against, rather than simply without, women, and argue that a gendered concept of virtue was central to that process. For more positive assessments of how discourses of feminine virtue offered a possibility of some empowerment for women, see Lynn Hunt, 'Male virtue and Republican motherhood', in Baker, *The French Revolution and the Creation of Modern Political Culture*, vol. 4, *The Terror*; Marisa Linton, 'Virtue rewarded? Women and the politics of virtue in eighteenth-century France', part I, *History of European Ideas*, 26, 1 (2000): 35–49, and part II, *History of European Ideas*, 26, 1 (2000): 51–65; Tracey Rizzo, *A Certain Emancipation of Women: Gender, Citizenship and the Causes Célèbres of Eighteenth-Century France* (Selinsgrove, PA: Susquehanna University Press, 2004); and Lesley H. Walker, *A Mother's Love: Crafting Feminine Virtue in Enlightenment France* (Lewisburg, PA: Bucknell University Press, 2008).

[59] On Jacobin concepts of masculine heroism, see Miguel Abensour, 'Saint-Just and the problem of heroism', in Ferenc Fehér (ed.), *The French Revolution and the Birth of Modernity* (Berkeley: University of California Press, 1990); Annie Jourdan, 'Robespierre and Revolutionary Heroism', in Colin Haydon and William Doyle (eds), *Robespierre* (Cambridge: Cambridge University Press, 1990).

choose terror? It is an unsettling problem, and not one to which I claim to have any definitive answers. I do think it important, however, that we approach this subject without complacency, and with open minds; nor should we be in a hurry to pass judgement unless we too have lived through the same circumstances in which they lived. The Terror was not inherent in an ideology: not in the Enlightenment, not even in the ideology of political virtue, though in retrospect we can see the risks of that ideology. Terror came about through the choices of individuals in a very specific set of circumstances. A series of small choices led to a changed outlook as, step by step, political leaders set out on a road that led to their acceptance of the deployment of violence against their opponents.[60] Chief in those circumstances were war and actual betrayal by a series of France's political and military leaders. These circumstances gave rise to a swelling tide of fear and suspicion, which in turn made revolutionary leaders readier to take measures that, in normal circumstances, they would have rejected.

Whilst this book focuses on the Jacobin leaders, it is important to bear in mind that terror was a collective choice in the Year Two. The idea of a specifically Robespierrist terror was a myth, invented by the Thermidoreans, the men who overthrew Robespierre, who themselves were very much implicated in the recourse to terror.[61] The pragmatic choice to use terror extended far beyond the Montagnards: to the deputies of the Convention who voted for it, and the many activists beyond the national representation who implemented it.

One of the problems in writing a book that aims to show how the Jacobin leaders 'chose terror' is the question where to begin. I do not take the view that terror had in some sense become inevitable from the early days of the Revolution. On the other hand, to begin at the end—with the Terror itself—would not show the process by which the Jacobins arrived at the point of choosing terror. In my view the path that led to terror was a complex and long-term process, involving contingent events and individual choices in the context of shifting circumstances. The structure of this book tries to reflect that complexity by beginning at a period long before the Terror itself came into place.

The process by which idealistic and humanitarian men made a series of choices that eventually led to their adopting terror was a complicated one, in the course of which they themselves struggled to respond to, and make sense of, a set of unprecedented circumstances that they could not have envisaged. The decision to choose terror was a gradual process, achieved through a series of steps. It came into being through several years of revolutionary and counter-revolutionary struggle, actual betrayals and conspiracies—as well as imagined ones, external war, and internal struggle. There is no one reason why it occurred; rather, it involved the

---

[60] Lucas takes a similar view in his study of the provincial terror, in which he argues that choosing terror was 'the cumulative result of a whole series of successive choices made during the proceeding years of the Revolution': Lucas, *The Structure of the Terror*, 335.

[61] On this point, see Jourdan, 'Les discours de la terreur'; and Mazeau, 'La "Terreur", laboratoire de la modernité', 83.

dynamic interaction of all these factors. In the end, choosing terror was a decision that individual revolutionaries had to come to in their own minds, before putting it into effect. Ironically, the consequences of choosing terror unleashed the events that led to the self-destruction of the Jacobins. This book will trace how that happened.

# 1

# The Eighteenth-Century Man of Virtue

You can hardly pay a man a greater compliment than to censure him for not knowing the ways of the court: that single phrase implies the possession of every sort of virtue.

La Bruyère, *Les Caractères* (1688).[1]

The soul takes fire, the mind raises itself up while speaking about virtue. Even the most perverse sometimes feels its divine transports, and there is no man so wicked who does not feel in his heart some sparks of that celestial fire, and who is not capable of heroic feelings and actions at least once in his life.

Rousseau, 'On Honour and Virtue'.[2]

There were no Jacobins before the French Revolution. It took the experience of the Revolution to bring them into being and breathe its fire into them. Consequently, there was no specific 'Jacobin' ideology before the Revolution. The Jacobins would draw on a whole wealth of existing ideas, based on principles of liberty, equality, and natural rights. Here we shall focus on the derivation of one key set of related ideas that informed the Jacobins' mental landscape: these were ideas about how politics *actually* worked, how it *ought* to work, and the responsibilities of political leaders who took on a public role to the public good. These ideas were not exclusive to future Jacobins: they were part of a common currency of thought in the later years of the eighteenth century. This way of thinking was not inherently 'revolutionary'. Thus, men who were prominent in the hierarchy of the old regime—ministers, military officers, higher clergy—were familiar with these political discourses, and could select them to make arguments that suited their own strategies. With the onset of the Revolution, these discourses would crystallize into a fixed ideology.[3]

---

[1] Jean de La Bruyère, *Characters*, trans. Jean Stewart (London: Penguin, 1970), 129,156.
[2] 'On Honour and Virtue', in *Political Fragments*, Jean-Jacques Rousseau, *The Collected Writings of Rousseau*, Roger D. Masters and Christopher Kelly (eds), 13 vols (Hanover, NH and London: University Press of New England, 1994–2009), 4: 39.
[3] On the relationship between ideologies, discourses, rhetorical strategies, and the intellectual origins of the Revolution, see Marisa Linton, 'The intellectual origins of the French Revolution', in Peter R. Campbell (ed.), *The Origins of the French Revolution* (Houndmills: Palgrave, 2005).

## THE THEORETICAL BASIS OF POLITICS
## IN THE OLD REGIME

The theoretical basis of politics in old regime France was fundamentally different from that of revolutionary politics: there were no politicians in the modern sense of men and women pursuing a career, voted into office, and subject to public opinion. According to the ideology of absolute monarchy, politics was the exclusive affair of the king. The king's right to be the sole arbiter of political policy on behalf of his people derived from divine authority. Sovereignty was located within the 'sacred' body of the king. The king was the only 'public' person in France, that is, the only person who was supposed to have the public good as his guiding principle. All public officials were responsible ultimately to the king. The king's ministers were answerable just to him. To 'get on' a minister had only to think about what would please the king. It was a very enclosed political world.[4] There was no place in this conception of power for a 'nation' to exist as an independent force outside the king's sovereign authority, that is, a 'nation' in the sense of the people as a collective sovereign body as opposed to the people as individuals or as corporate interests. Authority, law, and justice, all emanated from the monarch as the intermediary of God's will. Bossuet's *Politique tirée des propres paroles de l'Ecriture Sainte* (1709) set out the principles of absolute monarchy. Royal authority had four essential characteristics: it was 'sacred', 'paternal', 'absolute', and 'guided by reason'. 'Kings must respect their own authority and only use it for the public good.'[5] A king ought not to rule despotically, but his subjects had no legitimate right to intervene in the political realm.

There were periodic challenges to the absolute authority of the king: the main sources of contention being over the rights of religious minorities (Jansenists and Protestants); and the rights of the *parlements*. Nonetheless, right up to the Revolution Bossuet's argument remained the official line of the monarchy. There was to be no sharing of sovereign authority: the king embodied the moral authority of rule within himself. The king's ministers did not hold authority in their own right: they were subject to the king's will. In practice many minor decisions were delegated to the king's ministers, and the ministers could suggest policy to the king. Nonetheless, they were concerned with pleasing the king, rather than appealing to the public. Their task was to carry out the king's wishes, and if they lost royal favour they would lose their posts.[6]

---

[4] For an excellent analysis of how old regime politics worked and the relationship between the king, patronage, and political power, see Peter R. Campbell, *Power and Politics in Old Régime France, 1720–1745* (London: Routledge, 1996). See also James B. Collins, *The State in Early Modern Europe* (second edition, Cambridge: Cambridge University Press, 2009); and the case studies by Joël Félix, *Finances et politiques au siècle des lumières: le ministre l'Averdy, 1763–1768* (Paris: Imprimerie nationale, 1999); and Sara E. Chapman, *Private Ambition and Political Alliances: The Phélypeaux de Pontchartrain Family and Louis XIV's Government, 1650–1715* (Rochester, NY: University of Rochester Press, 2004).

[5] J-B. Bossuet, *Politique tirée des propres paroles de l'Ecriture sainte* (1709; this edition, Geneva: Librairie Droz, 1967), Book III, Article I, 64; 70–1.

[6] Julian Swann, 'Disgrace without dishonour: the political exile of French magistrates in the eighteenth century', 195, *Past and Present* (May 2007): 87–196.

## THE PRACTICE OF POLITICS IN THE OLD REGIME: REALITIES AND IMAGES

The actual practice of politics in the old regime contrasted sharply with the theory. Whilst the king was the ultimate ideological source of all political authority there were many people who exercised actual power—a power based upon hierarchy, noble status, wealth, and privilege.[7] The vast majority of the higher public offices were held by the nobility. There was a long tradition that maintained that noble office holders were devoted to the good of the state through their obligations of service: by serving the king, and carrying out the functions of their office, they were also benefiting France. According to this interpretation the nobility played their part in contributing to the public good.[8]

Yet it was accepted that in practice public officials should regard their offices as a means to further their self-interest. Venality, patronage, and clientage were fundamental to the functioning of the social elite of the old regime.[9] These were seen as legitimate ways by which to advance one's own and one's family interests. The practice of politics in the centre of government was a closed affair, largely confined to the manoeuvrings of the elite, as they disputed amongst themselves, seeking confirmation of their status, whether they were magistrates in the *parlements*, courtiers out of favour and conducting '*frondeur*' politics, or leading Jansenists denied the right to determine their religious loyalties. It has been argued that it was partly failure by Louis XVI and Marie-Antoinette to give the customary patronage to the oldest families of court nobility that fuelled the resentment of the latter in the last years of the old regime, with fatal consequences for the monarchy.[10] The court was at the epicentre of old regime politics. It was the place where people manoeuvred and jostled for power. The theory of absolute monarchy left little space for court nobles as legitimate wielders of power in their own right. The nature of court politics was for great families to seek the favour of the king to further their own family interests. Power in the old regime was mediated through informal structures that the great noble families used to deal with one another and to further the interest and ambition of themselves and

---

[7] See Campbell, *Power and Politics in Old Régime France*.

[8] On ideas about the nobility serving the public good through noble virtues, see Linton, *The Politics of Virtue*, 31–7; on the *parlementaires* and virtue, see Linton, 'The rhetoric of virtue and the *parlements*, 1770–1775', *French History*, 9, 2 (June 1995): 180–201; on nobility and patriotism, see Jay M. Smith, *Nobility Reimagined: The Patriotic Nation in Eighteenth-Century France* (Ithaca, NY: Cornell University Press, 2005).

[9] For patronage see Sharon Kettering, *Patrons, Brokers and Clients in Seventeenth-Century France* (Oxford: Oxford University Press, 1986); and Roger Mettam, *Power and Faction in Louis XIV's France* (Oxford: Blackwell, 1988). On venality, see William Doyle, *Venality: The Sale of Offices in Eighteenth-Century France* (Oxford: Oxford University Press, 1996); and Doyle, *Officers, Nobles and Revolutionaries: Essays on Eighteenth-Century France* (London: Hambledon Press, 1995), ch. 2–5. On privilege, see Gail Bossenga, *The Politics of Privilege: Old Regime and Revolution in Lille* (Cambridge: Cambridge University Press, 1991); and Michael Kwass, *Privilege and the Politics of Taxation in Eighteenth-Century France* (Cambridge: Cambridge University Press, 2000).

[10] Daniel L. Wick, *A Conspiracy of Well-Intentioned Men: The Society of Thirty and the French Revolution* (New York: Garland Publishing, 1987).

their families: patron–client relations, friendship, networks, and family connections. Court politics was seen to be about subterfuge, deceit, theatre, masks, and self-interest.[11] All actions of nobles not authorized by monarchy could be labelled as 'conspiratorial' interventions in politics.

From the time of Louis XIV the court was portrayed as a place of moral corruption—the antithesis of virtue. In *Les Caractères* (1688) La Bruyère claimed that luxury and wealth led to greed and moral corruption, while the studied politeness of the court cloaked intrigue, duplicity, and artificiality. The courtier was the very antithesis of virtue. La Bruyère looked instead to 'the people' as ignorant, but possessed of authentic morality: 'The people have no wit, and the nobility have no soul; the former are basically good, and lack veneer; the latter have veneer, and nothing underneath it. Am I to choose? I'll not hesitate; I'll belong to the common people.'[12] To many outside observers the court was about the pursuit of power, privilege, and position; courtiers were characterized as corrupt and self-serving. The court was the *locus* of personal ambition: the place where nobles congregated to further their individual and family interests through access to monarchical patronage. It was associated with personal glory, honours, and advancement. The pursuit of personal ambition and personal glory were seen as entirely compatible with a life at court.

Such an attitude was typified by a young courtier, Hérault de Séchelles. His family had been noble since 1390, and he himself owed his appointment as an *avocat-général* in the Paris *Parlement* to the patronage of his cousin, Yolande de Polignac, through her intimate friendship with Marie-Antoinette.[13] In 1788 he penned a *Theory of Ambition*, a book of epigrams containing advice for how to 'get on' in the world. He was unabashed about the goal of the ambitious man: 'It is not about how to be modest, but about how to be at the forefront.'[14] It was considered to be a shocking book, not for endorsing ambition, but for the calculated and cynical way in which he treated the subject. His own family suppressed his book. In those last years before the Revolution, the kind of naked espousal of self-interest he had expressed in his *Theory of Ambition* was beginning to go out of fashion. Ambition ran counter to the discourse of virtue.

In the later years of the old regime, therefore, there was a discrepancy between how the nobility presented their motives, and how they were perceived by the growing category of public opinion. This negative public image was particularly directed against the court nobility; it was couched in terms of their apparent immorality. This image appeared in fiction, where arrogant, predatory, exploitative nobles appeared as characters in Laclos's *Dangerous Liaisons,* and Beaumarchais's *The Marriage of Figaro*. Duplicitous, corrupt nobles also featured in some high-profile legal

---

[11] Henry C. Clark, *La Rochefoucauld and the Language of Unmasking in Seventeenth-Century France* (Geneva: Droz, 1994). Clark argues that the 'strategy of unmasking was an integral part of seventeenth-century absolutism', one of the many parallels between absolutism and Jacobinism: 19.

[12] La Bruyère, *Characters*, 129,156.

[13] See Georges Bernier, *Hérault de Séchelles: Biographie, suivie de Théorie de l'ambition* (Paris: Éditions Julliard, 1995).

[14] Hérault de Séchelles, *Théorie de l'ambition (Codicille politique et pratique d'un jeune habitant d'Épône)* (1802: this edition, Paris: Arthème Fayard, 2005), 53.

cases, which played out like a drama, with third-estate heroes and noble villains.[15] Nevertheless, nobles joined with commoners in enjoying these fictional portrayals as a form of entertainment; there is little sign that they were perceived as a threat. Even *The Marriage of Figaro* was eventually given permission to be performed, despite the reluctance of the king, who in this matter was more perspicacious than the queen. But the negative image of an immoral and self-serving nobility would be a constant theme in the political culture of the Revolution.

According to the discourse of political virtue, women who actively participated in court politics had a particularly corrupting influence. These aristocratic women were characterized as the epitome of self-interest; they schemed for themselves, their families, and their faction; they were incapable of high-minded political virtue. The most powerful women were those who were closest to the king: queens and royal mistresses had the potential to influence the king's political decisions. Madame de Pompadour and Madame du Barry were the subject of much speculation of this kind during the reign of Louis XV. Louis XVI, by contrast, took no mistress; consequently hostility was focused on the political influence of Marie-Antoinette. Many of these hostile accounts originated from rival court factions, but eventually found their way into salacious, clandestine pamphlets that spread stories of court women corrupting politics, and literally corrupting the king.

Salons were regarded as a *locus* for a particularly feminine version of aristocratic power. Most salons were presided over by women (the *salonnières*), and some historians have seen them as a force for Enlightenment empowered by the women who led them. This may have been true of certain salons (such as that of Julie de l'Espinasse, which was far from typical), but the chief purpose of the salons was not to assert the rights of women; rather, their primary function was to serve as a conduit for the promotion of aristocratic interests through patronage, sociability, and *politesse*. Some men of letters resented the power of the women who led these elite institutions, and took pride in retaining their independence by remaining outside the influence of the *salonnières*. The work of Antoine Lilti has shown that this hostile perception largely reflected the reality of the salons as bastions of aristocratic self-interest. Attendance at the salons was a semi-private activity, in that participation was by invitation only; 'social undesirables' would not be admitted. The salons were held in the intimate atmosphere of the home, rather than in the public spaces of a club or a café.[16]

---

[15] See Sarah Maza, *Private Lives and Public Affairs: The Causes Célèbres of Prerevolutionary France* (Berkeley: University of California Press, 1993); Maza, 'The Rose-Girl of Salency: representations of virtue in prerevolutionary France', *Eighteenth-Century Studies*, 22, 3 (Spring 1989): 395–412; on fictional portrayals of the nobility, see Smith, *Nobility Reimagined*, 242–5. On the deployment of the discourse of virtue in the pamphlets in the Kornmann affair, see Robert Darnton, 'Trends in radical propaganda on the eve of the French Revolution, 1782–1788' (DPhil thesis, University of Oxford, 1964), 316–56.

[16] On eighteenth-century salons as bastions of aristocracy, see Antoine Lilti, *Le Monde des salons. Sociabilité et mondanité à Paris au XVIIIe siècle* (Paris: Fayard, 2005). For the contrasting view of the salon as a republic, see Dena Goodman, *The Republic of Letters: A Cultural History of the Enlightenment* (Ithaca, NY: Cornell University Press, 1994). On the mockery of men of letters as 'lackeys' to the aristocratic women who ran the salons, see Michael Sonenscher, *Sans-Culottes; an Eighteenth-Century Emblem in the French Revolution* (Princeton, NJ: Princeton University Press, 2008), 57–77.

## THE RISE OF JOURNALISM AND THE GROWTH OF PUBLIC OPINION

In theory, under absolute monarchy information about politics did not belong in the public domain. There was no legitimate space within which to debate political issues of the day. All political matter was subject to official censorship. Permitted newspapers such as the *Mercure de France* and the *gazettes* were obliged to be circumspect, confining their discussion of the monarchy to lists of court engagements, rather than engaging in political criticism.[17] Nonetheless, there was a thriving literature of clandestine works that engaged in political discussion. More outspoken comments circulated in the form of clandestine pamphlets. Some of these works engaged in serious political discussions; others took the form of libels, featuring scurrilous stories about the financial and sexual corruption of the court. Ironically, some of the most scandalous stories were originally generated by disaffected court factions. These stories spread a narrative of a decadent and corrupted court, that took hold in the imagination of the reading public. When the Revolution broke out this narrative helped shape the way in which the new participants in politics viewed the political failures of the old regime. Occasionally the monarchy was caricatured in clandestine images. Such stories also circulated as oral rumours amongst the crowd.[18]

The critique of the closed world of court politics was facilitated by the development of a 'public sphere' within which it was legitimate to debate political subjects.[19] Several factors promoted this: the rise of a concept of public opinion; the growth of a reading public interested in national events; and the increasing readiness of political participants to appeal to public opinion by publishing their writings.[20] Public opinion was an invaluable linguistic weapon for the reading classes in a society characterized by censorship and lack of political representation: it provided 'a voice for the voiceless'. Members of the reading public legitimized their right to participate in the public sphere on the basis of their virtue: they were seen,

---

[17] On the press before the Revolution see Jack. R. Censer, *The French Press in the Age of Enlightenment* (London: Routledge, 1994); and Jeremy D. Popkin, *News and Politics in the Age of Revolution: Jean Luzac's* Gazette de Leyde (Ithaca, NY and London: Cornell University Press, 1989); and on the culture of print, Chartier, *The Cultural Origins of the French Revolution*, ch. 3.

[18] On clandestine political pamphlets before the Revolution, see Robert Darnton, *The Literary Underground of the Old Regime* (Cambridge, MA: Harvard University Press, 1982). On rumour in Paris, see Arlette Farge and Jacques Revel, *The Vanishing Children of Paris*, trans. Claudia Miéville (Cambridge, MA: Harvard University Press, 1991); and Thomas Manley Luckett, 'Hunting for spies and whores: a Parisian riot on the eve of the French Revolution', 156, *Past and Present* (1997): 116–43. On caricatures of the monarchy, see Annie Duprat, *Les Rois de papier: la caricature de Henri III à Louis XVI* (Paris: Belin, 2002).

[19] See Habermas, *The Structural Transformation of the Public Sphere*. Habermas's approach has generated much further discussion, including Dena Goodman, 'Public sphere and private life: toward a synthesis of current historiographical approaches to the old regime', *History and Theory*, 31 (1992): 1–20; Jon Cowans, 'Habermas and French history: the public sphere and the problem of political legitimacy', *French History*, 13 (1999): 134–60. The debate on the public sphere is summarized very effectively by Thomas E. Kaiser, 'The public sphere: in search of the "Shadowy Phantom"', in William Doyle (ed.), *The Oxford Handbook of the Ancien Régime* (Oxford: Oxford University Press, 2011).

[20] On public opinion see Introduction, note 6.

and saw themselves, as virtuous citizens who had the moral right to express their views because they were motivated by a concern for the public good. It was their virtue that gave them a voice.

## THE POLITICS OF VIRTUE IN THE OLD REGIME

François Furet claimed that 1789 saw the invention of a new 'political discourse'; one that for the first time conflated politics and morality: 'When politics becomes the realm of truth and falsehood, of good and evil, and when it is politics that separates the good from the wicked, we find ourselves in a historical universe whose dynamic is entirely new.'[21] He further claimed that it was the new revolutionary moral politics—the politics of virtue—that made the Terror not only possible, but inevitable from the moment the Revolution broke out. In recent years Furet's arguments have been challenged by a series of historians who have shown that a political vocabulary based on a rhetoric of moral politics was already current long before the collapse of the old regime. By 1789 a whole repertoire of words in circulation were readily available for use in political polemic by a wide section of new participants in the public arena. Terms such as nation, *patrie*, despotism, privilege, citizen, and virtue were being deployed as discourses that empowered the politically excluded.[22] Such words provided a common language and culture by means of which politics might be understood and contested as a matter of public concern. The participants who used this language extended through a wide range of literate society—from drafters of the *cahiers de doléances* to the elite of old regime society within the Assembly of Notables.[23] These participants by no means agreed on the kind of political model they wanted to see for their nation, but they now had a common language with which to debate the matter.

The idea of political virtue was fundamental to 'moral politics'.[24] Virtue had a number of complex, interconnected meanings, some of which were explicitly political. Political virtue was defined as selfless devotion to the public good. It entailed the abnegation of self-interest. A man of virtue should not attempt to use his post of public responsibility for his own private gain, nor for the advancement or advantage of his family or friends. Political virtue was an idealized concept in

---

[21] Furet, *Interpreting the French Revolution*, 26.

[22] On nation, *patrie*, and virtue, see Introduction, note 35. On 'citizen', see Pierre Rétat, 'The evolution of the citizen from the Ancien Régime to the Revolution', in Waldinger, Dawson, and Woloch, *The French Revolution and the Meaning of Citizenship*. On the discourse of anti-despotism as a means of attacking ministerial corruption, see John M. Burney, 'History, despotism, public opinion and the continuity of the radical attack on monarchy in the French Revolution, 1787–1792', *History of European Ideas*, 17, 2/3 (1993): 245–63.

[23] On the shared language of the Assembly of Notables, see Vivien R. Gruder, 'Paths to political consciousness: the Assembly of Notables of 1787 and the "pre-Revolution" in France', *French Historical Studies*, 13, 3 (1984), 323–55.

[24] Linton, *The Politics of Virtue*.

eighteenth-century thought, which provided a sharp contrast with the theory and practice of old regime court politics. It was conceived very much in opposition to the practice of court politics—to the idea of politics as self-serving and venal. The term was used across a wide spectrum of reformers, radicals, and polemicists; and they used it strategically, to pursue a range of arguments. It became a mainstream argument, adopted by anyone who wanted to criticize aspects of the old regime administration and social structure. In the context of the old regime the language of political virtue existed as a discourse, rather than an ideology. By discourse I mean a group of linked words by means of which a speaker gains authority and power. These linked words may be accessed by different groups, put together in different ways, and thus have different consequences.[25] The discourse of political virtue thus served as a weapon of rhetorical strategy. It was all the more compelling in that it provided a means to talk about politics in a way that outflanked the prohibition against writing about politics in the old regime. Thus the pre-revolutionary language of virtue was not confined to future revolutionaries; it could be met with everywhere in the last years of the old regime. There are many examples of it being used by the elite of the regime, including ministers, noble officers, and bishops.[26] It provided a rhetoric and justification which could be used to examine the existing political and social system. It was a political ideal, rather than a realistic programme for government; above all it was a means to criticize features of existing government, and to give a legitimizing voice to the men making the criticisms. All the features of the revolutionary concept of virtue were already in place; still, it had not yet taken on the form of an ideology, in the sense of a set of consciously held beliefs that were drawn together in support of a particular political stance. Moreover, in pre-revolutionary discourses the concept of virtue was still a long way from being linked with terror. Indeed, this link did not take place until the Terror itself was already under way.[27] Before the Revolution the word 'terror' was employed in a religious, judicial, or military sense, rather than a political one.[28]

The political meaning of virtue owed much to two major currents of thought: the classical republican tradition, and the concept of natural virtue.

---

[25] See Linton, 'The intellectual origins of the French Revolution'.

[26] On Necker's willingness to engage with public opinion by presenting himself as a virtuous and patriotic minister, see Julian Swann, 'From servant of the King to "Idol of the Nation": the breakdown of personal monarchy in Louis XVI's France', in Julian Swann and Joël Félix (eds.), *The Crisis of the Absolute Monarchy* (Oxford: Oxford University Press, 2013); and Linton, *The Politics of Virtue*, ch. 7. On the association of nobility with the idea of patriotism, see Smith, *Nobility Reimagined*; and on the growing preoccupation of the military nobility with the pursuit of soldierly merit as a quality opposed to courtly 'corruption', see Jay M. Smith, *The Culture of Merit: Nobility, Royal Service, and the Making of Absolute Monarchy in France, 1600–1789* (Ann Arbor: University of Michigan Press, 1996), 227–61.

[27] On the links between virtue and terror in Jacobin political language, see M. Linton, 'Robespierre's political principles', in Haydon and Doyle, *Robespierre*; and George Armstrong Kelly, 'Conceptual sources of the Terror', *Eighteenth-Century Studies*, 14 (1980), 18–36.

[28] On the long-term origins of and use of the term 'terror', see Jourdan, 'Les discours de la terreur', and on the relationship between terror and sovereignty, Ronald Schechter, 'The terror of their enemies: reflections on a trope in eighteenth-century historiography', *Historical Reflections*, 36, 1 (2010): 53–75.

## THE DERIVATION OF POLITICAL VIRTUE:
## CLASSICAL REPUBLICANISM

Ideas drawn from antiquity shaped the eighteenth-century perspective on the nature and purpose of politics.[29] Amongst the ideas derived from antiquity, the most important variant was that of classical republicanism whose influence, in its various guises, weighed heavily on the eighteenth century.[30] It provided a distinctive approach to political ideas, along with a characteristic political culture and a political vocabulary. It offered models of political conduct. Above all it imparted a narrative structure by means of which political players could make sense of events, through accounts of political leaders who played a heroic role in resisting the forces of corruption and malice.[31]

Within the French tradition of classical republican thought, Montesquieu was the key figure. Montesquieu's own loyalties were to the nobility and the *parlements*. Yet his intellectual association of virtue with republics, and honour with monarchy, combined with his depiction of the republic as the most superior form of government, became the framework through which subsequent generations conceptualized the political order.[32] For Montesquieu the monarchical form of government was characterized by court politics: the court was the place for the pursuit of self-interest, for honour and personal glory. A republic, by contrast, was founded on the virtue of its citizens. In *De l'Esprit des lois* (1748) Montesquieu defined virtue after the manner of the ancients as 'the love of the laws and of the *patrie*', a love which necessitated 'a continual preference for the public good over one's own good'. Political virtue was egalitarian and selfless: it was based on 'love of equality' and 'love of frugality'.[33] Political virtue was the highest form of morality: 'I speak here of political virtue, which is moral virtue in the sense that it directs itself

---

[29] On the legacy of classical antiquity, see Chantal Grell, *Le Dix-huitième siècle et l'antiquité en France, 1660–1789*, in *Studies on Voltaire and the Eighteenth Century* (Oxford, 1995), vols. 330–1. On the classical education of the revolutionary generation see H.T. Parker, *The Cult of Antiquity and the French Revolutionaries* (1937: republished, New York: Octagon Books, 1965), 8–36.

[30] Amongst the many works on classical republicanism in eighteenth-century France, see J.G.A. Pocock, *The Machiavellian Moment: Florentine Political Thought and the Atlantic Republican Tradition* (Princeton, NJ: Princeton University Press, 1975); Baker, *Inventing the French Revolution*, esp. ch. 6; Johnson Kent Wright, *A Classical Republican in Eighteenth-Century France: the Political Thought of Mably* (Stanford, CA: Stanford University Press, 1997); and the relevant sections in Martin van Gelderen and Quentin Skinner (eds), *Republicanism: a Shared European Heritage*, 2 vols (Cambridge: Cambridge University Press, 2002). On the relationship between classical republicanism and the revolution, see Keith Michael Baker, 'Transformations of classical republicanism in eighteenth-century France', *Journal of Modern History*, 73 (2001): 32–53; K.M. Baker, 'Political languages of the French Revolution', in Mark Goldie and Robert Wokler (eds), *The Cambridge History of Eighteenth-Century Political Thought* (Cambridge: Cambridge University Press, 2006), 626–59.

[31] For a case study of how the ancient republics offered an appealing political narrative to the revolutionaries, see Marisa Linton, 'The Man of Virtue: the role of antiquity in the political trajectory of L.A. Saint-Just', 24,3, *French History* (2010): 393–419.

[32] For a more detailed account of the place of political virtue in Montesquieu's thought, see Linton, *The Politics of Virtue*, ch. 1 and 2. On Montesquieu's republicanism, see Johnson Kent Wright. 'Montesquieuean moments: the "Spirit of the Laws" and republicanism', *Proceedings of the Western Society for French History* (2008).

[33] *De l'Esprit des lois*, in Montesquieu, *Oeuvres complètes*, 2: 255–6, 267–9, 274.

towards the general good....'[34] Montesquieu warned that such virtue was difficult to achieve, and impossible to sustain in the long term. This is why the ancient republics had been subject to decay, and that was why modern republics, too, would founder.

The democratic republic had outlived its historical moment. It was the political system that was most worthy of mankind, but one that was doomed to eventual failure. Montesquieu's primary purpose in depicting the 'republic of virtue' was not in order to call for its renewal, but to use it to practical effect, as a model of how politics ought to be, against which he could delineate the shortcomings of the actual political system.[35] His account of the inevitable decline of the political ideal served to illustrate his far more pressing political concern, which was to show how easily monarchy might lapse into despotism.

In *Considérations sur les causes de la grandeur des Romains et de leur décadence* (1734) Montesquieu explored this problem in a historical context. He saw the decline of virtue as a key factor in the fall of the Roman republic. The Romans' very success paved the way to their downfall. Military conquest led to the corruption of Roman virtue; replacing it with greed, luxury, inequality, and the personal ambition of political leaders.[36] The men of antiquity were possessed of superhuman virtue. As such they were superior to any other people that now walked the earth: '...they did such deeds as we no longer see today, and which amaze our little souls'.[37]

But such virtue came at a cost. There was a terrible aspect to political virtue, one that Montesquieu well understood. For a man who wished to be truly virtuous was obliged to make a *choice*. His duty was to put the public good—the good of all people in the republic—before the good of the people who were personally dear to him, his own self, his family and friends. A central concept of classical republicanism was that of self-sacrifice. Citizens should be prepared to put the good of all before their own good, and to sacrifice everything to it. Ultimately this might mean that a man should be prepared to sacrifice his own life for the public good, or even (and worse still perhaps) the lives of those who were personally dear to him—his family or friends.[38] This was the dual nature of political virtue: both 'divine' and 'terrible', because it entailed putting the greater good before personal loyalties.

Rousseau agreed, though for him the 'divine' aspect outweighed its 'terrible' potential. For Rousseau virtue was about self-mastery. No one should set out to rule over others who had not abnegated his personal passions and desires, and put himself at the service of the 'public good'. 'If some man were worthy of being the master of the others, it would be the one who knows how to be the master of

---

[34] Montesquieu, *De l'Esprit des lois*, 255, footnote a.

[35] Baker calls this method of using classical republicanism 'diagnostic', in that its primary purpose was to highlight shortcomings in political management, rather than to offer a programme for practicable change; see Baker, 'Transformations of Classical Republicanism'.

[36] Montesquieu, *Oeuvres complètes*, 1: 174.       [37] Montesquieu, *Oeuvres complètes*, 1: 266.

[38] Montesquieu, *Oeuvres complètes*, 1: 132.

himself the same way.'[39] To be worthy of public office one must not show favour-itism or self-interest. More than that, a man of virtue who held public office ought to be prepared to sacrifice even his personal friends, or the relatives he loved, if this sacrifice was necessary for the public good. Lucius Junius Brutus, who had (while consul) condemned his own sons to death for conspiring to over-throw the republic, had shown the kind of virtue essential for someone who held public office: 'After he absolved, or refused to condemn his son, how could Brutus have dared to face condemning another Citizen? O consul, this criminal would have said, did I do something worse than selling my fatherland, and am I not your son too?'[40]

For Rousseau the significance of Sparta lay primarily in the contrast that it offered with the political culture of his own time: the republics of antiquity were mirrors that could be held up to illuminate the pettiness and pointlessness of life as it was lived.[41] Unlike the present, antiquity was a land of heroes: 'But I take pleasure in turning my eyes towards those venerable images of antiquity where I see men raised up by sublime institutions to the highest degree of greatness and virtues that human wisdom can reach... in some way one participates in the heroic actions of these great men, it seems that meditation about their greatness communicates a part of it to us.'[42] One can know 'that there was a time' when such men existed.[43]

Most of the future Jacobin leaders learned about antiquity through their second-ary education at the *collèges,* where much of the instruction was in Latin and the favoured authors included such as Plutarch, Cicero, Livy, and Tacitus, all of whom encouraged the vision of the Roman Republic as a golden age of political virtue. Many of the revolutionary generation were taught by Oratorians, a more progres-sive order than the Jesuits who were expelled in 1764. As adolescents, future Jacob-ins imbibed important lessons for their careers as revolutionary leaders: they learned the classical methods of declamation, and how to use these rhetorical methods to win over an audience. Their very idea of having a political voice was modelled on an idealized view of the leaders of antiquity.[44]

Antiquity gave inspiration to the revolutionary imagination. Heroes out of Plutarch's *Lives* or Fénelon's reimagining of antiquity, *Télémaque,* gave future Jacobins a model they could use in order to envisage how they too might act in such circumstances; how they could see themselves differently; how they could fashion their own identities as men and women of virtue. Brissot would later

[39] 'History of Lacedaemonia', *Political Fragments*, in Rousseau, *The Collected Writings*, 4: 67.

[40] 'On honour and virtue', Rousseau, *Political Fragments*, 38.

[41] 'Parallel between the two republics of Sparta and Rome', Rousseau, *Political Fragments*, 59–60.

[42] 'Parallel between the two republics of Sparta and Rome', 60.

[43] 'History of Lacedaemonia', Rousseau, *Political Fragments,* 64.

[44] R.R. Palmer, *The School of the French Revolution. A Documentary History of the College of Louis-le-Grand and its Director, Jean-François Champagne 1762–1814* (Princeton, NJ: Princeton University Press, 1975). Regarding how antiquity was taught at schools attended by the revolutionary generation, see Parker, *The Cult of Antiquity*, 37–46; and Jacques Bouineau, *Les Toges du pouvoir: ou la Révolution du droit antique* (Toulouse: Éditions Eché, 1986), 21–31. On education as a whole, see Roger Chartier, Marie-Madeleine Compère, and Dominique Julia, *L'Education au France du XVIe au XVIIIe siècle* (Paris: Société d'édition d'enseignement supérieur, 1976).

recall how he imagined being a character from *Télémaque*. Madame Roland took pleasure in reading about 'the virtues of heroes'. She dreamed how she might take on the identity of one of Plutarch's characters: 'I never read of a beautiful action without saying to myself: "That is how I would have acted".'[45] Together with the written word, the growing cult of visual images of classical heroes heroically sacrificing themselves for the *patrie* also played its part in feeding the imaginations of the revolutionary generation.[46]

The classical authors condemned personal ambition and love of glory as a failing in public figures. Marcus Junius Brutus had killed Julius Caesar because Caesar succumbed to personal ambition. The best heroes were those who, like the Roman general Cincinnatus, accepted public office only in order to serve the *patrie*, and when their public service was over were content to retire into the obscurity of private life.[47] To combine virtue with self-interest was much more acceptable in the economic and commercial realm than in the sphere of politics: thus a merchant who pursued his own self-interest could be said to be generating wealth and commercial development that would also benefit the wider community.[48] There could be no such justification for a public official, whose acceptance of responsibility and funds was seen as a position of trust, which he should not abuse for private interest. As Rousseau put this: 'Self-interest corrupts the best actions. He who does good only for money only waits to be better paid to do what is bad.'[49]

## THE DERIVATION OF POLITICAL VIRTUE: NATURAL VIRTUE

Classical republican virtue might be a sublime quality, but it was also rather cold and abstract. There was an alternative tradition that made a much more direct appeal to the emotions: this was the concept of natural virtue. It was not confined to the dry texts of the ancients: natural virtue came directly from the heart. Natural virtue was closely related to the idea of sensibility, or sincere feeling. Both were believed to be a source of happiness. They brought people closer together as part of a community linked by sincere feeling. Two works played a key part in bringing this idea to a French readership: Shaftesbury's *An Inquiry Concerning Virtue and Merit*, translated by Diderot in 1745, and Toussaint's *Les Moeurs* (1748). Natural

[45] Marie-Jeanne Roland (née Phlipon), *Mémoires de Madame Roland*, ed. Paul de Roux (Paris: Mercure de France, 1966), 256; see also 212–14, 270–71. Jacques-Pierre Brissot, *Mémoires*, ed. Cl. Perroud, 2 vols (Paris: Picard et fils, 1912), 1: 3–4, 9.

[46] On visual depictions of classical heroes and the impact of this culture on pre-revolutionary politics, see Thomas E. Crow, *Painters and Public Life in Eighteenth-Century Paris* (New Haven, CT: Yale University Press, 1985); and T. E. Crow, '"The Oath of the Horatii" in 1785: painting and pre-revolutionary radicalism in France', *Art History*, I, 4 (December 1978): 424–71.

[47] On the influence of the model of Cincinnatus in the American Revolution, see William Doyle, *Aristocracy and Its Enemies in the Age of Revolution* (Oxford: Oxford University Press, 2009), ch. 4.

[48] On virtue in the field of economic and commercial development before the revolution, see John Shovlin, *The Political Economy of Virtue: Luxury, Patriotism, and the Origins of the French Revolution* (Ithaca, NY: Cornell University Press, 2006).

[49] Rousseau, 'On honour and virtue', in *Political Fragments*, 4: 36.

virtue had a practical application. It led to the desire to carry out acts of *bienfaisance* (philanthropy) to secure the well-being of others—especially the poorer and weaker members of the community. A truly virtuous man or woman would derive happiness from caring for his or her fellows. It was only by helping others that true happiness could be obtained.[50] Since natural virtue stemmed from the heart, rather than from education, it was a quality that could be found as much—or more—amongst the poor as amongst the rich, for the poor had not been corrupted by the corrosive effects of excessive wealth and self-regard.[51]

Natural virtue entailed the rejection of selfish egoism in favour of *bienfaisance*. Like classical republican virtue, natural virtue also entailed self-denial. Reference to self-sacrifice was a central theme in the sentimental literature of the day. Unlike the classical republican tradition, however, which painted self-sacrifice as a harsh, sometimes agonizing choice, natural virtue encouraged the idea that self-sacrifice was a way of achieving a sublime level of happiness and fulfilment, through being of benefit to others.[52]

Classical republicanism and natural virtue came at the problem from two different sides, but for both the conclusion was the same: the morally good man was devoted to his fellows, and by extension to his *patrie*. Virtue and *patrie* were intimately connected and interdependent: the *patrie* was made up of the virtuous individuals who loved and sustained it. The *patrie* was more than a physical or geographical community: it was the place to which people *belonged*. Like the related—but less emotive—term 'nation', the significance of *patrie* differed according to the context in which it was being deployed.[53] Thus, to the monarchical government attempting to mobilize public opinion in support of the Seven Years' War, it meant something different from its significance for revolutionaries in 1792 in the build-up to war with Austria.[54] At its most intense, as the Jacobins were to understand the term, it was a spiritual and emotional community in which people were bonded by fellow feeling and mutual sympathy. It was about identity, morality, and love. For the Jacobins the *patrie* was the heart of the moral republic, more important even than democracy or equality.

Though Rousseau himself thought that virtue was neither easy nor natural, he came to be identified as a major exponent of the cult of natural virtue.[55] There were

[50] On *bienfaisance* before the Revolution and the link with the *patrie*, see Catherine Duprat, *Le Temps des philanthropes*, vol. I (Paris: Comité des Travaux Historiques et Scientifiques, 1993); Daniel Mornet, *Les Origines intellectuelles de la Révolution française: 1715–1787* (Paris: Armand Colin, 1938), 258–66; Robert Mauzi, *L'Idée du bonheur dans la littérature et la pensée française au XVIIIe siècle* (1960: this edition, Paris: Albin Michel, 1994); and Linton, *The Politics of Virtue*, esp. 67–74, 184–6.

[51] On natural virtue and the poor, see Linton, *The Politics of Virtue*, esp. 186–92. On the urban poor, forerunners of the *sans-culottes*, as virtuous, see Jeremy Caradonna, 'The monarchy of virtue: the Prix de Vertu and the economy of emulation in France, 1777–1791', *Eighteenth-Century Studies*, 41, 4 (2008), 443–58. On the origins of the term '*sans-culotte*' as a salon joke, see Sonenscher, *Sans-Culottes*, 85.

[52] On natural virtue, see Linton, *The Politics of Virtue*, ch. 2, 4, and 7. On virtue, self-sacrifice, and happiness, see Mauzi, *L'Idée du bonheur*, 624–34.

[53] On 'nation', see Bell, *The Cult of the Nation*.

[54] On the changing use of the term *patrie*, see Campbell, 'The politics of patriotism'.

[55] On Rousseau's concept of virtue, and its relationship both to classical republicanism and to natural virtue, see Linton, *The Politics of Virtue*, 80–93.

innumerable other writers on this subject, but he was undoubtedly the most elo-quent.[56] One reason for the universality of his appeal is that he dealt not only—or even primarily—with political theory, but also with matters of the human heart. People felt that Rousseau spoke directly *to* them in his writings, though they had never met him.[57] His writings dealt with such themes as authenticity, loneliness, friendship, and the search for meaning in human existence, needs that concerned everyone—Jacobins included.[58] The Jacobins derived their political categories from Montesquieu, but they never adored him in the way that many did Rousseau. It is said that as a young man Robespierre visited him, as did Carnot—though Rous-seau gave the latter a hostile reception. After his death, Barère and many others made the pilgrimage to see Rousseau's tomb on the Isle of Poplars at Ermenon-ville.[59] For Madame Roland it was to Plutarch rather than to Rousseau that she owed her intellectual formation as a republican: '...he inspired in me the true enthusiasm for public virtues and for liberty'; but it was from Rousseau that she learned about personal happiness and self-fulfilment: 'Rousseau showed me how I could achieve domestic happiness and the sublime delights that I was able to experience'.[60]

On the other hand, the evidence for Rousseau's direct political—as opposed to emotional—influence on the early years of the Revolution is ambiguous. His ideas did not just influence future radicals; his cult was enthusiastically celebrated by a wide swathe of society.[61] Up until at least 1791 conservatives were just as likely to enlist Rousseau on their behalf as were the supporters of the revolution.[62] Rousseau may have been close to their hearts but the deputies of the Constituent Assembly

---

[56] There are too many studies of Rousseau's influence on the revolutionary generation to list here. They include Norman Hampson, *Will and Circumstance: Montesquieu, Rousseau and the French Revo-lution* (London: Duckworth, 1983); Blum, *Rousseau and the Republic of Virtue*; Roger Barny, *Prélude idéologique à la Révolution française: le Rousseauisme avant 1789* (Paris: Les Belles Lettres, 1985); Durand Echeverria, 'The pre-Revolutionary influence of Rousseau's *Contrat social*', *Journal of the His-tory of Ideas*, 33 (1972): 543–60; David Williams, 'The influence of Rousseau on political opinion, 1760–95', *English Historical Review*, 48 (1933): 414–30; and Boudon, *Les Jacobins: une traduction des principes de Jean-Jacques Rousseau* (Paris: Librairie Générale de Droit et de Jurisprudence, 2006), Intro-duction, 1–25.

[57] See, for example, Darnton, 'Readers respond to Rousseau', in Robert Darnton, *The Great Cat Massacre and Other Episodes in French Cultural History* (London: Penguin, 1984).

[58] By far the most popular of Rousseau's books before the Revolution was his novel *La Nouvelle Héloïse*, though *Emile* and the *Confessions* were also widely read by the revolutionary generation; see Daniel Mornet, 'Les Enseignements des bibliothèques privées (1750–80)', *Revue d'histoire littéraire*, 17 (1910): 449–96.

[59] Mornet, *Les Origines intellectuelles de la Révolution française*, 416–17.

[60] Madame Roland, *Mémoires*, 302; see also 270–71, 277. As McPhee points out, it is unlikely that Robespierre actually met Rousseau, but the important point is that he wanted to believe that he had because of his identification with the 'man of virtue': see McPhee, *Robespierre*, 107–8.

[61] Gordon H. McNeil, 'The anti-Revolutionary Rousseau', *American Historical Review*, 58/9 (1953), 808–23; and Gordon H. McNeil, 'The cult of Rousseau and the French Revolution', *Journal of the History of Ideas*, 6 (1947), 197–212.

[62] On the ways in which the ambiguity of Rousseau's writing led to his being appropriated by people of very different political persuasions, see James Swenson, *On Jean-Jacques Rousseau, Considered as One of the First Authors of the Revolution* (Stanford, CA: Stanford University Press, 2000); and Joan McDonald, *Rousseau and the French Revolution, 1762–1791* (London: Athlone Press, 1965).

made little reference to him in their diaries and letters when dealing with the actual business of politics.[63]

Natural virtue was based on the notion of an inner truth: authentic emotions written on the human heart and expressed by means of a sensibility that found an outlet in an active concern for others. Rousseau's *Confessions*, his self-revelatory autobiography, provided a literary and philosophical model for the exposure of this authentic self. This book spoke to a deep-seated need in the minds of eighteenth-century readers. It was symptomatic of this desire for inner truth that, of all Rousseau's works, it was the *Confessions* that the revolutionary generation admired the most, over and above his overtly political works; even *The Social Contract*.[64] The authentically virtuous self was familiar to eighteenth-century readers: they encountered it in the proliferation of novels, plays, and works of art composed in the language and imagery of sensibility.[65] Priests in the pulpit and lawyers at the bar pleading their cases also used this kind of language to examine the conduct of people in public life, and bring to light their true motives.[66]

There was, however, an underlying anxiety about the authenticity of virtue. What if a person's virtue was not, after all, authentic? If virtue were not natural, might it not be an assumed and artificial quality? The answer to this problem depended on one's view of human nature. The Jansenist theologians Nicole and Esprit, who took a sceptical view of humanity's capacity for inner integrity, regarded virtue with deep suspicion, seeing it as a manifestation of pride (*amour-propre*) and self-interest.[67] The language of virtue could be falsely appropriated by people who wore a mask of public-spiritedness, because it was in their self-interest to do so. Thus the question of the authenticity of a person's virtue was already problematic, long before the Revolution made it a matter of life of death.[68]

The model of the man of virtue in public life was seen as the reverse of the man of honour. Honour was closely associated with the values and status of

---

[63]  See Tackett, *Becoming a Revolutionary*, 65.

[64]  Brissot, for example, read Rousseau's *Confessions* at least six times. See Ellery, *Brissot*, 43.

[65]  On the literary cult of sensibility, see David. J. Denby, *Sentimental Narrative and the Social Order in France, 1760–1820* (Cambridge: Cambridge University Press, 2006). On visual depictions of sensibility and natural virtue, see in particular Emma Barker, *Greuze and the Painting of Sentiment* (Cambridge: Cambridge University Press, 2005); and Mark Ledbury, *Sedaine, Greuze and the Boundaries of Genre*, in *Studies on Voltaire and the Eighteenth Century*, vol. 380 (Oxford, The Voltaire Foundation, May 2000). On themes of natural virtue in the *drame bourgeois* see Linton, *The Politics of Virtue*, 116–21.

[66]  See Maza, *Private Lives and Public Affairs*; Marisa Linton, 'The unvirtuous King? Clerical rhetoric on the French monarchy, 1760–1774', *History of European Ideas*, 25, 1–2 (1999): 55–74; and Jeffrey Merrick, 'Politics in the pulpit: ecclesiastical discourse on the death of Louis XV', *History of European Ideas*, 1, 2 (1986): 149–60.

[67]  Jacques Esprit, *La Fausseté des vertus humaines. Par M. Esprit de l'Académie Françoise* (1677–8: this edition, Paris: André Pralard, 1693); Pierre Nicole, *Essais de Morale, contenus en divers Traités sur plusieurs Devoirs importants*, 14 vols (1715; this edition, Paris: G. Desprez, 1781).

[68]  See, for example, Charles-Joseph Mathon de la Cour, *Discours sur les meilleurs moyens de faire naître et d'encourager le patriotisme dans une monarchie* (Paris, 1787), 16–17. See also Michael Moriarty, *Disguised Vices: Theories of Virtue in Early Modern French Thought* (Oxford: Oxford University Press, 2011).

nobility. A man of honour openly sought to maintain his prestige, glory, wealth, and social status. If need be he was supposed to be ready to maintain his personal and family honour by duelling, or other acts of violence against anyone who threatened to 'dishonour' him in the eyes of the public.[69] Through much of the eighteenth century the distinction between virtue and honour, as defined by Montesquieu, continued to be addressed in debates over the role and status of the nobility.[70]

In theory virtue should be pursued for its own sake. The reality was far different. Virtue was not its own reward, because this was a society where luxury and corruption *did* prevail. People chose to portray their actions as virtuous, not only because they wanted others to think of them as morally good, but because they themselves also benefited in some tangible way. It was difficult, therefore, to know whether a man possessed genuine integrity, or if he was just faking the image for his own material gain. This way of thinking was not necessarily secular: some of the more radical members of the clergy thought the same way. Clerics such as the abbé Grégoire and Claude Fauchet saw natural virtue as a quality that could bring about a moral—and a political—regeneration of France. There was a strand of radical Catholic thought, that came from Jansenism and the radical Richerism that spread through the parish clergy on the eve of the Revolution, that strongly endorsed the view that wealth and privilege had a corrupting influence on society's leaders, which could make such people less fit to rule over others.[71]

The public man as a model of virtue found its way into an increasing number of treatises and eulogies of 'great men' that used their virtues as a way of making oblique points about contemporary politics. One such forum was the *Académie française* which, from 1759, offered prizes for eloquence in eulogies of 'great men'.[72]

---

[69] On the pre-revolutionary culture of calumny and honour and its relationship to the maintenance of noble prestige, see Charles Walton, *Policing Public Opinion: The Culture of Calumny and the Problem of Free Speech* (Oxford: Oxford University Press, 2009), 39–50.

[70] See Smith, *Nobility Reimagined*, esp. 1–25, 143–81; and Linton, *The Politics of Virtue*, esp. 31–7, 62–7.

[71] Much important work on the Jansenists has been carried out by Dale Van Kley. His writings on Jansenist thought as a means of critique of absolute authority are crystallized in Dale Van Kley, *The Religious Origins of the French Revolution: From Calvin to the Civil Consitution, 1560–1791* (New Haven, CT: Yale University Press, 1996). See also Edmond Préclin, *Les Jansénistes du XVIIIe siècle et la constitution civile du clergé: le développement du Richerisme, sa propagation dans le bas clergé, 1713–1791* (Paris, 1929); Maurice Hutt, 'The *curés* and the third estate: ideas of reform in the pamphlets of the French lower clergy in the period 1787–1789', *Journal of Ecclesiastical History*, 8 (1957), 74–92. There is helpful discussion of Richerism in Nigel Aston, *Religion and Revolution in France, 1780–1804* (Houndmills: Palgrave, 2000). On the political thought of Grégoire, see Alyssa Goldstein Sepinwall, *The Abbé Grégoire and the French Revolution: the Making of Modern Universalism* (Berkeley: University of California Press, 2005); on Fauchet's ideas about natural virtue as a means of political regeneration, see Linton, *The Politics of Virtue*, esp. 177–8, 191–2.

[72] On the eulogies promoted by the *Académie française*, and the political strategies behind this policy, see Linton, *The Politics of Virtue*, ch. 4; and, for a more detailed account, Marisa Linton, 'The concept of virtue in eighteenth-century France, 1745–1788' (DPhil thesis, University of Sussex, 1993), ch. 5, 'Virtue in the *Académie française*'. See also Andrew McClellan, 'D'Angiviller's "Great Men" of France and the politics of the *parlements*', *Art History*, 13, 2 (June 1990): 175–92.

## THE POLITICS OF FRIENDSHIP

The issue of friendship would be central to the theoretical, practical, and especially the personal dimensions of Jacobin politics.[73] Friendship occupied a complex and problematic place within eighteenth-century political thought. The central problem was how far individual friendships were compatible with the public good. Was a political leader justified in having friends if he put their interests before those of the public? Or, to put this another way, was public virtue compatible with private friendship? Like so much of eighteenth-century political thought, this question was familiar to the writers of antiquity.[74] In the small city states of ancient Greece where many citizens were personally known to one another, citizenship and friendship were closely connected. Friendship was a central concept in Aristotle's *Ethics*. Here the capacity for friendship was an admirable human quality: it was a form of virtue, and thus was important for the construction and stability of the *polis*. 'It is not only that friendship is necessary to the good life, it is in itself a good and beautiful thing.'[75] He associated friendship with egalitarian government: 'There is little of friendship in tyrannies but more in democracies.'[76]

Cicero's essay *On Friendship* pictured virtue and 'true' friendship as inextricably linked: 'It is virtue, yes, let me repeat it again, it is virtue alone that can give birth, strength, and permanency to friendship.'[77] He went further, claiming that 'true' friendship, precisely because it was founded in virtue, could not be seen as a justification for committing a crime, including the political crime of the betrayal of the *patrie*—for no virtuous man would ask his friend to commit such a crime.[78] By contrast, with their emphasis on the isolated individual, the Stoics put relatively little stress on friendships, either personal or political. According to Seneca the man of virtue could do without friendship.[79]

Friendship played an important, though often ambiguous, role in the emotional history of eighteenth-century France.[80] It was recognized as a sincere and fundamental

---

[73] On the Jacobins and friendship, see Linton, 'Fatal friendships'.

[74] On friendship and politics in ancient Greece, see David Konstan, *Friendship in the Classical World* (Cambridge: Cambridge University Press, 1997), 60–67, 72–8, 91–2; on the wide range of meanings of *philia*, which could denote various kinds of affectionate relationship, including, but not confined to, friendship in the modern sense, see David Konstan, 'Greek friendship', *The American Journal of Philology*, 117, 1 (1996): 71–94; on friendship across both ancient Greece and Republican Rome, see Dirk Baltzly and Nick Eliopoulos, 'The classical ideals of friendship', in Barbara Caine (ed.), *Friendship: A History* (London: Equinox, 2009); and Mark Vernon, *The Philosophy of Friendship* (Houndmills: Palgrave, 2005), 94–108.

[75] Aristotle, *Ethics*, trans. J.A.K. Thomson (London: Penguin, 1953), book 8, 227–8.

[76] Cited in Vernon, *The Philosophy of Friendship*, 94.

[77] Cicero, 'Laelius: or, an Essay on Friendship', in *Offices and Select Letters*, trans. W. Melmoth (London: Dent, 1909), 213.

[78] Cicero, 'Laelius', 187. For Cicero's view of friendship, see Konstan, *Friendship in the Classical World*, 122–37; Constant J. Mews, 'Cicero on friendship', in Caine, *Friendship: A History*; and more generally, Horst Hutter, *Politics as Friendship: the Origins of Classical Notions of Politics in the Theory and Practice of Friendship* (Waterloo, Ontario: Wilfrid Laurier University Press, 1978).

[79] Konstan, *Friendship in the Classical World*, 113–14; Vernon, *The Philosophy of Friendship*, 107.

[80] On friendship in eighteenth-century France, see Anne Vincent-Buffault, *L'Exercise de l'amitié: Pour une histoire des pratiques amicales aux XVIIIe et XIXe siècles* (Paris: Seuil, 1995); Maurice Aymard, 'Friends

human emotion.[81] The intensity of some friendships between men in the eighteenth century has made some historians speculate that they often involved a homoerotic dimension, but this can be difficult to ascertain from letters alone.[82] This was a society in which there were strict rules about social conduct, and limited mingling of the sexes; therefore male friendships (and female friendships) could serve a deep emotional need for closeness. The codes of letter writing in the eighteenth century allowed for friendship between men to be expressed in terms of love.[83] In many ways their understanding of love, friendship, and homosexual desire was different from ours, and differently expressed, which makes it a hard task to infer anything about the nature of that closeness in the absence of other evidence.[84] On a more concrete and ascertainable level, the growth of Masonic lodges and provincial academies and societies also provided a forum for friendship as a social and cultural institution, though here the friendships were collective and part of a rhetoric of fraternal, rather than individual, personal relationships. Such 'fraternal' societies provided a *habitus* where the ideas of public-spiritedness and *bienfaisance* were to the fore, and which would serve as models for the network of Jacobin Clubs. Fraternity would be a key idea of the Revolution.[85]

and neighbours', in Philippe Ariès and Georges Duby (eds), *A History of Private Life*, trans. Arthur Gold-hammer, 5 vols (Cambridge, MA: Harvard University Press, 1987), vol. 3, Roger Chartier (ed.), *Passions of the Renaissance*; and—on England as well as France—David Garrioch, 'From Christian friendship to secular sentimentality: Enlightenment re-evaluations', in Caine, *Friendship: A History*. Work on friendship in England and Europe includes: Alan Bray, *The Friend* (Chicago: University of Chicago Press, 1993); Alan Bray, 'Homosexuality and the signs of male friendship in Elizabethan England', *History Workshop*, 29 (1990): 1–19; Miri Rubin, Laura Gowing, and Michael Hunter (eds), *Love, Friendship and Faith in Europe* (Houndmills: Palgrave, 2005); Naomi Tadmor, *Family and Friends in Eighteenth-Century England: Household, Kinship and Patronage* (Cambridge: Cambridge University Press, 2001).

[81] See Montaigne's account of his friendship for Étienne de la Boétie, in Michel de Montaigne, 'On friendship', *Essays*, trans. J.M. Cohen (London: Penguin, 1958), 97. See also Barry Weller, 'The rhetoric of friendship in Montaigne's *Essais*', *New Literary History*, 9, 3 (Spring 1978): 503–23.

[82] For a thoughtful exploration of the connections between friendship and homoeroticism in the writings of future French revolutionaries, see Jeffrey Merrick, 'Male friendship in prerevolutionary France', *GLQ: A Journal of Lesbian and Gay Studies*, 10, 3 (2004): 407–32.

[83] See Marie-Claire Grassi, 'Friends and lovers (or the codification of intimacy)', *Yale French Studies*, 71 (1986): 77–92.

[84] There were, for example, occasional instances from the fourteenth to the nineteenth centuries of men being buried in the same tomb, in a 'marriage of souls'; but even here we should be cautious about how we interpret such a 'marriage', and wary of imposing our own understanding on the early modern context. See Alan Bray, 'A traditional rite for blessing friendship', in Katherine O'Donnell and Michael O'Rourke (eds), *Love, Sex, Intimacy and Friendship Between Men, 1550–1800* (Houndmills: Palgrave, 2003); and Bray, *The Friend*, ch. 4.

[85] On the politics of Freemasonry, see Margaret Jacob, *Living the Enlightenment: Freemasonry and Politics in Eighteenth-Century Europe* (Oxford: Oxford University Press, 1991); more recently, Kenneth Loiselle, 'Living the Enlightenment in an age of revolution: Freemasonry in Bordeaux, 1788–1794', *French History*, 24,1 (2009): 60–81; and Kenneth Loiselle, '"Nouveaux mais vrais amis": la Franc-maçonnerie et les rites de l'amitié au dix-huitième siècle,' *Dix-huitième siècle*, 39 (2007): 303–18. For statistics on the relationship between Masonic affiliations and revolutionary politics, see Harriet B. Applewhite, *Political Alignment in the French National Assembly, 1789–1791* (Baton Rouge: Louisiana State University Press, 1993), 45–6, 116. On provincial academies, see Daniel Roche, *Le siècle des lumières en province: Académies et académiciens provinciaux, 1680–1789*, 2 vols (Paris: École des Hautes Études en Sciences Sociales, 1989). On revolutionary fraternity see Marcel David, *Fraternité et Révolution française, 1789–1799* (Paris: Aubier, 1987); Mona Ozouf, 'La Révolution française et l'idée de fraternité,' in *L'Homme régénéré: essays sur la Révolution française* (Paris: Gallimard, 1989), 158–82.

During the later eighteenth century, the cult of sensibility and natural virtue encouraged a new emphasis on the validity and authenticity of friendship as a meeting of minds and hearts, based on the sincere affection of those who truly understood one another. Rousseau was the most influential of the writers to validate the cult of *sensible* (feeling) friendship. For Rousseau friendship sprang from natural virtue and was characterized by sincere feelings for others.[86] Such friendship could lead to virtue, as in the idealized friendships experienced by the characters of *La Nouvelle Héloïse*, particularly those of Claire and Julie, and of Saint-Preux and Milord Edouard. Friendship here imparted true contentment and a sublime sense of unity with one's fellow human beings, while also acting as a moral guide that led people to act virtuously. In contrast to his writings, on a personal level Rousseau later became much more embittered about friendship. The latter sections of the *Confessions* listed many former friends whom he felt had betrayed him. Notwithstanding, the model of friendship in *La Nouvelle Héloïse* had a profound effect on many of Rousseau's readers. The revolutionaries were no more immune from this influence than the rest of their generation. Many of the letters that future Jacobins wrote to one another had echoes of the letters exchanged by Rousseau's fictional characters.

In the very different world of court politics, friendship played an important part in the system of reciprocal favours between patron and client.[87] Patronage was central to the way in which old regime government and administration functioned. Peter Campbell, who has analysed this system in depth, defines patronage as 'the non-bureaucratic operation of power through a system of personal relations...'[88] Friendship at court was one such personal relationship and was seen as a means by which people could pursue self-advantage and social success (kinship was another). Even before the Revolution made the overt pursuit of self-advancement in politics unacceptable, friendship at the French court was tainted with associations of corruption, cynicism, and the pursuit of self-interest at the expense of the public good. French court politics were riven by faction, and friendships at court were characterized by factional allegiances.[89] In England, where the political system was much more developed, the practice of favouring the advantage of one's friends at the expense of those who possessed greater talent or merit, had its own derogatory

---

[86] See Joseph R. Reisert, *Jean-Jacques Rousseau: A Friend of Virtue* (Ithaca, NY: Cornell University Press, 2003), esp. ch. 4; and William Acher, *Jean-Jacques Rousseau, écrivain de l'amitié* (Paris: Nizet, 1971).

[87] On the historiography of patronage and its relationship to friendship, see Campbell, *Power and Politics*, 16–20. On friendship and the ways that courtiers used the language of friendship to 'soften' the way in which they addressed clients and patrons, see Sharon Kettering, 'Friendship and clientage in early modern France', *French History*, 6, 2 (1992): 139–58. For a consideration of how seventeenth-century male friendships in England could be linked to clientage, see Alan Bray and Michel Rey, 'The body of the friend: continuity and change in masculine friendship in the seventeenth century', in Tim Hitchcock and Michele Cohen (eds), *English Masculinities 1660–1800* (Harlow: Longman, 1999), 65–84; on the Renaissance period see also Guy Lytle, 'Friendship and patronage in Renaissance Europe' in F.W. Kent and Patricia Simons (eds), *Patronage, Art, and Society in Renaissance Italy* (Oxford: Clarendon Press, 1987).

[88] Campbell, *Power and Politics*, 16.     [89] Campbell, *Power and Politics*, 20–21.

name, 'cronyism'. The old regime link between political practice and informal personal relations such as friendship networks, is mirrored by anthropological studies of 'informal groupings'.[90] This gives a different, broader, take on politics, one more grounded in its practice.

Friendship was to play a key role in revolutionary politics, where it posed conflicts of loyalty for the Jacobins just as it had long before for the ancients. Was it possible to be both a good friend and a revolutionary leader of integrity, a man of virtue? On the other hand, could a man who betrayed his own friends ever be trusted with the well-being of people he did not know; for whom his feelings existed only in the abstract category, 'the public good'?

## POLITICS AS CONSPIRACY

Conspiracy was a familiar theme of old regime politics. Seen in this sense, conspiracy meant a group of people, linked by friendship or other personal ties, whose secret intention was to subvert the public good for their own personal interests. The idea that shadowy, ill-intentioned individuals were secretly plotting to undermine the stability and good order of the realm was a characteristic way of comprehending political opposition. It was particularly prominent in three forms of political and social rhetoric. The first of these was the popular preoccupation with the 'famine plot', a scheme supposedly hatched by the elite to starve the urban lower orders. During the Revolution this discourse would develop into characteristic *sans-culotte* themes: fear of profiteers, speculators, and hoarders.[91]

The second conspiratorial theme was much more literary, and was drawn from the classical republican model of politics. The discourse of classical republicanism was steeped in allusions to the dangers of conspiracy. The archetypal example of a classical conspirator was Catiline. The classical authors saw the denunciation of corrupt and conspiratorial office holders as a public duty, and a sign of the virtue of the denouncer. Cicero's polemics served as a model for this kind of patriotic denunciation.

The third theme owed much to political theorists, often spokesmen for the monarchy, who associated the factional politics of the court with duplicitous individuals who grouped together using clandestine tactics to pursue their own self-interest and self-advancement at the expense of the state and good government. Many groups and individuals—ranging from the Huguenots to the Cardinal de Retz—were characterized as forming cabals.[92] In the last years of the old regime

---

[90] See, for example, Eric R. Wolf, 'Kinship, friendship, and patron–client relations in complex societies', and Alex Weingrod, 'Patrons, patronage, and political parties', both in Steffen W. Schmidt *et al.*, *Friends, Followers and Factions: A Reader in Political Clientelism* (Berkeley: University of California Press, 1977); and Shmuel N. Eisenstadt and Luis Roniger (eds), *Patrons, Clients and Friends: Interpersonal Relations and the Structure of Trust in Society* (Cambridge: Cambridge University Press, 1984).

[91] See Hunt, *Politics, Culture and Class in the French Revolution*, 40.

[92] On fears of conspiracy in old regime France, see Peter R. Campbell, 'Perceptions of conspiracy on the eve of the French Revolution', in Campbell, Kaiser, and Linton, *Conspiracy and the French*

this discourse was frequently deployed by critics of monarchical policy, who used it to claim that the king's own ministers were conspiring against the people, indulging in ministerial despotism, and pursuing personal political ambition at the expense of the public good, either without the knowledge of the king, or occasionally, it was whispered, in collusion with the monarchy itself.[93]

## WHAT MAKES MEN INTO REVOLUTIONARIES?

'Do books make revolutions?' This question was posed by Roger Chartier; to which the answer has to be—no, or at least, not in an obvious way.[94] Future leaders of the Revolution thought much like their contemporaries. They did not adopt specific political ideas before the Revolution; indeed many, if not most, of them seem to have hardly thought about national politics at all prior to the collapse of the old regime.[95]

There is no easy way to trace the political development of individuals and predict the trajectory that they would take through revolutionary politics, simply by knowing what they read, or even what they wrote before the Revolution. According to Brinton the true Jacobin was a religious fanatic, by which he meant a fanatic without Catholic religion.[96] That might be one way of describing what some of the Jacobins became, but it is not how they began. The example of two future Jacobin leaders illustrates this point. Hérault de Séchelles belonged to the most privileged elite of the old regime. His world was that of the court and its values; but he was also an enthusiast for the cult of natural virtue; he kept a foot in both cultures simultaneously. He was, as we have seen, the author of the *Theory of Ambition*, a work which laid bare the under-workings of court politics, and advocated brazen tactics by which a man might manoeuvre to 'get on' in this world. Yet he also searched out and bought the manuscript of *La Nouvelle Héloïse*

---

*Revolution*; J.H.M. Salmon, *Cardinal de Retz: The Anatomy of a Conspirator* (London: Weidenfeld and Nicolson, 1969); also the chapters by Peter Campbell, Penny Roberts, and Stuart Carroll in Barry Coward and Julian Swann (eds), *Conspiracies and Conspiracy Theory in Early Modern Europe: From the Waldensians to the French Revolution* (Aldershot: Ashgate, 2004).

[93] On the origins of Billaud-Varenne's terrorist rhetoric in perceptions of ministerial politics of the old regime, see John M. Burney, 'The Fear of the Executive and the Threat of Conspiracy: Billaud-Varenne's Terrorist Rhetoric in the French Revolution, 1788–1794', *French History* 5, 2 (1991): 143–63. Burney argues that Billaud-Varenne's idea that the terror must be wielded to destroy conspiracy owed much to his earlier assimilation of old regime political arguments that ministerial politics were inherently factional, corrupt, secretive and prone to conspiracy. He derived this view from theorists as diverse as Necker and the Jansenist critics of executive power.

[94] Chartier, 'Do books make revolutions?' in Chartier, *The Cultural Origins of the French Revolution*, ch. 4; and Robert Darnton, *The Forbidden Best-Sellers of Pre-Revolutionary France* (London: Fontana, 1997), Part 3, 'Do books cause revolutions?'.

[95] A recent study by Tackett examines the pre-revolutionary reading of five future revolutionaries, and shows that it was not what they read that politicized them, but the experience of the early stages of the Revolution itself: Timothy Tackett, 'Paths to revolution: the old regime correspondence of five future revolutionaries', *French Historical Studies*, 32, 4 (2009): 531–54.

[96] Brinton, *The Jacobins*, 238–9.

for 24,000 *livres*—a book advocating values the very reverse of the ones he espoused in the *Theory of Ambition*. At the same time that he professed a profound admiration for Rousseau, he made notes on how to fake sensibility in order to get people to do what you want. Perhaps he was not the kind of man to espouse any set of beliefs wholeheartedly. People who knew him said he was both cynical and egotistical. He was, like many others, a complex and many-faceted man.

A very different kind of man, Louis-Antoine Saint-Just, from a relatively obscure background in a village in Picardy, occupied his time immediately before the Revolution in writing a pornographic, cynical, and satirical poem, *Organt*. This poem was written as a calculated attempt to further his ambitions to make something of himself in the world of the old regime. The poem reflected fashionable worldly taste of the time; it depicted the court as a place of glittering immorality; though it offered no alternative political vision. Unlike Hérault, Saint-Just had to imagine the world of the court from the position of an outsider, a provincial nobody. He was dissatisfied with the final result; he prefaced the poem with a self-critical epigraph: 'I am twenty, I have done badly, I could do better.'[97] It was published just as the Revolution broke out, that would make the culture that had inspired the poem obsolete. Saint-Just and Hérault reacted to the changed political order by making new choices, and by fashioning for themselves identities that would bring them together into the same world, that of Jacobin politics. Both men had a hand in the writing of the Jacobin constitution of June 1793—the most idealistic and egalitarian political constitution yet written. Both men became members of the Committee of Public Safety and thus had a responsibility for implementing the Jacobin policy of terror. What were their motives? It seems safe to say that in both cases ambition played a part; yet ambition was a motive that no revolutionary could publicly acknowledge. One cannot therefore know for sure what either man 'really thought'; one can only judge them by what they chose to do. In 1789 both chose revolution; but they were not yet 'opting for terror': that moment was still some way off, to be arrived at through a process of contingent choices in circumstances that no one could have foreseen.

---

[97] Preface to *Organt*, in Saint-Just, *Oeuvres complètes*, 50.

# 2

# 'How the Face of Things has Changed!'

This fortunate revolution, this regeneration will be accomplished; no power on earth is capable of hindering it. Sublime effect of philosophy, of liberty and of patriotism! We have become invincible. For myself I freely admit, I who used to be timid, now I feel I have become a different man...I feel I could joyfully die for so beautiful a cause, and, pierced by blows, I too would write in my blood *France is free*!

Camille Desmoulins, *La France Libre*, 1789.[1]

I had not realized the extent of the common bond that links us with the soil, with men who are our brothers; I learned it at that moment. I take this oath: beloved France...never will I betray the honourable trust of those who confided your interests to my hands; never shall my judgement or my will be determined by anything but the common good.

The marquis de Ferrières, in a letter to his wife on the opening of the Estates-General.[2]

The period 1786–9 saw the collapse of the old regime, and the rise of a revolution that would transform the nature and practice of politics.[3] The Revolution redefined political life, while bringing new men to the forefront of it. In 1789 the language of political virtue was almost universal; even political moderates and conservatives, many of whom were deeply sceptical about the value of moral politics, felt obliged to make some public show of conforming to it. But it was the leaders of the emerging radical Left, above all, who took the opportunity offered by this unprecedented circumstance to seize on the discourse of political virtue and shape it into their defining ideology. In the process they forged for themselves a new kind of political identity—that of 'the man of virtue' who would put this ideology into practice.

---

[1] Desmoulins, *La France Libre*, in Camille Desmoulins, *Oeuvres de Camille Desmoulins*, ed. J. Claretie, 2 vols (Paris: Charpentier et cie, 1874), 1:132.

[2] Cited in Hampson, *Prelude to Terror*, ix.

[3] On current historical thinking about the origins of the French Revolution, see Peter Campbell, 'Introduction' to Campbell, *The Origins of the French Revolution*; also the editors' 'Introduction' to Kaiser and Van Kley, *From Deficit to Deluge*. See also the classic Jean Egret, *La Pré-révolution française, 1787–1788* (Paris: Presses Universitaires de France, 1961). On the Assembly of Notables see Vivian R. Gruder, *The Notables and the Nation: The Political Schooling of the French, 1787–1788* (Cambridge, MA: Harvard University Press, 2007); and John Hardman, *Overture to Revolution: The 1787 Assembly of Notables and the Crisis of France's Old Regime* (Oxford: Oxford University Press, 2010). Hardman shows how much personal ambition motivated leading figures in the Notables, above all Brienne.

This chapter will look at how this new identity was formed in the crucible of politics during the first months of the Revolution.

The Revolution saw a transformation of the prevailing political culture from the enclosed and private world of old regime politics to the new and transparent political culture of revolutionary politics. Men who wanted to succeed in this new culture carved themselves out a space for political participation by identifying themselves with the ideology of political virtue. Political leaders would not be answerable to the king, but to public opinion: they therefore submitted their identities to the judgement of the public, inviting the public to decide whether or not their virtue was authentic. Public opinion would be embodied in the flood of pamphlets and other writings that appeared in the collapse of the old regime system of censorship.[4] The ideology of virtue provided the necessary justification for turning rebels into revolutionaries. It gave revolutionaries moral legitimacy from which sprang their claim to authority. To be a 'man of virtue' meant that one was engaging in revolution not to profit from it, not to overthrow one ruling class in order to replace it, but for the public good.

## PATRIOT NOBLES BECOME MEN OF VIRTUE

It was from the ranks of the nobility that the first leaders of the revolutionary movement emerged in 1787–8. They were not the only ones to want changes in the political structure, but they were the only ones with sufficient power and status to bring it about. They justified the blows they dealt to the old regime by appealing to public opinion; they presented themselves as men of integrity, fighting against the despotism and corruption of the king's ministers. Most of these nobles had only a very limited desire for change; many referred to 'custom' rather than revolutionary principles as their justification for opposing what they termed 'ministerial despotism'. These nobles had conflicting ideas about the kind of system that they wanted to see established; what they had in common was a desire that they themselves should play a bigger political role than had been possible in the old regime. What they did not envisage was that the consequence of their actions would be the onset of a revolution that would swell to encompass the transformation of the whole political and social system, and sweep away many things in the process, including the very existence of the French nobility itself.[5] Four years later, the

---

[4] On the origins of the revolutionary pamphlet press, see Kenneth Margerison, *Pamphlets and Public Opinion: The Campaign for a Union of Orders in the Early French Revolution* (West Lafayette, IN: Purdue University Press, 1998); Margerison, 'The pamphlet debate over the organisation of the Estates-General', in Campbell, *The Origins of the French Revolution*; Jeremy D. Popkin, 'The prerevolutionary origins of political journalism'; Jack R. Censer and Jeremy D. Popkin (eds), *Press and Politics in Pre-Revolutionary France* (Berkeley: University of California Press, 1987); and Jeremy D. Popkin, 'Pamphlet journalism at the end of the old regime', *Eighteenth-Century Studies*, 22, 3 (1989): 351–67.

[5] On the part played by nobles in the initiation of revolution, the classic account is in Georges Lefebvre, *The Coming of the French Revolution*, trans. R.R. Palmer (1939: this edition, Princeton, NJ: Princeton University Press, 2005); together with Elizabeth Eisenstein, 'Who intervened in 1788? A commentary on the coming of the French Revolution', *American Historical Review*, 71 (1965/6): 77–103.

revolutionary leader Vergniaud was to say that the Revolution was like Saturn—it devoured its own children. This was a process that began with the nobles who played a leading role in creating it.

Much of the more radical rhetoric that came out of the pre-revolutionary debates was hostile towards the power of the nobility as a privileged caste.[6] This attitude was encapsulated by the rhetoric of Sieyès's pamphlet, *What is the Third Estate?* where he warned: 'While the aristocrats talk of their honour yet watch out for their self-interest, the Third Estate, that is to say, the nation, will develop its virtue, for if corporate interest is egotism, national interest is virtue.'[7] Sieyès's intention was to ensure that the nobility could no longer claim separate representation, and make the case for the bourgeoisie to secure political representation.[8] It did not preclude individual nobles from embracing the cause of national politics and taking a leading role in the campaign for political transformation. The patriot nobles who spearheaded the early phases of the Revolution identified themselves with the ideology of political virtue. The core of this group was the Society of Thirty, whose members met in the Paris house of Adrien Duport, a *conseiller* in the Paris *Parlement*, between November 1788 and May 1789.[9] The Society sought to rally opinion around liberal reform projects and supported the publication of a number of the pamphlets that appeared in support of political change. Despite Sieyès's anti-noble rhetoric, it is generally accepted by historians that his pamphlet was sponsored by the Society of Thirty.[10] The great majority of the membership of the Society (91 per cent) were nobles, most of whom were both influential and well connected. They included the marquis de Lafayette, his brother-in-law, the vicomte de Noailles, and the three Lameth brothers, all of whom had been radicalized by their experiences fighting in the American War of Independence.[11] The Society included a few prominent non-nobles, men such as Target, a barrister and seasoned pro-*parlement* campaigner with a renowned reputation for outspoken views.[12] Most of the members had residences in Paris and formed part of an

---

[6] On the growing hostility towards aristocracy, see Doyle, *Aristocracy and Its Enemies*. On the negative image of both the aristocracy and, by extension, individual nobles, as a cornerstone of Jacobin ideology, see George Armstrong Kelly, *Victims, Authority, and Terror: The Parallel Deaths of d'Orléans, Custine, Bailly, and Malesherbes* (Chapel Hill: University of North Carolina Press, 1982); and André Découflé, 'L'aristocratie française devant l'opinion publique à la veille de la Révolution (1787–1789)', in André Découflé *et al.* (eds), *Études d'histoire économique et sociale du XVIIIe siècle* (Paris: Presses Universitaires de France, 1966).

[7] Emmanuel-Joseph Sieyès, *Qu'est-ce que le Tiers état?* (1789; this edition, Geneva: Droz, 1970), 195.

[8] See Murray Forsyth, *Reason and Revolution: the Political Thought of the Abbé Sieyès* (Leicester: Leicester University Press, 1987); and William H. Sewell, *A Rhetoric of Bourgeois Revolution: the Abbé Sieyès and* What is the Third Estate? (Durham, NC: Duke University Press, 1994).

[9] Duport's house was in the Rue du Grand Chantier, in the Marais quarter.

[10] Margerison expresses doubt about the extent of Sieyès's connections with the Society of Thirty, given that most of the latter were working for a union of orders. See Margerison, *Pamphlets and Public Opinion*, ch. 5, 'Sieyès and public opinion', esp. 94–5.

[11] Daniel L. Wick, *A Conspiracy of Well-Intentioned Men: The Society of Thirty and the French Revolution* (New York: Garland Publishing, 1989), 319.

[12] The principal study of the Society of Thirty is by Wick, *A Conspiracy of Well-Intentioned Men*; and Wick, 'The court nobility and the French Revolution: the example of the Society of Thirty',

informal network of liberal nobles based around the court and the *Parlement*. The renegade noble Mirabeau was a member for a while, but he disliked the fact that the Society met in Duport's own home as this gave Duport the opportunity to manipulate its direction and turn it to the advantage of *parlementaire* politics. Having tried, unsuccessfully, to change the venue to an 'independent location', Mirabeau ceased to participate.[13]

The members of the Society of Thirty presented themselves as motivated by their virtue: in criticizing the king's ministers they were engaging in the public-spirited defence of 'the social virtues, public morals' against the 'men of corruption'.[14] They thus took the lead in initiating this language of revolution and launching it onto the political stage. As individuals, too, some of them would go on to play a key role in the politics of the early stages of the Revolution. The members of the Society had differing political and constitutional goals. The conflicts among their views soon became apparent; even before the Revolution had begun the Society fragmented. Some members, like Duval d'Éprémesnil, withdrew in dismay when they realized the extent to which the whole old regime was in danger of collapse, and joined the reaction against the Revolution; while others stayed at the forefront of revolutionary politics. What occupies us here, though, is what motivated these men during the time that they worked together. They said that they were motivated by a desire to obtain the public good. That may have been the case. Another motive was personal resentment at the mismanagement of court patronage by the king and queen, above all resentment at the ascendancy of the Polignacs at the expense of the Noailles faction.[15]

Family and friendship networks were also a major influence. A high proportion of nobles in the Society were connected by ties of family or friendship to other members. This was not invariably the case, however; families did divide over political choices, and friendships fractured. The choice to become a revolutionary in many cases caused conflict with family members, and notables in their own localities. New ties had to be forged, with hitherto strangers, now 'brothers in revolution'. Amongst other factors we should not underestimate the emotional excitement of the revolutionary moment: it generated the heady sensation that the world was changing course all around them, and people wanted to be part of this. Younger heads were probably more attuned to this euphoric feeling than older ones. In the Society of Thirty there was a fairly high proportion of younger nobles, particularly amongst the military nobility who were mostly in their late twenties or, at most, early thirties. Personal ambition, whether acknowledged or not, played a part in

*Eighteenth-Century Studies*, 13 (Spring 1980): 263–84. See also Margerison, *Pamphlets and Public Opinion*, ch. 3. Margerison makes the point that some of the men who attended the meetings, like Duport, were pro-*parlement*, and were hoping to regain the popular initiative that the *Parlement* had lost in September 1788.

[13] Georges Michon, *Essai sur l'histoire du parti feuillant: Adrien Duport* (Paris: Payot, 1924), 31.

[14] These were words used by Duport to criticize the financial mismanagement of Calonne. Cited by Darnton, 'Trends in radical propaganda', 275–6.

[15] On the Polignacs, see Wick, 'Court nobility and the French Revolution'; and Thomas E. Kaiser, 'From fiscal crisis to revolution: the court and French foreign policy, 1787–1789', in Kaiser and Van Kley, *From Deficit to Deluge*, 150.

many cases, particularly for men whose ambitions were blocked because they were members of out-of-favour court factions. As men of the privileged elite, raised to be self-assured about their importance in the world, they assumed that if there was to be a regime change they were the natural men to lead the new order.

## SEIZING THE MOMENT: CAMPAIGNING FOR ELECTION TO THE ESTATES-GENERAL

Elections to the Estates-General were held in the spring of 1789. One of the problems faced in organizing these elections was whether to follow precedent, or to establish new methods for choosing representatives.[16] When the French looked about them for ways to conduct the new kind of politics an obvious candidate was the English model. They particularly admired the English constitution with its separation of powers. Some French theorists drew on the English republican tradition, though others were of the opinion that their own republican ideas were far superior to the English variety.[17] There was less admiration, however, of the English method of conducting politics, and the behaviour of English politicians, which the French looked down upon as rife with corruption and cronyism. French commentators were particularly suspicious of the English method of conducting elections through official candidatures that were open to corruption: French politicians would do their politics differently. French views of political representation derived partly from France's own electoral traditions, for the Estates-General, for the provincial estates, and religious institutional precedents.[18] There were also intellectual reasons to reject open candidacy and campaigning. According to the discourse of virtue, the very fact that a man openly stood for election indicated that he had an ulterior motive and intended to use his public position to further his own career; he was therefore unworthy of holding public office. From the outset it was accepted

---

[16] On the electoral system adopted see Malcolm Crook, *Elections in the French Revolution: an Apprenticeship in Democracy, 1789–1799* (Cambridge: Cambridge University Press, 1996); Patrice Gueniffey, *Le Nombre et la raison: la Révolution française et les élections* (Paris: École des Hautes Études en Sciences Sociales, 1993); Patrice Gueniffey, 'Revolutionary democracy and the elections', in Waldinger, Dawson, and Woloch, *The French Revolution and the Meaning of Citizenship*; and Bernard Gainot, 'Théorie et pratique(s) de la représentation politique', in Martin, *La Révolution à l'oeuvre*.

[17] When Arthur Young dined with members of the patriot party at the Duc de Liancourt's home in January 1790, he found that they had a low opinion of the English constitution as a safeguard of liberty: Arthur Young, *Travels in France During the Years 1787, 1788 and 1789* (1792: this edition, Cambridge: Cambridge University Press, 1929), 258. On English republicanism's influence in France, see Gueniffey, *La Politique de la Terreur*, 43–9. On French interest in English constitutional theory, see also the classic studies by Joseph Dédieu, *Montesquieu et la tradition politique anglaise en France* (Paris: J. Gabalda, 1909); and Elie Carcassonne, *Montesquieu et le problème de la constitution française au XVIIIe siècle* (1927: this edition, Geneva: Slatkine Reprints, 1970). On Mirabeau's English links, see Jean Bénétruy, *L'Atelier de Mirabeau: quatre proscrits génévois dans la tourmente révolutionnaire* (Paris: A. and J. Picard, 1962). For the argument that members of the Cordeliers Club were influenced by English republicanism, see Rachel Hammersley, *French Revolutionaries and English Republicans: the Cordeliers Club, 1790–1794* (Woodbridge: The Royal Historical Society, The Boydell Press, 2005).

[18] Léo Moulin, 'Les origines religieuses des techniques électorales et délibératives modernes', *Revue Internationale d'histoire politique et constitutionelle* (1953), 106–48.

that there should be no official candidates, no platforms, no manifestos, and no parties.

That at least was the theory. In fact, many nobles were already part of informal networks of friendship and more formal networks of power and patronage. Those nobles who had been at court already had their own networks; many more had secondary residences in Paris where they were accustomed to socializing with one another. The mass of the nobility disregarded the code against electioneering; they relied on the traditional means of patronage and networking to secure their election. Many of the higher clergy followed suit, campaigning and networking openly.[19] There were situations in which provincial nobles used the rhetoric of virtue, but this was the exception rather than the rule.[20]

The group of nobles who allied themselves with the new 'patriot party' (which included some of the more radical members of the Society of Thirty) took a different stance. They consciously and very deliberately presented themselves as men of virtue. They stated their formal opposition both to monarchical 'despotism' and to 'aristocracy'. They claimed to be concerned principally with the public good, and only incidentally with their own candidacy as a means of furthering that good. Alexandre de Lameth, who was elected as a noble deputy for Péronne, declared that he had been inspired by the new public spirit: 'It [the public spirit] spread the light, warmed men's hearts, and replaced selfishness and personal interests with general views; finally, it is to this principle, so beneficial, that we owe the happy revolution which is under way.'[21] In similar vein, Duport applauded the fact that the electoral assemblies had not listened to private considerations: 'the interest of all was the only thing that counted'.[22]

Amongst the electors of Third Estate deputies the rhetoric of political virtue had taken a strong hold. It was generally accepted that a man was unworthy of public office if he openly campaigned to get it. This put many would-be deputies into an awkward position for, in practice, there was little hope of getting elected if one was not already known to the eligible electors and did not have a reputation as a man engaged in public affairs. A few campaigned openly, but most Third Estate deputies embarked on the delicate business of signalling to the electorate their availability as prospective candidates without openly admitting that such was their desire.

---

[19] On the extent to which nobles in the Estates-General employed friendship networks and patronage to secure their places, see Timothy Tackett, 'Nobles and the Third Estate in the Revolutionary dynamic of the National Assembly, 1789–1790', republished in Peter Jones (ed.), *The French Revolution in Social and Political Perspective* (London: Arnold, 1996), 318. See also Tackett, *Becoming a Revolutionary*, 94–9.

[20] On the example of the nobles of Arras, see Norman Hampson, 'The Enlightenment and the language of the French nobility in 1789: the case of Arras', in D.J. Mossop, G.E. Rodmell, and D.B. Wilson (eds), *Studies in the French Eighteenth Century, Presented to John Lough* (Durham: University of Durham, 1978).

[21] Cited in Doina Pasca Harsanyi, 'The Memoirs of Lameth and the reconciliation of nobility and Revolution', in Jay M. Smith (ed.), *The French Nobility in the Eighteenth Century. Reassessments and New Approaches* (University Park: The University of Pennsylvania Press, 2006), 283.

[22] Cited in Michon, *Adrien Duport*, 37.

We can see how prospective Third Estate deputies negotiated these difficulties by looking at the example of Maximilien Robespierre's election as a representative of the Third Estate of Artois. His pre-revolutionary career had been notable partly for the shortage of patrons to smooth the path to success. With no network, and few family connections to help him, he had been obliged to shape his pre-revolutionary career largely through intelligence, determination, and hard work.[23] Robespierre was eager to secure a place in the Estates-General, but to do this he needed to make a public impression in his native province and was hampered by his own obscurity. He handled this dilemma partly by becoming active in local politics. He became known locally as an outspoken champion of the poor and oppressed. There is no reason to think that he was insincere in his concern for the social underclasses. On the contrary, in his legal career he had been known for his sympathy for the poor, the underdog, the victims of elitist injustice, whom he had supported long before the possibility of a career in revolutionary politics made it expedient to do so. On the other hand, he quickly learned how to shape his concern into the language of revolutionary politics, as witnessed by the fact that he was asked by the guild of lesser shoemakers in Arras to draft their *cahier de doléance*.[24]

He also wrote *À la Nation artésienne*, in which he presented himself as a man of virtue. The pamphlet contained a warning. Like many others, Robespierre suspected the activities of the privileged orders in the Estates of Artois, and feared that they would try to manipulate the process of election to the Estates-General for their own advantage. The effect of the despotic regime under which they had been living was 'a fatal indifference for the public interest'. The aristocratic party counted on being able to continue its tactical domination:

> ...this happy revolution, this ending of all the evils that crush us, depends on the virtue, the courage, and the sentiments of those to whom we shall confide the re-doubtable honour of defending our interests in the Assembly of the Nation; during these important choices we shall carefully avoid the snares that intrigue and ambition will lay on our path; above all we shall not entrust the reform of abuses to the zeal of those whose interest it is to retain them, through the most powerful of all motives, personal interest, *esprit de corps*, and the love and habit of domination. Imagine what you can expect at the hands of those who have not been able to cloak their ambitions, even under the mask of patriotism and disinterest whose language they are obliged to imitate sometimes by the force of public opinion...[25]

The success of the Revolution would depend on the virtue of the representatives, and their ability to stand against the aristocratic conspiracy. The choice was between deputies who were authentically virtuous, and those who imitated this

---

[23] This complex community, and Robespierre's development within it, are excellently described by McPhee, *Robespierre*, ch. 1–4.

[24] 'Doléances du Corps des Cordonniers Mineurs de la Ville d'Arras' (March 1789), in Maximilien Robespierre, *Oeuvres de Maximilien Robespierre*, eds Marc Bouloiseau, Albert Soboul, *et al.*, 11 vols (Paris: Société des études Robespierristes, 1910–2007), 11, *Compléments (1784–1794)*: 275–7.

[25] Maximilien Robespierre, *À la Nation artésienne* (1789), in *Oeuvres de Robespierre*, 11, *Compléments (1784–1794)*: 244–5.

language in order to further their own interests. Already he saw that the problem with the language of virtue was the gap between what men said and what they did. How then could one trust the integrity of men who sought public office?

It was common practice during the political campaigns of 1788–9 to publish pamphlets anonymously; not only did this help to deflect the enmity that might result from publishing contentious ideas openly but, in the run-up to the elections to the Estates-General, such a practice was in conformity with the code that frowned upon people standing as open candidates. For Robespierre, his anonymous pamphlets brought him to the notice of the electors to the Third Estate; the pamphlets helped to establish his reputation, while throwing down the gauntlet to the privileged elite. Robespierre went further in a second anonymous pamphlet in April 1789, *Les ennemis de la Patrie démasqués*. Here he took up the rhetoric of conspiracy to state that there was a plot by the 'ambitious men of the municipal and provincial administration to perpetuate their oppressive regime' by manipulating the elections. He closed with an account of what motivated him—his virtue. He was explicit that what he meant by virtue was not the classical republican version, but natural virtue, 'this generous sensibility' that was 'not confined to the Romans or the Greeks', but rather was a universal quality 'that men of all countries and all times were shaped to wield, in the same circumstances, all the virtues that honour human nature'. The pamphlet ended with him referring to his willingness to brave martyrdom as a 'defender of the people'.[26]

Robespierre's enemies pounced upon any evidence that he was contravening the embargo on electioneering. The abbé Proyart, Robespierre's early, hostile biographer, later accused Robespierre of 'playing a role', and of 'speaking the language' he thought most likely to win him supporters. According to Proyart, Robespierre sent his brother Augustin to promote his campaign for election in the countryside round Arras, and put pressure on distant relatives.[27] Robespierre's tactics seem to have been fairly standard practice in the run-up to the Estates-General.[28] But his opponents had latched onto what was to be both his political strength and his weakness—the wholeheartedness of his identification with virtue. Robespierre was particularly vulnerable to the accusation that he was electioneering (even if all around him people were busily doing much the same thing) precisely because he insisted so strongly that *he* was the candidate of authentic virtue, and therefore opposed to practices of corruption, patronage, and networking.[29]

[26] Maximilien Robespierre, *Les ennemis de la Patrie démasqués* (April 1789), in *Oeuvres de Robespierre*, 11, *Compléments (1784–1794)*: 248, 273–4. On Robespierre's debt to Rousseau, see McPhee, *Robespierre*, 108.

[27] Le Blond de Neuvéglise [pseudo. of Lievin-Bonaventure Proyart (abbé)], *La Vie et les crimes de Robespierre, surnommé le tyran, depuis sa naissance jusqu'à sa mort* (Augsburg, 1795), 69–72.

[28] Thompson agrees that there was nothing dishonest about Robespierre's election campaigning, not least because he was not very successful at it: Thompson, *Robespierre*, 201. See also McPhee, *Robespierre*, 59–60; and Bruno Decriem, '1788/1789 en Artois: un candidat en campagne électorale, Maximilien de Robespierre', in Jean-Pierre Jessenne *et al.* (eds), *Robespierre: De la Nation artésienne à la république et aux nations* (Lille: Centre d'Histoire de la Région du Nord, 1993).

[29] On the problem of Robespierre's authenticity, see also Marisa Linton, 'Robespierre et l'authenticité révolutionnaire', *Annales historiques de la Révolution française*, 371 (2013): 153–73.

## VERSAILLES: THIRD ESTATE ENCOUNTERS WITH COURT NOBLES

The new deputies came to the Estates-General with ideas informed by the many pamphlets they had read, and politicized by the process of elections to the Estates-General and the preparation of the *cahiers de doléance*. Many of the Third Estate deputies were hopeful of achieving a regeneration of the French state, yet they feared that the two privileged orders, nobles and clergy, would side against theirs, and that the king intended to add his weight to the forces of privilege. These fears were confirmed when the Third Estate deputies arrived at Versailles and were introduced to the stultified atmosphere at court. It looked as though nothing here had changed since the days of Louis XIV, and that the monarch had no intention of changing the way that politics was conducted, or widening the circle of men permitted access to politics. The rituals of the court, the orders of procession, even the clothes prescribed to the deputies to wear, all were set out according to the entrenched system of privilege and hierarchy that was at the heart of the old regime. Every kind of distinction was employed to reinforce social divisions and to demonstrate that whilst the deputies were all political representatives there was no equality in their status and social station. At every turn the deputies of the Third Estate were reminded of their inferior position.[30] It was a clear case of political mismanagement of a situation that was already far more explosive than the king or his ministers understood. Even some of the parish clergy who made up the lower ranks of the First Estate, were stung by the ritual humiliations that they were obliged to undergo. In allowing the socially hierarchy to be ritually enacted in this way, the king—whether he realized this or not—was dealing out a snub to the newly self-conscious nation. It appeared to observers from the Third Estate that the distinctions were indeed intentional. Rabaut Saint-Etienne, a Third Estate deputy for Nîmes, remarked 'all was prepared to make the distinction between the orders as marked as possible; because it was intended to maintain it'.[31]

Few of the men representing the Third Estate had previously encountered members of the court nobility at close hand, or experienced the enclosed world of Versailles. The overt arrogance of much of the nobility gave substance to the negative image of the Second Estate that had circulated so widely in the 1780s. The Third Estate deputies were deeply disappointed, too, by the attitude of many—not all—of the nobility who were more concerned with preserving the purity and status of their own caste, than working towards creating a more participatory and egalitarian political system. Many of the conservative nobles would never be reconciled to the Revolution and continued to obstruct and humiliate the Third Estate deputies, provoking a strong reaction, both tactical and emotional.[32]

---

[30] For much detail about the experiences of the deputies, see Edna Hindie Lemay, *La Vie quotidienne des députés aux états généraux, 1789* (Paris: Hachette, 1987).

[31] Cited in Lemay, *La Vie quotidienne des députés*, 85–6.

[32] For the evidence that fear was a powerful emotion amongst the deputies, especially between June and 4 August, see Tackett, *Becoming a Revolutionary*, 149–69. For insight into the psychological trauma suffered by the Third Estate deputies as a result of confrontation with the monarchy, see Shapiro, *Traumatic Politics*.

A small group of Third Estate deputies banded together on the far Left of the Assembly, advocating popular sovereignty: they were Robespierre, Jérome Pétion, François Buzot, and Pierre-Louis Prieur.[33] In such oppressive circumstances they could take pride in their identity as men of virtue. It became a kind of badge with which they recognized one another, and by means of which they could empower themselves and pass judgement in their turn on the court nobles who looked down upon them. Buzot later described his first impressions of the court from his perspective as a man of virtue:

> Born with an independent and proud character that never bent under the command of any person, how could I abide the idea of a hereditary master and an inviolable man? My head and my heart full of Greek and Roman history, and the great personages who, in the ancient republics, imparted most honour to humanity, I professed their maxims from the earliest age, I nourished myself on the study of their virtues.

He had never given himself up to 'libertinage' or 'debauchery'. His favourite authors had been Plutarch and Rousseau. When he arrived at Versailles his worst expectations were realized: '. . . the nobility, the clergy, the court the most dissolute in all Europe! I showed myself to be a friend of the people, an intrepid defender of the rights of humanity.' He soon found, however, that through his new persona as a moral politician, he gained access to a level of recognition and respect that he would never had reached in his home town of Evreux where he was just another obscure lawyer. He recalled in a moment of happiness: 'At Versailles I was considered, sought after, everywhere I was esteemed.'[34]

However, in maintaining their political careers many of the Third Estate deputies had more practical difficulties to contend with than the sneering of courtiers. Money—or lack it—was a pressing problem. At first representatives to the Estates-General were expected to pay their own expenses. But as the Estates-General transformed into a National Assembly the question of payment for deputies became more urgent.[35] Many, particularly Third Estate deputies and parish priests, had been getting into considerable financial difficulties through the cost of moving to Versailles, and struggling to live without earnings. It was apparent that men of humble means could not continue to be national representatives and that without payment their voices would be lost. The conservative nobles were content to see the same kind of principles applied in France as in England, where only a man of private means could afford to be a deputy. But on 1 September 1789 the Assembly agreed that deputies be remunerated at a rate of 18 *livres* a day (to be paid monthly, totalling 540 *livres* a month), and backdated to 27 April. This was a key step in enabling men who would otherwise have to work for a living to maintain a political career.

---

[33] On Buzot, see Jacques Herissay, *François Buzot: député de l'Eure à l'Assemblée Constituante et à la Convention, 1760–1794* (Paris: Perrin, 1907).

[34] François Buzot, *Mémoires sur la Révolution française par Buzot, député à la Convention Nationale* (Paris: Béchet ainé, 1823), 21–5.

[35] On the question of the collective identity of the new Assembly, see Robert H. Blackman, 'What's in a name? Possible names for a legislative body and the birth of national sovereignty during the French Revolution, 15–16 June 1789', *French History*, 21 (March 2007): 22–43.

In accordance with the principle of equality all deputies, regardless of private income or lack of it, would be paid at the same rate.[36]

## VIRTUE ASCENDANT: THE PATRIOT NOBLES AND THE EMOTIONAL POLITICS OF SACRIFICE

The Revolution began in June 1789 with the union of the three orders into a National Assembly. The welcome extended by the Third Estate deputies to the patriot nobles owed something to their pleasure at being accepted by nobles on equal terms. As Tackett comments, at this stage the Third Estate did not want to overthrow the nobles but to be treated as equals by them.[37] The new spirit of fraternity would encompass nobles and non-nobles alike. Indeed, the nobility could still retain their pre-eminent place—by abandoning exclusive privilege and embracing egalitarian virtue. Their natural leadership qualities would ensure their status.

A group of like-minded friends formed itself around the marquis de Lafayette, including the Lameths, Duport, Mounier, the marquis de Latour-Maubourg and the duc de la Rochefoucauld. Another prominent member was Antoine Barnave. He was a lawyer from an affluent family in Grenoble, with noble family (his mother was noble, his father had personal nobility) but his sympathies were very much with the Third Estate.[38] This group became the nucleus of the so-called 'patriot party' in the Assembly, though it was not a formal party in the English sense. The patriot nobles supported a much more radical position. They accepted that nobles would no longer have separate status within the Assembly, looking to a future where merit mattered more than caste. The patriot nobles embraced the idea of political virtue. In theory all men were equal. No group would dominate the new political order on the basis of hereditary right. Nevertheless, the patriot nobles saw themselves as natural leaders; their individual virtues and talents fitted them to become dominant figures in the Assembly.

Ironically, it was easier for a man like Alexandre de Lameth, with his wealth and privileged status, to be seen as an *authentic* man of virtue than it was for someone like Robespierre, or Buzot, or the other Third Estate deputies of humble means. In comparison with the patriot nobles, such men were relatively poor, in that they could not live indefinitely like gentlemen on the income from land or rents. The Revolution provided an obvious career opportunity for men like Robespierre. It was all too easy for his opponents to say that his radical politics were a cloak for his ambition. This could not be said about the patriot nobles. They all enjoyed status, and were in easy circumstances—in many cases extremely wealthy—before the Revolution. Such men had potentially a great deal to lose by supporting radical

---

[36] C.L. Benson, 'How the French deputies were paid in 1789–91', *Journal of Modern History*, 5, 1 (1933): 19–33.

[37] Tackett, 'Nobles and the Third Estate', 321.

[38] He was christened Antoine-Pierre-Joseph-Marie Barnave, but the name he commonly used was Joseph. On Barnave's political friendships, see Bradby, *The Life of Barnave*, I: 115–25. See also François Furet, 'Barnave', in Furet and Ozouf, *Dictionnaire critique de la Révolution française*, 206–15.

policies, and this made their claims that they acted out of a desire to further the public good more convincing.

The patriot nobles, however, were vulnerable to a different kind of accusation. This was that they had chosen to act recklessly in precipitating the events that would bring down the old regime, the nobility, and eventually the monarchy itself. According to the conservative nobles, men like the Lameths, Duport, Lafayette, d'Aiguillon, were far worse than Robespierre and his kind, for the patriot nobles bore a responsibility for the destruction of their own world, their own people. Robespierre had never met the king.[39] La Rochefoucauld, Lafayette, and the others had been at court, they knew the king personally, had been trusted by him. In the eyes of the monarchy and the nobility, this made them doubly treacherous, traitors to the world of the old regime that had sustained them, and to the people they knew.

Such accusations threw Alexandre de Lameth onto the defensive. Many years later, when in 1828 he published his *History of the Constituent Assembly*, he was still trying retrospectively to justify the choices that he, his brothers, and his friends amongst the patriot nobles had made in the far-off days of 1789. Lameth had been stung by the charge that Robespierre was less guilty than the old duc de la Roche-foucauld for his part in destroying the old regime, precisely because Robespierre had not been genuinely virtuous but 'had followed his own interest' which was 'a completely natural impulse' for someone of his low social origin; whereas la Roche-foucauld had 'betrayed his order'.[40] According to Lameth the motives of the patriot nobles had been impeccable: they had acted not out of ambition but out of devo-tion to the public good. Their actions were contrasted with those of the people he still saw as the villains of the piece, 'the class of such dangerous and pernicious courtiers'. Such people always had a harmful effect on the state, but it was 'during the epoch of revolutions that their influence became more fatal'. The courtiers he singled out for condemnation were 'a small number of families' who were inti-mates of the king and queen. In Lameth's view it was their egoism, greed, and political stupidity that had sparked off the Revolution: 'Taking up root close to the throne, they blocked off all avenues to it. They occupied all the principal posts, and entrenched themselves there in such a way that the monarch himself no longer had the power to make them give up their posts . . .' On the other hand, the nobility (and he includes most of the nobles who frequented the court in that category) 'regarded it as a duty to give the king disinterested homage'. Some obtained mili-tary advancement, but made 'considerable sacrifices to do so'. (This was possibly an oblique reference to a generous pension secured by his mother for her sons, after

---

[39] As a boy at the school of Louis-le-Grand, Robespierre was chosen to make a speech of welcome when the king and queen made a fleeting visit. But since the king neither replied nor left his coach, this was a distinctly one-sided encounter.

[40] Alexandre de Lameth, *Histoire de l'Assemblée Constituante*, 2 vols (Paris, Moutardier, 1828), 1: Avertissement, iv. Lameth's retrospective defence of his political choices should be seen in the light of the self-doubt felt by the nobility in the years following the Revolution: see Doyle, *Aristocracy and its Enemies*. For a persuasive account of Lameth's political agenda, see Harsanyi, 'The Memoirs of Lameth', 300–2.

the death of their father.) Almost the totality of the nobility that attended the court 'depleted their fortunes with enormous expenses and without obtaining any advantage'.[41] Unlike court nobles, military nobles such as Lameth had been ready to sacrifice their own lives for the good of the country, and this gave them added resonance as men of morality rather than egoism.

Lameth's arguments illuminate the emotional and rhetorical context of the extraordinary act of ritual self-sacrifice of 4 August 1789. On this momentous night the Assembly witnessed a wholesale repudiation of the old regime and the edifice of privilege on which it was built. The patriot nobles led the way in making a public show of their altruism by sacrificing material and financial advantages, posts, and positions. This event had a huge political and social impact. The self-sacrifice initiated by the patriot nobles took on a symbolic and emotional significance that became central to the meaning of the Revolution. It came about partly in response to the peasant uprisings in the movement known as the 'Great Fear' over the summer. Rumours spread through the countryside that the 'aristocratic' party were sending brigands to attack the peasantry. Peasants responded by rising against their noble overlords and the feudal dues exacted on them as part of noble privilege. Historians have debated whether pragmatic self-interest was the motive for the Assembly's actions—a 'damage control' response to peasants taking revolution into their own hands, burning the feudal records—so as to regain the initiative and recoup a situation that threatened to spiral outside the revolutionary leaders' control.[42] An alternative perspective is that events were spurred on by a genuine sense of injustice at the inequalities of the system of privilege and a desire to abolish an iniquitous regime.[43] In fact it was both ideological and tactical. The strategy was plotted out beforehand in the Breton Club (a group composed both of patriot nobles and of Third Estate deputies that was a forerunner of the Jacobin Club; it included most of the Society of Thirty).[44]

Bertrand Barère, a young, well-connected, and personable Third Estate deputy from Tarbes, gave a vivid account of how the strategy was worked out in the Club.[45] It was needful for these gestures to be made as an act of *personal* sacrifice in order to have validity and make it hard for anyone to argue against them. Le Chapelier, a leader of the Breton Club, was voted in as president of the Assembly

---

[41] Lameth, *Histoire de l'Assemblée Constituante*, 1: 323–4.

[42] On the peasant uprisings see John Markoff, *The Abolition of Feudalism: Peasants, Lords and Legislators in the French Revolution* (University Park: Pennsylvania State University Press, 1996). On 4 August as 'damage control' to regain the initiative from the peasantry, see Markoff, 'Peasants and their grievances', in Campbell, *Origins of the French Revolution*, 266.

[43] The fullest account of 4 August is by Michael P. Fitzsimmons, *The Night the Old Regime Ended: August 4, 1789, and the French Revolution* (University Park: Pennsylvania State University Press, 2003).

[44] On the Breton Club see François Aulard (ed.), *Société des Jacobins: recueil de documents pour l'histoire de club des Jacobins de Paris*, 6 vols (Paris: Léopold Cerf; Noblet; Quantin, 1889–97), 1: Introduction, ii–xvii; Lemay, *La Vie quotidienne des députés*, 209–16; and Applewhite, *Political Alignment in the French National Assembly*, 72–3, 119.

[45] Bertrand Barère, *Memoirs of Bertrand Barère*, trans. De V. Payen-Payne, 4 vols (London: H.S. Nichols, 1896), 1: 228.

on 3 August, which made it easier for the Left to take the initiative. To that end the plan was for the duc d'Aiguillon (the man who, after the king, had the greatest wealth in feudal properties in France) to initiate events by proposing to sacrifice noble privilege in a bid to restore order. This gesture would wrong-foot other privilege holders making it very difficult for them to argue that they should retain their privileges, without appearing themselves to be motivated by greed and egoism. In the event, the vicomte de Noailles, a well-connected, but considerably less affluent, patriot noble, got in with his renunciation of privilege before d'Aiguillon, in a bid for popularity. Nonetheless, d'Aiguillon's gesture had a great impact. He lost more than 100,000 *livres* in rents as a consequence. As Lameth said, 'this patriotic devotion became the signal for other sacrifices of the same kind'.[46] The outcome surpassed the wildest dreams of the men who planned it. The gesture of self-sacrifice escalated dramatically and sparked off a huge wave of genuine emotion inspired by the nobles' sacrifice, which moved events much further along than the Breton Club had envisaged.[47] Étienne Dumont, the Genevan democrat who at the time was working as speech-writer for Mirabeau, was an eyewitness to that extraordinary night, and saw 'good and worthy deputies who wept for joy in seeing the work advance so rapidly, and finding themselves from moment to moment borne on the wings of enthusiasm beyond all that they had hoped for'.[48] According to the young, impecunious lawyer-turned-journalist Camille Desmoulins, instead of customary shouts of 'long live the vicomte de Noailles, long live the duc d'Aiguillon', from all sides echoed the words 'we are all friends, all equals, all brothers'.[49] People came together with a sense of emotional fusion and shared purpose that overcame the rigid social barriers of the old regime. It was a key revolutionary moment. Despite some backtracking the following day regarding financial compensation for the loss of some key privileges, 4 August spelled the end of the old regime. To have any kind of privilege would soon become anathema. Such was the mood of rejection of the traditions of honour in the Assembly that when, on 12 August, Target read an address to the king as 'the restorer of French liberty', beginning with the formal words 'Sire, the Assembly has the honour . . .' he was interrupted by a storm of resounding cries: 'Not honour! Not honour! We don't want that word!'[50] The world of honour had been eclipsed. Virtue was ascendant.

On 4 August Barère was presented with a personal choice—one that would play a great part in determining his future. His background was one on the fringes of nobility. His mother was noble, his wife was noble (he had made an advantageous

---

[46] See Lameth's account, in *Histoire de l'Assemblée Constituante*, 1: 92–8.

[47] Tackett, 'Nobles and the Third Estate', 322.

[48] Étienne Dumont, *Souvenirs sur Mirabeau et sur les deux premières Assemblées Législatives, par Étienne Dumont*, ed. Jean Bénétruy (1832: this edition, Paris: Presses Universitaires de France, 1952), 99–100. By the time Dumont wrote this he had considerably modified his views on revolutionary politics, partly as a result of the Terror in France: see Bénétruy's Introduction, 29–30.

[49] Desmoulins, *Discours de la lanterne*, in *Oeuvres de Camille Desmoulins*, 1: 143.

[50] Desmoulins, *Discours de la lanterne*, 144, note.

though not very happy marriage), and he was entitled to claim nobility through having inherited the seigneury of Vieuzac in 1788. But he was a well-connected and affluent lawyer, and he identified himself with the Third Estate. Just prior to the Revolution he spent nearly a year in Paris and seems to have become radicalized by the friends he made there. He moved in elite revolutionary circles, both before and during the Revolution.[51] On 4 August Barère made the fateful choice to renounce his office as chief councillor of the *sénéchaussée* of Bigorre: a post valued at 12,000 *livres*. He even, which was more surprising, voluntarily renounced his claim to financial reimbursement for the loss of this post, though the Assembly had decreed that compensation should be paid for such losses. He was not a man of immense wealth: this was a considerable financial sacrifice for Barère. He was, he said, 'soundly blamed' by his fellow citizens for this gesture, and his family were furious with him. He did it to set an example of virtue to other office holders in the *parlements*, but not a single one of these men, though wealthier than himself, was prepared to make such a sacrifice.[52]

The sacrifice of the patriot nobles on 4 August helped to establish their political credentials as men of virtue. It was a tangible act that proved the authenticity of their commitment to the public good: it went some way to closing the gap between what they said and what they did. The act of sacrifice gave them moral legitimacy, establishing their entitlement to be leaders of the new regime. The reality was rather more ambiguous. The patriot nobles set a generous example in giving up privilege and noble entitlement. They genuinely wanted France to embrace a new future, by establishing a constitutional monarchy. And yet, by showing their strong commitment to the new regime and pioneering the deployment of the rhetoric of virtue as the ideology of that regime, they were also staking their claim to control the political agenda. What could be more natural than that these wealthy, well-connected, intelligent men, who had offered satisfactory proof of their integrity, should become the leaders of this new regime? Their attitude was that of men who knew their worth. They had given up their financial and judicial privileges; but they still had considerable wealth, social connections, and a power base that grew exponentially as they established political networks within the new regime, and courted public opinion. They were charming and affable. They established friendly relations with the Third Estate deputies and opened their homes to them, inviting them into that personal space. Even Robespierre was invited to dine at the home of Charles de Lameth, his colleague on the Arras delegation. They could afford to be generous: they would be France's new natural leaders, on the basis not of hereditary privilege but of their virtues and talents. The political culture of the Constituent Assembly was still dominated by the nobility.

---

[51] See Leo Gershoy, *Bertrand Barère: A Reluctant Terrorist* (Princeton, NJ: Princeton University Press, 1962), 76–80.

[52] Barère, *Memoirs*, 1: 229–31.

# REVOLUTIONARY POLITICAL CULTURE AND THE PERSISTENCE OF OLD REGIME PRACTICE

During the early stages of the Revolution politics was conducted in two cultural *milieux* or worlds. The first was the cultural *milieu* associated with old regime politics; the second was that of revolutionary politics. In theory the new culture had replaced the old. Yet the political culture of the old regime continued to thrive behind the public face of revolutionary politics. Old regime methods continued to play a central role in the way that the business of politics was actually practised. The cultural *milieu* of old regime politics was located 'behind closed doors': it took place in private, primarily in people's own homes. It was a world into which one could venture only by invitation: the public was excluded. Here the business of politics was done, not through ideological rhetoric (that was for the Assembly and the clubs and popular societies) but through personal connections. It was here that an ambitious young revolutionary could make contacts, establish political friendships, and strike deals. It was a *milieu* that at first was still dominated by the nobility, with their wealth, self-assurance, connections, and knowledge of the appropriate codes of behaviour. The primary location for this culture was the private home. In the case of the patriot nobles this meant their *hôtels*, fine, luxurious Parisian residences. Other venues included exclusive restaurants, at which one could avoid the popular classes who could not afford to eat there. Here, especially in private rooms, political actors were relatively free to discuss tactics, and strike deals. Another location was the political salon. The ultimate centre of 'behind closed doors' politics was the court. Political leaders who were seen to deal with the court laid themselves open to public suspicion of their integrity and independence.

There were implications involved in visiting someone's home, and especially in dining there. At the start of the Revolution these implications were less significant, but over time this would become more of an issue. To accept such an invitation was to accept the hand of friendship. According to the old regime codes of political friendship, such an acceptance signalled the opening of mutual obligation. This could be to the advantage of an ambitious politician: it could lead to the establishment of connections that might well benefit his career. It could also, however, be a disadvantage for the same reason. A Third Estate politician who crossed the threshold of a nobleman's home might be deemed to have compromised his independence, and let himself be co-opted by the old elite into its power networks. He could have entered into an obligation, the details of which remained secret, because carried out in private. In short, to accept an invitation was potentially to oppose virtue. Desmoulins experienced this dilemma at first-hand when Mirabeau, wanting to enlist his services as a revolutionary journalist, invited Desmoulins to stay with him in Versailles.[53] Mirabeau was well known for hiring the services of a stable

---

[53] On Desmoulins, see Gérard Bonn, *La Révolution française et Camille Desmoulins* (Paris: Éditions Glyphe, 2010). In English there is no study more recent than Jules Claretie, *Camille Desmoulins and his Wife: Passages from the History of the Dantonists*, trans. Mrs Cashel Hoey (London: Smith, Elder and Co., 1876).

of writers to prepare his speeches.[54] Desmoulins gave his father an account of the visit:

> For the last eight days I have been staying with Mirabeau, at Versailles. We have become great friends; at least, he calls me his dear friend. At each moment he takes my hand, he punches me playfully on the back; then he goes to the assembly, resumes his dignity as he gets to the vestibule, and achieves marvels; after which, he returns to dine with excellent company, and sometimes his mistress, and we drink excellent wines. I fear that his table, too laden with delicacies, is corrupting me. His Bordeaux wines and his *maraschino* come at a price which I try in vain to hide from myself, and I have all the difficulty in the world in resuming afterwards my republican austerity and to detest the aristocrats, whose crime is to give such excellent dinners.[55]

For revolutionary leaders the culture of dining with one another had a significance all its own. This was partly because of a very old idea, well understood by anthropologists, that to break bread with another person has a symbolic, cultural, and emotional significance. It indicates mutual trust. To subsequently break that trust is a taboo. There were other reasons besides, that were more specific to revolutionary politics. Fine dining was a characteristic of the luxurious living associated in the mind of the public with the nobility. For a deputy to be seen to eat well when the people he represented were hungry could be seen as an insult to them; it opened up the gap between what that deputy said, and what was done in private. On a practical level, dining generally entailed drinking alcohol—the temptations of Mirabeau's *maraschino* and fine wine—and a man who drank in dubious company was letting his guard down. He might let secrets slip and, again, be compromised.

For all these reasons the new newspapers and pamphlets abounded in revelations that political leaders were sealing private, friendly relations over dinner and wine. These allegations are revealing for what they say about the codes of eighteenth-century friendship, and the point at which genuine, rather than formal intimacy might be said to have been established: an intimacy in which social and political aims could coincide. In these circumstances to have visited the house of a man since designated 'counter-revolutionary', or to have had a private dinner with him, was seen as indicative of close intimacy and thus politically 'suspect'. In certain circumstances such an act could be open to interpretation as conspiracy. It thus played up to the fears of conspiracy that continued to simmer in the undercurrents of revolutionary politics.[56]

---

[54] On the Genevans who worked for Mirabeau, see Dumont, *Souvenirs sur Mirabeau*; and Jean Bénétruy, *L'Atelier de Mirabeau* (Geneva: Alex Jullien, 1962).

[55] Letter from Desmoulins to his father, 29 September 1789, Camille Desmoulins, *Correspondance inédite de Camille Desmoulins* (Paris: Ébrard, 1836), 40–41. In a pamphlet in 1793 Desmoulins gave a much more muted and careful account of this visit in which he made no mention of offers of *maraschino* or gestures of friendship from the now disgraced and dead Mirabeau: see Desmoulins, *Fragment de l'histoire secrète de la Révolution*, in *Oeuvres de Camille Desmoulins*, 1: 308.

[56] On fears of conspiracy during the Constituent Assembly, see Timothy Tackett, 'Conspiracy obsession in a time of revolution: French elites and the origins of the Terror, 1789–1792' *American Historical Review*, 105 (2000): 691–713; and Tackett, 'Collective panics in the early French Revolution, 1789–1791: a comparative perspective', *French History*, 17 (2003): 149–71.

The Revolution established a new political culture.[57] Political virtue was a fundamental ideological principle of this new culture. Revolutionary politics was meant to be a transparent process. In contrast to the secrecy of the old regime, the deputies were meant to conduct their politics openly, in the public gaze.[58] They were not supposed to form factions; still less to group themselves into the kind of formal parties that characterized the English system. French politicians were meant to take political decisions according to the dictates of their individual consciences, informed by their political virtue to consider only the public good. They answered directly to the people, though this itself could be ideologically problematic: were they representatives—or demagogues? The 'people' could convey very different notions: it was a term that might signify either Rousseau's idealized *locus* of civic virtue, or the dangerous crowds of militants on the streets of Paris.[59] In time, for the deputies on the radical Left the term 'the people' came to signify, amongst other groups, the organized Parisian militants who became known as the *sans-culottes*. It was to this audience that the Jacobins would direct much of their rhetoric.[60]

There were considerable advantages to a political leader who could successfully embody the identity of a 'man of virtue': it gave him legitimacy, it gave him a voice. It could, however, be a problematic identity. Article fifteen of the *Declaration of the Rights of Man and of the Citizen* stated 'Society has the right to hold accountable every public agent of the administration'. Politicians, too, were now public agents, responsible directly to the people. Their conduct, both public and private, could be held up to public scrutiny. A man who sought to adopt the persona of a 'man of virtue' was engaging in a risky strategy that might rebound upon him. His assumption of this identity invited public interest both in his inner motivation and in his private life, as a way of judging the authenticity of his public persona. Thus the putative 'man of virtue' risked seeing himself exposed as falling short of these high standards. Even worse, he might be suspected of deliberately manipulating his political image for his own private purposes. Authenticity, therefore, was paramount.

In contrast to the old regime political culture, the venues for the new revolutionary culture were open, accessible to all. The primary locations were the Assembly itself, the various clubs and popular societies, and the streets. Newspapers and pamphlets transmitted this culture in printed form. The public participated by cramming into the public galleries of the Assembly, the Jacobin Club, and other

---

[57] There is an extensive literature on the culture of the Revolution, much of it cited elsewhere in this book. For an overview see Emmet Kennedy, *A Cultural History of the French Revolution* (New Haven, CT: Yale University Press, 1989).

[58] On transparency, see Starobinski, *Jean-Jacques Rousseau*; and Hunt, *Politics, Culture, and Class in the French Revolution*.

[59] On the problem of the deputies as representatives of the people and of the nation, see Cowans, *To Speak for the People*; Baker, *Inventing the French Revolution*, ch. 10; and Paul Friedland, *Political Actors: Representative Bodies and Theatricality in the Age of the French Revolution* (Ithaca, NY: Cornell University Press, 2002).

[60] The term *sans-culotte* is problematic as it signified a political grouping in the Paris Commune and the Parisian sections rather than the Parisian popular classes as a whole. On the invention of the *sans-culottes* as a political category, and their relations with the Jacobins, see Burstin, *L'Invention du sans-culotte*.

venues; surging onto the streets and discussing in the cafés; and reading the newspapers and pamphlets. Would-be political leaders had to master this new culture if
they wanted to have any impact on events. It was not an easy task. Out of a total
of 1,315 men accredited as deputies of the Estates-General, according to Tackett
only about forty went on to become regular speakers when it became the Constituent Assembly. The Legislative Assembly, composed of different men, would pro-
duce a similar number of leading orators.[61] Most of the best speakers were lawyers,
who had received oratorical training. They employed the rhetorical style they had
learned from studying the methods of Cicero and other classical authors. Most
read from prepared speeches. The English observer Arthur Young was unimpressed:
'It can scarcely be conceived how flat this mode of debate renders the transactions
of the Assembly.' He considered the English House of Commons much better in
this respect than the French. On the other hand, the proceedings in the French
Assembly were unruly, and often chaotic. Young had commented on the tumultuous scenes in the Assembly at the outset of the Revolution. By January 1790 things
were little changed: 'The want of order, and every kind of confusion, prevails now
almost as much as when the Assembly sat at Versailles. The interruptions given are
frequent and long; and speakers who have no right by the rules to speak, will attempt it.' The spectators were numerous, vociferous, and influential, and deputies
could bring in their friends to act as *claques* and exert pressure on the debates.
Young described the atmosphere in the public galleries, and the pressure that spectators could exert on the politicians:

> ... there is a gallery at each end of the saloon which is open to all the world; and side
> ones for admission of the friends of the members by tickets: the audience in these gal-
> leries are very noisy: they clap, when anything pleases them, and they have been known
> to hiss; an indecorum which is utterly destructive of freedom of debate.[62]

The radical deputies in particular laid great stress on being able to move their audiences through their eloquence.[63] An orator who could succeed in stirring the emotions of his listeners was believed to be demonstrating his authenticity: his heart
spoke directly to theirs. Revolutionary politics played out like a theatrical drama
with continual interplay between the speakers, the listening deputies, and the
people in the galleries.[64] Revolutionary politicians were very aware of their audiences. Women in the public galleries could be particularly vociferous in giving

---

[61] See Tackett, *Becoming a Revolutionary*, 19–21, 321–2. On oratory in the Constituent Assembly
see also Patrick Brasart, *Paroles de la Révolution: Les Assemblées parlementaires, 1789–1794* (Paris: Minerve, 1988), Part 1, and on eloquence in the various revolutionary assemblies, ibid., 169–96. On the
forty-nine principal speakers of the Legislative Assembly, see Edna Hindie Lemay (ed.), *Dictionnaire
des Législateurs, 1791–1792*, 2 vols (Ferney-Voltaire: Centre International d'Étude du XVIIIe Siècle,
2007), 2: 787.
[62] These were Young's views on debates in the Constituent Assembly on 12 January 1790, in Young,
*Travels in France*, 253. In June 1789 he described the interventions of spectators as 'grossly indecent;
it is also dangerous', 144.
[63] See Hunt, *Politics, Culture, and Class in the French Revolution*, 45.
[64] Friedland argues that the theatricality of revolutionary politics reduced the audience to 'passivi-
zation': *Political Actors*, 295–300.

their opinions about the various revolutionary leaders. They had a notable influence on the public standing of various deputies, and whether a man was to be seen as a 'hero' of the Revolution. But the approbation of women spectators could be used against a political leader by his opponents, who would play on the popular masculine belief that women were gullible, and all too susceptible to a speaker's good looks, or his dashing 'gallantry'. A man who had too many female admirers could find that this undermined his 'man of virtue' image. A man of virtue, amongst other things, was not meant to act up for the benefit of women in the audience. Men like Robespierre and Lafayette, who both had considerable female followings (though probably for different reasons), were criticized for it by serious-minded revolutionaries, such as Brissot.[65]

The clubs were equally important as a venue within which a man could make his reputation. Here a rather different kind of oratory was called for. In the clubs impromptu debate and improvised responses were much more significant. The best orators knew how to adapt their discursive strategies to different audiences. Revolutionary rhetoric was not set in stone, but was played out in a context in which there were differences in how a politician might speak, depending partly on whether he was speaking to friends, or facing down his enemies.[66]

Revolutionary journalism played a key role in this new culture and the formation of public opinion. On a basic level the revolutionary journalists told their audiences about what was happening in the world of Parisian politics, keeping them informed about debates in the Assembly, about who were the key players, what they said, what they did. In addition, revolutionary journalists could wield ideological and tactical power by using a direct relationship with their readers to shape public opinion. They made sense of the complex and often confused events in Paris by forging them into a comprehensible narrative, with heroes and villains, and 'right' and 'wrong' views, according to the political allegiances of the journalist. Their newspapers praised men whose politics they admired, and poured scorn on their political opponents. Crucially, it was the newspapers that gave factional labels to the deputies in the Assembly. Throughout the revolutionary period newspapers would play a vital role in identifying and mobilizing factions.[67] A number of political activists, including some future Jacobin leaders, took an active role in these new media by founding their own newspapers. By this means they could establish a presence in politics, launch their careers, and gain direct access to an audience. Some—like Brissot, Marat, and Desmoulins—used their journalism to forge strong identities for themselves in the public mind, before ever being elected as national representatives.

---

[65] Brissot, *Mémoires*, 2: 138. Brissot had similarly harsh words for Bergasse, arguing that the 'idolatry' shown towards him by some 'women of *esprit*' encouraged his egoism: ibid., 55. See also the commentary in the Girondin press on the high proportion of women who came to hear Robespierre speak, discussed in Chapter Five.

[66] On Robespierre's discursive strategies, see Jourdan, 'Les discours de Robespierre'.

[67] Popkin, *Revolutionary News*, 41, 47, 114–16.

## LOOKING LIKE A MAN OF VIRTUE: THE VISUAL IMAGE OF POLITICAL LEADERS

One of the last acts of the Assembly before it left Versailles in October 1789 was to decree an end to distinctions in dress for deputies. This was a blow for freedom and individuality, and against old regime hierarchy. Thereafter deputies would dress in the same way; there would be no distinctions between nobles and the Third Estate; and there would be no distinctions between the deputies and the people they represented.

In January 1790 Arthur Young, invited to dine *chez* the duc de Liancourt in his apartments in the Tuileries where the duc gave twice-weekly dinners for twenty to forty deputies, noted the sudden transformation in dress from that expected of public figures of the old regime: 'At this dinner, according to custom, most of the deputies, especially the younger ones, were dressed *au polisson* [disreputably], many of them without powder in their hair, and some in boots; not above four or five were neatly dressed. How times are changed!' Young concluded: 'Everything in this world depends on government'—even fashion evidently.[68] Miss Mary Berry, a writer and friend of Horace Walpole who visited the Assembly in October 1790, was equally struck by the dishevelled look of the French deputies: 'Their appearance is not more gentlemanlike than their manner of debating—such a set of shabby, ill-dressed, strange-looking people I hardly ever saw together; our House of Commons is not half so bad.'[69]

For the deputies the new way of dressing denoted their rejection of the artificiality of the court and its values, and the intentness of their political purpose. Their simple outward apparel was intended to reflect the sincerity of the hearts that beat beneath. The question whether or not the deputies should adopt a uniform, or some sort of distinguishing mark such as an insignia or badge, was much discussed. For various practical reasons this would have been helpful, but it was repeatedly rejected, because for the deputies to distinguish themselves from other citizens would have implied that they were somehow superior to the people they represented. Only after the end of the Jacobin period would costume be used to enforce a clear distinction between politicians and the people they led.[70]

From the outset of the Revolution, clothing was a principal way in which people of all kinds—not only deputies—could show their political affiliations.[71] Yet from early on there was a growing realization that clothes could equally be used to *disguise* a person's true political identity: far from showing what was in a person's heart, external appearance could be a way of concealing it. Thus the idea of

---

[68]  Young, *Travels in France*, 248, 255.

[69]  J.M. Thompson (ed.), *English Witnesses of the French Revolution* (Oxford: Blackwell, 1938), 98.

[70]  On the clothes worn by deputies see Richard Wrigley, *The Politics of Appearances: Representations of Dress in Revolutionary France* (Oxford: Berg, 2002), 77–87; and Hunt, *Politics, Culture and Class in the French Revolution*, 74–86.

[71]  On the politics of clothing, see Wrigley, *Politics of Appearances*; and Nicole Pellegrin, *Les Vêtements de la liberté: Abécédaire des pratiques vestimentaires françaises de 1780 à 1800* (Aix: Éditions Alinéa, 1989).

authenticity could be played upon and manipulated. In revolutionary politics the wearing of masks—both metaphorically and literally—also provoked unease; so much so that in Paris traditional carnivals (that had involved much disguising and mask-wearing) were banned in January 1790.[72]

The ways in which visual portrayals of revolutionary politicians were portrayed constituted a clear break with the old regime portrayal of public figures. Whilst under the old regime there had been many images of the monarch, images of the king's ministers were rarely brought before the public in an individualized way.[73] This changed with the Revolution.[74] The new political leaders were keen for their images to be shown to the public: the extensive circulation of engravings derived from their portraits helped to establish their identities before a wider public than could see them in the flesh. Some portraits of political leaders were on display at the salon of 1791, including those of Mirabeau, d'Aiguillon, the Lameth brothers, and Robespierre, together with David's preliminary drawing of the deputies taking the Tennis Court Oath; though according to Leith these made up only a 'small fraction' of the works on public show there.[75] There were codes about how revolutionary politicians should, or should not, be displayed visually. These codes were in line with expectations of the 'man of virtue'. Thus, in contrast to the kings of the old regime, or indeed to the Napoleonic period, revolutionary leaders were not shown on horseback, which would have been seen as a sign of superiority, and of personal glory. Neither did they wear insignia or badges of office. Portraits of deputies were acceptable, if done in the intimate, understated style that was in vogue. Thus their portraits were modest and personal, designed to show the sitters' natural virtue and sensibility, their hard work as agents of the state. They were not surrounded by symbols or paraphernalia of power. Sometimes they were depicted speaking publicly, though not in a way that accentuated personal authority or glory. Two portraits of Robespierre at the salon of 1791, one of which was titled 'The Incorruptible', were very much in this style and were acknowledged as such by admiring spectators who spoke of Robespierre as 'the incorruptible legislator'.[76]

There was a particular problem associated with representing political leaders in stone, in the form of busts or full-length statues. Stone indicated permanence: a durability that lasted beyond death; an identity that was no longer subject to alteration by the human frailties and vicissitudes of a life still being lived. Busts recalled the heroes of antiquity. To allow oneself to be depicted in a way that self-consciously emulated the 'great men' of antiquity could be problematic.

---

[72] Wrigley, *Politics of Appearances*, 229–57.

[73] On pre-Revolutionary visual portrayals of the monarchy, see Mark Ledbury, 'The contested image: stage, canvas, and the origins of the French Revolution', in Campbell, *The Origins of the French Revolution*, 206–12.

[74] On the cult of 'great men' in the Revolution, see Annie Jourdan, *Les Monuments de la Révolution 1770–1804: une histoire de la représentation* (Paris: Honoré Champion, 1997), ch. 2.

[75] J.A. Leith, *The Idea of Art as Propaganda in France, 1750–1799: A Study in the History of Ideas* (Toronto: University of Toronto Press, 1965), 101.

[76] Thompson, *Robespierre*, 143–4.

Was this a sign of genuine virtue? Or was it rather a sign of the opposite qualities, of egoism and ambition? A living man who permitted himself to be represented in stone was understood to be fixing his identity in the public mind, and thereby making a bid for political power. Early in the Revolution this was still an acceptable tactic, though one to be pursued cautiously. During 1790 there was a small industry devoted to the manufacturing of busts of Mirabeau, many of which found their way into provincial Jacobin clubs. When, subsequently, evidence of Mirabeau's corruption began to pile up, this helped to discredit the whole idea of busts of living politicians.

## IN THE CRUCIBLE OF THE NEW CULTURE

During the early period of the Revolution politics and the accompanying political culture were in a state of flux. In theory a new political culture had replaced the old: everything was now about the public sphere. In practice, however, elements of these two political cultures, the old and the new, continued more or less side by side. Revolutionary politicians had to negotiate their way through both cultures, using differing strategies for each. Old regime culture, dominated by the nobility, still maintained a presence during the Constituent Assembly, and to some extent even up to the overthrow of the monarchy in August 1792. Though nobility was officially abolished in June 1790, nobles continued to wield unofficial power and influence, through their friendship and patronage networks which formed an established 'politics of connections'.[77] Old regime culture continued to set much of the tone in which the business of politics was conducted. This style of intimate and exclusive politics, conducted behind closed doors where select groups met to discuss and to plan policy and tactics, was still a very powerful force. Commoners brought into this world by revolutionary politics, and not brought up in it, could easily feel awkward, wrong-footed, not dressed properly, not knowing the right social codes of *politesse*.

The political salons, once bastions of aristocratic interest, enjoyed what Tackett has characterized as an 'Indian summer' at the start of the Revolution.[78] There were some changes, however. The patriot nobles recognized that they had to make some adaptation to the demands of the new politics in order to thrive. They invited some radical Third Estate deputies and journalists into their private space, partly as a way of co-opting these representatives and harnessing their popularity. Thus new men were allowed entry to the world of salons and fine dinners. In these private locations new networks were being established, and the ground being laid for the establishment of leading players in the new order. Jacques-Pierre Brissot, one of those 'up and coming' men (a journalist, though not yet a deputy), later described

---

[77] The phrase 'politics of connections' was used by Kelly, *Victims, Authority, and Terror*, 25. See also Gueniffey, *La Politique de la Terreur*, 108–10.

[78] See Tackett, *Becoming a Revolutionary*, 242–3; and Lemay, *La vie quotidienne des députés*, 94–105.

some of the political dinners and salons to which he was invited in the pre-revolutionary period and in 1789, along with men like Lafayette, Bergasse, and Clavière. Brissot quickly learned how effective a dinner could be as a venue for political decisions: 'It was during dinners that the most important political questions were thrashed out. There I preached the republic, but with the exception of Clavière, no one had a taste for it.'[79]

In the early months of the Revolution there were some awkward cultural encounters between people who would never have socialized on such intimate terms under the old regime. In 1789 Robespierre was invited to dine with Necker. Necker's daughter, Madame de Staël, met Robespierre there: 'I talked with him once at my father's house, at a time when he was known only as a lawyer from Artois.' She noted that he did not look like the usual kind of man to be allowed entrance to Necker's house, remarking disdainfully that 'his features were those of a commoner'. She did not like his political opinions any better than his face: 'he put forward the most absurd propositions with a *sang froid* that had the air of conviction . . . on the equality of fortunes, and the levelling of social rank'.[80]

One appreciable change, remarked upon by Arthur Young at yet another political dinner, is that the traditional role of aristocratic women in the 'behind closed doors' style of politics, was becoming much less acceptable:

> Dined with a large party, at the Duke de la Rochefoucauld's; ladies and gentlemen, and all equally politicians, but I may remark another feature of this revolution, by no means unnatural, which is, that of lessening, or rather reducing to nothing, the enormous influence of the sex: they mixed themselves before in everything, in order to govern everything; I think I see an end to it very clearly.[81]

English political attitudes of the time showed a similar hostility towards women 'meddling' in political matters. Young observed the change in France with great satisfaction: 'they are, in fact, sinking into what nature intended them for; they will become more amiable, and the nation better governed'.[82]

Friendship played an ambiguous role in the new culture of revolutionary politics.[83] The revolutionaries idealized friendship in Rousseau's sense of a communion of minds, emotional openness, and sympathy for others. On a tactical level, in politics friendship was fundamental to the development of revolutionary networks and unofficial factions. As in the old regime friendship could be a means of social advancement. It provided a way of making connections that that could give access

[79] Brissot, *Mémoires*, 2: 54.

[80] Cited in Louis Jacob (ed.), *Robespierre vu par ses contemporains* (Paris: Armand Colin, 1938), 213–15. She wrote this much later, however, when Robespierre's reputation had taken on a very different significance, and this may well have affected her memories of him in 1789.

[81] Young, *Travels in France*, 251–2.

[82] Young, *Travels in France*, 251–2. On contemporary attitudes towards elite women in English politics, see Elaine Chalus, *Elite Women in English Political Life, 1754–1790* (Oxford: Clarendon Press, 2005). On the part played by gender in conceptions of political virtue in English politics, see Matthew McCormack, *The Independent Man: Citizenship and Gender Politics in Georgian England* (Manchester: Manchester University Press, 2005).

[83] Linton, 'Fatal friendships'.

to administrative and governmental posts. It was also a natural way of conducting politics in a cultural world containing no formal party structure to bring people together. On a personal level, friendship played a part in shaping people's allegiances and choices. But there was a negative aspect to friendship in revolutionary ideology. It could be regarded with suspicion as a conduit for private self-advancement; thus in some ways it was inimical to political virtue.

The autumn of 1789 saw the fixing of the shape of the Constitutional monarchy. In September 1789 the form of the constitution was decided: a unicameral system, with the king to retain only a suspensive veto. It was during these debates on the veto that the terms 'Left' and 'Right' in politics first came into use. In the October Days, the king was forced by a new popular uprising to come to Paris, along with the Assembly, and to agree to the Declaration of the Rights of Man and the decrees of 4 August. Thereafter the political system stabilized. It remained for the new political leaders to consolidate their position and to establish their identity at the head of the new political regime. The Revolution, to all intents and purposes, appeared to be over. In fact, it had only begun.

# 3

## New Men for New Politics
### The First Jacobin Leaders

Enemies even more redoubtable in that they are more afraid to show themselves
and cover themselves beneath the mask of friendship. In this class must be
placed nearly all our mandataries, all the representatives of the people, all the
public functionaries, these infamous hypocrites in whom we have entrusted
the defence of our rights, of our goods, of our liberty and of ourselves who
turn our own weapons against us, and who are working solely to put us back
in chains, all the while assuring us that they are only occupied in making us
free and happy.

Marat, L'Ami du peuple, June 1791.[1]

I am accused of ambition. I have never had any other ambition than to attain
through *popularity* the places which are found to be appropriate to my
talents.

Barnave at his trial, November 1793.[2]

As relative stability returned the moment had arrived to embark on the task of
fashioning a new politics.[3] The intense exhilaration, drama, and fear of the summer
of 1789 dwindled, though they did not disappear. There is no sign that even the
most radical revolutionaries had any further intention of bringing about a renewal
of revolution. France without some sort of monarchy seemed unthinkable.

The Revolution was founded on a new bureaucracy. It has been estimated that,
by 1790, between 500,000 and 1 million new administrative positions had been
created, half of which were elected municipal posts.[4] Though many were honorific
and not paid, even the non-remunerated positions offered a public status and so
could be stepping-stones to more important posts. Thus the Revolution itself
became a career path. Access to public office was transformed. Article Six of the

---

[1] Jean-Paul Marat, *L'Ami du peuple*, No. 505, 27 June 1791, cited in Anne Simonin, *Le Déshonneur dans la République: une histoire de l'indignité 1791–1958* (Paris: Bernard-Grasset, 2008), 232.

[2] 'La défense de Barnave transcrite par son avocat', reproduced in *Actes du Tribunal révolutionnaire, recueillis et commentés par Gérard Walter* (Paris: Mercure de France, 1968), 422.

[3] On the Constituent Assembly, see Tackett, *Becoming a Revolutionary*; and Michael P. Fitzsimmons, *The Remaking of France: the National Assembly and the Constitution of 1791* (Cambridge: Cambridge University Press, 1994).

[4] For varying estimates, see Gueniffey, *Le Nombre et la raison*, esp. 418–28; and Crook, *Elections in the French Revolution*, 177.

Declaration of the Rights of Man stated that 'all citizens...are equally admissible to all public dignities, offices, and employments, according to their ability, and with no other distinction than that of their virtues and talents'. Robespierre argued that this should mean that there should be no property requirements for voting and holding office.[5] The Constituent Assembly was not willing to go that far, but the property qualification was set fairly low, allowing many men of moderate background access to public office. Other categories of people were excluded from the right to vote or hold office, including women and servants. In order to be eligible for local office the threshold was set at the payment of ten working days in taxation. Almost 2,500,000 Frenchmen were eligible.[6] Many offices were decided by elections. The new electoral system was established in December 1789. It was tacitly agreed that the principles applied to the elections for the Estates-General would be confirmed for the new political regime: there would be no official candidates, no canvassing for votes, no manifestos. Official candidacy was condemned, not by law, but by public opinion. It was unacceptable for a man to openly signal his desire to stand for office. It was believed that official candidacy would undermine popular sovereignty and encourage the formation of cabals or interest groups. This opinion was near universal amongst the political class.[7] Yet in practice, in the absence of an accepted structure of parties and campaigning, would-be candidates often relied on their friends and unofficial patrons to lobby on their behalf, exploiting existing connections and unofficial networks.[8] Representatives of the people were included in the new category of 'public functionary' and were publicly accountable for their integrity. As Anne Simonin has noted, during the Constituent Assembly any public official (including a deputy) who was found to be unworthy of his office was deemed to be guilty of a disciplinary fault and subject to public disgrace; yet he was not regarded as a criminal.[9]

It has been said that by breaking down the institutionalized power of birth and privilege the Revolution gave people the possibility of a career open to talent. Nowhere was this more evident than in the new world of politics. Those deputies of the Constituent Assembly who supported the gains made by the Revolution were on the whole hard-working, patriotic, enthusiastic, and idealistic. Yet their genuine commitment to revolutionary ideals does not preclude the fact that for many of them the Revolution also opened up an unprecedented opportunity to carve out a career in politics. Some of them aspired to play a leading role in the new political world. Since they could not openly avow their ambitions we can only speculate about what their unspoken desires may have been. Such unacknowledged goals might encompass a desire for wealth and material success, also undoubtedly for

---

[5]  22 October 1789, Robespierre, *Oeuvres*, 6: 130–3.

[6]  Crook, *Elections in the French Revolution*, 44.

[7]  Brissot was one of the few to call for official candidacies. See Gueniffey, *Le Nombre et la raison*, 316–21, 363–6.

[8]  Gueniffey, 'Revolutionary democracy and the elections', 94.

[9]  Simonin, *Le Déshonneur dans la République*, 232. Simonin points out that by the summer of 1791 Marat was already defining corrupt public officials as enemies of the Revolution, though at that time this was an extreme view, shared by few political participants.

power, but there was something more too, the burning desire to have a name that mattered, to count as someone, to be at the centre of events; perhaps, too, to achieve the 'immortality' of being remembered by posterity.

The new men who came to the fore of political life were obliged to negotiate this changed political landscape in which their own ambition was considered as inherently suspicious, their true identity subject to public scrutiny. They sought to establish their power bases through appropriating the identity of 'men of virtue', selflessly dedicated to the public good.

## THE FIRST LEADERS OF THE JACOBIN CLUB

The Jacobin Club was founded in late 1789 as a rallying point for radical revolutionary politics. From the outset, the identity of the Jacobins was formed in explicit opposition to the popular image of the 'aristocrats'. Aristocrats were seen as corrupt, self-interested, and profligate.[10] By contrast, the ideal Jacobin was a man of independence, courage, and heroism, who stood firm against the egoist 'vampires' and 'parasites' of the aristocracy and considered only the public good—in short, a 'man of virtue'. The question of who was designated by the term 'aristocrat' changed over time. In 1789 this anti-aristocratic Jacobin rhetoric was directed mostly against the courtiers who clustered round the skirts of the monarchy, but during the life of the Constituent Assembly it would be gradually extended to encompass any nobles and higher clergy who opposed the Revolution, and eventually to anyone whose political sympathies were not 'patriotic'—that is, anyone who opposed the Revolution.[11] Nevertheless, the Jacobin opposition to aristocracy was not just a rhetorical stance. Tackett makes the point that the Jacobin deputies were confronted by a tightly organized faction of bitterly hostile, 'genuine, genealogically certified aristocrats, swords at their sides, day after day in the Assembly itself'.[12]

Nine-tenths of the Jacobins were commoners, but their leaders were from the social elite of the old regime. The initiative to found the Jacobins came from a small group of patriot nobles in conjunction with a few leading Third Estate deputies. This founding group included Target, Le Chapelier, d'Aiguillon, Noailles, Mirabeau, Duport, Barnave, and the Lameth brothers.[13] Most of these men had been members of the Society of Thirty, and later of the Breton Club. For many months they dominated Jacobin politics, exercising a near monopoly over the offices of presidents and secretaries for the Jacobins.[14]

---

[10] See the account of the founding of the Jacobins given by Louis-Marie de La Revellière-Lépeaux, *Mémoires*, 3 vols (Paris: Plon, Nourrit, 1895), 1: 85–7. On the formation and early days of the Jacobin Club, see Aulard, *Société des Jacobins*, 1: xvii–xxi; and Lemay, *La Vie quotidienne des députés*, 216–22.

[11] On characterizations of the nobility as 'conspiratorial' see Thomas E. Kaiser, 'Nobles into aristocrats, or how an order became a conspiracy', in Smith, *The French Nobility in the Eighteenth Century*.

[12] On the impact of the hard-line Right on the foundation and rise of the Jacobins, see Tackett, 'Nobles and the Third Estate', 330–6.

[13] La Revellière-Lépeaux, *Mémoires*, 1: 83; and Tackett, *Becoming a Revolutionary*, 206–7.

[14] Edna Hindie Lemay, 'Poursuivre la Revolution: Robespierre et ses amis à la Constituante', in Jessenne *et al.*, *Robespierre*, 146, note 34.

Four men from this group—Alexandre de Lameth, Duport, and Barnave—became the effective leaders of the Jacobins, known as the 'triumvirate'.[15] They were united by shared political goals and close friendship. They drew strength, coherence, and unity of purpose from their friendships with one another; friendships that pre-dated their activity at the Jacobins. They were so closely united that Barnave lived with Alexandre de Lameth and his brothers during the period of their involvement at the Jacobins.[16] The name 'triumvirate' was a hostile term coined during the Constituent Assembly by their opponents to indicate that these men had appropriated the power of the Jacobins for the purposes of ambition.[17] Every man in the Assembly was familiar with the story of how Caesar, Pompey, and Crassus had formed the first triumvirate in order to share power between themselves, destroying the Roman Republic in the process. The guiding hand of the triumvirate in shaping the Jacobins' identity is evident in the Club's rulebook, which was written by Barnave in February 1790, together with the first manifesto to explain the objects of the society.[18] According to La Revellière-Lépeaux, who was present at the earliest meetings of the Jacobins, there were 'fifteen or twenty deputies…we received no strangers at that time. But soon the Lameths and their friends arrived in force and introduced a crowd of intriguers and ambitious men.'[19] He later recalled the Lameths' assumption of the identity of men of virtue in cynical terms, '…all the ambitious men in the Constituent Assembly told me each day in tones of sincerity that could easily impose upon people who didn't know them, that after the session they would refuse the offer of any post, whatever it might be, unless it was to serve as justice of the peace in their own village…Men are everywhere the same, and ambition and duplicity always go hand in hand with one another.'[20]

## RIVAL LEADERS: THE SOCIETY OF 1789 AND THE JACOBINS

The fragmentation of the patriot nobles was largely tactical, prompted by disagreements over who should form ministries to lead the new regime. The split between Lafayette and the Lameths and Duport began in September 1789, and rapidly deepened. What divided them was not differences in ideology or principles but personal ambition, and perhaps considerable self-belief. There was particular dissension over the involvement of the Mirabeau and the Orléans factions, and how far either should be trusted. Lafayette viewed the patriotism of the Lameths with

[15] See Ran Halévi, 'Feuillants', in Furet and Ozouf, *Dictionnaire critique*, 366–72. Charles de Lameth was an unofficial fourth member of the 'triumvirate'.

[16] Bradby, *Barnave*, 1: 181.

[17] Mirabeau referred to them mockingly as a 'triumgueusat' (a trio of shabby fellows): letter from Laporte to the king, 21 March 1791, *Réimpression de l'ancien Moniteur*, 31 vols (Paris, Plon Frères, 1847), 14: 658.

[18] Bradby, *Barnave*, 1: 213–15.

[19] La Revellière-Lépeaux, *Mémoires*, 1: 86. It should be noted that this was written many years after the events, with the benefit of hindsight.

[20] La Revellière-Lépeaux, *Mémoires*, 1: 86–7.

deep suspicion, and claimed that they were using their influence at the Jacobins as part of a strategy to increase their popularity and use it as a means to take over his post at the head of the National Guard.[21] But the split was also a personal one, dividing men who had been friends; it contained all the bitterness of that fractured friendship.[22] There was also a 'running feud' between Mirabeau and Duport, Barnave, and the Lameths in the Constituent Assembly. The enmity between Mirabeau and the triumvirate was personal as well as political. It had its origins in 1788 when Mirabeau had taken offence that the Society of Thirty had met in the home of Duport.[23]

Early in 1790 a group of patriot nobles led by Lafayette, withdrew from the Jacobins, and formed the Society of 1789. This group included leading nobles such as Mirabeau, Le Chapelier, Talleyrand, La Rochefoucauld, and Condorcet, and prominent non-nobles, including Sieyès and Duquesnoy. The Society occupied luxurious rooms in the Palais Royal, and fine dining was a regular feature of their political meetings, in the style of old regime political culture. The atmosphere was more intimate and exclusive than that of the Jacobins. The Society's members hoped to reap the harvest of their leadership of the Revolution of 1789 by positioning their leaders for ministerial roles. Barnave wrote a letter to his constituents in Grenoble in June 1790, in which he compared the identities and motives of the members of the Society of 1789 unfavourably with the Jacobins.[24] He described the Society as consisting of 40 to 50 deputies, and about 250 very wealthy and well-connected men: bankers, financiers, men of letters, and above all a large number of young men, either courtiers or very rich, 'who had left the party of the aristocracy' and attached themselves to the Society of 1789 in order 'to find themselves a place in the new system', whereas if they had joined the Jacobins they would have been personally disadvantaged by the hostility of the court. They wanted posts and advancement in the new regime. According to Barnave their leaders were motivated by 'personal perspectives of wealth and ambition' to manipulate the political process:

> It is said that this society was formed to be the cradle and support of the ministerial party in our legislative assemblies. It is said that because our representation has rejected corruption, either through the perfection of our electoral forms, or through the frequency of renewals of elections, this society, which is trying to set up affiliations in all the *départements*, will serve, by means of the credit, the talent, the wealth of its members, to take the place of the means that our constitution has removed from ministers, to assure them a constant majority in the legislative body.[25]

[21] Michon, *Adrien Duport*, 72–3.

[22] On disputes between Lafayette and Alexandre de Lameth over who could be trusted to form a ministry, see Louis Gottschalk and Margaret Maddox, *Lafayette in the French Revolution: From the October Days through the Federation* (Chicago: University of Chicago Press, 1973), 26–46; also Furet, 'Barnave', 208.

[23] On this running feud, see Barbara Luttrell, *Mirabeau* (Carbondale and Edwardsville: Southern Illinois University Press, 1990), 160–1; also Furet, 'Barnave', 208.

[24] 'Letter to the municipality of Grenoble', 25 June 1790, in Antoine-Pierre-Joseph-Marie Barnave, *Oeuvres de Barnave*, 4 vols (Paris: Jules Chapelle et Guiller, 1843), 4: 333–42.

[25] Barnave, 'Letter to the municipality of Grenoble', 337.

According to Barnave the aims of the Jacobins were diametrically opposed to those of the Society of 1789. While '... the action of the Government and the movement of the political machine require that men of talent and virtue should specially devote themselves, in various offices, to the direction of the executive power in the ministry', it was also essential for the preservation of liberty that a watchful eye be kept on ministers by upright men who avoided standing for office:

> ... it is no less necessary for the preservation of liberty that firm and capable men should devote themselves to a ceaseless watch on her behalf; that without being the enemies of the executive power they should stand strict sentinels over it; that in order to be perfectly sure of themselves they should even fortify themselves against every temptation by resolving never to wish for anything, never to accept anything... Our opposition must not be composed of men who want to overthrow the ministry in order that they may take its place... but of men detached from all ambition... This is, I think, the kind of men which the [Jacobin Club] ought to endeavour to form... in order to keep this character it is not enough to be honest and disinterested; one must be able to resist all kinds of error and seduction, to despise the calumnies one hears about oneself and to distrust those which people try to insinuate about others; to re-nounce the allurements of the most brilliant society in order to concentrate oneself among one's friends; one must not be afraid of seeing oneself torn to pieces by a swarm of libellous pamphlets, nor even of seeing the satisfaction one might receive from the affection of the people tarnished by the constant accusation of one's enemies, that one bribes them and incites them to riot.[26]

In reality the disparity between the Jacobins and the Society of 1789 was not so great as Barnave chose to claim, but the exclusivity of the Society told against its members. It failed to attract much support, partly because it was seen as the preserve of a wealthy elite. Though many of the principles held by its members (at least through till the summer of 1790) were similar to those espoused by the Jacobins, the Society of 1789 lacked a strong political language that would enlist more popular support. The language used there was that of enlightened reform, rather than that of virtue, egalitarianism, and demonstrative emotion adopted by the Jacobins.[27]

The contrast was pointed out by the English observer William Augustus Miles. He described in a letter how he had addressed the Society of 1789 on the dangers of anarchy and mob rule, using a rhetoric which would never have done before the Jacobins. 'If I had held this discourse at the Jacobins, I should have been expelled, or perhaps trampled under foot. There were, however, several of the Jacobins present, as many are members of both clubs.'[28] The fact that a number of men—such as Barère—regularly attended both clubs shows that these political groups were not fixed. There was considerable fluctuation in people's allegiances as they

---

[26] Cited by Bradby, *Barnave*, 1: 225–6.

[27] On the failure of the Society of 1789 to appeal to a wider audience, see Mark Olsen, 'A failure of enlightened politics in the French Revolution: the Société de 1789', *French History*, 6,3 (1992): 303–34.

[28] William Augustus Miles, letter of 25 February 1791, *Correspondence on the French Revolution, 1789–1817*, 2 vols (London: Longman, Green and Co., 1890), 1: 228–9.

sampled different kinds of political forum. Some of the same people were experimenting with different kinds of political aims and rhetoric. Ultimately, the choices that people made as to which club to attend, where to put their political allegiance, came down to a number of factors. Ideology was key—the Jacobins were committed to more populist politics. But other factors counted also: the informal networks with which people identified themselves; the geographical regions from which they came; and their friendships. Yet friendship, though important, was not enough in itself to counter the lure of ambition. Thus Lafayette and the Lameths, though long-term friends and political collaborators with many shared convictions, nevertheless chose opposing sides.

## JACOBIN IDEOLOGY

The nature of Jacobin ideology evolved within the changing context of revolutionary politics.[29] The Jacobinism of the Constituent Assembly was more tolerant of difference, more trusting, much more cosmopolitan than the Jacobinism after war began in 1792. Some beliefs, however, were consistent. The core tenets of Jacobinism were the belief in popular sovereignty, in equality, and in liberty. The Jacobins were against any form of privilege or hereditary right. They had a passionate desire for justice. They believed in individual rights and the importance of the self. They asserted the right to liberty of a people kept in perpetual childhood and dependency. Many of the Jacobins' policies reflect their determination to liberate individuals from the stifling authority of absolute monarchy, the Catholic Church, and the patriarchal rule of the family. At the same time they believed in the importance of the common good. Theirs was not to be an atavistic society in which 'liberty' meant the rights of a few to secure wealth, success, self-aggrandizement, at the expense of the sufferings of the many. They believed in patriotism—by which they meant love of their community—and the need for virtue to secure the good of the *patrie*. Jacobin 'patriotism' was the reverse of aristocratic 'egoism'.[30] The language of Jacobinism was strongly emotional—and emotive—imbued with sensibility and feeling for others. To be a Jacobin one was supposed to speak from the heart. Gestures, tears, were seen as signs that the speaker's emotions, his love of the *patrie*, were genuine. It was this voice of virtuous sensibility that was endlessly parodied in the many anti-Jacobin publications of the time, above all the *Actes des Apôtres*.

Despite the Jacobins' agreement on principles, there was much less consensus on how far these should be applied in practice. There were considerable divisions over such key issues as the extent of suffrage (a propertied franchise, or one for all men

---

[29] Many works address the subject of Jacobin ideology. Most are noted elsewhere in this work, but see especially Brinton, *The Jacobins*; Higonnet, *Goodness beyond Virtue*; and Boudon, *Les Jacobins*, in particular the Introduction, 1–25.

[30] On 'egoism' as a category to which the Jacobins were fundamentally opposed, see Isobel Brooks, 'Bienfaisance and empowerment in Old Regime and Revolutionary France', unpublished paper given at the Study of French History conference at the University of Aberystwyth, July 2008. I am grateful to Isobel Brooks for her sharing with me her work, and her many original insights on this subject.

regardless of wealth?); the rights and wrongs of slavery; and the ethics of capital punishment. On all these subjects the early leaders of the Jacobins took up significantly more conservative positions than Robespierre and the other radicals. In the early years of the Revolution, few Jacobins were in favour of establishing a republic. Desmoulins and Brissot were amongst the very few who were outright republicans. Even Robespierre considered that the fully fledged republican ideal was unsuitable for France. He endorsed the notion of a limited republic, a compromise that retained a constitutional monarchy.[31]

The Jacobins' ideology translated into the way in which they organized the Club and conducted politics. In contrast to the Society of 1789, the Jacobins were characterized by 'publicity', by equality and openness; all patriots had the right to be admitted to their membership. They were formally opposed to court-style politics, and the domination of a few leaders. Like the Assembly, the structure of which the Jacobins mirrored, they were organized around a regularly elected presidency and secretariat. In theory this meant that no individual or group of individuals ought to be able to dominate but, as we have seen, there were ways to circumvent that restriction, using 'behind closed doors' tactics. Members of the Club who were also deputies in the Assembly exerted considerable influence in the Club; as did the journalists who were members of the Club, and who acted as intermediaries between the Jacobins and public opinion. In theory the Club was predicated on liberty and equality, and no man was superior to any other; yet in practice unofficial leaders exerted considerable influence over the Jacobins.

A would-be leader who had the support of the Jacobins behind him could assert considerable sway over public opinion. There were also, however, certain risks, for he would be offering himself to the judgement of people who came from a very different background to his own. Not all the Jacobins, let alone their audiences, came from the social elite. To be a patriot was enough to ensure entry to the Jacobins, which in practice meant that anyone who declared himself to be a patriot could join so long as he could afford the membership fee of 12 *livres*, and the 24 *livres* annual fee, and could be vouched for by an existing member. One did not have to be a deputy, nor even French. In the early years the Jacobins were relaxed and cosmopolitan about their membership. Arthur Young was admitted easily, as was William Miles. Admittedly, the Jacobins were unaware that Miles was acting as Pitt's agent, and that he carried on a clandestine correspondence with the British Prime Minister during the years 1789 to 1791, by means of unsigned letters sent to intermediaries.[32] Miles was introduced to the Jacobins by the duc d'Aremberg de La Marck with whom he went to dine on his arrival in France. Fifteen days later Pétion wrote to advise him of his membership.[33] Miles's excellent connections with the leaders in this new political

---

[31] On Robespierre's changing attitude towards a republic, see Linton, 'Robespierre's political principles'.

[32] On Miles's career as a secret agent, see Howard V. Evans, 'William Pitt, William Miles and the French Revolution', *Historical Research*, 43, 108 (November 1970): 190–213; and Cobban, 'British Secret Service in France, 1784–92', in Alfred Cobban, *Aspects of the French Revolution* (London: Paladin, 1968), 209–11, 221–2.

[33] Lemay, *La Vie quotidienne des députés*, 221.

culture give his testimony particular interest. He was strongly opinionated, but he did know the people involved, and some of his assessments (though naturally prejudiced against the 'French style' of politics) were astute. Miles's political opinions were too republican, too pro-French, to find much favour with Pitt, but Miles prided himself on his independence: he spoke as he found. His private correspondence shows him to have had a very low opinion of the choices of the patriot nobles, chief amongst which was their decision to throw in their lot with the Jacobins:

> I am scarcely acquainted with one amiable character in the whole patriot party; but, however vain, vicious, and contemptible they may be, they are not the primary cause of the extensive ruin into which their country is fallen. They are mere subalterns in the dreadful havoc, plunder, and dissolution of the French monarchy, and are only entitled to half the odium of so much guilt. They found everything in disorder, and they have increased the general confusion. The power they possess is an usurpation, for it was never delegated to them; it is far from being permanent, for they now hold it at the pleasure of the Jacobins, who, on the slightest provocation, will perhaps dismiss them with as little ceremony as Cromwell dismissed the Parliament in the middle of the last century. This club, composed of men of all ranks and of every climate, faith, and description, has no bond of union—no common relation, and, meeting tumultuously four days in the week...they separate, and become as distinct and detached as the sand on the beach. From such an assemblage, from such a piebald crew of nobles, plebeians, priests, beggars, thieves and assassins, what good can possibly be expected! The Jacobins govern the kingdom, or rather, they carry everything before them.[34]

Miles was unwilling to give the patriot nobles any credit for integrity, but his assessment, harsh as it was, conveys some idea of their ambiguous position, caught between the Scylla of a discredited court politics, and the Charybdis of the Jacobins. Being a Jacobin leader necessitated winning popular support among the working people of Paris, people who had never before had a political voice. Miles considered this a dangerous game: 'The Lameths wish to supplant him [Lafayette], and they are leagued with those who wish the extinction of the royal family. There is a club underneath the Jacobin where women are admitted, and as they often mount the tribune I leave you to judge of the society, and of its principles and capacity.'[35] This was a reference to the Fraternal Society of Two Sexes, which met downstairs from the Jacobins, in the chapel under the library. Miles, who was clearly no champion of the political rights of women, described how he had ventured to go with Barnave underneath the Jacobins to pay these frightening women a visit. He noted with derision that Barnave courted their good opinion in the language of virtue:

> In the most abject manner [Barnave] concluded a fulsome address to this rabble, the refuse even of all that is infamous, in which he flattered their power and complemented their civic virtues. 'Your will is our duty,' he observed; 'we have no other; to please you, to obey you, will always be our glory, and your applause will be the greatest benefit that we can receive for our work for your well-being, for your happiness.'[36]

---

[34] Letter to Mr Henry James Pye, Paris, 5 January 1791, Miles, *Correspondence*, 1: 199.
[35] Letter to Mr T. Somers Cocks, Paris, 23 February 1791, Miles, *Correspondence*, 1: 220.
[36] Letter to Mr Somers Cocks, 25 February 1791, Miles, *Correspondence*, 1: 230.

In order to become a leader of the Jacobins, a man needed to acquire skills at three things: oratory, networking, and the projection of a Jacobin identity. To master the oratory of the Jacobins he had to speak as a patriot and a man of virtue, and convince his audience that he was not motivated by personal ambition. Duport and Alexandre de Lameth were skilled public speakers, but it was Barnave who was the outstanding orator, fluent and able to improvise on his feet. In addition, the triumvirate proved adept at networking and building up their power bases in the Jacobins. They had numerous friends and allies who could be trusted to act in their interests. They also controlled the all-important Correspondence Committee of the Paris Club. This meant that they could manipulate the public image of them that was sent out to the hundreds of affiliated clubs and societies. The triumvirate also used their power base in the Jacobins to help them to secure electoral support for prominent positions within the Constituent Assembly. Both Barnave and Alexandre de Lameth spoke in favour of the holding of multiple posts on committees. Lameth was elected on to seven committees. Of the prominent Jacobins only Robespierre was not given one committee. Perhaps Robespierre's watchful eyes always made the triumvirs uneasy. Other radical Jacobins, Pétion, Buzot, Prieur, did not speak so often as Robespierre, nor did they have such a high profile, but all three were members of several committees: Buzot of three, Prieur of four, and Pétion of five.[37]

The Lameths led the way in proposing the decree of 19 June 1790 by which nobility itself was abolished. As on 4 August 1789, it may well be that this event was secretly planned in advance, though proof of this is lacking. The actual proposal to abolish nobility was made by an obscure Third Estate deputy, Lambel, but it was greeted with such applause from the public gallery and the Left of the Assembly that the Lameths made haste to seize the initiative. Other patriot nobles followed the Lameths' lead, including Noailles, Lafayette, and Lepeletier de Saint-Fargeau. The exercise was staged in the absence of certain key right-wing nobles who would have tried to oppose it. Like 4 August, this was a dramatic event, and the highly emotional atmosphere was heightened by the powerful theme of self-sacrifice. Alexandre de Lameth's renunciation of nobility was a further sacrificial offering on the altar of the *patrie* that implicitly supported his right to power on the basis of his virtue, without his ever publicly admitting as much. It was an act that finally burnt the Lameths' bridges with a large proportion of the nobility, many of whom were more distressed at the abolition of their noble status than they had been at the ending of their privileges. More than one outraged noble attributed Alexandre de Lameth's very public stance against nobility to his political ambitions. It was also claimed that the Lameths made this dramatic gesture in order to distract attention from the revelation that they had benefited from a royal pension that paid for their education. This awkward fact had come to light with the publication in April 1790 of the *Red Book*, which contained a long list of court nobles who had been in

[37] Alison Patrick, 'The Second Estate in the Constituent Assembly, 1789–1791', *Journal of Modern History*, 62, 2 (1990): 223–52; Lemay, 'Poursuivre la Révolution', 145.

receipt of secret pensions from the monarchy. The scandal provoked highly embarrassing to the Lameths. Mocked by the Right, defended by the Left, they hastily borrowed money to pay the pension back.[38]

## PERSONAL CONDUCT OF THE MAN OF VIRTUE

In his private life a man of virtue was expected to conduct himself in a way that echoed his public pronouncements. If there was a mismatch between the public identity of a political leader and his conduct when he was off the political stage, then he risked losing credibility. A Jacobin was meant to live frugally, conduct himself with modesty, and never seek to put himself forward by ostentatious living. He was not expected to be sexually chaste, or never to drink, but the watchword was moderation. Anything that smacked of dissipation, sexual promiscuity, and self-indulgent hedonism was associated with 'aristocracy'; therefore these were attributes to be despised in a public figure. This was not because the Jacobins were puritans; rather, it was about what a politician owed to the people he represented. What was at stake here was the authenticity of his virtue. If a man said one thing publicly and did another privately, this was seen as evidence that he was a hypocrite, cynically manipulating the people with a lie about who he truly was in his heart. The Lameths had a reputation for self-assured seductive charm, something that did not play too well in the more austere revolutionary circles. When Madame Roland arrived in Paris she made haste to the Assembly to see the famous men of the day. She noted with satisfaction her own immunity to the masculine charms of the Lameths: 'The seductive Lameths did not seduce me at all.'[39] By that time her friends amongst the radical Jacobins were deeply suspicious of the triumvirs, which may help to explain Madame Roland's reaction. Alexandre de Lameth seems to have found conforming to the codes of bourgeois morality expected of a revolutionary leader something of a challenge. Later (during the Legislative Assembly) Barnave wrote a letter to Théodore de Lameth saying that Alexandre had a good opportunity to rally the troops, to make them love him, especially the volunteers, but warned that 'he must stay sober and chaste till the end of the Revolution'.[40]

It was far more important, however, that a public figure should not be financially corrupt. Venality was associated with the court, and everything to which the Revolution was opposed. The Jacobins began to suspect Mirabeau of being in the pay of the court. They were absolutely right. Revelations of Mirabeau's corruption did much to establish what came to be the primary fear of the

---

[38] See Fitzsimmons, *The Night the Old Regime Ended*, 124–34; and Doyle, *Aristocracy and its Enemies*, ch. 7, esp. 228–38.

[39] Madame Roland, *Mémoires*, 128. She used the same term 'the seductive Lameths' when she first encountered the brothers, characterizing them as 'ambitious' and comparing them unfavourably to 'the true patriots'. Letters to Bancal, 7 and 15 March 1791, in Madame Roland, *Lettres de Madame Roland*, ed. Claude Perroud, 2 vols (Paris: Imprimerie Nationale, 1902), 2: 241, 244.

[40] Barnave, *Oeuvres de Barnave*, 4: 338.

Jacobins—the man who claimed to be on their side, but whose allegiance could be bought, and who would work from within to undermine the Revolution. 'Mirabeau! Mirabeau! less talent and more virtue, or watch out for the lamppost!' was the ominous pronouncement of Fréron, Desmoulins' friend and fellow Jacobin, in his journal the *Orateur du peuple*.[41] Mirabeau had many friends amongst the Jacobins. As his reputation declined, so these friendships became seen as compromising, and some of his former friends hastened to dissociate themselves from the taint of having accepted Mirabeau's friendship. Attacking Mirabeau's morality was a good way of establishing one's own integrity. Desmoulins, conscious that he had once all too willingly succumbed to the temptations of Mirabeau's *maraschino*, was merciless in his journal, *Les Révolutions de France et de Brabant*, in holding Mirabeau up to mockery, referring to him ironically as 'Saint Mirabeau'.[42] Desmoulins seized on Mirabeau's dinners as a sign of his duplicity and double-dealing: 'Breakfasting with the Jacobins, dining with 89, and supping with La Mark and the Monarchists. Where he slept it is not for me to tell.' Desmoulins recounted how, after Mirabeau's speech on the king's right to declare peace and war, he himself reproached Mirabeau for his corruption: 'You have sold yourself for a hundred thousand crowns.' Mirabeau merely smiled ironically and replied: 'Come and dine.'[43]

Another former friend, Brissot, later gave a damning indictment of Mirabeau's integrity: 'I knew him too well to esteem his character; but for a long time I let myself be carried away by his seductive spirit. He was, when he wanted to be, the most amiable of all friends, but he was also the most egoist and the most depraved of all men...I did not need authentic proofs to be certain that the moment that he modified his opinions, it was because he had sold them.'[44]

The Jacobins' suspicion of Mirabeau's ambition was shared by many in the Assembly. It was pivotal to the passing of a decree on 7 November 1790 that barred deputies from serving as ministers. More broadly, the decree marked a conscious and decisive rejection of the British parliamentary system, which was seen as facilitating venality and corruption.[45]

[41]  Cited in Luttrell, *Mirabeau*, 218.

[42]  Desmoulins, *Les Révolutions de France et de Brabant*, No. 8: 362.

[43]  Claretie, *Camille Desmoulins*, 103–5.

[44]  Brissot, *Mémoires*, 2: 39. This assessment was made in retrospect, when Mirabeau's correspondence with the king had been uncovered.

[45]  On visceral suspicions of Mirabeau's ambition as part of a conspiratorial conception of politics that resulted in the decision of 7 November 1789, see Barry M. Shapiro, 'Conspiratorial thinking in the Constituent Assembly: Mirabeau and the exclusion of deputies from the ministry', in Campbell, Kaiser, and Linton, *Conspiracy in the French Revolution*. Shapiro draws the intriguing conclusion that fears of Mirabeau's 'conspiratorial' tendencies actually contributed to Mirabeau becoming a genuine conspirator, after his access to ministerial power was blocked. See also Shapiro, *Traumatic Politics*, 1–16. On the rejection of the 'balanced' form of separation of powers in favour of 'pure' republicanism, see Johnson Kent Wright, 'National sovereignty and the General Will', in Dale Van Kley (ed.), *The French Idea of Freedom: The Old Regime and the Declaration of Rights of 1789* (Stanford, CA: Stanford University Press, 1994).

## THE RADICAL JACOBINS

The three most radical deputies in the Jacobins were Robespierre, Buzot, and Pétion. They formed a nucleus around which others on the far Left gathered, both within and beyond the Assembly. Two more deputies, the abbé Grégoire and Prieur, gave them considerable support. Like Robespierre, Pétion was a lawyer, with a reputation for virtue.[46] He quickly allied himself with Robespierre, and the two became close personally as well as politically.

No one, however, made the language of virtue more his own than did Robespierre. He emerged out of obscurity to become, month by month, a more significant figure in revolutionary politics. He had no wealth, influence, or existing power networks to help him on his way. His success in revolutionary politics was achieved partly through what he said; for this reason Furet calls Robespierre 'the mouthpiece' of the purest revolutionary discourse.[47] Furet is right to identify the importance of the language; but he gives insufficient weight to the role of Robespierre's own agency, to his tactical abilities, and to the extent to which he actively contributed to the fashioning of his own political identity. Robespierre's reputation did not stem just from the fact that he spoke in the idiom of a 'man of virtue'—many people did that. It is that he voiced this with utter conviction. His characteristic use of the language of sensibility helped give him access to the aura of 'true feelings'.[48] Mirabeau is supposed to have said about Robespierre: 'That man will go far, he believes what he says.'[49] Moreover, Robespierre understood that words alone were not enough. There must be no gap between words and deeds. His manner of life—simple frugality and personal morality—bore witness to his political integrity. At different times in his career his numerous enemies tried to 'dig the dirt' about his private life, but the evidence they turned up was thin indeed. His virtue was tested in the crucible of revolutionary politics; he proved immune to the temptations of *maraschino* and other revolutionary hazards. The public gave him the title 'the Incorruptible'. Other revolutionaries, including Pétion and Brissot, were sometimes described by this name, but Robespierre was the only one to whom the soubriquet stuck. He had what came to count most in revolutionary politics—credibility.

Even so, Robespierre's rise to pre-eminence was slow, achieved through wholehearted effort and dogged persistence in the face of consistent mockery of his appearance and persona. One person who recognized something more to him than just another

---

[46] Despite Pétion's political importance, there are few works about him. See the entries in Soboul, *Dictionnaire historique*; Lemay, *Dictionnaire des Constituants*; Kuscinski, *Dictionnaire des Conventionnels*; and Leigh Whaley, 'Made to practice virtue in a republic: Jérome Pétion: a pre-Revolutionary radical advocate', *The Consortium of Revolutionary Europe Selected Papers* (Fort Lauderdale: Institute on Napoleon and the French Revolution, Florida State University, 1995): 167–76.

[47] Furet, *Interpreting the French Revolution,* 60–61.

[48] See Andress, 'Living the revolutionary melodrama'.

[49] According to Luttrell Mirabeau may have made this comment on 5 December 1790, when he himself was president of the Jacobins, having to stave off an attempt by the 'true Jacobins' (as Desmoulins called them) to rally round Robespierre's attempt to speak against the Assembly's decree that only 'active citizens' could enter the National Guard: Luttrell, *Mirabeau*, 236–7.

ambitious politician mouthing radical language, was the outsider, Miles. Immediately before the open break between Robespierre and the triumvirs Miles's testimony regarding Robespierre is all the more convincing as he was a hostile witness. What he saw in Robespierre was authenticity. In a letter dated 1 March 1791 Miles wrote:

> The man held of least account by Mirabeau, by Lafayette, and even by the Lameths, and all the Orléans faction, will soon be of the first consideration. He is cool, measured, and resolved. He is *in his heart* Republican, honestly so, not to pay court to the multitude, but from an opinion that it is the very best, if not the only form of government which men ought to admit. Upon this principle he acts, and the public voice is decidedly in favour of this system. He is a stern man, rigid in his principles, plain, unaffected in his manners, no foppery in his dress, certainly above corruption, despising wealth, and with none of the volatility of a Frenchman in his character. I do not enter into the question of the forms of government, but I say that Robespierre is *bonâ fide* a Republican and that nothing which the King could bestow on him, were his Majesty in a situation to bestow anything, could warp this man from his purpose. In this sense of the word, that is, *in his heart meaning well*, as to the destruction of the monarchy, he is an honest man. I watch him very closely every night. I read his countenance with eyes steadily fixed on him. He is really a character to be contemplated; he is growing every hour into consequence, and, strange to relate, the whole National Assembly hold him cheap, consider him as insignificant, and, when I mentioned to some of them my suspicions and said he would be the man of sway in a short time and govern the million, I was laughed at.[50]

Miles's assessment, written immediately before the open break between Robespierre and the Lameths, suggests that the latter thought that they were using Robespierre to increase their popularity with the lower orders, but that they seriously underestimated their man. For many months during the Constituent Assembly the radical Jacobins were on terms of friendship with the Lameths. Later this was a connection that both parties were anxious to disavow, though for different reasons. Many years later, Alexandre de Lameth wrote to deny the marquis de Ferrières' assertion that there had been an 'intimate friendship between Robespierre and the Lameths and Mirabeau'. Alexandre admitted that Robespierre had gone to the home of Charles de Lameth, where he had been invited to dine on several occasions, but claimed that this was only because they were in the same delegation from Arras; their political views had always been opposed in the Assembly: Robespierre was an 'audacious leveller' while the Lameths and Mirabeau were constitutional monarchists.[51] This attempt to put clear water between himself and his brother and Robespierre was a little misleading. Charles de Lameth had gone further than inviting Robespierre round to dinner: he publicly testified to his friendship for Robespierre.[52] Or more than one occasion Charles de Lameth paid

[50] Letter to Mr H.J. Pye, Paris, 1 March 1791, Miles, *Correspondence*, I, 245.

[51] Lameth, *Histoire de l'Assemblée Constituante*, 1: 193.

[52] See below, note 73. Lamartine put the Lameths on a list of friends who visited Robespierre. Elizabeth Le Bas wrote 'only at first'. But the timing does not fit, as Robespierre only went to live with Elizabeth's family in June 1791 after the Lameths had led the exodus from the Jacobins and formed the Feuillants. It does not seem likely that they would have been paying social calls on Robespierre at that point. Stéfane-Pol [pseudonym of Paul Coutant], (ed.), *Autour de Robespierre: le Conventionnel Le Bas, d'après des documents inédits et les mémoires de sa veuve* (Paris: Ernest Flammarion, 1901), 83–4.

tribute to Robespierre's integrity. In January 1790 he spoke in the Assembly of Robespierre's 'courage and zeal, which have always characterized him, and with which he has defended the interests of the least fortunate classes in society'.[53] When Briois de Beaumez, one of the noble deputies for Artois, repeated an allegation that Robespierre was stirring up popular unrest in Artois over taxation, Charles de Lameth, along with other Artois nobles, signed a testimonial in defence of Robespierre's integrity, which Robespierre then published in Arras: 'Although M. Robespierre needs no other testimony to his patriotism than that of his conduct, and of his public reputation, we have much pleasure in giving him proof of the esteem and affection with which he is regarded by all his colleagues... He has always zealously defended the cause of the people at large, and of public liberty, as well as the special interests of Artois.'[54] According to Fréron, when (in November 1790) Charles was wounded in a duel with the duc de Castries, Robespierre visited him twice a day.[55] It seems that the Lameths were happy to invite Robespierre into the circle of their friendship, to show him affable condescension, and to milk his growing popularity with the lower orders; never imagining that his reputation might one day eclipse their own.

A network of radical Jacobins developed, linked by shared ideology and by burgeoning friendships. This network extended well beyond the ranks of the Assembly, and included a growing number of revolutionary journalists. In these hothouse circumstances, it was natural that people who found they had much in common politically should soon become friends.[56] Desmoulins, with his journal *Les Révolutions de France et de Brabant*, was a prominent figure in this community; as was Georges Danton, a successful lawyer. These two men became intimate friends; and both of them were on very friendly terms with the Lameths and with Barnave.[57] Desmoulins also reactivated his friendship with Robespierre. The two men had known one another during their school days, when they were both at Louis-le-Grand, though not in the same class. There is no evidence that they were close at that time. Nor, despite their coming from similar backgrounds and regions, is there any evidence that they had kept up their friendship in the intervening years. The first proof of renewed contact between them is a letter that Robespierre sent to Desmoulins on 7 June 1790, in which he pointed out an inaccuracy in Desmoulins' reporting of him in *Les Révolutions de France et de Brabant*.[58] Evidence for their friendship having become a significant one is given by Robespierre's presence as a witness at Desmoulins' wedding in December 1790. Desmoulins was well

---

[53] *Le Moniteur*, 3: 228.

[54] Cited in Thompson, *Robespierre*, 82–3. On Briois de Beaumez's allegation and its consequences, see McPhee, *Robespierre*, 100–1.

[55] Fréron, 'Notes sur Robespierre', in *Papiers inédits trouvés chez Robespierre, Saint-Just, Payan, etc., supprimés ou omis par Courtois*, 3 vols (Paris: Baudouin Frères, 1828; republished Geneva, 1978), 1: 158.

[56] On these political friendship networks from 1789 to 1791, see Lemay, 'Poursuivre la Revolution', 139–56; and Whaley, *Radicals*.

[57] Bradby, *Barnave*, 1: 217.

[58] Letter from Robespierre to Camille Desmoulins, 7 June 1790, *Correspondance de Maximilien et Augustin Robespierre*, ed. Georges Michon (Paris: Librairie Felix Alcan, 1926), 83–4. Desmoulins' response is in a footnote, 84–5.

connected in revolutionary circles. His other witnesses were the writer Mercier, Pétion, and Brissot.

It was Pétion who brought Brissot to meet Robespierre, Desmoulins, and others in their circle. Brissot was Pétion's childhood friend from Chartres. Brissot had already made a name for himself in Parisian municipal politics, and for his journalism, and he was now the editor of the popular journal *Le Patriote français*.[59] Brissot was a consummate networker; the kind of man who knew 'everybody'. The core of his friendships stretched back before the Revolution, to men as diverse as his long-term collaborator, the Genevan financier Clavière, and the doctor, scientist, and writer Marat.[60] A number of men who would play a key part in Jacobin politics already knew Brissot before the Revolution; he became a point of mutual contact for many of the Paris radicals. Others in the network of Paris Jacobins included Robert and his wife, Louise de Kéralio, editors of the *Mercure National*; Gorsas, editor of the *Courrier des 83 départements*; and Carra, editor of the *Annales patriotiques*, which was by far the most popular journal with the provincial Jacobins.[61]

It was through Brissot that another important connection was made, to Monsieur and Madame Roland. Brissot's contact with them stretched back over several years; they had been introduced through mutual friends including Lanthénas and Bosc. The Rolands had conducted a long correspondence with Brissot; they also made contributions to *Le Patriote français*; though they did not actually meet him till after they came to Paris in February 1791. So important were these friendships to Brissot that—until politics intervened in 1791—he planned to buy land in America and set up a community of friends there, whose lives would be devoted to rustic virtue.[62] Madame Roland was an enthusiastic republican, and saw herself as a woman of virtue—in terms both of politics and of personal morality. She was articulate, clever, and opinionated, as her *Memoirs* testify, and more politically astute than most of the men around her. She was not the kind of woman to sit back and let her husband and the other men have all the excitement of being part of the new politics. It was Brissot who suggested an opportunity for her to become involved in Jacobin politics. For a time political friends

---

[59] On Brissot's life before the Revolution, the fullest account is in Ellery, *Brissot*. See also the contrasting interpretations of Brissot's character and motivations, by Frederick A. De Luna, 'The Dean Street style of revolution: J.P. Brissot, *Jeune Philosophe*', *French Historical Studies*, 17 (1991): 159–90; Robert Darnton, 'The Brissot dossier', *French Historical Studies*, 17 (1991): 191–205; and, with new material, Simon Burrows, 'The innocence of Jacques-Pierre Brissot', *The Historical Journal*, 46,4 (2003): 843–71.

[60] Brissot conceded that he and Marat had been close friends before the Revolution, though they were to become bitter enemies: see Brissot, *Mémoires*, 1: 196–7.

[61] On Louise de Kéralio and her husband, see Leigh Whaley, 'Partners in revolution: Louise de Kéralio and François Robert, editors of the *Mercure National*, 1789–1791', in Malcolm Crook, William Doyle, and Alan Forrest (eds), *Enlightenment and Revolution: Essays in Honour of Norman Hampson* (Aldershot: Ashgate, 2004). On Carra, see Michael L. Kennedy, '"L'Oracle des Jacobins des départements": Jean-Louis Carra et ses *Annales patriotiques*', in Albert Soboul (ed.), *Actes du colloque Girondins et Montagnards (Sorbonne, 14 décembre 1975)*, (Paris: Société des études Robespierristes, 1980); and Michael L. Kennedy, 'The best and the worst of times: the Jacobin Club network from October 1791 to June 1, 1793', *Journal of Modern History*, 56,4 (1984): 635–66, esp. 647–8. On Brissot's friendships, see also Whaley, *Radicals*, 19–20.

[62] Patrice Gueniffey, 'Brissot', in François Furet and Mona Ozouf (eds), *La Gironde et les Girondins* (Paris: Payot, 1991), 441–2; Ellery, *Brissot*, 151.

had been meeting at Brissot's house, but holding salons does not seem to have been Madame Brissot's forte.[63] So, acting on Brissot's advice and with his help, Madame Roland took on the role of a political *salonnière* for the radical Jacobins. Within a very short time of her arrival in Paris she was organizing regular gatherings for political friends at her home at the Hôtel Britannique in the Rue Guenegaud, which was spacious and conveniently situated for both the Assembly and the Jacobin Club.[64]

To call Madame Roland's political gatherings a 'salon' is something of an anachronism as Siân Reynolds points out; the word 'salon' originally meant the room in which the gatherings took place, and was not used to describe the gatherings themselves until the nineteenth century.[65] Yet the concept was a familiar one from the old regime, and Madame Roland's activities were *perceived* in this light, so I shall use the term here, albeit with caution. She herself did not refer to her group as a salon: tellingly, she called it 'the little committee', emphasizing its political purpose. We have seen that the eighteenth-century salons were viewed at the time as bastions of aristocratic interest, led by elite women. In revolutionary terms they were venues for 'behind closed doors' politics. A salon was a place where 'intrigue' could take place; where plots could be hatched. A salon was potentially, therefore, against virtue. Nonetheless, for tactical reasons the radical Jacobins needed a location at which they could network, and plan their strategies. Madame Roland's 'little committee' soon became an important venue for the radical Jacobins. Rousseau had opposed the involvement of women in politics and public life, associating this with the power of aristocratic women. Madame Roland conformed outwardly with this view. She herself was careful not to play too prominent a role. She provided the location, the sociability, the refreshments, and then sat back to let the men talk politics: she was careful not to speak herself. Nevertheless, the act of setting up a salon inevitably brought her more into the political spotlight.[66]

Madame Roland's 'little committee' was organized differently to one of the aristocratic salons. It met four times a week, after the sessions of the National Assembly, and before the meeting of the Jacobins, a strategy that facilitated regular discussion of business in the Assembly and the Club, and the planning of courses of action. It offered a place for sociability, where people could talk about politics with more privacy than in the Jacobin Club or another public place. Because it met in private and only men who had an invitation or *entrée* through a mutual friend would attend, it could potentially be seen as inimical to the required openness of revolutionary culture. Madame Roland described how meetings often involved 'proposing a course of action and agreeing how to go about it, or distributing roles to one another'.[67]

---

[63] Michael Sydenham, *The Girondins* (London: The Athlone Press, 1961), 63.

[64] On Madame Roland's first salon see Madame Roland, *Mémoires*, 62–4; and on her first encounters with political leaders at this time, 126–37.

[65] On Madame Roland's political gatherings at this period, see Reynolds, *Marriage and Revolution*, ch. 14; Gita May, *Madame Roland and the Age of Revolution* (New York: Columbia University Press, 1970), 180–99; and Sydenham, *The Girondins*, 86–91. See also Guy Chaussinand-Nogaret, *Madame Roland: une femme en revolution* (Paris: Éditions du Seuil, 1985); and Mona Ozouf, 'Madame Roland', in Furet and Ozouf, *La Gironde et les Girondins*.

[66] The gender politics of Madame Roland have attracted a considerable amount of analysis. See May, *Madame Roland and the Age of Revolution*, 180–99.

[67] Madame Roland, *Mémoires*, 133.

To this salon came numerous radical Jacobins, many of them introduced by the ever-active Brissot. It was he who brought the three deputies, Robespierre, Buzot, and Pétion. Robespierre soon became friends with the Rolands, and attended the salon, though not as regularly as some of the others in the group. Madame Roland mentioned Robespierre for the first time in a letter on 15 March 1791 in which she wrote of his courage in facing down intimidation in the Assembly. A few days later she wrote to Brissot characterizing the Jacobin deputies, with whom she already was on good terms, as 'your good friend Pétion...the vigorous Robespierre and the wise Buzot'.[68] Her letters written in 1791 show that at this time she thought highly of Robespierre and his courage in the Assembly.[69] Her *Memoirs* give a very different account of her attitude towards Robespierre. We must bear in mind, however, that when she wrote her *Memoirs* in 1793, she was imprisoned, under threat of death; the Jacobins had become her bitter enemies and her view of Robespierre had changed considerably from the days of their shared ideals and purpose; indeed, she was convinced that Robespierre had tried to have her husband murdered in the September Massacres of 1792. Thus, in 1793 she wrote that Robespierre, by acting in an egotistical way (that is, against virtue), had often undermined the collective strategies previously planned by the 'little committee' to sway the Assembly. She said he sometimes gave the game away, and would 'try to take the credit for himself, causing the whole plan to fail'.[70] She had not, however, said this at the time. Her memories of her own friendliness towards Robespierre had also dimmed when she implied that it was Robespierre who sought her out, rather than the other way round: '...even when Robespierre came only rarely to the little committee, he sometimes invited himself to dinner'.[71]

At the time, however, as the ties between radicals and the triumvirs fractured into open hostility, Madame Roland's 'little committee' became a venue for planning strategies to oppose the triumvirate. This group of radical Jacobins stuck together during the coming break with the Jacobin leadership and the dangerous time in July 1791 when it seemed that Jacobinism was in danger of collapse.

## IDENTITIES UNDER ATTACK: DENOUNCING MIRABEAU, DENOUNCING BARNAVE

From late 1790 the triumvirs began backing away from some of the more radical positions that they had previously supported. They were becoming increasingly fearful of the Parisian crowds whose support they had so assiduously courted. In

---

[68] Letter to Bancal, 15 March 1791; Letter to Brissot, 28 April 1791, in Madame Roland, *Lettres de Madame Roland*, 2: 244; 270.

[69] In Madame Roland's letter to Bancal of 22 June 1791 she recounted approvingly Robespierre's courage in saying in the Assembly what she herself was thinking. See Madame Roland, *Lettres de Madame Roland*, 2: 304. On the striking similarity between the views of Madame Roland and Robespierre on their own virtuous heroism and how this made them ready both to sacrifice themselves and to destroy political rivals, see Annie Jourdan, 'La guerre des dieux ou l'héroïsme révolutionnaire chez Madame Roland et Robespierre', *Romanticisme*, 85 (1994): 19–26.

[70] Madame Roland, *Mémoires*, 133.

[71] Madame Roland, *Mémoires*, 133.

November 1790 the triumvirs made secret overtures to the court. Barnave visited the house of the king's minister, Montmorin, where he was seen by Mirabeau. The radical Jacobins got wind of this development very quickly. Marat, who was always the first to sniff out a conspiracy, had already claimed in *L'Ami du people* that the triumvirs were following the example of Mirabeau who 'has prostituted himself to the executive power'.[72] Marat's dire warnings were borne out on 6 December in the Jacobin Club, when Mirabeau (serving as president) blocked an attempt by Robespierre to speak out against a decree passed that day in the Assembly forbidding passive citizens to be in the National Guard. The issue had important ramifications for whether the poor were to have a voice in the Revolution. In a significant turn of events the triumvirate sided with Mirabeau, against Robespierre. Desmoulins' account of this event is revealing of the changing attitude of the radical Jacobins towards their leaders. He described Mirabeau as supported by 'thirty honourable members', whereas 'Robespierre, always so pure, so incorruptible, and at this session so eloquent, was surrounded by all the true Jacobins, all the republican souls, all the elite of patriotism'. The ensuing tumult lasted for an hour and half, stated *Le Patriote français*. According to Desmoulins, the Lameths made use of a visible sign of their patriotism, 'Charles Lameth's arm in a sling' (evidence of the wound incurred in his recent duel) to impose silence on the indignant Jacobins. Charles then spoke; he was careful to praise Robespierre's 'love for the people', and emphasized that Robespierre was 'his very dear friend', yet made it clear that the triumvirate supported Mirabeau.[73] From this moment the radical Jacobins understood that their leaders were indeed deserting them and seeking a role for themselves as king's men. The triumvirs began to push through a series of more centrist decrees in the Assembly, swinging further to the Right, but many of the Right distrusted them, leaving the triumvirate in an awkward situation, caught between their desire to achieve political stability with themselves in a commanding position, and the popular militancy that they had done so much to encourage as a way of giving themselves a power base.

Barnave's reputation was further damaged by his active involvement in the defence of the French colonial interests in Saint-Domingue, and his resistance to political rights for mulattos.[74] Charles de Lameth owned extensive property in Saint-Domingue, and Barnave's involvement was seen as motivated by his personal friendship for the Lameths, though Barnave denied this. Barnave's chief attacker was Brissot. Brissot was a leader of the abolitionist *Société des Amis des Noirs*; he was outraged at what he saw as Barnave's betrayal of the principles underlying the rights of man. Charles had offered to sacrifice his colonial property early on, but according to Brissot this was a ruse to gain popularity amongst the Jacobins and Charles had not been in earnest.[75] In November 1790 Brissot published an open

---

[72] Marat, *L'Ami du peuple*, No. 279, 13 November 1790.

[73] 6 December 1790, Aulard, *Société des Jacobins*, 1: 404; and *Le Patriote français*, No. 486, 7 December 1790.

[74] There is an extensive literature on the abolition of slavery and the revolt in Saint-Domingue. A recent study is by Jeremy D. Popkin, *You Are All Free: The Haitian Revolution and the Abolition of Slavery* (Cambridge: Cambridge University Press, 2010).

[75] Brissot, *Mémoires*, 2: 121–3.

*Letter to Barnave*, in which he denounced the latter for having acted out of personal motives, and in support of the vested interests of his friends; in short for his lack of virtue. The open letter ended with a description of the characteristics of a true patriot. Such a man should 'want liberty for all men'; he should 'hate monarchy'; he must 'not allow a lie to sully his lips'; he does not 'manoeuvre to arrive at positions of pre-eminence'; he 'does not have a court of numerous clients in his anti-chamber'. A political leader should be like Cato, or Cincinnatus: 'He will stay in mediocrity even in the midst of the most brilliant places; and often he will leave to his children only his memory and the recognition of his fellow citizens.'[76] Brissot then went on to examine Barnave's conduct in detail, to show how, point by point, Barnave fell short of this model of political conduct, which he merely imitated, without actually achieving. Brissot's personal denunciation of a political leader who feigned an identity he did not possess was a tactic that would be employed repeatedly by the Jacobins. Denunciation was seen as a duty of Jacobins and *sans-culottes*. The whole idea of denunciation as a legitimate activity in revolutionary politics was based on the virtue of the denouncer. It was essential for Brissot, therefore—as for everyone else who subsequently denounced a fellow politician— that his own position be seen as that of a man of virtue, who was motivated only by his desire to further the public good, not by a personal grudge against the man he accused.[77]

Yet Brissot's attack on Barnave went beyond a tactical hit, or even a matter of principle; there was a personal venom in it. When, in 1793, both men were imprisoned under the Terror, Brissot was still reliving the battles of 1790. His *Memoirs*, written partly as a personal justification of his actions, presented an unforgiving portrait of Barnave's shortcomings: 'Barnave, as I reproached him, never had true patriotism, but only the vanity of the orator and the ambition of the tribune. It was not…a blind indignation that animated me against him. I had seen into the depths of his soul…'[78] Here, in prison, facing his own death, Brissot was still intent on establishing his own authenticity and Barnave's perfidy, both in his own eyes and in those of posterity. He remained proud of his *Letter to Barnave*, saying it was 'one of the best and most useful works to have come from my pen'.[79]

At his own trial, which took place after Brissot's death, Barnave, for his part, protested that the case against him was composed of calumnies invented by Brissot three years earlier. 'It is Brissot,' Barnave protested, 'it is Brissot almost alone who devised this notion of an alteration in my principles…'[80] The image of Barnave as an unprincipled turncoat had survived the man who had invented it.

---

[76] Brissot, *Lettre de J.P. Brissot à M. Barnave* (Paris, 20 November 1790).

[77] On virtue and denunciation see Lucas, 'The theory and practice of denunciation'. For a more detailed account of the fraught relationship between Brissot and Barnave and its political consequences, see Marisa Linton, 'Friends, enemies and the role of the individual', in Peter McPhee (ed.), *Companion to the History of the French Revolution* (Oxford: Wiley-Blackwell, 2012).

[78] Brissot, *Mémoires*, 2: 113.

[79] Brissot, *Mémoires*, 2: 111.

[80] 'La défense de Barnave transcrite par son avocat', in *Actes du Tribunal révolutionnaire*, 416–17.

The triumvirs for their part were equally prepared to deploy the language of virtue to inflict deep wounds on the reputations of their opponents. By February 1791, their attempts to work with the court, using Mirabeau as an intermediary, had fallen through. Their move to the Right had compromised their popularity with the rank and file of the Jacobins (their chief card), leaving them stranded. The triumvirs blamed Mirabeau for having used them for his own purposes, and the bitterness between them mounted again in the last months of Mirabeau's life.[81]

On 28 February 1791 an altercation arose in the Assembly over whether the king's aunts should be allowed to leave the country and go to Rome. This turned into a fierce debate on whether the emigration of potential opponents of the Revolution should be authorized. Mirabeau defended the legal right to freedom of movement, a view supported by the Right. The Jacobins led by Alexandre de Lameth protested loudly. Mirabeau turned towards the benches where the Jacobins sat. 'Silence those thirty men!' he cried, a phrase that was intended to humiliate them, by exposing them as a small factious group within the Assembly as a whole.

In the Assembly, the triumvirs were leaders of a small minority. In the Jacobin Club things were different. That night the triumvirs turned publicly on Lafayette and on Mirabeau in an attempt to reassert their own political credibility with the Jacobins. Earlier that evening Mirabeau, who had been invited to dine at the house of d'Aiguillon, Lameth's friend, had arrived there to find the door shut in his face. According to Desmoulins (who gleefully recounted the whole affair in his journal) twelve men had refused to come to the dinner if Mirabeau was present.[82] His humiliating exclusion from d'Aiguillon's home mirrored his political rejection by the Left. Nevertheless, Mirabeau came boldly to the Jacobin Club that same evening, in an attempt to regain some of his political credit. Earlier that evening, Duport had denounced Lafayette as a 'secret enemy' and 'a traitor', while he praised Robespierre and others for their patriotism.[83] When Mirabeau arrived at the packed Jacobins he too was met by a furious attack by the triumvirs. Duport looked Mirabeau in the eye and stated that 'our most dangerous enemies are here: these are the men in whom we have placed the greatest hopes'. Duport warned that the people had been too gullible in entrusting their political leaders with the very power that they were now turning to their own self-advantage, and against the good of the people. The Jacobins applauded him loudly.[84] Then Alexandre de Lameth took to the tribune and launched into a full-scale denunciation of Mirabeau, accusing him of private vice and public corruption. Worse still, Lameth denounced Mirabeau for having orchestrated a 'plot' against the Jacobins, going back to the start of the Revolution. According to Lameth, Mirabeau had been 'unable to corrupt or to "ministerialize"' the Jacobin deputies, so had schemed to destroy their reputation by depicting them as 'factious' in the Assembly, whereas they were the ones who were dedicated to the public good.[85] By all accounts Lameth had never spoken so eloquently. At

---

[81] Michon, *Adrien Duport*, 85–7, 183.

[82] Desmoulins' account in *Les Révolutions de France et de Brabant* is reproduced in Aulard, *Société des Jacobins*, 2: 95–110.

[83] Michon, *Adrien Duport*, 89–91.

[84] Aulard, *Société des Jacobins*, 2: 97–8.      [85] Aulard, *Société des Jacobins*, 2: 103.

the same time, the effect of his words, as he turned on a former friend and political ally, was terrifying. A German witness reported how for some time afterwards he had felt sickened as he recalled 'the cruelty' and 'the hatred' shown by Lameth, and the 'impetuous joy' with which the majority of the Jacobins greeted this display.[86]

William Miles was present. He saw how Mirabeau struggled to use the same language of virtue in reply:

> The same night—Monday last—Mirabeau himself was denounced as a traitor to his country by the two Lameths and Duport at the Jacobins. I sat next to Charles Lameth and opposite to Mirabeau. Never did a man defend a good cause so ill . . . The denunciation lasted two whole hours. I saw him ascend the tribune, dismayed and terrified. I never heard a man speak so badly in my life. In vice he is eloquent; in the cause of virtue and of justice he was abashed because he was not at home. We move awkwardly out of our sphere. He spoke only ten minutes, and half the time was consumed in fulsome and dishonourable panegyric on the zeal and patriotism of his accusers.[87]

Lameth and Duport had made a key step in the language of political virtue, corruption, and conspiracy: the most dangerous enemies were their own leaders, the men who dissembled their true identity. As Lameth said, 'it's no longer the aristocrats whom we fear, it is those who have gained the confidence of the people by a mask of patriotism'.[88] Their opponents replied in similar terms.[89] The language that they used to denounce politicians was not so far removed from that which would be used against politicians during the Terror. The difference is that during the Constituent Assembly it was a politician's personal reputation and career that were put at risk by revelations that he was feigning political virtue. During the Terror it would be his life that was at stake.

Robespierre took no part in these attacks. He seems to have seen behind the show of words, to the personal enmity and disappointed ambition they concealed. From his perspective, there was little to choose now between the triumvirs, Lafayette, and Mirabeau; all of them seemed to be pursuing their own interests.[90] There was some substance in this assessment, in that all these men, while sharing the same ideology and with no intention of destroying the monarchy, put personal ambition first, and did not collaborate with one another. They bear their own share of responsibility for all that followed. Had they put personal enmity and ambition aside and worked together then the monarchy might have survived, and war and terror been averted.

---

[86] Aulard, *Société des Jacobins*, 2: 112.

[87] Letter to Somers Cocks, Paris, 4 March 1791, Miles, *Correspondence*, 1: 251–2, also 270–4.

[88] Aulard, *Société des Jacobins*, 2: 107.

[89] In a formal address to the Jacobins Lafayette's associate, Duquesnoy, accused Lameth of 'hiding a profound ambition under the mask of patriotism, he regards the people as stepping stones by means of which to achieve power'. See the letter of Duquesnoy to the Jacobins, 2 March 1791, in Aulard, *Société des Jacobins*, 2: 152–4.

[90] Michon, *Adrien Duport*, 92.

## AMBITION DEFEATED

The death of Mirabeau on 2 April 1791 prompted a fresh opportunity for the triumvirate to negotiate an alliance with the monarchy. Within a matter of days Montmorin made secret overtures to the triumvirs, and found them amenable.[91] Naturally, this connection was not publicly admitted, but the actions of the triumvirate made it apparent that they had had a change of loyalties. Robespierre, Pétion, and the other radicals suspected it, without having absolute proof. The fact that they chose to act on the basis of suspicions that were later shown to have been well founded helped set up a precedent for the Jacobins to judge political leaders on the basis of what they were thought to be doing. Where absolute certainty could not be reached, a moral certainty must and would suffice.

This distrust emerged into open confrontation over the key issue of whether deputies could also serve as ministers, and thus potentially use their political capital to further their personal advancement and power. The Constitution Committee (dominated by friends of the triumvirate, particularly Thouret and Le Chapelier) tried to dismantle the decree which prevented deputies from also being ministers. On 7 April 1791 Robespierre rose to pre-empt this manoeuvre by reasserting the principle that 'the legislator should...free himself from all personal considerations'. He asked the Assembly not only to reaffirm that deputies could not serve as ministers, but to add a new provision, that no former deputy could ask for any place or pension until four years after he had ceased to be a deputy.[92] His aim was to keep the triumvirs out of ministerial power. The triumvirs, especially Duport, tried to oppose him, but they were caught in a difficult position. They could not speak openly against a measure couched in the language of virtue without exposing themselves to the serious allegation that they were self-interested. They were caught by the inexorable logic of the political identity that they themselves had adopted.

Though the triumvirs were not named, everybody knew who Robespierre had in mind. It proved a popular measure with the Assembly. The Right had their own reasons to want to block the ambitions of the triumvirs. Most of the press, too, supported the proposal. The *Journal universel* announced that Robespierre's proposal was directed against 'the intriguers and ambitious of the National Assembly...A number of very strong partisans of the cause of the people are accused of aspiring to be ministers. It is certain that the extreme facility with which they enabled the extension of the prerogatives of the throne, makes such accusations quite credible. This motion worthy of a true patriot [Robespierre]...has been accepted with acclamation. At last, we have seen a renewal of the superb scene of 4 August.'[93] According to Brissot's *Le Patriote français*, 'a vigorous patriot, M. Robespierre, who feared criminal influences on the achievement of the constitution' had succeeded

---

[91] Michon, *Adrien Duport*, 181–7.

[92] *Journal des Etats Généraux* ou *Journal Logographique*, in Robespierre, *Oeuvres*, 7: 201. See also Michon, *Adrien Duport*, 315–21. Buzot proposed that the interdiction be limited to two years, and it was in this form that it passed into the constitution.

[93] *Journal universel*, 11: 4011 and 4018, in Robespierre, *Oeuvres*, 7: 202.

in warding off a conspiracy. Robespierre's fears were shared by many others: 'The Assembly...enthusiastically applauded and welcomed this proposition.'[94] The *Journal de la Noblesse*, though it came from a political perspective very different from that of Brissot, agreed with him that no trust should be put in Barnave's political identity: 'It had escaped no one's attention that the Monsieur Barnave of 1789 was not the Monsieur Barnave of 1791. It is permitted to change one's opinion, but not to conceal the motives behind this change.'[95]

The decision that deputies could not serve as ministers was to have a great impact on revolutionary politics. The revolutionary ministers had access to considerable power and patronage. In closing off this avenue to the deputies the Constituent Assembly was acting in conformity with the ideology of virtue. In future deputies could not have direct access to these lucrative posts. One consequence would be that some deputies worked to get indirect access to ministerial power through securing the appointment of friends to ministries, who then owed them favours in return and could be lobbied for posts and patronage.

On 8 April Earl Gower reported the vote over ministers, seeing it as a decisive moment: 'The party of the Lameths and Barnave are visibly on the decline.' He also pointed out the damage that the personal nature of the enmity between the Lameths and Mirabeau had done to the political credibility of the former: 'Charles Lameth has given a severe blow to his popularity by refusing to attend a deputation to enquire after Mirabeau's health, who, when he heard it, said, "I knew him to be maladroit but I didn't believe he was such an idiot."'[96] By 15 April the split within the Jacobins had hardened. Earl Gower reported: '...there is a set of men whose object is the total annihilation of monarchy however limited. The heads of this party are: Robertspierre [*sic*], Péthion [*sic*], Buzot, and Prieur...as for Barnave and the Lameths their consequence as a party, is so much destroyed that they are wavering whether they should give themselves to the Republicans or the friends to a limited monarchy. The present constitution has no friends and cannot last.'[97]

On 11 May Brissot confronted his enemy, Barnave, openly in the Jacobins for the first and only time. The debate turned on the political rights of mulattos; the atmosphere grew heated. Each man made intimations of the other's corruption. A further stormy session took place two days later at which Robespierre too came out in open opposition against the triumvirs. Charles de Lameth tried to speak, but he was met by jeers and cries of 'they have betrayed us; they have turned their backs on us'.[98] The triumvirs' domination of the Jacobins was over. After that day Barnave ceased to attend the Club. Duport made a further attempt to talk about re-eligibility, but got a hostile reception.[99]

---

[94] *Le Patriote français*, No. 608, 8 April 1791; Robespierre, *Oeuvres*, 7: 203.

[95] Cited in Michon, *Adrien Duport*, 311.

[96] George Granville Leveson, Earl Gower, *The Despatches of Earl Gower, English Ambassador at Paris from June 1790 to August 1792* (Cambridge: Cambridge University Press, 1885), 77–8.

[97] *Despatches of Earl Gower*, 79–80.

[98] 13 May 1791, Aulard, *Société des Jacobins*, 2: 414–15.

[99] Bradby, *Barnave*, 2: 75–8; Michon, *Adrien Duport*, 204–5.

A few days later a further event took place that reinforced the consequences of the decisions taken over ministers. This was the self-denying ordinance of 16 May.[100] It was an extraordinary provision which had far-reaching consequences for the future of the Revolution. Once again, it was proposed by Robespierre, and again, its principal tactical purpose was to block the ambitions of the triumvirate. The proposal was for the deputies of the Constituent Assembly, having forged the constitution, to now voluntarily stand aside from politics, forgo the option to participate as deputies in the coming Legislative Assembly, and let others take the lead.

Robespierre's proposal was greeted with wild acclamation. Members of the Constitution Committee (where the triumvirs had many friends) tried to speak against it, to argue in general terms the importance of continuity and stability, but the Assembly was of no mind to listen. The moderate Jacobins could not argue openly on their own behalf against Robespierre's proposal because it would have made them look ambitious—which of course they were. They were stymied by the very language of virtue that they themselves had used so successfully on previous occasions. A triumphant Desmoulins wrote that Robespierre 'had one of the finest successes that any member has ever had in the assembly, and I saw those who had up till then acknowledged only his virtues, agree that on that day he showed his eloquence'. The ordinance was, he added, 'a master-stroke of our dear Robespierre' and the self-sacrifice of Robespierre and Pétion to achieve it (for they themselves would have been certain of re-election), was worthy of all praise.[101] Desmoulins' judgement was borne out by the royalist *L'Ami du Roi*, not usually a place where one looked for praise of Robespierre, which on this occasion proclaimed '...we can say, without exaggeration, that he astounded the entire assembly. Never had anyone spoken with more good sense, with more wisdom, and it would be difficult to surpass M. Robespierre's eloquence on this occasion.'[102]

Robespierre's tactic was indeed a masterstroke, for it brought together different factions of the Assembly, united in their desire to disempower the triumvirate, though for different reasons. The deputies of the Right (with a few exceptions such as the far-sighted Cazalès) embraced the proposal as a way of undermining the constitution to which they were so opposed. They saw only that such a measure would exclude from power the patriot nobles, men whom they hated. What most failed to realize was that the expulsion of the moderate Left from political power might usher in, not a return to the pre-Revolutionary regime that they so desired, but a swing towards the more radical Left.

---

[100] On the self-denying ordinance, see Barry M. Shapiro, 'Self-sacrifice, self-interest, or self-defence? The Constituent Assembly and the "Self-Denying Ordinance" of May 1791', *French Historical Studies*, 25, 4 (2002): 625–56. Whilst recognizing the importance of factional politics in the decree, Shapiro also explores the psychoanalytical dimensions of the deputies' motivation, particularly the possibility that deputies were projecting both their fear of conspiracy, and their sense of the inadequacy of their own virtues, onto the triumvirate. On the politics behind the ordinance, see Michon, *Adrien Duport*, 206–24.

[101] Desmoulins, *Les Révolutions de France et de Brabant*, No. 78: 599–601; and Robespierre, *Oeuvres*, 7: 398–9.

[102] Montjoie, *L'Ami du Roi*, 17 May 1791, 547, in Robespierre, *Oeuvres*, 7: 401.

The triumvirs reacted to the collapse of their ambitions with anger and horror. Desmoulins reported that he met the Lameths just before the decree when they were still 'patriots'; when he saw them afterwards they were no longer the same. Alexandre de Lameth refused to speak; Duport talked despairingly of emigration.[103] Robespierre had stripped them of their political identity. As Jacobins they were silenced.

In the days that followed Barnave tried to organize an attempt to repeal the ordinance, on the grounds that the triumvirs' desire to stay in politics was motivated solely by a determination to avoid anarchy and to stop the work of the Constituent Assembly being dismantled; thus in accordance with the public good. Few observers were inclined to find this argument a credible one. A contemptuous *L'Ami des Patriotes* declared that the triumvirs were desperate to reverse the self-denying ordinance; they 'desire it with an incredible ardour because they feel that outside the Assembly they will return to the nullity from which they ought never to have emerged; and they are taking the most astonishing steps to obtain it'.[104] Attempts were made to forge a tactical alliance between the triumvirs and the Society of 1789 in order to oppose this reverse, for both groups stood to lose by it. The attempt came to nothing for there was too much mutual distrust and personal enmity between the triumvirate and Lafayette for them to cooperate.[105]

Barry Shapiro's excellent study of the politics behind the self-denying ordinance shows that the motives for proposing it were inspired less by the radical Left's desire to make an altruistic gesture, on the lines of 4 August, than the fear that the radicals had of the 'conspiracies' of the triumvirate. Shapiro brings out the importance of the psychological dimension of this fear and distrust, demonstrating how this pervasive atmosphere affected people's political decisions at this key juncture.[106] He is surely right to emphasize the importance of this emotional reaction. At the same time, we should also remember that this fear was not illusory: on the contrary, the triumvirs were indeed engaged in secret negotiations with the monarchy. Moreover, the evidence for this 'conspiracy' was not dreamt up in the minds of the participants in Madame Roland's salon; rather, their suspicions were grounded on the gap between what the triumvirs were saying, and what they were actually doing. Crucially, deputies in the unaligned centre shared much of the radical Jacobins' suspicion of the motives of their leaders, and were quite as hostile to personal ambition in political leaders. Thus the moderate Thibaudeau wrote about Barnave and his friends: 'We have been put on our guard against proposals made by men who have always passed for good patriots, but who are now known to be intriguers, ambitious men who would like to revoke the decrees on the ministry and the eligibility of former deputies.'[107]

---

[103] *Les Révolutions de France et de Brabant*, No. 86: 31–4.

[104] Duquesnoy, *L'Ami des patriotes*, vol. II, 274, note (14 May 1791). Cited in Bradby, Barnave, 2: 86.

[105] Gouverneur Morris's diary recounted attempts to set up this alliance: 20 and 22 April 1791, Gouverneur Morris, *A Diary of the French Revolution, 1789–1793*, 2 vols (London: George G. Harrap and Co., 1939), 2: 166–8.

[106] Shapiro, 'Self-sacrifice, self-interest, or self-defence?'

[107] Letter from Thibaudeau to Plorry, 13 August 1791, in Antoine-René-Hyacinthe Thibaudeau, *Correspondance inédit du constituant Thibaudeau (1789–1791)* (Paris: Champion, 1898), 184. Thibaudeau wrote this in the light of the fall-out from Varennes, so might not have articulated his disapproval of the triumvirs so strongly the previous spring.

The circumstances around the passing of the ordinance illustrate how ideological, tactical, personal, and emotional factors came together at a key moment to have a decisive effect on the future path of the Revolution. The ordinance reflects how the ideology of virtue combined with tactical manoeuvring to outflank the moderate patriots, fed by very personal factors such as enmity, loyalty, and emotions of suspicion, fear, and distrust. The self-denying ordinance had a further consequence. Robespierre, Pétion, and the other deputies who planned this proposal were also depriving themselves of the chance to dominate the political agenda. Robespierre was not without the prospect of employment: he had an elected position as a public prosecutor in Paris to fall back on; but as far as political power went, he and those who backed him were giving up any personal ambitions they might have had. Robespierre was thus abiding by the demands of political virtue. By sacrificing his own political career he was giving tangible proof of the authenticity of his virtue, thus closing the gap between words and deeds. This would help to confirm his subsequent reputation as a 'man of virtue'. No one could have foreseen at that point that the Legislative Assembly was going to last a scant ten months. Not even Robespierre's fiercest detractors have said that he was corrupted by a desire for wealth. It has often been said, however, that he was corrupted by power. The self-denying ordinance should give pause to those who think so. He blocked the first Jacobin leaders at the price of sacrificing his own career too—or so he believed at the time.

The politics of virtue were about far more than one individual, however: the importance of the ordinance is not that Robespierre proposed it, but that many others in the Assembly agreed with his views, and also agreed to abide by its provisions. Not everyone was making a personal sacrifice in taking this stance: as Shapiro points out, many deputies had had enough of politics, and just wanted to go home. In his study of the Constituent Assembly as a collective project, Mike Fitzsimmons argues that its deputies, in voluntarily adopting this ordinance, demonstrated that they were not trying to impose their own rule on the future of the Revolution. The Constituent Assembly was not aiming to perpetuate its power and therefore it was very far from being a body that would cling to power through Terror.[108] On the other hand, the ordinance did have the serious consequence of destabilizing politics. It broke continuity and brought new and inexperienced men into politics who were in no mood to compromise with the monarchy.[109]

## VARENNES AND THE CHAMP DE MARS: DIVISIONS SEALED IN BLOOD

On the night of 20 June the king and his family fled the palace, aiming for the royalist garrison at Montmédy on the border with Austria. They were intercepted at Varennes and brought back to Paris. On the return journey they were accompanied

---

[108] Fitzsimmons, *The Night the Old Regime Ended*, 43.
[109] Fitzsimmons argues that, more than the royal family's flight to Varennes, the self-denying ordinance was the single issue that did most to destabilize the constitutional monarchy: Fitzsimmons, *The Remaking of France*, 253–8.

by two deputies, Barnave and Pétion. The Jacobins suspected—correctly as it turned out—that the queen and Barnave had seized this impromptu moment 'behind closed doors' to strike up an alliance that would have fateful consequences.[110] Barnave and Marie-Antoinette engaged in secret correspondence; nearly a hundred letters passed between them, despite his vehement denial at his trial in 1793. These secret letters did not come to light till 1912, but this is not the point: his actions at the time gave him away, not only to Robespierre and the extreme radicals, but to the unaligned centre. Barnave acknowledged to the queen that the law prohibiting deputies from becoming ministers had 'closed the door on all their ambitions'. He had not given up the hope of being a key player in events, though from now on his influence would be exerted not in the public arena of the Assembly, but 'behind closed doors', advising the queen, and through her the king.[111]

The consequences of Varennes for the fate of the Revolution—and the monarchy—were profound.[112]. For the radical Jacobins, it marked the moment when they began decisive moves towards rejecting the monarchy. In leaving his people, the king had acted with egoism. Robespierre reacted to Varennes with a deeply emotional speech in the Jacobins, to which his audience responded with similar feeling.[113] Varennes also galvanized Lafayette and the triumvirs into reconciling their differences.[114] For some time the triumvirs had abandoned the Jacobin Club, but the morning after the flight Alexandre de Lameth suddenly appeared at the Jacobins, arm in arm with Lafayette to signify both renewed friendship and political solidarity, and proceeded to speak in defence of Lafayette's integrity.[115]

The factional division of the Jacobins was sealed by the blood shed on 17 July. The Jacobins decided to draw up a petition to call for the deposition of the king. Brissot and Danton were included on the committee to draft it. At the last moment Robespierre, fearful of the consequences, persuaded the Jacobins to drop the petition. But by then the Cordeliers Club had taken it up, while the triumvirs deserted the Jacobins to found a rival club, the Feuillants, taking with them almost all the deputies, except Robespierre, Pétion, Buzot, and one or two others. The scene was thus set for a violent confrontation between the rival factions. Charles de Lameth, was who presiding in the Assembly, urged the authorities to use violence to suppress the unrest. In an act of loyalty to friendship, on the morning of the 17th Alexandre de Lameth, who clearly knew that violence was

[110] Jeanne-Louise-Henriette, Madame Campan, *Memoirs of Marie-Antoinette* (London: Hutchinson and Co, no date given), 264–7.

[111] 'Letter to the queen', 28 August 1791, in Alma Söderhjelm (ed.), *Marie-Antoinette et Barnave: Correspondance secrète (Juillet 1791–Janvier 1792)* (Paris: Armand Colin, 1934), 81.

[112] On the political consequences of Varennes see Timothy Tackett, *When the King Took Flight* (Cambridge, MA: Harvard University Press, 2003). See also, Munro Price, *The Fall of the French Monarchy: Louis XVI, Marie-Antoinette and the Baron de Breteuil* (Houndmills: Palgrave, 2002).

[113] Andress has an excellent account of this, in 'Living the revolutionary melodrama', 110–12.

[114] Gouverneur Morris's diary described attempts to set up this alliance: 20 and 22 April 1791, Morris, *A Diary of the French Revolution,* 2: 166–8. On the reconciliation of the Lameths and Lafayette over the crisis of Varennes, see Madame Roland, *Mémoires,* 134.

[115] 21 June 1791, Aulard, *Société des Jacobins,* 2: 533–7.

coming, sent a verbal message to Danton, Desmoulins, and Fréron warning them to absent themselves and go to dine in the country.[116] A crowd of 50,000, including many women and children, gathered at the Champ de Mars to sign the petition. Lafayette ordered the National Guard to fire on the unarmed crowd. It is estimated that about fifty people were killed and many others wounded. Jacobins withdrew at the last moment when Robespierre feared the consequences of confronting the moderates head on. After the massacre, Charles de Lameth and Barnave led praise of the conduct of Bailly and Lafayette in suppressing the demonstration at the Champ de Mars against what Charles termed 'the enemies of the happiness and liberty of France usurping the mask and language of patriotism...' to mislead the people.[117]

Barnave's influence with the queen depended on his continuing ability to sway men in the radical camp. After the Champ de Mars he provided the queen with 'a large volume in which the names of all those who were made to act at will by the power of gold alone were written', and who were to be paid to applaud when the king accepted the constitution. The following year, when France was embarking on war and Barnave himself no longer had any official post, he gave her a list of men whom he said should replace the king's Constitutional Guard (that had been denounced in the Assembly on 23 May 1792), stating that 'all who were set down in it passed for decided Jacobins, but were not so in fact; that they, as well as himself, were in despair at seeing the monarchical government attacked; that they had learned to dissemble their sentiments, and that it would be at least a fortnight before the Assembly could know them well, and certainly before it could succeed in making them unpopular', and that the monarchs could take advantage of this to get away from Paris. The queen did not take his advice on this occasion, either. Probably she had little confidence in Barnave's claim that he still had influence in radical circles; she preferred instead to put her reliance in the intervention of foreign powers.[118]

Unable to control the Jacobins the triumvirs walked out after Varennes, and founded a rival club, the Feuillants, across the street from the Jacobins. For a while the Jacobin Club had few leaders left; of the deputies only Pétion, Buzot, Robespierre, and a handful of others remained. Nevertheless the Feuillants continued to lack credibility, while the self-denying ordinance had destroyed the ambitions of their leaders; already, by the end of the Constituent Assembly, many deputies had returned to the Jacobins.

On 30 September 1791, the Constituent Assembly came to an end. As far as the crowds in Paris were concerned, Robespierre and Pétion had conclusively demonstrated their right to be seen as 'men of virtue'. When they emerged from the final session of the Assembly the waiting crowd went wild. They cried 'vive l'incorruptible!' Both men were crowned with oak leaves; and the crowd pulled their *fiacre* home through the streets.[119] By contrast the triumvirate's reputation as men of virtue was in tatters. When Barnave and the Lameths left the Assembly for

[116] Michon, *Adrien Duport*, 262–3.     [117] Michon, *Adrien Duport*, 261, 267.
[118] Campan, *Memoirs*, 269, 295.     [119] Thompson, *Robespierre*, 174–5.

the last time they were met with boos and hisses.[120] Barnave became known as 'Monsieur Double Visage' (Mr Two-Faced), a soubriquet that indicated the false-hood of his identity. When, however, he was put on trial during the Terror, after enduring a year of imprisonment, and found himself accused of such revolution-ary crimes as 'ambition' and friendship with the wrong kind of men—namely the Lameths—he was able to reply proudly 'never would I be so base as to disavow my friends'.[121] When his time came, Robespierre, the man of virtue, would not be able to say as much.

In conclusion, the co-founders and first leaders of the Jacobins, Barnave, the Lameths, and Duport, supported the constitutional monarchy, and manoeuvred tactically to become powerful figures in the new regime. In order to dominate the Jacobin Club and appeal to radical public opinion, they adopted the identity of men of virtue. They used this rhetoric to denounce their political opponents and personal rivals, above all Mirabeau, as men without virtue, and therefore secret enemies of the Revolution. According to Lameth, politicians who purported to be on the Left, but who were motivated by ambition, not virtue, were the Revolu-tion's most dangerous enemies, more dangerous than the 'aristocrats'. The language that the triumvirs used to attack Mirabeau's authenticity was essentially the same as that which would be used to denounce politicians during the Terror. The Jacobin leaders in their turn had their political ambitions blocked in a tactical and ideo-logical move spearheaded by a radical group in the Jacobins led by Robespierre and Brissot, who had come to suspect the authenticity of the Jacobin leaders' identity as 'men of virtue'. The language that the triumvirs had deployed was used against them in turn. The power of the language of virtue to make or break the reputation of a revolutionary politician was well established by the end of the Constituent Assembly. A politician who was seen to be personally ambitious and feigning political virtue was at severe risk of losing his reputation and his career—but not yet his life. It would take the very changed circumstances that began with the war, to make the politicians' terror possible.

---

[120] Bradby, *Barnave*, 2: 257.
[121] 'La défense de Barnave', 418–19.

# 4

# The Ascendancy of the Girondins and the Path to War

The post of legislator is often more perilous than that of a warrior: the courage needed by the public man is often even more demanding. His career is a continuous fight against envy, hatred, calumny, persecution and the black plots of all the enemies of equality...He must raise himself above all private interests, and generously risk his life for that of the State.

Address of the Jacobins to the Affiliated Societies,
16 July 1791.[1]

Messieurs, you are placed here between the security of a great nation and the interests of an individual: choose.

Brissot, denouncing Delessart to the Legislative Assembly,
10 March 1792.[2]

## BRISSOT: THE 'MAN OF VIRTUE'

The elections to the Legislative Assembly, coupled with the exclusion of the leaders of the Constituent Assembly by the self-denying ordinance, presented Brissot with the opportunity to forge a political career. He complained about the embargo on any man presenting himself as an open candidate; but in the event he managed to be elected as a deputy for Paris without much difficulty.[3] For his election strategy he used his power base at the Jacobins and *Le Patriote français*. At the Jacobins he declaimed against the new constitution. It had done nothing, he said, to change the old political system of corruption and patronage. The constitution was only 'a useless pedestal raised for the glory of ambitious men'. The constitution had left the civil list intact, with its corrupting effects; 'the right to nominate to so many posts,' he said, encouraged 'a crowd of adulators and corrupt men' to cluster round the corridors of power.[4] New men, men of virtue, could change that constitution.

---

[1] Published in *Le Patriote français*, No. 744, 23 August 1791.
[2] *Archives parlementaires*, 39: 544.
[3] See Patrice Gueniffey, 'Revolutionary democracy and the elections', in Waldinger *et al.*, *The French Revolution and the Meaning of Citizenship*.
[4] J.P. Brissot, *Discours sur les Conventions, Prononcé à la Société des Jacobins, le 8 Août 1791*.

Part of the difficulty in portraying oneself as a man of virtue suitable for election is that one could not openly lay claim to that persona without appearing arrogant or mendacious. There were ways round this difficulty, however, particularly for a newspaper editor with the means to speak directly to his public and convince them of his authenticity. Brissot wrote an exhortation to the electors, which appeared in *Le Patriote français*, in which he detailed the kind of qualities they should favour when deciding who to vote for: 'Proved patriotism, courage, good judgement, and probity.'[5] At about the same time *Le Patriote français* published a curious letter addressed to the editor of the journal (Brissot himself, of course, though he was not mentioned by name), which purported to be from the 'Haut-Rhin' though no name of the letter's author was provided. The letter was full of praise for the editor as the 'defender of liberty'. It concluded by asking for the editor's silhouette, 'in order to place it above the altar of liberty. The worms have eaten those of Barnave and company, so much so that they are no longer recognisable.' Below was printed Brissot's laconic response: 'Place the head of Cato or Sidney; no statues before death.'[6] It was a neat tactic: by publicly repudiating personal ambition, and refusing to accept praise directed at him, Brissot was obliquely indicating to the readers of his journal that if they were looking for a man of virtue to defend the public interest, they need look no further than—himself.

Brissot had had previous experience of dealing in this kind of discourse. In the 1780s, in common with many other future revolutionaries, he had earned his living writing under the patronage of powerful figures, including Calonne and d'Orléans. His acceptance of patronage had made him vulnerable to claims made by his personal enemies, of whom the most vindictive and persistent was Morande, that he was dependent on powerful political figures, therefore lacking virtue. Morande continued to make such allegations during Brissot's election campaign, against which Brissot was obliged to defend himself.[7]

Brissot grew rapidly in stature, to become one of the leading figures within the Legislative Assembly. He was also a key player in the Jacobin Club where his discrediting of Barnave's reputation had helped to reinforce his own.[8] Brissot himself was not a particularly original thinker, though he was quick to soak up the ideas of others.[9] He was a great enthusiast for natural virtue and sensibility, and he condemned noble arrogance, manners, corruption, and personal immorality; though he shared these views with many others.[10] According to the Genevan, Dumont,

[5] *Le Patriote français*, No. 744, 23 August 1791.

[6] *Le Patriote français*, No. 745, 24 August 1791.

[7] Burrows, 'The innocence of Brissot', 867–8. Morande continued to attack Brissot's reputation as a 'man of virtue': see Charles Théveneau de Morande, 'Réponse au dernier mot de J.P. Brissot et à tous les petits mots de ses camarades' *(Supplément au No. 25 de l'Argus Patriote)* (Paris, 1791).

[8] See the entry on Brissot in Lemay, *Dictionnaire des Législateurs*.

[9] Gueniffey, 'Brissot', 444. Loft, however, gives an altogether more generous assessment of Brissot's intellectual capacities: see Leonore Loft, 'The roots of Brissot's ideology', *Eighteenth-Century Life*, 13 (1989): 21–34.

[10] See for example Brissot's views on the corruption of d'Orléans and of Mirabeau. He condemned their personal immorality and lack of political virtue in the same breath: Brissot, *Mémoires*, 2: 32–40, 64–5.

Brissot's success at a political leader was owed not to his ideas, nor his eloquence, but rather to his activity and energy: 'Brissot was forever writing, running about, getting things together, getting things moving, but he didn't have a talent for the spoken word, and never had an impact as a orator. He lacked dignity, facility of expression, and aptness in his choice of words.'[11]

Around Brissot a group of new Jacobin deputies began to form that had a profound influence on the direction of politics in the Assembly. Out of the 768 members of the Legislative Assembly, only 49 deputies spoke very frequently; these men dominated the mood in the chamber. Many names associated with Brissot appear on this list.[12] Brissot's group became known variously as the 'Brissotins', 'the Rolandins', and 'the faction'. Eventually they took on the name of the 'Girondins'. Though this new name was only acquired in late 1792, we shall refer to them here as the Girondins, in order to avoid confusion. It should be borne in mind, however, that these men were members of the Jacobin Club, indeed were leading figures in it, throughout most of the period discussed in this chapter.

Historians have raised key questions about the identity of the Girondin group: who was part of it; what their ideology was; and even whether there was a group at all. We shall consider these questions in the following chapter in the context of political choices in the Convention. For this chapter, however, we shall confine ourselves to the relatively small group of figures around Brissot during the life of the Legislative Assembly, and look first at what they did. One thing we should briefly address, however, is the argument that Brissot and his faction were 'moderates' in contrast to the Jacobins of Robespierre's ilk. Whatever happened later, this was not the case in 1791, when Brissot was on the radical end of the spectrum of Jacobin ideology. It was he, not Robespierre, who was the first to argue that the king had forfeited his right to the throne, and that France should embark on a republic. By the summer of 1791 Brissot and his group were committed to the republic. During the months before the war, while Brissot spoke openly of his desire to see France become a republic, Robespierre was much more cautious. As late as March 1792 Robespierre argued that 'the word republic is nothing'. In his view, unless and until the 'general will' decided otherwise, France should keep to the constitution agreed with the king as a better choice than a hazardous and dangerous future.[13] Also, at this period the Girondins were no more squeamish about popular violence than were other Jacobins. They were eager to court the support of the Parisian militants (often referred to by their new political name—the '*sans-culottes*'). As Sonenscher has shown, it was Gorsas, along with other members of the group around Brissot, who first began to use the new apellation, *sans-culotte*, between September 1791 and May 1792, partly as a way of discrediting the Feuillants. There was a deep irony in the fact that the same men who fell victim to real *sans-culottes* in June 1793, had themselves invented this political term, profited by

---

[11] Dumont, *Souvenirs sur Mirabeau*, 207.

[12] Lemay, *Dictionnaire des Législateurs*, 2: 787.

[13] 2 March 1792, in Robespierre, *Oeuvres*, 8: 211–12; and on the context, Aulard, *Société des Jacobins*, 3: 419–21.

it, but then proved unable to control it.[14] Several of the Girondins frequented public dinners given by Pétion, now mayor of Paris, at which many of the *sans-culottes* congregated. The *sans-culottes*, who had probably read few novels of sensibility and natural virtue and even less classical literature, expected their political leaders to have a much more rough and ready demeanour than that of the refined 'man of virtue'. The Girondins were ready to adapt their own conduct to appeal to the militants of Paris. Dumont described the manners and language that the Girondins used on these occasions:

> They spoke endlessly about the conspiracies of Coblenz, the Austrian Committee, the treasons of the court, and the moderation of the Feuillants was subject to more abuse there than the anarchic fury of the Jacobins... Several of the personages there, whose names I have forgotten, displayed a coarseness that was truly shocking. I was amazed to see Condorcet at ease in a society so inappropriate for him. I know of nothing more repugnant in a popular party than the necessity of living alongside dissolute and crude people. Politeness and seemliness were aristocratic distinctions that one must trample underfoot in order to raise oneself to equality with the rabble.[15]

The ties between the group around Brissot were based more on personal choice and friendship groups than on an identifiable 'Girondin' ideology. In 1791, insofar as the Girondins had a collective identity, it was primarily through their friendships.[16] The Girondins were a 'clique' or 'faction' rather than a political party like those in the English parliament. Brissot was the central connecting point, rather than an official leader. He dominated partly by virtue of his great facility for networking and forging connections. He himself admitted: 'I have always loved to bring my friends together...'[17] He was, it was said, the life and soul of the social gatherings attended by the Girondins. All the Girondins were either his friends or were acquainted with him, even if they did not know one another, or even, in some circumstances, knew, but actively disliked one another. Brissot was the kind of man who operated very much in terms of friendships and personal connections. He worked tirelessly for the political advancement of his friends, and used *Le Patriote français* to promote their careers, particularly that of his former patron, the financial expert, Clavière.[18] Although this says something for his personal qualities, it says less for his political ones. The favouring of friends had adverse resonances of old regime culture and private loyalties over the public good. It was a path that needed to be trod with care by an aspiring revolutionary politician.

---

[14] Sonenscher, *Sans-Culottes*, 338–61. On Vergniaud's defence of the patriot perpetrators of a massacre at Avignon in October 1791, see *Archives Parlementaires*, 40: 152–3; and René Moulinas, *Les Massacres de la Glacière: Enquête sur un crime impuni: Avignon 16–17 octobre 1791* (Aix en Provence: Edisud, 2003), 175–7.

[15] Dumont, *Souvenirs sur Mirabeau*, 206–7.

[16] On the network of friends who formed the *Cercle Social*, and its relationship to the formation of a Girondin press, see Gary Kates, *The Cercle Social, the Girondins and the French Revolution* (Princeton, NJ: Princeton University Press, 1985), ch. 7, esp. 191.

[17] Brissot, *Mémoires*, 1: 176.

[18] Gueniffey, 'Brissot', 441; Ellery, *Brissot*, 181.

The core of the Girondin group was made up of several overlapping friendship networks. Firstly, there was the group of friends that Brissot had made before the Revolution, including Pétion, the Rolands, Lanthenas, and Clavière; then there were the Rolands' Lyonnais connections; thirdly, a group of deputies from Marseille; and fourthly, the group from the Gironde who gave their name to the 'Girondins', some of whom first made contact with Brissot over the anti-slavery issue. The Gironde group were particularly radical, and were early supporters of republicanism. Amongst this fourth group were Vergniaud, Guadet, Gensonné, and the brothers-in-law Ducos and Boyer-Fonfrède. The friendships between this last group of men antedated the Revolution. They had been members of the Musée, a literary society in Bordeaux, which had been an important feature of their intellectual and cultural formation.[19] Condorcet was only on the fringes of the core group of Girondins. Influence flowed from him to Brissot, and not the other way around. Though he was friendly with some of the Girondins, he was not an intimate of Brissot's; between Condorcet and Madame Roland there was mutual antipathy.[20]

## THE DRIVE TO WAR

By the time the Legislative Assembly met there was widespread anxiety that France was on the verge of invasion by a coalition led by Austria and the many *émigrés* gathered on France's borders. The Declarations of Padua and Pillnitz, and the Papacy's attack on the Revolution, all contributed to a growing fear that the foreign powers were preparing to declare war on the Revolution. Brissot and his group seized upon this general fear and used it to argue that France should pre-empt the anticipated invasion and seize the initiative by declaring war. The Girondins characterized the political situation confronting the new Assembly in terms of a plot, secretly directed by the monarchy, for the *émigrés*, Austria, and other foreign powers to destroy the Revolution.[21] Years later Louvet recalled the heady atmosphere of late 1791: 'The court had arrived at the point of conspiring openly against the accepted constitution...not content with fomenting interior revolts, it was calling on the foreign powers. A guilty king, who was violating all vows, released us from

[19] On relations between the Girondin deputies see the study by Guadet's nephew, which was based on considerable personal documentation: Joseph Guadet, *Les Girondins, Leur vie privée, leur vie publique, leur proscription et leur mort*, 2 vols (Paris: Librairie académique, 1862), esp. 1: 30–3. On the role of the Musée in the intellectual formation of these deputies, see Stephen Auerbach, 'Becoming the Girondins: the pre-Revolutionary careers of the Girondins from Bordeaux', unpublished paper given at the French Historical Studies conference, Rutgers University, April 2008. Cited with permission of the author.

[20] Elizabeth Badinter and Robert Badinter, *Condorcet (1743–1794): un intellectuel en politique* (Paris: Fayard, 1988), 354.

[21] For a quantitative analysis of language in the successive assemblies showing a marked increase in the language of conspiracy in the Assembly from late 1791, see Timothy Tackett and Nicolas Déplanche, 'L'idée du "complot" dans l'œuvre de Georges Lefebvre: une remise en cause à partir d'une nouvelle source', *La Révolution française* [online], Georges Lefebvre, 5 July 2010, available at <http://lrf.revues.org/index171.html> (accessed 3 February 2011).

our own. He wanted to return us to the old despotism: very well! We shall give him the republic!'[22] Brissot and his group argued that the Assembly must pre-empt this threat, and seize the initiative by embarking on a war against Austria. It was not, however, the Girondins who initiated the call for war; as Francesco Dendena has shown, the triumvirs had pursued a militarist rhetoric, using the threat of war as a way of reinforcing their own position and strengthening that of the king, though they did not want actual war.[23] In the case of Brissot and his friends, however, the rhetoric was employed with a very real intent. The Feuillant deputies continued to block Jacobin measures in the Assembly, but they had limited credibility with either the Left or the Right. Unlike the Jacobins the members of the Feuillant Club met in private, without spectators, and their power was not based on popular support. As emotions raised by the threat of war grew heated they found themselves increasingly marginalized.

The Girondins first began to work together as a group in order to promote the push to war.[24] By early 1792 Brissot, Condorcet, Vergniaud, and others were meeting privately at the salon set up by Vergniaud in the apartment of Madame Dodun in the Place Vendôme. Here they planned strategies for influencing the direction of the Assembly, and for out-manoeuvring Robespierre's influence in the Jacobins. Brissot also met with the comte de Narbonne, the Minister of War, and his faction at Madame de Staël's salon.[25] This group made common cause with Brissot's supporters in the spring of 1792, for both wanted war, though for different reasons. In the case of Narbonne, he and his royalist allies hoped that a war would rally support for the monarchy, and so strengthen it.[26]

Brissot's plan was very different. He set out deliberately to destabilize the political situation. He thought there were two possible outcomes to this. The first was that the monarchy would be forced to knuckle down before the revolutionary leaders and accept the constitution. The second was that the monarchy's opposition to the constitution would come out into the open, at which point Brissot envisaged that both the monarchy and the constitution could be brought down in a renewal of revolution. A third option, Narbonne's hope that the monarchy would have its hand strengthened, is not something that Brissot seems to have considered. It was a high-risk strategy, one that depended for success on the optimistic assumption

[22] Jean-Baptise Louvet, *Mémoires de Louvet de Couvray, député à la Convention Nationale* (Paris: Baudouin Frères, 1823), 31–2.

[23] Francesco Dendena, 'A new look at Feuillantism: the triumvirate and the movement for war in 1791', *French History*, 26,1 (2012): 6–33.

[24] As Blanning says, the Girondins were the only group to push unequivocally for war, seeking to subvert the constitution: see T.C.W. Blanning, *The Origins of the French Revolutionary Wars* (Harlow: Longman, 1986), 98–9. A similar view is taken by John Hardman, 'The real and imagined conspiracies of Louis XVI', in Campbell, Kaiser, and Linton, *Conspiracy in the French Revolution*.

[25] On Brissot's connection with Narbonne see H.A. Goetz-Bernstein, *La Diplomatie de la Gironde: Jacques-Pierre Brissot* (Paris: Hachette, 1912), esp. 40–41; also Sydenham, *The Girondins*, 102; and Georges Michon, *Robespierre et la guerre révolutionnaire 1791–1792* (Paris: Marcel Rivière, 1937), 30.

[26] On 11 January 1792 Narbonne gave a report to the Assembly on the army's preparedness for war, which was calculated to bolster the conviction that France could easily win: *Archives Parlementaires*, 37: 233–40.

that France's armies would be victorious in a war against Austria and her allies. Whether through war, or through a second revolution to overthrow the monarchy, it was likely that a great many people would die as a result of Brissot's callous plan. It may well be that Brissot believed his own rhetoric and genuinely thought that the French army would indeed be welcomed as 'armed liberators', signalling an international wave of revolution and liberation. But by choosing war, Brissot and the Girondins—whether they understood the risks or not—were taking a path that brought much closer the danger of unleashing internal terror.

It was in this bellicose context that the Girondins' identity was forged: they portrayed themselves as 'heroic patriots' who were valiantly leading the call for war. Not all those who later became Girondins started out by wanting war, but over the months of winter 1791 and spring 1792 they eventually coalesced into a war party. In the Assembly, Brissot and Isnard, along with the deputies from the Gironde (Vergniaud, Guadet, and Gensonné) became the chief spokesmen for the pro-war lobby. Curiously, Brissot claimed that the war would end terror rather than cause it: 'This war is necessary to France for her honour...to put an end to terrors, to treasons, to anarchy...This war would be a real benefit, a national benefit, and the only calamity that France has to dread, is not to have war.'[27] The following day Brissot anticipated that the king would side against his own people in the war; Brissot even seems to have desired this. He said to the Jacobins: 'I have only one fear, that we shall not be betrayed. We need great treasons, our safety lies there, because there are still great doses of poison within the heart of France and violent explosions are needed to expel them.'[28] There was something more too, an almost religious fervour for liberty. Brissot spoke of a 'crusade for universal liberty', to be waged to promote the Revolution, a means both of purging the nation, and of bringing the Revolution to other countries.[29] The Girondins were convinced, or convinced themselves, that the Revolution would be welcomed with open arms by benighted peoples who would be grateful for the introduction of French 'liberty'. It can be argued that the Girondins were the true revolutionary idealists; Robespierre's Jacobins were not more radical than the Girondins, but more pragmatic.[30] In the spring of 1792 it was the Girondins, buoyed up by their own conviction that they were right, who were more extreme.

The Girondins took the rhetoric of virtue and conspiracy to a new level of intensity and perceived threat. Guadet was greeted by repeated applause when, speaking on behalf of the Diplomatic Committee, he declared that it was no longer acceptable for 'men of good faith' to choose different parties. Now there was only one

---

[27] Brissot's speech to the Legislative Assembly, 29 December 1791, *Archives parlementaires*, 36: 607.

[28] Brissot, 'Second discours de J.P. Brissot sur la nécessité de faire la guerre', given in the Jacobins, 30 December 1791, 15.

[29] Brissot, 'Second discours de J.P. Brissot sur la nécessité de faire la guerre', 27.

[30] See Doyle, 'Thomas Paine and the Girondins', in William Doyle, *Officers, Nobles and Revolutionaries: Essays on Eighteenth-Century France* (London: Hambledon Press, 1995); a more favourable interpretation is by François Furet, 'Les Girondins et la guerre: les débuts de l'Assemblée législative', in Furet and Ozouf, *La Gironde et les Girondins*.

choice for all the French, 'between the old and the new regime'.[31] On 14 January there was a dramatic session in the Assembly; it was likened by excited deputies to the collective emotional fusion of the Tennis Court Oath, the moment at which the Revolution had been born, when the deputies had sworn to give France a constitution. But now, amidst the swirling rhetoric of war and patriotism, a new kind of revolution was born. Gensonné declared, to a wildly enthusiastic audience, that anyone who sought a reconciliation with Austria by means of a concert were 'traitors to the *patrie*' and therefore guilty of the crime of *lèse-nation*, treason against the nation.[32] In a further move it was decided that such a crime warranted the death penalty: 'Let us mark out in advance a place for traitors, and let this place be on the scaffold.' Deputies, ministers, ushers, spectators (including the women) alike all swore an oath to maintain the constitution, amidst cries of 'live free or die, the Constitution or death'.[33]

There was more to the war movement than the machinations of the Girondins. Many people were *genuinely* afraid of a conspiracy by the court to overthrow the constitution and destroy the Revolution. Marie-Antoinette became a chief target of this suspicion as the 'plotter in chief', the enemy within the heart of Versailles. There was considerable justification for their fear: a conspiracy at court actually existed, in which Marie-Antoinette was deeply implicated, to use the threat of intervention by Austria, in the form of an 'armed congress', to bring pressure to bear to overturn the constitution and crush the Revolution; though until early 1792 (the point at which war began to appear inevitable) she hoped to avoid an outright war, which could threaten the safety of the royal family.[34] The actions of Austria further inflamed the situation. From late 1791 to early 1792 Austria put increasing diplomatic pressure on France by threatening invasion. This intimidatory stance had a disastrous effect, for it gave credibility to the argument that France must act to pre-empt attack, and thus lent support to the pro-war lobby. Nevertheless, the revolutionary leaders still had a choice. The fact that this fear had some foundation to it does not mean that some better political alternative could not have been found than a declaration of war that resulted in so much spilling of blood. Despite

---

[31]  26 December 1791, *Archives parlementaires*, 36: 406.

[32]  The term *lèse-nation* was not invented by the revolutionaries. It circulated in *parlementaire* discourse before the Revolution, forming part of a linguistic transfer of authority from royal sovereignty to the sovereignty of the nation. As Dale Van Kley has shown, it had its origins in Jansenist constitutionalism: see Van Kley, *The Religious Origins of the French Revolution*, 325–6.

[33]  14 January 1792, *Archives parlementaires*, 37: 413–16.

[34]  A series of studies by Kaiser have cast much new light on the politics of Marie-Antoinette and the perception—and the extent of the reality—of the 'Austrian Committee' conspiracy. See Thomas E. Kaiser, 'Who's afraid of Marie-Antoinette? Diplomacy, Austrophobia, and the Queen', *French History*, 14 (2000): 241–71; Thomas E. Kaiser, 'From the Austrian Committee to the foreign plot: Marie-Antoinette, Austrophobia and the Terror', *French Historical Studies*, 26, 4 (Fall 2003): 579–617; Thomas E. Kaiser, 'Entre les mots et les choses: le fantôme du "Comité Autrichien"' in Anne Duprat (ed.), *Révolutions et mythes identitaires: mots, violences, mémoire* (Paris: CHCSC de l'université de Versailles Saint-Quentin-en-Yvelines, 2009); and Thomas E. Kaiser, 'Ambiguous identities: Marie-Antoinette and the house of Lorraine from the affair of the minuet to Lambesc's charge', in Dena Goodman (ed.), *Marie-Antoinette: Writings on the Body of a Queen* (New York and London: Routledge, 2003).

Austria's belligerent rhetoric the foreign powers were too divided amongst themselves to be eager for war. Even up to the last moment it is quite possible that a war could have been averted by the contrivance of 'politics', and conciliation of the king.[35]

Instead, Brissot and his allies played on the mingled emotions of fear and patriotism to stir up popular support for war. They seized on accounts of the Austrian Committee, and made this a central part of their case for declaring war against Austria.[36] The Austrian Committee was supposed to consist of a shadowy group of malevolent counter-revolutionaries, whose patroness was the queen herself. Marie-Antoinette was the proverbial enemy within; her loyalties were to her Austrian family dynasty, rather than to France and the Revolution. The Girondins did not invent the idea of the Austrian Committee. As Thomas Kaiser has shown, the fear of a conspiratorial 'Austrian Committee', nurturing Austrian interests within the French court, antedated the Revolution by many years. These rumours magnified in the tense atmosphere of late 1791 when the Austrian Committee served as the focal point for every kind of fear and suspicion. It was alleged that Marie-Antoinette, dressed as a man, crept out from the Tuileries at night to attend meetings of the Austrian Committee in the shadows of the Bois de Boulogne. Kaiser also demonstrates that, despite some of the unlikely—if picturesque—details, these stories had some foundation in the reality of Austrian foreign policy. Marie-Antoinette's activities at the French court were simply the latest in a long policy of the pursuit of Austrian interests at foreign courts. Marie-Antoinette was indeed playing a double game. Privately she rejoiced in the short-sightedness of the Girondins' policy of seeking a war, confident that it would play into the monarchy's hands, and that the old regime would be restored.[37] The revolutionaries could not know what the queen was writing in her private correspondence that circulated by courier to her allies in Vienna and Coblenz and that would have proved the extent of her double-dealing. They were operating in a climate of uncertainty, which encouraged them to act on the basis of suspicion alone.

## THE MOTIVES OF THE GIRONDIN LEADERS

We might ask ourselves, as Robespierre so pointedly did, what was the *real* motivation of the Girondins in seeking war? Ironically, to try to establish what they really thought, we have to do as their opponents did, and try to get behind the public

---

[35] For Dumont's opinion on this, which was similar to that of Delessart and the other anti-war ministers, see Dumont, *Souvenirs sur Mirabeau*, 216. See also Thomas E. Kaiser, 'La fin du renversement des alliances: la France, l'Autriche et la déclaration de guerre du 20 avril 1792', *Annales historiques de la Révolution française*, 551 (2008): 77–98.

[36] See Kaiser, 'From the Austrian Committee to the foreign plot', 587.

[37] For contrasting views on how far Louis XVI himself was complicit in the queen's strategy, see John Hardman, 'The real and imagined conspiracies of Louis XVI', in Campbell, Kaiser, and Linton, *Conspiracy in the French Revolution*; Price, *The Fall of the French Monarchy*; and Joël Félix, *Louis XVI et Marie-Antoinette: un couple en politique* (Paris: Payot, 2006).

face to find out what they were saying 'behind closed doors'. Evidence provided by the Girondins themselves, in their letters, and in memoirs, is invaluable; though we do have to be careful about interpreting this material, particularly the memoirs, as it was written by the Girondins to justify what they had done and inevitably puts their actions and motives in the best light. There is also evidence that was put together later from testimonies used against them for their indictment and trial. Much of this was assembled by their enemies in the Jacobins; and the things that the Girondins said at their trial, in fear of their lives, must also be approached with caution. For the period running up to war, Étienne Dumont is generally held to be a reliable witness, though in writing his retrospective account he was keen to distance himself from any suspicion that he had been compromised by being present at the Girondins' discussions on the war: he would hardly have been party to their decision making if he had not, at that time, shared some of their views. At this time he was friendly with the leading Girondins, especially Brissot, Clavière, and Condorcet, and admitted to their intimate circle. He was introduced to Vergniaud's salon. Here, over lunches attended by Brissot, Clavière, Roederer, Gensonné, Guadet, Vergniaud, Ducos, Condorcet, and others, plans were made to concert actions in advance of the meetings of the Assembly. According to Dumont they were not a well-organized group; there was 'more chatter and party gossip' than taking of clear decisions. It was Brissot who brought them together: 'Brissot became the doer. His activity sufficed for all.'[38]

The Girondins do seem to have been genuinely afraid that a conspiracy would be launched by the Austrian Committee. According to Dumont, fear of this scenario 'tormented Brissot's imagination'.[39] Even so, they deliberately talked up the potential danger. Following Brissot's lead in the spring of 1792 the Girondins were reckless of the consequences of their actions, carried away by the intoxication of power, their own rhetoric, and the drama of the situation. It is not clear whether at this point the Girondins actually wanted to overthrow the monarchy (as is sometimes claimed) or whether they hoped by means of their aggressive policy to come to an accommodation with the king that would see them installed in power. It may be that they were not themselves sure what would happen, but were prepared to run the risk of the monarchy being destroyed, the country thrown into renewed turmoil, and a republic established if the monarchy would not toe the line. Brissot himself, as the prime mover in all this, showed a singular lack of political judgement.[40] He declared that the court did not want war, and so could be pressured into acquiescence. Madame Roland, who was rather more politically astute than most of the men in her own faction, cautioned them that the court was making fools of them—but her warning fell on deaf ears. In her *Memoirs* she admitted that she had come to appreciate that Brissot was a political lightweight, out of his depth

---

[38] Dumont, *Souvenirs sur Mirabeau*, 201. On Dumont's reliability as a witness and his shifting political views, see Bénétruy's Introduction, 29–30.

[39] Dumont, *Souvenirs sur Mirabeau*, 216.

[40] Gueniffey, 'Brissot', 439.

in the struggles of revolutionary politics.[41] Saint-Just would later make the observation that Brissot's own friends called him 'a child' and 'inconsequential'.[42]

Robespierre eventually came to believe that the Girondins had been motivated by personal ambition, in direct contradiction of the ideology of political virtue. Other observers, outside the Jacobins, had already formed a similar view. The goal of the Girondins, according to Dumont, was to penetrate the secrets of the Austrian Committee by forming a ministry: 'The ambition to govern was at the heart of it.'[43] Barnave wrote to Alexandre and Théodore de Lameth to complain bitterly of the recklessness and personal ambition of the new leaders of the Assembly, and warned of the destabilizing impact of their policies on the country. But, like the Lameths, Barnave was now a spent force, observing futilely from the sidelines.[44] It is likely that Brissot saw no contradiction between his identity as a man of virtue and his ambition. It is probable that he genuinely assumed that he himself and his friends were the most virtuous patriots, and therefore the men best fitted to rule France, in place of men whose loyalties the Girondins considered to be 'suspect'. The pro-war policy thus chimed in with Brissot's own desire to be a major political player.[45]

## BRISSOT'S DENUNCIATION OF DELESSART

An essential part of the pro-war strategy was the plan to denounce and overthrow Delessart, the Minister for Foreign Affairs, and the king's other ministers along with him, and to replace these men with friends of Brissot. The downfall of Delessart was contrived by the Girondin leaders acting in concert with Narbonne and probably Dumouriez (a minor noble and professional soldier who played a leading role in the drive to war). Dumouriez and Delessart had been at school together. It was said that Dumouriez dined with Delessart in order to get information about foreign affairs out of him, which Dumouriez promptly shared with the Girondins, and which Brissot used to shape the act of accusation against Delessart.[46] Many years later in his *Memoirs* Dumouriez would cast the blame for Delessart's downfall and subsequent death on the 'report of the terrible Brissot'. Dumouriez himself had been confined to his room with a 'bad cold'.[47] In writing his *Memoirs* Dumouriez had every motive to downplay his political involvement with the Girondins. The reality is that the overthrow of Delessart was contrived through a collective strategy: Narbonne, who led the rival court faction to that of Delessart, had been dismissed by the latter and was eager for revenge; while Dumouriez was the man

[41]  Madame Roland, *Mémoires*, 129.

[42]  Saint-Just, 'Notes pour servir au rapport du 11 Germinal an II', *Oeuvres complètes*, 759.

[43]  Dumont, *Souvenirs sur Mirabeau*, 201–2, 216–17.

[44]  Barnave, *Oeuvres*, 4: 376.

[45]  See Sydenham, *The Girondins*, 103.

[46]  See Goetz-Bernstein, *La Diplomatie de la Gironde*, 162; Ellery, *Brissot*, 262.

[47]  Charles-François Dumouriez, *Mémoires du Général Dumouriez* (Paris: Firmin Didiot Frères, 1848), 426. On Narbonne's complicity, see Morris, *A Diary of the French Revolution*, 2: 384.

who would take Delessart's place. The strategy was plotted out privately before-hand, at the salon of Vergniaud. There seems also to have been a last-minute meeting at the home of Madame de Staël where Brissot, Narbonne, Guadet, Fauchet, and others gathered for dinner. Here, over dessert, the final details of the plot to bring down Delessart were worked out.[48] The next day, 10 March, Brissot rose in the Assembly to denounce Delessart for weakness in his dealings with the Austrians. Brissot accused the Minister outright, 'I declare that we are surrounded by treasons, that the traitors are not far from us, and that it is important to know them... I regard M. Delessart as a traitor.'[49] Brissot admitted that he lacked substantive proof of this accusation, but maintained that 'moral proofs' were sufficient. He examined Delessart's words and conduct, comparing them with what should be the conduct of a 'patriotic and skilful minister', and found Delessart to be lacking on every point. One of the Minister's chief offences had been to write to the Austrian emperor saying that France wanted peace in a way that Brissot maintained was humiliating for France: 'this thirst for peace is dishonouring for a nation that has been outraged, insulted by a prince who raises all the powers against her'. Brissot intimated that Delessart's motives were treasonous, that he too was part of the conspiracy: 'It is not a French minister who wrote this letter, it came from the pen of the Austrian ambassador.'[50] Brissot maintained that in denouncing the Minister he himself was motivated only by his (virtuous) concern for 'the safety of France'. Delessart might have been motivated by treason or by incapacity, but in a time of national crisis the effect on the country was the same, either way, and should incur the same punishment. Addressing the deputies, Brissot said:

> You must be just, but never forget too that indulgence can compromise the fate of 25 million men. Never forget that we are in critical circumstances, in which perversity or incapacity can cause incalculable evils, and consequently incapacity on its own becomes a veritable crime for a minister... I am told that if he is guilty... then his head may pay the forfeit for his faults. This consideration might give pause to men who are novices in matters of responsibility; but... would the death of this guilty man return to life the thousands of our fellow-citizens on the frontiers whose lives are endangered by his conduct? If the coalition raises its mask, if it breaks out, if it attacks, no, there is no torture sufficient to expiate the crime of ministers who will have brought this scourge on France, when it was so easy to bring it to the enemy's land![51]

Vergniaud spoke alongside Brissot in support. To repeated applause he spoke a language that would become all too familiar—the language of Terror. Indicating the royal palace, whose windows he could see from his place at the tribune, he said:

> The day has arrived, Messieurs, when you may put an end to so much audacity, so much insolence, and confound the conspirators at last. Dread and terror often

[48]  See Goetz-Bernstein, *La Diplomatie de la Gironde*, 145; and Sydenham, *The Girondins*, 102–5.
[49]  10 March 1792, *Archives parlementaires*, 39: 528.
[50]  10 March 1792, *Archives parlementaires*, 543.
[51]  10 March 1792, *Archives parlementaires*, 539, 541, 544.

issued...in the name of despotism, from this famous palace. Let them return there today in the name of the law. [Repeated applause]. Let them penetrate all hearts. Let everyone who lives there know that we accord inviolability only to the king. Let them know that the law will fall without distinction on all the guilty, and that there will not be a single head, convicted of being criminal, which can escape its blade.[52]

The following day Delessart resigned; but Brissot did not deem this sufficient; Delessart's disgrace and loss of office was not enough: he had to be eliminated altogether from the political scene. The Assembly charged Brissot with preparing a formal act of accusation against Delessart. Dumont recounted how he was given this document to read. When he was alone with Brissot and Clavière he attempted to reason with them, saying that the indictment was not written in a judicial way; it was a tissue of vague, unsubstantiated, and insidious allegations, containing personal calumny, and designed to whip up the maximum public hatred and prejudice against the disgraced minister. Dumont was horrified by Brissot's response: 'He smiled, gave a sardonic laugh and literally mocked at my simplicity. "It's a party tactic", he told me...' Brissot sought to justify his methods. He explained that such fabrications were necessary to outflank the Jacobins, and to prevent the king recalling Delessart, who no doubt would eventually be found not guilty. Thus evidence of wrong-doing by a public figure was not needed in order to show that he lacked virtue, and was an enemy within. From that moment Dumont said that he 'no longer saw Brissot with the same eyes'.[53] This revelation of Brissot's capacity for ruthlessness against a political rival made Dumont reconsider what it meant to be a 'man of virtue' operating in the world of factional revolutionary politics:

> It is during the times of faction that one discovers the justice of Helvétius's ideas about what constitutes virtue. Brissot was faithful to his party and faithless to probity. He manoeuvred through a kind of enthusiasm to which he was ready to sacrifice himself; and, because he felt in himself neither the desire for money nor ambition for place, he believed himself to be a pure and virtuous citizen. "Look at how simple my house is, how modest, look at my dinner table fit for a Spartan, observe my private morals, search out if you can reproach me for any dissipation, any frivolity; for two years I have never set foot in the theatre." Such was the basis of his confidence. He did not see that zeal for his party, love of power, hatred, and self-love are corrupters as dangerous as the thirst for gold, ministerial ambition and the taste for pleasures.[54]

Brissot's indictment of Delessart was adopted by the Assembly on 14 March.[55] Delessart was sent to Orléans, to be judged by the Haute Cour Nationale. He was imprisoned the following August, after the overthrow of the monarchy. He was subsequently murdered during the September Massacres.[56]

---

[52] 10 March 1792, *Archives parlementaires*, 549.

[53] Dumont, *Souvenirs sur Mirabeau*, 202–4; also 192, 207.

[54] Dumont, *Souvenirs sur Mirabeau*, 204. Dumont's judgement was written with the benefit of hindsight. It can be compared with his view of Brissot in a 'Letter to Romilly', dated 13 November 1793, in Dumont, *Souvenirs sur Mirabeau*, 305.

[55] Dumont, *Souvenirs sur Mirabeau*, 305, note 3.

[56] Lemay, *Dictionnaire des Législateurs*, 759.

## BRISSOT AND ROBESPIERRE: RIVALS AS MEN
## OF VIRTUE IN THE JACOBINS

It was left to Robespierre to provide the most determined voice against the war. Robespierre's opposition was hampered by the consequences of the self-denying ordinance that he himself had proposed, which meant he no longer had a voice in the Assembly: his principal forum was the Jacobin Club. Here he and Brissot confronted one another and did battle for the direction of the Club. The debate over the war became simultaneously a struggle over the direction and leadership of the Jacobins. Robespierre began the contest with numerous advantages. He was well respected in the Club, and had many supporters in the public gallery. He was also regarded as the man who had held the Jacobins together in the difficult time the previous summer when the defection of the Feuillants had left the Club diminished and in danger of collapse. True to form, Marat had been one of the first to speculate publicly about Brissot's real intentions. In December he wrote that Brissot was 'letting fall his mask in the hope of being a minister'.[57] However, Marat's newspaper, *L'Ami du peuple*, did not appear during most of the period of the war crisis; and Robespierre was more scrupulous about voicing such suspicions about a fellow Jacobin, at least in public. There is some evidence that attempts were being made at this time by the king's agents to buy the voices and influence of Brissot, Vergniaud, and their associates in the Assembly, though little indication that this attempt was successful.[58]

In contrast to Brissot's naïve assertion that war would 'put an end to terrors', Robespierre had a more realistic—and grimly prophetic—grasp of the relationship between war and terror: 'A war gives rise to terrors, to dangers, to plots, to reciprocal struggles, to treason, finally to casualties.'[59] He was not opposed to war as an absolute principle, and he shared the general anxiety regarding the court's secret intentions.[60] But he thought that *this* war was a naïve and reckless tactic that would play into the hands of the monarchy. He was opposed, too, to the expansionist side of Brissot's military plans. Robespierre thought that the need was to secure the Revolution within France, without seeking to export it abroad. He put his ideas in two keys speeches on 2 and 11 January. In a veiled allusion to his suspicions of Brissot's ambitions Robespierre said that his own right to speak on this question was not in doubt, as there could be no question of his having a personal interest in aspiring to the ministry, 'neither for myself, nor for my friends'.[61] In answer to Brissot's call for the principles of the Revolution to be taken to other countries by the French armies, as missionaries on a 'crusade' for liberty, Robespierre replied 'no one welcomes armed missionaries'.[62] He opposed Brissot's tactic of referring to war as necessary for the 'honour' of the French nation. 'Honour' invoked the old ideas

[57] Cited in Michon, *Robespierre et la guerre révolutionnaire*, 31–2, note 1.
[58] Olivier Blanc, *La Corruption sous la Terreur (1792–1794)* (Paris: Robert Laffont, 1992), 26–8.
[59] Robespierre to the Jacobins, 12 December 1791, in Robespierre, *Oeuvres*, 8: 41.
[60] On Robespierre's opposition to the war, see Michon, *Robespierre et la guerre révolutionnaire*.
[61] Speech of 2 January 1792, in Robespierre, *Oeuvres*, 8: 77.
[62] Speech of 2 January 1792, 81.

of aristocracy, and military glory; it had nothing to do with the new nation: 'Magnanimity, wisdom, liberty, happiness, virtue, these are our honour. The honour that you want to resuscitate is the friend, the support of despotism; it is the honour of the heroes of the aristocracy, of all the tyrants...'[63] He was appalled at the idea of hazarding the fate of the Revolution on the unpredictable consequences of a war. He warned that the French armies were in disarray and in no condition to fight, and that the loyalty of their officers (many of whom came from the former nobility) was doubtful. The Girondins' strategy would put France—and the Revolution—at the mercy of the military elite.

This speech brought an emotional response from the Jacobins. Its anti-belligerent rhetoric appealed particularly to women in the audience. Desmoulins wrote to his father describing the impact of Robespierre's eloquence: 'You could not imagine with what abandon, with what truth he threw himself into his argument. He reduced the audience to tears, not just the women on the benches, but half the members of the assembly.'[64] On this occasion Robespierre's ability to tap into themes of natural virtue and sensibility helped win over his audience to the idea that his was the voice of authentic virtue. Robespierre's friend Madame de Chalabre wrote to him describing 'the emotion that reading his interesting and useful discourse' caused her, and her anger that people who opposed the war were being cynically stigmatized by the Girondins as 'misled patriots...' when their desire was only 'to save the *patrie*'.[65]

While Robespierre became increasingly convinced that personal ambition was behind Brissot's drive to war, some observers were inclined to put a still more sinister interpretation on Brissot's behaviour. Rumours circulated that he was a British agent. Gouverneur Morris, the American ambassador, found the stories credible enough to report to President Washington: 'It is unnecessary to tell you that some Members of the national Assembly are in the Pay of England for that you will easily suppose. Brissot de Warville is said to be one of them, and indeed (whether from corrupt or other Motives I know not) his Conduct tends to injure his own Country and benefit that of the ancient Foes in a very eminent Degree.'[66]

At first Danton, Desmoulins, and a few newspapers including *L'Ami du peuple* supported the anti-war stance, but as the tide of patriotic militarism rose, opposition ebbed away.[67] Danton sensed which way the wind was blowing, and changed his tune accordingly, adopting a more conciliatory tone towards Brissot, 'this vigorous athlete of liberty'.[68] As the patriotic fervour and popular desire for war increased Robespierre became an ever more isolated figure in the Jacobin Club; yet he continued doggedly to speak out against the war through the winter of 1791

---

[63]  Speech of 2 January 1792, 85.

[64]  Speech of 2 January 1792, 115, note 21.

[65]  Letter from the comtesse de Chalabre, 11 January 1792, in *Papiers inédits*, 1: 175–6.

[66]  Morris, *A Diary of the French Revolution*, 2: 355.

[67]  For an account of the excited atmosphere and crowded galleries in the Jacobins on 18 December 1791, see Aulard, *Société des Jacobins*, 3: 290–2. See also Michon, *Robespierre et la guerre révolutionnaire*, 39–46.

[68]  Michon, *Robespierre et la guerre révolutionnaire*, 38–9.

and into the spring of 1792. Defeatism, caution, and Cassandra-type warnings of impending doom were not going to play very well alongside heroic, enthusiastic, and passionate defiance of the court and the Austrians. Dashing, military speeches were never Robespierre's forte, even if he had felt inclined to engage in them. He knew very well that support was ebbing away from him, but he stuck to his guns with grim determination. It is important to realize that, over this crucial issue of the war, he put his principles before his popularity as a politician. Subsequently, when the war went badly wrong people would remember that the Girondins had heedlessly brought them into this perilous situation, and that Robespierre had held fast to his principles and stood out against it. In the long run, then, the Girondins' attacks on Robespierre's integrity would backfire on them, and help to confirm his credibility as a man of virtue.

Relations between Brissot and Robespierre continued to be publicly fairly amicable, if not warm, despite their political differences, until 30 December 1791. On this date Brissot gave a major speech in the Jacobins. He closed it by strongly implying that opponents of the war were causing dissension in the Jacobins. They were thus being fractious and blocking the public good; and should 'submit to the law'. Robespierre and Danton both rose to protest on this occasion.[69]

The Girondins adjusted the tone and delivery of their speeches to the more militant and emotional tempo of the Jacobin Club. Here they took on the kind of rhetorical violence that appealed to the all-important Paris militants. The denunciation of Delessart played well to the militants, demonstrating that the Girondins were quite as 'hard line' and capable of embracing the language of popular suspicion as were Marat and other spokesmen for the Parisian militants. They deployed a variety of rhetorical tactics to outflank Robespierre and his dwindling band of supporters. For all the logic of Robespierre's rationale for avoiding war, he was outplayed by Brissot's recourse to the patriotism card. Brissot implied that Robespierre's argument that the French armies were not in a fit state to fight meant that he was not patriotic. Not surprisingly, Robespierre bridled at such an insinuation: his entire political persona was founded on his self-image as a man of impeccable patriotic virtue. This was a sensitive issue for him—it was how his admirers in the Jacobin Club saw him: it was also, and more crucially perhaps, how he saw himself.

Brissot stepped up his attack on Robespierre's political credibility, by emphasizing his own moral authenticity, depicting himself as an honest man who acted according in good faith in a manner truly worthy of Rousseau. On 20 January Brissot addressed the Jacobins to assert his good faith: 'If I am deceived on the necessity for war at least it is in accordance with my conscience.'[70] He was making a moral case for war, based on his identity as a man of integrity and authentic virtue, rather than one founded on strategy and judgement.

---

[69] 30 December 1791, in Aulard, *Société des Jacobins*, 3: 302–3.

[70] Brissot, 'Troisième discours de J.P. Brissot, député, sur la nécéssité de la guerre', given in the Jacobins, 20 January 1792, 17.

Following Brissot's emotive claim that he was motivated solely by his conscience, Dusaulx (described by Brissot as 'aged and venerable' which were code words for 'man of virtue') stepped forward. Dusaulx invited the two rivals 'to embrace one another' as a sign of continuing amity, despite their political differences. Before the eyes of the applauding—in some cases weeping—onlookers, they did so. It was a scene worthy of a novel by Rousseau. Dusaulx was on friendly terms with Brissot, so it is quite possible that the scene was a put-up job to manipulate Robespierre into going along with Brissot as a 'man of virtue' or risk losing credibility as a 'man of virtue' himself. The ritual enactment of this embrace had a highly symbolic value: it was a demonstration of the sensibility of the two political leaders; it was also a ritual enactment of the principle of revolutionary fraternity; additionally, it was a sign that each man recognized the integrity of the other. For Robespierre it meant that he still believed in Brissot's good faith: it did not mean he had conceded the argument.[71]

The weeks leading up to the declaration of war saw the development of a new stage in the tactical deployment of the ideology of political virtue. In the Jacobin Club the opposing groups in the issue of war began to accuse one another openly of corruption, and to challenge the integrity of one another's motivation. It was the first time that radical factions within the Jacobins had used this sort of tactic against one another, and it marked a significant stage in the process that led to the politicians' terror. It was Brissot and his group that took the initiative to attack Robespierre openly. They no longer confined themselves to debating the rights and wrongs of the war in terms that allowed for the good faith of their opponents. Now Brissot began to indicate that if Robespierre opposed him, it must be because Robespierre was corrupt. On 30 March Brissot, via *Le Patriote français*, strongly implied that the true motive for Robespierre's opposition to the war was that he was acting as a secret agent for the Austrian Committee.[72] In subsequent issues *Le Patriote français* stepped up the attack: 'Why is the conduct of M. Robespierre always such as would not have been different had it been fashioned by the Austrian Committee? We know nothing about it; but we attest that if it is just by chance, then this is a very strange chance.'[73] The Girondins used their considerable strengths in the new forms of revolutionary media to publicize their attacks on Robespierre's integrity. Since late 1791, several of the Girondins, including Brissot, Louvet, Roland, Lanthenas, and Bosc, had dominated the Correspondence Committee of the Jacobins. Through their weight on this institution they gained a decisive influence over the messages sent out to the provincial Jacobins, much as the triumvirate had before them. They used this influence to circulate the call for war to the provincial Jacobins, despite Robespierre's attempts to stop them and to have the case against war

---

[71] On the contrasting ways in which Robespierre and Gorsas subsequently portrayed the significance of this embrace, see Robespierre, *Oeuvres*, 8: 128–31. Brissot referred to Dusaulx as 'aged and venerable', in Brissot, *Mémoires*, 2: 245; and Robespierre, *Correspondance de Maximilien et Augustin Robespierre*, 135–6; 140–2.

[72] Michon, *Robespierre et la guerre révolutionnaire*, 96–7.

[73] Robespierre, *Oeuvres*, 8: 338–40, note 7.

also circulated.[74] They also had control of an extensive section of the radical press. Though Brissot had given up the editorship of *Le Patriote Français* after his election to the Assembly, he continued to keep control of its direction and had considerable behind-the-scenes involvement in it, thus maintaining his influence over public opinion. He used it increasingly to make the pro-war case, and to attack Robespierre. Several of the Girondin newspapers accused Robespierre outright of being paid for by the civil list: the 'Incorruptible', they alleged, had been corrupted by the Austrian Committee.[75]

Amongst the Paris Jacobins some members began to step off the sidelines to align themselves with the Girondins. One of the most prominent of these was Louvet, who first made contact with Brissot by beginning to make public pronouncements in favour of war. Louvet's choice, he later recounted, angered Robespierre, who began to 'write, write, write' against Louvet, and campaigned against him in the cafés and political groups.[76] The division between these two soon swelled into a particularly personal animosity. Louvet raged against Robespierre and his persistence as the thorn in the side of the Girondins' war policy: 'You despair of the *patrie*, your doubts insult the nation... You are almost alone, and almost alone you still hold in suspense the opinion of a great number of the people.'[77] In the Club on 2 March, when Louvet was acting as president he tried to block Robespierre from speaking at all.[78]

## ACHIEVING POWER: THE APPOINTMENT OF THE GIRONDIN MINISTRY

The Girondins reaped the rewards of their strategy by gaining the decisive voice in the formation of the new ministry to succeed that of Delessart.[79] This later became known as the 'patriot' ministry or, more revealingly, the Girondin ministry. The king went along with the ousting of his more moderate ministers who had been trying to maintain peace and the constitutional monarchy, and the appointment of men from Brissot's clique in the hope that this move would precipitate war and disaster for the Revolution. The monarchy was duping the Girondins, while flattering their vanity by appointing them to ministerial posts. Brissot himself could not serve as a minister, due to the law previously proposed by Robespierre to block the ministerial ambitions of the triumvirs. Nonetheless, Brissot was very active behind the scenes, pulling strings and acting as a power broker.

---

[74] See, for example, 26 February 1792, in Aulard, *Société des Jacobins*, 3: 410–11. See also Michon, *Robespierre et la guerre révolutionnaire*, 78–9; and Sydenham, *The Girondins*, 102.

[75] Michon, *Robespierre et la guerre révolutionnaire*, 96–7, 105–14; and Hugh Gough, 'Robespierre and the Press', in Haydon and Doyle, *Robespierre*, 114.

[76] Louvet, *Mémoires*, 36.

[77] Cited in Michon, *Robespierre et la guerre révolutionnaire*, 67, note 1.

[78] Robespierre, *Oeuvres*, 8: 210.

[79] See Sydenham, *The Girondins*, 104–6. Daniel Ligou, 'Le concept de participation ministrielle à l'époque du Ministère Roland Dumouriez et l'opposition de Robespierre', in Jessenne *et al.*, *Robespierre*, 167–74.

Brissot succeeded in getting his great friend Clavière, who had been a leading voice in the denunciation of Delessart, elevated to Minister of Finance, an ambition for which Clavière had striven for many years.[80] It was Brissot, too, who visited Madame Roland to sound out whether her husband would be prepared to serve as Minister of the Interior. Since the abolition of Roland's previous post as an inspector of manufactures the Rolands had been living in reduced circumstances, so the sudden change in their fortunes was very welcome.[81] Other Jacobins hoped for preferment, but were disappointed. Hérault de Séchelles had assured Louvet that he was to be made Minister of Justice but, 'over a dinner, attended by the ministers and several deputies' it was decided instead that Duranton should have the post. Years afterwards Louvet was still complaining that things would have turned out very differently if the position had gone to him.[82] There was talk of the radical Jacobin Collot d'Herbois for Minister of the Interior. When this came to nothing he turned against Brissot. It was said by *Révolutions de Paris* that Collot was motivated by 'disappointed ambition'.[83] Robert and his wife, for their part, hoped for an ambassadorial post in Constantinople, and when they were disappointed in this Robert took his revenge by writing a pamphlet that accused Brissot of being a 'distributor of places'.[84] There were rumours of Danton as Minister of Justice, though this too came to nothing. In the notes Robespierre was to write two years later for the denunciation of Danton he would intimate that it was motives of self-interest and personal ambition that made Danton switch sides in the debate on the war and support Brissot.[85]

A key appointment was that of Minister of Foreign Affairs: it went to Dumouriez. It was evident that Dumouriez's interest lay in furthering his military and political career rather than in politics. From the beginning Dumouriez's loyalty to the Jacobins was in doubt.[86] At first sight the Girondins and Dumouriez seem to have been unlikely allies. They were brought together not by a shared political ideology, but through the common aim of achieving war. A friendship also brought them together: though Dumouriez was not a part of Brissot's group, he was an intimate friend of Gensonné, who brought about the initial links between Dumouriez and the Girondins. Later the Jacobins would accuse Gensonné of having used this friendship to engineer Dumouriez's appointment to office.[87] Servan, who was a favourite with Madame Roland, became Minister of War, probably on her recommendation. There was an immense amount of work involved in these

---

[80] Dumont, *Souvenirs sur Mirabeau*, 205, 211.

[81] Madame Roland, *Mémoires*, 64–5. On the role of Roland and his wife in the 'patriot' ministry, see Reynolds, *Marriage and Revolution*, Part 4.

[82] Louvet, *Mémoires*, 39–41.

[83] On Collot, see Whaley, *Radicals*, 53.

[84] See Madame Roland, *Mémoires*, 115–20; and Linton, 'Fatal friendships', 63.

[85] Robespierre, 'Les notes contre les Dantonistes', in *Oeuvres*, 11: 433, 436.

[86] Morris to President Washington, 21 March 1792, in Morris, *A Diary of the French Revolution*, 2: 390.

[87] Dumouriez, *Mémoires du Général Dumouriez*, 424–5. On the friendship between Gensonné and Dumouriez see Linton, 'Fatal friendships'. For the case that the Girondins engineered the appointment of Dumouriez, see Ellery, *Brissot*, 261–2; and Sydenham, *The Girondins*, 79.

ministerial posts, especially that of the Minister of the Interior. The revolutionary ministers held a great deal of power in their hands, and with it the ability to dispense patronage. Gouverneur Morris in the autumn of 1792 said that 'the ministers [possess] far more patronage than any monarch since Louis the Fourteenth'.[88]

On 19 March Dumouriez put in an appearance at the Jacobins, wearing the *bonnet rouge* on his head as a sign of his sympathy with their politics. His adoption of this potent symbol of *sans-culottism* was greeted with lively applause; though there was unease in some quarters about how genuine was Dumouriez's new-found patriotism. As Collot d'Herbois put it, it was to be hoped that the new Minister would act as he had spoken. Robespierre was prepared to give him the benefit of the doubt on this occasion: 'I am not one of those who believes that it is absolutely impossible that a minister can be a patriot.' Once again, Robespierre went along with the desire in the Club that he should formally embrace Dumouriez as a sign of true feeling and fraternity. In reality it must have been a very frosty embrace: Robespierre was deeply suspicious of Dumouriez's true motives. Robespierre's distrust focused on the *bonnet rouge* that Dumouriez was sporting as an external sign of his compliance with Jacobin ideology. Someone attempted to put a similar *bonnet* on Robespierre's own head. In a revealing gesture he snatched it off and flung it away. Then a letter was read from Pétion (at that time he was still friendly with Robespierre, and probably the letter was written in collusion) that repudiated the *bonnet rouge* precisely because many 'aristocrats' were now wearing them; and this symbol could be used to frighten people about the intentions of the Jacobins, and to encourage factionalism. The very fact that a man like Dumouriez was wearing the *bonnet rouge* discredited it as a revolutionary symbol. Such was the influence of Robespierre and Pétion that the fashion for wearing the *bonnet rouge* at the Jacobins ceased at once.[89] What had begun as an indication of true revolutionary sentiment and a way for men of virtue to identify one another, had become no more than a means for men of ambition to feign an emotion they did not really feel. What mattered was the virtue in people's hearts. Robespierre's reaction is an indication of the increasing anxiety he felt about the motivation of the men who were now leading the Revolution. In principle, the Girondin ministry was a sign that the Jacobins had won; but the very act of winning power called into question what the Girondins really wanted.

In the eyes of Robespierre, Marat, and several other Jacobins, the ministerial appointments were a clear case of politics by means of patronage, not merit. As far as they were concerned the Girondins had 'sold out'. Robespierre began a new newspaper, *Le Défenseur de la Constitution*, partly to make his case against the Girondins. The gloves were now off. In Issue 3 he made an all-out attack on the integrity of Brissot and his friends, by recounting their conduct during the last few months as evidence of their self-serving politics. He accused Brissot of using *Le Patriote français* to procure places for his friends in the new ministry, thereby

---

[88] On the extent of the patronage to which Roland had access, see Reynolds, *Marriage and Revolution*, 168–9.

[89] 19 March 1792, in Aulard, *Société des Jacobins*, 3: 438–45; and Robespierre, *Oeuvres*, 7: 221–7.

circumventing the Constitution, which stipulated that as a deputy, Brissot could not obtain ministerial responsibility on his own account. Brissot had acted like an old regime politician.[90]

When the new ministers went to take their vows Robespierre still thought well enough of Roland's integrity to offer him a qualified public statement of support for his 'most upright intentions'.[91] Madame Roland wrote Robespierre a warm response, saying that they were still at the Hôtel Britannique, 'at least for a while; you will regularly find me there at dinner time, and I keep there, as I shall keep wherever I go, the simplicity which makes me worthy not to be disdained, despite the misfortune of finding myself the wife of a minister'.[92] Robespierre did go, but what took place between them is not known. At any events the last shreds of friendship between them were about to dissolve. The opacity of Girondin politics aroused all Robespierre's suspicions. He accused Brissot of secret meetings with Lafayette, of protecting the interests of Narbonne; while behind the web of secret politics Robespierre professed to find a 'female triumvirate' (Madame Roland, Madame Robert, and Madame Condorcet) corrupting the 'severe virtue' of the true patriots.[93]

The ascendancy of the Girondin faction made the pressure for an immediate declaration of war overwhelming. Dumont was present at some of the discussions behind closed doors in those final days. He later stated that Brissot and Dumouriez played a deciding role in the declaration of war. (In his *Memoirs* Dumouriez himself was, unsurprisingly, eager to deny his own responsibility for the decision to declare war, declaring that the blame lay with what he called the 'too ambitious' Girondin faction.)[94] Had Brissot and Dumouriez not given the lead, Dumont considered, things would have gone the other way, and the deputies would have voted for a delay, because people were indecisive, and many did not want a war, but they gave in to pressure, including the pressure to be seen to be a 'true patriot'. Viewed from Dumont's perspective, leadership played a critical role in revolutionary politics, both behind closed doors and in the forums of the Assembly and the Clubs: 'The way in which people's wills are swept away once the government takes a decision, when the party chiefs have made their resolution, is inconceivable for those who have never seen at close hand the playing out of popular passions'. At private dinners Dumont saw Clavière, Roland, the pacifist Condorcet, and other Girondins express their doubts about the advisability of going to war at that time, but then unite publicly to push for it.[95] The bonds of personal friendship and group loyalty held Brissot's friends together, so that they did as a collective things that they would not have done separately. In the Assembly the leadership provided by

[90] Robespierre, *Le Défenseur de la Constitution*, Issue 3, in *Oeuvres*, 4: 92–3.
[91] Cited in Reynolds, *Marriage and Revolution*, 176.
[92] Letter to Robespierre, 27 March 1792, in Madame Roland, *Lettres de Madame Roland*, 2: 413–14. She mentioned his subsequent visit to Bosc, but did not say what passed between them: Letter to Bosc, April 1792, in ibid., 2: 417.
[93] Robespierre, *Le Défenseur de la Constitution*, Issue 3, 79–99.
[94] Dumouriez, *Mémoires*, 433–5, 440–1, 445–9.
[95] Dumont, *Souvenirs sur Mirabeau*, 216–20.

this group influenced many of the waverers, and the risk involved in standing out against a tide of patriotic rhetoric and being identified as 'unpatriotic' brought almost all the rest on board. In the end, all but seven deputies voted for the war.

## THE CONDUCT OF THE GIRONDINS IN POWER

A new world of power now opened up to the Girondin leaders, and a different mode of life, with ministerial offices in fine buildings, assistants at their beck and call, regular face-to-face discussions with the king in the Tuileries palace, and public recognition of their new importance. Not all of them were interested in the material rewards of office. Clavière had a taste for luxury, but Dumont maintained that he was honest with public money. It was something even more exhilarating that seized and inspired them—the Girondin leaders found that they liked power. They relished being at the centre of things. They were now the movers and shakers in exciting times, with the public hanging on their words. Brissot, especially, was much changed by the experience. Dumont observed that 'the public reputation that Brissot enjoyed nearly turned his head, he spoke only in oracles, and could brook no contradiction'. The Girondins were ' . . . men who are pleased with themselves and flattered with their elevation. They arranged themselves in their ministerial residences as though they would stay there forever. Only Madame Roland, regarding the gilding of these apartments, declared that for her it was the luxury of an *hôtel*.' Dumont described their 'lively dinners', where the conversation ranged back and forth over the matters of the day. Dumouriez attended some of these dinners, telling risqué stories, and adding an air of courtly sophistication to the proceedings. But the austere 'republican morality' of the Girondins bored the General. He was a very different kind of man, not in the least interested in being a man of virtue.[96]

For the Girondins the moment in which they passed from being the opposition to being themselves part of government was a testing one. The way that they conducted themselves was observed by a number of interested parties: by the royalists, by the Feuillants, by the majority of the Jacobins who remained outside government, and by the *sans-culottes*. The Girondins were well aware of the importance of new forms of revolutionary culture, above all the press, for putting their case to public opinion. Roland, as minister, supported and funded the Girondin press, though such use of public funds in itself looked partisan. Thus Louvet was brought to meet Roland by a mutual friend, Lanthenas. Roland then recruited Louvet to be editor of a publication, *La Sentinelle*, financed by the ministry.[97]

Would the Girondins be absorbed into the ruling elite, or would they stand aloof from it? Any courting of the established political elite would give credibility to Marat's narrative that the Girondins sought only to be co-opted into the elite themselves. The Girondins were well aware of the need to distinguish their manner

[96] Dumont, *Souvenirs sur Mirabeau*, 213, 218. Madame Roland, *Mémoires*, 65, 67–8.
[97] Louvet, *Mémoires*, 37, 41.

and speech from that of the old regime style of the people with whom they now had to deal on a daily basis. The image of the Girondin ministers was subjected to scrutiny, especially in the press, and in the Jacobin Club. Their way of speaking, their manner of conducting themselves, even their mode of dress, all made a political statement about their identity as 'men of virtue'. They needed to distinguish themselves from figures whose loyalty to the Revolution was seen as tainted.

A 'man of virtue' could be identified from his style of writing. Brissot described Roland as using 'the noble and simple language of a republican' to write to Lafayette, whereas Lafayette's 'insolent response' showed 'the presumption of a former nobleman who had not sufficiently forgotten the haughty forms of the caste from which he came'.[98] The way in which a revolutionary leader dressed was also significant: a 'man of virtue' would dress in a plain way that signified his rejection of court fashion and everything it stood for. For a political leader, Roland seems to have had little interest in his own dress, and possessed few clothes suitable for public occasions. According to the English doctor John Moore, 'his dress, every time I have seen him has been the same, a drab-coloured suit lined with green silk, his grey hair hanging loose'.[99] Roland drew scandalized comments from the court valets when he appeared before the king in simple attire, in his round hat, and with laces rather than buckles on his shoes. The horrified master of ceremonies gasped: 'Eh! Monsieur, no buckles on his shoes!' to which Dumouriez gravely replied. 'Ah! Monsieur, all is lost!', making the onlookers laugh.[100] Brissot continued to dress in a style recalling the American Quakers or Benjamin Franklin. In his devastating attack on Brissot's political integrity, *Brissot Unmasked*, Desmoulins mocked Brissot's puritan style, with his flat hair and round head. He compared Brissot to the religious hypocrite Tartuffe, meaning that Brissot's manner of presenting himself, his austere clothes, his puritan hairstyle, drew people's attention to his assumption of a virtue he did not possess.[101] Brissot's and Roland's ostentatiously simple attire was a way of signalling that, despite the fact that they were now dealing with the king, the Girondin leaders' inner integrity was intact. The simplicity of their clothes signalled the purity of their inner selves; but it was also open to the interpretation that Desmoulins gave it—that this external simplicity was not a genuine sign, but its opposite—a mask, to conceal the fact that Brissot had been corrupted by old regime power.

Their behaviour was not just about presenting a particular face to the public; there was also the Girondins' own anxiety that they should not succumb to the seductions of the court. This anxiety was voiced in an argument that flared up one day between Brissot and Clavière at Roland's home. Clavière had told the company how the king had made him laugh by jokingly saying he knew the constitution better than Clavière, and producing a well-thumbed copy of his own. Brissot saw no humour in this story: a man of virtue must not be seduced into cordial relations with the king;

---

[98] Brissot, *Mémoires*, 2: 141.
[99] Cited in Thompson, *English Witnesses of the French Revolution*, 207.
[100] Madame Roland, *Mémoires*, 66.
[101] C. Desmoulins, *Jean-Pierre Brissot démasqué*, in *Oeuvres de Camille Desmoulins*, 1: 266, 268, 272–3.

even complicity in a private joke was the start of a slippery slope to corruption. The constitution was no laughing matter. The discussion between the two friends became heated. Roland feared to say anything in case he gave the impression that he too was being seduced by his proximity to the monarchy. It was Madame Roland who intervened, deftly changed the conversation, and gave both men time to calm down.[102]

## AT HOME WITH THE GIRONDINS: POLITICS AS A PRIVATE ACTIVITY

We have already seen that Vergniaud's salon played a part in the Girondins' strategy over the war and the fall of Delessart. Jacobins who were not part of the Girondin circle were not invited to attend. The Girondin leaders used the salon to drum up support, but also to exclude outsiders. It was a politics of co-optation. Chabot would later accuse Brissot of having issued him with a personal invitation to come and dine at Vergniaud's salon and discuss 'the progress to be made in the Assembly', an accusation which Brissot did not deny.[103] Attendance at a salon was a very personal decision, based partly on whether one had similar views to the people who attended, but also whether one liked them, and felt at ease in their company. Even Roland rarely attended Vergniaud's salon. Madame Roland said that this was because of the distance, but it was not in fact so far from where the Rolands were staying. A more likely explanation may be Madame Roland's dislike of Vergniaud—she spoke frankly of his 'egoism' and 'indolence'. She may well have resented, too, being supplanted as the *salonnière* of the Girondins by this rival establishment, set up when her own was in temporary abeyance.[104]

Madame Roland resumed her own salon some time after the Rolands' return to Paris in December 1791, though probably not straight away. Once Roland became Minister the nature of these gatherings altered, and friendship with the Roland household took on a new significance, as the Rolands were able to dispense patronage in a style reminiscent of old regime politics. Her great friend, Sophie Grandchamps, recalled how, immediately before Roland's elevation to the ministry, his wife had been unwell, suffering from a depression of spirits that her friend attributed 'to a secret ambition that she nourished'. On the day that Roland was appointed, Madame Roland recovered her spirits and set about acting the part of the Minister's wife. Sophie Grandchamps went to their apartment, which the previous day had consisted of 'a bedroom and a cabinet on the top floor, a simple country servant, the greatest abandon; a man who was anxious about his existence, a woman thinking of terminating her own...' But now a very different scene met her eyes:

> I thought I was dreaming as I entered the salon. My friend, who had been on the point of death that morning, had recovered her freshness and graces; she was surrounded by

---

[102] Dumont, *Souvenirs sur Mirabeau*, 214.
[103] Chabot's denunciation is in Walter, *Actes du Tribunal révolutionnaire*, 289–90.
[104] Madame Roland, *Mémoires*, 64, 109.

a numerous circle of people who loaded her with praises; Roland shared in the homage and seemed quite satisfied. I threw myself into an armchair near the fireplace, and there observed attentively the new personages; all the ministers, the chiefs of the State, the principal deputies, crowded out the room. Two lackeys stood behind the door, opening either one or two panels according to the rank of the person who presented himself and indicated to them the etiquette.[105]

The Rolands moved from their modest home to the ministerial *hôtel* that had once housed Calonne. Now Madame Roland gave weekly dinners to which the other ministers, together with selected deputies, were invited. According to her own account, 'the ministers agreed to eat together at one or the other's home on the days of the sessions; I received them every Friday...'[106] She used the dinners as an opportunity to bring together with the ministers selected deputies in the circle of Roland and Brissot, within her home: 'I often saw, with Brissot, several other members of the Legislative Assembly; from time to time they met at my home with the ministers and kept up with them the kind of liaison which is needful amongst men who, completely devoted to public affairs, need to maintain contacts and be well-informed in order to better serve the public.'[107]

She did not invite other women to the dinners, to avoid giving the impression that the dinners were about feminine sociability and 'feminine indiscretion'. To encourage male sociability and political networking, she herself avoided speaking as much as possible. As a consequence, she avowed, the male guests did not hold back from discussing political business. She herself occupied the smallest salon, using it as her bureau where friends could find her for political business and to ask her to speak to the Minister on their behalf.[108] During Roland's second ministry she kept up a similar tactic of giving regular dinners, which she organized with care:

Two days a week only I gave a dinner: one for the colleagues of my husband along with whom would be several deputies; the other for a variety of people, either deputies, or high-ranking officials, or others connected with public life or preoccupied with public affairs. Good taste and neatness reigned at my table, without profusion, and luxurious ornaments were never seen there; people were relaxed there, without consecrating a lot of time to the meal, because I served only one course and I never let anyone but myself do the honours. Fifteen was the usual number of guests, on rare occasions eighteen and once only twenty.[109]

She was highly indignant at the way the Jacobin press had represented her dinners as scenes of aristocratic opulence and conspiratorial politics, and furious at Desmoulins' characterization of her as a 'Circe':

---

[105] Sophie Grandchamps, 'Souvenirs de Sophie Grandchamps', in *Mémoires de Madame Roland*, ed. Cl. Perroud, 2 vols (Paris: Plon, 1905), 2: 475–8. Dumont gave a similar account of Clavière's wife being at death's door, until her husband's appointment brought about her spectacular recovery. Dumont remarked drily that he had witnessed 'one of the miracles effected by the royal sceptre': *Souvenirs sur Mirabeau*, 214–15.

[106] Sophie Grandchamps, 'Souvenirs de Sophie Grandchamps', 66. See also the perceptive account in Reynolds, *Marriage and Revolution*, 223–9.

[107] Madame Roland, *Mémoires*, 68.    [108] Madame Roland, *Mémoires*, 72; also 62–3, 168.

[109] Madame Roland, *Mémoires*, 168; see also 66, 72.

Such were the dinners that the popular orators at the Jacobins transformed into sumptuous feasts where I, a new Circe, corrupted all those who had the misfortune to attend. After the dinner we would talk for a while in the salon, and afterwards everyone would return to their own business. We sat down to dinner at around five o'clock, by nine everyone had left; such was the court of which they say I was the queen, this nest of conspiracy...[110]

Dumouriez's own perspective on these ministerial dinners was rather different. Despite the republican austerity of the comestibles, he saw their purpose as being one of political manipulation in the interests of the Girondin faction. He claimed that the other ministers (that is with the exception of the Girondin ministers, Clavière and Roland himself) resented the takeover staged by the Girondin network: 'the Friday ministerial dinner became the faction's dinner, at which members of the Gironde wanted to constrain the ministers to accept their counsel and guidance on policy'. He said that the other ministers tacitly agreed not to bring their ministerial briefs to discuss at these dinners. He further claimed that when he remonstrated with Roland about his political attachment to his friends, the Minister of the Interior was open about the extent to which his political decisions were influenced by his friendships: '...he declared that he would do nothing, either at the ministry, or at the council, without the advice of his friends...'[111]

Relations between Dumouriez and the Girondins had become somewhat chilly within a short time of the ministerial appointments and broke into outright hostility after the dismissal of Roland, for which the Girondins held Dumouriez responsible. This weakening of the Girondins' position culminated in the dismissal of their first ministry. In a tactic that recalled his public 'private' letter to Barnave, in which he had discredited Barnave's political identity, Brissot now wrote a public letter to Dumouriez, published in *Le Patriote français*, repudiating their friendship: 'The intimacy that has brought us together for several days must vanish before the truth, before public safety; you have deceived me as you have many other patriots, better informed and less trusting than myself. The memory of my prejudice in your favour is painful and will be for a long time...You have seen my soul bared in the outflowing of friendship...'[112] Brissot's intention was to dissociate himself publicly from Dumouriez. Rumours were circulating, both that Dumouriez was in collusion with the monarchy, and that he was involved in financial corruption: there were stories about secret funds to which, as Foreign Minister, Dumouriez had access. Brissot could not afford to be linked with either rumour. He used the language (taken from Rousseau) of the trusting man of virtue betrayed by the purveyor of false friendship to distance himself from Dumouriez's machinations.

Though Madame Roland was by far the most politically active of the women connected with the Girondin leaders, there were several other women who played a part in the Girondin network. They included Madame de Condorcet and

---

[110]   Madame Roland, *Mémoires*, 168, 255, and 404, note.
[111]   Dumouriez, *Mémoires du Général Dumouriez*, 440–1, 449–50.
[112]   'Première lettre de J.P. Brissot à Dumouriez, ministre de la guerre', in *Le Patriote Français*, No. 1041, 16 June 1792.

Madame Dodun, both of whom had political salons; Madame Clavière (who, according to Dumont, wanted to play a role as a political hostess after the manner of Madame Roland, but lacked her 'talent and strength'), and Madame Robert, a journalist and author in her own right.[113] The prevalent attitude of hostility towards women who were seen to be actively involved in the 'behind closed doors' culture of politics, was extended to women in the Girondin network. We have seen that Robespierre accused the Girondins of being directed by a shadowy 'female triumvirate' of Madame Roland, Madame Robert, and Madame Condorcet. Several Girondin women, including Madame Roland, Madame Clavière, and Madame Pétion, were alleged to have put pressure on their husbands to further their careers in ways that would act as conduits for the social ambitions of their wives. Thus these Girondin women were held indirectly responsible for corrupting their husbands' commitment to the public good.

The subsequent treatment of Madame Brissot shows how women could come under suspicion. It would be alleged by the Jacobins that many of the Girondins went to visit her at the chateau of Saint-Cloud where she held court, as the queen had formerly done.[114] In the *Memoirs* he wrote in prison Brissot vehemently denied these allegations. He insisted that his wife had taken the children there for their health, and that she concerned herself only with domestic matters, and the children's education, not at all with politics. They had stayed at first in the lodging of a *concierge* at Saint-Cloud; but calumny had spread that, like Marie-Antoinette before her, Madame Brissot was living in the chateau itself, and holding a political salon. Thereafter she had moved out, into a very small lodging, where she only had a daily help, and she prepared the children's meals with her own hand.[115] Madame Brissot herself, when she was later arrested and interrogated, denied that she had received members of the Girondin faction when she was at Saint-Cloud. In the face of repeated questioning she sought refuge in the defence that she occupied herself with the traditional roles of a woman, 'caring for my household and my children, without concerning myself with what my husband was doing in his study'.[116]

## *BRISSOT UNMASKED* AND THE SPLITTING OF THE JACOBINS

Though it was the Girondin leaders who began the tactic of attacking the integrity of their political enemies within the Jacobins, their opponents soon responded in kind. One of the earliest, most comprehensive, and most damagingly articulate of

[113] On Madame Clavière's frustrated political ambitions, see Dumont, *Souvenirs sur Mirabeau*, 214–15.

[114] Saint-Just, 'Rapport fait au nom du Comité du salut public sur les trente-deux membres de la Convention, détenus en vertu du décret du 2 juin', 8 July 1793, in Saint-Just, *Oeuvres complètes*, 472.

[115] Brissot, *Mémoires*, 2: 259–61.

[116] Interrogation of Madame Brissot, 11 August 1793, in J.P. Brissot, *Correspondance et papiers*, ed. Cl. Perroud (Paris: Picard, 1911), 373–6. See also Madame Roland, *Mémoires*, 185.

the attacks on Brissot was Camille Desmoulins' pamphlet, *Jean-Pierre Brissot Unmasked* (*Jean-Pierre Brissot démasqué*).[117] Though this pamphlet should be seen as a contribution to the growing divisions between Brissot's group and the Jacobins who were loyal to Robespierre, Desmoulins had an additional, personal motive to go all-out to get Brissot. Brissot prided himself on his own austerity, and contempt for fine dining—and gambling.[118] Brissot had been responsible for an article in *Le Patriote français* which had attacked Desmoulins as an unworthy patriot for his defence of people's rights to engage in gambling. Desmoulins used *Brissot Unmasked* to inflict a very personal revenge on the former friend who had slighted him. Desmoulins recast Brissot's role in the Revolution, turning him from patriotic hero to self-seeking and duplicitous villain. Despite abstract references to the Republic and the good of the people, the world Desmoulins wrote about here was relatively enclosed—a small group of people who knew one another, who liked or disliked one another, trusted or distrusted one another, and who chose sides accordingly. As part of this personalization of politics, Desmoulins addressed Brissot directly: 'I warn you that you shall not succeed in your attempt to *brissoter* my reputation: it is I who will tear the mask from your face...'[119] The term 'brissoter', first coined by Brissot's enemy Morande and given the meaning 'to steal', had earlier been taken up by the right-wing press and used against Brissot. Here Desmoulins was seizing upon this word and using it to discredit Brissot's reputation as a true Jacobin. It was a highly successful tactic. Brissot's devotion to the Revolution had always been highly questionable: 'you have been in the worst of bad faith, a true Tartuffe of patriotism and a traitor to the *patrie...*' Brissot's true motivation, according to Desmoulins, was 'your limitless ambition'.[120]

*Brissot Unmasked* was said to have made more stir than any other revolutionary pamphlet. It would set the tone and the style for the series of deadly attacks on political leaders that would be made during the period of the Terror. It unpicked Brissot's conduct since the beginning of the Revolution; mingling personal and political allegations; calling into question Brissot's claims to authentic virtue; and depicting him as a secret enemy of the Revolution. It appeared in February 1792, in the midst of the controversy over the war; and it included a defence of Robespierre, who may well have been involved with its production. The pamphlet stopped short of declaring Brissot to be a counter-revolutionary, nor was it directed against anyone other than himself. Nonetheless, it made him look a fool, self-interested,

---

[117] His name was Jacques-Pierre Brissot, but Desmoulins remembered it wrongly. Revolutionaries—even friends—were rarely on first-name terms with one another; a rule to which Desmoulins himself—who was often known more familiarly as Camille even to casual acquaintances—was an exception.

[118] See, for example, Brissot's disparaging comments on d'Orléans and Ducrest: Brissot, *Mémoires*, 64–70. On gambling as an activity centred on the court and Paris, see Olivier Grussi, *La Vie quotidienne des Joueurs sous l'ancien régime à Paris et à la cour* (Paris: Hachette, 1985).

[119] Desmoulins, *Brissot démasqué*, 1: 259. On the earlier use of 'brissoter' as a calumny against Brissot, see Ellery, *Brissot*, 218–19. In 1791 the word was used in the right-wing *Journal de la cour et de la ville*. Desmoulins' attack on Brissot is addressed in greater depth in Linton, 'Friends, enemies and the role of the individual'.

[120] Desmoulins, *Brissot démasqué*, 266–8.

and a false patriot, if not worse. He made little attempt to respond to the damaging allegations.[121] Here, as elsewhere in revolutionary politics, the personal friendship that had existed between Desmoulins and Brissot and that had soured into enmity had political consequences. Desmoulins' friendship with Brissot gave him inside information which Desmoulins did not scruple to use to attack his friend publicly. The allegations that Desmoulins made here, and the interpretation that he gave to Brissot's conduct, would subsequently form part of the basis of the case made against Brissot at his trial; thus these words were used to kill him.

Once the Girondin ministry was formed, Brissot ceased to attend the Jacobins as frequently as he had formerly done, but on 25 April he spoke at the tribune of the Club, before an angry and tumultuous audience, to defend his reputation against allegations that he had had a hand in appointing people as ministers. He was understandably vague about this, but he was also defiant—if he had, what of it? The people in question were patriots, so only counter-revolutionaries would say that was a bad thing. He also shrugged off accusations that the patriot ministers could corrupt the Jacobins by 'throwing all the favours' their way. This, he said, was the language of the Feuillants; how much better it would be '…if all the places were occupied only by Jacobins!'[122] He denied the allegations that he had cosied up to Narbonne and the aristocratic war party, 'the stories of dinners and suppers with Monsieur de Narbonne, whom I do not know at all'. As regards Madame de Staël, he said he did not even know what she looked like, and that he 'detested her impure morals'.[123]

The formation of the Girondin ministry began the reversal of Robespierre's temporary isolation in the Jacobins over the war question. Many of the Jacobins were fast becoming disillusioned with Brissot and his friends. The uncertain progress of the war would also give them pause. Robespierre was once more a dominant voice within the Jacobins. With Brissot's friends in the ministries, the question whether Jacobins were open to old regime-style corruption now began to assume a fresh importance. The new opportunities provided by the war heightened anxieties on this front. Entry to the Jacobins began to be tightened: Robespierre said it was no longer enough that people wish to be members, or profess to be patriots, there should be some evidence of their previous conduct. He feared that counter-revolutionaries would stage a takeover of the Club.[124] He also feared that men who cared nothing for the success of the Revolution were using the network of the Jacobins in an opportunistic way to secure their careers.

Robespierre himself had been chosen by the electors of Paris for the post of public prosecutor in the criminal tribunal of the Department of Paris. After several months he resigned. His enemies said that this was to better enable him to denounce his enemies.[125] In *Le Tribune des patriots,* a journal that ran briefly from the

---

[121] Ellery, *Brissot*, 242.
[122] 25 April 1792, in Aulard, *Société des Jacobins*, 3: 526–30.
[123] 25 April 1792, in Aulard, *Société des Jacobins*, 3: 526–30.
[124] Thompson, *Robespierre*, 198–9.        [125] Thompson, *Robespierre*, 147, 199–200.

end of April 1792, Desmoulins responded indignantly to the allegations. He declared that Robespierre's rejection of the post was a sign of his incorruptibility. Robespierre had 'sacrificed eight thousand livres, when he is without fortune' in order to preserve his independence and integrity as a journalist. If the post had been an attempt to buy Robespierre off, it failed. Desmoulins reminded his readers that it was Robespierre—not Brissot—who was his friend, 'my dear Robespierre, it is three years ago that I gave you this name!' He went on to assert that despite his having previously expressed admiration for revolutionary leaders such as Mirabeau, Lafayette, and the Lameths, all of whom had turned out to be not such patriotic heroes after all, it was Robespierre whose authenticity he had consistently praised.[126]

Robespierre used his independence to criticize Jacobins who wanted places. When the question was raised whether other societies should be able to affiliate to the Jacobins, he argued that some caution should be exercised, as some of the would-be patriots might be fair-weather Jacobins, intent on exploiting the network for themselves. He thought the Girondin-dominated Corresponding Committee was setting a bad example: '...when I see members of the committees obtain all of a sudden lucrative employments, henceforward I see them only as ambitious men who seek to separate themselves from the people. And well, what has happened? Of the men who were members of the correspondence committee, there are barely six who have not been appointed to posts; and paid patriotism is always suspect to me.' The Jacobins applauded this heartily. 'In the future,' he continued, the Jacobins should be 'entirely purged'.[127] At this time Robespierre saw the freedom of the press as the only way to ensure that political leaders did not forget their obligation to the public that they act as men of virtue.[128]

The divisions in the Jacobins were becoming ever deeper and more factional. The split was personal as well as political. The final step was the formal severing of friendship. On 25 April Madame Roland wrote a letter to Robespierre, this time taking him to task for his self-righteous assumption that anyone 'who thought differently to him about the war was not a good citizen'. He was not the only one who 'has good intentions, who is without any personal motives, without any hidden ambitions...' She defended her friends, denied that they were his 'mortal enemies', and denied that she 'received them on intimate terms in her home'. She finished by saying that her frank criticism of him was a sign of her own authenticity: '...I never know how to seem otherwise than who I am'. We do not know if he replied to her. They were equally strong-minded people, each convinced of the authenticity of their own virtue. This letter, repudiating the friendship that had existed between them, marked the moment of the open breach between the factions.[129]

[126] Desmoulins, 'Avertissement', *La Tribune des patriotes*, in Desmoulins, *Oeuvres*, 1: 248.
[127] Robespierre, speech to the Jacobins, 27 May 1792, *Oeuvres*, 8: 358–9.
[128] Robespierre, *Le Défenseur de la Constitution* in *Oeuvres*, 4: 146–7.
[129] Letter to Robespierre, 25 April 1792, Roland, *Lettres de Madame Roland*, 2: 418–20.

Contrary to Brissot's expectations, the war went badly from the outset, not least because of the defection of many of the officers, leaving the French armies in chaos. Popular fear and anger over the volatile situation led to renewed crisis. On 10 June Madame Roland took a leading role in another peremptory letter, written in her hand, and sent by Roland to the king, taking him to task for his seeming support of opponents of the Revolution, specifically his use of the veto against the Assembly's decrees, and warning him that he risked being seen as 'the friend and accomplice of conspirators'. These reproaches were justified by the contention that Roland's first responsibility was to the public good: 'the man in public life' must consider 'his duties above all'.[130] The king reacted predictably by dismissing the Girondin ministers. Yet the letter did its task in conveying the message that Roland was acting with ministerial virtue, and was not party to any dealings 'behind closed doors' with a tarnished king. As part of this strategy the letter was made public. The letter had dramatic consequences. As we have seen it provoked a temporary rift between Brissot and Dumouriez. It also brought about a resurgence of support for the dismissed Girondin ministers by the Parisian militants, which culminated in a demonstration of between 10,000 and 20,000 armed militants who invaded the Tuileries and intimidated the king. But the revelation that in July Vergniaud, Gensonné, and Guadet had written secret letters to the king, advising him that the only way to save the monarchy was to reinstate a Girondin ministry with Vergniaud himself as a member, further discredited the Girondins.[131]

## THE SECOND REVOLUTION: AUGUST 1792

In late July foreign troops crossed the frontiers of France. The allied commander, the Duke of Brunswick, issued a manifesto designed to bring terror to Paris. Faced with this situation, the Girondin leaders vacillated, unable or unwilling to follow through on the logic of their own argument that the monarchy was 'the enemy within'. The Parisian militants, in alliance with *fédérés* who had volunteered for the army, seized the initiative and turned their anger on the monarchy. On 10 August the monarchy was overthrown in a pitched battle at the Tuileries palace. This second revolution transformed the political landscape. The monarchy was suspended. The Legislative Assembly was disbanded, to be replaced by a new assembly, the National Convention. Between the fall of the monarchy and the meeting of the Convention, the Paris Commune became the dominant power in Paris. Because of their equivocal response to the crisis, the Girondin leaders lost what credibility they had regained with the militants. This time the split proved definitive. The Girondin ministers, Roland, Clavière, and (briefly) Servan, were

---

[130] The letter is printed, in translation, in John Hall Stewart (ed.), *A Documentary Survey of the French Revolution* (New York: Macmillan, 1951), 293–8. On Madame Roland's part in this letter see Reynolds, *Marriage and Revolution*, 181–4.

[131] The Jacobins disclosed the existence of these letters in January 1793, at the time of the king's trial, but had known about them earlier. See Sydenham, *The Girondins*, 110, 139.

reinstated, which caused resentment at their appearing to have profited personally from the fall of the monarchy without having dirtied their hands to achieve it. The Girondins' attitude towards the militants and the threat of popular violence changed dramatically: they themselves were now at risk of retaliatory popular violence.

Popular violence reached a horrific crescendo when, on 2 September, massacres broke out on the streets of Paris. Groups of men went from prison to prison dragging out prisoners suspected of being counter-revolutionaries, subjecting them to an impromptu 'trial', and butchering out of hand those that they found 'guilty'. This grim episode took place against the fear of foreign invasion; it followed the news of the fall of Verdun. It was a pivotal moment on the path to the Terror, for it demonstrated that the Parisian militants were ready to take the initiative in violent defence of the Revolution.[132] Revolutionary leaders had to decide very quickly where they stood on the question of popular violence. The Jacobins, however squeamish they may have felt over the realities of the bloodshed, chose to align themselves publicly with the Paris militants. The Girondins believed that the Jacobin leaders, including Marat, Danton, and Robespierre, had had some inside knowledge of the impending massacres.[133] Danton had been appointed Minister of Justice and his close friends Fréron and Fabre were amongst the Jacobin journalists to call for the killing of counter-revolutionaries in the prisons. His good friend Deforgues was known to have been a leader of the massacres. Hard evidence was lacking, but suspicion remained. Even so, while the September massacres were continuing, the Girondin leaders, including the ministers, took no more action than the Jacobins to try to stop them; while most of the Girondin press expressed solidarity with the massacres, seeing them as a regrettable necessity. In the heightened atmosphere of the moment they agreed with the perpetrators' view that the massacres were made needful by the danger that Paris might be overrun by the invaders, and the fear that the many counter-revolutionaries imprisoned after the overthrow of the monarchy were engaged in a conspiracy to break out of the prisons and themselves murder the patriots. Roland, whether out of fear or helplessness, did nothing either, and in the immediate aftermath even called what happened 'a kind of justice'.[134] What changed the Girondins' minds was their growing conviction that Brissot and Roland had also been targeted for massacre. The Girondins claimed that Robespierre had engaged in a Machiavellian scheme to have them arrested in the hope that they too would become victims of the killers. Robespierre's most recent biographer, Peter McPhee, argues that the evidence for this is dubious. Robespierre obtained warrants for the arrests of Brissot and Roland from the Commune before the massacres broke out, but this did not prove that he knew of the impending massacres beforehand, and he himself denied that

---

[132] There are contrasting accounts of the September massacres by Pierre Caron, *Les Massacres de septembre* (Paris: Maison du livre français, 1935); and Frédéric Bluche, *Septembre 1792, logiques d'un massacre* (Paris: Robert Laffont, 1986). See also Andress, *The Terror*, ch. 4.

[133] Madame Roland, *Mémoires*, 140–1.

[134] See Marcel Dorigny, 'Violence et Révolution: les Girondins et les massacres de Septembre', in Soboul, *Girondins et Montagnards;* and Ellery, *Brissot*, 412–13.

he had known.[135] Regardless of what his intention may have been, however, the Girondins believed it of him. The conviction that Robespierre had tried to have Brissot and Roland murdered sharpened the edge of the Girondins' enmity towards the Jacobin leaders, and made any hope of reconciliation between the two factions all but impossible. Fear also crystallized the Girondins' growing hostility towards Parisian militancy. For their part the Jacobins had chosen to position themselves as the apologists for popular violence, if not the instigators behind it.

For the revolutionary politicians the pressing question was how to achieve election to the Convention. The members of the Legislative Assembly had declined to pass a self-denying ordinance as the Constituent Assembly had done. Participation in the Convention was therefore open to all contenders. To some extent the convention of not campaigning for candidates broke down in the run-up to the elections, as some of the journalists, most notably Louvet and Marat, began to try openly to sway public opinion; to promote their own candidates and disparage those of the opposing faction.[136] The rules of the political game were changing, along with everything else.

In conclusion, Brissot and the other leaders of the new 'Girondin' faction within the Jacobins identified themselves as 'men of virtue' pitted against a conspiracy by the court. They used this narrative to bolster their efforts to obtain a declaration of war on Austria. The Girondins brought fears of internal betrayal and conspiracy up to a whole new level of intensity and danger. In the context of the build-up to war, the narrative of the 'men of virtue' mingled with the much more inflammatory language of war, enemies—and death. From January 1792 the rapid decline in tolerance of political opposition, together with the appearance of the crime of *lèse-nation*, made the position of political opponents to the leading group much more vulnerable. A link was forged between France's 'natural' and external enemies (Austria and the *émigrés*) and the enemy within, created by the Revolution itself, the 'false patriots' or 'false brothers' whose offences against the *patrie* were now recast as the crime of *lèse-nation*, making them traitors and so subject to execution.[137] The deployment of this language was one of the key steps in the process that led to terror. The Girondins' strategy in obtaining war brought terror much closer; the war created an unstable and fearful context in which terms like 'virtue', 'patriotism', 'enemy within', and 'conspiracy' became words that could kill. The tactics which the Girondins used to come to power—above all the denunciation of Delessart on the basis of a moral conviction of his guilt, without evidence— anticipated in many respects the tactics of denouncing political opponents used during the Terror. The ways in which Brissot and Robespierre confronted one another in the Jacobins over the question whether France should go to war reflect

---

[135] MPhee, *Robespierre*, 129–30.

[136] Crook, *Elections in the French Revolution*, 91–2.

[137] The phrase 'false brothers' is used by Simonin, who also points to how the new crime of *lèse-nation* was used to recategorize disgraced public officials as traitors: Simonin, *Le Déshonneur dans la République*, 232–40. On changing legal definitions of *lèse-nation* from 1789 to 1791, see Walton, *Policing Public Opinion*, 173–8.

the importance for both men of their identity as 'men of virtue'. It was the Girondins who initiated the practice of characterizing their political rivals as 'conspirators'. They used this tactic above all against Robespierre, to undermine his opposition to the war by suggesting that he was in the pay of the court. This tactic represented a key stage in the process whereby the ideology of virtue developed into an ideology of terror, to be used against politicians whose assumption of the identity of men of virtue was said to be a mask for their corruption. In the context of a war situation, this characterization of political opponents as 'the enemy within' put politicians themselves into a potentially dangerous position, and increased their anxieties over the need to maintain their credibility as authentic 'men of virtue'. The Jacobins responded in kind; thus escalating the split between the emerging 'Girondin' and 'Jacobin' factions.

The war policy of the Girondins would have major consequences for the way in which politicians' words and actions were interpreted in the future. The war that the Girondins had done so much to bring about dramatically increased the dangers inherent in using the language of virtue to attack the credibility of political leaders. Brissot in particular must bear some of the responsibility for this stage of the process that led to Terror.

# 5

## Choosing Sides
### Friends, Factions, and Conspirators in the new Republic

It is very difficult to make a revolution without becoming passionate about it; no one has ever made a revolution without that emotion; there are great obstacles to overcome: you can only achieve it by means of a sort of frenzy, a devotion which comes from exaltation or which produces it. But then you avidly seize on anything which can help your cause, and you lose the ability to foresee whether these things could be harmful.

Madame Roland, *Mémoires*.[1]

The Revolution has aroused such passions that it is impossible to see the truth about anybody. You must be prudent to avoid the traps of designing men. You must keep a lock on your lips and a key to your mouth, and not let a word escape that can be held against you...

Madame Jullien's advice to her son on being a Jacobin.[2]

The National Convention first met on 20 September 1792. Almost its first action was to abolish the monarchy and declare France a Republic. Its immediate task was to consolidate the Republic while ensuring that France remained undefeated by the invading foreign powers and the *émigrés* who fought alongside them. The deputies were united, albeit briefly, by a sense of shared mission, by the urgency of the ongoing war crisis, and by the adrenalin generated by their situation.[3] At the same time they were confronted by acute problems: the ongoing war and the threat of defeat and destruction at the hands of the foreign powers; the social and economic turmoil and shortages that ensued from the war, the depreciation of the *assignat*, and the second revolution; the fate of the king; the unrest of the Parisian militants who had played a crucial role in overthrowing the monarchy and now expected to be rewarded with a stake in the new regime; and the swelling numbers of people who, for different reasons, were opposed to the Revolution, some of whom ended by taking up arms against the revolutionary forces, above all in the Vendée, where a full-scale civil war broke out in March 1793.

---

[1] Madame Roland, *Mémoires*, 134.
[2] Madame Jullien's letter to her son, Marc-Antoine Jullien, cited by R.R. Palmer, *From Jacobin to Liberal: Marc-Antoine Jullien, 1775–1848* (Princeton, NJ: Princeton University Press, 1993), 4–5.
[3] See Patrick, *The Men of the First French Republic*.

These fraught, complex circumstances paved the way for a further stage in the process that led to the 'politicians' terror'. Whilst the language in which people denounced their political opponents remained largely unchanged, the trauma of war generated an atmosphere of mistrust and fear, in which this language took on an ever more dangerous resonance. The consequences of being seen as a 'dissembler' of political virtue had changed. Politicians who were exposed as 'self-serving', 'corrupt', or engaged in 'political cronyism' with their friends, were no longer at risk only of disgrace and loss of career and influence. They could now be characterized as conspirators who were in league with the *émigrés* and foreign powers—and therefore traitors. In such circumstances their very lives would be at stake. Thus it mattered more than ever for political leaders to be able to maintain their credibility as 'men of virtue'.

## DIVISIONS BETWEEN GIRONDINS AND JACOBINS IN THE CONVENTION

For the first four months of the Convention the Girondins monopolized its formal leadership. They also dominated executive power. They thus continued to be vulnerable to Jacobin charges of ambition and political tactics 'behind closed doors'. Despite the war situation, executive power remained relatively uncentralized, being shared between the council of ministers and various committees of the Convention. Ministers were now elected by the Convention itself, and achievement of ministerial office was thus an indication of support in the Assembly.[4] The Girondins had benefited from the overthrow of the monarchy, and held a number of ministerial posts in what became known as the second Girondin ministry. Roland was again Minister of the Interior, and Clavière Minister of Finance. Thanks partly to the way in which the Constituent Assembly had organized the ministries, these ministers held much more power than old regime ministers had done. The Minister of the Interior was a particularly powerful role, involving considerable scope for patronage. In their defence the Girondins could point to the fact that Danton, as Minister of Justice, had also been given access to patronage and funds. Indeed, Danton's friends Desmoulins and Fabre traded on their personal links with him to become his official secretaries and dispensers of patronage, albeit on a minor scale.[5] Other Jacobins, however, felt themselves to have been excluded from political power; while Danton was obliged to give up his ministerial role in order to stand as a deputy.

Even as the Republic was declared, divisions between factions of radical revolutionaries escalated into open confrontation. The Convention itself became the *locus* in which many of the struggles over revolutionary identity and control took place. The Girondins definitively split from the Jacobin Club in the autumn of 1792. Girondins and Jacobins confronted one another in the Convention. (Jacobins who

---

[4] On the voting figures, see Patrick, *The Men of the First French Republic*, 210–11.
[5] Desmoulins, *Correspondance*, 138–9.

took seats in the Convention were also known as Montagnards from the positions high up in which they sat as a group. However, switching between the names 'Jacobins' and 'Montagnards' is potentially confusing, so I shall continue to refer to them as Jacobins.) Neither the Girondins nor the Jacobins constituted a formal political party. Of the two, the Jacobins were the more unified group. The twenty-four deputies for Paris who formed the nucleus of the Jacobins in the Convention included Robespierre, Danton, Desmoulins, Marat, and lesser lights, Legendre, Fabre d'Eglantine, Billaud-Varenne, and Collot d'Herbois.[6] Aside from their leaders and members of their inner circles, identifying just who was a 'Girondin' and who was a 'Jacobin' could be a delicate affair, both for contemporaries and for historians. Most deputies remained politically unaligned and sat in a metaphorical and literal middle space known as the plain or marsh (*marais*). Some deputies sided with the Girondins on occasion—especially when the dominance of Paris was at issue; or with the Jacobins; or fluctuated between the groupings. Over the ensuing months the balance of power shifted as a sizeable section of unaligned deputies who started out by offering fairly consistent support to the Girondins gradually moved to supporting the Jacobins instead. This was not because they identified themselves as Jacobins, or were members of the Jacobin Club, but because they were increasingly sceptical of the Girondins' leadership, while the Jacobins had a more pragmatic grasp of the political and military realities of the situation. Without their support the Jacobins could not have come to power in June 1793 and would not have maintained power during the crucial year of the Terror.

All of this has caused difficulties for historians who have attempted to trace the distinctions between the Girondins and the Jacobins. It used to be claimed that there were major social, class, and ideological differences between them.[7] In recent years, the work of historians has tended to minimize those differences. Michael Sydenham argued that the idea of a unified political faction of Girondins was largely a myth, created retrospectively by the Jacobins in order to condemn the Girondins as a conspiratorial group. Its members were only loosely allied politically, and did not share a consistent political ideology clearly distinguishable from that of other Jacobins. In her detailed study of voting, tactical operations, and alignments in the Convention Alison Patrick took a slightly different view from Sydenham. She showed that there was an 'inner sixty' men whom she identified as 'Brissot and his friends', who often worked closely together, but who still exercised considerable independence over ideological positions.[8] I would go further in this,

---

[6] On the Jacobins and their supporters, see Patrick, *The Men of the First French Republic*, 17–33, 105–7; and Françoise Brunel, 'Les Députés montagnards', in Soboul, *Girondins et Montagnards*, 343–61. See also the individual entries in Kuscinski, *Dictionnaire des Conventionnels*.

[7] The classic social distinction between the Girondins (as representing 'commercial bourgeois' class interests) and the Jacobins (as 'lower middle class') was made most systematically by Soboul: see the Introduction to Soboul, *Girondins et Montagnards*.

[8] Sydenham, *The Girondins*, and Patrick, *The Men of the First French Republic*. See also the debate between Michael Sydenham, 'The Girondins and the question of revolutionary government: a new approach to the problem of political divisions in the National Convention', *French Historical Studies*, 10 (1977): 342–8, and Theodore A. Di Padova, 'The question of Girondin motives: a response to

nd argue that there was very little to distinguish between those Jacobins who became Girondins, and those who remained Jacobins. They came from similar social and cultural backgrounds, had many friendships in common, read the same books, and shared the same ideals. In 1792 both groups were committed republicans; both conceptualized revolutionary politics in terms of a struggle between men of virtue who defended the Republic, and conspirators who opposed it; and both sides would be prepared to break the ideological principle of immunity of deputies in order to eliminate their opponents.

Thus it is difficult to trace consistent ideological divisions between those Jacobins who remained in the Club, and those who left to side with Brissot's group. What distinguished them above all were the choices that they made over this critical period.[9] It has been said that the Girondins differed from the Jacobins in their hostility towards Paris and the Parisian militants. Although this was certainly the case during the period of the Convention, it was not an inherent ideological distinction. As we have seen, in 1791 the Girondin leaders had made considerable play to harness the power of the Paris crowd. Indeed, the links between the Girondins and popular militancy were still evident in the mass demonstration in support of the purged Girondin ministers on 20 June 1792.

It was above all the blood shed in the September massacres that swung the Girondins definitively against the Paris militants. That blood swelled to a river dividing the two factions. The Girondin leaders' conviction that their own lives had been endangered in the massacres added considerably to their fear and hostility. They were subject to growing fear that street violence would be turned on them, stirred up by journalists popular with the militants. Marat was their fiercest opponent; fuming at the Girondins' tactics to frustrate his attempts to speak in the Convention, he avenged himself in print by denouncing them as given over to 'egoism, to cupidity, to avarice, bent on ambitious designs...'[10] Equally hostile to the Girondins, and much more brutal in his language, was Hébert, editor of *Le Père Duchesne*. Hébert himself, like most of the spokesmen for the *sans-culottes*, was from a higher social class than the people he represented.[11] But in his journal he assumed the identity and language of a *sans-culotte* to appeal to the militants.

---

Sydenham', *French Historical Studies*, 10 (1977): 349–52. See also the forum in *French Historical Studies*: Frederick A. De Luna, 'The "Girondins" were Girondins after all'; and Michael S. Lewis-Beck, Anne Hildreth, and Alan B. Spitzer, 'Was there a Girondist faction in the National Convention?', with commentary by Sydenham, Patrick, and Kates, *French Historical Studies*, 15, 3 (1988): 519–36.

   [9]  Joseph Guadet (nephew of the revolutionary Guadet) stressed that the Girondins did not constitute a unified group. As individuals they retained 'their opinions, their sentiments, their interests'. He also emphasized the importance of understanding the Girondins not only in terms of 'public and parliamentary life' but also 'private life': Guadet, *Les Girondins*, 1: Preface, xiii–xvii.

   [10]  'Adresse de Marat à ses Commettants', in *Le Journal de la République Française*, No. 76, 17 December 1792, in Jean-Paul Marat, *Oeuvres de J.P. Marat (L'Ami du Peuple)*, ed. A. Vermorel (Paris: Décembre-Alonnier, 1869), 263–5.

   [11]  Hébert was the son of a goldsmith, and had attended a *collège*, though the family had since fallen on hard times. Marat, who had had a long career as a writer, scientist, and medical practitioner, was also from the class of 'gentlemen'; whilst Varlet (who was one of the leaders of the *sans-culotte* movement) received a private income, and had no need to work at all. See R.B. Rose, *The* Enragés*: Socialists of the French Revolution* (Melbourne: Melbourne University Press, 1965), 10–11.

The gulf between the Girondins and Paris escalated and hardened in the succeeding months. The Girondin leaders assumed the role of spokesmen for provincial France, making a federalist stand against the radicalism and domination of Paris. Many of the deputies new to national politics were attracted to the Girondins' banner by their anti-Paris stance. However other—more personal—factors were also significant in influencing individuals' choices of alignment between the two factions. It is to these that we shall now turn.

## FRIENDSHIP AND THE GIRONDINS

When it came to the tipping point in choosing between the Girondin and Jacobin factions, in many (though by no means all) cases a critical part was played by ties of friendship and personal loyalty on one hand, and distrust and enmity on the other. These ties particularly affected members and former members of the Jacobin Club. These men had been part of the same close network, joined by shared beliefs and friendship, for several years now. It was hard, therefore, for them to ignore the pull of personal ties. Often this proved to be a difficult choice. Some men retained bonds of sympathy and friendship with both factions, and hesitated for some time before choosing which side to support—and ultimately, perhaps, which to betray.

Another significant factor, though it could not be openly acknowledged, was personal ambition. Though there was no obligation for a deputy to choose sides, if he hoped to be a powerful player in revolutionary politics it was of considerable help to him to join forces with a group, and attach his star to theirs, rather than rely on his individual efforts. Though he could not admit to his own ambition, his enemies would not hesitate to accuse him of it. Accusations and counter-accusations of ambition were a central feature of the bitter verbal exchanges between the factions.

Some historians have acknowledged that friendships counted for a great deal in Girondin politics. Sydenham concedes that the Girondins operated largely through their friendships. Furthermore, he notes that they frequently did not agree on ideological principles or policy, even when it was expedient to do so. They were too individualistic and indecisive to operate as a coherent ideological group.[12] More recently, Leigh Whaley's detailed study of both Girondin and Jacobin networks argues that the two identifiable rival factions emerged in the Convention very late in the day, by the spring of 1793. Her work points to the important part played by personal friendships in bringing together individuals in both groups; she details a number of occasions when friendships overrode political differences.[13] Gary Kates situates friendship at the heart of the Girondin faction. He argues that the *locus* of the Girondin faction was 'in networks of friendships and personal alliances' that operated in clubs and salons

[12] Sydenham, *The Girondins*, 61–74, 98, 202–6.
[13] Whaley, *Radicals*, 122. On personal friendships outweighing ideology and tactical choices, she cites the examples of Gorsas and Carra: 99, 108–9.

outside the Convention and where 'ambitious politicians forged personal relation-ships that were crucial to their careers'.[14]

My argument is broadly in agreement with these views, but takes this perspec-tive a stage further.[15] Friendship was not only fundamental to the way in which the Girondins operated, it was also instrumental in their downfall. Robespierre and the Jacobins were not likely to forget—or forgive—either the personalized attacks on their own integrity by the Girondins, or the way in which Brissot had manipulated his friends into the Girondin ministry and political power. The Girondins' injudicious recourse to the 'behind closed doors' tactics of private connections and friendships played against them in the cultural *milieu* of trans-parent politics.

Thus there were two principal factors that divided the factions in 1792, deep-ening the division that had begun over the war and the first Girondin ministry. The first—divisions over popular violence and Parisian domination—has been well documented. The second—the importance of friendship and personal loyal-ties and enmities—needs to be understood better in order to appreciate how the revolutionaries themselves conceived of the differences between themselves; and just why these intense divisions developed into a rhetoric linking dissembling politicians with conspiracy and terror, a rhetoric which each group used to try to eliminate the other. Part of the unwritten story of the split between Girondin and Jacobin is one of how erstwhile friends became enemies, and confronted one another with the bitter sense of personal betrayal that only a fractured friendship can impart. The emotional enmity between the two groups, and the ways in which they identified both like-minded men and opponents, became part of an explanatory narrative of revolutionary politics that both sides told themselves and their audiences. According to this narrative politicians who dissembled virtue as a cloak for self-interest and ambition became secret conspirators in league with the external enemies of France. It was out of this narrative that the politicians' terror emerged.

## POLITICAL IMAGE, IDENTITY AND CALUMNY

The deputies were conscious of their own position at the centre of the drama of the new Republic. Speakers were keenly aware of their audiences, and shaped their words, their manner of speaking, their gestures accordingly. The great set pieces of debate, such as the trial of the king, were performed as political theatre, in which the participants played to the gallery as well as to one another, mindful of how their rhetoric and attitudes would be reported in the press.[16] Both Girondins and

---

[14] See Gary Kates in his commentary in *French Historical Studies* 15, 3 (1988), 544.
[15] See Linton, 'Fatal friendships'.
[16] See Peter France, 'Speakers and audience: the first days of the Convention', in Renwick, *Language and Rhetoric of the Revolution*, 50–68; and Brasart, *Paroles de la Révolution*, Part 3.

Jacobins struck self-conscious attitudes of heroic virtue, modelled on republican heroes from antiquity; favouring above all, Cicero, Cato, and the two Brutuses.[17]

Recently historians have drawn attention to the theatrical elements that characterized many of the scenes in the Convention, analysing the Revolution as drama, and drawing parallels between theatre and politics.[18] Nevertheless, an explicit engagement with the idea of politics as theatre was anathema to the revolutionaries themselves. Any intimation that they were 'actors' performing a role, wearing a mask, threatened to undermine their claims to authenticity. Much of the language was intensely emotional. The progress of the war racked up the tension and patriotic fervour, as regular dispatches arrived from the front, and were reported with rejoicing, or (more often in 1793) fear, depending on how the war was going. The best speakers such as Robespierre, Danton, and Vergniaud, with their very different oratorical styles, could whip up their audiences into excited outbursts of approbation or disapproval. For many months the Girondins were able to prevail over the right to speak in the Assembly, but as their power waned, their ability to influence the Convention diminished. They complained bitterly at the predominance of noisy and partisan Jacobin supporters in the public galleries. The struggle that the factions were engaged in was reflected beyond the walls of the Convention, in the public image of revolutionary leaders. All parties had learned much about the power of the press and how to negotiate it since the early days of the Revolution. They gave much thought to their own public images, and the images of their rivals. Some deputies were also editors of their own newspapers: they included the Girondin sympathizers Gorsas, Carra, Mercier, and Condorcet. If the Girondins were incensed at the antics of the Jacobin *claques* in the public galleries, the Jacobins were equally furious at the hostile reporting of the Girondin press. What outraged the Jacobins the most was that Roland was using his ministerial position and his access to 100,000 *livres* in public funds (granted him for government propaganda) to give his patronage to journalists who supported the Girondins.[19] One of the journalists financed by Roland was Louvet, editor of *La Sentinelle*, a newspaper in poster form that was fiercely anti-Jacobin. For the Jacobins this was a continuation of old regime-style politics in an underhand way, so as to manipulate the new politics based on public opinion.

There was a marked intensification in personal attacks to undermine the credibility of political opponents, not only in the newspapers, but conducted face to

[17] On Saint-Just's use of the image of both Brutuses, see Linton, 'The man of virtue'. For the varying significance of these two Brutuses and the conflict between virtue and sensibility, see Denise Amy Baxter, 'Two Brutuses: violence, virtue, and politics in the visual culture of the French Revolution', *Eighteenth-Century Life*, 30, 3 (Summer 2006): 51–77.

[18] For varied approaches to this field, see Friedland, *Political Actors*, 172–6; Susan Maslan, *Revolutionary Acts: Theater, Democracy and the French Revolution* (Baltimore, MD: The Johns Hopkins University Press, 2005); and Andress, 'Living the revolutionary melodrama'.

[19] Popkin, *Revolutionary News*, 172. For a detailed study of the extent to which Roland used government funds to finance pro-Girondin publications, see Reynolds, *Marriage and Revolution*, 234–41. On the fury that the Girondin press provoked amongst the Montagnards, see Whaley, *Radicals*, 111–13; and Marc Bouloiseau, 'Robespierre d'après les journaux Girondins', in Albert Soboul (ed.), *Actes du colloque Robespierre* (Paris: Société des études Robespierristes, 1967).

face on the floor of the Convention. On 28 October Robespierre spoke in the Jacobins on 'the influence of calumny on the Revolution'. Calumny, he said, was responsible for all the 'unhappy events' and 'bloodshed' since the origins of the Revolution. It undermined the Revolution itself, by attacking the reputations of the men of genuine virtue. It was 'the language of aristocrats', but was being used on their behalf by revolutionary factionalists. The situation in the Constituent Assembly, when the triumvirate and Lafayette had used personal attacks to undermine the patriots, was being replicated by a new group:

> Take away the word republic, and I see nothing that has changed. I see everywhere the same vices, the same cabals, the same methods, and above all the same calumny... There exists a coalition of *virtuous patriots*, of *austere republicans*, who are perfecting the criminal politics of Lafayette and his allies... I do not even need to name them to you, you will recognize them by their works. [Everyone knew he meant Brissot and his friends. Robespierre's real anger was directed at the press funded by Roland. This faction was serving the interests of all the forces opposed to the Revolution:] The rich, public officials, egoists, ambitious intriguers, men in positions of authority, they organize as a group under the banner of this hypocritical faction, known by the name *moderates*, they are the ones who have put the Revolution in peril. [Calumny was the new weapon of this faction. They used it to destroy the public reputations of the men of virtue. They reversed reality, by] painting each virtue in the colours of the vice opposed to it, and exaggerating it to look as bad as possible. [They painted a picture of] themselves as the honest men, the gentlemen of the republic; whilst we are the *sans-culottes* and the rabble... They accuse us of trying to set up a dictatorship, we, who have no army, no treasure, no places, no party. [The reality was thus the very reverse of what the faction maintained: it was this faction that held] all the power and all the riches. [Yet they found many who would believe their calumnies] because we know the power of words over the minds of men.[20]

Despite the extent of the double-dealing that Robespierre attributed to the Girondins, his conclusions were moderate; he counselled only watchfulness, patience: sooner or later the calumny writers would expose themselves. Robespierre had long held the conviction that freedom of the press was the best way of obliging political leaders to consider what they owed to the public in the way of integrity. Nevertheless, as Charles Walton demonstrates, this speech pointed to the beginnings of an ominous change in the Jacobin leaders' attitude towards the freedom of the press. In 1791 Robespierre had thought that probity and virtue were far stronger than the ability of the press to misrepresent them. He had learned since then to fear the power of the press.[21]

The following day, Louvet staged a dramatic denunciation of Robespierre in the Convention. It was a direct attack on Robespierre's persona as a man of virtue. Louvet had been planning it for several weeks, with the encouragement of Madame Roland. Louvet said he had come to reveal 'plots', the goal of which was

---

[20] 28 October 1792, Robespierre, 'Sur l'influence de la calomnie sur la Révolution', in Robespierre, *Oeuvres*, 9: 44–7, 51, 59.

[21] See the thoughtful discussion in Walton, *Policing Public Opinion*, 129.

'to subvert, subject to anarchy, to overcome and destroy the national representation'. Robespierre was at the head of these plots. He was using his public image to consolidate his political power: 'I accuse you of having continually presented yourself as an object of idolatry; of letting people say to your face that you are the only virtuous man in France.' Louvet went back over every move that Robespierre had made as a political leader, using a reading of Robespierre's motives that had been developed in the Girondin press. According to this narrative, Robespierre's involvement in revolutionary politics, all his actions and words, made under the cloak of his supposed devotion to the good of the people, had in reality served as a screen for his actual purpose—to further his own advancement to power. Louvet's denunciation culminated in the accusation that Robespierre was guilty of the ultimate crime in personal ambition, of secretly plotting to make himself a dictator: 'you have taken great strides, Robespierre, towards this dictatorial power, the thirst for which devours you'.[22]

Louvet's accusation went well beyond the evidence and did the Girondins few favours, prompting a fall in support for their group. It was a clear case of the kind of unsubstantiated calumny that Robespierre had spoken about the day before. Robespierre was indignant at the escalating attacks against him in the Girondin press where Louvet's allegation that Robespierre wanted to make himself a dictator was being regularly repeated. In the face of these attacks his belief in a free press began to waver.[23] The growing hostility to freedom of the press was another step in the process that made the position of political leaders more dangerous.

Robespierre's reply and his repudiation of Louvet's reading of his motivation strengthened his reputation and his power base at the Jacobins. On the day that Robespierre gave his response to Louvet's charges, the public galleries were packed with spectators. Again, witnesses commented on the large numbers of women who came to hear the Incorruptible defend his reputation. They included several wives of deputies, as well as many 'women of the people'. One of the things that the Girondin press used to attack Robespierre's political credibility was the high proportion of women amongst his supporters.[24] Condorcet's journal, the *Chronique de Paris*, counted between 700 and 800 women, and 200 men, and many more women obstructed the passageways. The account was also taken up and reproduced in *Le Patriote français*. The *Chronique de Paris* asked why Robespierre was so popular with women; why did so many come to hear him, 'at his home, at the tribune of the Jacobins, at the Cordeliers, at the Convention'? The answer, according to Condorcet, was that women were 'devout' and Robespierre was 'a priest of

---

[22]  29 October 1792, *Archives parlementaires*, 53: 52, 57.

[23]  Bouloiseau, 'Robespierre d'après les journaux Girondins'. On Robespierre's changing attitude towards freedom of the press, see Gough, 'Robespierre and the Press', in Haydon and Doyle, *Robespierre*, esp. 117–26.

[24]  Vilate described encounters with several of the Girondins in cafés and their homes, who grumbled about Robespierre's popularity with women, which they attributed to his priestly aura: Joachim Vilate, *Les Mystères de la mère de dieu dévoilés: troisième volume des Causes secrètes de la Révolution du 9 au 10 thermidor* (Paris: 1795), republished in *Collection des Mémoires relatifs à la Révolution Française: Desmoulins, Vilate et Méda* (Paris: Baudoin, 1825), 310–12.

the Revolution' who 'has his followers among women and the weak-minded'.[25] Women had no legitimate political role, and had the official status of 'passive citizens', so to assert that most of Robespierre's supporters were women was a considerable put-down. Condorcet was an eloquent supporter for the rights of women, so it is curious to hear his newspaper deliberately belittle women's intellectual powers, and mock their incapacity for making 'serious' political choices. Condorcet's narrative reminds us that the battle between Jacobins and Girondins had little to do with ideology and principles, and everything to do with political tactics and personal relationships of friendship and enmity. Condorcet at this point was trying to keep out of the factional infighting, but he loathed Robespierre.[26] Disparaging references by Robespierre's opponents to his multitude of female admirers was a way of informing readers of the journals that Robespierre's supporters were on the margins of the political body, without power, voice, or significance; therefore by extension so was Robespierre. Yet the disparaging attitude of the Girondin journalists towards Robespierre's enthusiastic female supporters indicates that they feared the—largely unacknowledged, yet substantial—part that women could play in shaping public perceptions about the image and credibility of revolutionary politicians. It is also likely that some of the women in the audience had links with the organized popular militants, the *sans-culottes*, and that fear of the militants gave additional fuel to Condorcet's hostility. Robespierre himself was uneasy at being identified with the *sans-culottes*. He was resolute in his support of them, but that did not mean that he wanted to be seen as one of them. His image was dignified and meticulous, far from that of a 'man of the people': rough, uncouth, prone to swearing, drinking—and violence. Robespierre kept himself aloof from the kind of persona adopted by many Jacobin deputies who imitated the dress, speech, and manners of the *sans-culottes*, the better to appeal to their support. Madame Roland described such antics in a contemptuous portrait she penned following her arrest, '...the deputies, after 31 May, dressed like navvies, in trousers, short jackets and bonnets, their shirts open on their chests, swearing and gesticulating like drunken *sans-culottes!*'[27]

Brissot described the popular militants as resembling religious hypocrites: 'The word Republic is imprinted on the cockades of our revolutionary cockroaches, on their buttons, on their snuffboxes; in their homes, on their persons, the Republic is everywhere...except in their hearts.' They were 'tormented by the need to denounce', but their greatest antagonism was reserved for one another: 'They detest the patriots who do not share all their ideas much more than they do the enemies of the Revolution.'[28] Ironically, Robespierre might have agreed with much of this

---

[25] The disparaging account of Robespierre's female admirers was taken up and reproduced in *Le Patriote français*, No. 1192, 14 November 1792. The extract from *La Chronique de Paris* is in Jacob, *Robespierre vu par ses contemporains*, 311. See also Robespierre, *Oeuvres*, 9: 77, note 2. Vilate claimed to see the hand of Rabaut Saint-Étienne in the article: *Collection des Mémoires relatifs à la Révolution Française*, 311. See also McPhee, *Robespierre*, 136–8.

[26] Badinter and Badinter, *Condorcet*, 503–4.

[27] Madame Roland, *Mémoires*, 169–70.

[28] Brissot, *Mémoires*, 2: 95.

characterization. To his way of thinking such activities were signs of the dissembling of patriotism, the reverse of authenticity.

One of Louvet's accusations against Robespierre was that he was the friend of Marat, and that he had engineered Marat's election to the Convention. No one had been more doggedly persistent than Marat in denouncing plots and corruption by revolutionary officials. Still, attitudes towards him within the Jacobins were decidedly ambivalent. So virulent were Marat's policies and his public persona that many Jacobins recoiled from friendship with 'the people's friend'. Robespierre was at pains to make it clear that there had been no personal relations between himself and Marat; he also denied that he had influenced the election process. He stated that Marat had come to see him in his home only once, in January 1792, and the conversation had been on 'public affairs'. Marat himself confirmed that there was no personal friendship between himself and Robespierre; as did Robert, in whose home Louvet alleged that the two Jacobin politicians had met. According to Robert, 'Marat has never come there'. Robespierre also had never visited, but in his case, continued Robert, 'he can come when he likes'.[29]

Both factions accused the other of instances of corruption. The Jacobins directed much of their fire at the Girondin ministers, especially Roland. The Jacobins used his reputation for austere republicanism against him, suggesting that he was hiding behind a manufactured public image to use his ministerial post for the benefit of himself and his faction. Merlin de Thionville, when accusing Roland of using immense sums of public money to circulate Girondin newspapers in the provinces, hammered home the point by turning Roland's reputation for virtue back on him, repeatedly referring to him with pointed irony as 'the virtuous, the eternally virtuous Roland'.[30] For their part the Girondins attacked Danton's reputation since he was the only Jacobin to have served as a minister. They found him a relatively easy target, homing in on his most vulnerable point—his flexible approach towards financial integrity. During his brief tenure as Minister of Justice, Danton had run up substantial costs for which the accounts were mysteriously missing. The Girondins reminded the Convention of this fact on every possible occasion. Whenever Danton stood up to speak in the Convention they would embarrass him by shouting out: 'The accounts!', a demand to which Danton had no effective answer.[31]

---

[29] 5 November 1792, Robespierre, 'Réponse de Maximilien Robespierre à l'accusation de J.B. Louvet', in Robespierre, *Oeuvres*, 9: 80–1; Robert's response is at 81, note 11. See also Marat, *L'Ami du Peuple*, No. 648, 7–8. The Jacobins were at pains to distinguish between the political personas of Robespierre and Marat; see, for example, 23 December 1792, Aulard, *Société des Jacobins*, 4: 612–15.

[30] *Journal des débats de la Société des Jacobins*, No. 296, cited in Louis Mortimer-Ternaux, *1792–1794, d'après des documents authentiques et des pièces inédites*, 8 vols (Paris: Michel Lévy Frères, 1869), 5: 130–1.

[31] Hampson, *Danton*, 89–90. The evidence for Danton having misappropriated ministerial funds is laid out in Albert Mathiez, *La Corruption sous la Terreur* (Paris: Armand Colin, 1927i), ch. 3.

## CHOOSING SIDES: GIRONDIN OR JACOBIN?

The definitive split came when Brissot and his group left the Jacobin Club. Brissot had ceased to attend the Jacobins after 10 August. When he was threatened with expulsion he was invited to come to the Jacobins and explain himself, but replied only that he would respond when he had time from his various occupations: he never appeared there. He was formally expelled in October 1792 after a discussion in which anyone who wanted to defend him was given the chance to speak.[32] As for the other Girondins (with the exception of Louvet, who was expelled following his denunciation of Robespierre, and one or two others) for the most part they seem not to have been expelled, but to have chosen to leave. On 11 January 1793 the Jacobins debated whether or not to expel Gensonné, Vergniaud, or Guadet, but Desfieux pointed out that it had been decreed that anyone who had not renewed their card for three months would be deemed excluded, '. . . it is [for] more than three months that the Girondistes, Brissotins, Rolandistes, Buzotistes and their accomplices, have not renewed their cards, therefore they are no longer Jacobins'.[33] Robespierre was now the undisputed leading figure in the Jacobin Club. It was still a place of many voices and many views, but no one knew how to work its mingled rhetoric of patriotism, sensibility, and virtue, and appeal to its public galleries, as Robespierre did. The Club was his power base: the heartland of his support.[34]

Members of the Jacobin Club would be obliged to choose sides as their own leaders quarrelled bitterly and irrevocably amongst themselves. Whilst the identity of most of the principal leaders of the two factions was established by the time the Convention met, many people wavered between the sides, and did not make their final choice until late in the day, not long before the Girondins' proscription. In many cases the tipping point in an individual's decision came down to personal factors, who his close friends were, and to which side he had the deepest emotional attachment. Some were driven by fear—fear of the *sans-culottes*, a fear exacerbated by the September massacres.

The *conventionnels* were faced by the urgent question of what to do with the king. One of the most prominent participants in the debate over the fate of the king was the young Saint-Just, a newcomer to national politics.[35] His intervention in this debate gave him the opportunity to make his mark, and he seized it with both hands. He chose that moment to abandon his earlier opposition to the death penalty; he argued that the king stood outside the nation, therefore he could be put to death for the crime of kingship itself, without need of a formal trial. The argument caused a considerable stir and made Saint-Just into

[32] 12 October 1792, Aulard, *Société des Jacobins*, 4: 376–8.

[33] 11 January 1793, Aulard, *Société des Jacobins*, 669.

[34] See Jacques Bernet, 'La perception de Robespierre dans les clubs de Jacobins de Champagne et de Picardie (1791–1795)', in Jessenne *et al.*, *Robespierre: De la nation artésienne*.

[35] Saint-Just spoke twice on this issue. The first speech (which made the most impact) was on 13 November 1792, the second on 26 December. On Saint-Just and the king's trial, see Linton, 'The man of virtue', 405–7.

a notable figure almost overnight (as I discuss below), but such abstract reasoning was unacceptable to most of the deputies, who continued to set great store by visible justice and the legal process. The three factors that carried most weight with the majority of the deputies (the great majority of whom were not Jacobins) were their conviction that the king really was guilty of treason; their ideological and emotional commitment to equality and the principle that justice should be the same for a king as for a commoner; the pragmatic assessment that his death was necessary for the *salut public*. It was decided to put the king on trial before the Convention itself.

The trial of the king obliged the deputies to make another choice that brought them closer to terror.[36] Since the deputies themselves were to judge the king's fate there was no evading that choice. The Convention was packed with spectators to see the trial take place, amidst an atmosphere of intense emotion and high drama. Every deputy had to decide for himself on a series of questions regarding the guilt of the king and the appropriate punishment. When it came to the moment to pronounce the sentence, each man had to state his choice—death, imprisonment, or banishment—and, if he chose death, give his reasons. There was no doubt that the king would be found guilty of treason: were it otherwise then the legality of the Convention and the Republic itself would be called into doubt. The question whether or not the king should be subject to an immediate death penalty was, however, much more divisive. Rightly or wrongly, some deputies feared that if they failed to vote for death the Paris militants might threaten the royal family and the Convention itself in a renewal of the September massacres.[37] In the end the verdict that the king should be put to death was carried, amidst scenes of knife-edge tension.

The debate on the trial further polarized the position of the Girondins and Jacobins. The Girondins had argued that the fate of the king should be determined by a national referendum (*appel au peuple*). This was held against them by the Jacobins who saw it as a sign either of royalism, or of weakness; an attempt to abnegate responsibility for a situation which the Girondins themselves had done so much to bring about, and to risk civil war if the provinces should reject the death sentence—as they almost certainly would have done. It was not only the Jacobins who took the view that the Girondins had been both inept and self-serving in their attitude towards the monarchy; a considerable number of deputies shared this view, even while also remaining uneasy at the Jacobins' commitment to the Paris militants.[38] Thus the king's trial further divided the factions, though not quite as much as is sometimes supposed; there was still some space for difference of opinion.[39]

---

[36] See David P. Jordan, *The King's Trial: Louis XVI vs. the French Revolution* (Berkeley: University of California Press, 1979). See also Patrick's detailed analysis, particularly her conclusions regarding why a majority of deputies came round to supporting the Jacobin position: Patrick, *The Men of the First French Republic*, chs. 3 and 4.

[37] On these rumours, see Jordan, *The King's Trial*, 178–80; and William Doyle, *The Oxford History of the French Revolution* (Oxford: Clarendon Press, 1989), 195–6.

[38] Patrick, *The Men of the First French Republic*, 65–6.

[39] On how the trial affected factional divisions see also Whaley, *Radicals*, 106–16.

The factors that drove deputies to gravitate towards one faction or another were complex. Not everyone who took sides was a veteran of the Paris Jacobins network. There was an influx into the Convention of new deputies from the provinces. For many of these men the horror of the September massacres put an impassable gulf between them and the Jacobin leaders. A number of them were drawn to the Girondins' anti-Parisian stance and became prominent spokesmen for the Girondins. They included such men as Barbaroux and his close friend Rebecqui (both from Marseille); and Lanjuinais, a founder of the Breton Club who, in the Convention, became one of the most outspoken opponents of the Paris militants.

There was a scattering of men of ancient noble pedigree who continued to align themselves with the Jacobins, even after the overthrow of the monarchy. These included Hérault de Séchelles and his intimate friend since early childhood, Lepeletier de Saint-Fargeau (both of whom had been leading members of the Paris *Parlement* before the Revolution). This select group also—and most notoriously— included the duc d'Orléans, along with his close friend and long-standing political associate, the marquis de Sillery. The majority of the prominent former nobles who remained active in politics after the overthrow of the monarchy aligned themselves with the extreme Left. The heavy price paid for this decision was that they were seen as traitors to their own caste; they experienced rejection by family and friends from their old lives. We might ask whether they made such a choice out of authentic conviction—their fellow revolutionaries certainly posed the same question. In their public declarations the former nobles maintained that they were motivated by a passionate commitment to Jacobin ideology. This may have been the case. We cannot be sure what they *really* thought. They may, however, have had other motives, as their enemies were not slow to point out. Ambition was one possibility. Personal motives such as disaffection from their own families may have been a factor in some cases, and probably affected the choices of Hérault de Séchelles. Fear was another incentive—for they had burnt their bridges with their old lives and were in danger of being politically isolated. In Madame Roland's scornful judgement both Lepeletier and Hérault were 'weak and rich' former nobles who aligned themselves with the Mountain 'out of fear'.[40] It may well be that they saw their best chance of self-preservation in the increasingly dangerous world of revolutionary politics as lying in being prominent members of the most egalitarian group. In any case, as wealthy members of the old elite, they were at risk of being characterized as 'conspirators', seeking to manipulate revolutionary politics for their own advantage. Thus, they could only participate in politics by distancing themselves as far as possible from their former identities, and being reborn as men of virtue, committed to the most egalitarian positions. D'Orléans even acquired a new name as part of his new identity, that of Philippe-Égalité.

The presence of such men amongst the Jacobin deputies, especially d'Orléans, could taint others by association. The Girondins repeatedly attacked the Jacobins for permitting d'Orléans to sit amongst them. Thus Louvet, writing long afterwards,

---

[40] Madame Roland, *Mémoires*, 360–1.

described Brissot, Roland, and Condorcet as the 'pure Jacobins who wanted a republic', while Robespierre, Danton, and (secretly) Marat were plotting to put d'Orléans on the throne. The accusation is revealing of how one of the Girondins would later choose to characterize the differences between the two factions, depicting the Girondins as the 'pure' or 'authentic' revolutionaries; their rivals as 'conspirators' against the Republic. [41] Condorcet for his part drew away from the Girondin faction; he disapproved of their infighting with Robespierre and Danton, considering this to be a tactical mistake, and was repelled by the 'affairism' of Brissot. But the Girondin leaders did not listen to him, and he was an ineffectual presence in the Convention. He was caught up in the Girondins' downfall largely because he sought to defend them when they were arrested. [42]

For many deputies the choice between Girondins and Jacobins was intensely difficult. A number of men had friends on both sides of the divide. Barère was a friend of several of the Girondins, and dined often with Vergniaud. He sympathized with their political ideas, but he did not share their readiness to make trouble, nor their intractability; and he extricated himself from those friendships, having no desire to be pulled down with them. In his case the choice was primarily about political tactics—and choosing what he thought would be the winning side. [43]

For Pétion the choice was particularly hard. Back in August, Pétion had written Robespierre a letter in which he asserted the sincerity of his feelings for his comrade in revolution: 'You know, my friend, what my sentiments are towards you…it would be useless to attempt to divide us…you and I will never be in opposing parties, we shall always hold to the same political faith. I have no need to say that I shall never join in any movement against you, by tastes, by character, by principles, I could not be party to it. I think that you do not aspire to my place, just as I do not aspire to that of the king…'[44] The fact that he needed to say this suggests that he was trying to paper over the cracks in their relationship. For as long as he could Pétion avoided choosing sides in the dispute, but on 7 November he sent a letter to the Jacobins making clear that he was aligning himself with the Girondins. For Pétion it came down to a choice between Brissot and Robespierre, both of whom were his good friends, and alongside whom he had fought many political battles during the three years of the Revolution. Yet he had known Brissot since childhood, and his feelings for Brissot ran deeper than his attachment to Robespierre; for that reason he trusted Brissot's integrity. In his letter he denied that there was a Brissotin faction, justifying himself by his intimate knowledge of Brissot's authentic nature: '…I have known him since his childhood. I have seen him in those moments where the soul shows itself in its entirety; when one gives oneself up without reservation, to friendship…I know his principles, I protest to you that

---

[41] Louvet, *Mémoires de Louvet*, 34–5.

[42] See Kuscinski, *Dictionnaire des Conventionnels*; and Badinter and Badinter, *Condorcet*.

[43] Gershoy, *Bertrand Barère*, 131.

[44] Pétion to Robespierre, 20 August 1792, in Robespierre, *Correspondance de Maximilien et Augustin Robespierre*, 152.

they are pure...'[45] Brissot, according to Pétion, was the kind of man who was simply incapable of leading a faction.

Immediately the Jacobins weighed in against Pétion for publicly defending his friend. One of the first was Chabot, who responded predictably by undermining Pétion's own integrity. He hesitated to attack Pétion outright, however, and imputed Pétion's weakness to succumbing to the ambition of Madame Pétion on his behalf. Chabot claimed that from her seat in the public gallery she had been seen to applaud Louvet's attack on Robespierre. Her motivation was jealousy of Robespierre's reputation as a man of virtue; she saw in him 'a rival for her husband's glory'.[46] Once again, according to Chabot's narrative, it was a woman who had come between the men of virtue, and with her concern only for self-interested ambition, had divided them from one another.

Pétion had laid bare what he said was Robespierre's *true* character, the side of him to which only those who had been close to him could have access: 'Robespierre takes offence readily and is very suspicious; he sees everywhere plots, treasons, impending disasters...listening to no one but himself, unable to tolerate contradiction, never pardoning anyone who has wounded his self-love, and never recognizing his own faults; denouncing on the basis of slender evidence and growing angry at the least suspicion; always thinking that everyone is preoccupied with him, is persecuting him...' Most damning of all was Pétion's assessment of Robespierre's longing for public applause as his *real* motive for pursuing a career in politics, a 'weakness...that is behind all his actions in public life'.[47] Pétion ended by reaffirming his support for the Jacobins—but only for as long as he considered 'their opinions...to be good'.[48] Pétion's revelations of Robespierre's *true* character can be seen in two ways. He could be giving an impartial assessment of Robespierre's personality, and certainly Pétion's description of Robespierre's propensity to suspect the true motives of all the other revolutionaries around him, and to treat any criticism of himself as equivalent to an attack on the Revolution itself, sounds convincing. But Pétion's tactical reasons for writing this should also be taken into account. Pétion's judgement of Robespierre's character and motives carried weight precisely because Pétion knew Robespierre well. This information could be used as a deliberate strategy to undermine Robespierre's reputation. It was the same kind of tactic that Brissot had deployed in his *Letter to Barnave*, and that Desmoulins in his turn had used to reveal his version of Brissot's true identity in *Brissot Unmasked*. The exposure of the 'true character' of a politician, based on inside information from a former friend or intimate, became a form of ritualized narrative, used by both Girondins and Jacobins to uncover the 'face behind the mask' and undermine publicly the credibility of friends who had become opponents.

---

[45] Jérome Pétion, *Discours de Jérome Pétion sur l'accusation intentée contre Maximilien Robespierre* (November 1792), 16.

[46] 7 November 1792, Aulard, *Société des Jacobins*, 4: 464–7. On the extent to which Pétion's choice was motivated by his friendship for Brissot, see Whaley, *Radicals*, 99, 103.

[47] Pétion, *Discours de Jérome Pétion*, 20–1.

[48] Pétion, *Discours de Jérome Pétion*, 28. Robespierre replied to this in his journal, *Lettres à ses commettans*, Robespierre, *Oeuvres*, 5: 97–115, 141–59.

A new Girondin group met from the time of the king's trial, in the home of Dufriche-Valazé, a large apartment in the rue d'Orléans-Saint-Honoré. It became known as the Valazé Committee. It was something like a salon, in that attendance was by personal invitation; though the membership was much larger than for the more exclusive salons of Madame Roland and Vergniaud. Between thirty and forty people attended it, most of them deputies; and it included some women, though the women do not seem to have been party to the political discussions. After their arrest, Brissot and Valazé both conceded that its aim was to formulate policy to be put before the Convention, particularly on the judgement of Louis XVI.[49] The desire to outmanoeuvre the Jacobins, rather than sympathy for the king, seems to have been a principal motive. Valazé himself had been rebuked by Barère for treating the king with offhand rudeness when he appeared at the bar of the Convention.[50] In his *Memoirs* Brissot underplayed his own role in Valazé's society, saying that he had attended 'only two or three times' and 'heard only political discussions', suggesting (not very plausibly) that his own role was a passive one. According to Brissot it was Valazé 'who was responsible for the invitations'. The Valazé Committee was seen by the Jacobins not just as another instance of 'behind closed doors' politics but also, and more seriously, as a conspiratorial group. Information against the group was provided by Réal. He had formerly been a supporter of Brissot, but had fallen out with him, exasperated at the Girondins' vacillations over whether or not to overthrow the monarchy. He lodged in the same house as Valazé, and was able to provide the names of some of the people who attended the meetings at Valazé's home.[51]

Another man who changed sides was Couthon. Though he was to become one of Robespierre's closest and most devoted colleagues, he began his career much closer to the Girondins. Couthon first entered national politics with the Legislative Assembly as a deputy from the Puy-de-Dôme. When he first arrived in Paris he became part of a network of deputies from the Puy-de-Dôme; he shared a house with Soubrany, and through him became friends with Soubrany's great friend Romme. All three would become Jacobin stalwarts. Couthon was a provincial lawyer, with a reputation for sensibility, and not much interest in money; he had little personal wealth.[52] He suffered from a progressive debilitating illness which made it hard for him to walk. He used this disability to dramatic effect when, on the day that Brissot was formally struck off the list of Jacobins, Couthon had himself carried into the Jacobin Club, to signal a change of his allegiance. Before a rapt audience he declared:

[49] Brissot's interrogation on 15 October 1793, is in *Correspondance et Papiers*, 384–5. See also Brissot, *Mémoires*, 2: 259.

[50] Sydenham, *The Girondins*, 91–7; Kuscinski, *Dictionnaire des conventionnels*, entry on Dufriche-Valazé.

[51] Walter, *Actes du Tribunal révolutionnaire*, 310; and Charles Vatel (ed.), *Charlotte Corday et les Girondins*, 3 vols (Paris: Henri Plon, 1872), 2: 403–4, note 2.

[52] Little has been written about Couthon, despite his key position on the Committee of Public Safety. For his political development up to the time of the king's execution, see Geoffrey Bruun, 'The evolution of a Terrorist: Georges Auguste Couthon', *Journal of Modern History*, 2, 3 (1930): 410–29.

There exist two parties in the Convention...One is a party of men with exaggerated principles, whose weak measures tend to anarchy; the other is a party of clever people, subtle, intent on intrigue, and above all extremely ambitious; they want the Republic, these people; they want it because public opinion has decreed it, but they want it to be aristocratic, they want to use it to perpetuate their influence, to have at their disposal the positions, employments, above all the riches of the Republic, and already don't we have the most convincing proofs? Look at the positions, they all flow from this faction; look at the composition of the Constitution Committee, it's that above all which has opened my eyes. It is upon this faction, that wants liberty only for itself, that we must turn all our energies. For that, citizens, we need the men who are truly pure, morally upright, to take a firm resolution, that they should meet, where? Here, to devise the means.[53]

Couthon made it clear that he had hesitated between the factions; neither was without flaws; there was a certain disapproval in his use of the term 'anarchy' to describe the Jacobins. He continued that at first he had supported the Girondins, trusting in their good faith, and had supported the project for an armed guard for the Convention, but his 'eyes had been opened' by the announcement of the membership of the Constitution Committee (most of whom were to be Girondins): 'I see nothing other in this project than the design of forming a nucleus of forces.' His words were greeted with acclamation. Couthon's reputation for integrity and the fact that hitherto he had kept out of the factional infighting, gave his views greater authority. His physical weakness served to emphasize the strength of his reputation as a man of virtue whose words carried conviction. According to Collot, 'Couthon is a respected man: he will be the guide of patriotism; his name will attract all the patriotic deputies in the Society'. To loud applause the Jacobins decreed that Couthon's words should be printed, and that all the members present should sign it.[54]

Madame Roland saw the danger of this at once. Two days later she wrote to Bancal:

Go and see Couthon and reason with him; it is incredible that a man of such intelligence should let himself be prejudiced in so strange a manner against the best citizens. He speaks absolutely like one of the faction, and supports it at the Jacobins with the weight of his integrity.

What an extraordinary craze this is for making perpetual accusations of intrigue and ambition against men who have only ever used their souls and their talents to serve public affairs with the greatest devotion, and to serve this alone![55]

Her intervention came too late. There would be no going back for Couthon from such a public transfer of loyalties. The reasons why he repudiated the Girondins are not entirely clear: it looks as though disappointment at the Girondins' failure to give him an important post was a factor, though this certainly does not preclude

---

[53] 12 October 1792. Aulard, *Société des Jacobins*, 4: 380.
[54] 12 October 1792. Aulard, *Société des Jacobins*, 4: 381–3.
[55] Madame Roland, *Lettres de Madame Roland*, 1: 438.

the likelihood that he genuinely thought the Jacobins to be the group that was more committed to the public good.

The artist, David, a close personal friend of Robespierre, who would become a hard-line Jacobin and member of the Committee of General Security, nevertheless hesitated before taking sides against the Girondins. On 17 October he wrote a letter to Roland, welcoming him back into office with the words 'at last a virtuous minister'. David also took the opportunity to ask for—and receive—lodgings in the Louvre for some of his students.[56] Another future Robespierrist who started out with some sympathies for the Girondins' federalism was Philippe Le Bas. In January 1793 he took the Girondins' side in advocating federalist proposals to defend the Convention from Parisian militants.[57] Yet he too was to become Robespierre's loyal friend and share his convictions.

Another rising talent in the Jacobins was Saint-Just.[58] He had written a flattering letter introducing himself to Robespierre in 1790. He also knew Desmoulins (who was from the same region) and at one time was on friendly terms with him. Before Saint-Just arrived in the Convention, however, he had come to despise Desmoulins, confiding to a mutual friend, 'I have penetrated his soul, and he fears that I will betray him'. What was it that Saint-Just thought he saw in Desmoulins' soul? Not false patriotism, evidently: 'I esteem his patriotism'. What Desmoulins lacked, according to Saint-Just, was 'the courage that comes from magnanimous virtue'.[59] Other than this, little is known for sure of Saint-Just's direct links with the Jacobin leaders before he arrived in the Convention, nor of the factors that drew him towards them, rather than the Girondins, with whom most of his fellow deputies from the Aisne sympathized.

Saint-Just forged a considerable reputation within just a few weeks of the opening of the Convention through astute, carefully judged speeches. At this time Brissot thought highly of him and praised his speech calling for the death of the king, saying that, despite some youthful errors, it showed 'a talent which can honour France'.[60] Brissot was particularly impressed by Saint-Just's speech on economics and free trade: 'Saint-Just treats the fundamental nature of the question, both in its political and moral aspects; he shows spirit, warmth and philosophy, and honours his talent in defending liberty of commerce'.[61] Brissot's appreciation of Saint-Just's economic ideas illustrates how little fundamental difference there was between the ideas of the Girondins and the Jacobins on the subject. It was the Jacobins who changed direction on this when they decided to support price controls, which they did for tactical rather than ideological reasons, to retain the support of the *sans-culottes*. If Brissot's overtures were an attempt to entice Saint-Just into the Girondin camp, the younger man proved unresponsive. Brissot and the other Girondins

---

[56] Cited in Reynolds, *Marriage and Revolution*, 216.
[57] 16 January 1793. Kuscinki, *Dictionnaires des conventionnels*, entry on Le Bas.
[58] On Saint-Just's career before his election see Vinot, *Saint-Just*.
[59] Letter to Robespierre, 19 August 1790, Saint-Just, *Oeuvres complètes*, 267. For Saint-Just's low opinion of Desmoulins' virtue, 'Letter to Daubigny', ibid., 363–4.
[60] *Le Patriote Français*, No. 1192, 14 November 1792.
[61] *Le Patriote Français*, No. 1207, 30 November 1792.

would soon reverse their good opinion of Saint-Just when he became one of their most unflinching opponents. Nevertheless, it is apparent that Saint-Just, Le Bas, and Couthon, all of whom were to identify themselves closely with Robespierre, began from political outlooks not appreciably different to those of the Girondins. Saint-Just himself remarked on this shared ideology in his first speech at the Jacobins, where he responded to Buzot on the nature of the Republic:

> And I also, like Buzot, define the republic as a holy confederation of men who acknowledge one another as fellows and brothers, as men who are equal, independent, but wise, and who recognize no master but the law which emanated from the general will, freely expressed by the representatives of the entire republic. The principle is common to us both; the consequences to us are different.[62]

According to Saint-Just, it was not on principles or the nature of the Republic that he and the Girondins diverged—but on the consequences of their choices.

Of all the Girondin leaders, Madame Roland had perhaps the most acute political intelligence; she certainly had admirable strength of character and courage. Yet she had weaknesses also. She made up her mind about people very rapidly, and was as quick to make enemies as friends, relying largely on her own judgement and impressions of their character, comparing their 'language' with their 'conduct', and doing her best to further the careers of men whose ideas seemed to coincide with her own.[63] The social conventions of the day (which she was careful to endorse) prohibited a 'respectable' bourgeois woman from playing a public role in revolutionary politics. Yet she was a key figure in the private dimension of Girondin politics, and her judgements about people's virtue, or lack of it, had significant consequences for the conflict between the Girondins and the Jacobins, and the fate of individuals—including her own. When Danton was first made Minister of Justice he gave no sign of holding a grudge for the fact that Roland and the other Girondins had kept him out of office the previous March. On the contrary, in the latter half of August he came to the Rolands' home regularly, bringing along his sidekick Fabre; the two men casually invited themselves to dinner on almost a daily basis. This was Danton's way of inveigling Roland and his friends into forging an alliance with him, and thereby to bring about some *rapprochement* between the estranged factions. It was largely due to Madame Roland's personal antipathy for Danton that the opportunity was rejected. Many of the personal attacks on Danton's conduct as a minister originated with her and her husband.[64] The other Girondin leaders were considerably more relaxed about Danton's lack of integrity, and thought they could strike a deal with him that would 'flatter his *amour-propre* and satisfy his ambition'. She retorted to her friends '... you reason like little boys in politics'. She could not bring herself to make an intimate of a man whom she

[62] Saint-Just, 'Discours sur la proposition d'entourer la Convention nationale d'un garde armée prise dans les quatre-vingt-trois départements, prononcé aux Jacobins dans la séance du 22 octobre 1792', in Saint-Just, *Oeuvres complètes*, 369–70.

[63] See Dumont's assessment of Madame Roland's character: Dumont, *Souvenirs sur Mirabeau*, 209–11.

[64] Whaley, *Radicals*, 93–5.

found physically and morally repugnant, and who conducted himself so little in accordance with her ideas about the proper behaviour of a man of virtue (admittedly Danton was probably not anyone's idea of a man of virtue). As for Fabre, the former actor and poet, she judged him to be a hypocrite—a 'tartuffe'—who played the role of a virtuous politician, while cynically exploiting the opportunities his position brought him for corruption and outright theft; she regarded him with open distaste. She prided herself on the 'Roman' way in which she spoke the truth as she saw it, saying repeatedly that transparency was the hallmark of her character, and that she had nothing to hide; but she and her husband showed a lack of political judgement in their rejection of Danton, the consequences of which would rebound on them both.[65]

Though Madame Roland could not bring herself to warmly welcome Danton and Fabre into her home, other political figures whom she found more congenial congregated there. She resumed her weekly ministerial dinners, and also held a second weekly dinner which was for deputies, senior officials, and other men in public life.[66] Again, there was a tacit understanding that part of the purpose of these intimate evenings *chez* the Rolands was to network and to secure places. These dinners were subject to attack as venues for immoral politics by Jacobin journalists. The most savage characterization of her salon was that by Hébert, who used a stylized argot of the streets to depict an evening *chez* the Rolands when the 'virtuous female Roland, in the arms of her little negro, Lanthenas, was relaxing from the moral pleasures which her bald husband procures for her'. This narrative was familiar from scurrilous accounts of the corruption of the court. In another issue Hébert compared Madame Roland explicitly to the queen and to Louis XV's mistresses, Madame de Pompadour and Madame du Barry. Leading Girondins, Brissot, Buzot, Barbaroux, and others were depicted as Madame Roland's 'courtiers'. Hébert used this narrative strategy to portray Madame Roland and her fellow Girondins as operating a continuation of the corrupt politics of the court, dominated by unscrupulous, amoral women. Hébert repeatedly deployed the phrase 'virtuous Roland' as part of his vicious caricature of the Minister and his wife, to hammer home the point that the Rolands were presenting a false persona to the public, and that Roland was a sanctimonious but weak figure, the dupe of a woman.[67]

Roland resigned as minister on 22 January 1793, in part at least because he and his wife could no longer stand the strain of living with verbal attacks on his integrity in the press and at the Jacobins, or—and far more worrying—the threats of violence from the *sans-culottes*. His wife described how in the final days of his ministry she slept with a pistol under her pillow, intending to use it on herself should a crowd break into the ministerial *hôtel* and lay hands on her.[68] His resignation did little to ease the pressure. His papers were confiscated, and scoured for signs that

[65] Madame Roland, *Mémoires*, 75–80, 138–45.    [66] Madame Roland, *Mémoires*, 168.
[67] Hébert, *Le Père Duchesne*, Issue 202: 4–5; Issue 203: 2.
[68] Madame Roland, *Mémoires*, 41.

he had abused his ministerial powers. Anything that gave a whiff of corruption to Roland's ministry would be used against him.[69]

## THE DANGERS INCURRED BY A CAREER
## IN POLITICS IN 1793

It is hard to appreciate just why revolutionary politics became so polarized and bitter, if we do not take into account the extent to which the leaders, Girondins and Jacobins alike, were driven on by emotions. By 1793 the euphoric emotions of 1789 had long since dwindled. Patriotic fervour had not abated, though war had affected its character, making it more nationalist, less cosmopolitan. But by 1793 one emotion was fast assuming ever greater importance—this was fear. The revolutionary leaders were afraid the Revolution would fail (an emotion they could acknowledge to an extent, so long as it did not sound like defeatism) and afraid for their own lives (something they could not admit, certainly not publicly, and perhaps not even to themselves). These feelings coloured what they said and what they did. They stared blindly into the dark, anticipating attack from different quarters; uncertain from which direction the blow would fall, but increasingly sure that, sooner or later, fall it would.

The most obvious source of danger was reprisals and revenge attacks from royalists. The republican deputies were surrounded by hostility, both hidden and open. On the evening of the day in which the Convention condemned the king to death, one of the Jacobin deputies, Lepeletier de Saint-Fargeau, went to dine at *chez* Février, a modest restaurant at the former Palais-Royal. As he went to the counter to pay he encountered a stranger who asked him if he had been one of those who had voted for the death of the king. When Lepeletier answered yes, and declared he had voted according to his conscience, the man pulled out a sabre hidden under his great-coat and stabbed him; Lepeletier died some hours later. What particularly troubled the deputies was the semi-complicity of people in the restaurant. The restaurant had been packed; yet no one there had lifted a finger to apprehend the assassin, and he stayed there for some time, at his ease, talking to other customers. Later that evening he was even seen mingling with the crowd at the café de Foy (a centre of revolutionary fervour back in 1789 and where Desmoulins had once made the stirring speech urging the onlookers on to storm the Bastille) and again, no one had challenged him or seemed to have felt the need to call the authorities to apprehend the killer of the deputy. It was an incident that exposed the vulnerability of the deputies both to secret enemies in the crowd, and to the potential indifference—even hostility—of that same public which they ritually invoked.[70] An obvious precaution would have been to give deputies armed protection, but

---

[69] On the continuation of attacks on Roland after his resignation, see Reynolds, *Marriage and Revolution*, ch. 24.

[70] See Edmond Biré, *Journal d'un bourgeois de Paris pendant la terreur*, 5 vols (Paris: Perrin, 1895), 2: 1–20.

this would have made them inaccessible to the people, and therefore was seen as against virtue.

At the same time the assassination of a Jacobin deputy could be exploited polit-ically as a narrative of self-sacrifice for the public good, and thus evidence of the authenticity of the Jacobins' virtue. Madame Roland said that the most useful thing that Lepeletier ever did for the Jacobins was getting himself assassinated, en-abling them to make a patriotic martyr of him—she even intimated that the Jacobins themselves might have been behind his assassination in order to create a martyr out of a man they would not otherwise miss. She had every reason to resent the Jacobins' manipulation of their own public image, but this seems a little harsh. It is true that the Jacobins made political capital out of Lepeletier's death, and that Robespierre praised Lepeletier as a dead hero of virtue, along lines that recalled the old regime academies' eulogies of great men of virtue, but he could not bring him-self to do the same when Marat (a man he personally disliked) was murdered in his turn.[71] Moreover, when Basire proposed that anyone who harboured Lepeletier's assassin should be liable to the death penalty Robespierre strongly opposed him, and succeeded in having the proposal rejected. Despite his support for the execu-tion of the king, Robespierre was still opposed to the death penalty as a general principle, and particularly emphatic that no exception should be made on the grounds that the victim had been a deputy. There should be no special protection for deputies:

> I attack the basis of the motion itself; it is contrary to all principles. What, at the moment when you are effacing the death penalty from your penal code, you would reinstate it for a particular case! The eternal principles of justice are opposed to it. Moreover, why would you set aside the law to avenge a representative of the people? You would not do it for a simple citizen; and yet the assassination of a citizen is equal, in the eyes of the law, to the assassination of a public official.[72]

Enemies might also come in other guises. The Girondins were caught between the royalists who considered them to be ruthless Jacobins who had brought about the fall of the monarchy, and the *sans-culottes* who regarded them as traitors to the popular cause who had exploited their former leadership of the Jacobins to satisfy their thirst for power. The Earl of Lauderdale reported that he had entertained a large number of Girondins at his house at the time of the king's trial. In the course of a general discussion about pocket pistols several of them had produced their own concealed pistols for inspection. It transpired that all of them—with the exception of Brissot himself—were carrying arms with which to defend themselves.[73] In the early months of the Convention it was the Girondins who suffered most from fear of the *sans-culottes*. Yet in riding the tiger of popular militancy the Jacobins, too, were running a risk that popular violence might rebound on their heads, if they failed to satisfy the expectations of their key supporters amongst the popular militants.

---

[71] Robespierre, *Oeuvres*, 9: 249–52; Madame Roland, *Mémoires*, 360–1.
[72] Robespierre to the Convention, 21 January 1793, Robespierre, *Oeuvres*, 9: 255.
[73] Sydenham, *The Girondins*, 201–2.

But enemies could come from even closer to home. After the September massacres an ambitious deputy's most dangerous enemies might not be the soldiers of the enemy; nor the royalists, both open and hidden; nor even the militants of the Commune; but the so-called 'men of virtue', his fellow deputies, and in many cases, his former friends, whom he had to confront daily within the Convention itself. These, it seemed now, were potentially the most dangerous enemies of all—the enemies within. It was this knowledge that sharpened the edge of hostilities between the warring factions as they had to look in the eye men whom they believed were prepared to kill them.

## BEGINNINGS OF A LEGALIZED TERROR

It is against the backdrop of rising panic that the legislation that enabled the recourse to Terror began to be put into place. It was decreed in response to the outbreak of civil war in the Vendée, and the news of the crushing defeat of the French armies at Neerwinden. Days earlier the Revolutionary Tribunal was created, to try suspected counter-revolutionaries. The purpose of the Revolutionary Tribunal was, in the words of Danton, 'to frighten the conspirators'.[74] In the same month the first deputies *en mission* were sent out, and *comités de surveillance* were set up to monitor the movements of foreigners and to issue *certificats de civisme*; to be followed early the following month by the establishment of a Committee of Public Safety. On 19 March 1793 a decree was instituted which stated that anyone who engaged in armed rebellion and was found with 'arms in their hands' would be decreed an outlaw (*hors la loi*), brought before a military commission, and subject to execution without appeal. This was the single piece of legislation under which the great majority of the people who were executed during the Terror were condemned. It was a brutal law, but one that was in line with contemporary attitudes towards treason and the treatment of armed rebels in time of war. These were all provisions which the Jacobins wanted, but which were also backed by the Convention. The law of 19 March was drafted by the Committee of Legislation, led by Cambacérès, who was no Jacobin. A number of the Girondins voted for the decree of 19 March, a law which was subsequently used to arrest many of their number who had engaged in the federalist revolt.[75]

Godfrey's detailed study of the Revolutionary Tribunal points out that, on the first occasion when the creation of such a tribunal was raised in the Jacobins, Bentabole suggested that it could be used to try 'the former minister [Roland] and his accomplices'.[76] The indication that the Revolutionary Tribunal originated, at least in part, in suspicion of the Girondin ministry offers some support to the

---

[74] 6 April, *Archives parlementaires*, 61: 334. Strictly speaking the Tribunal was re-created, as one had operated from August to November 1792.

[75] Greer, *The Incidence of the Terror*, 14–15; 153. See also Jourdan, 'Les discours de la terreur'.

[76] 3 March 1793, Aulard, *Société des Jacobins*, 5: 64–5. See James Logan Godfrey, *Revolutionary Justice: A Study in the Organisation and Procedures of the Paris Tribunal, 1793–95* (Chapel Hill: University of North Carolina Press, 1951). Edelstein, *The Terror of Natural Right*, 136, and Reynolds, *Marriage and Revolution*, 253, both pick up on this point.

argument that the mutual distrust between the political factions had a significant impact on the origins of the Terror. Even so, it was a complex situation. The origins of the Revolutionary Tribunal must be seen in the context of the wider crisis; of popular pressure from the Paris militants who fully shared the Jacobins' suspicions; and the rising panic at the internal and external crisis, all of which were inextricable from the context of the war. If the Jacobins wanted Roland to be called to account it was partly because they attributed France's precarious situation to the policies of its leaders. It was also because they needed to demonstrate to the Paris militants the authenticity of their own dedication to the public good, by taking a hard line on politicians whom the militants themselves had found wanting. The holding of Roland personally responsible for the political failures of the previous months was a harsh and unfair judgement, but in time of war not so inexplicable. As Desfieux said in support of Bentabole's proposal, 'It is necessary to make laws that accord with the circumstances, and modify them in time of peace.'[77] The fact that the creation of the Revolutionary Tribunal was about something more fundamental than factional grudges is apparent from the readiness with which the deputies of the Convention accepted it. The Jacobins were in no position to force the creation of a judicial forum for their personal grievances on an unwilling Convention. Again, the Committee of Legislation was much involved in the process of creating the Revolutionary Tribunal. The establishment of the Revolutionary Tribunal took place in an atmosphere of fear and crisis, emotions which coloured the decisions of the Convention itself.[78]

[77] 3 March 1793, Aulard, *Société des Jacobins*, 5: 64–5.
[78] Godfrey stresses the context, pointing out that the establishment of the Tribunal took place against the backdrop of 'one of the critical periods of revolutionary history', a time of acute 'fear and anxiety': Godfrey, *Revolutionary Justice*, 4–7.

# 6

# A Conspiracy of Girondins

> Robespierre, in 1791 and 1792, had the most intimate friendships with Pétion, with Buzot, and even with Roland; how could he accuse them today without accusing himself?
>
> Gensonné, in preparation for his trial, 'Relations with Dumouriez'.[1]
>
> He was a good father, good husband, good citizen.
>
> Pétion on his childhood friend, Brissot.[2]

Here we turn to the final steps in the process that led to the politicians' terror. It was a process that culminated in the trial and execution of leading members of the Girondin faction, charged with having conspired with the monarchy and the foreign powers, and therefore of being guilty of *lèse-nation*.

## THE MOST FATAL FRIEND: GENERAL DUMOURIEZ

The fall of the monarchy was followed by a series of emigrations; many of the moderate leaders abandoned the political contest and fled for their lives across the frontiers. They included the Lameths and Duport; their defection gave confirmation to the view that they had been playing a double game all along. Henceforth, anyone seen to have been personally close to them during the time of their ascendancy in the Jacobins risked being tainted by association. Worse still was the defection of political leaders who had been entrusted with military roles. The most prominent of these were Lafayette and Dumouriez; their transformation from leaders of the Revolution to counter-revolutionaries had serious implications for the new French Republic. Treason in time of war has meant death in most times and cultures; the French revolutionary wars were no exception. The treasonous generals' actions appeared to confirm Robespierre's warning that war would empower military leaders whose loyalties would not be given to the Republic but to their own self-interest. Actual betrayals fed into the expectation of further betrayals to come. These events reinforced the narrative analysed by Kaiser, according to which the Revolution was bound to an endless

---

[1] Gensonné, 'Relations with Dumouriez', written in his hand, no date, in *Papiers inédits*, 2: 436–7.
[2] Jérome Pétion, 'Notice sur Brissot', in Brissot, *Mémoires*, 2: 370.

cycle of conspiracy.[3] The Jacobins' anxiety led them to subject the conduct of their current leaders to ever more intensive scrutiny, looking for the gap between their words and their conduct, trying to establish what they *truly* thought.

The most shattering betrayal of all was that of Dumouriez, who had been made commander-in-chief of the French army. After losing the battle of Neerwinden he changed sides, and attempted to march the army with which he had been entrusted on Paris to overthrow the Convention. Disaster was averted only by chance and the patriotism of the army. When his soldiers refused to follow him he fled across the frontier and joined France's enemies, taking with him a number of officers and nobles including the duc de Chartres, son of the duc d'Orléans. Dumouriez's choice bolstered the conviction that France's most dangerous enemies were not to be found amongst the invading armies, but amongst their own leaders, in positions of trust and authority. Because, prior to his military promotion, Dumouriez had been a political leader, the question of his conduct while a minister— and its lack of authenticity—became central. Never had the need to know the authentic motives of politicians been so intense, so pressing. Political leaders who had previously supported Dumouriez were now in a dangerous position, as the fallout from his defection ratcheted up the fear that they too would be called 'conspirators'. Dumouriez's treachery had a critical impact on the genesis of the politicians' terror.

Confirmation of Dumouriez's treachery reached Paris on the night of 31 March 1793. It added to the anxiety already raised by the successes of the rebels in the Vendée. On 1 April, Marat declared to the panicked Convention that the 'conduct of the members of the Convention, generals, ministers who have been denounced should be examined'. It was Birotteau, a Girondin supporter, who supported Marat's proposal and demanded that the Convention formalize it, on the grounds that 'at a moment in which liberty is menaced on all sides, all forms of inviolability cease'. Birotteau proposed, and the Convention agreed, that all deputies who came under suspicion should be liable to arrest.[4] It was this decree that ended the immunity of the politicians from arrest. Danton managed to get this decision modified somewhat a few days later, on 6 April, at a time when his own relations with Dumouriez were in question. It was agreed that the assent of the Convention itself would be needed to authorize the arrest of anyone serving as a deputy, general, or minister.[5]

The Girondins were the first to use this decree against their political rivals. They used it to denounce Sillery and d'Orléans—both of whom sat with the Montagnards—as accomplices of Dumouriez. The Girondins succeeded in obtaining their arrest, despite both men's frantic efforts to defend their conduct, and despite

---

[3] On the idea of an endless cycle of conspiracy, see Thomas Kaiser, 'Catilina's revenge: conspiracy, revolution, and historical consciousness from the Old Regime to the Consulate', in Campbell, Kaiser, and Linton, *Conspiracy in the French Revolution*.

[4] 1 April 1793, *Archives parlementaires*, 61: 63.

[5] 5 April 1793, *Archives parlementaires*, 61: 335.

support (unexpectedly) from Marat, who said there was no proof against them.[6] As the Jacobin Levasseur later pointed out, it was the Girondins who set the precedent for attacking the inviolability of the deputies by acting against d'Orléans—a motion proposed by Buzot and supported by Louvet and Lanjuinais. It was the Girondins, too, who used the new decree to send Marat before the Revolutionary Tribunal for an incendiary address put forward by the Jacobin Club which he had signed as president. The Girondins' action signalled the opening move of the struggle to the death between the factions. Had the Girondins succeeded, Marat could well have been the first deputy put to death; but he was acquitted, amidst scenes of enthusiastic support by the Parisian crowds.[7] The Girondins' attempt to eliminate Marat was a serious blunder. It set a precedent for deputies to use terror against one another; thus heightening the stakes in the factional stand-off. Henceforward the factions understood that if they were to hesitate to seek the death of their opponents, their opponents might not feel similar scruples.

The Girondins escalated hostilities by claiming that Danton had been in league with Dumouriez. There was some evidence to support this allegation. Danton had visited Dumouriez in Belgium in the final days before the general changed sides; he must have had some indication of what was in the wind, yet he said nothing to the Convention; he lay low until news of Dumouriez's betrayal emerged from other Jacobins. It looked to people at the time—and to historians since—as though Danton had been forewarned by Dumouriez of what he meant to do, and had delayed reporting this to the Convention until he knew which side would win before committing himself. Waiting for the cat to jump was hardly likely to be seen as an appropriate action for a 'man of virtue'. Over the previous year there had been a close connection between Danton and Dumouriez. A cloud of suspected corruption hung over Danton's dealings, and those of some of his friends, in the lucrative business of army contracting. There was evidence too of Danton, Delacroix, and other associates having engaged in plunder and theft in the wake of the army in Belgium; there were signs of a cover-up, the proof of which mysteriously disappeared. The men implicated with Danton—Fabre, Delacroix, Westermann—were to form the nucleus of the so-called Dantonist faction the following year. Madame Roland was convinced that, when a minister, Danton and his friend Fabre were involved in both corruption and larceny, and she did not trouble to hide her feelings from them.[8]

---

[6] 3 April 1793, *Archives parlementaires*, 61: 300–1; 6 April 1793, ibid., 61: 381. Ironically, Marat spoke in defence of Sillery and d'Orléans on the grounds that there was no proof that they were conspirators. Sillery attempted to defend himself on the grounds that his conduct was 'pure', but his position was made difficult by the emigration of his son-in-law, just as d'Orléans' credibility was fatally undermined by the emigration of his son. Ibid., 383.

[7] René Levasseur, *Mémoires de R. Levasseur (de la Sarthe) Ex-Conventionnel* (1829–31: this edition, Paris, Messidor/Éditions Sociales, 1989), 106–7. See also Mathiez, 'L'Immunité parlementaire sous la Révolution', in Albert Mathiez, *La Conspiration de l'étranger* (Paris: Armand Colin, 1918).

[8] On Danton's relations with Dumouriez and his activities in Belgium, see Hampson, *Danton*, 96–116. On Madame Roland's view of the involvement of Danton and Fabre in corruption, see Madame Roland, *Mémoires*, 75–81, 88–9, 138–45.

Unsurprisingly, Danton denied the Girondins' accusations; he countered with the charge that the true conspiracy had been between Roland and Dumouriez. The Rolands had consistently snubbed Danton, and repudiated his efforts at a *rapprochement*. Danton may have had it in mind that Roland was party to the Girondins' decision to thwart Danton's desire for a place on the patriot ministry. Perhaps his incrimination of Roland was motivated in part by revenge, but this seems unlikely: Danton was not a petty kind of person. It is more likely that the sticking point was fear for himself and the desire to protect his own reputation with the Jacobins and the Paris militants. Whaley suggests that Danton's mysterious disappearance during the days before Dumouriez's attempts to turn the army failed, was due to his positioning himself to come up on top as 'Dumouriez's right-hand man'.[9] If true (and Danton's silence has never been explained) then Danton was genuinely party to a treasonous conspiracy. Whatever the truth of this, fear for his own safety gave him every incentive to distract attention from his conduct by fastening the blame on the Girondins.

Nevertheless, it was the Girondins themselves who were the most vulnerable to the charge of complicity with Dumouriez, for they had supported him up to the eve of his defection.[10] In their defence they argued that they had been deceived by the general, that he had imposed upon their trust with a false persona, as he had deceived others; they had been guilty of misjudgement, no more. Hard evidence of the Girondins' complicity was lacking, yet doubts lingered. The Girondins' association with the general was capable of sinister interpretations for those who were prepared to believe the worst of them. Marat was at the head of their accusers; for him the Girondins were stained indelibly by their association with Dumouriez: 'it is Dumouriez who has impressed upon their foreheads this indelible mark'.[11] In the absence of any solid evidence that the Girondins had been party to Dumouriez's treachery, suspicion focused on ties of personal friendship between them, as indicative of a secret understanding. Brissot, who had so publicly repudiated both his political alliance and his personal friendship with Dumouriez the previous June, had patched matters up with him by October. Dumouriez was too important a man to have on-side for Brissot to let personal considerations get in the way of a mutually useful collaboration. After this date Brissot wrote at least three private letters to the general. The letters themselves, though friendly, were far from proof of any 'conspiracy' or even of an intimate friendship. Nor does Dumouriez seem to have responded to these overtures. Yet the very existence of these letters would be enough to damage Brissot's credibility.[12] After his arrest Brissot denied that such a

---

[9] See Whaley, *Radicals*, 130–6, esp. 136; also Sydenham, *The Girondins*, 159–62.

[10] See Richard Munthe Brace, 'General Dumouriez and the Girondins, 1792–1793', *American Historical Review*, 56, 3 (1951): 493–509; also Linton, 'Fatal friendships'.

[11] J.P. Marat, *Le Publiciste de la République française, par Marat l'ami du peuple, député à la Convention*, No. 201, 24 May 1793.

[12] The three existing letters from Brissot to Dumouriez while the latter was a general, dated 28 November, 2 December, and 9 December 1792, are in Brissot, *Correspondance et Papiers*, 314–20. In the first two letters Brissot refers to Dumouriez several times as 'my friend' and invokes their mutual friend, Gensonné. By the third letter it does not appear that Dumouriez has replied and Brissot's tone, though still amicable, is notably more constrained.

correspondence existed, stating that he had had 'no correspondence, no particular relations' with Dumouriez since the public break in their friendship in June 1792.[13] Ironically, in later years Dumouriez himself was just as keen to dissociate himself from any suggestion that he had been a friend of the 'terrible Brissot'.[14]

On 3 April, the day when the Convention heard that Dumouriez had arrested its emissaries and handed them over to the Austrians, Robespierre made an impassioned denunciation of Brissot as an accomplice in the 'plots' of Dumouriez: 'I declare that the interests of the *patrie* demand that Brissot must be unmasked'. An essential component of that complicity, as Robespierre envisaged it, was personal friendship: 'I have stated that I was absolutely unwilling to deliberate with the counsellors, the friends of Dumouriez. Well then, never has Dumouriez, never have the enemies of liberty, had a more faithful friend, a more useful defender than Brissot...I will prove that Brissot and Dumouriez were bonded together by their shared self-interest.'[15] Robespierre was heard amidst angry scenes and threats of dagger-blows, to which he responded by turning and indicating David's painting of the martyred body of Lepeletier, which hung on the wall behind and above where Robespierre stood. The point of the gesture was to demonstrate his own authenticity as a man of virtue, which he was ready to prove by sacrificing his life if necessary.

Immediately Brissot jumped up to counter the accusations of complicity with 'the crimes of Dumouriez'. He denied having had any personal relationship with Dumouriez, or that he had known Dumouriez prior to the general's appointment as a minister, or that he had had a hand in that appointment. It was, he said, the queen who had been responsible for all ministerial appointments, 'and assuredly Robespierre will not maintain that I had liaisons with that woman'.[16] Later Brissot composed a written denial, in which he sought to turn the allegation of corruption back on the Jacobins:

> He [Robespierre] accuses me of distributing places, and I affirm that it is Roberspierre [sic], Danton and their party who have been distributing them since 10 August...I defy anyone to give the names of six people who owe their places to my supposed favour; whereas the Jacobins have swarmed over everything, money and places...As a republican since I reached the age of reason, I have devoted myself to that moral austerity which requires that everything be given to talent and virtue, and nothing through favour.

---

[13] Brissot, 'Réponse au Rapport de Saint-Just', in *Mémoires*, 2: 259. When he was subsequently interrogated Brissot admitted writing one letter to Dumouriez when he was a general, but stated that this was an official document on behalf of the Diplomatic Committee, in November 1792: 'Interrogatoire de Brissot', in Brissot, *Correspondance et Papiers*, 381.

[14] Dumouriez, *Mémoires du Général Dumouriez*, 11: 426.

[15] 3 April 1793, *Archives parlementaires*, 62: 271–2.

[16] 3 April 1793, *Archives parlementaires*, 61: 275–6. A week later Vergniaud also defended himself against Robespierre's allegations. Like Brissot, Vergniaud was at pains to deny that he had met Dumouriez privately. Vergniaud admitted to having been present at a private dinner with the general on his return from Belgium but said that the meeting had been by chance. Nor had he and Dumouriez written letters to one another. 10 April, *Archives parlementaires*, 61: 545–6.

Still Roberspierre [*sic*] accuses me of being the leader of a party, when no such party or leader exists.

Leader of a party! Me, a solitary man, who knows barely forty members of the assembly, rarely appears at the tribune, doesn't frequent the clubs, the sections or the committees, doesn't receive or visit anyone, confined to the society of three or four friends who are as incorruptible as they are enlightened...[17]

This self-portrait of Brissot as an aloof and self-contained loner bears little resemblance to the man his contemporaries described as gregarious and an inveterate networker. Yet to have admitted that he was a man with many friends in the Convention would have been tantamount to a confession that he was exploiting the Revolution for his own benefit.

Though Brissot was not an intimate of the general, Gensonné was, and their friendship came under intense scrutiny. Even before Dumouriez's final defection, Desfieux had denounced Gensonné's correspondence with Dumouriez in the Jacobin Club. For Desfieux, the mere fact that the correspondence existed suggested that Gensonné was incriminated in Dumouriez's machinations:

You know of Dumouriez's liaisons with the Girondin faction. Gensonné is an intimate friend of this general; he corresponds with him, I do not know the contents of the correspondence between Gensonné and Dumouriez, but Ducos assured me that these two men are connected by a close friendship, and that they write to one another.

For the rest, would Gensonné have abruptly left the Convention, to join with Dumouriez, if a plot had not been hatched against liberty?[18]

In this correspondence, later seized, Gensonné had addressed Dumouriez as 'my dear general' and signed himself off by embracing him 'with all his soul, with all his heart'.[19] In fact this correspondence seems to have ceased several months before, at the time of the king's trial. Notwithstanding this, in Amar's official indictment of the Girondins, which would later form the basis of the case against them, Gensonné's letters to the general were to be exaggerated into a 'daily correspondence' and cited as evidence of the Girondins' 'intimate relations with Dumouriez'.[20] Although Gensonné himself was one of the most subdued of the Girondin network in the months leading up to their arrest, the fact of his friendship with Dumouriez in itself ensured that he came under particular suspicion.

---

[17] Brissot, *J.P. Brissot, député à la Convention, sur la dénonciation de Roberspierre* [*sic*], *et sur l'Adresse prêtée aux 48 Sections de Paris*, 8–9. The text of Brissot's defence was also published in *Le Patriote Français*, No. 1346, Saturday 20 April 1793. The journal was at that point being edited by Brissot's friend Girey. Brissot had previously replied in the journal to allegations that he was still dictating its opinions, by stating that Girey was independent in his editorial decisions: No. 1329, Wednesday 3 April 1793.

[18] 17 March 1793, Aulard, *Société des Jacobins*, 5: 92.

[19] See Roger Brouillard, 'Dumouriez et les Girondins: correspondance inedité de Gensonné', *Revue historique de Bordeaux et du department de la Gironde*, 36 (1943): 35–47; and Bertrand Favreau, 'Gensonné ou la fatalité de la Gironde', in Furet and Ozouf, *La Gironde et les Girondins*, 426.

[20] 3 October 1793, *Archives parlementaires*, 75: 529. See also Billaud-Varenne's speech against the Girondins, in which he claimed that Gensonné was 'the most intimate friend of Dumouriez'; that he had conducted a secret correspondence with the general, and had (with the help of Lebrun at the War Office) removed incriminating parts of Dumouriez's correspondence: 13 July 1793, *Le Moniteur*, 17, 200.

On 2 June 1793 his name headed the list of those accused, coming even before that of Brissot. [21]

From his prison cell Gensonné wrote a defence of his friendship with Dumouriez. He said it had dated from the time when he, like many others, believed in the good faith of the general. He did not seek to deny their friendship, but he countered with a challenge to the idea that friendship was evidence of conspiracy. He said that if sincere—though as it transpired, misguided—friendship was a crime, then all citizens equally should be held guilty if they had ever been friends with someone who later turned out to be a counter-revolutionary. Gensonné pointed out that Robespierre himself had once been the intimate friend of Brissot and Pétion, so that to accuse them of friendship as a sign of bad faith was to accuse himself:

> It is evident that this kind of censure on the basis of connections founded on affection and confidence which a man may have during the course of his life, should weigh equally on the heads of all citizens. To invoke this with regard to some, when one wants to liberate others from its constraints, that would be to add to the immorality of the principle in itself all the most odious absurdity and the most atrocious privilege.
>
> Ah indeed! Robespierre was for a long time the intimate friend and confidant of the Lameths; he knew all the stratagems that they put into play at the beginning of the revolution; he was party to the secrets of their intrigues, and he became the heir of the popularity which they had acquired. Would he want his liaisons of that earlier time to expose him at a later time to suspicions that he had conspired with them?…Would he also wish, because he was the dupe of Mirabeau, because he asked for and obtained the honours of the Panthéon [for Mirabeau], even at a time when [Mirabeau's] immorality was well known to him, and when he must have at least had doubts about [Mirabeau's] corruption, that he could be considered today as [Mirabeau's] accomplice? [22]

Did Robespierre's conscience prick him when he read this reminder that these men had once been his friends? We do not know; but we do know that Gensonné's defence of friendship was found amongst Robespierre's personal papers.

## THE SECRET HISTORY OF THE GIRONDINS

On 17 May 1793 Desmoulins published a *Fragment of the Secret History of the Revolution* (later also known as *L'Histoire des Brissotins*) with the assistance, possibly the collaboration, of Robespierre. This was a much more comprehensive attack than Desmoulin's *Brissot Unmasked* of the previous year. It purported to be an exposé of the real motives behind the words and actions of Brissot and his friends. The political failings of the Girondins were depicted as something much more than the result of incompetence or recklessness: Desmoulins saw a more sinister purpose at work. Whereas *Brissot Unmasked* had focused on the supposed perfidy

---

[21] See Favreau, 'Gensonné ou la fatalité de la Gironde', 426–9.

[22] Gensonné, 'Relations with Dumouriez', 436–7.

of one individual, this new attack went beyond Brissot himself, to include the network of Brissotins: all were implicated in what Desmoulins openly characterized as a conspiracy. Brissot, of course, would deny that there was any proof of such a plot, yet, as Desmoulins pointed out, turning Brissot's own tactics against him, Brissot himself had not been so particular when he argued for the existence of the Austrian Committee on the basis of little hard evidence. The point about conspiracies, as Brissot himself had said, was that few conspirators were so inept as to leave compromising materials lying around. 'It is absurd to ask for hard evidence and judicial proofs that one has never had. Not even in the conspiracy of Catiline, for conspirators have never been in the habit of letting evidence against themselves be open to discovery.'[23] To give substance to his claims, Desmoulins recounted a new narrative of the history of the whole Revolution, one that turned on a rereading of the words and actions of Brissot's group, to uncover their secret meaning. Many of the specific allegations, such as the claim that the Brissotins were in league with the foreign powers, were already familiar, but now Desmoulins wove all these together to construct a collective meaning for seemingly disparate events. Step by step, he reinterpreted past events of the Revolution in the light of his revelations. According to his account, the Girondins were dissembling when they claimed to be motivated by a love of virtue. On the contrary, their approach to politics was characteristic of the most suspect style of old regime politics: they conducted their politics in private; they used their positions of power to further their own self-interest and that of their friends, dispensing patronage and places and using money from public funds to support their nefarious activities; their activities were evidence of corruption, ambition, and egoism.

Desmoulins was given access to Roland's confiscated papers to help give substance to his attack. One such piece of evidence was a letter from Brissot to Madame Roland when her husband was serving for the second time as Minister of the Interior. In it Brissot excused himself from coming to dinner, on the grounds that he himself was giving a regular dinner on Thursdays, to which Clavière would come, and that he hoped Roland also would be able to attend. Brissot had added, 'I send [Madame Roland], for her husband and for Lanthenas, a list of patriots to place: because one should always have such a list ready to hand'.[24] Desmoulins used this letter as proof that the Girondins were resorting to 'behind closed doors' politics based on patronage and the influence of friends. He rephrased the letter to make Brissot's action appear worse by having him state that no one but the people recommended by him should be given posts.[25]

No one was better placed than Desmoulins to give the 'inside story' of his former fellow revolutionaries, now his enemies, for they had worked closely together, shared the same political experiences, and even attended the same private dinners—such as those at the home of Sillery, in the salon of Apollo, which

---

[23] Desmoulins, *Fragment de l'histoire secrète de la Révolution (Histoire des Brissotins)*, in *Oeuvres de Camille Desmoulins*, 305.

[24] Brissot, *Correspondance et Papiers*, 293.

[25] Desmoulins, *Histoire des Brissotins*, 326, note 1.

Desmoulins (once a frequent visitor himself) now depicted as a den of Orléanist intrigue.[26] If Desmoulins remembered, as his pen traced the damning words, that Brissot had once been his good friend and a witness at his wedding, he adroitly avoided any mention of that awkward fact. Instead he dwelt on Brissot's friendships with tainted men such as Dumouriez, Lafayette, Bailly, and d'Orléans, men who had all now been recast as counter-revolutionaries. These friendships pointed to the guilt of the Girondins by association. Most damning of all was Desmoulins' allegation that Brissot and his friends were secretly working for Pitt and the foreign powers, and that all along they had secretly been working for the overthrow of the very Revolution that they purported to serve. In time of war this was tantamount to treason:

> I bring to light that the party of the Right in the Convention, and principally the leaders, are nearly all partisans of royalty, accomplices in the treasons of Dumouriez and Beurnonville, directed by the agents of Pitt, of d'Orléans and of Prussia, and of having wanted to divide France into twenty or thirty federalist republics, or rather to overturn it, for never in history has there been a conspiracy for which there is more proof, and with a host of [still] more violent presumptions, than this Conspiracy, which I call that of the Brissotins because Brissot has been at the heart of it. [27]

With the *Fragment of the Secret History of the Revolution*, the outlines of the case against the Girondins were brought into being. The subsequent charges made against them when they were eventually brought before the Revolutionary Tribunal would owe much to Desmoulins' narrative.

## THE FALL OF THE GIRONDINS

After the disaster of Dumouriez's defection, attacks on the Girondins increased. During April the sections continuously petitioned both the Convention and the Jacobin Club with two main demands: the removal of the deputies associated with Dumouriez and the setting of a maximum price on essential supplies, above all bread. Threats and denunciations of the Right in the Convention were being made daily by the political leaders of the Commune and the sections. For their part the Girondins fought back with attempts to curb the popular movement, impeaching Marat, setting up a Commission of Twelve to look into the activities of the Commune, and issuing incendiary challenges in the Convention and the press. Robespierre played a leading role in the Jacobins' war of words with the Girondin leaders. Louvet's denunciation of him appears to have destroyed any lingering scruples Robespierre had felt about engaging in personal attacks. He denounced Roland as the source of corruption, a man who 'had immense sums in his hands', exercised government on behalf of his friends, and manipulated public opinion; all without public accountability. As so often with Robespierre, he pitched his attack in emotive

---

[26] Desmoulins, *Fragment de l'histoire secrète*, 309.
[27] Desmoulins, *Fragment de l'histoire secrète*, 306.

terms, emphasizing the danger to himself, and his willingness to suffer martyrdom in the cause of the Revolution. He declared that Brissot, Roland, and their friends were ready to assassinate him for his resolution in exposing their perfidy. The Jacobins responded with enthusiastic applause and cries of 'we shall perish with you under the blades of the Brissotins'.[28]

As the May days passed the Girondins felt under intense threat. In late May Valazé urged the group attending his salon to arm themselves. He wrote notes to upwards of thirty-eight men, one of which, unfortunately for him, was seized by the Committee of General Security and found its way into the hands of Marat, who used it to denounce 'a plot' hatched at Valazé's salon. Valazé was confronted by the note, which had been intended for Lacaze, and in which was written: 'Come in arms to the Convention at precisely ten in the morning; warn as many of your colleagues as you can. Only cowards will not come.' Valazé admitted that he had written the note, claiming that his motive had been self-defence against the *sans-culottes*. Lacaze then said that he had not received the note; it had been obtained by corrupting the porter at his house, but that regardless of the note he had independently resolved to come to the Convention armed with pistols, as he would do on any occasion when he was threatened by scoundrels.[29] It was a wild plan, motivated by fear, but it gave some credibility to the claim that the Girondins were prepared to use violence against the Jacobin leaders.

The Girondins were not the only deputies under pressure from the popular movement. The sections and popular societies were beside themselves with anger at the continuing food shortages, and were ready to turn on Jacobin deputies too if their private conduct did not tally with their public utterances. It was particularly injudicious to be seen to be eating well while the people were hungry. Not even the leading Jacobins were immune from this kind of criticism. On 12 February Saint-Just was embarrassed by a petition from the sections of Paris that singled him out as a *bon viveur*, living a life at odds with his public persona: 'When the people know that in the popular assemblies, the orators who harangue and deliver the finest discourses and the best lessons, dine well every day... Of this number is the citizen Saint-Just, lift high the odious mask with which he covers himself.'[30] It was further suggested that Saint-Just, as a way of regaining the militants' approbation, had encouraged them to insist on the Convention bowing to their demands. He stepped forward quickly to defend himself against such an allegation. Hardly any of the Jacobins condoned the threat of popular violence against the deputies. Even Marat took a dim view of intimidation of the Convention by the protestors.[31]

---

[28] 12 December 1792, Aulard, *Société des Jacobins*, 4: 574–5.

[29] Mortimer-Ternaux, *Histoire de la terreur*, 7: 252–4. At the trial of the Girondins Valazé spoke of how he had acted out of fear of assassination by the Parisian militants, only to be counter-attacked by Hébert, who accused him of spreading a 'calumny' against the Commune: Walter, *Actes du Tribunal révolutionnaire*, 286–7.

[30] Saint-Just, *Oeuvres complètes*, 408–9; *Archives parlementaires*, 58: 480.

[31] See Marat's interventions on this occasion, and his attribution of the petition to 'aristocratic intrigue', *Archives parlementaires*, 58: 476, 479–80.

Nevertheless, as a police spy reported, 'the Jacobins know only too well that the people cannot be resisted when one needs them'.[32]

On 31 May and 2 June militants from the sections organized a full-scale insurrection to pressurize the Convention to agree to the exclusion and arrest of the Girondins. Despite protests from deputies at the use of intimidation to violate the national representation, the insurrection culminated in the purging of twenty-nine Girondin deputies from the Convention, along with two ministers, Clavière and Lebrun. Garat, then Minister of the Interior, attributed the masterminding of the insurrection to a secret group that met at the café Corazza, though others ridiculed him for this conspiracy theory.[33] The Jacobin deputies did not take an active part in these events. On the contrary, there is evidence that they, too, were in fear of the Paris militants that day.[34] For Robespierre and the Jacobins it was another moment of choice. They might disapprove of the violence of the militants, but were they prepared to profit from it, to come to power themselves? On 7 June Camille Desmoulins read an official address to the Paris Jacobins which he had composed on their behalf to be sent to the provincial clubs, explaining the reasons why the arrest of the Girondins had been necessary for the public good. In it he repeated many of the allegations that he had previously made in the *Fragment of the Secret History of the Revolution* about the extent of the Girondins' conspiracy. He brushed aside the difficulty of there being little proof by citing the example of Dumouriez, who had acted so fast that had the revolutionaries waited to gather evidence of his perfidy they would have been overwhelmed. He also referred to the Girondins themselves, who had not scrupled to act without proof when making the case for war on the basis of unsubstantiated stories of a conspiracy by the Austrian Committee. He furthermore accused the Girondins of alienating France from the foreign powers, and 'having pitched us into war with all Europe, having covered France in mourning, the colonies in ruins, and caused the deaths of two hundred thousand men'.[35]

By 14 June Robespierre had revised his view of the significance of the insurrection when he stated at the Jacobins that on 31 May a pact had been sealed between the people and the 'patriotic part' of the Convention. 'The people', for its part, 'must defend the pure part of the Convention, at a time when it still has obstacles to overcome'. As for the role of the Convention, he continued, 'the Convention has spoken, it has proved that it is free, that it has taken the people of Paris under its protection against those who have been led astray by tyranny'.[36]

The excluded Girondin deputies were placed under loose house arrest. There was considerable uncertainty as to what should be done with them. At this stage

---

[32] Cited by Doyle, *Oxford History of the French Revolution*, 229.

[33] Morris Slavin, *The Making of an Insurrection: Parisian Sections and the Gironde* (Cambridge, MA Harvard University Press, 1986), 87.

[34] Slavin concludes not only that the militants in the sections took a leading role in events, but that their threat to Jacobins should they too fail to fulfil the militants' demands was not an idle one: Slavin, *The Making of an Insurrection*, 162. See also Whaley, *Radicals*, 150–6.

[35] Desmoulins, 'La Société des amis de la liberté et de l'égalité de Paris, aux citoyens des départements sur l'insurrection du 31 mai', in Aulard, *Société des Jacobins*, 5: 235–41.

[36] Robespierre, *Oeuvres*, 9: 559.

there was still room for negotiation, and there seemed good reason to hope that the Girondins would eventually be readmitted to the Convention. The initial report on the arrest of the Girondins, given by Barère on 6 June on behalf of the newly-formed Committee of Public Safety, was relatively moderate, deliberately vague and judicious. The culpability of the men arrested 'was still uncertain', he said, and it was not for the 'men of the Mountain' to put themselves above the truth, and pass premature judgement on the accused. 'It is for France, it is for the entire republic, to judge their case.'[37] But the flight of some of the deputies, and the reckless involvement of several of them in an armed revolt against the Convention, were to make any compromise highly unlikely.

A more comprehensive report was made by Saint-Just on 8 July. He too was now an associate member of the newly formed Committee of Public Safety. This report went a little further than that of Barère in accepting the idea of a Girondin conspiracy. The Girondins, Saint-Just said, had been prepared to use violence against the Jacobin deputies. He referred darkly to 'the secret meetings at the home of Valazé, where the detainees met, where the project was formed to assassinate a part of the Convention'.[38] Yet the report was still relatively moderate in that it made an attempt to prove the charges. It was also careful to limit the numbers of men accused of actual involvement in the conspiracy. Saint-Just said: 'You must distinguish between those detained: most were misled; and who amongst us can flatter himself that he has never been deceived? The true culprits are those who fled, and you owe them nothing more, for they have brought desolation on their *patrie*.' The final advice to the Convention was notably pragmatic: 'Proscribe them, not for what they said but for what they did; pass judgement on the others and pardon the greater number.'[39] Nine men who had fled from arrest to instigate the revolt were decreed *hors la loi*. These were Buzot, Barbaroux, Gorsas, Lanjuinais, Salle, Louvet, Bergoeing, Birotteau, and Pétion. There were grounds of accusation against a further five men who were 'suspected of complicity with those who had fled and engaged in rebellion': Gensonné, Guadet, Vergniaud, Mollevault, and Gardien. Roland was not mentioned in the list of those to be accused. Nor was Brissot: he had escaped arrest but not been involved in the armed uprising. He had been under arrest since his recapture at Moulin. Saint-Just's conclusions were fairly conciliatory. The deputies who had engaged in an armed uprising against the Convention were to be proscribed, possibly also some of the men associated with them. Yet the overall concern was to limit the numbers. Half the excluded deputies should be brought back into the Convention. The view amongst some in the Jacobins was that Saint-Just had not gone far enough: the report was too moderate.[40]

---

[37]  Barère's report on the Girondins, 6 June 1793. *Moniteur*, 16: 585. See Sydenham, *The Girondins*, 21.

[38]  Saint-Just, 'Rapport au nom du Comité de salut public sur les trente-deux membres de la Convention détenus en vertu du décret du 2 juin', in Saint-Just, *Oeuvres complètes*, 472, 477.

[39]  Saint-Just, 'Rapport sur les trente-deux membres', 476–8.

[40]  Châles complained that, in their reports to the Convention, Saint-Just (also Lindet and Billaud-Varenne) had forgotten the two men most implicated in the 'counter-revolutionary plot', Roland and Gensonné. 22 July 1793, Aulard, *Société des Jacobins*, 5: 310.

## THE POLITICIANS' TERROR BEGINS

The Jacobins of the summer of 1793 used the same rhetorical strategies previously employed by the triumvirate and the Girondins themselves: the denunciation of a fellow revolutionary for duplicity, lack of virtue, secret ambition—and complicity with the enemies of the Revolution. This was the rhetoric that Lameth had once used to rip Mirabeau's reputation to shreds; the same that Brissot had used to savage Barnave's credibility as a patriot; the same that Brissot and his friends had used to undermine Robespierre's opposition to the war by intimating that he was in the pay of the 'Austrian Committee'. The Jacobins of 1793 simply did it more efficiently, comprehensively, and to more devastating effect.

Still the Jacobins hesitated to use this rhetoric to kill. What happened to change the attitude of the Jacobins, who up till then had seemed capable of distinguishing between the leaders amongst their political enemies and the rank and file who were 'misled'? In early July the fate of the rank and file of the Girondins (if not those involved in the revolt) still hung in the balance. It was sealed by an act of violence—the assassination of Marat by Charlotte Corday.[41] This took place on 13 July, five days after Saint-Just's report; it changed the whole tenor of the prosecution of the Girondins. Corday had initially planned to assassinate Marat at the Convention. Not finding him there, she gained entry to his home by posing as a 'patriot' and took advantage of his trust to stab him. Corday believed her action would end the violence and terror. It had the opposite effect. It generated more fear in the minds of the Jacobin leaders, fear for their own lives, and fear for the survival of the Revolution. (They did not necessarily distinguish between the two.) This made them pitiless in using the weapons of terror to destroy their enemies.

At the same time, the Jacobin leaders immediately recognized the possibility of making political capital out of Marat's reputation. Augustin Robespierre wrote that the Jacobins should seize the chance to 'demaratize Marat' in the eyes of the public, for it had now been demonstrated that Marat 'lived in a Spartan manner, that he spent nothing on himself and that he gave all that he had to those who asked him for help'.[42] These revelations about his private life thus *proved* his authentic virtue. Death froze Marat's identity. There was no longer any risk that he would tarnish his own reputation by ambition or corruption. The embargo against visual depictions of political leaders that might glorify them did not apply to a dead man. In death Marat was transfigured: he became a revolutionary martyr. Like Lepeletier before him, Marat's dead body was painted by David. The iconic

---

[41] See Mazeau's study of the assassination of Marat and how this was represented: Guillaume Mazeau, *Le Bain de l'histoire: Charlotte Corday et l'attentat contre Marat, 1793–2009* (Seyssel: Champ Vallon, 2009). Mazeau argues (107–9) that the impact of this event has been underestimated, and that the reaction of the Jacobins and the *sans-culottes* to the murder of Marat should be interpreted in terms of a 'politics of emotions', pointing to the way in which men like Hébert used different registers of emotive language in two separate spheres of politics: as an official of the Commune he sought to temper the anger of the *sans-culottes*, as editor of *Le Père Duchesne* he sought to whip up their fury.

[42] Augustin Robespierre to Buissart, Paris, 15 July 1793, Robespierre, *Correspondance de Maximilien et Augustin Robespierre*, 174–5.

painting would hang alongside the image of the dead Lepeletier, in the Convention, behind the tribune for speakers.[43]

The ongoing federalist revolt also had serious consequences for the fate of the Girondins. On 13 July the Girondin insurgents at Caen had been defeated with relative ease. But federalist protests were spreading to other parts of the country, and in some areas, most notably Lyon, Marseille, and Toulon, were shading into outright counter-revolution.[44] The fact that escaped Girondins were inciting an armed uprising appeared to Jacobins, at a time of war and civil war, to be an act of treason. This explains their hard-line attitude towards the leaders of the revolt, including Pétion, Barbaroux, and Buzot, but not the inclusion on the list of the accused deputies who had not fled—including Gensonné and Vergniaud. Lauze-Deperret and Fauchet were implicated by Corday, who had sought their help when she arrived in Paris to pursue her plan to assassinate Marat. Though neither man, nor indeed Barbaroux, who had recommended her from Caen, seems to have had any idea of what Corday intended: to the Jacobins it appeared that a plot was afoot to assassinate Jacobin leaders, and that Corday (being a mere woman) must have been acting at the instigation of the rebels. Barbaroux had written a letter for Corday to give to Lauze-Deperret. It was nothing to do with Marat; rather, it was a letter of patronage with a view to obtaining a pension for an *émigré* nun. Yet patronage itself was viewed as suspicious, particularly when it was exercised on behalf of an *émigré*, so the letter was viewed as implicating Barbaroux as a patron of Corday.[45] Lauze-Deperret and Fauchet denied involvement, but their pleas were ignored.[46] Thus two new and serious allegations, of federalist revolt and assassination plots, were added to the other claims about conspiracy.

A week is a long time in politics. In revolutionary politics it can be an eternity. By the time that Billaud-Varenne spoke on 15 July, two days after Marat's assassination, his account of the Girondin conspiracy had become much more sinister than the one given by Saint-Just the previous week. Billaud-Varenne identified a concerted, active, and long-standing conspiracy, and included the names of more suspects. He traced 'the plan of a conspiracy which appears to embrace the whole republic'. He conceded that there were few formal proofs since 'conspirators work in the shadows' but their plots could be uncovered by means of 'a simple moral conviction', and by observing how far their plans were in conformity with those of other conspirators.[47]

---

[43] The deputies frequently invoked the deaths of Lepeletier and of Marat. On Lepeletier's portrait see Donna M. Hunter, 'Swordplay: Jacques-Louis David's painting of Le Peletier de Saint-Fargeau on his deathbed', in James A.W. Heffernan (ed.), *Representing the French Revolution: Literature, Historiography, and Art* (Lebanon, NH: University Press of New England, 1992). On the death of Marat see the documents in Jacques Guilhaumou (ed.), *La Mort de Marat* (Paris: Éditions complexe, 1989). On the representation of the dead Marat, see Mazeau, *Le Bain de l'histoire*.

[44] On the federalist revolt see Paul R. Hanson, *The Jacobin Republic Under Fire: the Federalist Revolt in the French Revolution* (University Park: Pennsylvania State University Press, 2003).

[45] Letter from Barbaroux, 7 July, *Archives parlementaires*, 68, 720.

[46] Fauchet vehemently denied having even met Corday, but his protests were ignored. See his letter to the Convention, in *Papiers inédits*, 3: 255–7.

[47] Billaud-Varenne's report 'sur les trente-deux membres décrétés d'arrestation dans la journée du 2 juin', 15 July 1793, *Moniteur*, 17, 198–9.

Nevertheless, for some time the Jacobin leaders remained reluctant to cross the Rubicon and send the Girondins to their deaths. The Girondin leaders continued in prison for four months, over the summer and early autumn. During that time the Republic struggled under a series of military disasters, together with the expansion of the federalist revolt. On 2 September news arrived in Paris that Toulon with its naval bases had been delivered up to the British by French royalists; an event that offered confirmation of the links between (some) federalists and royalism. The Jacobin leaders were under intense pressure from the Paris militants and the radical journalists led by Hébert to demonstrate their own commitment by taking a hard line on the 'Girondin conspirators'. On 20 August Hébert was defeated in an attempt to become Minister of the Interior. He thereafter redoubled his efforts to be the leading spokesman for the Paris militants. Through his domination of the Commune, the Cordeliers Club, and his journal *Le Père Duchesne*, Hébert was rapidly becoming a force to be reckoned with in Paris politics. On 4 September a renewed demonstration by thousands of militants used threats and intimidation to coerce the Convention into imposing economic controls, using terror on those deemed to be the Revolution's enemies, and putting the imprisoned deputies on trial. In response the Convention voted through a series of measures that would be used to implement terrorist practices, which we shall look at more closely in the following chapter. It was in large part to appease the militants that the decision was taken to put the Girondins on trial.

Thus the Jacobins embarked on what was to be the first of the trials of revolutionary factions. The factional trials were the place where the Jacobin leaders intervened directly in the legal process. They were the accusers. They were witnesses to the conduct of the accused. They wrote the narratives that characterized the accused as conspirators. They knew personally the people they accused; they had worked with them over several years; shared the same intense patriotic fervour; in many cases they had once been friends. The trial of the Girondins was the moment at which the Jacobins chose terror in a very direct and personal sense; looking into the eyes of people they knew; people whom they now sought to condemn to death. The accused, for their part, used the same narrative themes, the same language of virtue and conspiracy; conceiving of revolutionary politics in the same way, as a matter of the culpability or innocence of the leaders. It is hard to speculate with any certainty on what might have happened had the Girondins and not the Jacobins been the victors in the political struggle; but the previous attacks of the Girondins on Marat, Sillery, and d'Orléans suggest that a similar scenario might well have developed, though one in which the identities of accused and accusers would have been reversed.

The trial of the Girondin leaders was a 'political trial' in that the members of one faction decided to destroy another, for the 'public good'. It was characterized by fear shared by the men carrying it out. If the Jacobins failed to convict their own lives could be at stake. Rival politicians whose virtue was vindicated could easily retaliate by turning the tables and accusing their accusers. This had happened when Marat had been acquitted by the Revolutionary Tribunal; the verdict in his favour rebounded on the Girondins who had engineered his arrest. This knowledge made the Jacobins ruthless. It also led to an increase in the number of people included in the trial. Once the Jacobins decided to embark on terror and to exterminate their political enemies, any friend of their enemies who was left alive was likely to seek revenge. It could be safer, then, to kill anyone who might pose a threat in the future. This was the brutal logic behind the trial of the Girondins. A similar rationale would characterize all the decimations of political factions during the period of the Terror. The point of the trial was not to prove the guilt of the Girondins, but to bring about their deaths, and to make the case look vaguely credible.

It remained to decide who was to appear on the list of those to be sent for trial. There was considerable uncertainty about whom to include, with names added and struck off even up to the last minute. Several of the men who figured late in the day as members of the 'Girondin party' had had limited political connections with the Girondin leaders.[48] In some instances friendship (above all the decision to be publicly loyal to proscribed Girondins) was a factor in whether or not individuals were listed among the 'Girondins'. This seems to have been the case, for example, with Ducos and his brother-in-law Boyer-Fonfrède, both of whom were intimate friends of Vergniaud from Bordeaux. By temperament both men were closer to the Jacobins than the Girondins, and had often voted against Girondin measures, with no diminution of their friendship. It seems to have been primarily their courageous and outspoken personal loyalty to Vergniaud that led to their being included on the list of Girondins, and sharing his fate.[49]

Friendship alone, however, did not necessarily result in conspiracy allegations and execution. Brissot's friend Souque accompanied Brissot on his flight from imprisonment and tried to help him escape; they were caught together. Brissot wrote asking for Souque's life to be spared, claiming that Souque had acted out of friendship alone, and 'a generous friend should not be punished for his devotion'.[50] Souque had known Brissot from the Jacobin Club, yet he was not a political activist. He was interrogated, imprisoned, yet escaped the guillotine and was released after 9 Thermidor. Lanthenas, a good friend of Roland and of Brissot, was also arrested. Yet he too escaped death, in large part because he would not support the federalist revolt. Friendship alone was not enough for people to be put on the proscription lists by the Jacobins, if it was unaccompanied by any political involvement, especially any attempt to attack the credibility of the Girondins' accusers.

Did the Jacobins genuinely believe that the Girondins were involved in a conspiracy against the Revolution? To some extent they probably did, as did the Paris militants. To understand why clever men who had seen only a limited conspiracy in early June claimed to have uncovered a much more extensive one a month later, we need to acknowledge that they were driven more by fear and anxiety than by

[48] Sydenham, *The Girondins*, 20–38.

[49] See Claude G. Bowers, *Pierre Vergniaud, Voice of the French Revolution* (New York: Macmillan, 1950).

[50] 'Letter from Brissot to the Convention', Moulin, 10 June 1793, in Vatel, *Charlotte Corday et les Girondins*, 2: 247–50.

reasoned judgement.[51] The intense atmosphere of 1793 contributed enormously to the sinister interpretation of the Girondins' actions and motives. The judgement of the Jacobin Levasseur, looking back on those events thirty years later when most of the protagonists had gone to their graves, offered a more dispassionate insight than was possible at the time. He deplored the trial and stated that most of the Girondins had been sincere republicans. But he also sought to exonerate his old Jacobin colleagues who, he said, had been driven by circumstances and the actions of the Girondins to take this fatal step.[52] The Girondins had brought their fate on themselves by stirring up revolt and civil war. Levasseur acknowledged that the charge that they were secret royalists was untrue; however, their reckless actions had lent support to the royalists, '...the Girondins were not cut out to be conspirators: they were simply elegant sophists, marked by a radical nonentity...' Their 'lack of political skills' and their 'errors, in the course of discussions on matters of the gravest national interest, gave the appearance of concerted treachery'.[53] But the point is also that the Jacobins believed in the idea of a concerted conspiracy because that was the way in which they understood politics, as a matter of morality and immorality, guilt and innocence, virtue and corruption.

## THE TRIAL OF THE GIRONDINS

Amar's speech on 3 October on behalf of the Committee of General Security was the culmination of the case for a Girondin conspiracy. This was the formal *acte d'accusation* that would form the basis of the legal case brought against the Girondins at their trial. The key charges against the Girondins were that they had tried secretly to save the monarchy; that they had made a catastrophic mess of the war that they themselves had brought into being; and lastly (and most crucially) they had taken up arms in the federalist revolt.[54] The charges against the Girondin leaders of recklessness and even criminal incompetence in wartime were serious ones. In the matter of the federalist revolt there was a case for saying that the actions of the participants had been treasonous. But the report went further than this: it depicted the Girondins collectively and systematically as conspirators, who had always been against the Revolution. It also included a number of people who had not evaded the arrest ordered by the Convention, and had not been party to the federalist revolt.[55] Amar stressed their unity: 'they are all part of the conspiracy'.[56] Thirty-six more men were now implicated than in Saint-Just's report. The additional

---

[51] The surviving Girondins used a similar language and way of conceiving politics to characterize the Jacobins. Louvet, for example, commented on the suspiciously large numbers of foreigners in the Commune. He claimed that the Jacobins were conspiring against the Girondins and were themselves engaged in the Foreign Plot, but that most of the Girondins were too honest themselves to appreciate the extent of the conspiracy against them: Louvet, *Mémoires de Louvet*, 56–61, 95.

[52] Levasseur, *Mémoires*, 339–45.     [53] Levasseur, *Mémoires*, 341–2.

[54] 3 October 1793, *Archives parlementaires*, 75: 532.

[55] See Sydenham, *The Girondins*, 25–8.

[56] 3 October 1793, *Archives parlementaires*, 75: 534.

names were those of men who had not been involved in the federalist revolt, and who were only marginally associated with the Girondins' inner network. They were accused of being agents in the service of Pitt—an altogether more nebulous charge, hard either to prove or to disprove. Amar listed ways in which Girondin politics corresponded with Pitt's aim to destroy France. The ills of the present war and political disasters were attributed to malevolent machinations by the Girondins, including the declaration of war against the leading powers of Europe, the scourge of civil war, the putting in place of treacherous generals at the head of the armies, the loss of French colonies, and the assassinations of Marat and Lepeletier.[57] No plausible evidence was offered for these allegations beyond the fact that Pitt would evidently be pleased at France's disastrous situation.

Some of the decisions to place men on the list of suspects in the Girondin conspiracy were arbitrary in the extreme. The unfortunate marquis de Sillery found himself on trial alongside the Girondins in large part thanks to Desmoulins' portrayal of him in the *Fragment of the Secret History of the Revolution* as an inveterate conspirator. Yet Sillery and the Girondins had been enemies for some time. It had been the Girondin leaders themselves who had denounced him and secured his arrest, and he had nothing in common with them. Yet he died along with them, caught up in the pell-mell narrative of the Girondins as an *über*-conspiracy; sharing the horrible enforced intimacy of the dock, the prison cell, the tumbrel, the scaffold; finally to be laid in the same communal grave; friends and enemies together.

There were however limits beyond which Robespierre refused to go. He opposed Billaud-Varenne's demand that there be a vote by *appel nominel* on the fate of the Girondins, on the grounds that it would polarize the Convention into those for and against conspiracy. On 3 October Robespierre defended seventy-five deputies who had signed a secret protest at the arrests, saying that the Convention should not seek to multiply the numbers of the guilty. He laid his credibility on the line to defend them, persisting through shouts of disapproval from the public galleries that threatened to drown out his voice.[58] His stance on that day probably saved their lives. He continued to defend them subsequently: though they were arrested and remained in prison, they were not put on trial. Some of these men would seek retributive vengeance on surviving Jacobins after Thermidor.

The culpability of the Girondins who had been involved in armed revolt was a fairly straightforward matter—they were condemned under the terms of the decree that prescribed the death penalty for armed rebels. The question of the guilt of the Girondins who had not fled, and remained in prison awaiting judgement, was a different matter.[59] There was little evidence to link them to the federalist revolt. Yet

---

[57] 3 October 1793, *Archives parlementaires*, 75: 533.

[58] 3 October 1793, *Archives parlementaires*, 75: 535–7; Robespierre, *Oeuvres*, 10: 134–6. On the figures for who signed the protest and whether they can be categorized as 'Girondin sympathizers', see Sydenham, *The Girondins*, 41, 44–8, 219.

[59] For a more detailed account of the depiction of the Girondins at their trial as 'conspirators', see Linton, 'Do you believe that we're conspirators?' On the trial of the Girondins and their defence, see Hanson, *The Jacobin Republic Under Fire*, ch. 1.

it was a political trial, and at the moment their names had been included on the list the decision to kill them had already been taken. In order to make a case even vaguely credible, their political conduct was raked up and used against them. Their private lives and connections with other suspects were produced as evidence of their conspiratorial aims. Much use was made of their personal letters. It was a tactic that rightly horrifies us. However, as Carla Hesse points out, rather than comparing the revolutionary judicial system with modern procedure, it can be better understood in the context of old regime judicial procedures that permitted torture in cases of treason to find a suspect's authentic views. The revolutionaries were struggling to establish less brutal ways of finding out the truth.[60] The use of private letters, while invasive and distasteful to us, also attests to a genuine anxiety on the part of the Girondins' interrogators to discover what the Girondins truly thought and the extent of the 'conspiracy'.

In the absence of more substantive evidence, instances of the Girondins having used 'behind closed doors' political methods were presented as 'proof' of a conspiracy against the Republic. Amongst the witnesses who gave evidence against the Girondins were several of their former colleagues and friends amongst the Jacobins, including Fabre d'Eglantine, Chabot, and Léonard Bourdon, all of whom used their personal acquaintance with the Girondins to inform against them. They accused Brissot and his friends of being motivated by personal ambition, and of having held secret meetings to procure the appointment of ministers and to 'rule through them'. Chabot accused Gensonné of being 'an aristocrat who made himself into a patriot in order to secure posts'; and claimed that Guadet had originally 'aspired to a place as the king's commissary' and only took on the persona of an 'enemy of the court' when this post was refused him.[61] The conduct of Brissot and the Rolands in particular came under scrutiny for signs of ambition, self-interest, and corruption. The Girondin ministers were accused of having dispensed patronage. As a deputy Brissot had not held office himself, so his accusers examined evidence that he had used his friendship with Roland and other ministers to exert indirect patronage. During his interrogation Brissot was asked if he had contributed to giving commissions and places to Blancheland, Sonthonax, Polverel, and Genet. He agreed that he had recommended all but Blancheland.[62] The letter that had been sent by Brissot to Madame Roland recommending men to places, and which Desmoulins cited in his *Fragment of the Secret History of the Revolution*, was produced at Brissot's interrogation.[63] Brissot admitted writing it, but said the list had been compiled at the request of Roland.[64] Private dinners and other social

---

[60] Carla Hesse, 'La preuve par la lettre: pratiques juridiques au tribunal révolutionnaire de Paris (1793–1794)', *Annales: Histoire, Sciences Sociales*, 3 (1996): 629–42; see also Laura Mason, 'The "bosom of proof": criminal justice and the renewal of oral culture during the French Revolution', *Journal of Modern History*, 76, 1 (2004): 29–61.

[61] Walter, *Actes du Tribunal révolutionnaire*, 290–91.

[62] Brissot's interrogation on 15 October is in Brissot, *Correspondance et Papiers*, 380.

[63] Brissot, *Correspondance et Papiers*, 293. Another letter he wrote to Madame Roland, asking for a place for his friend Goussier, was also brought as evidence against Brissot in the report by Brival on 19 May: ibid., 292.

[64] Brissot, *Correspondance et Papiers*, 384.

gatherings were also used to incriminate the Girondins. Under interrogation Brissot was asked about his social relations with Lafayette. He replied that he had eaten at Lafayette's house on two occasions at most, and that at a time when Lafayette had seemed to be 'a friend of Liberty'. In his much longer written defence, Brissot claimed that he had seen Lafayette continually in the course of their official responsibilities, but that 'I rarely went to his house, and I never ate there'.[65]

Attendance at the salons of Madame Roland and Vergniaud, and at Valazé's Committee, were all depicted as signs of conspiracy. Valazé admitted to the meetings in his home, but attested that they were for the purpose of conferring on 'the interests of the Republic'.[66] The focal point for many of these allegations was Madame Roland herself. She had been imprisoned since early June, and in the absence of her husband (who had fled) she was interrogated several times about the political engagements of her salons, and her own involvement in patronage. She was told that her salon amounted to 'a horrible conspiracy against the security of the Republic', and that in place of the present government the Girondins wanted to set up their own (federalist) government with places reserved for 'their good friends' in each department. She was questioned as to whether she had presided at her dinner table over private conversations amongst the Girondin leaders. In her defence she argued that as a woman she had been concerned with domestic matters, not public affairs; that the only guests at her home were those whom her husband as a minister was obliged to see, or 'old friends', and that none of these had come to her home 'in secret'. The Jacobins would have none of it.[67] She was asked to name friends who were welcomed to their house: she refused to implicate anyone.[68] But when her servants were also questioned, her daughter's piano teacher provided many names of men who came to the salon. Madame Roland's political involvement had been much greater than she admitted in her interrogation—she was, after all, fighting for her life. As the Minister's wife she had been very active in politics 'behind closed doors', even running agents for the ministry to report on public opinion. Above all, there was her prominent role in the letter sent by Roland to Louis XVI.[69] None of this amounted to conspiracy—yet conspiracy, along with inciting the federalist revolt, were the crimes for which she was indicted. Apart from some injudicious notes to Lauze-Deperret that were produced at her trial, the evidence of her complicity in the federalist revolt was minimal.[70] It was her friendships and her participation in politics 'behind closed doors' that constituted the

[65] Brissot, *Correspondance et Papiers*, 379. See also Brissot, 'Défense devant le Tribunal révolutionnaire', in Brissot, *Mémoires*, 2: 280.

[66] Walter, *Actes du Tribunal révolutionnaire*, 287.

[67] 'Dénonciation à la Section du Panthéon', 1 June 1793, in Madame Roland, *Mémoires de Madame Roland*, ed. Cl. Perroud, 2 vols (Paris: Plon, 1905), 2: 424–6. For Madame Roland's defence, see 'Premier interrogation subi par la citoyenne Roland pendant sa detention à l'Abbaye', 12 June 1793, in ibid, 2: 427–31.

[68] She wrote notes on her interrogation, reproduced in Madame Roland, *Mémoires*, ed. Paul de Roux (Paris: Mercure de France, 1966), 95–7.

[69] On the extent of Madame Roland's political involvement see Reynolds, *Marriage and Revolution*, esp. 220–45; 255–7.

[70] Reynolds, *Marriage and Revolution*, 273.

primary evidence of her guilt. She recognized this in the spirited defence that she wrote, while emphatically denying that her 'friendships' amounted to conspiracy. She declared that these friendships 'predate by a long way the political circumstances which now make them be considered as culpable'.[71] She was only allowed to deliver a few sentences of her defence before the Revolutionary Tribunal. She was condemned to die that same afternoon.

Madame Roland was not alone in being condemned for suspicious friendships and political manipulation 'behind closed doors'. Vergniaud admitted to having 'dined five or six times' at the Rolands' home, but denied that this constituted a 'coalition'. He also denied being an 'intimate' friend of Brissot and Gensonné.[72] Sillery was accused of friendship with several men who, for different reasons, were now identified as conspirators: d'Orléans, Lafayette, Dumouriez, and Pétion.[73] Fabre testified to a dinner that he and Danton had attended *chez* Pétion at which 'a great number of the accused were present' and where the guests showed a hostile attitude to the revolution of 10 August. He was asked to name who was present at the dinner, and recalled that Brissot was not there at the start 'but when he arrived we judged by the reception he received the influence that he had over this reunion'. Danton and Fabre seem to have been using the dinner to sound out whether the Girondins would accept Danton as minister. At the trial Brissot said he had been agreeable, though according to Fabre, Pétion was against it.[74] Other 'signs' of conspiracy that emerged under interrogation included gestures such as a fist shaken at the Jacobins and positions where people chose to sit in the Convention, together with more tangible points of difference, such as attitudes towards the invasion of the Tuileries by Parisian militants on 20 June, and the overthrow of the monarchy on 10 August.[75]

The meetings at Valazé's home came under intense scrutiny, and anyone who had information about them was questioned to see if they would implicate other 'conspirators'. One of these was Boilleau. He was only loosely attached to the Girondins and had been put on the proscription list largely for his outspoken opposition to the Commune and membership of the Commission of Twelve (which had been set up to investigate the activities of the Commune). He was the only one of the defendants to give the judges what they wanted to hear and admit to a real conspiracy. He wrote a letter to that effect to the staunch Jacobin Léonard Bourdon, who produced it at the trial. In it Boilleau wrote:

> It is clear to my eyes that there was a conspiracy against the unity of the Republic, just as it is clear that the Jacobins have always served the Republic…I declare that I have never been to Valazé's home, although he invited me many times.[76]

---

[71] Walter, *Actes du Tribunal révolutionnaire*, 371–2, 377.
[72] Walter, *Actes du Tribunal révolutionnaire*, 273–4.
[73] Walter, *Actes du Tribunal révolutionnaire*, 334–7.
[74] Walter, *Actes du Tribunal révolutionnaire*, 311–12.
[75] See the questions put to Lesterpt-Beauvais, Antiboul, and Lehardi at the trial of the Girondins, in Walter, *Actes du Tribunal révolutionnaire*, 330–2.
[76] Henri Wallon, *Histoire du Tribunal révolutionnaire*, 6 vols (Paris: Plon, 1880–1), 1: 401–3.

It was a desperate attempt to extricate himself, but it did not save him. Under questioning he was invited to name names. With the reproachful eyes of his fellow-accused upon him he faltered and said he could not identify any conspirators.

The other Girondins vehemently denied that they had been party to a conspiracy. Brissot wrote a lengthy defence, in which he dealt point by point with the accusations made in the reports of Saint-Just and Amar. He challenged their interpretation of his motives and actions, claiming that throughout his revolutionary career he had acted with integrity and solely in the public interest. Yet even in these extreme circumstances it is notable that he continued to speak a similar language to that employed by his accusers. Whilst he denied that he himself had been a conspirator, he spoke of his own old adversaries as conspirators; thus Lafayette had engaged in an 'infamous coalition' and 'conspiracy' with the Lameths. Brissot referred to Delessart, the minister whose overthrow had been the means by which the Girondins had achieved political power, and who had been murdered in the September massacres, as 'the traitor Delessart'.[77] He expressed his satisfaction at the destruction of Barnave's public reputation that he had wrought with the 'Letter to Barnave', though Barnave himself was currently in prison awaiting his own appearance before the Revolutionary Tribunal.

Vergniaud, too, wrote frantic notes for a defence of himself and his friends that he was never allowed to give. In these notes he insisted that what linked the prisoners was friendship, not conspiracy, nor, revealingly, a shared policy or ideology. What brought the Girondins together had been '[r]elations based on mutual esteem, never coalitions of opinion'. He wrote 'I knew B[rissot] at the Jacobins. We were unknown to one another: how therefore to form a coalition? ... I sometimes voted with the Mountain, sometimes etc...'[78] In their defence, the Girondins did not deny their mutual friendships; for the most part they showed considerable courage in standing by their friends. Rather than depicting their friendships as a means of networking and political advancement, still less as a sign of conspiracy, they presented them in terms that Rousseau might have used, as evidence of their own sensibility—and genuine virtue.

It was a hopeless effort. The Girondins were not permitted to put forward any substantive defence against the charge of complicity in a 'conspiracy against the unity, the indivisibility of the Republic, against the liberty and safety of the French people'; and the jurors on the Revolutionary Tribunal were not interested in hearing that the Girondins considered themselves to be virtuous.[79] In the end all

---

[77] Brissot, 'Défense devant le Tribunal révolutionnaire'.

[78] 'Projét de Défense de Vergniaud', in Wallon, *Histoire du Tribunal révolutionnaire*, 1: 480–2. When the remainder of the seventy-five deputies who had signed a secret protest at the arrest of the Girondins were reinstated into the Convention after Thermidor, they too insisted on the integrity of their motives, and their abhorrence of faction and conspiracy: see Sydenham, *The Girondins*, 34–6.

[79] Walter, *Actes du Tribunal révolutionnaire*, 338–40.

twenty-one of the men put on trial were found guilty. When the verdict against the Girondins was pronounced, Camille Desmoulins, who was present, cried out in anguish. According to one witness he collapsed in shock and belated remorse, crying out 'it is my *Brissot Unmasked* that is killing them!' Desmoulins' own account of how he acted at that moment did not mention any personal guilt he might have felt for his part in characterizing the Girondins as conspirators. He did, however, acknowledge his grief at the condemnation of men who had been his friends: 'they were true republicans…they will die like Brutus', he is reported to have said.[80] Perhaps he meant that, once they were safely dead, they could be 'men of virtue' once again.

[80] This account was given by Vilate, a Jacobin who witnessed the trial. See Wallon, *Histoire du Tribunal révolutionnaire*, 1: 418. Desmoulins was obliged to justify his show of 'sensibility' at the sentencing of the Girondins, when questioned over his conduct at the Jacobin Club. He admitted that he had said that they would die 'like republicans', but denied that he had added the words 'like Brutus', claiming he had said they would die as republicans, but 'federalist republicans': 14 December 1793, Aulard, *Société des Jacobins*, 5: 559.

# 7

## Being Cincinnatus
### The Jacobins in Power

Believe us, Legislators, four years of misfortunes have taught us enough to know how to discern ambition even under the cloak of patriotism; we no longer believe in the virtue of these men who are reduced to praising themselves; finally, more than words are necessary if we are to believe that ambition does not rule your committees...

> Petition from the Revolutionary Republican Women to the Convention,
> August 1793.[1]

It is on the basis of probity, of morality, that you want to establish the Republic; since you yourselves are the architects of this edifice you must be pure, and the whole of France must witness your purity. Let the mask of charlatanism fall; let virtue show itself entirely naked. Let the people know whether all those who call themselves their friends, really work for their happiness. But let us begin by being severe towards ourselves.

> Philippeaux addressing the deputies of the Convention, November 1793.[2]

The leap from opposition to ruling group brought about a decisive change for the leading Jacobins. Robespierre himself had always been more at home criticizing the shortcomings of others than being the man at the helm of the ship. Being in power offered new opportunities for forging a successful career in revolutionary politics; it also entailed hard choices. Many Jacobins expected to be rewarded for their devotion by material and career benefits. Like the triumvirs and the Girondin leaders before them, the Jacobin leaders were faced by a conflict between the ideology of political virtue, and the realities of power. Having witnessed the fate of the Girondins, the revolutionary leaders understood that their own position in the public eye was precarious. The Jacobin leaders were subject to constant scrutiny, not least by the Paris militants and by their fellow Jacobins. Would these men of virtue succumb to the temptations of office and 'sell out' as had former leaders of the Jacobins? If not, how could they prove to their supporters, and perhaps even to themselves, that their virtue was authentic? To explore this issue we shall look at

---

[1] Petition from the Revolutionary Republican Women to the Convention on the Leadership of the Armies and the Law of Suspects, August 1793. Cited and translated in Darline Gay Levy, Harriet Branson Applewhite, and Mary Durham Johnson (eds), *Women in Revolutionary Paris, 1789–1795: Selected Documents* (Chicago: University of Illinois Press, 1979), 172–4.

[2] 20 Brumaire (10 November 1793), *Archives parlementaires*, 78: 703.

how the Jacobins presented their own identity in the new context of revolutionary government, and how the need to maintain this identity led some of them to choose terror. Tensions over questions of political integrity and corruption need to be understood against the backdrop of the renewal of factional division within the Jacobins. These tensions generated a new and ominous narrative, that of the so-called 'Foreign Plot' that linked Jacobins in a web of financial corruption and political conspiracy with foreign powers. Factional divisions within the Jacobins and ensuing conflicts over identity and integrity would launch a new stage of the politicians' terror.

## THE JACOBINS IN GOVERNMENT

In accordance with the revolutionary calendar that had recently been adopted, a new year began in September 1793: the Year Two of the Republic.[3] This was the year of the Jacobin Republic. It was also to go down in history as the year of the Terror. The fall of the Girondins brought about the transformation of the fortunes of the Jacobins; no longer the opponents and critics of the Revolution's leaders, they themselves were now the ones in power. They dominated the leading institution of revolutionary government, the Committee of Public Safety. This Committee was first set up in April. Its role increased subsequently until it shouldered many of the responsibilities of government. It was formed to deal with the critical circumstances of the external war now being fought with all the major foreign powers of western Europe, and the internal struggle with counter-revolutionaries and federalists. The Committee became what was effectively a war cabinet. It assumed many of the executive powers formerly held by the ministries.[4] Part of its role was to ensure the integrity and good behaviour of the leading civil and military officials of the Republic: ministers, functionaries, and generals were all directly accountable to the Committee and had to report to it regularly. As a measure of the trust given by the Convention to the Committee, it was entrusted with substantial funds (in August it was granted 50 million *livres* for secret expenses). Its members could claim expenses, but otherwise they continued on their modest 18 *livres* a day salary as deputies. The only areas over which the Committee did not have direct control were the police, arrests, and revolutionary justice, all of which were regulated by its sister committee, the Committee of General Security. The Committee of Public Safety was accountable to the Convention; its membership was subject to monthly renewal by means of elections, but for many months the Convention put its trust in the Committee to take executive actions on its behalf. From July 1793 to July 1794 the membership of this ruling Committee remained largely unchanged.

---

[3] On the revolutionary calendar, see Matthew Shaw, *Time and the French Revolution: the Republican Calendar, 1789–Year XIV* (Woodbridge: The Royal Historical Society, The Boydell Press, 2005).

[4] The powers of the ministries were whittled away over succeeding months. On 1 April 1794 ministries were abolished, to be replaced by twelve administrative commissions, the chairmen of which reported daily to the Committee of Public Safety.

The monthly re-election of its members became a matter of form, to which no open opposition was voiced. It was a delicate situation. Stability and strong government were needed, but there was a fine line between recognizing necessity and intimidation.

What kind of man was needed for such a position? The task required a Cincinnatus: someone who, like the legendary Roman general, would accept the task out of love of the public good, not for personal glory; someone who would not take advantage of his position to extend favouritism and patronage to his friends, or to destroy his personal enemies; who would keep his hands out of the public purse; who would not abuse his power by setting himself up as a dictator; and who would, when all was over (and if he still lived), retire gracefully from public life to live a life of rural tranquillity. In short, men of virtue were needed. But did such paragons of antique heroism actually exist?

When the renewal of the membership of the Committee was discussed in the Jacobins on 8 July the attitude of many members was bullish. They were now the winners. It remained to make good and consolidate the Jacobin victory; but what kind of men should lead them now? According to Bourdon de l'Oise, the friend of Danton, 'what we need today are revolutionary men, the kind of men to whom, without fear, we can entrust the fate of the Republic, men who will answer for it body and soul'.[5] Chabot followed this up, noting that fearlessness was an essential quality for the post: 'Guyton-Morveau is a perfectly honest man: but he's a quaker, he's always trembling'. Chabot went on to detail ways in which other current members of the Committee fell short of the high standards needed: 'the smallest stain should be a motive for exclusion'.

It was then that Robespierre stepped in, and it is revealing that he had a more realistic understanding of what political qualities France could expect of her leaders than did some of his fellow Jacobins: 'Chabot appears to me to be too exalted; he is indignant to see that the Committee of Public Safety has not achieved the degree of perfection that he ceaselessly envisages. He believes it then to be possible? In that case he deludes himself.' For himself, Robespierre continued, four years of experience of the 'changing vicissitudes' of revolutionary politics had taught him the necessity of 'adapting things to fit the circumstances'. He then spoke up for Saint-Just, who had proved his revolutionary credentials and his 'great talent and truly republican soul', by means of the report he had given earlier that day against the Girondins. Some Jacobins thought Saint-Just's report on the Girondins had not gone far enough but, according to Robespierre, it had proved his readiness to do whatever was necessary for the patriotic cause.[6]

Two days later, on 10 July, Robespierre acted to stop some of the more excitable Jacobins opening up the whole can of worms regarding the extent of corruption amongst their own people. A self-important Rossignol denounced a man presented to the Minister of the Marine by Danton, implying Danton too was

---

[5] 8 July 1793, Aulard, *Société des Jacobins*, 5: 291.
[6] 8 July 1793, Aulard, *Société des Jacobins*, 5: 293–5.

'infected'. Rossignol continued: 'I have many other counter-revolutionaries to denounce to you. All the bureaux are infected by aristocracy, and their clerks too are conspirators.' Robespierre was desperate to preserve the unity of the Jacobins, and understood all too well the direction in which such talk could lead. He intervened promptly to shut Rossignol up: 'I ask that this farce should cease, and the session commence'.[7] He went on to defend Danton's reputation, not for the first or for the last time; though privately he must have had doubts, for the odour of corruption had clung to Danton for a long time now. Earlier that day Danton had been voted off the Committee of Public Safety. Two days later, Danton defended himself on the specifics of the allegations, but his days in power had come to an end.[8] He does not seem to have regretted this. Years of intense engagement in revolutionary politics had exhausted him. Nonetheless, he continued to help his friends to attain advantageous posts. It was through his aid that Deforgues became Foreign Minister in June and Paré Minister of the Interior in August. Both of them had known Danton before the Revolution when they worked for him as clerks in his office; while Paré and Danton had been at school together in the Oratorian *collège* of Troyes. Through his protégés Danton still retained an indirect access to the circuits of power and patronage.

A few days after Danton left the Committee of Public Safety, Robespierre entered it, on 27 July. There is a sense of inevitability about the moment when Robespierre crossed the threshold of the Committee of Public Safety. In retrospect, it had all been building up to this. This does not mean that he had secretly been manoeuvring to get himself into power; some commentators have assumed so, but the evidence does not bear this out. Above all, the self-denying ordinance and his opposition to the war were not the actions of a man who was motivated by personal ambition. Rather, in the end both he—and the Convention—accepted that if men of virtue were needed, no one had a better track record than the 'Incorruptible'.

## CHOOSING TERROR?

Was there ever a definitive moment when the Jacobins 'chose terror' or was it something that they came to by a gradual process? I have argued that it was the latter. Nor were the Jacobin leaders alone responsible: it was a collective choice. That process reached its culmination over the summer and autumn of 1793 when the deputies of the Convention made a series of key choices that enabled a form of state terror to be put in place. One of these decisions was to shelve the egalitarian and libertarian constitution drawn up by the Jacobins in June 1793, on the grounds that in time of war the priority was to ensure the survival of the Republic. A principal piece of terrorist legislation was the Law of Suspects, passed on 17 September

---

[7]  10 July 1793, Aulard, *Société des Jacobins*, 5: 297.
[8]  10 July 1793, Aulard, *Société des Jacobins*, 5: 297–8, 298–300.

1793. It was voted in, partly in response to renewed pressure from the Paris militants, grown restive at the shortage of revolutionary measures since the overthrow of the Girondins. The deputies bowed to the pressure of popular demands, though they also took the precaution of arresting a group of leaders of the *sans-culotte* movement, the *enragés*, including the so-called 'red priest', Jacques Roux. Two representatives of the extreme militant wing of Jacobinism, Collot d'Herbois and Billaud-Varenne, were voted onto the Committee of Public Safety, to help stiffen the resolve of its existing members. Before the Revolution Billaud-Varenne had worked as a clerk in Danton's legal office, but their political views were now taking them on diverging paths. The Law of Suspects defined 'suspects' in very broad terms and gave sweeping powers of arrest. The Paris militants spoke at the time of making 'terror the order of the day'. Jean-Clément Martin, however, has pointed out that the Convention did not use this phrase when it responded to the militants' call for terror: for the Jacobins the rhetoric of terror was in part a way of manipulating and appeasing the militants.[9]

Though what took place is often referred to as the 'Jacobin Terror', this is somewhat misleading. Firstly, it was not simply 'Jacobin': though Jacobin leaders played a prominent part, they were by no means acting alone; and they had the support of the Convention. Secondly, to call it 'the Terror' implies a coherent intellectual whole, that there was a collective and conscious choice to institute 'the Terror' as a system of government. The reality was something much closer to the ad hoc process Martin has described: an improvised set of responses to a shifting situation, in which war and civil war played a critical part, not least in evoking an atmosphere of panic. The form of terror instituted by the revolutionary government in the Year Two was swift, harsh, and often brutal but it was a legal terror, founded for the most part on contemporary ideas of justice in a war situation.

The Jacobins did not have a monopoly on power even during the time of the so-called 'Jacobin Republic'. Only some of the members of the Committee of Public Safety identified themselves as members of the Jacobin group. These were Robespierre, Couthon, Saint-Just, Prieur de la Marne, Jean Bon Saint-André, and (from their entry to the Committee in September) Collot d'Herbois and Billaud-Varenne. Yet all the members of the Committee set their hands to the required tasks: dealing with a range of measures related to the war, to government—and to terror. At the time they did not distinguish: it was all about maintaining revolutionary government and the *salut public*.[10] Despite the scramble that took place after Robespierre's overthrow to attribute sole responsibility for implementing the Terror onto him and the men who died with him (Couthon and Saint-Just), the Committee's members bore a collective responsibility for measures that we could call those of 'state terror'. Nor was support for terror confined to the ruling Committees. The principal laws enabling terror, including the Law of Suspects, the

[9] Martin, *Violence et révolution*, 86–93. On discourses of terror as a rhetorical strategy, see Jourdan, 'Les discours de la terreur'.

[10] On the Committee of Public Safety, see Palmer, *Twelve Who Ruled*.

Decree on Emergency Government in October 1793 (which authorized revolutionary government to pass beyond accepted constraints and limits until the ending of the war), even the notorious Law of Prairial (enacted the following June), were all ratified by the Convention. The Jacobins chose to use terror, but this choice was equally made by non-Jacobin deputies who voted in support of legislation that enabled terror to take place.

Several Jacobin leaders played a principal role as front men for the revolutionary government. Robespierre and Saint-Just along with, to a lesser extent, Billaud-Varenne, Couthon, and Barère (the latter only very marginally associated with the Jacobin Club), were the men who most frequently acted as intermediaries, relaying the policy of the Committee of Public Safety to the Convention and securing the assent of the deputies. They used their oratory to justify policy. Part of that policy was the use of terror. Increasingly, these men—above all Robespierre—became the public face of terror. In speaking they gave the appearance of being in control of events, and in control of the Terror, but that appearance was to some extent illusory. No individual, no group of individuals, not even the Committee of Public Safety, could be said to have controlled the Terror. Nevertheless, Robespierre and the other spokesmen tried to impose an intellectual coherence on the revolutionary project. They had taken over from the acts of retributive street violence carried out by the *sans-culottes* and had tried to place the direction of violence against counter-revolutionaries on a legal footing, to be directed by the nation's representatives. Now they needed to justify what was already taking place. On 17 Pluviôse Robespierre spoke on 'the moral principles that should guide the Convention'. At the heart of those principles was virtue:

> If the mainspring of popular government in peacetime is virtue, the mainspring of popular government during a revolution is both virtue and terror; virtue, without which terror is baneful; terror, without which virtue is powerless. Terror is nothing more than speedy, severe and inflexible justice; it is thus an emanation of virtue; it is less a principle in itself, than a consequence of the general principle of democracy, applied to the most pressing needs of the *patrie*.[11]

Thus Robespierre tried to justify terror as an aspect of virtue. This notorious passage has been much discussed. But what has not been sufficiently recognized is the extent to which Robespierre, in talking of virtue, literally meant his own personal virtue. The legitimacy of his argument rested on the authenticity of his own commitment to the public good, and that of his fellow Jacobins. Because the Jacobins were genuinely virtuous they could be entrusted with power as they would use it not for themselves—not for personal motives such as self-aggrandizement, vengeance, or envy—but for the *patrie*. So long as terror was wielded by men of authentic virtue then it would be morally right, no longer terror but a form of justice. The

---

[11] 'Sur les principes de morale politique qui doivent guider la Convention Nationale dans l'administration intérieur de la République', 17 Pluviôse (5 February 1794), in Robespierre, *Oeuvres*, 10: 357. For the intellectual sources of Robespierre's ideas in this speech, and the changes incurred by his assumption of a leadership role, see Linton, 'Robespierre's political principles'.

'pressing needs of the *patrie*' required the use of terror. It was all for the *salut public* (literally 'public safety'). In this way he sought to rationalize and justify the use of terror to the public. He was also—and this is critical to understanding Robespierre—trying to justify it to himself. This was not the argument of a cynical man, using a specious form of words to keep himself in power. This was a man who believed in what he said—even though that effort of self-belief was becoming harder. He really needed to believe in it. The alternative for a man so committed as Robespierre was unbearable—that the Revolution could fail; or that it might not have been worth the struggle and sacrifice that it had already cost.

Yet the reality was that the fear that Robespierre wanted to use to intimidate the enemies of the Revolution was already in the Convention itself. It hung like a shadow over the heads of the deputies. After the death of the Girondins every deputy knew that their fate might be his own also. The deputies, however, could not admit publicly to their fear, since nervousness in a national representative was seen as a possible sign of hidden guilt: authentic virtue was fearless. The deputies' knowledge that they themselves had no immunity, indeed were particularly subject to scrutiny of their conduct for signs of corruption and conspiracy, increased the atmosphere of anxiety in the Convention, and stifled dissent to the government's policy.

This fear was more intense amongst the most politically active deputies—those who drew attention to themselves, and neglected to take the precaution of keeping their heads down. It was particularly rife amongst the Montagnards, that small group of men, brought together by years of common purpose, but increasingly uneasy now, and wary even of one another. Neither were the members of the Committee of Public Safety immune from fear. They knew the politicians' terror might be turned on them. That fear made it difficult *not* to choose terror. There were considerable risks incurred, not least from the anger of the Paris militants, if the men in charge were seen to be weak, corrupt, or personally ambitious rather than entirely dedicated to the good of the people.

Of all the cases that came before the Revolutionary Tribunal there were none more ruthless than those involving politicians. In most cases brought before the Revolutionary Tribunal, people had some chance to mount a legal defence, and overall, slightly over half the people brought before the Revolutionary Tribunal were sentenced to death. Even after the Law of Prairial was passed on 10 June 1794, one in four of the people who appeared before the Tribunal escaped death.[12] This was not the case with the terror that politicians dealt to one another. None of the deputies who were brought before the Revolutionary Tribunal during the Year Two, and virtually none of the other prominent political figures who appeared before it in that time, escaped the death sentence.

---

[12] For a detailed analysis of the statistics on the variety of verdicts given by the Revolutionary Tribunal, see Godfrey, *Revolutionary Justice*, 136–50. For an interesting analysis of why some people escaped death after the Law of Prairial was passed, see Anne Simonin, 'Les acquittés de la Grande Terreur: Réflexions sur l'amitié dans la République', in Biard, *Les Politiques de la Terreur*. On the importance to the Jacobins of maintaining justice, see Jourdan, 'Les discours de la terreur'.

## THE ZENITH OF THE JACOBINS: VIRTUE REWARDED?

The Jacobin Club reached the height of its influence during the Year Two. The Club was the emotional heartland of the radical Revolution. Its members constituted a brotherhood that had been through many shared experiences, hopes, dangers—and divisions. [13] Previous factions, the Feuillants, the Girondins, which had been exposed as 'false' Jacobins, had gone. The 'true' Jacobins remained. It was the moment of their triumph—or rather it should have been. The reality was rather different. Now that their leaders dominated executive power, controlling posts, patronage, and the wealth of the state, many rank and file Jacobins hoped for, indeed expected, rewards for their years of loyalty and sacrifice to the revolutionary cause in the form of career advancement and personal success. To some extent this was fulfilled: the Republic needed men who had the appropriate patriotism and could be trusted to undertake administrative tasks. In November the Committee of Public Safety formally requested the Jacobins to nominate men 'suitable for public functions'. There was considerable anxiety about the integrity of such men, as shown when, in December, on the proposal of Couthon, the Jacobins asked that two representatives of the Committee of Public Safety be deputed to undertake the Herculean task of uncovering 'exact information regarding the moral and political conduct' of the employees of all the offices and administrations of the Republic.[14] The problem of finding appropriate recompense did not arise only in relation to rank and file officials, but extended to the senior roles, which fast became a battleground. Leading Jacobins expected real power through the top posts in government. Those who were disappointed in their expectations were often angry and resentful of more successful revolutionaries. Instead of unity, there was a renewal of the infighting within the Jacobins. This time the divisions went deeper.

It is one of the ironies of the Jacobins' politics that they reserved their bitterest antagonism not for royalists, nor *émigrés*, nor politicians who did not frequent the Club, but for one another. Of the deputies of the Convention who perished in the Year Two, a very high proportion had at some time been members of the Jacobin Club. Most of the other deputies were left alone so long as they kept out of the ferocious disputes within this group.[15] A similar rate of attrition is apparent amongst Jacobins who filled other activist roles, or were journalists, members of the Commune, or other holders of official posts in the new regime. It is no coincidence that they were men who had bought heavily into the identity of virtue. In many cases these were former colleagues, or friends, now become enemies. They had the kind of personal knowledge of one another's failings to be well positioned to put the knife into one another; to strip off 'the mask of patriotism' and reveal the face of self-interest and corruption that lay beneath.

---

[13] On the psychology of revolutionary brotherhood, see Hunt, *The Family Romance*, ch. 3.

[14] 29 Brumaire (19 November 1793), Aulard, *Société des Jacobins*, 5: 523;
24 Frimaire (14 December 1793), *Aulard, Société des Jacobins*, 5: 558.

[15] As Patrick says, 'even under the Terror, it was very rare for men to be penalised for political independence': Patrick, *The Men of the First French Republic*, 32.

Corruption was a deep-seated problem. The many official positions necessary to govern civilian life, and to conduct the war, offered ample opportunities for those men who did not scruple to help themselves to public funds. For years the Jacobins had attacked other revolutionary leaders who had fallen short of their own high standards. More than any other group they had insisted on the need for transparency of political conduct. How would they conduct themselves now that they were the ones in power? Robespierre was particularly concerned that public officials should be virtuous.[16] Many Jacobins did take pride in conducting themselves with honour in positions of trust, and were scrupulous about the money that passed through their hands. Others seemed to have succumbed, more or less willingly, to the opportunities that lay open to them to acquire wealth and office. Some engaged in outright theft. Hard evidence is difficult to come by, but there are strong indications that financial corruption was endemic in some areas, especially in the War Office.[17] The escalation of the war on all fronts, together with the increasing centralization of administration meant that, ironically, opportunities for officials to abuse their position expanded at a rate that far outstripped such possibilities under the old regime. The deputies on mission, sent out by the Convention to supervise the armies, provisioning, and hostile civilians, were entrusted with very large sums: not all acted with probity. Most lucrative of all were the contracts to supply the ever-expanding needs of the armies.

Ironically, on more than one occasion those deputies that were most uneasy about personal exposure made the most dramatic gestures in the Convention to prove their own probity, and denounce the shortcomings of others. In November 1793 Philippeaux declared to the deputies that they must set an example of 'purity' and 'virtue' to the people by submitting within ten days a statement of their finances before the start of the Revolution, and accounting for any increase in their wealth since that date. He continued: 'For every law there must be a penalty.' Any deputy who failed to satisfy the Convention regarding his financial integrity 'should be declared a traitor to the *patrie*, and pursued as such...'[18] Since Philippeaux was close to Danton (whose financial dealings when in office had already aroused suspicion from the Girondins) and eventually was to perish with him, it may be that his draconian proposal was a double bluff, designed to draw attention to his own identity as a man of virtue, and away from his actual activities and those of his friends. Philippeaux's proposal was so extreme that few deputies were likely to have been genuinely keen to put it into effect, but they feared to be seen to oppose it in

---

[16] Jordan points out that a quarter of Robespierre's constitutional proposals were 'devoted to forcing officials to be virtuous, or at least outwardly honest'. See David Jordan, *The Revolutionary Career of Maximilien Robespierre* (New York: The Free Press, 1985), 156.

[17] On the evidence for financial corruption amongst the Jacobins—particularly Danton—see Albert Mathiez, *La Corruption parlementaire sous la Terreur* (Paris: Armand Colin, 1927); also Blanc, *La Corruption sous la Terreur*; and Arnaud de Lestapis, *La Conspiration de Batz* (Paris: Société des études robespierristes, 1969). For a long-term study of men who continued to be major profiteers, see Michel Bruguière, *Gestionnaires et Profiteurs de la Révolution: L'administration des finances françaises de Louis XVI à Bonaparte* (Paris: Olivier Orban, 1986), ch. 3 'Financiers, sans-culottes, thermidoreans', 75–108.

[18] 20 Brumaire (10 November 1793), *Archives parlementaires*, 78: 703.

case people thought that they themselves had something to hide. It was Basire (who knew he was already a marked man under suspicion of corruption while he had sat on the Committee of General Security) that found the courage to speak against the proposal. Such a piece of legislation, he said, could easily be manipulated by people who had a vindictive personal motive to attack a deputy. He continued:

> It is time, citizens, that you return to yourselves, it is time that the life of a public man should no longer be exposed to the will of the intriguers, of the malevolent; it is time that you deliver the patriots from this terror which destroys magnanimous virtues, generous sentiments, and flights of the imagination, that crushes the efforts of patriotism and renders the legislator incapable of making good laws.[19]

Basire finished by characterizing Philippeaux's proposal, as part of a 'system of terror' which could destroy the patriots.[20] The openness of Basire's speech met with a stony reception. He said he knew that he could lose his head for saying such things, but that he was prepared to pay this price. In the event the proposal was dropped on the grounds that a Commission had already been set up to look into the deputies' finances, though at a more leisurely pace, and without the same penalty.

In the autumn of 1793 two new factions formed amongst the Jacobins; they became known respectively as the Hébertists and the Dantonists, after their leaders, Hébert and Danton. Both these factions, for different reasons, opposed the rule of the Committees. Hébert, together with Ronsin, Vincent, and Chaumette, were the new spokesmen for the *sans-culottes*, and on the extreme radical edge of the Revolution. They called for intensification of the Terror against counter-revolutionaries and 'aristocrats', support for *sans-culotte* economic and political measures, and a policy of forcible dechristianization.[21] They had personal grudges too. After Danton left the Committee of Public Safety Hébert attacked his reputation, returning to the personal charges made against Danton by the Girondins—corruption, and complicity with Dumouriez. Hébert had coveted the post of Minister of the Interior, once held by Roland (whom he had attacked without mercy). He was bitterly resentful when Danton had ensured that the Ministry was given to Paré. Robespierre had also supported Paré's election. The factional activities of the Hébertist leaders were as much about personal power politics and frustrated ambition as they were about sympathy for the economic plight of the ordinary people of Paris.[22] These men had been disappointed in their attempts to be elected as deputies to the Convention, but they had established their own rival

[19] 20 Brumaire, *Archives parlementaires*, 78: 703.

[20] 20 Brumaire, *Archives parlementaires*, 78: 704.

[21] On the Hébertists see Morris Slavin, *The Hébertistes to the Guillotine: Anatomy of a 'Conspiracy' in Revolutionary France* (Baton Rouge: Louisiana State University Press, 1994). On the part played by Hébertist functionaries in the War Office Ministry and the power struggle between the Committee of Public Safety and the War Office, see Howard G. Brown, *War, Revolution, and the Bureaucratic State: Politics and Army Administration in France, 1791–1799* (Oxford: Clarendon Press, 1995), ch. 3.

[22] Albert Soboul attributes the motivation of the Hébertist leaders principally to ambition and personal spite: Albert Soboul, *Les Sans-culottes parisiens en l'an II* (Paris: Librairie Clavreuil, 1958), 149, 726–7, 723–59. See also Hampson, *Danton*, 127; and Slavin, The *Hébertistes to the Guillotine*, 100–101.

power base in the Cordeliers Club, once the territory of Danton and Desmoulins. In addition, through Hébert and Chaumette, they dominated the Commune; they had close connections with the Ministry of War, and Hébert had *Le Père Duchesne*. This journal was now enjoying an even greater circulation: its distribution in the army was being financed by large subsidies from the War Office. Week after week Hébert used his journalistic voice to command fear, if not respect, from all parties, as he urged the Jacobin leaders to stop prevaricating and to guillotine more traitors, expressing his satisfaction in ferocious terms whenever he saw more heads fall.

The Dantonists began to pursue the reverse policy. They wanted the Terror to be wound down, and the power of the Paris militants to be curbed. In late 1793 they called for a policy of clemency towards and amnesty for counter-revolutionaries. The alternative names given to this group indicate something of the ambiguity of their identity. They were known as the 'Indulgents' because they called for 'indulgence' for people identified as counter-revolutionaries; but they were also known as the 'Pourris'—a name which meant 'the corrupt ones'. Though Danton was their acknowledged leader he did not play a prominent public role in the faction's activities; as far as he could he remained in the background. It is hard to say with certainty exactly what were Danton's motives in forming a faction, and his reasons for opposing the Committee of Public Safety. Stories of Danton's financial corruption had circulated for several years, and there is compelling evidence to substantiate the rumours.[23] His tactic (learned through long years of revolutionary politics) was to keep a low profile over such matters, and to say nothing that could be used to incriminate him. Nevertheless, people continued to speculate openly about his venality. On 3 December Robespierre publicly came to the support of Danton once again. He summarized what people were saying 'in groups, in the cafés', that Danton was a conspirator, that his actions at the time of Dumouriez's treachery had been suspicious, but Robespierre said that Danton 'when seen amidst his family merited only eulogies', that is, that Danton's private life demonstrated the integrity of his heart. After this time, however, Robespierre went quiet on the subject.[24]

The real question was, did Danton's financial corruption indicate that he was also politically corrupt—that is, was he prepared to accept bribes from agents of the foreign powers to pursue the policies they required of him? For this the evidence is circumstantial and less conclusive, though the scenario has some plausibility. He was always something of a political adventurer. As far back as November 1789, when Danton was on a visit to London, the French foreign ambassador to London had reported that he and his friend Paré were known to be British agents. There is no proof that this was true, though it is a curious feature of Danton's career that these stories began so early and clung to his reputation so persistently. This tale was told at a time when Danton was a person of no political significance so it is

---

[23] On the evidence for Danton's corruption see Mathiez, *La Corruption parlementaire sous la Terreur*, ch. 2 and 3; Blanc, *La Corruption sous la Terreur*, 28–30; and Hampson, *Danton*, 55–66.

[24] Robespierre denied that Danton inclined towards 'treason', on 13 Frimaire (3 December 1793), in Robespierre, *Oeuvres*, 10: 223.

unclear why the French ambassador would have bothered to make it up.[25] The clearest indication that Danton was playing his own game in revolutionary politics was his curious inactivity and failure to warn the Convention when he learned of Dumouriez's intention to turn his army on the deputies. On that occasion he had distracted attention from himself by accusing the Girondin leaders of conspiring with the renegade general. But doubts lingered.

Members of Danton's faction included his close and trusted friends. Most of them had reputations for financial corruption. Fabre and Desmoulins were widely believed to have lined their own pockets when they served as Danton's secretaries during his time as Minister of Justice.[26] Delacroix had accompanied Danton on his mission to Belgium and was heavily implicated in allegations that the two had been engaging in plunder on a substantial scale there. There was little hard proof of all this, and in itself it was not enough to endanger Danton. What caused the Jacobin leaders alarm and suspicion was the way that the Dantonists were threatening the ruling Committees themselves.

## THE FOREIGN PLOT

Before we look at the factional fighting and what came of it, we must turn to the story that exploded over the Jacobins in late 1793, known as the Foreign Plot. It was a tale of conspiracy on a scale that outstripped anything they had hitherto imagined. This narrative of deep-rooted internal and external conspiracy was put together by Fabre. Whether he talked it over first with Danton is not known, though some of the men named as part of the Foreign Plot were Danton's enemies. It was Fabre who brought this tale to the Committees and convinced them of its reality. This incendiary narrative sparked off the series of events that led to the destruction of the Jacobins.

According to Fabre, the Foreign Plot was a conspiracy among certain leading revolutionaries, members of the Jacobin and Cordeliers Clubs, who were secretly in league with the British and the Austrians to bring down the Jacobin government and destroy the Republic. At its heart was Pitt, who was masterminding a network of enemies of the French Republic, open and secret. Pitt had his tentacles deep into the Jacobins themselves. Some of the most extreme Jacobins were in the pay of the British government. They were attempting to discredit and destroy the Republic by proposing ever more violent and destabilizing measures. Fabre accused men who were part of the Hébertist network at the Cordeliers Club. There were a number of foreign men in Paris, committed to extreme politics and linked to the Hébertists. They included the Prussian deputy, and devotee of the universal republic, Anacharsis Clootz; the Spaniard Guzman; the Austrian Proli; and the Portuguese Jew Pereira. War with the foreign powers had soured the openness

---

[25] See Hampson, *Danton*, 29–30.
[26] Hampson, *Life and Opinions of Maximilien Robespierre*, 204.

towards foreign supporters that had once characterized revolutionary ideology.[27] It was all too easy in that atmosphere of suspicion to plant the idea that these men were spies for the foreign powers. Fabre also implicated French Jacobins, including Hérault de Séchelles of the Committee of Public Safety. Despite Hérault's aristocratic background, he was linked to the Hébertists. He was also an intimate friend of Proli, who lived in his house. Fabre's account raised suspicions that Hérault was passing on secret information from the Committee to the Austrians. Fabre's accusations were to lead directly to Hérault's death.[28]

Fabre's motives for concocting this tale were unedifying, but like so much else that happened in the Year Two, they were driven by fear. He himself was deeply implicated in what became known as the East India Company affair, in which several deputies, including Fabre, participated in the forgery of a decree forcing the Company into liquidation in order to profit from its assets and shares. It was probably out of terror that his part in this would be disclosed that Fabre went to the Committees. He hoped by throwing suspicion onto the integrity of other Jacobins to divert attention away from his own activities. Robespierre and the other Committee members believed his allegations; they accorded all too well with the conspiracy fears that had long haunted them. Also Fabre himself seems to have been a convincing liar; he had that all-important air of authenticity. He was also, as Robespierre was to recall later, a former professional actor. Fabre's revelations were a bitter blow for the Committee. His allegations chipped away at the authenticity of the Jacobins. But worse was to follow.

Another prominent Jacobin had also come under suspicion. This was Chabot, who had been a member of the Committee of General Security, until he was expelled in September for suspected corruption.[29] There was considerable evidence against Chabot. He was linked to the Frey brothers (Austrian bankers operating in Paris who had also come under suspicion); he had recently married their sister for an implausibly large dowry of 200,000 *livres*, an action that looked very much like some form of money laundering. Feeling the weight of suspicion bearing down on him, Chabot panicked. He and his friend Basire succeeded in persuading the Convention that deputies should not be arrested without being heard. The leaders of the Girondins had been executed a few days before. The sight had understandably unnerved Basire.[30] Chabot made the point that the law that had allowed for the arrest of deputies could be used to destroy the Jacobin leaders themselves:

---

[27] On the treatment of foreigners, which generally remained positive except for those who incurred suspicion as a consequence of the war, see Michael Rapport, *Nationality and Citizenship in Revolutionary France: the Treatment of Foreigners, 1789–1799* (Oxford: Oxford University Press, 2000).

[28] See Mathiez, 'Hérault de Séchelles', in Mathiez, *La Conspiration de l'étranger*, 222–60.

[29] The most detailed attempt to unravel Chabot's revelations and the evidence for a conspiracy is by Norman Hampson, 'François Chabot and his plot', in *Transactions of the Royal Historical Society*, 5th Series, 26 (1976): 1–14.

[30] Dufourny later complained that Basire had been heard to ask 'when will this butchery of deputies cease?' 21 Brumaire (11 November 1793), Aulard, *Société des Jacobins*, 5: 506. On Chabot's own involvement in the arrest of the Girondins, see Mathiez, 'L'Immunité parlementaire', 307. Basire had been a secretary of the Committee of General Security, and in a private letter repented of his role in having been an 'instrument of the people's vengeance … perpetually obliged to bring trouble and desolation into families'. Cited in Mathiez, 'Recherches sur la famille et la vie privée du conventionnel Basire', in Albert Mathiez, *Autour de Danton* (Paris: Payot, 1926), 47.

Who is telling you, citizens, that the counter-revolutionaries aren't counting on sending *your* heads to the guillotine? One of your colleagues overheard someone say: today
it's the turn of that one, tomorrow it's Danton's turn; the day after tomorrow Billaud-
Varenne; we'll finish with Robespierre...[31]

With hindsight Chabot's words have an air of prescience, but his intention was to
use the implied threat to intimidate the Jacobin leaders. Instead of being cowed the
Jacobins responded with anger and defiance; they turned on Chabot and Basire.
The next day in the Jacobins, Dufourny, a friend of Danton, denounced the decision to restore immunity as being due to 'an excess of sensibility' amongst the
deputies. Tellingly, he pointed out the danger to the Jacobin leaders themselves if
they allowed the Terror to be relaxed: 'If the Convention softens, soon it will be
inundated by petitions from relatives and partisans of the people who are currently
in prison, and then those who have contributed to the arrest of these individuals
will themselves be put in prison, and may be taken for execution.' Other Jacobins
took this up, and the mood against Chabot and Basire turned ugly. Hébert made
the ominous proposal that their 'conduct be examined'.[32] Two days later, urged on
by the Committees, the Convention revoked its decision and reaffirmed that deputies should not have immunity, on the grounds that the nation's representatives
should not have a 'privilege' denied to other citizens. Deputies threatened with
arrest should not have the automatic right to be heard in the Convention, though
the Convention would consider the motives for the arrest. These guidelines stayed
in place throughout the rest of the period of the Terror.[33] It may be that Dufourny
later regretted his part in the reversal of the Convention's decision, for it would
enable the arrest of Danton to take place.[34]

Chabot was unaware of Fabre's denunciations, which had been made secretly,
but in an effort to save himself he made the same choice as Fabre had done—he
decided to throw the blame onto other Jacobins. He went to Robespierre's home
early on the morning of 14 November, where he too revealed a tale of a vast conspiracy; this time by royalists to corrupt leading Jacobins financially—and politically—using assets siphoned off from the East India Company. He presented a
horrified Robespierre with 100,000 *livres* in *assignats*, which he said had been
given him to effect this bribery. The plan, he said, was masterminded by counter-
revolutionaries including Benoît d'Angers. Later Chabot elaborated on the plotters'
motives: '...their goal is the dissolution of the Convention. And all those who work
to undermine it, to corrupt it or to defame its members who have given service to

[31] 20 Brumaire (10 November 1793), *Archives parlementaires*, 78: 704.

[32] 21 Brumaire (11 November 1793), Aulard, *Société des Jacobins*, 5: 505–8.

[33] See Mathiez, 'L'Immunité parlementaire', 303–7. On the immunity of deputies throughout this
period, see also Mette Harder, 'A "deputy's honour"—the impact of arrest and imprisonment on
French Revolutionary legislators, 1789–1799', unpublished paper given at the Consortium on the
Revolutionary Era conference, Baton Rouge, LA, February 2012.

[34] In notes on deputies of the Convention, Robespierre later described Dufourny as 'the friend of
Danton and of the foreigner', in *Papiers inédits*, 2: 17. On Dufourny's loyalty to Danton, see Hampson, *Danton*, 139, 166–7.

the Republic appear to me to be involved in this plot.'[35] Chabot himself was soon arrested, implicated in his turn by Fabre. Chabot spent several months in prison where he wrote frantic letters to Robespierre, Danton, and anyone else he thought might have influence, naming more names and giving more elaborate versions of the conspiracy. His account of a royalist plot became inextricably entangled with the Foreign Plot. Most of the evidence for the subsequent trials of those accused of participating in the Foreign Plot stemmed from the denunciations of Fabre and Chabot. Their separate testimonies implicated the Hébertists and the Dantonists in complicated allegations of a vast plot involving financial speculation, duplicitous foreigners, dechristianizers, British secret agents, and French royalists. Sinister figures such as Pitt himself, and the Gascon adventurer the baron de Batz, were portrayed as puppeteers who pulled the strings of the venal Jacobins.

One of the principal questions for us is whether there was any substance to the corruption and Foreign Plot allegations, but we are unlikely ever to have a definitive answer.[36] By the summer of 1794 most of the main protagonists were dead, having exterminated one another. Those that survived had every incentive to conceal evidence of their own financial corruption and even more their political corruption, and had every opportunity to do so. As an instance of this, the interrogation of Chabot has not been seen since 1795. It was conducted by Amar of the Committee of General Security, one of the men whom Chabot had accused—probably rightly—of involvement in the East India Company fraud.[37] Fabre, though not a member of the Committee of General Security, was deputed to help Amar in Chabot's interrogation; then twisted Chabot's evidence to help his own reputation. Chabot protested repeatedly about this, but to no avail. Another man who had opportunity and motive to dispose of awkward evidence was Courtois. He was another friend of Danton, and yet another man with a reputation for corruption; he was the person entrusted with sifting through Robespierre's papers after his death to look for material that could be included in the report that Courtois subsequently wrote to blacken Robespierre's reputation. It is virtually certain that many incriminating documents went missing at that time.

As for evidence of outright complicity with foreign powers, undercover espionage leaves few written sources, either for people at the time, or for subsequent investigators.[38] There was a scattering of British agents in France during the

---

[35] Cited in Lestapis, *La Conspiration de Batz*, 28–9.

[36] Much of the available evidence was examined in Mathiez, *La Conspiration de l'étranger*; see also Hampson, *The Life and Opinions of Maximilien Robespierre*, 201–23; Hampson, *Danton*, 173; and Michel Eude, 'Une Interprétation «non-Mathiézienne» de l'affaire de la Compagnie des Indes', *Annales historiques de la révolution française*, 244 (1981): 239–61 which takes a perspective that seeks to exonerate Fabre from financial wrongdoing, but leaves much unanswered, particularly the question how far Amar of the Committee of General Security may have been implicated in the financial malpractice that he was investigating. On Amar's possible involvement see Hampson, 'François Chabot and his plot', 6–7, 10–11. Kaiser has argued convincingly that there was probably some substance to the idea of a 'foreign plot': Kaiser, 'From the Austrian Committee to the Foreign Plot', 579–617.

[37] Hampson, *The Life and Opinions of Maximilien Robespierre*, 207–8, 219, 52. On Amar's corruption see also Linton, 'Do you believe that we're conspirators?'.

[38] The British secret service was still a rudimentary institution in the early years of the revolutionary and Napoleonic wars: see Elizabeth Sparrow, *Secret Service: British Agents in France, 1792–1815* (Woodbridge: The Boydell Press, 1999).

Revolution, including Miles, who, during the Constituent Assembly, had been welcomed into the Jacobin Club. Once the war began such manoeuvres on the part of the British government became much more difficult to engineer, hence the plausibility of the idea that Pitt would try to use French revolutionaries as double agents. There are indications of the existence of some kind of political plot. With regard to spies for the counter-revolution, Proli probably was genuinely an Austrian agent, although purportedly a Hébertist. The British government did have paid agents in the Jacobin Club. It is probable that some Jacobins had been bought by Batz.[39] On the other hand, there is little sign that there was a concerted plot, still less that the Hébertists and Dantonists (who were implacably opposed to one another) would be secretly in collusion. Much of the narrative of the Foreign Plot was evidently a fabrication. Yet it is apparent now, as it was to the Jacobins themselves, that they faced considerable opposition and profound hostility, both open and covert: they had innumerable enemies. It is not so surprising therefore that they acted with brutal speed against anyone that they felt threatened them, and that they did not trouble over-much about proving guilt in any particular case, tragic though the consequences were for the people concerned. Fear of conspiracy undermined the Jacobins from within.[40] The revelation of the Foreign Plot shook the Jacobins as nothing else had done, for it undermined their trust in one another. The narrative threatened to strip away their identity as men of virtue, to disclose men who were not just financially corrupt, but enemy agents.

As an insight into Jacobin thinking, these conspiracy fears are highly significant. Most importantly, much of Jacobin politics from the autumn of 1793 to July 1794 has to be understood in relation to conspiracy—both real and imagined. Terror was not only something that the Jacobins wielded, they themselves were also susceptible to it. As their fear increased, they themselves became more ruthless and pitiless. By the autumn of 1793 they faced attack from different directions. Their enemies were innumerable: counter-revolutionaries, royalists, foreign invaders, federalists, assassins, dissatisfied *sans-culottes* threatening renewed insurrection. Now to these categories must be added fellow Jacobins, their former friends—the enemy within. Fear of a conspiracy involving some or all of these groups swelled to alarming proportions. What added to the Jacobin leaders' stress was that they did not know from what direction attack would come. The fear of a knife in the back is more terrifying than that of an open attack. Uncertainty over the identity of 'the enemy within' was perhaps the most difficult thing of all. The traumatic events of the Year Two and the way in which the Jacobins tore one another apart cannot be understood without an appreciation that their fear of conspiracy was genuine, all-encompassing, and had some basis in reality.

---

[39] On the baron de Batz, see Lestapis, *La Conspiration de Batz*; and Munro Price, 'The "Foreign Plot" and the French Revolution: a reappraisal', in Coward and Swann, *Conspiracies and Conspiracy Theory in Early Modern Europe*, 255–68.

[40] On the impact of the fear of conspiracy in 1793 to 1794, see Linton, 'Do you believe that we're conspirators?', and Kaiser, 'Catilina's revenge'; on Robespierre, see also Geoff Cubitt, 'Robespierre and conspiracy theories', in Haydon and Doyle, *Robespierre*.

# 8

# The Enemy Within

When will this butchery of deputies cease?

> Basire's reported words, November 1793.[1]

I was always the first to denounce my own friends.

> Desmoulins, defending his conduct before the Jacobins, December 1793.[2]

Here we come to the climax of the fight between the Jacobin factions: the Dantonists, the Hébertists, and the Jacobins on the ruling Committees. This internal battle culminated in the destruction of both splinter groups in the spring of 1794. Through this struggle we can trace how familiar themes of virtue, corruption, conspiracy, friendship, and enmity played out in forms that were at once ideological, tactical, and personal; waged against the vertiginous backdrop of the continuing war crisis and the Terror. All these men had chosen to support terror in the past, but would they now choose to draw back, and would they be able to do so, even if they willed it?

## DESMOULINS' CHOICE: *LE VIEUX CORDELIER*

On 5 December Camille Desmoulins began publication of a new journal, *Le Vieux Cordelier*. It became the most prominent vehicle for the Dantonist faction. It was a perilous venture for Desmoulins: anyone who openly attacked the revolutionary government was incurring a considerable risk. For this reason the precise policies of the Dantonists and the true extent of their aims are hard to determine. Judging from passages in *Le Vieux Cordelier* those aims included repealing the Law of Suspects; setting up a commission of clemency to release people imprisoned as 'counter-revolutionaries'; curbing the Paris militants; and purging some members of the Committees and replacing them with others sympathetic to the Dantonists' position. The precise motivation of the Dantonists remains more problematic. It is hard to say whether they acted most out of human compassion, guilt, self-interest, fear for themselves and their friends, or perhaps for all these reasons.

By means of his journal Desmoulins would secure his place in history. His identity was frozen as that of the Jacobin who publicly chose to reject the Terror,

---

[1] 21 Brumaire (11 November 1793), Aulard, *Société des Jacobins*, 5: 506.
[2] 24 Frimaire (14 December 1793), Aulard, *Société des Jacobins*, 559.

and lost his own life as a consequence. To some extent this image of Desmoulins was part of a mythology created after his death. As we shall see, his own attitude to the ethics of denunciation and terror was not consistent. He himself was as implicated as anyone. This uncomfortable fact does not detract from his courage in writing *Le Vieux Cordelier*, but it does remind us of the perpetual gap between myth and reality, and that people—including those who resort to terror—have complex motives for what they do. Moreover, the fact that Desmoulins could reverse his position on the use of violence against opponents shows the importance of individual agency. Opting to use terror was not an ideological imperative: it was something that individual Jacobins thought about, and agonized over, taking into account competing influences—ideological, polemical, personal, and emotional. The consequences of these pressures were not necessarily predictable. Desmoulins was in many ways an unlikely hero to make a stand against terror. For one thing, there is the inescapable fact that, since the days of 1789 when he rejoiced in the name 'Procurator of the Lamp-post', he had enjoyed the reputation of being someone who endorsed popular street violence. Thereafter he had frequently led the way in denouncing leading political figures from Mirabeau to Barnave, Brissot to Madame Roland, for falling short of the standards of political virtue. It was he who with his *Brissot Unmasked* and the *Fragment of the Secret History of the Revolution* had done much to develop the narrative of former Jacobins taking part in a secret counter-revolutionary conspiracy since the beginning of the Revolution. This theme was integral to the politicians' terror, and he himself had played a notable part in that struggle. Despite the impact of his journalism, he showed little consciousness of the deadly potential of revolutionary politics until August 1793 when, in a sudden attack of conscience, he wrote to his father:

> Life is so mingled with good and bad things in proportion, and for several years the bad has overflowed all around me, without reaching me, *that it seems to me all the time that my turn will come to be submerged in it* . . . I can't stop thinking that those men who are being killed in their thousands have children, have fathers too. At least I do not have any of these murders to reproach myself with, nor any of these wars against which I have always spoken . . . [As for] those who govern the Republic, I see in them only ambition against ambition, cupidity against cupidity.[3]

He was somewhat disingenuous here, particularly about his part in constructing the case against the Girondins, for which he did have 'something to reproach himself' had he been prepared to acknowledge it. Still, it is evident that, like other Jacobin leaders, Desmoulins had moments of feeling oppressed by the presence of death all around him, wondering if his turn would come. Was he right to fear that he was a target? Though Desmoulins had embraced the Revolution from the beginning, he had always found living like an austere man of virtue something of a challenge. Since his first encounter with Mirabeau's dinner table and the temptations of *maraschino*, Desmoulins had acknowledged to himself—and often to his readers—that he enjoyed the things that a successful career in politics could give, relative affluence,

---

[3] Desmoulins, letter to his father, 10 August 1793, Desmoulins, *Correspondance*, 175–8.

fine dining, and hobnobbing with leading power players in revolutionary politics. He had been on intimate terms with a number of men who were now seen as traitors, some of whom were already dead. His fellow Jacobins were well aware of this: he had always been indiscreet.[4] In the Year Two (thanks in part to Desmoulins' own portrayal of the Girondins) such activities by a political leader could look 'suspect'; but in itself this was not a particularly serious matter. All the Jacobins had such potential skeletons in their closets. Yet Desmoulins was regarded with an almost unique indulgence by his fellow Jacobins. They saw him as a political lightweight; a judgement made apparent by the way in which they habitually called him in public by his personal name, 'Camille', as though he were not yet grown up, not yet to be held accountable for his words and actions as one would judge a man. The ingenuousness of the persona he put across in his revolutionary journalism and his unguarded disclosures contributed to this view of him, both amused and mildly disparaging. He was looked upon with condescension, and he was not entrusted with any of the more responsible posts in the revolutionary government.

However, in the Year Two even Desmoulins needed to be careful about who he regarded as his friends. He ignored this precaution. One of his great friends was the noble general Arthur Dillon. In the early summer of 1793 Desmoulins pressured the Committee of Public Safety in an attempt to obtain for Dillon the post of commander-in-chief on the northern front. At the start of July Dillon came under suspicion of royalism and was arrested. He wrote to Desmoulins appealing to their friendship and asking him to intervene with Fouquier-Tinville, Desmoulins' cousin, for whom Desmoulins had obtained the post of public prosecutor on the Revolutionary Tribunal.[5] Desmoulins defended Dillon in a public 'Letter to General Dillon'. In the course of this witty but injudicious letter, Desmoulins made pointed jokes at the expense of Billaud-Varenne and Saint-Just. He depicted Billaud-Varenne as a physical coward; while his satirical portrait of Saint-Just became notorious for its debunking of Saint-Just's persona as a man of virtue:

> After Legendre, the member of the Convention who has the greatest idea of himself, is Saint-Just. You can see by the way he moves and holds himself, that he regards his own head as the foundation stone of the Republic, and he carries it on his shoulders with as much respect as if it were a holy sacrament. But what is so killingly funny about his vanity, is that this is the man who a few years ago published an epic poem in 24 cantos, entitled *Argant* [sic].[6]

Desmoulins had known Saint-Just in the days of his obscurity, and was privy to something Saint-Just preferred to forget—that he, a leading figure in the Jacobin

[4] The journalist Prudhomme, for example, took Desmoulins to task for a meal he had consumed at the home of General Dillon which had been altogether lacking in 'republican sobriety and frugality': see Bonn, *La Révolution française et Camille Desmoulins*, 43.

[5] Dillon's letters to Desmoulins, on 8 and 26 July, and 2 August 1793, Desmoulins, *Correspondance*, 167–9, 174, 178–9. Fouquier-Tinville had written to Desmoulins to ask for his patronage to obtain a post when Desmoulins was acting as Danton's official secretary: 20 August 1792, ibid., 144.

[6] Camille Desmoulins, *Lettre de Camille Desmoulins au général Dillon, en prison aux Madelonettes* (1793), 52.

government, who took his own political identity as a man of virtue so very seriously, had once been the author of the cynical and licentious epic *Organt*. Desmoulins misremembered the title (possibly deliberately), yet the point struck home. There was no more effective way to undermine the image of a revolutionary leader than to make him look publicly ridiculous, but during the Terror this was a risky game to play.

In the letter (quoted earlier) in which Desmoulins had confided his anguish about the future to his father, he could not resist boasting about the public impact of his *Letter to General Dillon*, even while, hand in his mouth, he wondered at his own temerity: 'Its prodigious success in the past two days makes me fearful that I have avenged myself too much. I need to look into my heart and find there the same patriotism, to excuse myself in my eyes, when I see how much the aristocrats are laughing at it: and to appreciate why I am attacked with such indignity.'[7] Up until the overthrow of the monarchy (when they had been forced underground), royalist newspapers had continually satirized the Jacobins and sneered at their assumption of the status of men of virtue. Desmoulins' mockery, however, was of a different order, precisely because he was himself one of the 'insiders' and was writing about people whom he knew personally, so that his character portraits had credibility. He feared that this time he had gone too far. He was probably right. Even so, Desmoulins had considerable support in the Jacobins. Above all, he had the friendship of Robespierre. He had only to keep silent and in all likelihood the 'bad things' would not have touched him. But he did not.

Why then, did Desmoulins choose to write *Le Vieux Cordelier*? Key passages in the journal would show his ideological opposition to the practice of terror, and his revulsion against it, as we shall see below. Yet as to what actually motivated him to take the considerable risk of writing it, his reasons, in part at least, were personal— at any event, this was how he himself conceived of them. Later, in prison, antici- pating the fate that loomed over him, he would write: 'I do not conceal from myself that I die victimized for a few pleasantries and for my friendship for Danton.'[8] The 'pleasantries' referred to his jokes at the expense of Saint-Just, Billaud-Varenne, and other leading Jacobins, and his ridicule of the Committee of Public Safety in *Le Vieux Cordelier*, particularly in Issue Three. However, the second reason, the friendship with Danton, was much more important. Desmoulins' connection with Danton was a pivotal force in his life. They had been good friends since the early days of the Revolution, when they and their families moved into the same building on the left bank, and frequented the Cordeliers Club and the café Procope.

Not all of *Le Vieux Cordelier* was against terror. Extensive sections were devoted to savage attacks on Danton's enemies, the Hébertists, at a time when allegations of corruption and complicity with foreign powers were likely to lead to their

---

[7] *Correspondance de Camille Desmoulins*, 176.

[8] Last letter of Camille Desmoulins to his wife, 12 Germinal, 'at five o'clock in the morning', P.J.B. Buchez and P.C. Roux (eds), *Histoire parlementaire de la Révolution française depuis 1789 jusqu'à l'Empire*, 40 vols (Paris: Paulin, 1833–1838), 32: 220.

deaths. But there is more to *Le Vieux Cordelier* than the bitter quarrels between the Jacobin factions. There were passages in which Desmoulins spoke out eloquently on the futility of using terror to build a republic of virtue. Robespierre wanted the Republic to be loved, but the Terror was ensuring that it would be hated. There was a simple authenticity in these passages which ensured that *Le Vieux Cordelier* would be remembered as one of the most powerful and moving documents of the Revolution. At the time, however, it also served a strategic political purpose—to challenge the political group in power, and try to bring about the overthrow of at least some of its members, most notably Saint-Just and Billaud-Varenne. While Danton remained for much of this time in the shadows, *Le Vieux Cordelier* came out onto the front line of the attack on the domination exerted by the Committees. It was a brave endeavour, though it was perhaps foolhardy for a man who had a family to consider. Desmoulins' anxieties gave him nightmares that centred on his infant son, but this did not deflect him from his purpose.

After all, Desmoulins was not entirely without support within the Committee of Public Safety, as he was well aware—in fact he was counting on it. Robespierre himself sympathized with the Dantonists' fears that the extremists who wanted more deaths and enforced dechristianization were gaining the upper hand, and that this would only reinforce resentment of the Republic among the majority of the population. Robespierre too would have liked to end the recourse to terror. But he feared that such a movement could bring about the fall of the Jacobin government, which to his way of thinking was the only force sustaining the Republic of Virtue and stopping it from falling into the abyss of reactionary politics. The practice of terror was a dreadful, unwieldy weapon; yet without it what power did the Jacobins have? In the country as a whole support for the Revolution had plummeted. Robespierre was well aware that, behind the rhetoric of terror, the Jacobins were vulnerable. Desmoulins' decision to embark on *Le Vieux Cordelier* forced Robespierre himself into making a choice; though for a considerable time he wavered as to what that would be. Robespierre read the first two issues of *Le Vieux Cordelier* while they were still in manuscript, and gave them his approval. In the first issue (5 December) Desmoulins used the narrative of the Foreign Plot, as invented by his close friend Fabre, to say that Danton's enemies, the Hébertists, were the paid agents of Pitt. On 12 December Danton followed this up by mounting an oblique attack on the Committee of Public Safety, in which he induced the Convention to vote for the renewal of the Committee's membership. The Committee rallied its support and got the decision reversed the following day.

In a move that illustrates the depth of the Jacobins' anxieties over their own authenticity it had been decided that the Club's members should go through a 'purifying scrutiny' before having their membership reconfirmed. Each man was to submit to having his past conduct and his motives examined publicly before the Jacobins. On 14 December it was the turn of Fabre and Desmoulins. Fabre was questioned about the source of his wealth, but his response that he owed his easy circumstances to his literary talents satisfied his audience and he passed his scrutiny with flying colours. Desmoulins, on the other hand, was questioned closely about his friendships. Lefort wanted Desmoulins to explain both his connection with Dillon (who was still in prison), and his reported words at the Revolutionary Tribunal when the Girondins had been condemned, that 'they were true republicans' and that 'they would die like Brutus'. Before the eyes of the watching Jacobins Desmoulins writhed as he pleaded extenuating circumstances. He admitted to having been 'deceived' by Dillon, with whom he said he had not communicated in the last three months. As for his show of grief at the condemnation of the 'twenty-two' Girondins,[9] in extenuation he said, 'of the sixty people who signed my marriage contract, I only have two friends left, Robespierre and Danton. All the others have either emigrated or been guillotined. Seven of the twenty-two were amongst these friends. It is surely pardonable therefore that I showed my sensibility on this occasion.' He further conceded that, though he 'cherished the Republic', he had often made a poor choice of his friends, including Mirabeau and the Lameths. In his justification Desmoulins said: 'I was always the first to denounce my own friends; from the moment that I realized that they were conducting themselves badly, I resisted the most dazzling offers, and I stifled the voice of friendship that their great talents had inspired in me'.[10]

Then Robespierre spoke up in defence of Desmoulins, acknowledging that he had 'both virtues and weaknesses'. Desmoulins had poor judgement and the tendency to choose the wrong kind of friends, but that did not make him a counter-revolutionary. Desmoulins had made good by 'sacrificing [his friends] on the altar he had raised to them, as soon as he understood their perfidy'. Robespierre went on to issue a warning; that Desmoulins 'should pursue his career, but avoid being so versatile, and make an effort not to let himself be deceived any more by the men who play a major role on the political scene'.[11]

Desmoulins does not appear to have been daunted by the intimidating scene at the Jacobins, for the following day a third issue of *Le Vieux Cordelier* appeared. Issue Three went much further than the previous numbers. It made a sweeping attack on the recourse to terror, and parodied the Law of Suspects, under the guise of a translation of Tacitus.[12] He followed it up with Issue Four, on 20 December, in which he called for the recourse to terror to be wound down, and a 'committee of clemency' to be set up to examine and release the people now crowded into the revolutionary prisons. He mocked at the twisted logic behind killing political opponents: 'You want to exterminate all your enemies by means of the guillotine! Has there ever been such great folly? Can you make a single man perish on the scaffold, without making ten enemies for yourself from his family or his friends?'[13]

---

[9] Twenty-one men were put on trial as Girondin leaders in October 1793. 'Twenty-two' originally referred to the number of Girondin deputies whose removal was demanded in a petition from the sections on 15 April. The number quickly became symbolic and was used to refer to the condemned leaders: Sydenham, *The Girondins*, 166.

[10] 24 Frimaire (14 December 1793), Aulard, *Société des Jacobins*, 5: 559.

[11] 24 Frimaire (14 December 1793), Aulard, *Société des Jacobins*, 5: 560.

[12] In 1933 Calvet realized that the 'translation' had been derived from an English adaptation of the original Latin text: see Palmer, *Twelve Who Ruled*, 259–60; and Hammersley, *French Revolutionaries and English Republicans*, ch. 5.

[13] Desmoulins, *Le Vieux Cordelier*, ed. Pierre Pachet (Alençon: Belin, 1987), Issue 4: 62.

Then Desmoulins addressed himself directly to Robespierre, reminding him of the hopes they had shared in 1789 for the Revolution:

> At these words *committee of clemency* what patriot would not feel himself to be moved? Because patriotism is the plenitude of all the virtues, and consequently cannot exist where there is no humanity, no philanthropy, but only a soul that is arid and dried out with egoism. Oh! My dear Robespierre! It is to you that I address these words; for I have seen the time when Pitt had none left but you to conquer, when, without you, our Argo would have foundered, the Republic would have fallen into chaos, and the society of Jacobins and the Mountain would have become a tower of Babel. O my old college comrade, you whose eloquent speeches will be read by posterity, remember well these lessons of history and of philosophy: that love is stronger and more lasting than fear...[14]

This time Desmoulins had definitely gone too far. The following day Nicolas (a *sans-culotte* who had previously constituted himself as Robespierre's bodyguard, and was now serving on the Revolutionary Tribunal) denounced Desmoulins in the Jacobins as a 'counter-revolutionary' who was risking the guillotine. He also accused Desmoulins of having tried to save another aristocratic friend, Vaillant, from prison. Hébert joined the attack. He accused Desmoulins of having been corrupted by wealth, aristocratic friends—and his wife: 'Since he married a rich woman, he spends his time only with aristocrats, whose protector he has often been.'[15] Both Nicolas and Hébert demanded that Desmoulins be expelled from the Jacobins. That Desmoulins remained (though called to give an account of his writings) is a measure of how far he could still call upon Robespierre's protection.

As regards the question whether the laws enabling terror could be relaxed, Robespierre himself showed signs that he was wavering at this point. On the very day that Issue Four appeared, a deputation of women from Lyon came to ask for mercy for their menfolk, arrested as a consequence of the revolt there. Robespierre was suspicious of their motives, and found it hard to believe that patriots could have arrested men who did not deserve it; but under intense emotional pressure from the women he suggested that a secret commission be set up to examine the cases of the Lyon rebels, to see if injustices had been committed. This was the closest he came to adopting a public position against the use of terror. However the members of the Committee of Public Safety disagreed about the form such a commission should take. Several days later in the Convention Billaud-Varenne weighed in against the whole idea. The Committee members rarely disagreed with one another in public, so Billaud-Varenne's open hostility was a measure of the seriousness of the division. Robespierre backed down, and the idea was abandoned.[16] That same evening, 26 December, Robespierre appealed for unity in the Jacobin Club. He warned that the factional infighting would 'give great

---

[14] Desmoulins, *Le Vieux Cordelier*, Issue 4: 66–7.
[15] 1 Nivôse (21 December 1793), Aulard, *Société des Jacobins*, 5: 569–73.
[16] Robespierre, *Oeuvres*, 10: 262–5, 283–4. On the commission, see also McPhee, *Robespierre*, 179; and Hampson, *Life and Opinions of Maximilien Robespierre*, 242–3.

pleasure to Monsieur Pitt'; but the dispute between the factions was intensifying and neither side was inclined to listen to him.[17]

On 5 January Desmoulins returned to the fray, with a fifth issue of *Le Vieux Cordelier*. After the latest skirmish in the Jacobins he was wary of taking on the Committees again. Instead, he devoted much of Issue Five to devising scathing replies to Nicolas and Hébert. He accused Nicolas of the cardinal revolutionary 'sin' of being self-interested, having profited from his role as printer to the Revolutionary Tribunal. He reminded Nicolas that Robespierre (Nicolas' patron) had spoken up in Desmoulins' defence.[18] Desmoulins also returned to his compromising defence of Dillon, asserting that if he were guilty of defending his friend, Dillon, then Robespierre was equally guilty of defending *his* friend, Desmoulins, for having defended Dillon. He cannily reminded his readers that 'there is no deputy of the Mountain who is not open to reproach for some error and for his Dillon'—that is, for having a friend whose political allegiances were an embarrassment.[19] His real venom, however, was directed at Hébert. Whether or not Desmoulins had felt remorse at the fatal consequences of his *Brissot Unmasked*, he gave no sign of that here; rather he boasted of how, having destroyed one fellow revolutionary through his words, he would now destroy another. Desmoulins issued a direct threat to Hébert that he would reveal Hébert's true identity as a conspirator: 'I shall unmask you as I unmasked Brissot'.[20] Using the same tactic he had deployed with Brissot, Desmoulins savaged Hébert's personal integrity. He accused Hébert of having pocketed a sizeable proportion of the large sums that he had received from Bouchotte of the War Ministry to subsidize the distribution of his paper through the army, in support of which accusation Desmoulins provided detailed figures. Desmoulins went on to denounce Hébert for fulfilling the role that had previously been Brissot's—that of working as an agent for the British, and conspiring with the counter-revolutionaries.[21] Hébert's alter ego as that epitome of the *sans-culottes*, the plebeian, uncouth, hard-swearing Père Duchesne, who viciously denounced traitors and openly rejoiced in the blood-letting of the guillotine, had given him considerable influence with the Paris militants (though not as much influence as he himself claimed to have). Yet his very success in adopting this persona could easily rebound on him. The real Hébert was quite as bourgeois and 'respectable' as Robespierre, Desmoulins, and the rest of them. What if, to this mismatch between public and private identities, were added charges of personal corruption and ambition? What if it were disclosed that Hébert was using the *sans-culottes* for his own self-advancement? How would the Paris militants feel if their self-appointed spokesman was unmasked as a fraud? Hébert was terrified and angered by Desmoulins' allegations: he had every reason to be.

---

[17] Robespierre, *Oeuvres*, 10: 289.
[18] Desmoulins, *Le Vieux Cordelier*, Issue 5: 71–2.
[19] Desmoulins, *Le Vieux Cordelier*, Issue 5: 75–6. He was careful to add, however, that he had not defended Dillon, only asked that Dillon be brought to judgement: ibid., 78.
[20] Desmoulins, *Le Vieux Cordelier*, Issue 5: 81.
[21] Desmoulins, *Le Vieux Cordelier*, Issue 5: 83.

Despite Robespierre's efforts to defend Desmoulins, there was open hostility towards him in the Jacobins. On 23 December an unnamed 'citizen' in the Club publicly protested about Desmoulins having been allowed to pass his 'purifying scrutiny'. He referred to Desmoulins as 'this man who dared say he pitied the fate of the Girondins'.[22] Hébert continued to denounce Desmoulins—for his friendship with Dillon and attempts to make him a 'generalissimo', and for 'ridiculing patriots'.[23] It was partly in self-defence that Desmoulins used this same edition of *Le Vieux Cordelier* to defend his record for putting the Revolution before his attachment to individuals: '... can anyone cite me a single conspirator whose mask I haven't raised well before it fell. I have always been six months, and even eighteen months ahead of public opinion.' He then gave a list of former political leaders of the Revolution whose integrity he had challenged long before they had been formally accused, including Lafayette, Mirabeau, the Lameths, Pétion, d'Orléans, Sillery, Brissot, and Dumouriez. He admitted that these men had been his friends: 'I had been personally connected with the majority of these men whom I denounced', but his determination to expose them from the moment 'that they changed their party' showed his own political virtue. 'I have been more faithful to the *patrie* than to friendship; and they had to be condemned to death before I would hold out my hand to them, as with Barnave'. This was a reference to Desmoulins' self-publicized refusal to shake the hand of his former friend, Barnave, until the latter had been condemned to death.[24]

On the evening of 5 January, Hébert, Desmoulins, and their respective supporters confronted one another amidst extraordinary scenes at the Jacobins. Both sides denounced the other. Augustin Robespierre warned of the destructive effects of the infighting on Jacobin unity, as his brother had previously done. Augustin had recently returned from service as a deputy *en mission*, and was shocked at the changed atmosphere: 'In the five months that I have been absent the Society seems to me to be strangely altered. At the time of my departure everyone was occupied with the great interests of the Republic. Today everything is taken up by the miserable quarrels of individuals.'[25]

The elder Robespierre was still trying to maintain unity, but his certainty appeared to be waning and he suffered ill-health. He tried to rally the Jacobins round the conviction of their own virtuous identities once again, by urging them

---

[22] 3 Nivôse (23 December 1793), Aulard, *Société des Jacobins*, 5: 574.

[23] 11 Nivôse (31 December 1793), Aulard, *Société des Jacobins*, 5: 589.

[24] Desmoulins, *Le Vieux Cordelier*, Issue 5: 74. See also the letter from Fréron to Lucille Desmoulins congratulating her husband on his stance regarding Barnave, which was 'worthy of Brutus'. 11 September 1793, in Desmoulins, *Correspondance Inédite de Camille Desmoulins*, 190.

[25] 16 Nivôse (5 January 1794), Aulard, *Société des Jacobins*, 5: 593. Hébert had previously been on friendly terms with at least some of the Robespierrists. On 26 August 1793 he was a guest at the wedding of Le Bas with Elizabeth Duplay, at which Robespierre and David were also present: see Alexandre Cousin, *Philippe Lebas et Augustin Robespierre: Deux météores dans la Révolution française* (Paris: Bérénice, 2010), 79.

to engage in lengthy discussions of the 'crimes of the English government and the vices of British society'. This was duly done, but without much sign of real enthusiasm or conviction.[26] The spectacle of revolutionary leaders fighting amongst themselves, in a vituperative war of words and mutual recrimination, threatened to cast into doubt the credibility of the Jacobins as a whole. Robespierre warned repeatedly that 'aristocrats' would be able to sit back and laugh at the spectacle of the Jacobins destroying one another. Talk on the streets and in the cafés was all of this, contributing to the confusion, and eventually the disillusionment of popular militants. It was increasingly hard for the most ardent revolutionaries to know which leaders to believe, whom to trust. Police spies warned of the negative reaction on the streets to the quarrels in the Jacobin leadership.[27]

Even those politically 'in the know' and close to the ruling group were confused by the twists and turns. Thus Gatteau, a protégé and loyal friend of Saint-Just, who was also a great supporter of Vincent at that time, wrote a letter to his friend Daubigny in support of Vincent, and against the Dantonists: 'The devil take me if I can help laughing with pity and indignation when I see all the Bourdon de l'Oises, the Fabres who call themselves d'Eglantine, the Thuriots etc... preach[ing] morality, virtue and disinterestedness.' Gatteau went on to accuse them of trying to destroy 'all the patriots of any vigour who are clear-sighted enough not to believe in the virtue of certain men who want to force our respect for their immorality itself because they want to wield the mace of the Republic in their own interest, or rather, in that of their base and disgusting passions'.[28] Gatteau was at this time in Alsace, and trying to work out what was happening in distant Paris. Meanwhile, in the capital itself, things were shaping up differently as all parties began to take sides in the power struggle within the Jacobins. Things had moved on for the recipient of this letter, Daubigny, who was in the complicated position of having close ties to all three groups of Jacobins. He was simultaneously an official at the War Office and close to Vincent (thus linked to the Hébertists), a friend of Danton, and a friend and protégé of Saint-Just and Robespierre. Daubigny had become involved in fraudulent army contracts, putting him in a vulnerable position. He settled the problem of his divided loyalties by moving away from the dangerous company of Vincent (a development unknown to Gatteau when he wrote that letter). When it became expedient to do so Daubigny would betray Danton to align himself with Robespierre; and after the fall of Robespierre and Saint-Just he would betray them too.[29] Many men made similar choices, based on the pragmatic desire to keep themselves alive in the tangled mass of friendships, suspicions, enmities, and betrayals that characterized the maelstrom of Jacobin politics in the Year Two.

---

[26] 18 Nivôse (7 January 1794), Aulard, *Société des Jacobins*, 5: 595.
[27] See Slavin, *The Hébertistes to the Guillotine*, 22–5.
[28] Cited and translated in Hampson, *Life and Opinions of Maximilien Robespierre*, 241.
[29] For a more detailed discussion of the relationship between friendships and political choices for Daubigny and Gatteau, see Linton, 'Fatal friendships'.

## ROBESPIERRE'S CHOICES: BETWEEN FRIENDSHIP, VIRTUE—AND TERROR

Desmoulins thought that Robespierre's friendship would be enough to protect him from the consequences of his choice. He was wrong. Calls for the arrest of the Dantonist faction were mounting in the Jacobin Club. Leading members of both Committees, above all Billaud-Varenne, pressured Robespierre into condoning the elimination of the Dantonists. For some time Robespierre had tried to defend Desmoulins. But the time was fast approaching when Robespierre would have to choose between revolutionary unity and individual rights, or to put this another way, between virtue and friendship. A connecting theme of this book has been Robespierre's political education, and how the experience of living through the Revolution caused him to change his mind about many political principles that he had previously thought indispensable. He expressed this dilemma in a statement of his beliefs about revolutionary government, in which he distinguished the role of government in peacetime from that of government at a time of war. He knew himself to be feeling his way: there was no precedent for what was happening: 'The theory of revolutionary government is as new as the revolution that has led to it. We should not search for it in the books of political theorists...who did not foresee this revolution...' He went on to compare normal constitutional government with the exceptional circumstances of revolutionary government:

> The goal of constitutional government is to maintain the Republic; that of revolutionary government is to found it. The Revolution is the war of liberty against its enemies: the Constitution is the regime of victorious and peaceful liberty...Under a constitutional regime, it is sufficient to protect individuals against the abuses of public power: under a revolutionary regime, public power is obliged to defend itself against all the factions that attack it.[30]

This statement gave an indication of why, if it came to a choice between sustaining the Jacobin government and defending the Dantonists, Robespierre would pick the former. Another event occurred, however, that was to prove a decisive factor in Robespierre's final choice. This was the revelation to the Committee of Public Safety that Fabre had been party to the East India Company embezzlement. Robespierre understood at last that he had been duped by Fabre: he felt both humiliated and betrayed. Curiously, neither he nor the other Committee members rejected Fabre's narrative of the Foreign Plot upon finding that the man who had spun them this story was himself a liar. On the contrary, the idea of a super-conspiracy, involving both foreign powers and Jacobin traitors, seems to have become more entrenched in their minds as a result. Fabre's duplicity also had a further consequence, which was to taint by association the Dantonists' policy. Danton and Desmoulins were Fabre's intimate friends. This raised an inevitable question: had they, too, been misled by Fabre, or were they both party to a conspiracy to overthrow the Committees and thereby cover up the extent of their own complicity in corruption?

---

[30] Robespierre, 'Rapport sur les principes du gouvernement révolutionnaire', before the Convention, 5 Nivôse (25 December 1793), Robespierre, *Oeuvres*, 10: 274.

These political and personal tensions came into the open at a meeting of the Jacobin Club on 8 January, when Desmoulins took to the tribune to respond to the denunciations made against him. Robespierre said what everyone knew, that the passages in *Le Vieux Cordelier* purporting to be translations of Tacitus were actually 'piquant satires of the actual government and the Convention'. Desmoulins' writings 'had been bought up eagerly by the aristocrats...and become weapons in the hands of the enemies of liberty'. Robespierre tried once more to extricate Desmoulins himself from blame, putting responsibility onto Desmoulins' choice of friends. He characterized Desmoulins as '...a thoughtless child, of a happy disposition, who has been led astray by bad company...' Robespierre continued that Desmoulins 'should prove his repentance by quitting the company that has caused him to be lost'. He further proposed that the issues of *Le Vieux Cordelier* be burned in the brazier of the Jacobin Club—a punishment that recalled old regime penalties for 'bad books'. The rebuke was clumsily done; yet there is no doubt that Robespierre was trying to hold out a lifeline to Desmoulins, to save him at the price of Desmoulins' repudiation of both his friends and his writings. Desmoulins' reply changed that:

> Robespierre's intention is to reproach me using the language of friendship; I am inclined to reply to all his proposals in the same tone. I will start with the first line. Robespierre said my issues must be burned; I reply to him, in the words of Rousseau: Burning is not an answer!

One can almost hear the collective gasp of breath as the audience took in what Desmoulins had said. To humiliate Robespierre in front of the Jacobins by using his beloved Rousseau against him, was an act of either great courage or great foolishness. Desmoulins was forcing Robespierre to make a public choice. Could Robespierre afford to be seen by the Jacobins as doing the very thing a 'man of virtue' must not do —put private friendship before the good of the Republic? He would risk losing his own political credibility; with both Dantonists and Hébertists standing ready to make political capital if he showed public sympathy to the Dantonist faction. Robespierre's response was a swift, emphatic retraction of his offer. 'Very well...I retract my last motion! I ask that Camille's issues should not be burned, but that they should be answered. Since he wills it so, let him be covered in ignominy.'

In reply Desmoulins, sounding more uneasy now, publicly invoked Robespierre's friendship once again, and tried to trade on that friendship to make Robespierre complicit in the stance Desmoulins had taken in *Le Vieux Cordelier*: 'You condemn me here, but wasn't I at your home? Didn't I read my issues to you, asking you, in the name of friendship, to give me your help, in advising me of the road that I should take?' Backed into a corner over whether he would publicly support the campaign to end the Terror and challenge the power of the Committees, Robespierre's response was a defensive denial: 'You didn't show me all the issues; I've only seen one or two. Since I will not support any particular quarrel, I didn't want to read the others; it would have been said that I dictated them.'[31]

---

[31]  18 Nivôse (7 January 1794), Aulard, *Société des Jacobins,* 5: 595–600.

This brief but significant exchange between the two men shows something of the dilemma in Robespierre's mind. It may have been the moment at which he began to take the fateful decision as to how to resolve it. A further revealing exchange took place in the Jacobins on the following day. Robespierre was speaking, having chosen to align himself with the Committees and outside the dispute between the two Jacobin factions, which he was depicting as a 'personal quarrel', when he spotted Fabre moving across the floor of the Club. Robespierre let loose a tirade of words on Fabre that showed his sense of personal betrayal at having been strung along by Fabre: '...I ask that this man, whom one never sees without a lorgnette in his hand, and who knows so well how to expose intrigues at the theatre, to explain himself here; we shall see how he wriggles out of that'. The wretched Fabre at first claimed not to know what he was being accused of; then went on to deny that he had influenced Desmoulins in the writing of *Le Vieux Cordelier*. He also denied that he was friendly with Philippeaux and Bourdon de l'Oise (both of whom had come under suspicion as connected with the Dantonists, while Philippeaux had been critical of the Committee). Despite Fabre's attempts to extricate himself the atmosphere in the Jacobins was extremely hostile. Someone shouted 'to the guillotine!'.[32] Robespierre had that person ejected, but it was clear to everyone, including Fabre himself, that Fabre was a marked man.

The realization that he had been duped by Fabre seems to have traumatized Robespierre, and hardened all his suspicions into certainties. His shock and anger was all the greater, since he felt that he had been imposed upon by a man who was exceptionally good at acting the role of a man of virtue. It was with this image of Fabre as a consummate dissembler in mind that Robespierre wrote a draft of a speech (it was never delivered) that depicted Fabre himself as the leader of the conspiracy to destroy the Revolution by undermining the integrity of the Jacobins. Robespierre described the two factions—Dantonists and Hébertists, 'moderates' and 'extremists'—as acting in concert. He characterized the struggle in the Jacobins as being one in which both factions feigned patriotism in order 'to sacrifice the Republic to their own self-interest. Their vaunted patriotism, is neither absolute nor universal; it is only displayed in particular circumstances, and is bound up with the interests of the sect. There is nothing in common here with public virtue. It resembles hatred, vengeance, intrigue and ambition.'[33] He gave a bitter portrait of Fabre as the man at the heart of this conspiracy, manipulating his fellow conspirators, and playing the rhetoric of the Jacobins to his advantage, '...skilful in the art of depicting men, much more skilful in the art of deceiving them, he only observed them perhaps in order to portray them successfully on the dramatic stage; he wanted to put them into play for his personal profit, in the theatre of the Revolution...' Robespierre now maintained that the Dantonists' policy of clemency had only been set up to weaken the Jacobins, to 'extinguish revolutionary energy' by encouraging 'moderation', to overthrow the

---

[32] 19 Nivôse (8 January 1794), Aulard, *Société des Jacobins*, 5: 600–604.
[33] End of Nivôse, 'Discours non prononcé sur la faction Fabre-d'Eglantine', in Robespierre, *Oeuvres*, 10: 326.

Committee of Public Safety and the War Ministry, and to put themselves and their friends at the head of government.[34] In a turn-around from his own previous proposal that a commission of clemency be set up in response to the petitioning of the women of Lyon, he criticized the indulgence of the Dantonists towards women who were menacing patriots at the bar of the Convention, and wanting amnesty, indulgence, for counter-revolutionaries and their families. Only Desmoulins and Danton were treated as not entirely given over to the conspiracy.[35] This undelivered speech gives an insight into Robespierre's altered state of mind, which lasted from this time to the end of what remained of his life. He no longer desired above all to preserve the unity of the Jacobins. Instead he had adopted the idea of the 'enemy within', naming and accusing many of the inner circle of the Club.[36]

It is evident from this that Robespierre had made a political and emotional decision to align himself with the Jacobin government and against the Dantonists. On a personal level, however, he had not yet abandoned Desmoulins or Danton. In the Jacobin Club he intervened to oppose the expulsion of Desmoulins that had been decreed. His carefully worded justification for this was that the Jacobins should not concern themselves with individual cases but with the public interest as a whole. Robespierre would no longer come out into the open to defend Desmoulins, in fact Robespierre explicitly said that he was not defending him, but the Jacobins understood his meaning—that he wanted Desmoulins reinstated, and Robespierre succeeded in obtaining this, though not without a struggle.[37] So cautious was Robespierre's wording that some historians have thought this meant that it was he who supported, and obtained, Desmoulins' expulsion; but in fact the reverse was true. Under the Terror even Robespierre had to be very cautious about what he actually put into words, especially at the Jacobin Club. He was not all-powerful there when he went against the tide of Jacobin opinion. In the toxic atmosphere of the Jacobins even Robespierre's authentic identity would have been at risk if he had been seen to put friendship before virtue. His contradictory attitude was recounted by Lucille Desmoulins in a panicky letter she wrote to Fréron, who was far away from the tumultuous Parisian situation, in Toulon. She described the fraught scenes in the Jacobins, and how Robespierre 'over two consecutive days railed at, or rather cried out against, Camille'. Yet when Desmoulins' expulsion was decreed, 'by a truly bizarre stroke', Robespierre 'made inconceivable efforts' to have Desmoulins reinstated. He succeeded, but in the course of the struggle he had seen that 'when he didn't think or act according to...the will of a certain number of individuals, he did not have all power'. Even Robespierre's power in the Jacobins had its limits. If he had continued to support the Dantonists he would have been running a far from negligible risk himself. As for Danton, Lucille continued sadly, '...they no longer listen to him, he loses courage, he grows weak'.[38]

---

[34] 'Discours non prononcé sur la faction Fabre-d'Eglantine', 332–3.

[35] 'Discours non prononcé sur la faction Fabre-d'Eglantine', 338–9.

[36] See the insightful comments that Hampson made about Robespierre's state of mind in this speech, in Hampson, *The Life and Opinions of Robespierre*, 245–6.

[37] 21 Nivôse (10 January 1794), Aulard, *Société des Jacobins*, 5: 604–8.

[38] Lucille Desmoulins' letter is reproduced in Jules Claretie, *Camille Desmoulins, Lucille Desmoulins: étude sur les Dantonistes, d'après des documents nouveaux et inédits* (Paris: Plon, 1875), 296–8.

## DESTROYING THE JACOBIN FACTIONS

Robespierre's intervention on Desmoulins' behalf had not gone unnoticed by hostile eyes. On 14 Ventôse (4 March) the Hébertists attempted to incite the Cordeliers into an insurrection against the Committees. The threatened insurrection itself did not go much beyond a lot of bluster in the Cordeliers Club; but words during the Terror were dangerous in themselves, particularly when Hébert himself seized the moment to denounce Robespierre's intervention on Desmoulins' behalf after his expulsion from the Jacobins: '...one man, misled no doubt...I do not know how to qualify it otherwise, found the nerve to have him reinstated, despite the will of the people who had expressed themselves clearly on this traitor'.[39] Though Hébert did not go so far as to name Robespierre, everyone knew who he meant. According to Morris Slavin, it was this implied threat to Robespierre that 'sealed Hébert's doom'.[40] In calling for an uprising against the ruling Jacobins, Hébert and the other Hébertist leaders seem to have been motivated as much by personal vindictiveness as by any ideological policy. This was also the conclusion of a police spy, Grivel, sent to observe the Hébertists, and the public reaction to them: 'It seems to me that Vincent, Hébert, Momoro who lead the Cordeliers, have united their interests and their efforts to employ this society in order to achieve the ambitious plans they have formed and to serve their particular passions.' Grivel went on to discuss Hébert's resentment at having his ministerial ambitions frustrated by Danton and by Robespierre in the matter of the appointment of Paré. At that same insurrectionary meeting of the Cordeliers Club, Hébert had declared that the men who were most to be feared were 'the ambitious, the ambitious', and went on to denounce Paré and Deforgues.[41] Of all the Hébertists, it was Hébert himself whom the Committees most feared. Since he failed to get the Ministry he had been using *Le Père Duchesne* to criticize the Committees' leadership.[42] The Committee of Public Safety sent Collot to act as an intermediary and issue a warning to the Hébertists, but this initiative failed. There is some evidence that Collot may have been playing a double game and that he considered using the Cordeliers as a springboard to personal power.[43] Vincent spoke out against Robespierre's continued defence of the men who had signed the

---

[39] 14 Ventôse (4 March 1794), Session of the Cordeliers Club, *Moniteur*, 19: 630, and footnote.

[40] See Slavin, *The Hébertistes to the Guillotine*, 100–101, 112; and Louis Jacob, *Hébert Le Père Duchesne, Chef des sans-culottes* (Paris: Gallimard, 1960), 305–24.

[41] *Moniteur*, 19: 630.

[42] Soboul, *Les Sans-culottes parisiens en l'an II*, 726–7. Soboul thinks that Grivel overestimated the extent to which the leaders of the Cordeliers dominated the popular movement, but does not contest Grivel's account of the leaders being motivated by ambition. See also Slavin, *The Hébertistes to the Guillotine*, 87–8, 101–102, 225–6.

[43] The stakes were high, and there was reason for subterfuge; thus Palmer, *Twelve Who Ruled*, 281–2, suggested that Collot was involved with the Hébertists' action and that he may have been playing a double game here, which, if he had succeeded, could have made him 'master of the Republic'; but in the end he decided that he was safer siding with the Committee. Madame Hébert said that Collot was playing a theatrical part when speaking to the Cordeliers and was not sincere; cited in Slavin, *The Hébertistes to the Guillotine*, 113.

petition against the arrest of the Girondins, and his refusal to send them before the Revolutionary Tribunal. Vincent did not name Robespierre, but the threat was obvious.[44] There were credible indications that renewed insurrection was brewing.[45] Previously, when the *sans-culottes* had staged a major protest against the deputies of the Convention it had culminated in the arrest and eventual deaths of the Girondins. The threat of a repeat of this happening may have been talked up a little, but the Jacobin leaders were not prepared to take the risk; they decided that the safest policy was to eliminate the Hébertists.

On 23 Ventôse Saint-Just delivered on behalf of the Committee of Public Safety the official account of 'the foreign faction'. The purpose of this speech was to implicate the Hébertists in the Foreign Plot. Saint-Just had travelled a long way since his much more conciliatory account of the Girondins' plot the previous summer; this speech was an object lesson in how to kill people with words. The men under accusation were not named. Instead Saint-Just adopted Fabre's narrative of the Foreign Plot to paint a portrait of the Republic threatened by the enemy within, who were in league with foreign powers. Saint-Just had a very clear, laconic style—when he chose to use it. This speech, by contrast, employed a rhetoric that was often cloudy, repetitive, and lacking focus. This strategy was entirely deliberate on his part, designed to sow uncertainty and confusion in the minds of his audience: '...there is in the Republic a conspiracy organized by the foreigner, which prepares for the people famine and new chains. A large number of people appear to serve this conspiracy.'[46] The speech used themes that had been familiar from the start of the Revolution. It was based on the contention that there were many officials and politicians in public life, motivated by self-interest and ambition rather than virtue, who were damaging the interests of the Revolution. Yet the crucial difference between the rhetoric of virtue and corruption in 1790 and this terrorist rhetoric of the Year Two, is that these self-interested men were now said to be secretly party to the Foreign Plot, making them traitors to the Republic, deserving of death. The conspirators were dissemblers; their supposed patriotism a mask: 'The nobles, the foreigners, the idle, the orators who had sold themselves. We declare war on these tartuffes of patriotism.'[47] There could be no toleration of political division: 'Every faction is therefore criminal, because it tends to divide the citizens; every faction is therefore criminal, because it neutralizes the power of public virtue.'[48]

Saint-Just warned that self-interest itself encouraged officials to take on the identity of men concerned with the public interest: 'If Pitt came to France to spy on the government, he would take on the appearance of an honest man, so as not to be recognized. There are even those who modestly usurp the names of great men of antiquity... The character of conspiracies is disguise.' Saint-Just contrasted true men of virtue with the counterfeit version: 'The hero kills a tyrant, and lives

[44] Jacob, *Hébert*, 319–20.
[45] Slavin, *The Hébertistes to the Guillotine*, 117–20.
[46] Saint-Just, 'Rapport sur les factions de l'étranger', 23 Ventôse (13 March 1794), in Saint-Just, *Oeuvres complètes*, 724.
[47] Saint-Just, 'Rapport sur les factions de l'étranger', 725.
[48] Saint-Just, 'Rapport sur les factions de l'étranger', 734.

modestly; he defends the people; he leaves public office poor…', whereas there were men who copied the English parliamentary style of '…acting with insolence, so as to become ministers. Amongst us, a class of men assume a haggard air, and affect to get worked up in debates, either so that the foreign powers will buy them, or that the government will give them a position.'[49] The Republic was being smothered by those who saw it as a means to a lucrative career, a way to enrich themselves and achieve power and status. Saint-Just addressed himself to these men:

> Do you want employments? Defend the unfortunate in the courts. Do you want riches? Learn how to pass on to others your superfluity. We see your tables, your draperies. Are you seen to speak to the people about civil virtues? Are you examples of probity?…Where are the oppressed whose tears you have dried? Woe betide you who know the paths that lead to fortune, and do not know the obscure paths that lead to the dwelling-places of misery! You pursue relentlessly the power which is above you, you despise the rest…[50]

So many men were passing themselves off as virtuous; how was it possible to discover an official's true self? A panoply of exterior signs could be invoked to identify conspirators from 'true patriots'.[51] 'The conspirators have signs whereby they recognize one another, at the theatre, in the places where they encounter one another, in the places where they go to eat.' Self-indulgent over-eating, especially when flaunted in public, was an indication of suspect political loyalties. In a time of dearth and war shortages, men could be seen consuming meals in restaurants at '100 *écus* a head'.[52]

A new generation of bureaucrats were exploiting revolutionary government for their own, corrupt purposes. Saint-Just imitated the wife of such a civil servant complaining that it was simply impossible 'to procure ermine and jewels at a good price' or 'to obtain table delicacies…a revolt is required so that they can procure pheasants'.[53] These vignettes were calculated to undermine the credibility of Hébert and the Cordeliers in the eyes of the Paris militants. The rhetoric of conspiracy was familiar to the urban populace, partly through the denunciations of men like Marat and Hébert himself. Now, that language was being turned against the very men who had employed it as spokesmen for the *sans-culottes*.

Once the Committee members had taken the decision to denounce the Hébertists in the Convention there could be no going back from it without danger to themselves. The Hébertists were arrested that same night, collected together with disparate individuals, and subjected to the *form* of a trial, in which the

---

[49] Saint-Just, 'Rapport sur les factions de l'étranger', 726–7.

[50] Saint-Just, 'Rapport sur les factions de l'étranger', 727.

[51] On the Jacobins' obsession with external signs of conspiracy and their anxieties regarding theatrical dissimulation, see Marisa Linton, 'The Tartuffes of patriotism: fears of conspiracy in the political language of revolutionary government, France 1793–94', in Coward and Swann, *Conspiracies and Conspiracy Theory in Early Modern Europe*.

[52] Saint-Just, 'Rapport sur les factions de l'étranger', 724. On the revolutionaries' distrust of masks and disguise, see James H. Johnson, 'Versailles, meet Les Halles: masks, carnival, and the French Revolution', *Representations*, 73 (2001): 89–116.

[53] Saint-Just, 'Rapport sur les factions de l'étranger', 731.

intention was to avoid giving them any chance to defend themselves. Along with the Cordeliers' leaders were tried several 'suspect' foreigners, including Clootz. Several of the Cordeliers' former friends and associates testified against them, including Dufourny and Legendre, friends of Danton who were described on the streets where the trial was avidly discussed as two of the Hébertists' most 'vigorous' accusers. The evidence presented against them was vague and contradictory. Thus Dufourny alleged that Ronsin and Vincent had wanted 'to assassinate the *patrie*'; he also described a dinner to which Clootz had invited him in order 'to corrupt him'.[54] One of the most damning witnesses was another friend of Danton's, General Westermann, who accused Ronsin of having deliberately prolonged the war in the Vendée during his time there as a leader of the *sans-culotte* internal military units, the *armée révolutionnaire*.[55] The reaction of the popular classes to the arrest and trial of the 'Père Duchesne' was one of confusion, which mirrored their response the previous autumn to the arrest of the leading *enragés*. After the initial shock, the sections chose to profess loyalty to the Convention. But the militants were unsure who to believe and increasingly doubtful about the trustworthiness of any of the Revolution's professed leaders.[56]

The arrest and execution of the Hébertists lulled the Dantonists into thinking that they had prevailed and were in a strong position. In fact the reverse was the case. Pressure had increased for the Committee of Public Safety to demonstrate its integrity, impartiality, and commitment to the public good rather than to any faction—by destroying the Dantonist faction as well as that of the Hébertists. Collot d'Herbois and Billaud-Varenne, who had both been close to the Cordeliers, argued fiercely that the Committee should strike down the Dantonists. For a long time Billaud-Varenne and Robespierre had been at loggerheads over this. For several months Robespierre resisted killing Danton. This is evident from the testimony of Billaud-Varenne when he subsequently denounced Robespierre on 9 Thermidor. He said that Robespierre had been 'soft' towards Danton: 'The first time I denounced Danton in the Committee, Robespierre rose up in a fury, saying he knew my intentions, that I wanted to ruin the best patriots.'[57]

Robespierre had already made a political choice—to dissociate himself from the campaign for clemency. He now had a personal choice ahead of him—whether or not to be a party to the deaths of the Dantonists. Billaud-Varenne, Collot d'Herbois, Saint-Just, along with leading members of the Committee of General Security, pushed hard to close in on Danton, but Robespierre did not cave in to their pressure until about two weeks before Danton's arrest. There was at least one final meeting between Robespierre and Danton, probably organized through Daubigny, a friend of both men.[58] It seems likely that Danton would not accept Robespierre's

[54] Wallon, *Histoire du Tribunal révolutionnaire*, 3: 51–3, 59.
[55] Wallon, *Histoire du Tribunal révolutionnaire*, 3: 54–5.
[56] Slavin, *The Hébertistes to the Guillotine*, ch. 6.
[57] 9 Thermidor (27 July 1794), *Le Moniteur*, 21: 332.
[58] Norman Hampson, who wrote excellent biographies of both Robespierre and Danton, provides a detailed and even-handed account of the evidence for the final breakdown of relations between them in *Life and Opinions of Maximilien Robespierre*, 254–5, and *Danton*, 150–60.

efforts to broker a compromise with the Committees and keep quiet. Danton now had the additional motive of wanting to defend his close friend Fabre, who was still awaiting trial on serious corruption charges,

Robespierre shrank from complicity in Desmoulins' arrest. His friendship for Danton had run less deep; even so, they had been through a great deal together and there was a letter that Robespierre wrote to Danton on the occasion of his wife's death that contained the words: 'I love you more than ever and until death'.[59] That emotion, too, was to be discarded now. The ideology of virtue backed him into a corner—he could not be seen to defend people purely because they were his friends. He would lose credibility—and to lose credibility as a revolutionary leader during the Terror was dangerous in itself. He still had a choice, though. Why then did he do it? His motives were partly ideological—the cause of revolutionary unity, public good over personal loyalty. He had come round to the belief that *at all costs* the revolutionary government must remain in power, as the best force to sustain the Republic of Virtue, a belief that he clung to in the final months of his life. His motives were also tactical. In common with other Jacobins, five years of experience of revolutionary vicissitudes had taught him that clemency towards leaders in time of war was a potentially costly mistake. The Jacobins were hardest on themselves. In his mind the fall of the Committee of Public Safety would risk the fall of the Republic. Up to a point he had supported the policy of indulgence; but he disapproved of the Dantonists' tactics, and became suspicious of the integrity of their motives. According to Norman Hampson, Robespierre was partly at least on the side of the Dantonists, but threw in his weight against Danton because he knew Danton was unlikely to defeat the Committees. Danton's group had challenged the power of the Committee of Public Safety, and threatened three of its most radical members, Billaud-Varenne, Collot d'Herbois, and Saint-Just. The revelation of Fabre's duplicity had stripped Robespierre of any remaining illusions about the Jacobins, and led him to suspect that Danton, and even Desmoulins, were also fooling him. He had emotional reasons also, of which the primary one was fear: Tissot (a contemporary historian present at the denunciation of Danton in the Convention) said that 'Robespierre did not want Danton's death, but he was easily frightened'.[60] Taking a decision to kill men who had been his friends left its mark on Robespierre.[61] From the time he agreed to the death of the Dantonists he was a changed man.

The Dantonists had not ceased their campaign. Desmoulins wrote a seventh issue of *Le Vieux Cordelier*. It contained an all-out attack on the integrity of the Committee of Public Safety. According to Desmoulins, whether they willed it so or not, the men of the Committee had become agents of corruption and fear:

[59] Letter from Robespierre to Danton, 15 February 1793, *Correspondance de Maximilien et Augustin Robespierre*, 160.

[60] Cited in Hampson, *Life and Opinions of Maximilien Robespierre*, 254.

[61] McPhee has investigated evidence from Robespierre's doctor Souberbielle regarding the effect that stress had caused on Robespierre, and argues that the confrontation with Danton and Desmoulins took a serious toll on both Robespierre's health and his political capacity: see McPhee, *Robespierre*, 186–8, 194–5.

Already the Committee nominates all the places; even including the committees of the Convention, the officials that are sent to the *départements* and to the armies. It has in its hands one of the great political resources, hope, by means of which the government attracts to itself all the ambitions, all the interests. What does it lack in order to master or rather destroy the Convention and to exercise the fullness of power of a decemvirate, if those deputies whom it cannot attract into its antechamber by dazzling their eyes with the tricolour plumes, recompense for their pliability and adulation, it can control by means of the fear of being sent to the Luxembourg, in the eventuality that they should cause displeasure? Are there many deputies, are there many men, who are entirely without either hope or fear? Even in the republic, history does not count more than one Cato in a million men.[62]

Desmoulins went on to confront the ideology of political virtue head on. Significantly, it was explicitly Montesquieu's conception of political virtue, the one that was used by Robespierre as the basis of revolutionary republican government, that Desmoulins challenged:

But if virtue were the sole spirit of government, if you suppose all men to be virtuous, then the form of government is a matter of indifference, and all serve equally well. Why, then, are some governments detestable and others good? Why do we hold monarchy in horror and cherish the republic? It is because, as one justly concludes, that not all men being equally virtuous, it is necessary for the efficacy of government that it should fill the place of that virtue and that the excellence of the republic consists in precisely this, that it supplements virtue...if the nation lacks virtue as in the monarchies, at least a balance of vices is established, the nature of the government opposes them to one another; and in this equilibrium it is the general interest which decides between them.

This series of simple and incontestable propositions makes palpable Montesquieu's error. Virtue is by no means the foundation of the republic.[63]

Desmoulins counselled Robespierre not to attempt to build the Republic on such a rare quality as virtue. As for the Committee of Public Safety, 'however free its members were of ambition' since they had taken power no one had dared oppose them, not in the Convention, nor in the newspapers, 'no contradictor, not the shadow of a discussion, even for the sake of form'.[64] This issue went unpublished. Desmoulins' publisher took fright at so open an attack, not only on the Committee but also on one of the founding principles of the Revolution, and would not go ahead with it. Before Desmoulins could formulate his next move the two Committees acting in concert had decided to strike down the Dantonists. The final blow fell only a few days after the execution of the Hébertists.

Once the decision was taken to proceed with the arrest of the Dantonists the Committee members were embroiled in the inexorable logic of their own choices. From their perspective they could not afford to lose. The trial of the Dantonists, like that of the Hébertists, would be political; for Danton, and the deputies arrested

---

[62] Desmoulins, *Le Vieux Cordelier*, Issue 7: 141.
[63] Desmoulins, *Le Vieux Cordelier*, Issue 7: 141–2.
[64] Desmoulins, *Le Vieux Cordelier*, Issue 7: 142.

with him, Desmoulins, Delacroix, and Philippeaux, it was about killing, not justice. Other men already under arrest for suspicion of involvement in the Foreign Plot (including Fabre, Hérault de Séchelles, and Guzman) were to be linked with Danton so as to make more credible the charge that they had all been part of the Foreign Plot. Westermann (dubbed 'the butcher of the Vendée'), who had been a key witness against Ronsin at the Hébertists' trial only a few days before, was now himself to be included on the list of conspirators. When Robespierre ventured to maintain that it would be the decent thing to do to denounce the Dantonists before arresting them, Vadier of the Committee of General Security answered, 'you can run the risk of getting guillotined, if such is your will; for myself, I prefer to avoid this risk, by getting them arrested at once, because we shouldn't be under any illusions about what we're doing here...'[65] Robespierre, it appears, was convinced by this brutal logic.

The case against the Dantonists was put together secretly and at great speed. They would be arrested without warning, followed by a speech in the Convention that would denounce the deputies as conspirators, part of the ubiquitous Foreign Plot. The delivery of the speech was entrusted to Saint-Just. Once again he would be the front man for the Committee of Public Safety in the denunciation of a faction. This time he had help in his grim task. Robespierre, who had so long resisted the proscription of the Dantonists, now threw himself into the endeavour. He preferred not to be the public denouncer of his former friends, leaving that role to Saint-Just. But he drew up a list of notes to provide Saint-Just with material to use against the Dantonists. These notes contained details about the political and personal failings of the men to be accused; all held up as evidence of 'conspiracy'. These tactics mirrored those developed over several years of Jacobin denunciations, fine-honed so as to bring about the deaths of the men accused. No one was better placed to carry this out effectively than Robespierre. He knew all the men concerned well, having worked closely with them over several years and been a personal friend to Danton and Desmoulins. Who better than he to unpick their identity as patriots in both public and private, and to show that every move they had made had been self-interested rather than virtuous? The paucity of the case Robespierre made against them demonstrates more conclusively than anything else that this was a factional quarrel (based on suspicion, fear, enmity) not a difference of principles. When Robespierre had defended Danton's reputation a few months earlier he had deplored the fact that Jacobins were making vague allegations against Danton without proof; now he was doing the same thing. It was not that he had become less capable of appreciating the arguments that he himself had previously made, but that other pressures had changed his mind over what course to take, and the consequences of having made those choices led to his making others, still more ruthless.

Robespierre was still trying to see himself as a man of virtue in that he would not go so far as actually to fabricate evidence against Danton. The case against the

---

[65] *P.A. Taschereau-Fargues, à Maximilien Robespierre aux enfers* (Paris: Year III, 1795). The author of this Thermidorean pamphlet said that Vadier gave him this account two days after the events.

Dantonists could have been made to look much stronger had he done so. On the contrary, Robespierre scrupulously corrected an error in Saint-Just's original draft.[66] What Robespierre did do, however, is attack the authenticity of the suspects by giving the blackest interpretation to words and actions that he had witnessed from the privileged position of being a trusted friend. The aim was to sow enough doubt in the minds of the deputies regarding Danton's political integrity to make it possible to proceed against him.

The version of the speech that Saint-Just finally delivered read like an amalgamation of all the previous denunciations of Jacobin leaders. Saint-Just employed a similar tactic to that used by Desmoulins against Brissot and his group, on a scale that was still more devastating, and with different characters cast in the roles of chief conspirators, including Desmoulins himself. Saint-Just retold the history of the Revolution as a narrative in which the role of the Dantonists was that of secret conspirators, who had sought to corrupt and subvert the very thing they were meant to defend—the public good. For 'the past five years' they had been leading a double life, pretending to be true revolutionaries, when in reality they were 'the last partisans of royalism'.[67] They had been in league, Saint-Just said, with a long line of former Jacobins who had already been exposed as traitors—Mirabeau, the Lameths, Duport, d'Orléans, Brissot, Hérault, Hébert. The Dantonists were 'the last friends of Dumouriez'. In fact Danton was still Dumouriez's friend. The Dantonists had been bought long ago by the British government; they were at the heart of the Foreign Plot. Fabre (the man who fabricated the story of the Foreign Plot) was now described as the man at the centre of it; he was 'at the head of this party'.[68]

Offering any kind of credible evidence of these vague and insidious allegations was not going to be easy. The 'evidence' that Robespierre provided in his notes lingered even more heavily than in the case of the Hébertists on outward signs of conspiracy observed in the conduct of the suspects. Robespierre remembered unwary words, uttered in confidence, sometimes several years before. Thus he wrote: 'I recall an anecdote which seemed of little importance at the time. During the first months of the Revolution I was at dinner with Danton, Danton reproached me with hindering our good cause, by not following the line taken by Barnave and Lameth who were at that time starting to deviate from popular principles.'[69] Thus Robespierre recalled something said in friendship over dinner four years earlier, and viewed it retrospectively as evidence of conspiracy. According to Robespierre's notes, Danton mingled conspiracy with the overt hedonism of a man who, on his own admission, knew no virtue better than that 'which he practised every night

---

[66] Robespierre, 'Les notes contre les Dantonistes', published in Albert Mathiez, *Études sur Robespierre (1758–1794)* (Paris: Éditions Sociales, 1958), 126, note 1.

[67] Saint-Just, 'Rapport sur la conjuration ourdie pour obtenir un changement de dynastie, et contre Danton...', delivered before the Convention, 11 Germinal an II (31 March 1794), in Saint-Just, *Oeuvres complètes*, 761.

[68] Saint-Just, 'Rapport contre Danton', 764–5, 768–70.

[69] Robespierre, 'Les notes contre les Dantonistes', 134. See also Saint-Just, 'Rapport contre Danton', 768.

with his wife'.[70] It is not clear whether the greater crime in Robespierre's eyes was Danton's ignorance of true virtue, or his having made a joke about it.

Once again lavish and expensive dinners were seen as the occasion for private plotting. This was reflected in Saint-Just's final version of the report. In the summer of 1793, he said, there was a plot to make the little Capet, son of Louis XVI, king. 'At that time Danton often dined in the rue Grange-Batelière, with some English people; he dined with Guzman, the Spaniard, three times a week, and with the infamous Sainte-Amaranthe, the son of Sartine, and Lacroix. It's on these occasions that some people partook of dinners that cost a hundred *écus* a head.' (Evidently the Dantonists were meant to have attended the same dinners as the Hébertists.)[71] Robespierre's notes refer only in passing to this particular accusation, though later, after Danton's death, he was to go into these 'conspiratorial dinners' at greater length in some private notes he compiled on deputies he suspected of counter-revolution, showing that he took these allegations seriously.[72] Robespierre's notes for the trial of the Dantonists also recounted how Fabre had continued to take both lunch and dinner with Proli, even after secretly denouncing him, thus showing the extent of Fabre's hypocrisy. Robespierre recalled other social gatherings, involving 'known' conspirators. 'One must not forget Robert's tea parties, where d'Orléans himself made the punch, and Fabre, Danton and Wimpffen were in attendance. It was there that attempts were made to attract the largest possible number of deputies of the Mountain, either to seduce or to compromise them.'[73] Robespierre even used Danton's well-fed look (*embonpoint*) against him, saying that Danton and his friends used it to justify his idleness and inaction at key revolutionary moments.[74]

Signs of emotion, such as tears or laughter, might indicate duplicity. In the language of Rousseau tears were the outpouring of authentic emotion, a sign of true sensibility. But in the context of fears of conspiracy, tears might be employed to disguise authentic emotions, offering the feigned appearance of sincere feeling.[75] Robespierre described the occasion when Fabre (that consummate actor again) had seen the issues of *Le Vieux Cordelier* that asked for a policy of clemency, and had wept tears, deceiving the gullible Desmoulins into thinking that he had

---

[70] Robespierre, 'Les notes contre les Dantonistes', 138.

[71] Saint-Just, 'Rapport contre Danton', 776–7. To situate this accusation within the wider context of the development of the restaurant as a 'public/private' space where secrets might be discussed, see Rebecca Spang, *The Invention of the Restaurant: Paris and Modern Gastronomic Culture* (Cambridge, MA: Harvard University Press, 2000).

[72] Robespierre, 'Les notes contre les Dantonistes', 131. In Robespierre's subsequent notes regarding one of the deputies he regarded with suspicion, Thuriot, Robespierre mentioned as grounds for suspicion the fact that Thuriot, too, had attended the dinners with Danton, Guzman, and Lacroix: see *Papiers inédits*, 2: 18–19.

[73] Robespierre, 'Les notes contre les Dantonistes', 138 and 151. Saint-Just referred to these 'confabulations' briefly in the final report, 'Rapport contre Danton', 770.

[74] Robespierre, 'Les notes contre les Dantonistes', 143. The *embonpoint* did not feature in the final version of the report, possibly because Saint-Just thought it too petty to be a serious accusation.

[75] On the growing suspicion of tears during the Revolution, see Anne Vincent-Buffault, *The History of Tears: Sensibility and Sentimentality in France* (Houndmills: Macmillan, 1991), 92–6.

'an excellent heart' and was, in consequence, 'a patriot'. 'Crocodiles weep too,' observed Saint-Just laconically in his version of this story. Still more cruelly, Robespierre recalled that Danton had attempted to copy this tactic, in the tribune of the Jacobins, and at Robespierre's home. According to Robespierre, 'he tried to imitate Fabre's talents' but he was unable even to make a pretence of authentic feeling: his tears were unconvincing and he succeeded only in making himself ridiculous.[76]

Even laughter might conceal duplicitous thoughts—a point that was used against both Danton and Hérault de Sechelles. According to Saint-Just, 'Hérault was serious within the Convention, elsewhere he played the buffoon, and would laugh incessantly to cover up the fact that he never said anything'.[77] It is not clear why Hérault's tendency to laugh should so have infuriated Saint-Just, yet it is not hard to imagine that Hérault might have been laughing out of sheer nervousness, feeling the eyes of his colleagues upon him, scrutinizing him for signs of noble mannerisms indicating suspect allegiances.

The very fear that successive factions had shown could be a sign of conspiracy. If they were not hiding their guilt, why should they be afraid of revolutionary justice?

> Those people who, for four years have conspired under the veil of patriotism, now that justice is closing in on them, repeat the words of Vergniaud: *The Revolution is like Saturn, it will devour its own children.* Hébert repeated these words during his trial; they are repeated by all those who tremble as they see themselves unmasked. No. The Revolution will not devour its children, but its enemies; no matter with what impenetrable mask they have concealed themselves. Were the conspirators who perished the children of liberty because for a moment they resembled them?[78]

Showing fear, suspect friendships, unguarded words, disguised appearances, private dinners, tears, laughter, inappropriate jokes, even facial expressions, all these might be invoked as external signs that called into question inner revolutionary integrity. Possibly one of the most revealing images was that of the conspirator as actor, the 'tartuffe' who emulated the words, the appearance, even the emotions of the genuine 'patriot' but did not share them in his heart. It is an image that suggests an underlying anxiety in the revolutionary mentality, a profound, though unvoiced, uncertainty that anyone could ever entirely prove their revolutionary virtue.

Saint-Just's accusation of Danton's personal as well as political shortcomings, his idleness at key moments and self-indulgence, invoked the classical model of denunciation of failures in private as well as public virtues. It recalled Cicero's indictment of the degrading behaviour of Mark Antony, his neglect of politics and abandonment of the soldiers fighting on his behalf in order to

---

[76] Robespierre, 'Les notes contre les Dantonistes', 135. Saint-Just, 'Rapport contre Danton', 774–5.

[77] Saint-Just, 'Rapport contre Danton', 774.

[78] Saint-Just, 'Rapport contre Danton', 777.

engage in dissipation with Cleopatra. At the same time, however, it is notable that some of the pettier charges made by Robespierre were either toned down considerably or omitted from Saint-Just's final version of the report, probably because the report writer thought they seemed so personally vindictive as to undermine the virtuous image of the man making it. Thus Saint-Just made no mention of Danton's inability to weep, nor his joke about virtue and sleeping with his wife; neither did he mention Danton's well-fed appearance, nor his penchant for wine.

The first intimation that Desmoulins had that the net was closing in on him was when Robespierre rejected a private appeal to their former friendship. Desmoulins said to a friend, 'I am done for: I have been to call on Robespierre, and he has refused to see me'.[79]

When news broke in the Convention that the Dantonists had been arrested the previous night, Legendre, a friend of Danton, spoke up against the deputies having been arrested without a chance to be heard in the Convention. It was a key moment: the issue was in doubt. The deputies watched, fearful for themselves, undecided, as Robespierre stepped in to save the situation for the Committees, and to condemn the Dantonists. He pointed out that one of the deputies, whose name Legendre pretended not to know, but according to Robespierre he surely did, was his own friend, Philippeaux. Robespierre thus intimated that, in trying to defend the right of the accused men to be heard by the Convention, Legendre was putting a personal friendship before the public good. Robespierre's argument was that the deputies who had been arrested had no right to a legal privilege that had been denied to others.

> We shall see on this day if the Convention knows how to break a false idol that has been corrupt for a long time, or whether in its fall this idol will crush the Convention and the French people. Cannot what has been said about Danton not have been equally applicable to Brissot, to Pétion, to Chabot, even to Hébert, and to so many others who have filled France with the lavish clamour of their dissimulated patriotism? What privilege would he have then? In what way is Danton superior to his colleagues, to Chabot, to Fabre d'Eglantine, his friend and confidant, whose ardent defender he has been?[80]

Robespierre declared that Danton's friends had appealed to him, reminding him of his own friendship for Danton, but that he put his 'zeal and passion for liberty' before 'the memory of a former liaison...' Virtue and the Revolution must come before 'false friendship'. Even the knowledge that the same danger now looming over Danton might one day threaten Robespierre himself had not stopped him: 'What do dangers matter to me! My life is the *patrie*; my heart is without fear; if I die it will be without reproach and without ignominy.'[81] He thus used his declaration that he was willing to sacrifice his own life to justify the

---

[79] Thompson, *Robespierre*, 463.

[80] 11 Germinal (31 March 1794), *Archives parlementaires*, 87: 627.

[81] 11 Germinal (31 March 1794), *Archives parlementaires*, 87: 628.

use of terror against others. Robespierre's eloquence—and much more than that, the fear his words evoked—won the day. His words were greeted with repeated applause. No one supported Legendre, who made haste to back down, terrified for his own life. No friend of the Dantonists dared speak up in case he too should be accused of putting friendship before virtue.[82] Shortly after, the Convention voted in support of Robespierre, and settled down to hear Saint-Just's report. For the Dantonists it was over.

[82] See for example the letter that the terrified Deforgues wrote to Robespierre, denying that he had been a friend of Danton: Deforgues to Robespierre, 14 Germinal, *Papiers inédits*, 2: 189–93.

# 9

# The Robespierrists and the Republic of Virtue

> ...the sacrifice of egoism, of self-love, this constant contempt for death, this equality of souls, this lofty courage which makes one always ready to sacrifice oneself for the truth and the good of the *patrie*; for myself who knows no other political virtue than this, and who thinks that this kind is infinitely rare, I by no means counsel Robespierre to build the republic on this foundation...
>
> Desmoulins, *Le Vieux Cordelier*, Issue 7.[1]

> My reason, not my heart, is on the point of doubting this virtuous republic whose image I had traced for myself.
>
> Robespierre, final speech to the Convention, 8 Thermidor.[2]

In this chapter we turn to Robespierre and the group around him during the last months of the Jacobin Republic. This group included Saint-Just and Couthon on the Committee of Public Safety, and Le Bas on the Committee of General Security. These men were linked to Robespierre by ties of personal friendship as well as political conviction. Beyond this inner group Robespierre had numerous allies who, especially since the fall of the Hébertists, were serving in administrative posts for the revolutionary government, above all on the Commune. As with previous Jacobin factions, much of the coherence of this group was imposed upon them retrospectively by their opponents at the time of their overthrow; it was only then that they were given the collective name of the 'Robespierrist' faction.

## FEAR INTERNALIZED: THE POLITICIANS' TERROR

By the summer of the Year Two the euphoria that had characterized the start of the Revolution had been largely worn away by nearly five years of political struggle and many months of war. One of the characteristics of a regime of terror is that people rarely venture to say what they really think. Nevertheless, there is much evidence, particularly from private sources, to indicate that for many participants in revolutionary politics, the rhetoric of virtue and patriotism had been eroded of much of its meaning: for them it was a manner of speaking, nothing

---

[1] Desmoulins, *Le Vieux Cordelier*, Issue 7, 142.
[2] Robespierre, 'Contre les factions nouvelles et les députés corrompus', 8 Thermidor l'an II, 26 July 1794, in *Oeuvres*, 10: 566.

more. Trust had been undermined by years of revolution, by a series of actual betrayals, and by the use of terror. Revolutionaries still talked about their patriotic fervour and formally enacted it in the revolutionary festivals, but on all sides this seems to have been increasingly an artificial emotion; only with an effort could it be attained, even for a few moments. The predominant emotion now was fear.

There is no doubt that during the Year Two the Jacobin leaders were afraid and that this anxiety affected their decision making. They were genuinely afraid of conspiracies and with good cause—even though not all the conspiracies they envisaged were actual ones. They were fearful of losing the war. They were afraid of the counter-revolution winning, of the monarchy being restored, and the advances of the Revolution being lost, along with their own lives. They were frightened of the *sans-culottes* and the popular violence that they themselves had benefited from but which, now unleashed, might be turned on them if they lost their credibility. They were anxious about the risks of being assassinated, a danger that might confront them at any moment, in public places, or even in their homes. They were worried about being misled by people with platitudes about virtue on their lips and corruption and enmity in their hearts. They were afraid of each other, with good reason; after the destruction of the Jacobin factions in the spring it was evident that any renewal of open conflict within the Jacobins would almost certainly lead to the extermination of whichever was the losing group. Some of them, at least, were *genuinely* filled with foreboding that, as the men of virtue entrusted with the defence of the Revolution, they were too few and that they would be overwhelmed by the self-interest and ambition of others, united in conspiracy. They were prey to uncertainty about themselves; apprehensive about the mismatch between what they had believed would happen in 1789 and what was happening now. Finally, they themselves were subject to the Terror, and dreaded that at any moment it might be turned against them. Many years later, Levasseur described the experience of the Jacobin leaders: 'The terror that we inspired crept over the benches of the Mountain, as it did into the *hôtels* of the faubourg Saint-Germain. It sat on the benches of the tribunal and taught its members that they could at any moment change from the role of judge to that of the accused.'[3] Thus the Jacobin leaders were beset by fears. Yet even to show their unease could be interpreted as a sign of their own guilt. It is against this background of anxiety, extreme stress, sleeplessness, suspicion, that we should seek, not to exonerate, but to understand what people are capable of when fear coupled with strong belief drives them forward.

The extent of Robespierre's own role in instituting and supporting terror has always been subject to debate, and there is contradictory evidence. The image of Robespierre as the sole initiator of Jacobin ideology and the Terror was encouraged by the group of Jacobins who joined forces to overthrow him. These men became known as the Thermidoreans after the (revolutionary calendar) month in which the fall of Robespierre took place. It was to their advantage to load the blame for

[3] Levasseur, *Mémoires*, 347.

the Terror onto Robespierre while downplaying their own involvement. Yet in reality the Committee of Public Safety took collective responsibility for its political decisions and there was much common ground between the Committee members. Robespierre and Saint-Just were prominent members of the Committee, but they were by no means the sole proponents of terrorist practices.[4] The chief thing laid at Robespierre's door was the infamous Law of Prairial, though even here he was by no means solely responsible. The Law of Prairial was partly modelled on the procedures of the Commission at Orange; it was championed in the Convention by Couthon, working closely with Robespierre; it tightened up considerably the procedures of the Revolutionary Tribunal and increased the proportion of convictions, for which the sentence of death was made the only possible verdict. Although the sullen and intimidated deputies passed this law it added to their sense of insecurity, for they understood that it could be used to expedite the arrest of members of the Convention.[5] Whilst Robespierre had sponsored the Law of Prairial he did little to put it into practice. Its implementation was carried out by other members of the Committees, whatever they might say later about having deplored it. It was put into place against a backdrop of fear both of assassination, and of a plot staged within the overcrowded prisons of Paris. The principal victims of the Law of Prairial were in those overcrowded prisons, many suspected of involvement in prison plots, especially a group of leading figures in the Luxembourg prison. The revolutionaries dreaded that the prisoners would break out and assassinate the patriots.

There is evidence that some of the Jacobins were looking for a way out of terror in the spring of 1794, but one of the things that made this difficult was the atmosphere of fear itself.[6] Robespierre himself seemed increasingly to be a man who was not in control of events, and was uncertain about what he was doing. The one constant that he clung to was his belief in the ideology of political virtue. Yet his actions were increasingly contradictory. His continued suspicion of the Jacobins led him to call for more purges of 'false' Jacobins. On the other hand, he continued to protect a number of people from the Terror, including the seventy-five deputies who had protested against the arrest of the Girondins, and who had been arrested. Robespierre remained steadfast in opposing any attempt to send them before the Revolutionary Tribunal. Many wrote to him to express their gratitude, and to encourage him, of course, to remain firm in their defence.[7]

One question which persists is why Robespierre and his allies on the Committees did not act immediately after the major victory at the battle of Fleurus on 26 June 1794 effectively ended the danger of the Revolution's destruction at the hands of foreign powers. Why did they not dismantle the emergency government and the

---

[4] Palmer, *Twelve who Ruled*, 333.

[5] On the Law of Prairial, see Lefebvre, 'Sur la loi du 22 Prairial an II', in Georges Lefebvre, *Études sur la Révolution française* (Paris: Presses Universitaires de France, 1954); Godfrey, *Revolutionary Justice*, 134–5; Martin, *Violence et Révolution*, 223–5.

[6] Martin, *Violence et Révolution* takes this view. See also some thoughtful reflection by Hampson, *Life and Opinions of Maximilien Robespierre*, 268–70.

[7] Letters from the imprisoned Girondin deputies are in Jacob, *Robespierre vu par ses contemporains*, 130–1. See also McPhee, *Robespierre*, 211.

laws enabling terror, and install the Jacobin constitution? One reason is that the impact of Fleurus on the international situation took a while to become apparent. Another reason, much closer to home, stemmed from Robespierre's horrified reaction to news of the atrocities committed in the name of the Convention by certain members of the Jacobins *en mission*. These included Collot d'Herbois and Fouché in Lyon, and Fréron and Barras in Marseille and Toulon. Their brutality towards local populations, and their involvement in the imposition of forcible dechristianization (which outraged Robespierre's own beliefs), convinced Robespierre that these men, far from being men of virtue, were corrupt and hypocritical, and that they were discrediting the Revolution with their recourse to excessive violence. Fréron and Barras had also come under suspicion for personal corruption: 800,000 *livres* entrusted to them for their mission had mysteriously disappeared.[8] In July 1794 Robespierre planned to conduct a further purge of these Jacobin deputies, giving them every reason to fear for their own lives, and to resolve to destroy him first.

Though the legal powers given to the revolutionary government were certainly very sweeping, not everyone was cowering in fear during the period of the Terror. Undoubtedly the Law of Suspects was a vague and horrible piece of legislation; nor was everyone who was executed guilty of the crimes with which they were charged. But the Jacobin government was primarily a war government. It ruled through coercion and intimidation rather than wholesale terror. Certainly the revolutionary leaders talked of a wholesale terror. The words of Saint-Just for example are much quoted: 'That which constitutes a Republic is the total destruction of everything that is opposed to it.'[9] Yet in large part this terrorist rhetoric remained exactly that—a rhetoric, designed to intimidate the external enemy, and counter-revolutionaries within France. The Jacobins did not embark on wholesale extermination of everyone opposed to them. Saint-Just and Le Bas, when *en mission* in Alsace, were relatively restrained considering that Alsace was at the front line of the war, and that many of its inhabitants were overtly hostile to the Revolution.[10] The work of recent scholars such as Martin and especially Jourdan bears out this view of a Jacobin government that used a rhetoric of terror to maintain its authority and to whip up defiance of the enemy, while in practice people put on trial still had recourse to a system of justice, and a considerable proportion of those charged with crimes under the revolutionary legislation were able to muster a successful legal defence. Having said this, we should remember that the civil war situation in the Vendée was very different to the rest of France.[11] Terror was for the most part directed against very specific groups of people: prominent amongst these were the political leaders of the Revolution themselves.

---

[8] In their defence Fréron and Barras claimed that the money had been lost in an accident when the coach in which they were travelling fell into a pond: Kuscinski, *Dictionnaire des conventionnels*, 274.

[9] 'Rapport...sur les personnes incarcérées, 8 ventôse', Saint-Just, *Oeuvres complètes*, 700.

[10] Saint-Just and Le Bas changed the military court to a special revolutionary commission which executed sixty-four people, mostly for military misconduct. See Jean-Pierre Gross, *Saint-Just: sa politique et ses missions* (Paris: Bibliothèque Nationale, 1976), 180–96; see also Gough, *The Terror in the French Revolution*, second edition, 46.

[11] Martin, *Violence et Révolution*; and Jourdan, 'Le discours de la terreur'.

As the English historian J.M. Thompson pointed out long ago, 'it is often forgotten that the Terror was mainly directed, not against the people, but against the Government'.[12] The watchful eye of terror was directed at revolutionary leaders, government officials, and other public functionaries. As we have seen, even after the Law of Prairial among politicians who appeared before the Revolutionary Tribunal during the Year Two the proportion of death sentences handed out was much higher than among other classes of defendant.[13] The corruption of politicians and government officials was an immense problem for the Jacobin leaders. With little previous administrative experience of any kind, they suddenly found themselves directing a population of over 28 million people, beset by war and civil war. The only governmental system with which they were familiar was that of the old regime, a system in which venality was central to the structure and function of government. Government still had to continue; men must be found to carry out administrative tasks. The changes to the system, together with the war itself, opened up for men from relatively modest backgrounds new opportunities to enrich themselves. There were considerable temptations; how then could the Jacobin leadership ensure that men entrusted with government posts remained honest? To this question Robespierre would reply—by using terror to keep them in check. Yet who could guarantee that the men administering the Terror were themselves motivated by genuine virtue? In a key speech on the need to purify the government, delivered during the previous October, Saint-Just expressed this problem in these terms: 'A people has only one dangerous enemy; its government.'[14] Government was intrinsically corrupt. It was ambition, not virtue, that motivated the great majority of people who held public office. He continued, '...public service, in the way it is practised, is not virtue, it is a career'.[15] The only thing that could make government work for the people rather than against them was the authentic virtue of the people who oversaw the running of government—the Jacobin leaders themselves.

From the outset of the Revolution a fundamental problem had been the impossibility of proving that would-be politicians were worthy of trust. In the Year Two this problem had taken on a further dimension—that is, how could a revolutionary politician *prove* that he was virtuous enough to be entrusted with the authority to wield terror in defence of the Revolution? We shall turn now to an exploration of how the Robespierrists were obliged to confront this problem within their own identities, as 'men of virtue' at the heart of the Terror.

## 'ONE CANNOT GOVERN WITHOUT FRIENDS'

We have seen the extent to which revolutionary politics was marked by deep-seated suspicions of leaders who appointed their friends to official posts. Now it was the

---

[12] J.M. Thompson, *Leaders of the French Revolution* (1929: republished, Oxford: Basil Blackwell, 1968), 196–200.

[13] See Chapter 7, p. 191 of this work.

[14] 'Rapport fait au nom du Comité de salut public sur la nécessité de déclarer le gouvernement révolutionnaire jusqu'à la paix', 10 October 1793, Saint-Just, *Oeuvres complètes*, 521.

[15] 'Rapport sur la nécessité de déclarer le gouvernement révolutionnaire jusqu'à la paix', 529.

turn of the Robespierrists to experience this problem at first hand as they struggled to be men of virtue in an inherently corrupt situation. The Robespierrists were constantly being importuned for posts and privileges. Robespierre's correspondence contained a number of such letters, couched in the language of virtue combined with unabashed flattery. There was no shortage of self-professed patriots. The problem was whether one could believe in the integrity of any man simply because he spoke the language of virtue at a time when it had become expedient to do so.

The fundamental problem was one of trust: by 1794 any ambitious man knew how to adopt the language of selfless patriotism, to present himself as a man of virtue. Nonetheless, most men's motives were much more self-interested than they could openly admit. According to the ideology of virtue all men were of equal value. In practice, in revolutionary politics, and particularly during the Terror, leaders put a premium on men whom they knew personally and on whose commitment they felt they could rely. Like the Jacobins, political activists from the lower orders of Paris were quite capable of adopting strategic identities to further their own prestige. In the spring of 1794 many activists at grass-roots level had adopted the appearance and language of 'Robespierrists' yet this could just as easily be due to expediency as to conviction. Whilst Robespierre was ideologically and emotionally dedicated to 'the people', he was often awkward with individuals. He seems to have felt uncomfortable amongst some of the Parisian militants and often used intermediaries to remain in contact with them and gain their support.[16] The Robespierrist friendship network gave rise to resentment amongst other Jacobins who felt excluded from power by their position outside this network. Robespierre referred to this resentment in his last speech: 'And what tyranny is more odious than that which punishes the people in the person of its defenders? For isn't friendship the freest thing in the world, even under the reign of despotism. But you, who have made it a crime on our part, are you jealous of it? No, you prize only gold and the perishable benefits that the tyrants lavish on those who serve them.'[17] The problem for the Robespierrists can be summed up by Saint-Just's observation: 'one cannot govern without friends'.[18] Yet Saint-Just confided this admission only to his private notebook—it was in direct contravention of the Jacobins' public rhetoric. After the deaths of the Robespierrists, Courtois, going through their personal papers to look for incriminating material, seized upon Saint-Just's phrase and used it as evidence that the Robespierrists' politics were conspiratorial and against virtue.[19]

In his private papers Robespierre compiled lists of 'patriots possessing greater or lesser talents'.[20] These were men whom he trusted to fill political posts. In each case the crucial factor in getting onto the list was that these were men in whom

[16] Burstin, *L'invention du sans-culotte*, 97–102.

[17] Speech of 8 Thermidor, Robespierre, *Oeuvres*, 10: 556.

[18] Saint-Just, *Oeuvres complètes*, 'fragments divers', 960.

[19] E.B. Courtois, *Rapport fait au nom de la Commission chargée de l'examen des papiers trouvés chez Robespierre et ses complices* (Paris, Nivôse, l'an III de la République), 30.

[20] *Papiers inédits*, 2: 7–13.

Robespierre or Saint-Just had confidence. A personal introduction and recommendation from someone in Robespierre's inner circle of intimates was necessary to overcome his wariness. In the labyrinth of revolutionary politics, only men whose hearts you felt you knew could be relied upon. Thus, in drawing up his lists, Robespierre adopted some of the tactics of the old regime ministers whose politics he so detested: the ends justified the means. Though at first sight these lists resembled an old regime list of preferment for patronage, the men named in them gained little financial advantage from serving as appointees of the Robespierrists; nor were they chosen from the social elite of the old regime. By the final months of the Jacobin regime it was increasingly apparent that there were considerable personal risks involved in being an agent of Robespierre and that these had to be offset against any potential career advantages that might ensue. This pessimistic assessment was fully borne out by the events of Thermidor when so many of Robespierre's friends and political associates were to perish. These men served in administrative posts, particularly in army administration and supplies; in the administrative commissions that in April replaced the ministries, the biggest of which was the War Office; in the Commune (these last two staffed largely by Robespierrist nominees after the purging of the Hébertists); and on the Revolutionary Tribunal. Others became agents of the Committee of Public Safety, some of them replacing more 'Dantonist' and therefore suspect agents.

Long-standing friends, men from one's own locality or region, were more readily to be trusted than recent acquaintances, or men from remote regions, who lacked local recommendations. Their virtue was deemed to be more authentic because it could be vouched for as antedating the time when adopting the rhetoric of virtue could be a means to career advancement. Some, such as Adrian Bayard (described by Robespierre simply as 'Saint-Just's brother-in-law, energetic patriot, pure, enlightened'), were recommendations from men whom Robespierre trusted. The lists included men long known to Robespierre, from his home town of Arras. Herman, who served as the president of the Revolutionary Tribunal until April 1794, was one of these; his background was in the upper echelons of the judicial system of Arras.[21] Herman attempted to conduct himself as a 'man of virtue', opposing the appointment of his own brother to an advantageous administrative post, preferring another older and better qualified candidate; though in Thermidor he was to disavow any personal connection with Robespierre, denying that he had been to Robespierre's house.[22] There were also friends of Saint-Just, from his own, small, home town of Blérancourt, including Gatteau and Thuillier. These two served in the army commissary, and oversaw supplies to the army in Alsace and later for the army of the North. Some of the men on the list recommended others in turn; thus,

---

[21] Hardman emphasizes the importance of patronage in revolutionary politics, linking it to old regime styles of preferment. He has also unearthed interesting new evidence about Robespierre's power base, in particular, about Herman and the Payan brothers: see John Hardman, *Robespierre* (London: Pearson, 1999), ch. 7–9.

[22] A. Mathiez, *The Fall of Robespierre and Other Essays* (first English version 1927; this edition, New York: Augustus M. Kelley, 1968), 132–7. Hardman takes a more sceptical view of Herman's moral integrity: see Hardman, *Robespierre*, 161–4.

Robespierre added the name Mercier to the list, and put in brackets after it 'indicated by Gatteau for the administration'.[23] Leroux and Bouthillier, both from Béthune, were friends of Le Bas, Robespierre's trusted friend, who himself became Duplay's son-in-law.

Not all the men in Robespierre's network had been known to him or Saint-Just before the Revolution. Couthon, who had become one of Robespierre's closest friends, was from the Auvergne. Claude Payan came from a borderline noble family in the Dauphiné and had served as an artillery officer before he embraced Jacobin politics and became a loyal supporter of Robespierre. Political choices divided his family. Claude himself, in common with many other Robespierrists, was particularly young, only 27 years old. His brother François also became part of Robespierre's network. Payan, who was appointed as national agent of the (Robespierrist) Commune after the overthrow of the Hébertists, also made recommendations to Robespierre. Payan in turn used his local knowledge to provide Maignet, a Jacobin in Valence, with a list of men he believed to have the requisite degree of the right 'republican attitude' of 'probity and moral virtues' to be suitable for administrative responsibilities.[24] A number of patriots from Lyon also entered Robespierre's network. One of these, who also featured on Robespierre's lists of patriots, was Achard. He had been recommended to Robespierre by another Lyonnais, Gravier, who was a next-door neighbour and friend of Duplay and had by this means entered the domestic circle of the 'Incorruptible'. Both Duplay and Gravier also served as jurors on the Revolutionary Tribunal; as did Souberbielle, Robespierre's doctor. Couthon, too, had for a time in the summer of 1792 been a tenant in the Duplays' house.[25]

Jacques Duplay (son of Robespierre's friend and landlord, Maurice Duplay, and brother-in-law of Le Bas) accompanied Saint-Just and Le Bas to the northern front; and Simon Duplay (nephew of Maurice) acted as an adjunct to Lejeune (Saint-Just's appointment to the Police Bureau), handling administration and correspondence for the Police Bureau. Physical disability was no barrier—neither Simon Duplay's wooden leg (he was injured at the battle of Valmy), nor Couthon's growing paralysis precluded them from taking on administrative responsibilities. Nor was youth and inexperience: Simon Duplay was 20 in 1794, his cousin Jacques only 16. Robespierre and Saint-Just tried to choose men who would be immune to corruption. Some at least of their appointees made it a point of honour to refuse bribes. Saint-Just described how, when serving as army commissaries, Gatteau and Thuillier denounced a storekeeper who offered them a 50,000-*écu* bribe; though the financial integrity of others, such as Daubigny (Saint-Just's friend from Blérancourt) was rather more doubtful.[26] The same names from the same small network

---

[23] *Papiers inédits*, 2: 8.

[24] *Papiers inédits*, 2: 11, 354–9.

[25] Thompson, *Robespierre*, 185, note 3.

[26] 'Rapport au nom du Comité de salut public…sur la police générale…', 26 Germinal, an II, Saint-Just, *Oeuvres complètes*, 817. On Robespierre's and Saint-Just's defence of Saint-Just's compatriot Daubigny, who was the subject of persistent allegations of corruption and theft, see Linton, 'Fatal friendships'.

turn up repeatedly. The Robespierrists were too few to fill all the jobs needed. Indeed, in the last months they were doubling up, tripling up, the posts on which they served.[27] Robespierre himself was acutely aware of this problem, and complained bitterly about the difficulty of finding reliable political administrators whose actual virtue was as great as their mastery of the rhetoric.

The members of the Committee of Public Safety (not just the Robespierrists) were not themselves implicated in corruption, at least as far as the surviving evidence shows. Long years afterwards, as an old man, Barère prided himself on his integrity as a member of the ruling Committee. The members of the Committee had not, he said, been motivated by 'ambition for fortune, nor for political position... nor for an increase of pay, honours, and distinctions'. Immense amounts of money had passed through his hands, but he had lived just on his deputy's salary of 18 *livres* a day (paid in *assignats* and so worth much less than the face value) and had not accepted bribes.[28]

There was much more of an aura of corruption clinging to some of the members of the Committee of General Security and its agents. Chabot's allegations had implicated several of them. As the police committee, responsible for arrests and the prisons, there were many opportunities for its agents to exploit their situation in a way that had political implications. One of its key agents, Dossonville, worked closely with a prison informer, Armand, who denounced fellow prisoners in the hope of remission for himself. Together these two constituted the principal source of the accusations against the fifty-four people executed in red shirts (as parricides) on 17 June as alleged conspirators in the Foreign Plot; some of them convicted (on the basis of flimsy evidence) of participation in the assassination attempts on Robespierre.[29]

There were two friends and supporters of Robespierre on the Committee of General Security. One of these was the artist David, organizer of a number of the revolutionary festivals. The other was Philippe Le Bas, who had been a lawyer at St-Pol, subsequently at Arras where he knew Robespierre.[30] Apart from these two men Robespierre and Saint-Just were increasingly distrustful of the members of the Committee of General Security. It was partly for this reason that Saint-Just set up a Police Bureau under the aegis of the Committee of Public Safety. The original role of the Police Bureau was to supervise public officials and financiers, and to root out corruption. Due to Saint-Just's prolonged absences *en mission* with the army of the north, Robespierre took over the running of it and expanded its remit; using it

---

[27] See, for example, the range of posts given in rapid succession to Gatteau and Thuillier, listed in Gross, *Saint-Just*, 34–2.

[28] Barère, *Memoirs*, 2: 116–17; and François Aulard, 'Une Interview de Bertrand Barère en 1840', *Révolution française*, 61 (1911). According to Blanc, Barère was not quite so lacking in corruption at this time as he liked to claim in after years: see Blanc, *La Corruption sous la Terreur*. Nonetheless, Chabot, who accused several of the Committee of General Security members of corruption, did not say anything about there being corruption in the Committee of Public Safety.

[29] See A. Goodwin, 'The underworld of the French Revolutionary Terror', in *Memoirs and Proceedings of the Manchester Literary and Philosophical Society* (Manchester, 1954–5): 38–56.

[30] M. Billet, *Philippe Le Bas, membre de l'institut de France (inscriptions et belles lettres). Lecture faite à l'Académie d'Arras, le 20 juillet 1866* (Arras: A. Courtin, 1866), 2.

to take over some of the surveillance functions that were seen as the prerogative of the Committee of General Security. The Bureau thus became one of the causes of the growing divisions between the two Committees. It was later attacked as a vehicle of the Robespierrist 'conspiracy'. To some extent this hostile perception was engineered by the Thermidoreans. The historian Ording showed that the activities of the Bureau were not confined solely to the Robespierrists; other members of the Committee also signed orders empowering the Bureau's agents.[31] Nonetheless, the Bureau was the particular project of Saint-Just and Robespierre.

Almost all of the Police Bureau's agents either were friends of Saint-Just, or had some personal connection with him. Most came from Saint-Just's locality; either from his home town of Blérancourt in the department of the Aisne; Soissons, where he went to school; or Reims, where he had attended university. One such agent was Eve Demaillot, a former tutor of Saint-Just. Another was Vieille, who had been at school with Saint-Just, and was later mayor of Soissons. Others included Étienne Lambert, an illiterate shepherd from Étoges, who was known to Saint-Just from his time at Reims; and Garnerin who knew Gatteau, who was himself a long-standing friend of Saint-Just's from Blérancourt.[32] These agents were appointed to various provincial postings, where their responsibilities included surveying ex-nobles, denouncing public officials suspected of corruption, intrigues, or incompetence, and the sending of information on the public mood. From April the head of the Police Bureau was another of Saint-Just's appointments, Augustin Lejeune. He too came from the same region as Saint-Just, and their acquaintance antedated Saint-Just's election as a deputy. Like all of these men (and like Saint-Just himself less than two years earlier) Lejeune had had negligible administrative experience at a national level prior to his appointment, so this was a considerable advancement for him. After Thermidor, when to have been involved with the Police Bureau was seen as tantamount to terrorism, Lejeune asserted that he had taken on the post with the utmost reluctance, and only after Saint-Just came to his home to insist, but that hardly seems likely.[33]

Many of Saint-Just's appointments were his contemporaries from his own generation. Lejeune, for example, was 23. Their lack of administrative experience was not a problem in Saint-Just's eyes. He himself had had to fight to overcome the doubts raised over the fact that he was the youngest member of the Convention. His political enemies had made much of this, dismissing him as not yet ready for the responsibility of public office. This characterization had dogged him since his first attempt at election into national politics, when he was below the legal age. After Saint-Just's

---

[31] Arne Ording, *Le Bureau de police du Comité de salut public* (Oslo, 1930), esp.139–52. On the division of labour between the two Committees, see also Jacques Godechot, *Les Institutions de la France* (Paris: Presses Universitaires de France, 1968), 308–14.

[32] Ording, *Le Bureau de Police du Comité de Salut Public*, 139–52; and Gross, *Saint-Just*, 340–42.

[33] By 1812 when the pressure had considerably lessened, Lejeune said (much more vaguely than he had after Thermidor) that his appointment took place 'by chance'. See A. Bégis (ed.), *Curiosités révolutionnaires: Saint-Just et les bureaux de la police générale au Comité de salut public en 1794: Notice historique par Augustin Lejeune, chef des bureaux: Documents inédits* (Paris: Imprimé pour les amis des livres, 1896), 32.

death Courtois mocked him as having been too young to be entrusted with the responsibilities of political leadership, describing him as '...only just escaped from the chalk dust of school'.[34] Saint-Just himself had argued, however, that the contrary was true. Back in 1791 he had characterized his political identity in these terms: 'I am very young...but because I was young, it seemed to me that I was closer to nature'.[35] Proximity to nature made a man more authentically virtuous. Thus youth and lack of experience were advantages in revolutionary politics, for they meant that one had not been corrupted by the power institutions of the old regime.

If youth was not a barrier to virtue, neither was the lack of a formal education. On the contrary: a number of the Robespierrists' appointees came from a low social status; several had little or no literacy. Robespierre argued that such men could have more authentic patriotism than more educated men who were better at constructing glib statements about their virtue in order to get posts.[36] One such man was a haberdasher named Deschamps. Robespierre obtained for him a post, first as agent of the Commission of Commerce and Supplies, later as *aide de camp* of Hanriot. In 1792 Robespierre became godfather to Deschamps' son, named appropriately enough, Maximilien-François.[37] Another humble figure on Robespierre's list was Guilain Villers, who in Thermidor stated that he had only worked as a servant for Saint-Just, though in fact he was employed in a political capacity. Courtois would later refer to the social obscurity of such men when he described Robespierre's lists of patriots as 'ignorant men, corrupt men, raised to office'.[38]

A particular problem was how to get reliable information about what was going on in the provinces. Robespierre himself was particularly reliant on information from others. Unlike his brother Augustin, Saint-Just, Le Bas, or even Couthon, he never acted as a deputy *en mission*. There is no evidence that Robespierre went further afield in his entire life than Artois, Paris, and the journey between them. The Committee itself received many official reports from areas of war or unrest, but when Robespierre or Saint-Just wanted the opinion of someone they could rely on they used their own agents. Robespierre's brother Augustin, who was *en mission* in the far south, wrote in response to a request from his brother: 'You ask me for the list of patriots whom I have been able to discover on my route. These are indeed rare, or maybe torpor hindered the pure men from coming forward because of the danger and oppression in which virtue was placed.' Ironically, one of the 'patriots' whom Augustin recommended to his brother was Bonaparte, whom Augustin considered a man of 'great merit'.[39] In contrast to the 'pure men'

---

[34] Courtois, *Rapport...de l'examen des papiers trouvés chez Robespierre et ses complices*, 5.

[35] Saint-Just, *Esprit de la Révolution*, Avant-propos, in Saint-Just, *Oeuvres complètes*, 276–7.

[36] See, for example, Robespierre's defence of an uncouth speaker in the Jacobins who was getting a poor hearing from his audience: 23 Germinal an II (12 April 1794) in Robespierre, *Oeuvres*, 10: 432–4.

[37] See Sabine Dupuy, 'Du parrainage d'un enfant du people aux conciliabules de Charenton: itinéraire d'une amitié chez Robespierre', in Jessenne *et al.*, *Robespierre*, 117–24.

[38] Courtois, *Rapport...de l'examen des papiers trouvés chez Robespierre*, 16–17.

[39] Letter from Augustin Robespierre to his brother, Nice, 16 Germinal an II, *Correspondance de Maximilien et Augustin Robespierre*, 271–4.

in whose integrity Augustin had confidence, he reported that he had also 'met thousands of intriguers, who repeat your name with emphasis, who call themselves your most intimate friends'.[40] Augustin wrote this letter from Lyon, scene of a major revolt against the Jacobins, which had been bloodily repressed. Another of Robespierre's trusted sources of information was Jullien, only 18 years old, with whose family Robespierre was on friendly terms. His mother was a strong figure, who had set out to instil in her son the need to 'be good and virtuous' since his early boyhood.[41] He too featured on Robespierre's list of trusted patriots. He went on a mission to Bordeaux and the west, from where he wrote to Robespierre and to Saint-Just, though he also wrote to the rest of the Committee, and said nothing to Robespierre that he did not share with the others. Jullien's mission included the task of keeping a watchful eye on the public conduct of the deputies *en mission* in the region; indeed, this seemed to preoccupy him more than the murderous reprisals being carried out against the Vendéan rebels. In his letters he complained of the behaviour of the deputy Ysabeau, whose activities were inappropriate for a Jacobin on public view. Everywhere Ysabeau went, said Jullien, 'people applauded even at the glimpse of his shadow', crying 'long live Ysabeau, our friend, our father!' Ysabeau had 'several coaches, a coachman, and horses, the *équipage* of a *ci-devant* noble, guards preceded him everywhere'. He was the idol of the people, especially the aristocrats. He accepted as a reward for his services 'a thousand presents which were lavished upon him by skilled seduction, which called itself *friendship*'. Jullien said he had been deceived in Ysabeau, whom he had long thought to be 'a patriot and virtuous'. According to Jullien, Ysabeau 'was always speaking about his tender concern for the people', but in truth he was exploiting them, as the aristocrats had done.[42]

## THE PRIVATE CONDUCT OF THE ROBESPIERRISTS

During the Terror it was vital that the Jacobin leaders' private lives should be seen to reflect the authenticity of their political principles. The politicians' terror meant that this was no longer just to stay in power; it was also to defend themselves against denunciation. Robespierre had used Danton's self-indulgent lifestyle as evidence that Danton was a conspirator; who better than Robespierre, then, to appreciate how dangerous it was in the Year Two for a Jacobin politician to be seen to live on the fat of the land? It does not seem to have been a hardship for Robespierre himself to stick to a frugal, moderate, and quiet home life, in conformity with the strictures of domestic virtue; according to the testimony of his sister Charlotte, he had always lived in this way. Admittedly Charlotte was partisan and presented Maximilien as the epitome of virtue in every circumstance, but there is no creditable

---

[40] Letter from Augustin Robespierre to his brother, Commune affranchie, 7 Ventôse an II, *Correspondance de Maximilien et Augustin Robespierre*, 262.
[41] See Madame Jullien's letter to her son, cited by Palmer, *From Jacobin to Liberal*, 4–5.
[42] Letter from Jullien to Saint-Just, Bordeaux, 25 Prairial, *Papiers inédits*, 3: 37–43.

evidence that contradicts her account of his earlier life.[43] Other Jacobins may have found it harder to maintain his standards of domestic virtue, including Maximilien's own brother Augustin, who had a penchant for gambling, a pastime associated with 'aristocratic' values. Nor was Augustin immune from the charms of women: he had a close connection, probably a love affair, with Madame Ricord, the wife of his fellow deputy when *en mission* to the Army of Italy. He shocked his sister Charlotte, who had accompanied the party, but no one else seemed that troubled about Augustin's *amours*, including Maximilien. However, Augustin complained bitterly to their brother about Charlotte's behaviour. What angered him is that Charlotte had been publicly besmirching his reputation. Augustin warned his brother that she 'threatens to make a scandal, in order to compromise us'. Augustin did not specify what Charlotte had said, but it looks as though he felt defensive about his connection with Madame Ricord, and afraid that Charlotte's revelations might damage his political persona and, by extension, that of Maximilien also.[44] Augustin's resentment provoked an estrangement between the siblings that was still ongoing when the brothers died. There was little reaction, however, to a subsequent mistress of Augustin's, Madame de La Soudraye, a Creole heiress who had married a much older man. When she went with Augustin to Besançon the local Jacobins reacted indignantly. What shocked them, however, was not the liaison itself, but that she accompanied Augustin to the Popular Society, where she took an active role despite their cries of 'no women!', and that he listened to her opinion about politics.[45] Augustin thought well enough of Madame de La Soudraye's political understanding to recommend that his brother pay attention to her views, in particular her local knowledge of 'certain people who play a role in the revolution' who hide 'their shame and immorality'.[46]

The Robespierrists do not seem to have been particularly puritanical about sex, though, like other Jacobins, they were careful not to flagrantly infringe the sexual codes of their time. It would not do their political image any good if they appeared to resemble the kind of dissolute sexual predators who—at least according to such fictional accounts as *Les Liaisons Dangereuses*—had been rife amongst the old regime nobility. Saint-Just, once the author of a licentious poem, now seemed to live a life of moral rectitude. When his former mistress from Blérancourt left her husband and came to join him he repudiated her. His friend Thuillier wrote to

[43] For Charlotte's account of Robespierre's abstemious and hard-working daily life before the Revolution, his numerous friends, and charming way with women, see Charlotte Robespierre, *Mémoires* (1834: this edition, Paris: Nouveau Monde Éditions, 2006), 57–9.

[44] Letter from Augustin Robespierre to his brother, no date, *Correspondance de Maximilien et Augustin Robespierre*, 293.

[45] McPhee, *Robespierre*, writes with considerable insight about Maximilien's relationships with women. On Augustin's private life, which was rather less staid than his brother's, see Mary Young, *Augustin: The Younger Robespierre* (London: Core Publications, 2011), 117–19, 139, 153–4, 162–6. Young's book is also available online at <http://fass.kingston.ac.uk/research/historical-record/publications/>. See also Cousin, *Philippe Lebas et Augustin Robespierre*, 130–2; and Sergio Luzzatto, *Bonbon Robespierre: la terreur à visage humain*, trans. Simone Carpentari Messina (Paris: Arléa, 2010), 94–6.

[46] Letter from Augustin Robespierre to his brother, Commune affranchie 7 Ventôse an II; Letter from Augustin Robespierre to his brother, undated, *Correspondance de Maximilien et Augustin Robespierre*, 262, 293.

warn him that the affair was causing a scandal back in Blérancourt. Saint-Just replied that he was not involved in her flight, 'you will oblige me by telling everyone who talks to you about this that I had nothing to do with it', though whether he was more concerned with trying to protect his own political image, or her reputation—or both—is unclear.[47] In principle, however—if not in his own life—Saint-Just condoned the rights of men and women to find sexual fulfilment outside marriage, 'the man and the woman who love one another are married, if they have no children they can keep their engagement secret'.[48]

Five years of engagement in revolutionary politics had increased Robespierre's caution about socializing in a way that could be construed as 'old regime'. A few sedate dinners are described, organized by women who sympathized with Robespierre's politics, but did not themselves take an active part in politics in the way that Madame Roland had done. One of these was Madame de Chalabre; another was Madame Jullien; she described the home life of Robespierre and his sister as 'all openness and simplicity'.[49] It is striking to see how Madame Jullien, as a Jacobin woman, explicitly identified herself with political virtue, to which she gave a feminine and maternal twist, to the extent of saying that it would be right to denounce corrupt family members.[50]

For Robespierre, even such temperate outings declined. During his time on the Committee he rarely went out into society, or ate with fellow revolutionaries as he had once done at the home of the Lameths, or later with the Rolands. There are occasional accounts of more political dinners, in the style of the Dantonists, but most of the evidence for these is from dubious sources. Barère described how, with difficulty, he had inveigled the 'unsociable and distrustful' Robespierre to dine at Meot's restaurant, promising him that he would meet only with deputies, and Barère's friends and relations. Barère had organized the dinner at the behest of M. Loménie, nephew of Brienne, who hoped that Robespierre would intervene on his behalf. Though the dinner was 'gay enough' Robespierre seems to have felt he had been manipulated into dining with Loménie, for according to Barère when he heard the identity of the guest he left without a word.[51]

Since the time of the Champ de Mars (except for a brief period spent with Charlotte) Robespierre had lived as a lodger at the home of the master carpenter

[47] Letter to Thuillier, September 1793, Saint-Just, *Oeuvres complètes*, 506–7.

[48] For Saint-Just's libertarian attitude towards sex outside the confines of marriage, see *Fragments d'institutions républicaines*, *Oeuvres complètes*, 984. In his unpublished *De la Nature, de l'état civil, de la cité ou les règles de l'indépendance du gouvernement*, Saint-Just went further in defending women's freedom of choice, and equality between men and women in marriage: 'No one should command on the earth, all power is illegitimate, neither sex should be superior to the other', ibid., 943.

[49] Robespierre accepted invitations to dinner from Madame de Chalabre, his political admirer, who became his friend. They seem to have been simple meals. Her letters to him are in *Papiers inédits*, 1: 171–8. Madame Jullien's account of a dinner she had with Robespierre and his sister in February 1793 is cited in Palmer, *From Jacobin to Liberal*, 28.

[50] See the thoughtful analysis of Madame Jullien's politics in Lindsay A.H. Parker, 'Family and feminism in the French Revolution: the case of Rosalie Ducrollay Jullien', *Journal of Women's Studies*, 24, 3 (Autumn 2012): 39–61. Parker is currently completing a full-length study based on the wealth of material in Madame Jullien's letters.

[51] Barère, *Memoirs*, 2: 164–5.

Maurice Duplay, whose family was devoted to Robespierre.[52] Many years later Elizabeth Le Bas, one of the four daughters of Maurice, provided descriptions of life in the Duplay household that show Robespierre as a man of private virtue and sensibility in an exemplary bourgeois setting. The Duplay women ministered to Robespierre's domestic comfort, providing simple family meals. He joined the family in the day-to-day pleasures of family life: walks in the country, impromptu singing and making music, and discussions about the daily matters of family life, love and suitors, and family disagreements.

In many ways the Duplay household carried out the functions of a traditional bourgeois family of the old regime, in which links were forged through patronage and friendships that led to employments for the men, and through marriage with the daughters. The Duplay household was the centre both of Robespierre's private world and of his political network. The men of the family (Maurice, his son, and nephew) were all actively involved in official duties thanks to Robespierre's patronage. The women tightened political connections through marriage: Elizabeth married one of Robespierre's closest friends, Philippe Le Bas. Her sister Éléonore was understood in the family to be engaged to Robespierre: they were seen to hold hands which was a traditional sign of betrothal. There was even a plan on the part of Le Bas and his young wife to bring Saint-Just more closely into this family and political network through a marriage to Le Bas' sister Henriette, though this matrimonial project foundered on the rock of Saint-Just's 'difficult' temperament.[53]

The Duplay household was central to Robespierre and to his political identity on a number of levels. On a personal level the Duplay family offered Robespierre a private refuge, a place of emotional security, along with the happy home life that had been denied him since the death of his mother and the departure of his father. It is to one of the Duplay daughters, Elizabeth Le Bas—as well as to his sister Charlotte—that we owe many of the details of the personal side of Robespierre's life. Both women depicted Robespierre as a man of private virtue and sensibility. Whatever it was that Robespierre wanted out of revolutionary politics it was not material gain. For the loyal Elizabeth the virtue of the Robespierrists was demonstrated by the incontrovertible fact that none of them had profited personally from their time in power: 'They all died poor.'[54]

---

[52] Thompson, *Robespierre* considers much of the surviving evidence for Robespierre's private life. For this period, see also McPhee, *Robespierre*, ch. 11. On the devotion of the Duplays to Robespierre, see Marc-Antoine Baudot, *Notes historiques sur la Convention nationale, l'Empire et l'exil des votants* (Paris: D. Jouaust, 1893), 242–3. Elizabeth Le Bas (née Duplay) is the source for much of what is known about Robespierre's private life in this period: see 'Manuscrit de Mme Le Bas', in Stéfane-Pol, *Autour de Robespierre*, 102–50). As an extraordinary testimony to the longevity of the devotion of the Duplay/Le Bas family, it was only in 2011 that documents (including draft speeches by Robespierre) were put on sale that had been kept hidden in the family since July 1794. Some of these documents had previously been used by Paul Coutant (related to the family by marriage) in *Autour de Robespierre*.

[53] See Le Bas' letters to his wife about Saint-Just's 'singular' personality, reproduced in Stéfane-Pol, *Autour de Robespierre*, 250, 253–4.

[54] Elizabeth Le Bas, 'Manuscrit de Mme Le Bas', 147. Elizabeth's account was given many years later, to Lamartine. Charlotte Robespierre's memories of her long-dead brother were also given to a man to write up, in her case Laponneraye: Charlotte Robespierre, *Mémoires*.

On a tactical level the Duplay household gave Robespierre a stable base from which he could operate politically, conveniently close to the Tuileries and the Jacobins. It provided him with a place at which he could meet political visitors in privacy, outside the public venues, or the restaurants. Visitors on political matters could climb the stairs to his rooms without going through the family home; though this relatively easy accessibility could occasionally prove awkward, making Robespierre vulnerable to visits from people he feared and would much rather avoid, such as when Fréron and Barras (two deputies he had had recalled for their excessive actions when *en mission*) evaded Éléonore Duplay and her mother and cornered him one morning. On that occasion Robespierre was reduced to refusing to acknowledge their presence.[55]

According to Charlotte Robespierre, before the Revolution her brother had had warm relationships with his friends: 'He had many friends whom he greatly loved.'[56] Back in 1791 Robespierre had had a wide circle of friends who were on intimate enough terms to visit him at his lodging in the Duplay house. But by the time he entered the Committee of Public Safety this circle had narrowed considerably. In the last months of his life he was much more guarded, trusting fewer people, particularly after the attempts made to assassinate him. Commentators noted how difficult it had become to get access to Robespierre. When not at the Convention, the Committee of Public Safety, or the Jacobins, he remained largely inaccessible at the Duplays' house. In the last weeks of his life he ceased to attend the Committee, returning only for the attempt to patch up a reconciliation with his fellow Committee members that collapsed in Thermidor. Only Le Bas, Saint-Just, Couthon, David, and the Italian patriot Buonarotti seem to have been frequent visitors to his home.[57]

According to the attitude of the time, any private visits to Robespierre's home could be construed as 'conspiratorial'. Thus, in the Year Three when anxious to explore the complicity of surviving members of the Committee of Public Safety with Robespierre, the Thermidoreans interrogated the imprisoned Duplays as to whether the Committee members had come to dinner at the Duplays' house in the summer of 1794. Both Jacques and Simon Duplay confirmed that—except for Saint-Just—visits from the other Committee members had all but ceased; though Simon did recall a final visit from Barère, who came to dinner a few days before Thermidor.[58]

On the level of political ideology, the fact that Robespierre lived as a lodger in another man's house enabled him to demonstrate the depth of his private virtue. His domestic arrangements had a notable effect on how public opinion viewed his reputation. He did not make the mistake that Roland had done, of accepting a

---

[55] Barras' account of this strange interview is reproduced in George Rudé (ed.), *Robespierre* (New Jersey: Prentice-Hall, 1967), 84–6.

[56] Charlotte Robespierre, *Mémoires*, 57–9.

[57] Lamartine made a list of friends who visited Robespierre at home, a list corrected by Elizabeth Duplay. See Stéfane-Pol, *Autour de Robespierre*, 83–4. There is a more comprehensive list in Thompson, *Robespierre*, 185.

[58] Mathiez, *The Fall of Robespierre*, 162–5.

ministerial mansion to live in. He had to be careful about maintaining his credibility—it was the only thing standing between him and disaster. Doubts about the authenticity of a political leader's integrity were dangerous, particularly when voiced by the popular militants of Paris. At the end of March (shortly after the execution of the Hébertists) a police spy amongst the crowds in Paris reported a 'patriot' as saying 'although Robespierre had rendered services to his country, if he happened to change it would be the duty of a republican to forget what he had done and from then on consider only his crime and demand that the law strike him down'.[59] Likewise, in Prairial a gardener, Jean Lamarche, was sent before the Revolutionary Tribunal by the Comité de sûreté de Clamart for having said that 'Robespierre was very poor before the Revolution and now he is very rich...his time will come, as it did for Danton who also had the appearance of being a good patriot...he will be judged by those who will come after him and he'll be guillotined'.[60]

Robespierre was not alone in living such an exemplary private life. In the Year Two other members of the Committee of Public Safety were careful to avoid being seen to live lavishly or to dine out ostentatiously. This was both a result of necessity—they worked all the time—and an outward sign of an identity that they had appropriated. If Saint-Just had once engaged in fine dining, as a *sans-culotte* deputation had complained, there was no sign of that now. He was pleased to report that he regularly dined on bread, sausage, and a little wine at his desk; noting the marked contrast between his own conduct and that of Pitt, who was notorious for partaking in what might now be called 'liquid lunches'. Sometimes the Committee members took their evening meal at neighbouring restaurants; though Prieur described how he and the other Committee members were regularly reduced to dining on 'a morsel of dried bread' while working at their desks. Barère would make jokes about it, to cheer them up. To be always thus virtuously working and snatching a little food in isolation at one's desk left scant time for plotting over extended meals shared with convivial friends.[61] For those in service to the Committee there was little time even for sleep. They sometimes slept in camp beds in the offices of the Committee. It was an uncomfortable, exhausting life. A plaintive Barère requested that the maintenance staff find him a more comfortable camp bed, such as that with which Saint-Just had recently been provided.[62]

In the last weeks of his life Robespierre quarrelled with the other members of the Committee and withdrew from the communal labour of the Committee. Later, under interrogation by the Thermidoreans, Simon and Jacques Duplay testified that Robespierre, far from staying late at the Committee, remained at home, had

---

[59] Report by Pourvoyeur, 30 March 1794, cited in Richard T. Bienvenu (ed.), *The Ninth of Thermidor: the Fall of Robespierre* (Oxford: Oxford University Press, 1968), 88.

[60] Wallon, *Histoire du Tribunal révolutionnaire*, 4: 207.

[61] Prieur's memories of this time are recounted in Hipployte Carnot, *Mémoires sur Carnot par son fils* (Paris: Pagnerre, 1861–3), 527–8.

[62] Gershoy, *Bertrand Barère*, 200.

work brought to him, saw very few people, and went to bed early—a sign perhaps of an incipient breakdown.[63] Week by week he was losing his grip.

## AMBITION OR AUTHENTICITY? SAINT-JUST'S CHOICES

Even Saint-Just seems to have found it an almost impossible task to live up to the Jacobins' concept of austere self-abnegation, though the sources for this are suggestive rather than conclusive. Saint-Just's political enemies—of whom he had many—planted the seeds of doubt in the public mind about whether this self-professed man of virtue was really all he seemed. Despite his well-known antagonism towards the nobility, he was the subject of persistent rumours that he himself was really a noble. In some versions he was even said to be a marquis.[64] These stories had first surfaced in print in the writings of several of the Girondins—Louvet, Salle, and Buzot—all of whom were on the run at the time, and understandably resentful of Saint-Just, who had presented the formal report against them. Their satirical portrayal of Saint-Just was based on first-hand observation. At the time of his proscription Salle was living in the same lodging house as Saint-Just, and had opportunity to observe Saint-Just's 'aristocratic' manners up close. There was something in his manner, presumably reflecting his sense of his own self-worth, that recalled the hauteur of the old regime elite. The Girondins delighted in baiting him by referring to him as 'Monsieur le Chevalier de Saint-Just'.[65]

Almost the final thing that Desmoulins wrote in his prison cell was an attack on 'Monsieur le Chevalier de Saint-Just', whose speech denouncing the Dantonists had put Desmoulins in his present plight. Desmoulins himself (rather than the Girondins) may well have been the original source for some of these stories, since he had known Saint-Just before he assumed his revolutionary identity.[66] Such an accusation threatened to discredit Saint-Just, especially in the eyes of the *sans-culottes*, and potentially could be disastrous, even for someone as eminent as himself.

[63] The interrogations of Simon and Jacques Duplay by the police section of the Committee of General Security on 12 Nivôse, Year Three are reproduced in Mathiez, *The Fall of Robespierre*, 160–67. On Robespierre's psychological state, see McPhee, *Robespierre*, esp. 207–8, 212–13.

[64] Though Saint-Just's father, before his premature death, had succeeded in hoisting the family into the fringes of noble status, the family thereafter had lived in relatively straitened financial circumstances in a social limbo below the local notables. So persistent were the stories that Saint-Just was a marquis that at least one recent scholarly study of the French Revolution refers to them as true. See Peter Jones, *The French Revolution* (Harlow: Pearson Education, 2003), 53, 141. On Saint-Just's suggestion that the nobility be forced to perform the task of the *corvée*, formerly the work of peasants, and Barère's shocked response, see Barère, *Memoirs*, 2: 139–40.

[65] Saint-Just was referred to variously as 'Monsieur le Chevalier de Saint-Just' and 'Monsieur le ci-devant' by J.B. Salle, *Observations sur le rapport de Saint-Just contre les trente-deux proscrits, par une Société de Girondins*, Caen, 13 July 1793. From Caen, Salle sent Saint-Just a letter couched in similar terms. The text of this letter is in Vatel, *Charlotte Corday et les Girondins*, 1: xcv–xcvi. Buzot referred to Saint-Just as a marquis who had written some poetic verses: Buzot, *Mémoires*, 165–6.

[66] 'Notes de Camille Desmoulins sur le rapport de Saint-Just', in Buchez and Roux, *Histoire parlementaire de la Révolution*, 32: 221–9, esp. 225–7. Desmoulins may well have known that Saint-Just's father had achieved the status of a chevalier de Saint-Louis (the highest honour available to a non-noble cavalry officer).

On 2 Thermidor these rumours resurfaced in a dangerous way when Legray, a member of the Revolutionary Committee of the Museum section, was arrested for criticizing the Committee of Public Safety, and in particular for having claimed that Saint-Just and Barère were nobles.[67] In a draft passage of his final speech Robespierre declared that a politically damaging rumour was in circulation that Saint-Just was a noble, and that he wanted to save the nobles. Saint-Just himself spoke about Legray's involvement in a plot 'to destroy the revolutionary government' in his last (undelivered) speech, though without mentioning the personal accusation Legray had made against himself.[68]

From his prison cell Desmoulins had one more damaging allegation that he could make, one small piece of revenge for the loss of his life—that Saint-Just was ambitious: 'There are witnesses that the ambitious Saint-Just said: "I know where I'm going".' Prieur also refered to him as the 'ambitious Saint-Just'.[69] Naturally, Saint-Just himself denied it: if he harboured personal ambitions they could not be acknowledged—even, perhaps, to himself. An account by Augustin Lejeune, who worked closely with Saint-Just and knew him from before his arrival in revolutionary politics, indicates that he too found Saint-Just's motivation puzzling. After Thermidor, Lejeune was anxious to extricate himself from suspicions that he himself had been a 'Robespierrist', so much of his testimony, particularly with regard to the Police Bureau itself, is dubious. But there is a ring of authenticity in his claim (made some years later in 1812 when he was under less pressure to vilify his former patron) that it was hard to make out what Saint-Just really thought. Lejeune said that, in contrast to Robespierre, who was constant in his views, Saint-Just seemed often to change his personality. Sometimes he wept at the misfortunes of others; at other times he was appallingly cruel. According to notions of sensibility drawn from Rousseau, tears were a sign of genuine emotion, but under the Terror tears themselves came to be seen as 'suspect'—none more so, perhaps, than the tears of a terrorist. Were the tears real, Lejeune wondered?[70] The Jacobins partook of the contemporary cult of sensibility in private life, as witnessed by letters and other personal documents. Sensibility in the course of public duties, however, was much more problematic.[71] The Jacobins were constantly stating that, in order to be prepared to use terror, to sign the arrest warrants of people whom they knew, people who had families, it was necessary for them to stifle their innate sensibility. The man of virtue must be the master of his feelings. A year before Saint-Just was elected to the Convention, Lejeune had encountered him at an inn at Laon. At that far-off time Saint-Just had said: 'For myself, my ambition is limited to living

[67] The denunciations of Legray by Fabrègue and Richard are reproduced in Albert Mathiez, *Girondins et Montagnards* (Paris: Firmin-Didot, 1930), 189–93.

[68] Speech of 8 Thermidor, Robespierre, *Oeuvres*, 10: 563; Saint-Just, 'Discours du 9 Thermidor, an II', in Saint-Just, *Oeuvres complètes*, 908–9.

[69] Buchez and Roux, *Histoire parlementaire de la Révolution*, 32: 229; Carnot, *Mémoires sur Carnot par son fils*, 1: 522.

[70] See Vincent-Buffault, *The History of Tears*, 92–6.

[71] Reddy sees Jacobin sensibility differently, arguing that sensibility and terror were intrinsically linked. See Reddy, *The Navigation of Feeling*.

in the country one day, within the limits marked out by nature. A wife, children for my heart, study for my leisure, my superfluity for my neighbours, if they are poor.'

By the time their paths crossed once again, in the midst of revolutionary politics, Saint-Just had adopted a different identity. Now he told Lejeune that he had renounced the bucolic life, 'to regenerate, he said, a people corrupted by centuries of barbarity and slavery'. When Lejeune reminded him of the rural idyll which Saint-Just had once imagined, Saint-Just replied: 'Other times, other discourses... when it is necessary to model oneself on the enemy of the Tarquins, one no longer reads the *Idylls* of Gesner.'[72] Brutus or Rousseau? What did Saint-Just really want? Lejeune's description of Saint-Just's abrupt changes of mood suggests that perhaps Saint-Just himself did not know, or that he was subject to conflicting emotions. Nor can we know ourselves; like the Jacobins we are reduced to looking at outward signs and trying to interpret them as indications of what people truly thought.

Despite Saint-Just's lofty words, Lejeune had no doubt that Saint-Just's choice of a career in revolutionary politics was prompted by 'the perfidious voice of ambition', which took the form of a blind devotion to Robespierre, whom Saint-Just took as 'a model to follow', because he desired to have the kind of public celebrity that Robespierre had achieved. This would seem to suggest that the political model that *truly* influenced Saint-Just, the one he chose to emulate, was that of Robespierre himself; the obscure man from the provinces who forged his revolutionary career out of the wholeheartedness of his commitment to the good of the people. By contrast, Robespierre himself never seems to have been conflicted about his identity, either in public or in private life; in that authentic identity lay the secret of his popularity with the revolutionary public. It was a rare political quality, which even Saint-Just, it seems, struggled to maintain.

## THE THREAT OF ASSASSINATION

In the oppressive atmosphere of mistrust and personal enmity that characterized revolutionary politics in the Year Two, it was not only Saint-Just who attracted the unwelcome epithet 'ambitious'. It was a term that the Jacobin leaders readily used to sabotage their opponents; knowing that, in the context of the Terror, to be publicly identified as an 'ambitious politician' was now tantamount to a death sentence. How then could they shake off this unwelcome adjective, and demonstrate their authenticity in the eyes of public opinion? Ultimately the only way to prove beyond all doubt that one's virtue was authentic was to be prepared to make the ultimate sacrifice for the public good—to give up one's own life. It was politics as self-sacrifice rather than self-advancement. Ironically, the offer of self-sacrifice also became a justification for using terror: since one was prepared to die oneself

---

[72] Bégis, *Curiosités révolutionnaires*, 27–36.

for the good of the Republic one was also justified in taking the lives of others. This readiness to sacrifice themselves was apparent in the way in which the Jacobin leaders confronted the dangers of assassination. Since the beginning of the Revolution the most committed revolutionaries had lived close to the Assembly, at the heart of politics, the clubs, the cafés, the atmosphere, and culture. This put them close to the public, but might also expose them to greater danger from hostile crowds or individuals. In the polarized landscape of the Year Two the peril had increased dramatically. Yet the Jacobin leaders defied the danger of assassination, refusing to hide behind high palace walls and armed bodyguards. If they were to maintain credibility as men of virtue then they had to be accessible to the public; which meant they had to be prepared to risk their lives. So they were afraid—with good reason. But being politicians to their fingertips they still made political capital out of their own vulnerability.

Lest the deputies ever felt inclined to forget the risks of assassination, they could contemplate David's iconic paintings of the deaths of Marat and of Lepeletier, as they hung in the Convention, ever before their eyes. The message was clear: the blades of assassins could be close at hand.[73] Martyrdom was not just a rhetoric: death was a very real possibility. The paintings were intended to inspire the deputies with thoughts of heroic virtue, but the daily sight of them may also have helped to make the deputies anxious and uneasy, though this must remain unacknowledged, or sublimated into rhetoric about devotion to the *patrie*. In addition, both these paintings served as a constant visual reminder that the deputies, as public officials, were obliged to be accessible to the public, and therefore to continue to run the risk that someone would seize an opportunity to kill them.[74]

Given the unpopularity in many quarters of the Jacobin leaders in the Year Two, it is remarkable to note, firstly, how few people did make attempts on their lives, and secondly, how relatively unprotected they were, particularly in comparison with the kings of the old regime, or with Napoleon.[75] Two attempts were made to assassinate Robespierre in May 1794. The first, on 3 Prairial (22 May), was when a man named Admiral (or Admirat), armed with two pistols, tried to find Robespierre to shoot him. He first went in the morning to Robespierre's lodgings, where in the courtyard a woman and an injured soldier told him that Robespierre was busy and could not speak to him. He then sat in the public gallery of the Convention and hung about the gallery that led to the offices of the Committee of Public

---

[73] On the different ways in which dead heroes of the Revolution were represented and commemorated, see Jourdan, *Les Monuments de la Révolution*, ch. 3; Antoine de Baecque, 'Le sang des héros: figures du corps dans l'imaginaire politique de la Révolution française', *Revue d'histoire moderne et contemporaine* 34 (1987): 553–86; Baecque, *Glory and Terror*; Avner Ben-Amos, *Funerals, Politics, and Memory in Modern France, 1789–1996* (Oxford: Oxford University Press, 2000), ch. 1; Joseph Clarke, *Commemorating the Dead in Revolutionary France: Revolution and Remembrance, 1789–1799* (Cambridge: Cambridge University Press, 2007).

[74] The deputies frequently invoked the deaths of Lepeletier and of Marat. See Chapter 6, note 41 of this work.

[75] On the ways that the Jacobin leaders reacted to the risks of assassination, see Marisa Linton, 'The stuff of nightmares: plots, assassinations, and duplicity in the mental world of the Jacobin leaders, 1793–1794', in Andress, *Experiencing the French Revolution*.

Safety in the hope of encountering Robespierre, but Robespierre did not take his customary route.[76] That evening Admiral returned by way of various cafés to the building in which he lived, which was also where Collot d'Herbois lodged. When Collot returned home that night Admiral attempted to shoot him, but both his pistols misfired. Admiral went into his own lodging, reloaded his pistols, and succeeded in wounding a locksmith, Geffroy, who had come to Collot's aid.

On 5 Prairial, a 20-year-old woman, Cécile Renault, was arrested at the home of Robespierre at nine in the evening. She had been trying to get to see Robespierre and had acted suspiciously. The citizens who apprehended her said that she had expressed anger when told she could not meet Robespierre 'and said that he was a public official, answerable to all those who presented themselves at his home'.[77] It is evident that she expected Robespierre, as a revolutionary politician, to be transparent and approachable. Under interrogation she said she had wanted to see what a tyrant looked like, but refused to say whether she had intended to kill Robespierre. She did say, however, that she would 'shed all her blood to bring about the return of the king'. As an assassination attempt it looks to have been fairly feeble. The Jacobins, however, saw it in a different light, for they remembered how the resourceful Charlotte Corday had bluffed her way into Marat's home and, armed only with a kitchen knife, put paid both to his revolutionary career and to his life. Robespierre, like Marat, was guarded by little more than his devoted women-folk. When Robespierre went to the Convention he was probably accompanied by one or two friends, and that was all.

On 6 Prairial (25 May) the attempted assassinations were discussed, in dramatic scenes, at the Jacobin Club.[78] It had been suggested that the Jacobin leaders, above all Robespierre, should be protected by guards. Legendre—trying to make good for his attempt to save Danton and his friends—spoke up, and 'invited the patriots to redouble their vigilance and not to let the representatives of the people go out alone, their existence is so useful to the Republic'.[79] He offered to place himself between the revolutionary leaders and the blades of their would-be assassins.

Legendre's proposal was countered first by Dumas, president of the Revolutionary Tribunal, who said that never would the representatives of the people countenance 'the proposal to provide them with bodyguards...even "a guard of

---

[76] According to Couthon, Admiral was waiting at the entrance to the Committee that Robespierre usually took, but thanks to Robespierre's 'génie conservateur' on that occasion he went by a different way. See his letter of 5 Prairial to the municipality of Orcet, in *Correspondance de Georges Couthon, suivie de L'Aristocrate converti* (Paris: A. Aubry, 1872), 342–4.

[77] Alexandre Tuetey, *Répertoire général des sources manuscrites de l'histoire de Paris pendant la Révolution française*, 11 vols (Paris: Imprimerie Nouvelle, 1914), 11: 604. The interrogators found that Admiral was a former lottery official, and had worked in the service of members of the Bertin family, who had since become *émigrés*. He had been a volunteer in the army. He spent a lot of time in bars and cafés.

[78] First Collot d'Herbois spoke. He made a stirring speech on how conspirators, at the instigation of 'the agents of Pitt and Austria', were attempting to assassinate the virtuous men. He also praised the heroic actions of Geffroy, meeting with huge applause. Then Robespierre entered, to renewed applause: 6 Prairial an II (25 May 1794), in Aulard, *Société des Jacobins*, 6: 146–50.

[79] Aulard, *Société des Jacobins*, 6: 150.

friendship" '. The representatives, he said, knew that they were already protected—
by the people.[80] Couthon also spoke to counter the proposal, but went further in
attacking the motives of the men behind it:

> People have spoken about giving us guards. I would love to believe that this proposal
> stems from pure intentions; but I would say that only despots have guards... We have
> no need of guards to defend ourselves; it is virtue, it is the confidence of the people,
> and Providence that watch over us; and we have friends who are there to support us.
> It would be an affront to our friends, to the people, and to Providence, to believe that
> we could have guards that are more sure.[81]

Couthon said that the greatest dangers stemmed from those 'men who surround
us, and who wish to appear the most ardent patriots, [but] are often our most cruel
enemies'. He claimed that they were 'directed by the British cabinet', thus part of
the 'Foreign Plot'. He added, though, that basic precautions could be taken, and it
would be prudent for deputies not to admit people into their homes unless their
good intentions had been proved.[82]

Why were the Jacobin leaders so determined not to have bodyguards when they
knew perfectly well that many people (whether agents of Pitt or acting on their
own initiative) hated them? The answer lies in the importance to them of maintaining their authenticity. If they accepted palaces and bodyguards then they were
no longer virtuous officials in their own eyes or in those of the public. Couthon
explained something of this in a letter he wrote to his constituents, members of the
municipality of Orcet. Here he expressed himself in much more measured language than in the Jacobin Club:

> We did not doubt that we were surrounded by assassins, above all us, members of the
> Committee of Public Safety... The patriots from all sides offer us guards. We will be
> very glad to have near us some friends on whom we can rely, but no other guards; it is
> the testimony of our consciences, it is the esteem of the public, it is the Supreme
> Being, that guard us. If distressing things happen to us, it is no doubt because it is
> necessary for liberty, since Providence will have permitted this to happen, and we
> should glory in doing our duty in serving the *patrie* by our deaths.[83]

Robespierre's enemies amongst the Jacobin leadership used the assassination attempts
to blacken his public image, depicting him as a would-be king, who was personally
vindictive towards his enemies.[84] As for Robespierre, once so acute and capable of
moderation in judgement, he had lost his capacity for political judgement. He interpreted everything that happened in revolutionary politics in terms of himself. He
drew the following chilling conclusions from the assassination attempts:

[80] Aulard, *Société des Jacobins*, 6: 151.
[81] Aulard, *Société des Jacobins*, 6: 152.
[82] Aulard, *Société des Jacobins*, 6: 153.
[83] Letter of Couthon to the municipality of Orcet, 5 Prairial (24 May 1794), *Correspondance de Couthon*, 342–4.
[84] For a cogent discussion of the ways in which Robespierre's enemies amongst the Jacobins used the assassination attempts against him, see Martin, *Violence et révolution*, 219–36.

The situation in which the enemies of the Republic have placed me is not without its advantages; because, the more uncertain and precarious become the lives of defenders of liberty, the more they detach themselves from the wickedness of men. Surrounded by their assassins, I have already placed myself in the new order of things where they wish to send me; the only things that still tie me to a fleeting life, are love of the *patrie*, and the thirst for justice; and disengaged more than ever from every personal consideration, I feel myself increasingly disposed to attack with energy the scoundrels who conspire against my country and against humanity.[85]

This passage made a key link—at least as far as Robespierre was concerned—between the trauma caused by fear of assassination and the decision to intensify the Terror in an effort to destroy the opponents of the Revolution.

Increasingly, Robespierre had cause to fear that the biggest danger to him was posed by other deputies, who encountered him every day he attended the Convention. One of a number of anonymous letters that Robespierre received was written with a view to making Robespierre believe—if he did not think it already—that in the Convention itself he was surrounded by secret enemies, determined to kill him. The writer claimed that Robespierre could not evade 'the blow delivered by my hand, or that of twenty-two others, like myself, determined Brutuses and Scaevolas...Surround yourself with guards, satellites, blacks and slaves; I shall be amongst them, don't doubt it.' The writer said he would have killed Robespierre already but had decided that, as a 'new Brutus', he will 'share that glory with others'.[86] Twenty-two was a reference to the Girondins, suggesting that the author of the letter was a deputy bent on revenge for their deaths.[87] Tallien, on 9 Thermidor, said that he was armed with a dagger to assassinate Robespierre on the floor of the Convention. Others felt as he did: several deputies were emboldened at the festival of the Supreme Being to shout threats at Robespierre as he walked before them, some at least of which he heard. Lecointre later stated that he had actually planned to lead a group of deputies to assassinate Robespierre at the festival.[88] Amongst the things of which the deputies accused Robespierre on that day were pride and ambition—both qualities that were the antithesis of virtue, and therefore probably wounded him most.[89] That abuse must have been a particular shock to him as (certainly by Vilate's account) he had genuinely been very moved when he saw the assembled crowds of people on that day. For Robespierre, these threats provided confirmation that the biggest danger to him was posed by the 'enemy within', that is, by other deputies who sat with the Mountain. The stage was thus set for the *dénouement* of Thermidor.

[85]  7 Prairial, in Robespierre, *Oeuvres*, 10: 475.
[86]  Anonymous letter to Robespierre, in *Papiers inédits*, 2: 151–4.
[87]  On the symbolic significance of 'twenty-two' Girondins, see Chapter 8, note 9 of this work.
[88]  See Bouloiseau, *The Jacobin Republic*, 205–7.
[89]  Buchez and Roux, *Histoire parlementaire de la Révolution*, 33: 178.

# 10

# Final Choices
## Thermidor

For the rest, for a long time now I have seen nothing but indifference, forgetfulness of the public good, ambition, hypocrisy.

Saint-Just, final line of his private notes.[1]

...in the battle of 9 Thermidor it was not a question of principles, but of killing.

Baudot, *Notes historiques*.[2]

We turn now to the political tensions in the summer of 1794 that culminated in the political coup of Thermidor. On 8 Thermidor (26 July) Robespierre declared in what was to be his final speech to the Convention that a conspiracy existed in the heart of revolutionary government. This time he had identified a genuine plot. Robespierre's own fears had been instrumental in bringing this conspiracy into existence, for it was led by men who banded together in fear of their lives to protect themselves against Robespierre's desire to purge the Convention of 'suspect' deputies amongst the Jacobins. Robespierre's own action in coming to the Convention to denounce a plot amongst the Jacobins without specifying who he meant, proved to be the trigger that precipitated the conspiracy into action. The conspiracy culminated the following day in the denunciation and arrest of Robespierre and those men who chose to stand alongside him, his brother Augustin, Saint-Just, Couthon, and Le Bas. The following day they were executed. Many others who sided with Robespierre also paid the ultimate price for their loyalty. Over 100 of his friends, colleagues, and appointees, including the General Council of the Commune, which was staffed by his supporters, were sent to the guillotine on 10, 11, and 12 Thermidor.[3]

## THERMIDOR: A REAL CONSPIRACY

The dramatic events of Thermidor changed the whole direction of the Revolution. Thermidor signalled the end of its radical phase. It resulted in the overthrow of Jacobin rule, of the Republic of Virtue, and the end of the Terror as a state-organized

[1] Saint-Just, 'Fragments d'institutions républicaines', in Saint-Just, *Oeuvres complètes*, 1009.
[2] Baudot, *Notes historiques sur la Convention nationale*, 125.
[3] Wallon, *Histoire du Tribunal Révolutionnaire*, 5: 252–60.

system of government. It also meant effectively the collapse of a politics based on the notion that the 'poor are the powers of the earth'. The following year, Year Three, a new constitution ended the democratic franchise and confined the vote to men who paid a sufficient rate of taxes to be judged fit to have a political voice, as well as limiting political rights by age, education, and marital status. It did not take long for a shift in political direction to become apparent. However, these consequences were not the intention of the men who actually carried out the Thermidor coup. The men who overthrew Robespierre were his fellow Jacobins. They were also supporters of the Terror; in many cases they were more unscrupulous and hard-line terrorists than he was himself. They destroyed Robespierre because they feared him—not because they wanted a change of political direction. Yet a change of direction came about, largely as a result of the self-immolation of the Jacobins.

The truth about what happened in Thermidor is almost impossible to disentangle. The systematic construction of a narrative that identified Robespierre himself as having been the arch-conspirator against the Revolution began in the hours that followed his arrest, even before he had been put to death. When it became apparent that public opinion had revolted against the Terror, the men who had carried out the coup scrambled to conceal their own part in the system of terror, and load all the responsibility onto Robespierre and the men who died with him. A few men were still held accountable, including Billaud-Varenne and Collot d'Herbois, both of whom were transported to Guiana in 1795, a destination that became known as the 'dry guillotine'. The majority of the Jacobin leaders, however, had time and opportunity to distance themselves from the newly coined word 'terrorist' and to wash the blood from their hands. When the survivors came to give their account of their actions in Thermidor they presented their own motives as having been pure and anti-terrorist, and those of the Robespierrists as having been pro-terrorist, conspiratorial, and against virtue. The evidence that comes from the survivors of Thermidor, therefore, has to be treated with considerable caution.

The complexities of Thermidor have been the subject of considerable debate amongst historians.[4] My own approach seeks to contribute to that debate by indicating three different—but interrelated—ways in which we can think about the meaning of Thermidor. Firstly, we can consider the impact of Thermidor on the ideology of the Revolution. By the summer of 1794 the ideology of political virtue had reached an impasse. As Saint-Just (and perhaps even Robespierre) recognized, it was impossible to maintain the Republic on the basis of the strength of will of its leaders alone. Stabilizing the regime, however, proved difficult in the

---

[4] There is an extensive historiography on Thermidor. On the politics the best study is by Françoise Brunel, *Thermidor: La chute de Robespierre* (Paris: Éditions Complexe, 1989). Translations of key documents are in Bienvenu, *The Ninth of Thermidor*. On the background to Thermidor and the politics of the Committees see Martin, *Révolution et violence*, 219–36. For the case that Thermidor emerged largely out of ideological conflicts amongst the Montagnards, especially over religion, see Martyn Lyons, 'The 9 Thermidor: motives and effects', *European History Quarterly*, 5, 2 (1975): 123–46. On the deeper significance of Thermidor there is an illuminating analysis in Bronislaw Baczko, *Ending the Terror: The French Revolution After Robespierre* (Cambridge: Cambridge University Press, 1994), esp. 25–32.

poisonous environment of the politicians' terror. Eventually the tensions inherent in maintaining an identity as a 'man of virtue' imploded into a bloodbath in which the Jacobins destroyed one another for lacking virtue, for having succumbed to ambition, corruption, and conspiracy. Secondly, Thermidor was also a contingent and tactical event, fought on several fronts: in the Convention, in the offices of the Committee of Public Safety, in the Jacobin Club, and in the Commune. For many hours the outcome was in doubt. Each of the leading players was obliged to make hard choices—whether to align himself with a particular group, gambling on which side would win; whether to support a friend, or to abandon him; whether to fight, or to make himself scarce and hope thereby to save himself. Life and death for himself and others turned on these decisions. Lastly, the drama was driven by intense emotions: fear, stress, suspicion, hatred, anger, despair; though there was also loyalty and extraordinary courage. These gut emotions operated on a different level to that of ideology. They affected the judgement and decision making of the leading players, and had a significant impact on the outcome. Thermidor shows as nothing else does the level of psychological stress the Jacobin leaders were under, and how this affected their choices, and their readiness to use terror against one another.

## VIRTUE OR FRIENDSHIP? *REPUBLICAN INSTITUTIONS*

Robespierre appears to have finally made up his mind where he stood on the republic of virtue and terror in the weeks leading up to the arrest of the Dantonists. Thereafter he clung rigidly to the same position for what remained of his life, unwilling or unable to think things through differently. In terms of Jacobin ideology it was Saint-Just, rather than Robespierre, who proved better able to adapt his ideas to fit the changed circumstances. Saint-Just left a number of personal notes that were later collected up and published under the title *Fragments on Republican Institutions*. Some passages appear to have been first drafts of speeches; other sections were evidently intended for himself alone. Together the notes formed a very open text, full of crossings-out, drafts, and alternative versions. There was a rawness about the words: they were not yet fashioned to sway an audience. They offer a unique insight into his actual state of mind, one that is much more open than his public words.[5]

Parts of the text addressed the problem of how to sustain the Republic. Saint-Just came to the striking conclusion that it was inevitable that the government would fail—because the virtue of revolutionary leaders and functionaries was not in itself sufficient to ensure the survival of the Republic, or rather there were not enough

---

[5] Saint-Just's recourse to antiquity in the *Fragments* is discussed in Linton, 'L'Antiquité, l'amitié et la nature dans la pensée de Saint-Just', unpublished paper given at the international conference on 'Images de l'Antiquité dans la Révolution Française', at the Université de Versailles-Saint-Quentin, June 2009. On Saint-Just's political ideas, see also Miguel Abensour, 'La Philosophie politique de Saint-Just', *Annales historiques de la révolution française*, 38 (1966): 1–32; and Linton, 'The Man of Virtue'.

such men who were truly virtuous. Sooner or later a conspiracy would overthrow them.[6] Saint-Just recognized that power had a tendency to corrupt even those revolutionary leaders who had set out with high principles to overthrow the old regime: 'One tries to be rigorous in one's principles, when one destroys a bad government; but it is rare that, if one governs in one's turn, one does not soon reject these same principles in order to substitute one's own will.'[7] He had lost faith (if he had ever had it) in political leaders, governments, and their ability to make effective laws and constitutions:

> Long laws are public calamities. Wisdom is in children. The majority of things that seem great to us only appear so because we measure them against our own littleness and our own vanity...In this condition in which we live, it is civil life that is the most natural, it is this which must be cultivated with the most care.[8]

Rather than rely on the fragile virtue of individual leaders, the republic must be secured on a new basis. The *Fragments* show Saint-Just trying to feel his way towards a model for a republic that would *not* involve terror, but would instead be grounded in social institutions; institutions that would establish a more natural and moral community—the *patrie*.[9] Saint-Just's faith in the natural virtue of the people had become equally problematic. Society had been corrupted by the old regime, and its influence still lingered, tainting the natural virtue of the people. Therefore their natural virtue must be reinvigorated. The notes disclosed his vision for a future that would be founded not upon terror, but upon social institutions, of which one of the most important was friendship.

His concept of friendship went beyond private sentiments to address social relationships.[10] For ordinary citizens friendship would fulfil the function that political virtue had for revolutionary leaders. In contrast to the almost superhuman efforts of self-denial required to sustain political virtue, friendship is aligned with natural feelings, and therefore easier to maintain. Friends forge ties of affection that are based on their mutual love and altruistic concern for one another. If friendship could be extended through society, then this would strengthen the bonds uniting people with one another; by this means a 'community of affections' could be achieved. Saint-Just's argument recalled that of Aristotle and Cicero, that friendship could be a form of political virtue. If friendship was to work as an institution of the Revolution it must be based on equality and free choice. Thus,

---

[6] Saint-Just, *Fragments d'institutions républicaines*, 966–7.

[7] Saint-Just, *Fragments d'institutions républicaines*, 969.

[8] Saint-Just, *Fragments d'institutions républicaines*, 968.

[9] It is the specific ideas of Saint-Just in this text on the self-regulating community that come closest to a Jacobin articulation of the 'natural republic' interestingly described by Edelstein, *The Terror of Natural Right*, 202–6; though how far Saint-Just's ideas reflected a wider desire on the part of other Jacobin leaders to set 'their sights on an ideal republic of natural right', as Edelstein contends (206), is perhaps more doubtful.

[10] See Françoise Fortunet, 'L'Amitié et le droit selon Saint-Just', *Annales historiques de la révolution française*, 248 (1982), 181–95. For a thought-provoking argument about Saint-Just's concept of friendship and its relationship to the pattern of acquittals made by the Revolutionary Tribunal during the 'Great Terror', see Simonin, 'Les acquittés de la Grande Terreur', 203–205.

his conception of the *patrie* was grounded in reciprocal emotional attachments between its citizens: 'The *patrie* is not the earth, it is the community of affections, with the effect that, each person fighting for the safety and liberty of that which is dear to him, the *patrie* is defended.'[11] Friendship would attach citizens to the *patrie* by the most powerful of bonds, those of love.

Yet to achieve this model Saint-Just's concept of friendship was stretched painfully thin, made to cover glaring holes in this idealized depiction of a community at one with itself.[12] In his notes he tended to express himself in brief aphorisms that left little space for development of meaning. Some of the aphorisms he wrote on friendship in the *Fragments* have surprised, baffled, and even horrified subsequent readers.[13] The following are examples:

> Whoever says that he does not believe in friendship is banished. Every man from the age of 21 must declare in the temple who his friends are, and renew this declaration every year... Those who have stayed friends all their lives are buried in the same tomb... If a man leaves a friend, he must give an account to the people, in the temple, of his motives for relinquishing him. Friends dig the grave, prepare the funeral rites for one another, together with children they scatter flowers on the tomb. If a man has no friends, he is banished.[14]

All of this may appear a fantasy, out of touch with political reality, and at first sight a long way from the betrayal of friends that took place in the politicians' terror. What makes this all the more thought-provoking is that these ideas came from a leading revolutionary who was, in other respects, politically astute and hard-headed.[15] Rather than dismiss passages that seem naïve to us, the text is well worth taking seriously, for it casts further light on some of the problems we have addressed in this book: the tensions between virtue and friendship; the failures of revolutionary government; and the underlying problem of alienation and social fragmentation in a society that was supposedly 'one and indivisible'. In addition, Saint-Just's text gives an extraordinary insight into the emotional isolation—even despair—of the Jacobin leaders in the Year Two.

One concern that was particularly apparent in the *Fragments* was the need to make friendship subject to transparency. There was to be no demarcation between the public world and the private. Rather, every man would publicly commit himself to his friends. This preoccupation may well reflect an underlying anxiety about the difficulty in revolutionary politics of knowing who one's real friends were. Behind

---

[11] Saint-Just, *Fragments d'institutions républicaines*, 977.

[12] On friendship and the community of affections in Saint-Just's writing, see also Pierre-Yves Glasser and Anne Quennedey, 'De la haine du roi à la communauté des affections: les resorts d'un politique républicaine selon Saint-Just', in Josiane Barnier, Monique Cottret, and Lydwine Scordia (eds), *Amour et désamour du prince du Haut Moyen Age à la Révolution française* (Paris: Kimé, 2011).

[13] See for example, Hampson, *Will and Circumstance*, 262–4.

[14] Saint-Just, *Fragments d'institutions républicaines*, 983–4. On the practice of burying male friends in the same tomb, see Bray, 'A traditional rite for blessing friendship'.

[15] See Lucien Febvre, who, when commenting on the *Fragments d'institutions républicaines*, was particularly struck by Saint-Just's account of friendship: 'Les texts curieux abondent. Parmi les plus intéressants, ceux qui traitent de l'amitié' in Lucien Febvre, 'En lisant Saint-Just', *A.E.S.C.* (1951), 120–22.

the idealized account of the man in the temple who testifies openly as to who his friends are, stands the contrasting reality of the Convention, where the deputies paid lip service to the notion of transparency, but where the toxic atmosphere of fear, distrust, and enmity had so seeped into the fabric of politics that no one could be trusted.

Some historians have interpreted several references to Spartan institutions in the text as meaning that Saint-Just wanted to impose the political model of Sparta on France.[16] The reality was more complex: the *Fragments* marked the rejection of politics in the sense of a government run by politicians who would exert power over others. Saint-Just's community would be a self-policing society. Functionaries were to be subject to scrutiny by citizens.[17] In this way it was the citizens themselves who would ensure that the functionaries served the *patrie*, rather than their own ambition, or the desire for personal glory: 'Those who are charged with governing the republic should give an example of virtues and modesty.'[18]

In between these visions of the future were interposed passages in which, like Robespierre, Saint-Just anticipated that his own death was drawing near. Several times he raised the question of whether or not he had succeeded in his self-appointed task as a revolutionary leader.[19] Arguably, these thoughts go to the heart of what this document is about. At points he spoke of his achievement in giving himself a life in people's memory. Elsewhere, however, he talked of being a powerless observer of 'crime', and spoke of the internal collapse of the revolutionary government—internal because it began with the bad faith of officials who had chosen corruption over virtue. There were even occasional moments of bitter disillusionment with the republic of virtue, as expressed in one of his most powerful aphorisms: 'The revolution is frozen: all its principles are weakened; there is nothing left but *bonnets rouges* immersed in intrigue.'[20]

There was a growing urgency in the *Fragments*—a sense that time was running out, both for the Republic and its leaders. Several times Saint-Just referred to his fear that, before these institutions could be put into place, the men of virtue would fail, and the revolutionary project would be destroyed along with them. Saint-Just coped with this fear by seeing his own identity and fate as paralleling those of virtuous heroes of antiquity. He recalled the names of men who had been put to death for their political ideals: Scipio, the Gracchi, and others such as Demosthenes who had chosen suicide rather than capitulation to their enemies.[21] Several passages in the *Fragments* made it clear that he expected to meet a similar fate. He consoled himself by invoking the stoicism of antiquity, his emotional attachment to the

---

[16]  This is considered in greater depth in Linton, 'The Man of Virtue'.

[17]  Saint-Just, *Fragments d'institutions républicaines*, 987.

[18]  Saint-Just, *Fragments d'institutions républicaines*, 999–1000.

[19]  Saint-Just, *Fragments d'institutions républicaines*, 967, 977, 986, 1007, 1008.

[20]  Saint-Just, *Fragments d'institutions républicaines*, 979.

[21]  Saint-Just, *Fragments d'institutions républicaines*, 966. Saint-Just also referred to other 'great men' who had made enemies through 'an incorruptible courage' and been put to death, including Sidney, Barneveldt, Chalier, and Marat.

*patrie*, and the model of heroic self-sacrifice. Saint-Just had played a principal role in the destruction of the factions in his successive speeches denouncing the Girondins, the Hébertists, the Dantonists. Yet there was no sign that he felt any remorse for his part in the politicians' terror or those men's deaths. On the contrary, he referred to his role in attacking Danton and other 'conspirators' against the Revolution as proof of the authenticity of his own virtue: '...I have attacked men whom no one dared attack...it is for the youngest to die and to prove his courage and his virtue'.[22] This pessimistic frame of mind probably influenced his conduct and decisions when Robespierre's last speech precipitated the final breakdown of the unity of the Committees.

## CHOOSING SIDES IN THERMIDOR

Any investigation of Thermidor has to take into account the internal politics of the Committee of Public Safety. For nearly a year the men on the Committee had worked together and cooperated more or less amicably, but from early summer these working relationships begin to break down under the pressure of growing tension and mutual mistrust. It is hard to judge what was really happening. The Committee kept no minutes; its members met in private, and allowed little of their internal discussions to escape publicly until they broke ranks in Thermidor. The evidence given afterwards is unreliable for many reasons: each of the survivors had an interest in lying. We do know that there were bitter quarrels over tactics. As the French armies amassed military successes, the need for governmental unity in the face of a threatened invasion by the foreign powers began to wane. Carnot was keen for the French armies to go on the offensive in a war of conquest: Robespierre and Saint-Just took the opposing viewpoint.[23] Carnot quarrelled furiously with Saint-Just on matters of army policy. The two men exchanged such threatening words that, according to Prieur, the rest of the Committee were left 'stupefied'.[24] Robespierre withdrew from the Committee altogether in late June. Thereafter we know little of what was in his mind until the day he went to address the Convention.

Much about what happened in Thermidor makes little sense unless we understand how far events were driven by virulent emotions, above all suspicion, dread—and despair. During the final months of the Jacobin government there is considerable evidence that the leaders were suffering from stress, exhaustion, and acute anxiety. According to the Jacobin Thibaudeau: 'The terror did not end because its leaders were weary of bloodletting, but because they were terrified of one another, and divided amongst themselves. You had to get your

---

[22] Saint-Just, *Fragments d'institutions républicaines*, 1007. On Saint-Just's conviction that he would shortly die, and how he confronted this, see also 977, 986, 1008.

[23] For the argument that Robespierre's opposition to a 'war of conquest' played an important part in the pre-Thermidor conflicts in the Committee, see Marc Belissa, 'Robespierre et la guerre de conquête', in Jessenne, *Robespierre*, 357.

[24] Prieur's account is in Carnot, *Mémoires sur Carnot par son fils*, 523–5.

attack in first, because if you were on the defensive, you were lost.'[25] The members of the Committee of Public Safety had particular cause to fear the politicians' terror. They had themselves brought about the arrest and deaths of other Jacobin factions. Most of the members of the Committee of Public Safety along with the Committee of General Security had actually signed the arrest warrant for the Dantonists. They had been complicit in the construction of the narrative that designated the Girondins, the Hébertists, and the Dantonists as 'conspirators' against the Revolution, and thus deserving death. Now they feared that such tactics might be used against themselves. Several of them were eyeing Robespierre warily, afraid that he was about to precipitate another purge of ambitious, corrupt, conspiratorial deputies who feigned virtue, and that their own names might be on his list. Prieur described the suffocating atmosphere in the Committee:

> Storm clouds banked up over our heads, and at each moment we came closer to an inevitable crisis. However the work of the Committee did not suffer. In the midst of our anguish, uncertain whether the hour would come that would see us sent before the Revolutionary Tribunal, to go from there to the scaffold, without perhaps having the time to say goodbye to our families and our friends...
>
> We ended by becoming so accustomed to these inextricable situations, that we pursued our daily task, so that business should not be left pending, as though we had a whole lifetime before us, when it was perfectly likely that we would not see the sun rise tomorrow.[26]

Vilate described a conversation with Barère, who was in such anguish over the situation that he talked of suicide. During the final days Billaud-Varenne's whole body expressed his tension: according to Prieur, 'Billaud-Varenne kept silent, his arms crossed, his head lowered on his chest during our deliberations'. Saint-Just too was struck by Billaud-Varenne's moodiness and pointed silences: he would 'close his eyes and feign sleep' in the midst of the Committee meetings. Saint-Just recalled Billaud-Varenne's use of the phrase 'we are walking on a volcano', which Saint-Just thought revealed his inward state of mind. At a meeting that had been set up to reconcile Robespierre with the other Committee members, Billaud-Varenne said to Robespierre: 'We are your friends: we have always gone forward together,' which Saint-Just interpreted—correctly as it turned out—as a sign that Billaud-Varenne was plotting against Robespierre.[27]

---

[25] Antoine-Claire Thibaudeau, *Mémoires sur la Convention, et le Directoire, par. A.C. Thibaudeau*, 2 vols (Paris: Badouin Frères, 1824), I: 58. On his view of Thermidor as a contingent event, and on the politicians' terror, see also I: 50, 86–7.

[26] Carnot, *Mémoires sur Carnot*, 1: 527–8.

[27] See Joachim Vilate, *Causes secrètes de la Révolution du 9 au 10 thermidor* (Paris, an III), republished in *Collection des Mémoires relatifs à la Révolution Française*, 194–5. For Prieur's description of the moody Billaud-Varenne, see Carnot, *Mémoires sur Carnot*, 535. Saint-Just's account of Billaud-Varenne's behaviour is in Saint-Just, 'Discours du 9 Thermidor an II', *Oeuvres Complètes*, 909–10, 914. On volcanic imagery as an expression of the violence of nature playing out in the revolutionary imagination, see Mary Ashburn Miller, *A Natural History of Revolution: Violence and Nature in the French Revolutionary Imagination, 1789–1794* (Ithaca, NY: Cornell University Press, 2011), 148–9.

There is less evidence for the state of mind of the Robespierrists. They were the losers in the battle of Thermidor, so were packed off to their deaths within hours, leaving no time for final words, still less to rewrite the past. Their papers were left at the mercy of the Thermidoreans to manipulate or suppress.[28] Still, there are signs that the Robespierrists, too, were struggling under extreme stress, and feared some kind of blow, whether from royalists, assassins, foreign agents—or their fellow Jacobins. There was, as we have seen, evidence in the writings of Saint-Just and Robespierre that both were struggling to repress despair. The people who were near to them were also very close to the edge. Philippe Le Bas had a young wife, and a baby son just six weeks old; but in his misery he talked over committing suicide with his wife. Many years later his widow, Elizabeth, now an old lady, recalled his words: 'In the Marbeuf garden, perhaps four or five days before Thermidor, Philippe said to me "If it wasn't a crime, I would blow your brains out, and myself too; at least we would die together...But no! there's our poor baby!" '[29]

Much of our judgement of the meaning of Thermidor derives from our understanding of the role that Robespierre himself played in it. Put crudely, was he a tyrant or a victim? Was he destroyed by heroic men; or was he laid low by the machinations of his duplicitous enemies? This is a subject that has been dogged by controversy for over two hundred years. There is never likely to be a definitive answer to that question, because historians (like anyone else) have their own political opinions, and their final judgement of the significance of Thermidor will depend in large part on their views about the value of revolution. Our problems are compounded by the lack of reliable evidence and Robespierre's guardedness about revealing what he was thinking. But some consideration of Robespierre's psychological and emotional state, as well as that of his fellow Jacobins, helps us to better understand the tactical decisions that he took in that chaotic situation. We have seen that, since the days when Barnave and the Lameths had dominated the Jacobins, Robespierre had suspected that not all Club members were as devoted to the public good as they claimed. Hitherto he had been able to exercise judgement and restraint in dealing with colleagues. He had always put the unity of the Jacobins first. He had maintained his ascendancy through five years of revolutionary struggle by his ability to temper his political idealism with acute tactical skills. But since his decision to engage in the destruction of the Jacobin factions in the spring of 1794, and particularly after he played a key role in the destruction of the Dantonists, that judgement and ability to step

---

[28] Amongst the men who had access to the Robespierrists' papers was Courtois, a friend of Danton, known for his corruption. Courtois made a very selective use of the Robespierrists' papers in order to write the official report on their activities. Lecointre, who was part of the same Dantonist group, and who hated Robespierre, also had access to the papers. A third man was Guffroy, who had once been a friend and colleague of Robespierre in Arras, but had fallen out with him when Guffroy embraced the most extremist form of revolutionary politics. Guffroy's newspaper, *Le Rougyff*, went beyond even the *Père Duchesne* in its brutality and violence. On 3 March 1794 this newspaper was denounced at the Jacobins, and Guffroy himself excluded from the Club: Aulard, *Société des Jacobins*, 5: 669–71. These men, and many others, had cause to be selective in what they retained of the Robespierrist papers, and to remove anything that might prove awkward.

[29] Elizabeth Le Bas, 'Manuscrit de Mme Le Bas', 136.

back from a situation had left him. He was burnt out, exhausted, and close to a breakdown.[30] He had lost all ability to distinguish between his personal enemies and the enemies of the Revolution. Speaking of his enemies, he said: 'It is you whom they persecute, it is the *patrie*, it is all the friends of the *patrie*.'[31] His identification with the Revolution was complete. In this condition he posed a danger to his fellow Jacobins as never before.

He began to suspect a further conspiracy amongst the Jacobins themselves. There were a number of Jacobin deputies who feared Robespierre and wanted to destroy him. One such group consisted of several men who had incurred Robespierre's hostility for their corruption, brutality, violent excesses, and policy of dechristianization when they had served as deputies *en mission*. They had been recalled from their posts, and now lived in fear that Robespierre intended to have them arrested for having brought the Jacobins and thereby the Revolution into disrepute by their conduct. These men included Fouché, Fréron, Barras, Tallien, Dubois-Crancé, and Carrier. Robespierre had other enemies too, notably some of the friends of Danton who were not likely to forgive or forget Robespierre's part in Danton's destruction. They included Bourdon de l'Oise, Lecointre, Legendre, Thuriot, and Dufourny. Bourdon de l'Oise and Lecointre were among the deputies who shouted threats at Robespierre on the day of the festival of the Supreme Being.[32] There were still more, too, who were less prominent, but who bided their time, waiting for others to take the lead, intent on revenge. The Law of Prairial contributed to the atmosphere of fear in the Convention, making the deputies acutely conscious of their own increased vulnerability.

Robespierre also had enemies amongst the ruling Committees. His enemies on the Committee of General Security included its leading figures, Vadier and Amar. Robespierre had come into conflict with the Committee of General Security over its corruption. He was wary of confronting the Committee members openly, but in a notebook he denounced the corruption of its clerks, under the patronage of Amar and Jagot.[33] Robespierre also fell out with the Committee of General Security over control of the Police Bureau, which some of the Committee resented as a rival that trespassed on their area of power. Again, Robespierre and the leading members of the Committee of General Security took very different views over religious policy: Robespierre was vehemently opposed to dechristianization, while Vadier, Amar, and others were militantly atheist. They were strongly antagonistic to Robespierre's attempt at religious reconciliation through the festival of the Supreme Being. Finally, and most dangerously for Robespierre, he had come into conflict

---

[30] This is the judgement of McPhee as well as myself. He discusses Robespierre's psychological state in *Robespierre*, ch. 12. To my mind this is one of the most perceptive accounts to have been written of Robespierre's state of mind in his final months.

[31] 'Contre les factions nouvelles et les députés corrompus', 8 Thermidor (26 July 1794), Robespierre, *Oeuvres*, 10: 555.

[32] Laurent Lecointre, *Robespierre peint par lui-même, et condamné par ses propres principes, ou dénonciation des crimes de…Robespierre, et projét d'acte d'accusation* (De l'Imprimérie de Rougyff, 1794), 3.

[33] 'Contre les factions nouvelles et les députés corrompus', 8 Thermidor (26 July 1794), Robespierre, *Oeuvres*, 10: 551–2, footnote 2.

with members of the Committee of Public Safety, particularly with the extremists Collot d'Herbois and Billaud-Varenne, together with Carnot (though Carnot was careful to keep a low public profile regarding his part in the conspiracy to destroy Robespierre). Previously, Robespierre had triumphed over the other Jacobin factions by working collectively with the other Committee members. That collective relationship had now broken down, owing partly to mutual distrust, but also to Robespierre's excessive self-righteousness, which set other men against him. Saint-Just's final speech spoke of some Committee members harbouring personal jealousy of Robespierre's high profile and eloquence, and it is perfectly possible that resentment of Robespierre's persona as *the* man of virtue did indeed fuel the hostility of his colleagues.[34] There is some evidence that members of the two Committees took advantage of Robespierre's absence from the Committee to damage his reputation by deliberately taking to excess the application of the Law of Prairial (the so-called 'Great Terror' in the last seven weeks of the Jacobin Republic), and carrying out vindictive acts of terror that they set to his personal account; above all the mass execution of the 'parricides' who had been incriminated in the assassination attempts against him.[35]

Robespierre made painstaking notes on the conduct of some of these deputies as he tried to piece together to his own satisfaction evidence of a conspiracy. He assessed their integrity in terms of signs that, since the beginning of the Revolution, had been used to analyse the conduct of political men. He noted that Dubois-Crancé had been 'intimately connected' with Danton; that Thuriot 'had dined with Delacroix and Danton, at the home of Guzman and other places of the same kind'.[36] Robespierre also received missives from Guérin and other agents, who spied on suspected deputies and wrote detailed reports of how they had observed the deputies engage in what looked like conspiratorial meetings with unknown individuals, both men and women, over dinners, in cafés, in public gardens, and in the streets; who referred to one another as 'my friend' and had furtive but animated conversations which the agents could not overhear.[37]

Men who felt threatened by the awareness that Robespierre's gaze was turned suspiciously upon them, responded with the rhetoric of virtue, desperately asserting the transparency of their conduct. Thus Tallien, who had been implicated in corruption and accepting bribes when he had been *en mission* in Bordeaux, wrote a letter to Robespierre in which he defended his identity as a man of virtue, after the approved fashion. Tallien said that he had acted with justice in Bordeaux. He denied that he was an immoral man as some had alleged. On the contrary, he lived with his 'aged and respectable' mother. He and his mother were not wealthy, they eschewed luxury: 'Living alone and isolated, I have few friends.' He declared

---

[34] See Anne Quennedey, 'Le talent oratoire est-il un danger pour la liberté? la controverse sur l'éloquence dans le discours de Saint-Just du 9 thermidor an II', in Cyril Triolaire (ed.), *La Révolution française au miroir des recherches actuelles* (Paris: Société des études robespierristes, 2011).

[35] Martin, *Violence et révolution*, 226–33, esp. 229; see also the discussion in McPhee, *Robespierre*, 205, 212–13.

[36] *Papiers inédits*, 2: 16–21.

[37] *Papiers inédits*, 1: 366–81, esp. 368–9.

himself to be a true defender of the people.[38] Whatever the truth about Tallien's home life and his respectable and aged mother, he was a chief instigator of the conspiracy against Robespierre; fearful both for himself and for the life of his mistress, Thérèse Cabarrus, who was about to be put on trial.[39]

Though some of these men disagreed with Robespierre on ideology—particularly on dechristianization and Robespierre's belief in the Supreme Being—the crucial factor that drove them to make up their minds to join the conspiracy seems in most cases to have been emotional rather than ideological—fear of Robespierre's intentions towards them, or enmity, or revenge. It looks as though several members of the Committee of Public Safety only made up their minds to throw in their weight with the other conspirators at the last moment.[40] Their intervention was to prove decisive. One of these was Billaud-Varenne, who would play a key role in the *dénouement* of Thermidor by denouncing Robespierre at a critical moment. Billaud-Varenne's ideological beliefs were close to those of the Robespierrists, particularly Saint-Just. The similarities can be seen in Billaud-Varenne's thereoretical treatise, the *Principes régénérateurs du système social*, which he wrote the following year. In this text he tried to devise a means whereby the corrupting influence of power and ambition on public functionaries could be overcome through the development of a civil space within which a democratic politics could develop.[41]

Collot d'Herbois, who also took a leading role in the conspiracy, seems to have made his choice at the eleventh hour. His fears for his own life had been stoked by Fouché, who wrote to him warning that their actions in the repression of the counter-revolution in Lyon were being investigated at the instigation of Robespierre for whether their conduct confirmed with 'justice and the most austere public probity'.[42] A letter by Voulland of the Committee of General Security on 9 Thermidor played down the significance of the events of 8 Thermidor in the Convention, which he attributed to the development in the two Committees of 'petty wounded vanities that have grown bitter with time'. From the evidence of this letter he was far from anticipating the dramatic events that took place the following day.[43]

It was Robespierre himself who provoked the final breakdown of the Jacobins, by going to the Convention on 8 Thermidor to disclose the divisions in the

---

[38] *Papiers inédits*, 1: 115–17.

[39] On Tallien's political career, see Mette Harder, 'Reacting to revolution—the political career(s) of J-L. Tallien', in Andress, *Experiencing the French Revolution*.

[40] Lecointre's account, written on 11 Thermidor, bears out the view that for many of the men on the Committees this was a last-minute decision. Lecointre also emphasized the role of Guffroy, Robespierre's former friend from Arras: Lecointre, *Robespierre, peint par lui-même*, 4. Brunel, *Thermidor*, 85–7, takes the view that until May the Committee of Public Safety was closely united, and that of all the Committee members at this time it was Carnot, who wanted France to embark on a 'war of conquest', that was pulling away from the others.

[41] Jacques-Nicolas Billaud-Varenne, *Principes régénérateurs du système social*, edited and with an introduction by Françoise Brunel (Paris: Publications de la Sorbonne, 1992).

[42] Cited in Michel Biard, *Collot d'Herbois: Légendes noires et révolution* (Lyon: Presses universitaires de Lyon, 1995), 176. Biard argues that Collot made up his mind at the last moment, 175–9.

[43] Lettter of Voulland to his constituents in Uzès, 9 Thermidor, cited in Bienvenu, *The Ninth of Thermidor*, 184–5.

Committees. He thus rejected the compromise which Saint-Just and Barère had been attempting to broker with the other Committee members and declared open war on his enemies in the Jacobins. Much of this long and intense speech consisted of an anguished protest at how his integrity had been undermined by his enemies. He said that they had tried to label him with a false identity—that of a 'tyrant'. At times he showed flashes of the insight that had stood him in good stead over several years of revolutionary struggle. One of these came when he gave a prescient warning about prolonging the war. 'Without reason', he said, 'victory is nothing but a conduit for ambition and a danger for liberty itself.'[44] Had he left it at that, Robespierre might have avoided the fate that befell him the following day but, acting on his own initiative, he called for a renewed purge of Jacobins who, by their excesses, had brought the Revolution into disrepute. At the same time he accused several of his fellow Committee members, more or less openly, of being part of the plot against him. He compounded this extraordinarily dangerous public declaration by refusing to give the names of the men on the list of those whose arrest he sought, leaving many of his terrified listeners to speculate whether they themselves, or their friends, appeared on it. Yet he took no precautions to protect himself against a conspiracy, relying only on the authenticity of his own virtue, and the 'virtuous men' in the Convention to defend him.

Baudot, a Jacobin who had been a friend of Danton and was an eyewitness to 9 Thermidor, conceded that the conspiracy against Robespierre was carefully planned. Despite his antipathy for Robespierre, Baudot affirmed that neither Robespierre nor his friends tried to organize a conspiracy. According to Baudot, on the morning of 9 Thermidor Duplay, who had heard rumours of the impending political storm, warned Robespierre to take precautions before speaking to the Convention, to which Robespierre replied: 'No, no...there is still enough virtue in the Convention to support me.'[45] The words suggest that, naïve or not, Robespierre believed what he said. Baudot, despite being an enemy of Robespierre, acknowledged as much. According to Baudot, the conspirators withdrew from Robespierre 'all his supports and he found himself isolated, lost and doomed to death whilst appealing to pretended virtue' to defend him.[46]

Since on this occasion Robespierre was correct in his judgement, in that there actually was a conspiracy amongst a number of the Jacobins poised to destroy him, this action was verging on suicidal. Why then did he do it? I think it says even more about his state of mind than about a political impasse. His speech of 8 Thermidor was intensely personal: emotional, disjointed, painfully sincere, full of grief, and despair. His need to identify himself as a lone man of virtue, surrounded by unnamed and shadowy men who were ambitious, self-serving conspirators against the Republic of Virtue, was complete. He had lost sight of anything else, including how his speech would be heard by his listeners, amongst whom were many enemies waiting for just such a sign of confusion and lack of capacity. At

---

[44] Robespierre, *Oeuvres*, 10: 572.
[45] Baudot, *Notes historiques sur la Convention nationale*, 242.
[46] Baudot, *Notes historiques sur la Convention nationale*, 152.

times he seemed to be on the point of conceding that the Revolution as an intellectual project had failed: 'My reason, not my heart, is on the point of doubting this virtuous republic whose image I had traced for myself'.[47] He was also confronted by an ideological dilemma. If he had organized his friends to resist he would, by his own standards maintained over five years of revolutionary conflict, have been engaging in a conspiracy. Robespierre made it evident that maintaining his authenticity as a man of virtue mattered more to him than anything at that moment—even more than staying alive.

When Robespierre was challenged after the speech by frightened deputies who wanted to know if their names were on the list of those he wanted proscribed, he refused to answer—a miscalculation that showed the extent to which he had lost all ability to appreciate the effect of his words on his listeners. Desperation for their own lives gave men the courage they had lacked when the Dantonists were arrested. Now, spurred on by fear for themselves, they found the courage to stand up to Robespierre. They denied him the endorsement of having his speech printed by order of the Convention. Robespierre was thrown onto the defensive. His final words in the Convention that day were to reassert his identity as a man of virtue, acting alone, choosing virtue over friendship: 'I do not desire the support, nor the friendship of anyone; I do not seek to form a party ... I have done my duty, it is for others to do theirs'.[48] Robespierre had been predicting his own death since the start of the Revolution. The assassination attempts had shaken him badly. Now he felt death closing in on him. In the Jacobins that night, he read the speech again, before an emotional audience. Collot d'Herbois and Billaud-Varenne were driven out of the Jacobin Club amidst shouts of 'to the guillotine!', leaving them in no doubt that either they—or Robespierre—were about to die, and therefore bent on killing him. It was said that Collot d'Herbois threw himself at Robespierre's feet to beg him to be reconciled with the Committees. For Robespierre to allow this exclusion to take place was tantamount to a declaration of war on his fellow Committee members. Indeed, he declared his speech to have been his last testament: he was ready to drink the hemlock. In the heat of the moment David cried out that he would drink it too, though the next day he thought better of it, and stayed away from the Convention.[49]

At this moment Robespierre was acting in a way that a psychologist now might be tempted to call clinically paranoid, but the point is debatable: he *was* facing a genuine conspiracy; on the other hand he himself had done much to provoke it. What is evident though is that even if he was indeed suffering from a nervous breakdown he was no less dangerous, in fact more so, because he had lost his political judgement.[50] The other deputies knew this, though they had no psychological

---

[47] Robespierre, *Oeuvres*, 10: 566.

[48] Robespierre, *Oeuvres*, 10: 586.

[49] Aulard, *Société des Jacobins*, 6: 289. On David's attitude towards Robespierre and the Republic of Virtue, see Philippe Bordes, 'Le robespierrisme de Jacques-Louis David', in Jourdan, *Robespierre—Figure-Réputation*, 121–41.

[50] For a psychoanalytical approach to Robespierre's thinking, see Jacques André, 'L'Incorruptible. Considérations psychoanalytiques', in Jourdan, *Robespierre—Figure-Réputation*, 143–52.

term for it. Saint-Just had been entrusted with a compromise speech by the other members of the Committee, which was meant to present them to the public as united. When, the following day, Saint-Just broke his agreement with the other Committee members, changed his speech at the last moment, and went to the Convention to defend Robespierre, he did this in the knowledge that Robespierre was a broken man who had lost his grip. Saint-Just referred to Robespierre's confused state of mind:

> If you think over carefully what happened in yesterday's session, you will find the point of all I have said; he who has been excluded from the Committee by the most bitter treatment, at a time when it was composed, in effect only of the two or three members who were present, this man justifies himself before you; to be honest, he by no means explained himself clearly enough, but his isolation and his bitterness of heart may give him some excuse; he understands nothing of the reasons for his persecution; he knows only his misery.[51]

Saint-Just's speech returned to the key tactical point: 'The deputy who spoke for a long time yesterday in this tribune did not distinguish clearly enough whom it was he was accusing.' Saint-Just intimated that Robespierre had been manipulated by Carnot into taking up this defensive position, in order to isolate him.[52]

In the event, Saint-Just was given no chance to deliver his speech. As he began Tallien interrupted him as part of the prearranged signal to launch the attack. Robespierre's unilateral choice to precipitate the crisis of Thermidor left his friends, colleagues, and associates scrambling to make their own decisions about what to do. Thus Robespierre forced the other Jacobin leaders to make a choice themselves—either to join in the conspiracy against him, or to go down with him. For Saint-Just this does not seem to have been a calculated decision. He made up his mind at the last moment, in fact the previous night. He wrote, 'someone this night has blighted my heart', referring to the explosion of furious words and physical violence directed at him by the terrified Billaud-Varenne and Collot d'Herbois after their expulsion from the Jacobins.[53] Saint-Just was evidently well aware that defending Robespierre put him in 'a delicate and difficult situation', but we cannot know whether he acted more out of conscious friendship for the mentor he had outgrown, or out of the conviction that this was how a 'man of virtue' should act.[54] Saint-Just was careful to assert, however, that his friendship for Robespierre would last only as long as Robespierre's virtue: 'I defend him because he seemed to me to be irreproachable; and I would accuse him myself if he became criminal'.[55] Saint-Just was not alone in making this choice. When Robespierre's arrest was decreed his brother Augustin voluntarily identified himself as a man of virtue, saying: 'I am as guilty as my brother is; I share his virtues. I ask the decree of arrest against myself as well'. Le Bas, whom no one had mentioned or thought

[51] Saint-Just, 'Discours du 9 Thermidor an II', Saint-Just, *Oeuvres Complètes*, 914–15.
[52] Saint-Just, 'Discours du 9 Thermidor an II', 911, 915.
[53] Saint-Just, 'Discours du 9 Thermidor an II', 907.
[54] Saint-Just, 'Discours du 9 Thermidor an II', 908.
[55] Saint-Just, 'Discours du 9 Thermidor an II', 909.

of, tore himself free of friends who tried to restrain him, and insisted on being arrested too, rather than share the guilt of being part of an assembly that voted for the arrest of his friends.[56]

The conspirators opened their attack by using the language of virtue and corruption to denounce Robespierre. Following hard on Tallien's heels, Billaud-Varenne spoke up to disclose that Robespierre had shown a lack of virtue in defending a secretary of the Committee who had stolen 114,000 *livres*. He then accused Robespierre and his friends of having refused to abandon Hébert for as long as possible, and Robespierre in particular of having tried to protect Danton. Through these actions, according to Billaud-Varenne, the Robespierrists had shown themselves as lacking true virtue because they had been reluctant to use terror against duplicitous politicians and corrupt public officials.[57] Speaker followed speaker to join the attack, while the Robespierrists were shouted down, held back, and forcibly prevented from speaking in their defence. The offensive moved swiftly on to the next stage, that of accusing the Robespierrists of being implicated collectively in a conspiracy. Tallien declared that the Convention had seen the 'conspirators unmasked'. The next moment he moved on to calling it 'this vast conspiracy'. Fréron leaped into the fray to call Robespierre, Saint-Just, and Couthon 'a new triumvirate', thus assigning them to the same narrative as the past leaders of the Jacobins, Barnave and his friends.[58] All this was accompanied by an extraordinary outcry as men who had been silent so long now joined in, unleashing the tension and fear of many months in an explosion of abuse and imprecations hurled at the Robespierrists. All the while Robespierre himself, his brother, and Le Bas were systematically prevented from speaking; while Saint-Just made no attempt to do so. The language used to bring down Robespierre and his friends was the same as that which had previously been deployed in the politicians' terror against other Jacobin factions. What was different about Thermidor was how fast this tumultuous transformation took place. At dizzying speed the identity of the Robespierrists was changed from that of leaders of the Revolution to traitors conspiring against it. Within two hours it was over and the Robespierrists placed under arrest.

The Robespierrists made no attempt to organize a conspiracy of their own as is evident from their own actions, and lack of any concerted policy. They do not even seem to have conferred with one another and had no clear plan for what to do, except to present themselves as men of virtue, and hope for the best; but the Convention was not in a pitying mood: the deputies were too fearful for their own lives for that. It was, therefore, as Baudot said: the death of Robespierre had become necessary: '...in the battle of 9 Thermidor it was not a question of principles, but of killing'.[59] There was, Baudot said, no way out of the 'inextricable and sanguinary state of the Republic before the 9 Thermidor except through the death or ostracism of Robespierre'.[60]

---

[56] 9 Thermidor, *Le Moniteur*, 21: 335. On the arrest of Augustin Robespierre and of Le Bas, see Stéfane-Pol, *Autour de Robespierre*, 278–83. See also Cousin, *Philippe Lebas et Augustin Robespierre*.
[57] 9 Thermidor, *Le Moniteur*, 21: 332.
[58] 9 Thermidor, *Le Moniteur*, 21: 332–3, 335.
[59] Baudot, *Notes historiques sur la Convention nationale*, 125.
[60] Baudot, *Notes historiques sur la Convention nationale*, 148.

## CONSTRUCTING A ROBESPIERRIST CONSPIRACY

In the immediate aftermath of Thermidor, the men who overthrew Robespierre systematically portrayed the Robespierrists as men without genuine political virtue. In the early hours of 10 Thermidor Legendre rushed to the Jacobin Club with a detachment of the National Guard to quell the disturbance in support of the Robespierrists. He told the women crowding the public galleries, who had long been amongst Robespierre's most vociferous supporters, that the Incorruptible had deceived them: 'You have been misled.'[61] He locked the Jacobins out of the Club, and handed the keys to the Convention. The day after Robespierre's death, a remnant of the Jacobins gathered at the Club, in a session presided over by Élie Lacoste of the Committee of General Security, who told the Jacobins that Robespierre was a criminal who had imposed upon them with his faked virtue, 'he had the words of virtue and probity forever on his lips' to conceal the fact that he was 'devoured by ambition'. Collot d'Herbois and Billaud-Varenne informed the remaining Jacobins that Robespierre, Saint-Just, and Couthon had conspired to divide France's territory between them in a new triumvirate: Couthon would rule the south, Saint-Just the north, Robespierre the centre.[62] Robespierre himself was described as a would-be 'dictator'. According to the deputy Roux, in one of the many exposés of the Robespierrist 'conspiracy' that appeared in 1794, 'the idea of the virtue of the pretended incorruptible Robespierre' had served as a screen to hide the fact that he was choosing men for positions of power who would serve his interests and his 'passion to rule'.[63] This was a similar narrative to that constructed for previous victims of the politicians' terror. The Thermidoreans were less scrupulous about this than Robespierre himself had been. He had made vague allegations against the Dantonists, many of which hinged on the interpretation of signs and outward conduct. The Thermidoreans went further and deliberately manufactured evidence where none existed. Many years later Vadier admitted that the *fleur-de-lys* seal found in the Commune where the Robespierrists made their last stand had been planted there by agents of the Committee of General Security, an action supervised by himself: 'the danger of losing one's head made one imaginative', he conceded. Within hours of Robespierre's arrest a story was already circulating that he had planned to marry the daughter of Louis XVI and thus make himself king.[64]

---

[61] Aulard, *Société des Jacobins*, 6: 297–8, note 2.

[62] 11 Thermidor (29 July 1794), Aulard, *Société des Jacobins*, 6: 295–300.

[63] Louis-Félix Roux, *Rélation de l'événement des 8, 9 et 10 Thermidor, Sur la conspiration des Triumvirs, Robespierre, Couthon et St Just* (Paris, Poignée et Volland, 1794), 5–7; L. Duperron, *Vie secrette, politique et curieuse de M.J. Maximilien Robespierre* (Paris: Prévost, 1794), also depicted Robespierre as calculatedly and hypocritically trading on his image as a man of virtue to bluff his way into power: 'He knew that people would not speak of him unless it was to consider him as virtuous, a man of integrity, of incorruptibility, and it was by decking himself in these virtues that he believed himself to be certain to succeed', 10.

[64] See the admission by Barras that these stories were circulated in order to convince the people that Robespierre was a traitor, cited in Baczko, *Ending the Terror*, 17–8. See also Baczko's account of the fabrication of these stories, esp. 16–25.

Fréron, who had been at school with Robespierre (though four years his senior), provided Courtois with an account of his private life that portrayed Robespierre as, amongst other unlikely allegations, an excessive drinker, who renounced this vice in the last months of his life as he was 'afraid of giving away secrets'. Fréron asserted that Robespierre was 'surrounded by avid bodyguards wherever he went; whilst some placed themselves in readiness in the streets where he would pass, in order to give him prompt help if he should be attacked'.[65] Fréron's account became part of the myth of Robespierre's posthumous reputation. The Thermidoreans fabricated a series of imaginative stories designed to show that the private lives of the Robespierrists had been characterized by vice and corruption. Sexual immorality featured strongly in these stories. Thus, Barras asserted that Robespierre had kept numerous 'concubines'; furthermore, Robespierre, Saint-Just, and Couthon had maintained secret palaces in the countryside round Paris, where they engaged in wild dissipation and orgies.[66]

This depiction of the Robespierrists as immoral schemers (begun by the Thermidoreans) was taken up and amplified by a whole series of royalist writers eager to expose the tawdry underside of 'Jacobin virtue'. The most comprehensive of these accounts was by Montjoie, *Histoire de la Conjuration de Maximilien Robespierre* in 1795. Amidst a catalogue of accusations Montjoie made the startling assertion that Robespierre 'had a taste for libertinage': in addition to conducting a liaison with his landlord's daughter which 'everyone knew about', he had recourse to prostitutes whom he procured with 'terror or money'.[67] All Robespierre's relationships were cold and without emotion. He was incapable of friendship, 'he had accomplices, and not a single friend'.[68] Montjoie's portrayal of a hypocritical, predatory, friendless Robespierre was intended to demonstrate the falsity of his political persona; the emptiness of his dream of a republic of virtue. According to Montjoie the key to understanding Robespierre was that he possessed 'ambition' (which Montjoie considered to be a natural quality) but was without 'virtue': thus 'he covered himself with the mask of hypocrisy' in pursuit of his secret ambition to become a 'dictator'.[69] Montjoie claimed that the faults of

---

[65] Fréron, 'Notes sur Robespierre', *Papiers inédits*, 1: 154–9. On the unreliability of Fréron, see Thompson, *Robespierre*, 9–10; and McPhee, *Robespierre*, 225.

[66] See the claims made by Barras, *Moniteur*, 29 Thermidor, 21: 497. Barras' imaginative account of Robespierre at the centre of a 'sex and vice scandal' formed the basis for many similar allegations, for example J. Leblanc, *Vies secrètes et politiques de Couthon, Saint-Just, Robespierre jeune, complices du tyran Robespierre, et assassins de la république* (Paris: Prévost, l'an II de la république française), 29–30. See also Baczko, *Ending the Terror*, 12–13; and Brunel, *Thermidor*, 117–20.

[67] Montjoie (F.L.C. Ventre de la Touloubre, known as Galart de Montjoie), *Histoire de la Conjuration de Maximilien Robespierre* (Paris: Chez les marchands de nouveautés, 1795), 216. The marquis de Ferrières gave a more credible picture of Robespierre, saying he was 'austere in his morals', yet 'a rogue, devoured by hidden ambition': Charles-Elie Ferrières, *Mémoires du marquis de Ferrières, avec une notice sur sa vie, des notes et des éclaircissements historiques*, eds Berville and Barrière, 3 vols (Paris: Badouin Frères, 1822), 1: 342–5.

[68] Montjoie, *Histoire de la Conjuration de Robespierre*. On Montjoie's account of Robespierre's supposedly sinister physiognomy and mannerisms and how they were interpreted as evidence of his psychology, see Julia Douthwaite, *The Frankenstein of 1790 and Other Lost Chapters from Revolutionary France* (Chicago: University of Chicago Press, 2012), 200–201.

[69] Montjoie, *Histoire de la Conjuration de Robespierre*, 7–9, 188–9.

Robespierre and the Jacobins stemmed from this misunderstanding of the classical authors, a misunderstanding which he attributed to the faults of their education. 'Robespierre retained from his reading of classical literature only errors that were the cause of his infamy and his torment...' The Roman republic of virtue was no fit subject for impressionable young minds who might be deceived into seeing the Romans as heroes, and grieve that 'they were not born Romans'.[70]

When it became evident that public opinion had tired of the Terror the initial allegation that the Robespierrists had been reluctant to enforce terror against other politicians was dropped. In its place arose the myth that the Robespierrists alone had been responsible for the Terror. So effectively did the Thermidoreans put together this narrative that to this day the image of Robespierre as a dictator, a hypocrite, and the mastermind behind the Terror is one that carries credibility in the minds of the public despite all the evidence to the contrary.

The death of Robespierre began a process of reaction against both Jacobinism and the Terror. In the provinces the events of Thermidor sparked off first panic and confusion in the Jacobin clubs, then an atmosphere of *sauve qui peut* as people scrambled to dissociate themselves from any taint of sympathy with 'Robespierrism'. The Jacobin Republic fell, and in November the Jacobin Club was closed. The laws and institutions that had enabled terror began to be dismantled, though this process did not happen as quickly as the Thermidorean myth would suggest. Whilst the Law of Prairial was quickly repealed and—after the bloodbath of Robespierre's supporters—the rate of executions declined dramatically, the Revolutionary Tribunal was maintained until 12 Prairial, Year Three.[71] Many Jacobins fell victim to the retributive White Terror. The Jacobins who survived Thermidor had to adapt to the new political circumstances.[72] The politicians' terror did not end with the fall of Robespierre. On the contrary, though there were fewer death sentences, the number of deputies arrested was greater in the Year Three than it had been in the Year Two. Sixty-five deputies (mostly Jacobins) were arrested for supporting the desperate popular uprisings by hungry crowds in Paris in Germinal and Prairial of Year Three.[73] According to Mette Harder almost a third of the deputies in the National Convention (220 out of 749) underwent arrest at some

---

[70] Montjoie, *Histoire de la Conjuration de Robespierre*, 17–20.

[71] On this process, see Jourdan, 'Les discours de la terreur'.

[72] The transformations of Jacobinism after the Terror are beyond the scope of this book, but see Isser Woloch, *Jacobin Legacy: the Democratic Movement Under the Directory* (Princeton, NJ: Princeton University Press, 1970); Pierre Serna, *Antonelle, aristocrate révolutionnaire, 1747–1817* (Paris: Éditions du Félin, 1997); and Bernard Gainot, *1799, un nouveau jacobinisme? La démocratie representative, une alternative à Brumaire* (Paris: CTHS, 2001). On changes in the Jacobin idea of the legitimacy of 'conspiracy' in the cause of liberty, see Laura Mason, 'Never was a plot so holy: Gracchus Babeuf and the end of the French Revolution', in Campbell, Kaiser, and Linton, *Conspiracy in the French Revolution*. On the struggle to achieve a stable government in the years after Thermidor, see Howard G. Brown, *Ending the French Revolution: Violence, Justice, and Repression from the Terror to Napoleon* (Charlottesville: University of Virginia Press, 2006).

[73] These figures are from Harder, 'Crisis of representation', 90–1. See also her perceptive comments on the significance of these continuing arrests. According to Brunel, of 'the last 100 Montagnards', a total of 74 were either imprisoned, deported, or put to death: Françoise Brunel, 'Montagnards', in Soboul, *Dictionnaire historique de la Révolution française*, 760.

point between 1792 and the dissolution of the Convention in October 1795.[74] Even after Thermidor, some were still put to death, victims of the failure to find a stable form of politics. Harder's work is particularly important for showing that the purging of deputies was a sign of a long-term problem with finding a stable form of politics. It was not just about the period of 'the Terror' or a specific 'Jacobin mentality'.

The ideology adopted by the Revolution's new leaders showed marked differences to what had gone before. Less than a year after Thermidor Lanne, a friend of Le Bas and former judge on the Revolutionary Tribunal, condemned to death in Floréal, Year Three, wrote to his wife: 'My judges have condemned me. Why? Because they are more misled than guilty; because what was virtue a year ago, is a crime today.—A year ago to love the people, pursue their enemies, pursue the enemies of equality, was a virtue. Today, to insult the people, insult their misery, is a virtue. Do not lose sight of these truths.'[75]

Former Jacobins who had chosen to take part in the overthrow of Robespierre and had thus precipitated the circumstances that led to the fall of the Jacobin Republic also had to deal with their past choices. Some, like Fouché, found it easy to adapt to successive regimes and forge a successful career in a very different political culture, one where glory, ambition, and desire for material success would be seen as entirely compatible with public office. Others, like Lanne, found it more problematic to reconcile themselves to the ending of the Republic of Virtue. Some Jacobins reflected on the time when they, too, had chosen terror. Deciding how to remember this, and how to construct the narrative of their own past involvement, was a difficult and painful process.[76] When he looked back on the Jacobin Republic from a distance of many years Levasseur deplored the loss of life that had stemmed from the Terror. But he insisted that the Terror had not been the creation of the Jacobins. They were not monsters, but ordinary men in extraordinary circumstances. The Terror was a collective response to a desperate situation, born out 'of circumstances and not the will of men'. Of those circumstances, the need to 'win battles, and chase the enemy from our territory' had been the most important. Levasseur also pointed out how big a part conflicting emotions had played in the genesis of the Terror. He recalled:

> The agitation of so many men who were all moved by the most delirious enthusiasm, the memory of the Old Regime, their certainty that it was against this that they must fight, the hatred and fear that the aristocrats inspired... [There were other emotions too:] Suspicion was born with the love of liberty; suspicion became then a route to the scaffold. [The revolutionary leaders were themselves subject to terror: the Terror that] crept over the benches of the Mountain. [Experiences of actual betrayals hardened the

---

[74] See Harder, 'Crisis of representation', 165, and appendix 2.1.
[75] This letter is reproduced in Stéfane-Pol, *Autour de Robespierre*, 252–3.
[76] On the different ways in which Jacobins remembered the past, see Sergio Luzzatto, *Mémoire de la Terreur: vieux montagnards et jeunes républicains au XIXe siècle*, trans. Simone Carpentari-Messina (Lyon: Presses Universitaires de Lyon, 1991).

revolutionary leaders:] They became unjust because they had often been deceived; they became cruel because they believed they had many reasons to be alarmed.[77]

For Levasseur, and some of the other surviving Jacobins looking back on the Year Two from a distance of years, the reasons for their having chosen terror had sprung from a collective emotional response to an extraordinary situation, impossible even for them to understand, once the conflicting emotions that had led to it had abated.

[77] Levasseur, *Mémoires*, 346–7.

# 11

## Achieving Authenticity

...whoever counts their life as having a value in time of revolution will never value virtue, honour and *patrie*.

Madame Roland, *Mémoires*.[1]

To be great, it is necessary only to become master of oneself. Our most formidable enemies are within ourselves... Strength, then, is the virtue that characterizes Heroism.

Jean-Jacques Rousseau.[2]

When Roland in hiding heard the news that his wife had been guillotined, he quietly slipped away from the shelter of his friends' house. He walked through the night down a country lane, seeking a place far enough from his friends not to compromise them. Then, in the dark and alone, he stabbed himself. In the sense of worldly advantage, it no longer signified whether people thought of him as having been an authentic man of virtue. There was no more political power or influence to be gained from maintaining that identity. But to him it still mattered. He left a suicide note, brief and to the point. In it he asked whoever found his body to treat it with respect, as that of 'a man who has died as he has lived, virtuous and honest'.[3]

The idea of self-sacrifice was fundamental to the revolutionary cause. It was a core belief of Jacobinism, one that transcended the factional politics of 1792 to 1794: it applied equally to Girondins and Jacobins. We shall focus here on revolutionary leaders who had been Jacobins in 1791 before the factional divisions of the following year. There was no appreciable difference in the ways that these Jacobins faced death or in how they conceived of their motives for having engaged in revolutionary politics.

Like Lucius Junius Brutus, the Jacobins had shown their virtue by being prepared to sacrifice for the good of the *patrie* those people they held personally dear. By an extension of the logic of political virtue they were also meant to be prepared to sacrifice themselves. It was almost a commonplace for revolutionary leaders to

[1] Madame Roland, *Mémoires*, 41.
[2] Rousseau, 'Discourse on this question: which is the virtue most necessary for a Hero and which are the Heroes who lacked this virtue?', Rousseau, *Collected Writings of Rousseau*, 7: 10.
[3] Wallon, *Histoire du Tribunal révolutionnaire*, 2: 44–5.

refer to their readiness to give up their own lives for the cause of the Revolution. This kind of claim served as a rhetorical strategy by which they could empower their political identities. But such words were not necessarily confined to play-acting. For some of the Jacobin leaders this idea meant something much more than simply posturing as Cato or some other hero out of the antique past as a means to achieve popularity: for them the rhetoric became a reality.

For those revolutionary leaders who faced death as a consequence of the politicians' terror it was possible, by the way in which they confronted their own deaths, to rewrite the significance of their fate. Instead of traitors sent to an ignominious death, they could be transfigured in the judgement of posterity into 'heroes' or 'heroines' of the Revolution—or at least so they hoped. It was the last consolation that remained to them, when everything else was lost. Ironically, for the Jacobin leaders, death could confer the proof of authenticity that had proved so elusive when they were pursuing their worldly careers in revolutionary politics. Death closed up the gap between their words and their actions. It provided formidable evidence that they had not embarked on their careers in revolutionary politics out of ambition or a desire for worldly success, but because they were genuinely devoted to the public good. Their self-sacrifice was the incontrovertible proof of the authenticity of their political identities. Moreover, the whole question of how they faced death was crucial in giving a retrospective meaning to all that had gone before when they had been men of power—their actions, their choices, the blood of others on their own hands. To die as authentic men of virtue provided some justification for the choices they had made in life—including having chosen terror. There was a close connection between the willingness to sacrifice oneself to a cause and being prepared to sacrifice other people to it also. The Jacobins could use the fact that they themselves were ready to die for the revolutionary cause to legitimize their acceptance of terror. Just as being a man of virtue legitimized denouncing others for their lack of virtue, so being willing to die for the Revolution legitimized killing others for the same cause.

The imminent prospect of death also affected choices about friendship. Some people hurried to disengage themselves from friendships that were now endangering their lives, while others showed extraordinary loyalty to their friends. In some cases—such as that of Philippe Le Bas—that loyalty led directly to their sharing the fate of their friends. Such choices offered proof of the compatibility of friendship with virtue.

With this in mind, we shall address the problem of how individual revolutionary leaders acted when confronting defeat and death, and consider how they made up their minds about what final choices they should make out of the few options available to them. Many of them, despite the fear and anguish they felt, were still able to give considerable attention to their own conduct. Even in these bleak circumstances they used the path to death as a political act fashioned to give the ultimate proof of the authenticity of their identities as men and women of virtue.

The rest of this book has looked at how leading revolutionaries saw their role and how they presented themselves to others in the course of their political careers. Much of this material has necessarily involved the public face of politics: speeches, journalism, polemics, infighting at the Jacobin Club and in the Assemblies. To some extent this kind of material has dealt with artifice—words used by the revolutionaries to fashion their public personas. But the material the Jacobins wrote when confronted with the immediate threat of death was rather different. Much of this material was confined to more personal places: notebooks; scraps of paper hidden from jailors if they were already in prison, or from their pursuers if they were on the run; letters to people they trusted and loved; memoirs in which they desperately scribbled out a justification for what they had done, and the choices they had made. Much of the artifice was stripped away. Everything that they might have stood to gain from participation in the Revolution—career, wealth, power—no longer had a significance. From such sources it is possible to see what they felt strongly about, strongly enough to be prepared to die for.

## HEROES OR CONSPIRATORS? THE JUDGEMENT OF POSTERITY

Many revolutionary leaders were hustled off to death too fast to have a chance to speak, especially those who died in the final months of the Terror when the whole process was speeded up. Those leaders who could do so often went to extraordinary lengths to give their side of the story. These included several of the Girondin deputies, most notably Pétion, Barbaroux, and Buzot, who went on the run after the collapse of the federalist revolts.[4] Though they were frequently on the move, or in hiding, and in constant fear for their lives, they were determined that the truth as they saw it should be told. In their prison cells Brissot and Madame Roland also found some solace in writing memoirs.[5] These Girondins scrutinized their own conduct, their motives, and their choices during their time in revolutionary politics, in much the same way as the Jacobins had done when putting them on trial. The Girondins used the same ideological and conceptual concepts as their accusers, but came to very different conclusions. In the Girondins' own judgement they were not conspirators, but men of virtue. Buzot called the proscribed deputies the nation's 'most virtuous representatives'.[6] He described his present predicament, hunted, hated, in constant fear of death, 'reduced to misery, without bread, without clothes, without shelter'. Yet his mind went back to those first days of the Revolution when he had been a deputy in Versailles; he reaffirmed that his political

---

[4] See Bette W. Oliver, *Orphans on the Earth: Girondin Fugitives from the Terror, 1793–1794* (Lanham, MD: Lexington Books, 2009).

[5] Brissot's gave an account of his motivation in a self-portrait entitled 'Portrait de Phédor', Brissot, *Mémoires*, 1: 12–23. For other examples of the Girondins' accounts of themselves and their friends as motivated by virtue and sensibility, see Madame Roland, *Mémoires*, 33, 98–102 (on M. Roland, Buzot, and Pétion), 108 (on Guadet and Gensonné), 129 (on Brissot); C. Barbaroux, *Correspondance et Mémoires de Barbaroux*, ed. Cl. Perroud (Paris: Au siège de la Société, 1928), 413; Buzot, *Mémoires*, 126, 131, 138, 148, 171. Louvet, who survived the Terror, also portrayed his fellow Girondins as motivated by virtue: see Louvet, *Mémoires de Louvet*, 56.

[6] Buzot, *Mémoires*, 126.

career had been inspired by his principles.[7] If ambition had indeed been a motive for what the Girondins had done, they had paid a heavy price for it. They were also concerned to defend their friends' memories. Thus Pétion wrote a posthumous defence of Brissot's integrity, based on his personal knowledge of his childhood friend. Brissot was 'of all men, the one who was the least avid for glory'.[8] Madame Roland described her fellow Girondins as virtuous and 'sensible' citizens. The papers of the fugitive Girondins Barbaroux, Buzot, and Pétion, including their statements of principles, were gathered up and hidden in a latrine by the people who risked their lives hiding the escaped deputies. The papers were eventually found by their pursuers.[9]

Many revolutionaries appealed to the judgement of posterity, hoping that this would vindicate them, demonstrate their good faith, and uphold their claims to have acted from motives of virtue. Madame Roland entitled her memoirs *An Impartial Appeal to Posterity*. Posterity would judge who had been the men of virtue. Buzot recited the list of his friends who had died, like 'Phocion' and 'Sidney' for liberty, and announced defiantly: 'One day posterity will utter your names with nothing but veneration and recognition.'[10] Barbaroux wrote to Madame Bouquey, to whom he had entrusted his memoirs and who was subsequently guillotined for having sheltered the deputies, '...it is you we entrust with making known to our children, to our friends, to the French people now so cruelly deceived...what we have done for Liberty, for Virtue...'[11] Brissot wrote from his prison cell of how he had found himself thinking back to other 'martyrs' of the past, to Sidney and Russell, and he returned to his boyhood love of *Télémaque*.

> I recalled the fate of Phocion and, in my sad plight, I congratulated myself on sharing the destiny of these great men. I was certain that posterity would avenge my memory.[12]

In such circumstances it was only by making appeals to a remote, idealized past, or to an equally distant, imagined future, that revolutionaries could construct a narrative that would make sense of their present.

Few of the victims of the politicians' terror in 1794 were given time to write more than brief letters between arrest and execution. Robespierre and Saint-Just had no time for memoirs or last letters, but their writings had already given intimations of how they thought about the future—with increasing pessimism and a brooding sense of inevitable death. In an undated note (written shortly before his death) Saint-Just was defiant:

---

[7] Buzot, *Mémoires*, 21–5.
[8] Pétion, 'Notice sur Brissot', 369.
[9] Guadet, *Les Girondins*, 2: 382–5. See also Oliver, *Orphans on the Earth*, 95–8. On the impoverished circumstances of the fugitive Girondin deputies as a proof of the integrity of their principles, see Guadet, *Les Girondins*, 2: 460–7.
[10] Buzot, *Mémoires*, 131.
[11] Barbaroux, *Correspondance et Mémoires*, 413.
[12] Brissot, *Mémoires*, 1: 9.

Circumstances are only difficult for those who recoil before the tomb. Myself I implore the tomb as a gift of providence in order that I shall no longer be obliged to witness crimes committed with impunity against my *patrie* and against humanity.

Certainly it is no great thing to leave an unhappy life in which one is condemned to die either as the accomplice or the powerless witness of crime.[13]

It is striking that Saint-Just saw his own role in revolutionary politics as that of a powerless and innocent man. The people who crowded the prisons under the Terror were hardly likely to concur. Yet this was how he expressed his situation. It suggests in the last months of the Terror that even men at the forefront of the Jacobin government were subject to personal despair, and felt helpless to alter events.

Robespierre had been anticipating his own martyrdom for the revolutionary cause for years. He too envisaged that posterity would vindicate his authenticity. Thus, in a speech against war, at the Jacobins on 10 February 1792, he had declaimed:

If the men of virtue despair of the assembly; if they can no longer fight against the torrent of intrigue and prejudice, they can die at the tribune, defending the rights of humanity; they can denounce the traitors to their constituents, freely unveil to them the cause of our difficulties, and at least leave a great example to posterity...[14]

He made many such rhetorical references to his readiness to die for the Revolution, until in July 1794 he was called upon to confront the reality, and to make one final choice.

## CHOOSING HOW TO DIE

As successive revolutionary leaders faced defeat and the trauma of the politicians' terror, they had one more choice to make—how to meet their deaths, and how to comport themselves in their last moments. Political ideologies and factions had no place in this kind of decision: Jacobins, Hébertists, Girondins, and Feuillants alike had similar views. For most the choice was a simple, albeit harrowing, one—how to behave in the face of public execution. Some, however, considered the alternative, that of taking their own lives, and forestalling the executioners.[15] Although

---

[13] Saint-Just, Fragments d'institutions républicaines, *Oeuvres Complètes*, 1008. He put the last two lines into his undelivered speech on 9 Thermidor, ibid., 908.

[14] Robespierre, *Oeuvres*, 8: 183.

[15] Amongst the works on attitudes to suicide in eighteenth-century France, see Patrice Higonnet, 'Du suicide sentimental au suicide politique', in Elizabeth Liris and Jean Maurice Bizière (eds), *La Révolution et la mort* (Toulouse: Presses Universitaires du Mirail, 1991); Jeffrey Merrick, 'Suicide and politics in pre-Revolutionary France', *Eighteenth-Century Life*, 30 (2006): 32–47; and Jeremy L. Caradonna, 'Grub Street and suicide: a view from the literary press in late eighteenth-century France', *Journal for Eighteenth-Century Studies*, 33, 1 (2010): 23–36. For the wider history of suicide, see Georges Minois, *History of Suicide: Voluntary Death in Western Culture*, trans. Lydia G. Cochrane (Baltimore, MD: Johns Hopkins University Press, 1999).

suicide was forbidden by the Catholic Church, for the ancients (from Socrates to Cato) suicide was an honourable and admirable response to political defeat. The tradition of stoicism, in particular, offered a way of dealing with defeat and death with dignity and courage, or at least the assumption of courage, that came to much the same thing.[16] Several of the *philosophes*, including Montesquieu and Rousseau, had also reflected on the ethics of suicide. Arguments for suicide in specific circumstances were set out in Saint-Preux's letter on suicide in Rousseau's *La Nouvelle Héloïse* (though elsewhere Rousseau himself was much more guarded about seeing suicide as a virtuous act). Roxanne, in Montesquieu's *Persian Letters*, resorted to suicide as an act of personal empowerment and political liberation, her means to escape from the prison of the harem.[17] Similarly, for the revolutionary leaders suicide could be seen as a blow for individual liberty—in that one could at least choose the manner and time of one's death. It gave back one final choice into their hands, that of choosing to sacrifice their own lives, rather than letting their lives be taken from them by the imposition of a revolutionary judgement that they were traitors against the *patrie* and deserving of death. Suicide gave the strongest possible message that the perpetrator did not accept the justice of the judgement of the Revolutionary Tribunal. Amongst the leading revolutionaries who pre-empted the guillotine by taking their own lives were Jacques Roux, Condorcet (his death in prison was a probable suicide), Clavière, Le Bas, and Valazé, who stabbed himself in the dock rather than mount the scaffold. Others attempted suicide including, possibly, Robespierre himself. The symbolic significance of their rejection of the judgement of the Revolutionary Tribunal by committing suicide was shown by the fact that, in some cases including that of Valazé, the Tribunal ordered that the dead bodies of deputies who had committed suicide be taken to the guillotine so that its judgement should not be evaded. Others, including Barbaroux and Augustin Robespierre, both of whom were already close to death, were nevertheless patched up and sent to the guillotine in an act of ritualized retribution by the state.

Another choice was that of shared suicide as a final act of collective defiance and of emotional union between friends. The Girondin deputies had the opportunity to reflect as a group beforehand, and considered the merits of shared suicide or waiting for execution. This discussion took place during the coup of June 1793 as they gathered at the house of Meillan in order to await the results of the stand-off in the Convention. Brissot, in his *Memoirs* written in the prison of the Abbaye, described how they had debated what to do, whether to try to use force to reassert

---

[16] On stoicism as a philosophy to which revolutionaries turned for consolation when nothing else remained to them, see Parker, *The Cult of Antiquity*, 171–7. On stoicism in the Directory, see Judith A. Miller, 'After sentiment: the stoic "real" of the Directory', unpublished paper given at the Western Society for French History, November 2007, Albuquerque, New Mexico. Cited with permission of the author.

[17] Rousseau, *Julie, ou La Nouvelle Héloïse*, Part 3, Letter xxi, together with Edouard's response, Letter xxii. Montesquieu, *Lettres persanes*, Letter clxi. See also J.M. Goulemot, 'Montesquieu: du suicide légitimé à l'apologie du suicide héroïque', and Michel Launay, 'Contribution à l'étude du suicide vertueux selon Rousseau', both in *Gilbert Romme (1750–1795) et son temps: actes du colloque tenu à Riom et Clermont les 10 et 11 juin 1965* (Paris: Presses Universitaires de France, 1966).

themselves, or to attempt to stir up a revolt in the provinces. They could not decide on this, and so fell to discussing whether, in the event of their arrest being decreed, suicide would not be preferable to 'the ignominy of climbing the scaffold'. Buzot, with great energy, argued that they should choose the scaffold. According to Brissot:

> Buzot argued for the latter, and showed us that death on the scaffold was more coura-geous, more worthy of patriots, and above all that it would be more useful to the cause of liberty.
>
> We were in the middle of discussing these two forms of death, when the news of the decree of our arrest arrived. We separated without having taken a decision.[18]

In the event, the Girondins faced this decision as individuals. Brissot fled immediately afterwards, making for his home town of Chartres. Some of them, including Vergniaud, Gensonné, and Lehardy, carried out Buzot's idea, and awaited their fate at the hands of the Jacobins. Others, including Buzot himself, fled, and did their best to incite an armed revolt. Ironically, he was one of the few Girondins who eventually committed suicide.[19] The practical logistics of how to commit suicide worried Pétion when he was on the run. He was afraid of being taken alive, no longer able to use his hands. 'More than once I feared that I would be surprised in my hiding place. Then the most sombre thoughts took hold of me. I familiarized myself with the idea of blowing my brains out. A hundred times I placed my pistols, one at my temple, the other in my mouth, to assure myself that I would not fail.'[20] He did not fail. Buzot and Pétion eventually committed suicide together, rather than face recapture. Their bodies were discovered partially eaten by wild animals.

For Madame Roland, as one of very few republican women held in prison, even the solace of sharing her feelings with a community of like-minded friends (as the other imprisoned Girondins could do) was denied her. In her isolation she hesitated over whether to take her own life:

> Two months ago I was ambitious for the honour of going to the scaffold; it was still possible to speak, and the energy of a great courage could have done service to the truth; now all is lost...
>
> Should I wait then for when it pleases my executioners to choose the moment of my death and to augment their triumph by the insolent clamours of the mob to which I would be exposed? Certainly! I could brave them, if my courage could instruct the imbecilic people; but they are no longer ready to feel anything other than the canni-balistic joy of watching the flow of blood which they themselves run no risk in shedding?[21]

---

[18] Brissot, *Mémoires*, 2: 215–16.

[19] Ellery's account describes this—a little harshly—as being typical of the indecision that character-ized the politics of the Girondins. Ellery, *Brissot*, 351–2.

[20] Jérôme Pétion de Villeneuve, *Mémoires inédits de Pétion, et mémoires de Buzot et de Barbaroux* (Paris: Henri Plon, 1866), 133.

[21] Madame Roland, *Mémoires*, 341–3.

At one point she went on a hunger strike, but in the end she decided to await revolutionary justice, inspired in part by the example of Brissot and the other Girondin deputies who had faced execution together. In the event, most of the revolutionary leaders did likewise, and waited for the Revolution itself—in the form of the Revolutionary Tribunal and ultimately the public executioners—to take their lives. In the Year Three, however, a group of Jacobins chose collective suicide at the moment of their condemnation for their involvement in the uprising of Prairial. They used knives, kept hidden until the decisive moment, then passed from one to another. They became known as 'the martyrs of Prairial', some of the last Jacobin martyrs.[22]

## FACING EXECUTION: VIRTUE VINDICATED

How the revolutionary leaders confronted the prospect of public execution was an individual matter that each person had to meet in his or her own way. Some dissolved in terror; some kept a stoical silence; some showed personal courage, while expressing cynical contempt for the political game that had brought them there; some even managed to make macabre jokes about the irony of their situation. Some looked death in the face with contempt, and supreme courage—or at least the assumption of courage, which in these circumstances was much the same thing. Under this category one might put the iconic last words of Danton to the executioner: 'Don't forget to show my head to the people: it's worth it.'[23] Here the focus was on preserving one's pride, and not showing weakness in front of witnesses. It was in this frame of mind that Hérault de Séchelles addressed Desmoulins, who went to pieces when they were condemned to death: 'My friend, let us show that we know how to die.'[24]

As Rousseau had said, however, 'bravery' was not the same thing as 'virtue'; for virtue one needed 'strength of soul', which required something more than courage.[25] Some revolutionaries made a conscious decision to die a 'virtuous' death. This was death as a political act. A 'virtuous' death encompassed more than dying with courage. To die with courage meant to maintain one's personal dignity, and not give way to futile struggling or visible weakness, such as tears or the degradation of pleading with the indifferent watching crowds. For the revolutionary leaders a 'virtuous' death entailed all this, but they also wanted to show something more—their

---

[22] On the suicide of the Jacobin 'martyrs of Prairial', see R. Andrews, 'Le Néo-stoïcisme et le législateur Montagnard: considerations sur le suicide de Gilbert Romme'; and J. Dautry, 'Réflexions sur les martyrs de Prairial: sacrifice heroïque et mentalité révolutionnaire' in *Gilbert Romme (1750–1795) et son temps*. In the same volume, on revolutionary suicides after Thermidor as examples of self-sacrifice and heroism, see the account of the circumstances around the death of Rühl, a few days prior to the 'martyrs of Prairial', by Michel Eude, 'Le "suicide héroïque" d'un Montagnard en prairial an III: Jacques-Philippe Rühl (1737–1795)'. See also Françoise Brunel, 'Les derniers Montagnards et l'unité révolutionnaire', in Soboul, *Girondins et Montagnards*.

[23] Walter, *Actes du Tribunal révolutionnaire*, 584.

[24] Kuscinski, *Dictionnaire des Conventionnels*, 333.

[25] Rousseau, 'Which is the virtue most necessary for a hero?', 7–9.

consciousness of their own innocence. They saw themselves—and sought to present themselves to the spectators—not as traitors justly condemned to an ignominious death, but as heroes sacrificing their lives for the *patrie*. It was their last political gesture. Virtuous death stamped a retrospective meaning on all their political actions and choices. To 'die a good death' was the final sacrifice of self for the *patrie*. By this means revolutionary leaders might close the gap between their words and actions, and bring about a resolution to the lived contradiction of their revolutionary careers. It was the ultimate proof of the authenticity of their political identity.

Executions under the old regime were ritualized dramas. Everyone had a prescribed role: executioners, crowd, priests, and victim. Penitence was an integral part of the event. This was formally expressed through the ritual of the *amende honorable*, where the condemned person knelt, candle in hand, before the priests to express contrition, and to hope for God's mercy in the next life. Since the killing was often protracted and agonizingly painful, there were many opportunities for victims to repent their sins, and beg for mercy. But these ritualized executions were also concerned with courage. Observers were interested in the demeanour of the condemned, and how well they faced up to death. People commented, for example, on the bravery with which Damiens, who had attempted to assassinate Louis XV, bore himself during the four hours of ritualized torture that preceded his death. This kind of courage was about facing death bravely, rather than making a point about one's innocence. There was little space in these formalized rituals to challenge the justice of the condemnation.

The execution of leading revolutionaries during the height of the Revolution was a very different affair. The guillotine, too, had its rituals. Yet since the actual killing was over so quickly, attention was concentrated on the attitude of the victims on their journey in the tumbrels, and while awaiting their turn to climb the steps of the scaffold. The rituals of the Church, with their emphasis on prayer and repentance, did not feature in revolutionary executions. There was no consolation to be had from that quarter. Penitence also seems to have been absent from the thoughts of most revolutionaries: they were angry, stupefied, distraught, revengeful, despairing, or resigned—but very few were sorry. (An exception was the constitutional bishop Claude Fauchet, who died as a penitent Catholic and apparently spent the night before his death asking God's forgiveness.) They refused to accept the humiliation intended by the treatment handed out to 'traitors'. They saw their condemnation not as revolutionary justice, but as a consequence of crime, conspiracy, counter-revolution, personal enmity, and the ignorance of the people.

One thing they could do was choose between a repertoire of models of behaviour that could sustain them in the last moments. Perhaps the most consistent and intellectually coherent model available was that derived from men of virtue of the past who had died at the hands of their enemies.[26] Antiquity offered many

---

[26] For the influence of antiquity on ideas about death, see Parker, *The Cult of Antiquity*, 171–7. George Armstrong Kelly, *Mortal Politics in Eighteenth-Century France* (Ontario: University of Waterloo Press, 1986), 260–80, discusses the profound influence of classical antiquity on funerary practices in the Revolution.

examples of men who were stoical in defeat, such as Phocion, the Gracchus brothers, or Socrates. The revolutionaries recalled that many great heroes of antiquity,
from Solon to the Gracchi, were unappreciated by the very people they had sought
to help, and that it is rarely given to heroes to die a natural death. The revolutionaries also took examples from the turbulent history of seventeenth-century England,
of men such as Sidney, to teach themselves how to die. Thus Madame Roland
wrote that the Girondins were likely to suffer the same fate 'as that of other true
friends of humanity, such as Dion, Socrates and Phocion and so many others from
antiquity, and Barnevelt and Sidney in modern times'.[27]

Heroic identity was closely connected with the idea of virtue.[28] The Revolution
had many official ceremonies, and hundreds of speeches, devoted to men (and
occasionally women) who were depicted as having died as heroes of the Revolution.[29] Political leaders condemned by the Revolutionary Tribunal would be given
no such ceremonies or memorials by a grateful Republic: instead they would die
labelled as counter-revolutionaries and conspirators. All they could do was recast
this situation in their own minds: instead they became the heroes. Their heroism
was demonstrated by their virtue and self-sacrifice. Their demeanour—the one
thing left to them over which they had control—provided the evidence of their
virtue.

The revolutionary leaders knew that their conduct on the way to execution
would be observed and commented on by the large crowds that turned up to watch
the show. There were a number of eyewitness accounts of the executions in which
the conduct and final words of the condemned were recounted. Not all these accounts are reliable; many grew in the telling. Final gestures and words were embel-
lished, or in some cases entirely fabricated. The myth-making began on the route
to the guillotine. Some of the revolutionary journalists played up to this ritualized
recounting, writing commentaries on the demeanour of victims en route to the
scaffold. Conversely, revolutionary journalists were often quick to disparage the
conduct of people whose politics they disagreed with, and to attribute even a display of courage to something other than the consciousness of integrity. Thus
Camille Desmoulins described the marquis de Favras (the only person to be executed for conspiracy during the Constituent Assembly) as having died with a pretence of courage, his attitude 'that of a gladiator, who, being mortally wounded,
strives to fall with decency and dignity'.[30] Hébert in *Le Père Duchesne* asserted that
the apparent stoicism Gorsas showed on his way to execution was due to his being
drunk, having consumed 'three or four bottles of wine' to block out the raucous

---

[27]  Madame Roland, *Mémoires*, 336.

[28]  See Abensour, 'Saint-Just and the problem of heroism'; and Jourdan, 'Robespierre and revolutionary heroism'.

[29]  On the commemoration of dead revolutionaries, in addition to works already cited, see Antoine
de Baecque, 'Le corps des martyrs et le discours politique', in Elizabeth Liris and Jean Maurice Bizière
(eds), *La Révolution et la mort* (Toulouse : Presses Universitaires du Mirail, 1991); Dominique Poulot,
'La révolution des ancêtres à Paris: corps privés et corps publics, entre Panthéon et musée', in Raymonde Monnier (ed.), *À Paris sous la Révolution: nouvelles approches de la ville* (Paris: Publications de
la Sorbonne, 2008), 213–21.

[30]  Cited in Claretie, *Camille Desmoulins*, 85.

mockery of the *sans-culottes*.[31] According to the police reports when Hébert himself was put to death he and his companions died as cowards. People in the crowd were heard to comment: 'We thought that Hébert would have shown more courage... The Brissotins went to the guillotine more bravely.'[32] This was a reference to the Girondins, who went to the guillotine singing 'La Marseillaise' as a proof of their patriotism and innocence of the crime of conspiracy against the Republic.

Heroism at the scaffold was a model that transcended gender. Women could participate in this final political drama as well and effectively as men or even more so. Observers commented on the conduct of many of the women who paid the ultimate penalty for their political views or for supporting those of their menfolk, and demonstrated a striking degree of courage. The widows of Camille Desmoulins and Hébert went to their deaths showing much more courage than their husbands had been able to muster. The two women embraced at the foot of the guillotine, a supreme expression perhaps of the futility of the Jacobins' warring factional politics. Charlotte Corday was not a Jacobin, yet she too prepared her response to death as a political event, with meticulous care and apparently a complete lack of fear. She knew that people would interpret the meaning of her assassination of Marat by the way in which she met her own death. The day before her trial she analysed her own response and planned how she would act: 'As for the rest, I do not know how my last moments shall be, and it is the ending that crowns the work.'[33] Both she and Madame Roland compared themselves to that very masculine figure of virtue, Brutus.[34]

Madame Roland prepared for her own death with the conscious intention of establishing her authentic identity before witnesses. She asked her friend Sophie Grandchamp to come and see her on the way to her execution: 'Would you have the courage to be present at my last moments, in order that you can give an authentic testimony of how they were?'[35] When Sophie assented, Madame Roland gave precise instructions, that Sophie stand on the route that the tumbrel would take, at the end of the Pont-Neuf, near the first step, dressed in the same clothes that she was wearing that day, so that Madame Roland could pick her out of the crowd. It was crucially important to Madame Roland that her friend could bear witness to her demeanour; that she been seen to be courageous, conscious of her own innocence and self-sacrifice, a woman of virtue. This transfiguration was particularly important for Madame Roland because women were meant to be shamed by appearing in public as the object of the crowd's gaze.[36] Helen Maria Williams,

---

[31]  Hébert, *Le Père Duchesne*, Issue 296: 7.

[32]  Report by Bacon, 24 March 1794, Bienvenu, *The Ninth of Thermidor*, 85.

[33]  Charlotte Corday, 'Letter to Barbaroux, deputy, at Caen', reproduced in Guilhaumou, *La Mort de Marat*, 149.

[34]  Corday, 'Letter to Barbaroux', 146–50; Madame Roland, *Mémoires*, 235. Madame Roland also spoke of how reading Rousseau in her early life had inspired her to be capable of sacrifice: ibid., 277, 302.

[35]  Cited in Chaussinand-Nogaret, *Madame Roland*, 299–301, 308–9.

[36]  For the argument that Madame Roland's political identity focused on the concept of virtue as maternal self-sacrifice, see Lesley H. Walker, 'Sweet and consoling virtue: the Memoirs of Madame Roland', *Eighteenth-Century Studies*, 34, 3 (2001): 403–19.

who visited Madame Roland in prison, found her reading Plutarch and resigned to a brave death. Only when her visitor spoke of her daughter did Madame Roland's resolve falter, and she began to cry.[37]

## FROZEN IDENTITIES: THE BEGINNING OF MYTH

Robespierre was unable to speak after the traumatic last scenes in the Hôtel de Ville that climaxed with a bullet shattering his jaw; his last thoughts remained unrecorded. His brother Augustin, however, having either thrown himself or fallen from the window of the Hôtel, was taken to the section of the Maison Commune and questioned about his motives by the section committee. He told his interrogators that he had known his death was inevitable since he heard the decree outlawing the deputies. He was grievously wounded, and kept losing consciousness, but he still insisted on the purity of his brother's motives and his own, claiming that 'neither he nor his brother had ever ceased to do their duty in the Convention, and that no one could reproach him with anything'.[38] Like Roland, and in common with so many others, Augustin Robespierre's last recorded concern was that people should know that he—and his brother—had acted from motives of virtue.

The chaotic scenes around the last stand of the Robespierrists ended with the suicide of Le Bas, and with several others, including both the Robespierres and Couthon, incapacitated and already half dead. Of the Robespierrist deputies only Saint-Just was able to go to his death with his dignity still intact. Even that was undermined by Courtois, who subsequently wrote that Saint-Just's failure to kill himself was motivated by loss of nerve. According to Courtois, 'Saint-Just entreated Le Bas to kill him. The latter called him a coward and told him he had something else to do, after which he killed himself. Why was it not said to Saint-Just as to Nero: "Is it then so difficult to die?"'[39] Since, of the witnesses to those last moments in the Hôtel de Ville before the entry of the Convention's forces, all were dead, it was a transparent lie. Courtois' purpose was to undermine Saint-Just's authenticity. Courtois' story shows the Thermidoreans' awareness of the significance of a 'good' or 'bad' death, and how this could be appropriated to take on a particular political meaning. In contrast to the Thermidoreans, the nineteenth-century Romantic historians Michelet and Lamartine interpreted Saint-Just's choice to wait for death as an act of courage, rather than cowardice. The voluntary silence with which Saint-Just faced the closing acts of his life thus became part of

---

[37] Thompson, *English Witnesses of the French Revolution*, 239–40.

[38] Cited in John Wilson Croker, *Essays on the Early Period of the French Revolution* (1857: republished: New York: AMS Press, 1970), 422–3. See also Brunel, *Thermidor*, 107; and Young, *Augustin*, 239–41.

[39] 'Notes of Courtois (de l'Aube)', cited in Claretie, *Camille Desmoulins*, 455. Levasseur repeated this story as though it were true: see Levasseur, *Mémoires*, 506. Montjoie gave a similar fictitious account. In his version Le Bas, like Saint-Just, was captured alive. Montjoie asserted that both men 'trembled' and 'wept like children' at their fate: Montjoie, *Histoire de la conjuration de Robespierre*, 206.

the enigma of his posthumous reputation, its meaning disputed on all sides. As for the enforced silence in which the maimed Robespierre passed his final hours, the meaning of this was speculated over, interpreted, and reinterpreted by countless narrators from the Thermidoreans onwards.[40] As the revolutionary politicians had themselves anticipated, the manner of their deaths contributed to their posthumous reputations. The moment of death froze their identities, and allowed the invention of myth to begin. For the revolutionary leaders, to take the choice of execution rather than suicide gave them a chance to contribute to that myth. It offered them one last public appearance, and with it a chance to demonstrate to eyewitnesses the authenticity of their virtue.

After it was over, Jacobins, Dantonists, Robespierrists, Hébertists, Girondins, Feuillants; bitter enemies, loyal friends; innocent and guilty, executioners and executed; their bodies lay in the earth together in their hastily prepared communal graves beneath the streets of a city where few people now know much about the reality of their lives: it is the myths that prove resilient, after all. They had chosen terror; they had killed, and they too had been put to death. In the end, though the Jacobin leaders had long since abandoned devout observance of the Catholic faith in which they had been raised, there was a fundamental idea in it with which they would have been familiar—that of atonement.

---

[40] On the contrasting symbolic interpretations given to Robespierre's last hours by Thermidoreans and supporters of Robespierre, see Antoine de Baecque, 'Robespierre; or, The Terrible Tableau', in Baecque, *Glory and Terror*.

# Conclusion
## Experiencing Revolutionary Politics:
## The Lived Contradictions of Virtue, Friendship,
## and Authenticity

The successive leaders of the Jacobins from 1789 to 1794 were the first modern politicians in France. They came to prominence in a new political culture of democratic politics. To play a part in this politics they had to fashion their identities in a way that would have an impact on public opinion. In order to understand the nature and experience of Jacobin politics more fully we need to reconstruct the landscape within which the new revolutionary politics was situated. It was a terrain that encompassed three dimensions: ideological, tactical, and personal. These three dimensions, though distinct, were closely related at the level of revolutionary politics as a lived experience. The Jacobin leaders operated simultaneously in these interacting dimensions.

The Jacobin leaders took on a set of ideas familiar from the oppositional rhetoric of the old regime about the need for virtue and transparency in politics, and the incompatibility of private friendship with political virtue. With the outbreak of the Revolution this oppositional rhetoric became an intrinsic part of revolutionary ideology. Revolutionary politics were constructed against old regime politics, and characterized in terms of polarities: virtue and corruption, transparency and secrecy, authenticity and duplicity. Most Jacobins were undoubtedly genuine in their commitment to revolutionary ideals (at least in the early years); but that does not preclude the fact that for many the Revolution also opened up the possibility to forge a career in the new regime. Revolutionary politicians vied with each other to present themselves as 'men of virtue' in the new realm of revolutionary political culture. In their public statements they consciously rejected old regime methods of doing politics 'behind closed doors', even while they—of necessity—continued to practise such methods.

It was not only the Jacobins who accepted the premise that politics should be based on virtue. The wide acceptance of this political ideal was indicated by the revolutionaries' adoption of an electoral system based on the principle that men could not put themselves forward as candidates for public office since this would indicate that they were ambitious and motivated by self-interest. Would-be politicians were only worthy of a career in politics if, like Cincinnatus, they did not seek it out. Thus the politics of virtue were not exclusive to the Jacobins, nor part of a specifically 'Jacobin mindset'. Nevertheless, the Jacobin leaders bought heavily into the ideology of political virtue, and many of them were to pay a high price for it.

This book dispels one of the most persistent myths of the Revolution—that the politics of virtue were specific to Robespierre, part of a warped way in which he, as an individual, viewed the political landscape. Robespierre was far from unique in assuming the identity of a man of virtue; he was just better at it than most of his contemporaries. He carried conviction. The triumvirs who helped found the Jacobin Club and were its first leaders presented themselves as men of virtue to win over radical public opinion and legitimize their desire to be major players in the new political order. Brissot and his friends, the Girondins who succeeded the triumvirs as leading voices in the Jacobin Club, also portrayed themselves as motivated by their virtue. Like the triumvirs before them, however, the Girondins suffered the consequences of this empowering rhetoric when their success in achieving ministerial power opened up a visible gap between their words and their actions. Henceforward they were portrayed by Paris militants and opposing Jacobins as men of inauthentic virtue, dissemblers, who had used the rhetoric of virtue for their own advantage.

Whilst the ideology of political virtue was an intrinsic part of the public face of revolutionary politics, Jacobin politics did not operate only in terms of ideology. The personal and emotional dimension of Jacobin politics is vital to an understanding of how it worked. Individual choices and agency counted for a great deal. The Jacobin leaders were not simply spokesmen for Jacobin ideology. They believed passionately in what they were doing, but they were also trying to establish their individual careers in the new world of opportunities opened up by the Revolution. The Jacobin leaders' strategies were informed by their personal circumstances as well as their convictions.

An intrinsic part of the personal dimension of Jacobin politics was experienced at an emotional level. To paraphrase Rousseau, the politics of the Revolution were 'felt' before they were 'thought'. Of all the conflicting emotions that influenced the Jacobins, the most important were patriotic fervour and—especially during the Terror—fear. There were others too: both acknowledged and unacknowledged. Emotions that could not be openly avowed because they conflicted with the ideology of virtue included ambition, self-interest, and enmity. In some cases these unacknowledged emotions had a decisive impact on the Jacobins' choices.

Friendship played an important part in the personal dimension of Jacobin politics. The leaders of the Paris Jacobins were united by a complicated network of friendships. Some of these friendships antedated the Revolution; others were forged in the intense atmosphere of the Revolution's early stages when the rigid social structures of the old regime broke down. The process which led to the gradual disintegration of some of these friendships, amidst growing enmity, mutual suspicions and denunciations, gave a particularly claustrophobic and toxic atmosphere to revolutionary politics in the Year Two.

## CHOOSING TERROR: THE DOUBLE BIND

Choosing terror was part of a gradual and collective process that took place in the years between 1789 and 1794. This book does not deal directly with the factors that led to terror as a whole; that would necessitate a much longer study which could take into account the whole scope of the impact of the counter-revolution, religious polarization, war, civil war, and much else besides. Rather, this book has focused on the specific form of terror that the revolutionary leaders directed at one another—what I have termed the 'politicians' terror'—and the steps that led to it. The politicians' terror culminated with the factional trials of Jacobins and former Jacobins in the Year Two. Participants in these trials—both accusers and accused—used similar narratives of virtue and conspiracy, and saw the success or failure of the Revolution in terms of the culpability or innocence of its leaders. Although small in overall numbers, this was one of the most ruthless forms of terror, since it was characterized not by the rules of justice—albeit harsh justice—employed in most cases heard by the Revolutionary Tribunal, but by vague allegations of duplicity, ambition, and conspiracy, given a merciless edge by the mutual fears of the protagonists.

The models of the man of virtue and of his alter ego—the corrupt politician who was ambitious, self-interested, deceitful, who used friendship as a form of political advancement, and who would sell himself to the highest bidder—were central to the way in which the politicians' terror was articulated. This rhetoric was used to denounce political opponents from early in the Revolution: the triumvirs used it to denounce Mirabeau for plotting to corrupt the Jacobins. In 1791 being labelled a corrupt politician could lead to disgrace: it did not yet lead to death. That came later, in the context of the critical circumstances of concerted opposition from mid-1791 onwards, the build-up to war, and actual and suspected betrayal by a series of political and military leaders. All these circumstances mitigated against the adoption of a more pragmatic form of politics that would have made the idea of a viable opposition acceptable. A critical moment came in the debates on the war when the Girondins put forward the argument that corruption and duplicity in a public official were signs of conspiracy with the external enemy, and therefore such an official was guilty of the crime of *lèse-nation*. In a process which began with Brissot and Robespierre adopting opposing stances over the declaration of war, factional quarrels between Jacobins and Girondins were increasingly articulated in terms of mutual accusations of bad faith, inauthentic virtue, and conspiracy. Brissot played a significant role, both in his active involvement in the declaration of a war that destabilized politics and brought terror closer; and in the deployment of the tactic of characterizing his opponents as conspirators against the Revolution. A further step was taken when the choice was made to remove the immunity that had protected deputies from arrest, leaving them vulnerable to denunciation by their opponents, and thus to death. It was Brissot and the Girondins who first used the ending of immunity to attempt to destroy political opponents, setting an example which their rivals, the Jacobins, were quick to follow.

The Jacobin leaders of the Year Two were obliged to confront the question of 'choosing terror' in a very concrete sense, when it came to the politicians' terror. Their opponents were men whom they knew personally, and with whom they had cooperated in the same intense cause over several years. Some of them, at least, had been friends. Several factors influenced those choices, amongst which three in particular stand out.

The first factor was ideological. The Jacobin leaders were constrained by the ideology of political virtue. Under the Terror the necessity of maintaining that identity became a destructive force. It was closely linked to the idea of the *salut public*, to which cause all else must, if necessary, be sacrificed. The close identification of the Jacobin leaders with the persona of 'men of virtue' caught them in a double bind in which, in order to demonstrate their own authenticity, they had to be seen to act *virtuously* and be prepared, if the public safety demanded it, to denounce and destroy their friends, and even to sacrifice their own lives.

The second factor was about human relationships, the importance of which in revolutionary politics has been greatly underestimated. The conflicting ties of friendship and enmity, loyalty and mistrust, pulled people in opposing directions. Very often these were the tipping points that led to protagonists making the final choice to align themselves with one group or another.

The third factor was emotion, especially—in the context of terror—the emotion of fear. We need to understand that the Jacobin leaders' fear was genuine—even if often misdirected. That is, they genuinely feared a plot between political leaders and foreign powers; they genuinely feared that their enemies, both internal and external, had come together in a concerted conspiracy, the 'Foreign Plot'. The Jacobin leaders feared the Paris militants who had put them in power, and they feared, perhaps even more, their political rivals within the Convention, the Jacobin Club, and the Commune. Ironically, the politicians' terror was given a merciless edge by the fears of the men wielding it that they too would fall victim to it. It was the abyss at the feet of all the political activists who spoke in the Year Two. They were well aware of it. It coloured their words, their actions. Yet they could not publicly acknowledge their awareness of the danger in which they stood, as to do so showed that they were conscious of not being virtuous, or that—unthinkable to admit publicly in the Year Two—they had lost faith in the Revolution.

Fear made it difficult for Jacobin activists in the Year Two to choose *not* to support terror. Danton, Desmoulins—and even Robespierre with his brief support for a commission of clemency—knew that in publicly siding against terror they were making themselves vulnerable to denunciation by the Paris militants and more hard-line Jacobins. So the politicians' terror also hung over the heads of the men who supposedly directed it.

It was not the Jacobin leaders alone who were responsible for the decision to put the laws enabling terror into place: on the contrary, that was a collective choice taken by the Convention. But the Jacobin leaders of the Year Two were the most high-profile defenders of the recourse to terror. Above all, Robespierre and Saint-Just, through their oratory and position as intermediaries between the Committee of Public Safety and the Convention, became the public face of the Terror, its front men and chief apologists. In his speech 'Sur les principes de morale politique' (5 February 1794) Robespierre offered a legitimation of terror, based on his identity as a man of virtue. In the hands of a man of virtue, terror would be used, not for personal motives, but to defend public safety; it was therefore a form of justice.

Robespierre's choice to turn terror on his friends served as a sign of the authenticity of his virtue. As with Brutus, who condemned his own sons to death, the relentless logic of political virtue meant that in order to demonstrate to the watching public that one was worthy of public office one had to be prepared to crush 'the enemy within', even if that entailed the deaths of people one held dear. Only by this means could one demonstrate that one's motives were not founded on personal revenge, but on devotion to the *salut public*. Being prepared to sacrifice one's friends and, if necessary, oneself legitimized the use of terror on others—made it an act of virtue. To prove the authenticity of their identity as men of virtue the Jacobins destroyed the 'enemy within'; in so doing, they destroyed themselves.

This book has addressed the struggle of France's first politicians to find a stable way of doing politics in which a balance could be found between the limitations of human nature and the need for leaders who would do their best for the public good, without succumbing to personal corruption. Men without previous experience of national politics conducted before public opinion had to find a way of doing that. Had it not been for the massive destabilization brought by the war they might well have managed it. It was a problem that continued after Thermidor. The politicians' terror did not end with the fall of the Jacobin Republic. It continued on in a modified form into the Thermidorean period. The problems of how to achieve a form of stable representative politics that was not mired in corruption continued through the troubled years of the Directory. It was an attempt that climaxed in the collapse of politics in Napoleon's *coup d'état*, and the rise of a militarist regime in which glory, not virtue, was at the ideological forefront. Many more would die for Napoleon's glory than ever died for the Jacobins' virtue. Robespierre had long warned of the danger of letting generals take political power. But that, as they say, is another story.

# Principal Victims of the Politicians' Terror in the Year Two (between 22 September 1793 and 21 September 1794)

Of the twenty-one Girondin deputies who were put on trial by the Revolutionary Tribunal, Brissot, Vergniaud, Gensonné, Lauze-Deperret, Carra, Gardien, Duprat, Fauchet, Ducos, Boyer-Fonfrède, Lasource, Lesterpt-Beauvais, Duchastel, Minvielle, Lacaze, Lehardy, Boilleau, Antiboul, Viger, and Sillery (though no Girondin), were all executed on 31 October 1793. The twenty-first, Valazé, committed suicide when sentence was passed.

If captured alive, other Girondins who had fled and engaged in the federalist revolt were executed on the order of military commissions, on the basis of having already been declared 'traitors' by the Convention, so did not appear before the Revolutionary Tribunal. These included Grangeneuve (deputy) executed 21 December 1793; Rebecqui (deputy) committed suicide 1 May 1794; Guadet and Salle (deputies) executed 20 June 1794; and Barbaroux (deputy) executed 25 June 1794. Pétion and Buzot (both deputies) committed suicide, June 1794.

A number of people associated with the Girondins also met their deaths either following an appearance before the Revolutionary Tribunal or through suicide. These were Gorsas (deputy) executed 7 October 1793; Madame Roland (minister's wife) executed 8 November 1793; Manuel (deputy) executed 14 November 1793; Roland (Girondin minister) committed suicide 15 November 1793; Rabaut Sainte-Étienne (deputy) executed 5 December 1793; Condorcet (deputy) committed suicide in prison 29 March 1794: Clavière (Girondin minister) committed suicide in prison 8 December 1793; Lebrun (Girondin minister) executed 28 December 1793.

Hébert and other Commune activists and *sans-culotte* spokesmen, including Momoro, Ronsin, and Vincent, along with the deputy Clootz, were put on trial, accused of conspiracy and complicity in the Foreign Plot. Of a total of twenty men, all but one, Laboureau, were found guilty and executed the same day, 24 March 1794.

Five Dantonist deputies were sent before the Revolutionary Tribunal: Danton, Desmoulins, Philippeaux, Delacroix, and Fabre d'Églantine. Several other deputies were put on trial with them, including Hérault de Séchelles (member of the Committee of Public Safety), Delaunay, Chabot, and Basire; together with General Westermann. They were joined in the dock by several other accused men, who were not politically active but were either involved in the East India Company fraud, or suspected of complicity in the Foreign Plot. All (with the exception of Lulier) were condemned to death—a total of fifteen—and executed on 5 April 1794.

Chaumette (*procureur* of the Commune), Simond (a deputy associated with Hérault de Séchelles), and the widows of Desmoulins and Hébert were all executed on 13 April 1794.

Of the five Robespierrist deputies, Maximilien Robespierre, Saint-Just, Couthon (all members of the Committee of Public Safety), and Augustin Robespierre, after a brief appearance before the Revolutionary Tribunal to confirm their identities, were executed on 28

July 1794. The fifth, Philippe Le Bas (member of the Committee of General Security), pre-empted execution by suicide. Along with Robespierre, and over the two ensuing days, 107 of his friends and allies perished in what became the biggest mass execution that took place in Paris.

Other high-profile revolutionary politicians who also perished included d'Orléans (deputy) executed 6 November 1793; Bailly (former deputy) executed 12 November 1793; Barnave (former deputy) executed 29 November 1793; Kersaint (former deputy) executed 5 December 1793; Thouret, Le Chapelier, and d'Epresménil (former deputies) executed 24 April 1794; and Jacques Roux, *sans-culotte* spokesman who, on hearing that he was to be sent before the Revolutionary Tribunal, stabbed himself in a courtroom on 14 January 1794; he died on 10 February.

This is by no means an exhaustive list. Other people died as an indirect consequence of the politicians' terror; some implicated as 'fellow conspirators'; some killed in the federalist revolts; some died in prison. The families of the victims, mostly women and children, suffered the loss of a parent or spouse, a brother or a son. Many were later accorded small pensions in recognition of what they had suffered, though a few were left in penury and had to live the rest of their lives under the stigma of their relatives' reputations. Of all the victims of the politicians' terror, it was these survivors, perhaps, who paid the highest price.

# Select Bibliography

## PRIMARY SOURCES

**Newspapers and Unattributed Sources**

*Archives Parlementaires de 1787 à 1860*, ed. M.J. Madival *et al.*, 127 vols (Paris: Librairie administrative de P. Dupont, 1862–1972).

Brissot de Warville, Jacques-Pierre (ed.), *Le Patriote français: journal libre, impartial et national, par une société de citoyens* (Paris, 1789–93).

Desmoulins, Camille (ed.), *Les Révolutions de France et de Brabant* (Paris, 1789–91).

Desmoulins, Camille, (ed.) *Le Vieux Cordelier* (Paris, 1793–4), this edition, ed. Pierre Pachet (Alençon: Belin, 1987).

Hébert, Jacques-René (ed.), *Le Père Duchesne* (Paris, 1790–4).

Marat, Jean-Paul (ed.), *L'Ami du Peuple, ou le publiciste parisien et impartial* (1789–92).

Marat, Jean-Paul (ed.), *Le Publiciste de la République française, par Marat l'ami du peuple, député à la Convention* (1793).

[Moniteur (Le)], *Réimpression de l'ancien Moniteur*, 31 vols (Paris, Plon Frères, 1847).

## ATTRIBUTED SOURCES

Aristotle, *Ethics*, trans. J.A.K. Thomson (London: Penguin, 1953).

Aulard, François (ed.), *Recueil des actes du Comité du Salut Public*, 27 vols (Paris: Imprimerie Nationale, 1889–1923).

Aulard, François (ed.), *La Société des Jacobins: recueil de documents pour l'histoire de club des Jacobins de Paris*, 6 vols (Paris: Léopold Cerf; Noblet; Quantin, 1889–97).

Barère, Bertrand, *Memoirs of Bertrand Barère*, trans. De V. Payen-Payne, 4 vols (London: H.S. Nichols, 1896).

Barnave, Antoine-Pierre-Joseph-Marie, *Oeuvres de Barnave*, 4 vols (Paris: Jules Chapelle et Guiller, 1843).

Baudot, Marc-Antoine, *Notes historiques sur la Convention nationale, l'Empire et l'exil des votants* (Paris: D. Jouaust, 1893).

Bégis, A. (ed.), *Curiosités révolutionnaires: Saint-Just et les bureaux de la police générale au Comité de salut public en 1794: Notice historique par Augustin Lejeune, chef des bureaux: Documents inédits* (Paris: Imprimé pour les amis des livres, 1896).

Bienvenu, Richard T. (ed.), *The Ninth of Thermidor: the Fall of Robespierre* (Oxford: Oxford University Press, 1968).

Billaud-Varenne, Jacques-Nicolas, *Principes régénérateurs du système social*, edited and with an introduction by Françoise Brunel (Paris: Publications de la Sorbonne, 1992).

Biré, Edmond, *Journal d'un bourgeois de Paris pendant la Terreur*, 5 vols (Paris: Perrin, 1895).

Bossuet, Jacques-Bénigne, *Politique tirée des propres paroles de l'Ecriture sainte* (1709; this edition, Geneva: Librairie Droz, 1967).

Brissot de Warville, Jacques-Pierre, *Mémoires*, ed. Claude Perroud, 2 vols (Paris: Alphonse Picard et fils, 1912).

Brissot de Warville, Jacques-Pierre, *Lettre de J.P. Brissot à M. Barnave* (Paris, 20 November 1790).

Brissot de Warville, Jacques-Pierre, 'Second discours de J.P. Brissot sur la nécéssité de faire la guerre', given in the Jacobins, 30 December 1791.

Brissot de Warville, Jacques-Pierre, 'Troisième discours de J.P. Brissot, député, sur la nécéssité de la guerre', given in the Jacobins, 20 January 1792.

Brissot de Warville, Jacques-Pierre, 'Discours sur les Conventions', given in the Jacobins, 8 August 1791.

Brissot de Warville, Jacques-Pierre, *J.P. Brissot, député à la Convention, sur la dénonciation de Roberspierre [sic], et sur l'Adresse prêtée aux 48 Sections de Paris.*

Buchez, P.J.B. and Roux, P.C. (eds), *Histoire parlementaire de la Révolution française depuis 1789 jusqu'à l'Empire*, 40 vols (Paris: Paulin, 1833–8).

Buzot, François, *Mémoires sur la Révolution française par Buzot, député à la Convention Nationale* (Paris: Béchet ainé, 1823).

Carnot, Hipployte, *Mémoires sur Carnot par son fils* (Paris: Pagnerre, 1861–3).

Cicero, 'Laelius: or, an Essay on Friendship', in *Offices and Select Letters*, trans. W. Melmoth (London: Dent, 1909).

*Collection des Mémoires relatifs à la Révolution Française: Desmoulins, Vilate et Méda* (Paris: Baudoin, 1825).

Courtois, Edmé-Bonaventure, *Rapport fait au nom de la Commission chargée de l'examen des papiers trouvés chez Robespierre et ses complices* (Paris, Nivôse, l'an III de la République).

Couthon, Georges, *Correspondance de Georges Couthon, suivie de* L'Aristocrate converti (Paris: A. Aubry, 1872).

Desmoulins, Camille, *Lettre de Camille Desmoulins au général Dillon, en prison aux Madelonettes* (1793).

Desmoulins, Camille, *Correspondance inédite de Camille Desmoulins* (Paris: Ébrard, 1836).

Desmoulins, Camille, *Oeuvres de Camille Desmoulins*, ed. J. Claretie, 2 vols (Paris: Charpentier et cie, 1874).

Dumont, Étienne, *Souvenirs sur Mirabeau et sur les deux premières Assemblées Législatives, par Étienne Dumont*, ed. Jean Bénétruy (1832: this edition, Paris: Presses Universitaires de France, 1952).

Dumouriez, Charles-François, *Mémoires du Général Dumouriez* (Paris: Firmin Didiot Frères, 1848).

Duperron, L., *Vie secrète, politique et curieuse de M.J. Maximilien Robespierre* (Paris: Prévost, 1794).

Esprit, Jacques, *La Fausseté des vertus humaines. Par M. Esprit de l'Académie Françoise* (1677–8: this edition, Paris: André Pralard, 1693).

Fénelon, François de Salignac de la Mothe, *Oeuvres*, 2 vols (Paris: Bibliothèque de la Pléiade, 1983).

Ferrières, Charles-Elie (marquis de), *Mémoires du marquis de Ferrières, avec une notice sur sa vie, des notes et des éclaircissements historiques*, eds Berville and Barrière, 3 vols (Paris: Baudouin Frères, 1822).

Gower, George Granville Leveson (earl), *The Despatches of Earl Gower, English Ambassador at Paris from June 1790 to August 1792* (Cambridge: Cambridge University Press, 1885).

Grandchamps, Sophie, 'Souvenirs de Sophie Grandchamps', in *Mémoires de Madame Roland*, ed. Cl. Perroud, 2 vols (Paris: Plon, 1905).

Guadet, Joseph, *Les Girondins, Leur vie privée, leur vie publique, leur proscription et leur mort*, 2 vols (Paris: Librairie académique, 1862).

Jacob, Louis (ed.), *Robespierre vu par ses contemporains* (Paris: Armand Colin, 1938).

La Bruyère, Jean de, *Characters*, trans. Jean Stewart (London: Penguin, 1970).

Lameth, Alexandre de, *Histoire de l'Assemblée Constituante*, 2 vols (Paris: Moutardier, 1828).

La Revellière-Lépeaux, Louis-Marie, *Mémoires*, 3 vols (Paris: Plon, Nourrit, 1895).

Leblanc, J., *Vies secrètes et politiques de Couthon, Saint-Just, Robespierre jeune, complices du tyran Robespierre, et assassins de la république* (Paris: Prévost, l'an II de la république française).

Le Blond de Neuvéglise [pseudonym of Lievin-Bonaventure Proyart (abbé)], *La Vie et les crimes de Robespierre, surnommé le tyran, depuis sa naissance jusqu'à sa mort* (Augsburg, 1795).

Lecointre, Laurent, *Robespierre peint par lui-même, et condamné par ses propres principes, ou dénonciation des crimes de... Robespierre, et projét d'acte d'accusation* (Paris: De l'Imprimérie de Rougyff, 1794).

Levasseur, René, *Mémoires de R. Levasseur (de la Sarthe) Ex-Conventionnel* (1829–31: this edition, Paris, Messidor/Éditions Sociales, 1989).

Levy, Darline Gay, Harriet Branson Applewhite, and Mary Durham Johnson (eds), *Women in Revolutionary Paris, 1789–1795: Selected Documents* (Chicago: University of Illinois Press, 1979).

Louvet, Jean-Baptiste, *Mémoires de Louvet de Couvray, député à la Convention Nationale* (Paris: Baudouin Frères, 1823).

Marat, Jean-Paul, *Oeuvres de J.P. Marat (L'Ami du Peuple)*, ed. A. Vermorel (Paris: Décembre-Alonnier, 1869).

Marat, Jean-Paul, *Oeuvres politiques, 1789–1793* (Brussels: Pole Nord, 1993).

Mathon de la Cour, Charles-Joseph, *Discours sur les meilleurs moyens de faire naître et d'encourager le patriotisme dans une monarchie* (Paris, 1787).

Miles, William Augustus, *Correspondence on the French Revolution, 1789–1817*, 2 vols (London: Longman, Green and Co., 1890).

Montaigne, Michel de, *Essays*, trans. J.M. Cohen (London: Penguin, 1958).

Montesquieu, Charles-Louis de Secondat (baron de), *Oeuvres complètes*, Roger Caillois ed., 2 vols (Paris: Bibliothèque de la Pléiade, 1949–51).

Montjoie, Christophe-Félix-Louis Ventre de la Touloubre [called Galart de], *Histoire de la Conjuration de Maximilien Robespierre* (Paris: Chez les marchands de nouveautés, 1795).

Morris, Gouverneur, *A Diary of the French Revolution, 1789–1793*, 2 vols (London: George G. Harrap and Co., 1939).

Morande, Charles Théveneau de, 'Réponse au dernier mot de J.P. Brissot et à tous les petits mots de ses camarades' (*Supplément au No. 25 de l'Argus Patriote*) (Paris, 1791).

Mortimer-Ternaux, Louis, *Histoire de la terreur, 1792–1794, d'après des documents authentiques et des pièces inédites*, 8 vols (Paris: Michel Lévy Frères, 1869).

Nicole, Pierre, *Essais de Morale, contenus en divers Traités sur plusieurs Devoirs importants*, 14 vols (1715; this edition, Paris: G. Desprez, 1781).

Nodier, Charles, *Souvenirs, épisodes et portraits pour servir à l'histoire de la Révolution et de l'Empire*, 2 vols (Brussels: Louis Hauman and Co., 1831).

*Papiers inédits trouvés chez Robespierre, Saint-Just, Payan, etc., supprimés ou omis par Courtois*, 3 vols (Paris: Baudouin Frères, 1828; republished Geneva, 1978).

Pétion de Villeneuve, Jérome, *Discours de Jérome Pétion sur l'accusation intentée contre Maximilien Robespierre* (November 1792).

Pétion de Villeneuve, Jérome, *Mémoires inédits de Pétion, et mémoires de Buzot et de Barbaroux* (Paris: Henri Plon, 1866).

Robespierre, Charlotte, *Mémoires*, with the introduction by Albert Laponeraye to the first edition (1834; this edition, Paris: Nouveau monde, 2006).

Robespierre, Maximilien, *Oeuvres de Maximilien Robespierre*, eds Marc Bouloiseau, Albert Soboul, *et al.*, 11 vols (Paris: Société des études robespierristes, 1910–2007*)*.

Robespierre, Maximilien, *Correspondance de Maximilien et Augustin Robespierre*, ed. Georges Michon (Paris: Librairie Felix Alcan, 1926).

Roland, Marie-Jeanne (née Phlipon), *Lettres de Madame Roland*, ed. Claude Perroud, 2 vols (Paris: Imprimerie Nationale, 1902).

Roland, Marie-Jeanne (née Phlipon), *Mémoires de Madame Roland*, ed. Cl. Perroud, 2 vols (Paris: Plon, 1905).

Roland, Marie-Jeanne (née Phlipon), *Mémoires de Madame Roland*, ed. Paul de Roux (Paris: Mercure de France, 1966).

Rousseau, Jean-Jacques, *The Collected Writings of Rousseau*, Roger D. Masters and Christopher Kelly (eds), 13 vols (Hanover, NH and London: University Press of New England, 1994–2009).

Roux, Louis-Félix, *Rélation de l'événement des 8, 9 et 10 Thermidor, Sur la conspiration des Triumvirs, Robespierre, Couthon et St Just* (Paris, Poignée et Volland, 1794).

Rudé, George (ed.), *Robespierre* (New Jersey: Prentice-Hall, 1967).

Saint-Just, Louis-Antoine, *Oeuvres complètes*, ed. Michèle Duval (Paris: Éditions Ivrea, 1989).

Salle, J.B., *Observations sur le rapport de Saint-Just contre les trente-deux proscrits, par une Société de Girondins*, Caen, 13 July 1793.

Sieyès, Emmanuel-Joseph, *Qu'est-ce que le Tiers état?* (1789; this edition, Geneva: Droz, 1970).

Söderhjelm, Alma (ed.), *Marie-Antoinette et Barnave: Correspondance secrète (Juillet 1791–Janvier 1792)* (Paris: Armand Colin, 1934).

Stéfane-Pol [pseudonym of Paul Coutant] (ed.), *Autour de Robespierre: le Conventionnel Le Bas, d'après des documents inédits et les mémoires de sa veuve* (Paris: Ernest Flammarion, 1901).

Stewart, John Hall (ed.), *A Documentary Survey of the French Revolution* (New York: Macmillan, 1951).

Taschereau-Fargues, P.A., *P.A. Taschereau-Fargues, à Maximilien Robespierre aux enfers* (Paris: Year III, 1795).

Thibaudeau, Antoine-René-Hyacinthe, *Correspondance inédit du constituant Thibaudeau (1789–1791)* (Paris: Champion, 1898).

Thibaudeau, Antoine-Claire, *Mémoires sur la Convention, et le Directoire, par. A.C. Thibaudeau*, 2 vols (Paris: Badouin Frères, 1824).

Thomas, Antoine-Léonard, *Oeuvres de M. Thomas de l'Académie Françoise. Nouvelle édition revue, corrigée et augmentée*, 4 vols (Amsterdam and Paris: Moutard, 'Librairie de Madame la Dauphine', 1773).

Thompson, J.M. (ed.), *English Witnesses of the French Revolution* (Oxford: Blackwell, 1938).

Tuetey, Alexandre, *Répertoire général des sources manuscrites de l'histoire de Paris pendant la Révolution française*, 11 vols (Paris: Imprimerie Nouvelle, 1914).

Vatel, Charles (ed.), *Charlotte Corday et les Girondins*, 3 vols (Paris: Henri Plon, 1872).

Walter, Gérard (ed.), *Actes du Tribunal révolutionnaire, recueillis et commentés par Gérard Walter* (Paris: Mercure de France, 1968).

Young, Arthur, *Travels in France during the Years 1787, 1788 and 1789* (1792: this edition, Cambridge: Cambridge University Press, 1929).

## SECONDARY WORKS

Abensour, Miguel, 'La philosophie politique de Saint-Just', *Annales historiques de la révolution française*, 38 (1966): 1–32.

Acher, William, *Jean-Jacques Rousseau, écrivain de l'amitié* (Paris: Nizet, 1971).

Andress, David, *The Terror: Civil War in the French Revolution* (London; Little, Brown, 2005).

Andress, David, 'Living the revolutionary melodrama: Robespierre's sensibility and the construction of political commitment in the French Revolution', *Representations*, 114, 1 (Spring 2011): 103–28.

Andress, David (ed.), *Experiencing the French Revolution* (Oxford: Studies on Voltaire and the Eighteenth Century, 2013).

Applewhite, Harriet B., *Political Alignment in the French National Assembly, 1789–1791* (Baton Rouge: Louisiana State University Press, 1993).

Ariès, Philippe and Georges Duby (eds), *A History of Private Life*, trans. Arthur Goldhammer, 5 vols (Cambridge, MA: Harvard University Press, 1987).

Astbury, Katherine and Marie-Emmanuelle Plagnol-Diéval (eds), *Le mâle en France, 1715–1830 représentations de la masculinité* (Oxford: Peter Lang, 2004).

Aston, Nigel, *Religion and Revolution in France, 1780–1804* (Houndmills: Palgrave, 2000).

Aulard, François, 'Une interview de Bertrand Barère en 1840', *Révolution française*, 61 (1911).

Baczko, Bronislaw, *Ending the Terror: The French Revolution After Robespierre* (Cambridge: Cambridge University Press, 1994).

Baecque, Antoine de, 'Le sang des héros: figures du corps dans l'imaginaire politique de la Révolution française', *Revue d'histoire moderne et contemporaine* 34 (1987): 553–86.

Baecque, Antoine de, *Glory and Terror: Seven Deaths under the French Revolution*, trans. Charlotte Mandell (London: Routledge, 2001).

Baker, Keith Michael, *Inventing the French Revolution* (Cambridge: Cambridge University Press, 1990).

Baker, Keith Michael (ed.), *The French Revolution and the Creation of Modern Political Culture*, vol. 4, *The Terror* (Oxford: Pergamon, 1994).

Baker, Keith Michael, 'Transformations of classical republicanism in eighteenth-century France', *Journal of Modern History*, 73 (2001): 32–53.

Barker, Emma, *Greuze and the Painting of Sentiment* (Cambridge: Cambridge University Press, 2005).

Barny, Roger, *Prélude idéologique à la Révolution française: le Rousseauisme avant 1789* (Paris: Les Belles Lettres, 1985).

Baxter, Denise Amy, 'Two Brutuses: violence, virtue, and politics in the visual culture of the French Revolution', *Eighteenth-Century Life*, 30, 3 (Summer 2006): 51–77.

Bell, David A., *The Cult of the Nation in France: Inventing Nationalism, 1680–1800* (Cambridge, MA: Harvard University Press, 2001).

Ben-Amos, Avner, *Funerals, Politics, and Memory in Modern France, 1789–1996* (Oxford: Oxford University Press, 2000).

Bénétruy, Jean, *L'Atelier de Mirabeau: quatre proscrits génévois dans la tourmente révolutionnaire* (Paris: A. and J. Picard, 1962).

Bernier, Georges, *Hérault de Séchelles: Biographie, suivie de* Théorie de l'ambition (Paris: Editions Julliard, 1995).

Biard, Michel, *Collot d'Herbois: Légendes noires et révolution* (Lyon: Presses universitaires de Lyon, 1995).

Biard, Michel (ed.), *Les Politiques de la Terreur, 1793–1794* (Rennes: Presses Universitaires de Rennes, and the Société des études Robespierristes, 2008).

Billet, M., *Philippe Le Bas, membre de l'institut de France (inscriptions et belles lettres). Lecture faite à l'Académie d'Arras, le 20 juillet 1866* (Arras: A. Courtin, 1866).

Blackman, Robert H., 'What's in a name? Possible names for a legislative body and the birth of national sovereignty during the French Revolution, 15–16 June 1789', *French History*, 21 (March 2007): 22–43.

Blanc, Olivier, *La Corruption sous la Terreur (1792–1794)* (Paris: Robert Laffont, 1992).

Blanning, T.C.W., *The Origins of the French Revolutionary Wars* (Harlow: Longman, 1986).

Bluche, Frédéric, *Septembre 1792, logiques d'un massacre* (Paris: Robert Laffont, 1986).

Bonn, Gérard, *La Révolution française et Camille Desmoulins* (Paris: Éditions Glyphe, 2010).

Boudon, Julien, *Les Jacobins: une traduction des principes de Jean-Jacques Rousseau* (Paris: Librairie Générale de Droit et de Jurisprudence, 2006).

Bouineau, Jacques, *Les Toges du pouvoir: ou la Révolution du droit antique* (Toulouse: Éditions Eché, 1986).

Bouloiseau, Marc, *The Jacobin Republic, 1792–1794*, trans. Jonathan Mandelbaum (Cambridge: Cambridge University Press, 1983).

Bowers, Claude G., *Pierre Vergniaud, Voice of the French Revolution* (New York: Macmillan, 1950).

Brace, Richard Munthe, 'General Dumouriez and the Girondins, 1792–1793', *American Historical Review*, 56, 3 (1951): 493–509.

Bradby, Eliza Dorothy, *The Life of Barnave*, 2 vols (Oxford: Clarendon Press, 1915).

Brasart, Patrick, *Paroles de la Révolution: Les Assemblées parlementaires, 1789–1794* (Paris: Minerve, 1988).

Bray, Alan, *The Friend* (Chicago: University of Chicago Press, 1993).

Brinton, Crane, *The Jacobins: an Essay in the New History* (1930: this edition, New York: Russell and Russell, 1961).

Brouillard, Roger, 'Dumouriez et les Girondins: correspondance inedité de Gensonné', *Revue historique de Bordeaux et du departement de la Gironde* 36 (1943): 35–47.

Brown, Howard G., *War, Revolution, and the Bureaucratic State: Politics and Army Administration in France, 1791–1799* (Oxford: Clarendon Press, 1995).

Brown, Howard G., *Ending the French Revolution: Violence, Justice, and Repression from the Terror to Napoleon* (Charlottesville: University of Virginia Press, 2006).

Brown, Howard G. and Judith A. Miller (eds), *Problems of a New Order From the French Revolution to Napoleon* (Manchester: Manchester University Press, 2002).

Bruguière, Michel, *Gestionnaires et Profiteurs de la Révolution: L'administration des finances françaises de Louis XVI à Bonaparte* (Paris: Olivier Orban, 1986).

Brunel, Françoise, *Thermidor: La chute de Robespierre* (Paris: Éditions Complexe, 1989).

Bruun, Geoffrey, 'The evolution of a Terrorist: Georges Auguste Couthon', *Journal of Modern History*, 2, 3 (1930): 410–29.

Burney, John M., 'The Fear of the Executive and the Threat of Conspiracy: Billaud-Varenne's Terrorist Rhetoric in the French Revolution, 1788–1794', *French History*, 5, 2 (1991): 143–63.

Burney, John M., 'History, despotism, public opinion and the continuity of the radical attack on monarchy in the French Revolution, 1787–1792', *History of European Ideas*, 17, 2/3 (1993): 245–63.

Burrows, Simon, 'The innocence of Jacques-Pierre Brissot', *The Historical Journal*, 46, 4 (2003): 843–71.

Burstin, Haim, *L'Invention du sans-culotte: regard sur le Paris révolutionnaire* (Paris: Odile Jacob, 2005).

Caine, Barbara (ed.), *Friendship: A History* (London: Equinox, 2009).

Campbell, Peter R., *Power and Politics in Old Régime France, 1720–1745* (London: Routledge, 1996).

Campbell, Peter R. (ed.), *The Origins of the French Revolution* (Houndmills: Palgrave, 2005).

Campbell, Peter R., 'The language of patriotism in France, 1750–1770', *Journal of French Studies, e-France,* 1: 1 (2007) 1–43.

Campbell, Peter R., 'The politics of patriotism in France (1770–1788)', *French History,* 24, 4 (2010): 550–75.

Campbell, Peter R., Thomas E. Kaiser, and Marisa Linton (eds), *Conspiracy in the French Revolution* (Manchester: Manchester University Press, 2007).

Caradonna, Jeremy, 'The monarchy of virtue: the *Prix de Vertu* and the economy of emulation in France, 1777–1791', *Eighteenth-Century Studies,* 41, 4 (2008): 443–58.

Caradonna, Jeremy, 'Grub Street and suicide: a view from the literary press in late eighteenth-century France', *Journal for Eighteenth-Century Studies,* 33, 1 (2010): 23–36.

Censer, Jack. R., *The French Press in the Age of Enlightenment* (London: Routledge, 1994).

Censer, Jack R. and Jeremy D. Popkin (eds), *Press and Politics in Pre-Revolutionary France* (Berkeley: University of California Press, 1987).

Chappey, Jean-Luc *et al.* (eds), *Pour quoi faire la Révolution* (Marseilles: Agone, 2012).

Chartier, Roger, *The Cultural Origins of the French Revolution,* trans. Lydia C. Cochrane (Durham, NC and London: Duke University Press, 1991).

Chisick, Harvey, 'Public opinion and political culture in France during the second half of the eighteenth century', *English Historical Review,* 117, issue 470 (February. 2002): 48–77.

Claretie, Jules, *Camille Desmoulins, Lucille Desmoulins: étude sur les Dantonistes, d'après des documents nouveaux et inédits* (Paris: Plon, 1875).

Claretie, Jules, *Camille Desmoulins and his Wife: Passages from the History of the Dantonists,* trans. Mrs Cashel Hoey (London: Smith, Elder and Co., 1876).

Clark, Henry C., *La Rochefoucauld and the Language of Unmasking in Seventeenth-Century France* (Geneva: Droz, 1994).

Clarke, Joseph, *Commemorating the Dead in Revolutionary France: Revolution and Remembrance, 1789–1799* (Cambridge: Cambridge University Press, 2007).

Clay, Stephen, 'Vengeance, justice and the reactions in the revolutionary Midi', *French History,* 23, 1 (2009): 22–46.

Cobban, Alfred, *Aspects of the French Revolution* (London: Paladin, 1968).

Collins, James B., *The State in Early Modern Europe* (second edition, Cambridge: Cambridge University Press, 2009).

Conner, Susan P., 'Public virtue and public women: prostitution in revolutionary Paris, 1793–1794', *Eighteenth-Century Studies,* 28, 2 (1994–5): 221–40.

Cousin, Alexandre, *Philippe Lebas et Augustin Robespierre: Deux météores dans la Révolution française* (Paris: Bérénice, 2010).

Cowans, Jon, *To Speak for the People: Public Opinion and the Problem of Legitimacy in the French Revolution* (London: Routledge, 2001).

Coward, Barry and Julian Swann (eds), *Conspiracies and Conspiracy Theory in Early Modern Europe: From the Waldensians to the French Revolution* (Aldershot: Ashgate, 2004).

Croker, John Wilson, *Essays on the Early Period of the French Revolution* (1857: republished: New York, AMS Press, 1970).

Crook, Malcolm, *Elections in the French Revolution: an Apprenticeship in Democracy, 1789–1799* (Cambridge: Cambridge University Press, 1996).

Crook, Malcolm, William Doyle, and Alan Forrest (eds), *Enlightenment and Revolution: Essays in Honour of Norman Hampson* (Aldershot: Ashgate, 2004).

Crow, Thomas E., '"The Oath of the Horatii" in 1785: painting and pre-revolutionary radicalism in France', *Art History*, I, 4 (1978): 424–71.

Crow, Thomas E., *Painters and Public Life in Eighteenth-Century Paris* (New Haven, CT: Yale University Press, 1985).

Curtis, Eugene Newton, *Saint-Just, Colleague of Robespierre* (New York: Columbia University Press, 1935).

Darnton, Robert, *The Forbidden Best-Sellers of Pre-Revolutionary France* (London: Fontana, 1997).

Darnton, Robert, *The Literary Underground of the Old Regime* (Cambridge, MA: Harvard University Press, 1982).

Darnton, Robert, 'The Brissot dossier', *French Historical Studies*, 17 (1991): 191–205.

David, Marcel, *Fraternité et Révolution française, 1789–1799* (Paris: Aubier, 1987).

Delaporte, André, *L'Idée d'égalité en France au XVIIIe* (Paris: Presses Universitaires de France, 1987).

De Luna, Frederick A., 'The Dean Street style of revolution: J.P. Brissot, *Jeune Philosophe*', *French Historical Studies*, 17 (1991): 159–90.

Denby, David J., *Sentimental Narrative and the Social Order in France, 1760–1820* (Cambridge: Cambridge University Press, 2006).

Dendena, Francesco, 'A new look at Feuillantism: the triumvirate and the movement for war in 1791', *French History*, 26, 1 (2012): 6–33.

Desan, Suzanne, *The Family on Trial in Revolutionary France* (Berkeley: University of California Press, 2004).

Di Padova, Theodore A., 'The question of Girondin motives: a response to Sydenham', *French Historical Studies*, 10 (1977): 349–52.

Douthwaite, Julia, *The Frankenstein of 1790 and Other Lost Chapters from Revolutionary France* (Chicago: University of Chicago Press, 2012).

Doyle, William, *Aristocracy and Its Enemies in the Age of Revolution* (Oxford: Oxford University Press, 2009).

Doyle, William (ed.), *The Oxford Handbook of the Ancien Régime* (Oxford: Oxford University Press, 2011).

Duprat, Annie (ed.), *Révolutions et myths identitaires: mots, violences, mémoire* (Paris: CHCSC de l'université de Versailles Saint-Quentin-en-Yvelines, 2009).

Edelstein, Dan, *The Terror of Natural Right: Republicanism, the Cult of Nature, and the French Revolution* (Chicago: University of Chicago Press: Chicago, 2009).

Edelstein, Dan, 'Do we want a Revolution without revolution? Reflections on political authority', *French Historical Studies*, 35, 2 (2012): 269–89.

Edmonds, William, *Jacobinism and the Revolt of Lyon, 1789–1793* (Oxford: Clarendon Press, 1990).

Ellery, Eloise, *Brissot de Warville: A Study in the History of the French Revolution* (1915: republished, New York: AMS Press, 1970).

Farge, Arlette, *Subversive Words: Public Opinion in Eighteenth-Century France* (Oxford: Polity Press, 1995).

Fehér, Ferenc (ed.), *The French Revolution and the Birth of Modernity* (Berkeley: University of California Press, 1990).

Félix, Joël, *Finances et politiques au siècle des lumières: le ministre l'Averdy, 1763–1768* (Paris, Imprimerie nationale, 1999).

Félix, Joël, *Louis XVI et Marie-Antoinette: un couple en politique* (Paris: Payot, 2006).

Fitzsimmons, Michael P., *The Remaking of France: the National Assembly and the Constitution of 1791* (Cambridge: Cambridge University Press, 1994).

Fitzsimmons, Michael P., *The Night the Old Regime Ended: August 4, 1789, and the French Revolution* (University Park: Pennsylvania State University Press, 2003).

Forsyth, Murray, *Reason and Revolution: the Political Thought of the Abbé Sieyès* (Leicester: Leicester University Press, 1987).

*French Historical Studies* forum: Frederick A. De Luna, 'The "Girondins" were Girondins after all'; and Michael S. Lewis-Beck, Anne Hildreth, and Alan B. Spitzer, 'Was there a Girondist faction in the National Convention?', with commentary by Sydenham, Patrick, and Kates. *French Historical Studies*, 15, 3 (1988): 519–36.

Forth, Christopher E. and Bertrand Taithe (eds), *French Masculinities: History, Culture and Politics* (Houndmills: Palgrave, 2007).

Fortunet, Françoise, 'l'amitié et le droit selon Saint-Just', *Annales historiques de la révolution française*, 248 (1982): 181–95.

Friedland, Paul, *Political Actors: Representative Bodies and Theatricality in the Age of the French Revolution* (Ithaca, NY: Cornell University Press, 2002).

Furet, François, *Interpreting the French Revolution*, trans. Elborg Forster (1978: this edition, Cambridge: Cambridge University Press, 1981).

Furet, François and Mona Ozouf (eds), *Dictionnaire critique de la Révolution française* (Paris: Flammarion, 1988).

Furet, François and Mona Ozouf (eds), *La Gironde et les Girondins* (Paris: Payot, 1991).

Gainot, Bernard, *1799, un nouveau jacobinisme? La démocratie representative, une alternative à Brumaire* (Paris: CTHS, 2001).

Gallo, Max, *Robespierre the Incorruptible: A Psycho-Biography* (New York: Herder and Herder, 1971).

Gauthier, Florence, *Triomphe et mort du droit naturel en Révolution 1789–1795–1802* (Paris: Presses Universitaires de France, 1992).

Gershoy, Leo, *Bertrand Barère: A Reluctant Terrorist* (Princeton, NJ: Princeton University Press, 1962).

*Gilbert Romme (1750–1795) et son temps: actes du colloque tenu à Riom et Clermont les 10 et 11 juin 1965* (Presses Universitaires de France, Paris, 1966).

Godechot, Jacques, *Les Institutions de la France* (Paris: Presses Universitaires de France, 1968).

Godfrey, James Logan, *Revolutionary Justice: A Study in the Organisation and Procedures of the Paris Tribunal, 1793–95* (Chapel Hill: University of North Carolina Press, 1951).

Godineau, Dominique, *Citoyennes Tricoteuses: Les femmes du peuple à Paris pendant la Révolution française* (Aix-en-Provence: Alinea, 1988).

Goetz-Bernstein, H.A., *La Diplomatie de la Gironde: Jacques-Pierre Brissot* (Paris: Hachette, 1912).

Goldie, Mark and Robert Wokler (eds), *The Cambridge History of Eighteenth-Century Political Thought* (Cambridge: Cambridge University Press, 2006).

Goldstein, Jan, *The Post-Revolutionary Self: Politics and Psyche in France, 1750–1850* (Cambridge, MA: Harvard University Press, 2008).

Goodman, Dena (ed.), *Marie-Antoinette: Writings on the Body of a Queen* (London: Routledge, 2003).

Goodwin, A., 'The underworld of the French Revolutionary Terror', in *Memoirs and Proceedings of the Manchester Literary and Philosophical Society* (Manchester, 1954–5): 38–56.

Gottschalk, Louis and Margaret Maddox, *Lafayette in the French Revolution: From the October Days through the Federation* (Chicago: University of Chicago Press, 1973).

Gough, Hugh, *The Newspaper Press in the French Revolution* (London: Routledge, 1988).

Gough, Hugh, *The Terror in the French Revolution* (second edition, Houndmills: Palgrave, 2010).

Grassi, Marie-Claire, 'Friends and lovers (or the codification of intimacy)', *Yale French Studies*, 71 (1986): 77–92.

Greer, Donald, *The Incidence of the Terror During the French Revolution: A Statistical Interpretation* (Cambridge, MA: Harvard University Press, 1935).

Gross, Jean-Pierre, *Saint-Just: sa politique et ses missions* (Paris: Bibliothèque Nationale, 1976).

Gross, Jean-Pierre, *Fair Shares for All: Jacobin Egalitarianism in Practice* (Cambridge: Cambridge University Press, 1997).

Gruder, Vivien R., *The Notables and the Nation: The Political Schooling of the French, 1787–1788* (Cambridge, MA: Harvard University Press, 2007).

Gueniffey, Patrice, *Le Nombre et la raison: la Révolution française et les élections* (Paris: École des Hautes Études en Sciences Sociales, 1993).

Gueniffey, Patrice, *La Politique de la Terreur: essai sur la violence révolutionnaire, 1789–1794* (Paris: Fayard, 2000).

Gueniffey, Patrice, 'La Terreur: circonstances exceptionnelles, idéologie et dynamique révolutionnaire', *Historical Reflections/Réflexions Historiques*, 29, 3 (2003): 433–50.

Guilhaumou, Jacques and Raymonde Monnier (eds), *Des notions-concepts en revolution. Autour de la liberté politique à la fin du XVIIIe siècle* (Paris: Société des études Robespierristes, 2003).

Gunn, J.A.W., 'Queen of the world: opinion in the public life of France from the Renaissance to the Revolution', in *Studies on Voltaire and the Eighteenth Century*, 328 (1995).

Gutwirth, Madelyn, *The Twilight of the Goddesses: Women and Representation in the French Revolutionary Era* (New Brunswick, NJ: Rutgers University Press, 1992).

Habermas, Jürgen, *The Structural Transformation of the Public Sphere: An Inquiry into a Category of Bourgeois Society* (Cambridge: Polity Press, 1989).

Hammersley, Rachel, *French Revolutionaries and English Republicans: the Cordeliers Club, 1790–1794* (Woodbridge: The Royal Historical Society, The Boydell Press, 2005).

Hampson, Norman, *The Life and Opinions of Maximilien Robespierre* (London: Duckworth, 1974).

Hampson, Norman, 'François Chabot and his plot', in *Transactions of the Royal Historical Society*, 5th Series, 26 (1976): 1–14.

Hampson, Norman, *Danton* (London: Duckworth, 1978).

Hampson, Norman, *Saint-Just* (Oxford: Blackwell, 1991).

Hanson, Paul R., *The Jacobin Republic Under Fire: the Federalist Revolt in the French Revolution* (University Park, : Pennsylvania State University Press, 2003).

Hanson, Paul R., *Contesting the French Revolution* (Oxford: Wiley-Blackwell, 2009).

Hardman, John, *Robespierre* (London: Pearson Education, 1999).

Hardman, John, *Overture to Revolution: The 1787 Assembly of Notables and the Crisis of France's Old Regime* (Oxford: Oxford University Press, 2010).

Haydon, Colin and William Doyle (eds), *Robespierre* (Cambridge: Cambridge University Press, 1990).

Herissay, Jacques, *François Buzot: député de l'Eure à l'Assemblée Constituante et à la Convention, 1760–1794* (Paris: Perrin, 1907).

Hesse, Carla, 'La preuve par la lettre: pratiques juridiques au tribunal révolutionnaire de Paris (1793–1794)', *Annales: Histoire, Sciences Sociales*, 3 (1996): 629–42.

Hesse, Carla, *The Other Enlightenment: How French Women Became Modern* (Princeton, NJ: Princeton University Press, 2001).

Heuer, Jennifer, *The Family and the Nation: Gender and Citizenship in Revolutionary France* (Ithaca, NY: Cornell University Press, 2005).

Higonnet, Patrice, *Goodness Beyond Virtue: Jacobins During the French Revolution* (Cambridge, MA: Harvard University Press, 1998).

Huet, Marie-Hélène, *Mourning Glory: the Will of the French Revolution* (Philadelphia: University of Pennsylvania Press, 1997).

Hufton, Olwen H., *Women and the Limits of Citizenship in the French Revolution* (Toronto: University of Toronto Press, 1992).

Hunt, Lynn, *Politics, Culture, and Class in the French Revolution* (Berkeley: University of California Press, 1984).

Hunt, Lynn, *The Family Romance of the French Revolution* (London: Routledge, 1992).

Hunt, Lynn, 'The experience of revolution', *French Historical Studies*, 32, 4 (Fall 2009): 671–8.

Jacob, Louis, *Hébert Le Père Duchesne, Chef des sans-culottes* (Paris: Gallimard, 1960).

Jainchill, Andrew, *Reimagining Politics After the Terror: the Republican Origins of French Liberalism* (Ithaca, NY: Cornell University Press, 2008).

Jaume, Lucien, *Le Discours Jacobin et la démocratie* (Paris: Fayard, 1989).

Jessenne, Jean-Pierre *et al.* (eds), *Robespierre: De la Nation artésienne à la république et aux nations* (Lille: Centre d'Histoire de la Région du Nord, 1993).

Johnson, James H., 'Versailles, meet Les Halles: masks, carnival, and the French Revolution', *Representations*, 73 (2001): 89–116.

Jones, Peter (ed.), *The French Revolution in Social and Political Perspective* (London: Arnold, 1996).

Jordan, David P., *The King's Trial: Louis XVI vs. the French Revolution* (Berkeley: University of California Press, 1979).

Jordan, David P., *The Revolutionary Career of Maximilien Robespierre* (New York: The Free Press, 1985).

Jourdan, Annie, 'La guerre des dieux ou l'héroïsme révolutionnaire chez Madame Roland et Robespierre', *Romanticisme*, 85 (1994): 19–26.

Jourdan, Annie (ed.), *Robespierre—Figure-Réputation* (Yearbook of European Studies, 9: Amsterdam, 1996).

Jourdan, Annie, *Les Monuments de la Révolution 1770–1804: une histoire de la représentation* (Paris: Honoré Champion, 1997).

Jourdan, Annie, 'Les discours de la terreur à l'époque révolutionnaire', *French Historical Studies*, 36, 1 (Winter 2013): 52–81.

Kaiser, Thomas E., 'Who's Afraid of Marie-Antoinette? Diplomacy, Austrophobia, and the Queen', *French History*, 14 (2000): 241–71.

Kaiser, Thomas E., 'From the Austrian Committee to the Foreign Plot: Marie-Antoinette, Austrophobia and the Terror', *French Historical Studies*, 26, 4 (Fall 2003): 579–617.

Kaiser, Thomas E., 'La fin du renversement des alliances: la France, l'Autriche et la déclaration de guerre du 20 avril 1792', *Annales historiques de la Révolution française*, 551 (2008): 77–98.

Kaiser, Thomas E. and Dale K. Van Kley (eds), *From Deficit to Deluge: The Origins of the French Revolution* (Stanford, CA: Stanford University Press, 2011).

Kelly, George Armstrong, *Mortal Politics in Eighteenth-Century France* (Ontario: University of Waterloo Press, 1986).

Kelly, George Armstrong, 'The machine of the duc d'Orléans and the new politics', *Journal of Modern History*, 51 (1979): 667–84.

Kelly, George Armstrong, 'Conceptual sources of the Terror', *Eighteenth-Century Studies*, 14, 1 (1980): 18–36.

Kennedy, Emmet, *A Cultural History of the French Revolution* (New Haven, CT: Yale University Press, 1989).

Kennedy, Michael L., *The Jacobin Clubs in the French Revolution: the First Years* (Princeton, NJ: Princeton University Press, 1982).

Kennedy, Michael L., *The Jacobin Clubs in the French Revolution: the Middle Years* (Princeton, NJ: Princeton University Press, 1988).

Kennedy, Michael L., *The Jacobin Clubs in the French Revolution, 1793 to 1795* (New York: Berghahn Books, 2000).

Kates, Gary, *The Cercle Social, the Girondins and the French Revolution* (Princeton, NJ: Princeton University Press, 1985),

Kettering, Sharon, *Patrons, Brokers and Clients in Seventeenth-Century France* (Oxford: Oxford University Press, 1986).

Kettering, Sharon, 'Friendship and clientage in early modern France', *French History*, 6, 2 (1992): 139–58.

Kuscinski, A., *Dictionnaire des Conventionnels* (Yvelines: Éditions du Vexin Français, 1973).

Lefebvre, Georges, *Études sur la Révolution française* (Paris: Presses Universitaires de France, 1954).

Lemay, Edna Hindie, *La Vie quotidienne des députés aux états généraux, 1789* (Paris: Hachette, 1987).

Lemay, Edna Hindie (ed.), *Dictionnaire des Constituants, 1789–1791*, 2 vols (Oxford: Voltaire Foundation, 1991).

Lemay, Edna Hindie (ed.), *Dictionnaire des Législateurs, 1791–1792*, 2 vols (Ferney-Voltaire: Centre International d'Etude du XVIIIe Siècle, 2007).

Lestapis, Arnaud de, *La Conspiration de Batz* (Paris: Société des études robespierristes, 1969).

Lilti, Antoine, *Le Monde des salons. Sociabilité et mondanité à Paris au XVIIIe siècle* (Paris: Fayard, 2005).

Linton, Marisa, 'The rhetoric of virtue and the *Parlements*, 1770–1775', *French History*, 9, 2 (June 1995): 180–201.

Linton, Marisa, 'The unvirtuous king? Clerical rhetoric on the French monarchy, 1760–1774', *History of European Ideas*, 25, 1–2 (1999): 55–74.

Linton, Marisa, 'Virtue rewarded? Women and the politics of virtue in eighteenth-century France', part I, *History of European Ideas*, 26, 1 (2000): 35–49.

Linton, Marisa, 'Virtue rewarded? Women and the politics of virtue in eighteenth-century France', part 2, *History of European Ideas*, 26, 1 (2000): 51–65.

Linton, Marisa, *The Politics of Virtue in Enlightenment France* (Houndmills: Palgrave, 2001).

Linton, Marisa, 'Fatal friendships: the politics of Jacobin friendship', *French Historical Studies*, 31, 1 (2008): 51–76.

Linton, Marisa, 'The Man of Virtue: the role of antiquity in the political trajectory of L. A. Saint-Just', 24, 3, *French History* (2010): 393–419.

Linton, Marisa, 'Robespierre et l'authenticité révolutionnaire', *Annales historiques de la Révolution française*, 371 (2013): 153–73.

Liris, Elizabeth and Jean Maurice Bizière (eds), *La Révolution et la mort* (Toulouse: Presses Universitaires du Mirail, 1991).

Loft, Leonore, 'The roots of Brissot's ideology', *Eighteenth-Century Life*, 13 (1989): 21–34.

Loiselle, Kenneth, ' "Nouveaux mais vrais amis:" la Franc-maçonnerie et les rites de l'amitié au dix-huitième siècle', *Dix-huitième siècle*, 39 (2007): 303–18.

Lucas, Colin, *The Structure of the Terror: the Example of Javogues and the Loire* (Oxford: Oxford University Press, 1973).

Lucas, Colin, 'The theory and practice of denunciation in the French Revolution', *Journal of Modern History*, 68, 4 (1996): 768–85.

Luckett, Thomas Manley, 'Hunting for spies and whores: a parisian riot on the eve of the French Revolution', 156, *Past and Present* (1997): 116–43.

Luttrell, Barbara, *Mirabeau* (Carbondale and Edwardsville: Southern Illinois University Press, 1990).

Luzatto, Sergio, *Bonbon Robespierre: la terreur à visage humain*, trans. Simone Carpentari Messina (Paris: Arléa, 2010).

Luzzatto, Sergio, *Mémoire de la Terreur: vieux montagnards et jeunes républicains au XIXe siècle*, trans. Simone Carpentari-Messina (Lyon: Presses Universitaires de Lyon, 1991).

Lyons, Martyn, 'The 9 Thermidor: motives and effects', *European History Quarterly*, 5, 2 (1975): 123–46.

Lyons, Martyn, 'M.G.A.Vadier (1736–1828): the formation of the Jacobin mentality', *French Historical Studies*, 10, 1 (Spring 1977): 74–100.

Margerison, Kenneth, *Pamphlets and Public Opinion: the Campaign for a Union of Orders in the Early French Revolution* (West Lafayette, IN: Purdue University Press, 1998).

Markoff, John, *The Abolition of Feudalism: Peasants, Lords and Legislators in the French Revolution* (University Park: Pennsylvania State University Press, 1996).

Martin, Jean-Clément (ed.), *La Révolution à l'oeuvre: perspectives actuelles dans l'histoire de la Révolution française* (Rennes: Presses Universitaires de Rennes, 2005).

Martin, Jean-Clément, *Violence et révolution: essais sur la naissance d'un mythe national* (Paris: Sueil, 2006).

Mason, Laura, 'The "bosom of proof": criminal justice and the renewal of oral culture during the French Revolution', *Journal of Modern History*, 76, 1 (2004): 29–61.

Mathiez, Albert, *La Conspiration de l'étranger* (Paris: Armand Colin, 1918).

Mathiez, Albert, *Autour de Danton* (Paris: Payot, 1926).

Mathiez, Albert, *La Corruption sous la Terreur* (Paris: Armand Colin, 1927).

Mathiez, Albert, *Girondins et Montagnards* (Paris: Firmin-Didot, 1930).

Mathiez, Albert, *Études sur Robespierre (1758–1794)* (Paris: Éditions Sociales, 1958).

Mauzi, Robert, *L'Idée du bonheur dans la littérature et la pensée française au XVIIIe siècle* (1960: this edition, Paris: Albin Michel, 1994).

May, Gita, *Madame Roland and the Age of Revolution* (New York: Columbia University Press, 1970).

Mayer, Arno, *The Furies: Violence and Terror in the French and Russian Revolutions* (Princeton, NJ: Princeton University Press, 2000).

Maza, Sarah, *Private Lives and Public Affairs: The* Causes Célèbres *of Prerevolutionary France* (Berkeley: University of California Press, 1993).

Mazeau, Guillaume, *Le Bain de l'histoire: Charlotte Corday et l'attentat contre Marat, 1793–2009* (Seyssel: Champ Vallon, 2009).

McDonald, Joan, *Rousseau and the French Revolution, 1762–1791* (London: Athlone, 1965).

McPhee, Peter, *Robespierre—a Revolutionary Life* (New Haven, CT: Yale University Press, 2012).

McPhee, Peter (ed.), *Companion to the History of the French Revolution* (Oxford: Wiley-Blackwell, 2012).

Melzer, Sara E. and Leslie W. Rabine, *Rebel Daughters: Women and the French Revolution* (Oxford: Oxford University Press, 1992).

Merrick, Jeffrey, 'Male friendship in pre-Revolutionary France', *GLQ: A Journal of Lesbian and Gay Studies*, 10, 3 (2004): 407–32.

Merrick, Jeffrey, 'Suicide and politics in pre-Revolutionary France', *Eighteenth-Century Life*, 30 (2006): 32–47.

Michon, Georges, *Essai sur l'histoire du parti feuillant: Adrien Duport* (Paris: Pavot, 1924).

Michon, Georges, *Robespierre et la guerre révolutionnaire 1791–1792* (Paris: Marcel Rivière, 1937).

Miller, Mary Ashburn, *A Natural History of Revolution: Violence and Nature in the French Revolutionary Imagination, 1789–1794* (Ithaca, NY: Cornell University Press, 2011).

Monnier, Raymonde, 'Républicanisme et révolution française', *French Historical Studies*, 26, 1 (2003): 87–118.

Monnier, Raymonde, *Républicanisme, patriotisme et révolution française* (Paris: L'Harmattan, 2005).

Moriarty, Michael, *Disguised Vices: Theories of Virtue in Early Modern French Thought* (Oxford: Oxford University Press, 2011).

Mornet, Daniel, *Les Origines intellectuelles de la Révolution française: 1715–1787* (Paris: Armand Colin, 1938).

Morrissey, Robert, *Napoléon et l'héritage de la gloire* (Paris: Presses Universitaires de France, 2010).

Oliver, Bette W., *Orphans on the Earth: Girondin Fugitives from the Terror, 1793–1794* (Lanham, MD: Lexington Books, 2009).

Olsen, Mark, 'A failure of enlightened politics in the French Revolution: the Société de 1789', *French History*, 6, 3 (1992): 303–34.

Ording, Arne, *Le Bureau de police du Comité de salut public* (Oslo: J. Dybwad, 1930).

Outram, Dorinda, *The Body and the French Revolution* (New Haven, CT: Yale University Press, 1989).

Ozouf, Mona, *La Fête révolutionnaire, 1789–1799* (Paris: Gallimard, 1976).

Ozouf, Mona, 'War and Terror in French revolutionary discourse (1792–1794)', *Journal of Modern History*, 56 (December 1984): 579–97.

Ozouf, Mona, *L'Homme régénéré: essais sur la Révolution française* (Paris: Gallimard, 1989).

Palmer, R.R., *Twelve who Ruled: the Year of the Terror in the French Revolution* (1941: this edition, Princeton, NJ: Princeton University Press, 1973).

Palmer, R.R., *From Jacobin to Liberal: Marc-Antoine Jullien, 1775–1848* (Princeton, NJ: Princeton University Press, 1993).

Parker, Harold T., *The Cult of Antiquity and the French Revolutionaries* (1937: this edition, New York: Octagon Books, 1965).

Parker, Lindsay A.H., 'Family and feminism in the French Revolution: the case of Rosalie Ducrollay Jullien', *Journal of Women's Studies*, 24, 3 (Autumn, 2012): 39–61.

Patrick, Alison, *The Men of the First French Republic* (Baltimore, MD: Johns Hopkins University Press, 1972).

Pellegrin, Nicole, *Les Vêtements de la liberté: Abécédaire des pratiques vestimentaires françaises de 1780 à 1800* (Aix: Éditions Alinéa, 1989).

Pocock, J.G.A., *The Machiavellian Moment: Florentine Political Thought and the Atlantic Republican Tradition* (Princeton, NJ: Princeton University Press, 1975).

Popkin, Jeremy D., *Revolutionary News: the Press in France, 1789–1799* (Durham, NC and London: Duke University Press, 1990).

Price, Munro, *The Fall of the French Monarchy: Louis XVI, Marie-Antoinette and the Baron de Breteuil* (Houndmills: Palgrave, 2002).

Rapport, Michael, *Nationality and Citizenship in Revolutionary France: the Treatment of Foreigners, 1789–1799* (Oxford: Oxford University Press, 2000).

Reddy, William, *The Navigation of Feeling: A Framework for the History of the Emotions* (Cambridge: Cambridge University Press, 2001).

Reisert, Joseph R., *Jean-Jacques Rousseau: A Friend of Virtue* (Ithaca, NY: Cornell University Press, 2003).

Renwick, John (ed.), *Language and Rhetoric of the Revolution* (Edinburgh: Edinburgh University Press, 1990).

Rétat, Pierre (ed.), *La Révolution du journal 1788–1794* (Paris: CNRS, 1998).

Reynolds, Siân, *Marriage and Revolution: Monsieur and Madame Roland* (Oxford: Oxford University Press, 2012).

Rizzo, Tracey, *A Certain Emancipation of Women: Gender, Citizenship and the Causes Célèbres of Eighteenth-Century France* (Selinsgrove, PA: Susquehanna University Press, 2004).

Robinet, Jean-François-Eugene, *Danton: Mémoire sur sa vie privée* (Paris: Charavay Frères, 1884).

Rose, R.B., *The Making of the Sans-Culottes: Democratic Ideas and Institutions in Paris, 1789–92* (Manchester: Manchester University Press, 1983).

Rosenfeld, Sophia, 'Thinking about feeling, 1789–1799', *French Historical Studies*, 32, 4 (Fall 2009): 697–706.

Rosenvallon, Pierre, *La Démocratie inachevée. Histoire de la souveraineté du peuple en France* (Paris: Gallimard, 2003).

Schechter, Ronald, 'The terror of their enemies: reflections on a trope in eighteenth-century historiography', *Historical Reflections*, 36, 1 (2010): 53–75.

Scott, Joan Wallach, 'The evidence of experience', *Critical Inquiry*, 17 (1991): 773–97.

Scott, Joan Wallach, *Only Paradoxes to Offer: French Feminists and the Rights of Man* (Cambridge, MA: Harvard University Press, 1996).

Scurr, Ruth, *Fatal Purity: Robespierre and the French Revolution* (London: Chatto and Windus, 2006).

Sepinwall, Alyssa Goldstein, *The Abbé Grégoire and the French Revolution: the Making of Modern Universalism* (Berkeley: University of California Press, 2005).

Serna, Pierre, *Antonelle, aristocrate révolutionnaire, 1747–1817* (Paris: Éditions du Félin, 1997).

Sewell, William H., *A Rhetoric of Bourgeois Revolution: the Abbé Sieyès and What is the Third Estate?* (Durham, NC: Duke University Press, 1994).

Shapiro, Barry M., 'Self-sacrifice, self-interest, or self-defence? The Constituent Assembly and the "Self-Denying Ordinance" of May 1791', *French Historical Studies*, 25, 4 (2002): 625–56.

Shapiro, Barry M., *Traumatic Politics: the Deputies and the King in the Early French Revolution* (University Park: Pennsylvania State University Press, 2009).

Shapiro, Gilbert and John Markoff, *Revolutionary Demands: a Content Analysis of the Cahiers de Doléances of 1789* (Stanford, CA: Stanford University Press, 1998).

Shaw, Matthew, *Time and the French Revolution: the Republican Calendar, 1789–Year XIV* (Woodbridge: The Royal Historical Society, The Boydell Press, 2005).

Shovlin, John, *The Political Economy of Virtue: Luxury, Patriotism, and the Origins of the French Revolution* (Ithaca, NY: Cornell University Press, 2006).

Simonin, Anne, *Le Déshonneur dans la République: une histoire de l'indignité 1791–1958* (Paris: Bernard-Grasset, 2008).

Slavin, Morris, *The Making of an Insurrection: Parisian Sections and the Gironde* (Cambridge, MA: Harvard University Press, 1986).

Slavin, Morris, *The Hébertistes to the Guillotine: Anatomy of a 'Conspiracy' in Revolutionary France* (Baton Rouge: Louisiana State University Press, 1994).

Smith, Jay M., *The Culture of Merit: Nobility, Royal Service, and the Making of Absolute Monarchy in France, 1600–1789* (Ann Arbor: University of Michigan Press, 1996).

Smith, Jay M., 'Between *discourse* and *experience*: agency and ideas in the French pre-Revolution', *History and Theory*, 40 (2001): 116–42.

Smith, Jay M., *Nobility Reimagined: The Patriotic Nation in Eighteenth-Century France* (Ithaca, NY: Cornell University Press, 2005).

Smith, Jay M. (ed.), *The French Nobility in the Eighteenth Century: Reassessments and New Approaches* (University Park: Pennsylvania State University Press, 2006).

Soboul, Albert (ed.), *Actes du colloque Robespierre* (Paris: Société des études robespierristes, 1967).

Soboul, Albert (ed.), *Actes du colloque Girondins et Montagnards (Sorbonne, 14 décembre 1975)* (Paris: Société des études Robespierristes, 1980).

Sonenscher, Michael, *Sans-Culottes; an Eighteenth-Century Emblem in the French Revolution* (Princeton, NJ: Princeton University Press, 2008).

Spang, Rebecca, *The Invention of the Restaurant: Paris and Modern Gastronomic Culture* (Cambridge, MA: Harvard University Press, 2000).

Spang, Rebecca, 'Paradigms and paranoias: how modern is the French Revolution?', *American Historical Review*, 108, 1 (2003): 119–47.

Sparrow, Elizabeth, *Secret Service: British Agents in France, 1792–1815* (Woodbridge: The Boydell Press, 1999).

Starobinski, Jean, *Jean-Jacques Rousseau: Transparency and Obstruction* (1971: this edition, Chicago: University of Chicago Press, 1988).

Sutherland, D.M.G., *Murder in Aubagne: Lynching, Law and Justice During the French Revolution, 1789–1801* (Cambridge: Cambridge University Press, 2009).

Swann, Julian, 'Disgrace without dishonour: the political exile of French magistrates in the eighteenth century', 195, *Past and Present* (May 2007): 87–196.

Swann, Julian and Joël, Félix (eds), *The Crisis of the Absolute Monarchy: From the Old Regime to the French Revolution* (Oxford: Oxford University Press, 2013).

Swenson, James, *On Jean-Jacques Rousseau, Considered as One of the First Authors of the Revolution* (Stanford, CA: Stanford University Press, 2000).

Sydenham, Michael, *The Girondins* (London: The Athlone Press, 1961).

Sydenham, Michael, 'The Girondins and the question of revolutionary government: a new approach to the problem of political divisions in the National Convention', *French Historical Studies*, 10 (1977): 342–8.

Tackett, Timothy, *Becoming a Revolutionary: the Deputies of the French National Assembly and the Emergence of a Revolutionary Culture (1789–1790)* (Princeton, NJ: Princeton University Press, 1996).

Tackett, Timothy, 'Conspiracy obsession in a time of revolution: French elites and the origins of the Terror, 1789–1792' *American Historical Review*, 105 (2000): 691–713.

Tackett, Timothy, 'Interpreting the Terror', *French Historical Studies*, 24, 4 (2001): 569–78.

Tackett, Timothy, 'Collective panics in the early French Revolution, 1789–1791: a comparative perspective', *French History*, 17 (2003): 149–71.

Tackett, Timothy, 'Paths to revolution: the old regime correspondence of five future revolutionaries', *French Historical Studies*, 32, 4 (2009): 531–54.

Thompson, J.M., *Robespierre* (1935: this edition, Oxford: Basil Blackwell, 1988).

Trahard, Pierre, *La Sensibilité révolutionnaire, 1789–1794* (Paris: Boivin, 1936).

Triolaire, Cyril (ed.), *La Révolution française au miroir des recherches actuelles* (Paris: Société des études robespierristes, 2011).

Van Kley, Dale (ed.), *The French Idea of Freedom: The Old Regime and the Declaration of Rights of 1789* (Stanford, CA: Stanford University Press, 1994).

Van Kley, Dale, *The Religious Origins of the French Revolution: From Calvinism to the Civil Constitution, 1560–1791* (New Haven, CT: Yale University Press, 1996).

Vincent-Buffault, Anne, *The History of Tears: Sensibility and Sentimentality in France* (Houndmills: Macmillan, 1991).

Vincent-Buffault, Anne, *L'Exercise de l'amitié: Pour une histoire des pratiques amicales aux XVIIIe et XIXe siécles* (Paris: Seuil, 1995).

Vinot, Bernard, *Saint-Just* (Paris: Fayard, 1985).

Wahnich, Sophie, *La Liberté ou la mort: essai sur la Terreur et le terrorisme* (Paris: La Fabrique Éditions, 2003).

Waldinger, Renée, Philip Dawson, and Isser Woloch (eds), *The French Revolution and the Meaning of Citizenship* (Westport, CT: Greenwood Press, 1993).

Walker, Lesley H., *A Mother's Love: Crafting Feminine Virtue in Enlightenment France* (Lewisburg, PA: Bucknell University Press, 2008).

Wallon, Henri, *Histoire du Tribunal révolutionnaire*, 6 vols (Paris: Plon, 1880–81).

Walter, Gérard, *Maximilien de Robespierre* (1961: this edition, Paris: Gallimard, 1989).

Walton, Charles, *Policing Public Opinion: The Culture of Calumny and the Problem of Free Speech* (Oxford: Oxford University Press, 2009).

Whaley, Leigh, *Radicals, Politics and Republicanism in the French Revolution* (Stroud: Sutton Publishing, 2000).

Wick, Daniel L., *A Conspiracy of Well-Intentioned Men: The Society of Thirty and the French Revolution* (New York: Garland Publishing, 1987).

Woloch, Isser, *Jacobin Legacy: the Democratic Movement Under the Directory* (Princeton, NJ: Princeton University Press, 1970).

Woloch, Isser, *The New Regime: Transformations of the French Civic Order, 1789–1820s* (New York: W.W. Norton and Co., 1994).

Wright, Johnson Kent, *A Classical Republican in Eighteenth-Century France: the Political Thought of Mably* (Stanford, CA: Stanford University Press, 1997).

Wright, Johnson Kent, 'Montesquieuean moments: the 'Spirit of the Laws' and republicanism', *Proceedings of the Western Society for French History* (2008).

Wrigley, Richard, *The Politics of Appearances: Representations of Dress in Revolutionary France* (Oxford: Berg, 2002).

Young, Mary, *Augustin: The Younger Robespierre* (London: Core Publications, 2011).

## UNPUBLISHED DISSERTATIONS

Darnton, Robert, 'Trends in radical propaganda on the eve of the French Revolution, 1782–1788' (DPhil, University of Oxford, 1964).

Harder, Mette, 'Crisis of representation: the National Convention and the search for politssical legitimacy, 1792–1795' (PhD, University of York, July 2010).

Linton, Marisa, 'The concept of virtue in eighteenth-century France, 1745–1788' (DPhil, University of Sussex, 1993).

# Index

Printed and bound by CPI Group (UK) Ltd, Croydon, CR0 4YY